797,885 Books
are available to read at

Forgotten Books

www.ForgottenBooks.com

Forgotten Books' App
Available for mobile, tablet & eReader

ISBN 978-1-5277-2784-7
PIBN 10884932

This book is a reproduction of an important historical work. Forgotten Books uses state-of-the-art technology to digitally reconstruct the work, preserving the original format whilst repairing imperfections present in the aged copy. In rare cases, an imperfection in the original, such as a blemish or missing page, may be replicated in our edition. We do, however, repair the vast majority of imperfections successfully; any imperfections that remain are intentionally left to preserve the state of such historical works.

Forgotten Books is a registered trademark of FB &c Ltd.
Copyright © 2017 FB &c Ltd.
FB &c Ltd, Dalton House, 60 Windsor Avenue, London, SW19 2RR.
Company number 08720141. Registered in England and Wales.

For support please visit www.forgottenbooks.com

1 MONTH OF FREE READING

at
www.ForgottenBooks.com

By purchasing this book you are eligible for one month membership to ForgottenBooks.com, giving you unlimited access to our entire collection of over 700,000 titles via our web site and mobile apps.

To claim your free month visit:
www.forgottenbooks.com/free884932

* Offer is valid for 45 days from date of purchase. Terms and conditions apply.

English
Français
Deutsche
Italiano
Español
Português

www.forgottenbooks.com

Mythology Photography **Fiction**
Fishing Christianity **Art** Cooking
Essays Buddhism Freemasonry
Medicine **Biology** Music **Ancient Egypt** Evolution Carpentry Physics
Dance Geology **Mathematics** Fitness
Shakespeare **Folklore** Yoga Marketing
Confidence Immortality Biographies
Poetry **Psychology** Witchcraft
Electronics Chemistry History **Law**
Accounting **Philosophy** Anthropology
Alchemy Drama Quantum Mechanics
Atheism Sexual Health **Ancient History**
Entrepreneurship Languages Sport
Paleontology Needlework Islam
Metaphysics Investment Archaeology
Parenting Statistics Criminology
Motivational

THE
ANNALS OF BRISTOL

IN THE EIGHTEENTH CENTURY.

BY

JOHN LATIMER,

Author of "Annals of Bristol in the Nineteenth Century."

PRINTED FOR THE AUTHOR.
1893.

BY THE SAME AUTHOR.

Demy 8vo, Price 18s. 6d., Large Paper, 22s. 6d. Net.

THE ANNALS OF BRISTOL IN THE NINETEENTH CENTURY.

PREFACE.

THE compiler must plead "extenuating circumstances" for making a further addition to the numerous histories of Bristol.

Whilst materials were being gathered for the Annals of the present century, facts frequently cropped up relating to its predecessor which were found to be either ignored or misreported in existing works. The number of such incidents became at length so great as to suggest a systematic search for others. By the courtesy of Mr. D. T. Burges, Town Clerk, and Mr. J. T. Lane, City Treasurer, the vast collection of documents preserved at the Council House was thoroughly examined for the first time, and yielded large returns. The late Archdeacon Norris kindly permitted access to the minute books of the Dean and Chapter, and to the mass of papers in the old Consistory Court, and the facts thus brought to light proved highly interesting. The extensive collection of local books and manuscripts made by the late Mr. C. T. Jefferies afforded another bountiful harvest. Much was gathered from the noble library of Mr. Alderman Fox, to whom sincere thanks are offered for his hospitality during the research. The valuable collection of local books, maps and manuscripts belonging to Mr. William George furnished original matter of great interest. An examination of the Bristol Wills preserved in the Probate Office, and at the Central Registry in London, supplied numerous instructive facts. Curious entries, again, were found in the vestry books of Christ Church, St. Nicholas, St. Stephen, Temple and St. Philip, and the courtesy of their custodians merits especial acknowledgment. At the Bodleian Library, in addition to various minor treasures, was found a manuscript "History of Bristol," compiled by a local schoolmaster early in the last century, containing many original notes. And in the State Papers from 1700 to 1760, to which access was obtained, were found much correspondence relating to city affairs.

The almost overwhelming stores of the British Museum embraced material requiring mention in a little more detail.

The local history of the last century has been hitherto chiefly based on so-called "Calendars," kept by private citizens, and very briefly recording the notable events of the time. From discrepancies existing in those manuscripts, some of them appear to have been written from memory, long after the incidents they record had passed away. In any case, it is obvious that such jottings are not to be compared, as regards trustworthiness, with the reports of local events published in contemporary newspapers. Yet the latter source of information has been neglected by the historians of the city, in despite of the baldness and inadequacy that characterise their later annals. Thanks to the usual kindness of Mr. T. D. Taylor, the volumes of early Bristol newspapers in his possession were made available. Mr. W. J. Phelps, of Chestal, Dursley, kindly permitted an examination of his fine set of Gloucester Journals, commencing in 1722. To supply the deficiencies still remaining, recourse was had to the piles of early newspapers in the British Museum, and although the inspection of many thousands of the pigmy sheets involved much time and labour, the facts brought to light amply repaid their cost.

With the mass of material thus accumulated, the compiler felt himself in a position to lay aside previous works, and to produce the story of the century entirely from new sources of information. How far this has been satisfactorily accomplished must be left to the judgment of the reader.

In addition to the gentlemen whose services have been acknowledged above, the compiler has to return grateful thanks for assistance received from the Earl of Ducie, Lord Lieutenant, Sir Charles Wathen, Mr. W. J. Braikenridge, Bath, the Rev. S. W. Wayte, Mr. G. H. Pope, Treasurer of the Merchants' Society, Colonel Bramble, Mr. W. H. Wills, Mr. J. J. Simpson, Clerk to the Corporation of the Poor, Mr. John Taylor, City Librarian, Mr. Harold B. Bowles, Mr. W. W. Hughes, Mr. R. Hall Warren, Mr. Walter Frost, Mr. F. G. Powell, Mr. G. E. Weare, Weston-super-Mare, and the Rev. A. B. Beaven, Preston.

TRELAWNY PLACE,
    January, 1893.

THE ANNALS OF BRISTOL

IN THE

EIGHTEENTH CENTURY.

MR. DALLAWAY, in one of his essays on local antiquities, expressed his sorrow at being unable to conjure up, for the benefit of his contemporaries, a vivid picture of Bristol in the time of William Worcester. A similar regret may be acknowledged that a perfect description of the city and its inhabitants about two hundred years ago is not to be obtained from the materials now available. Those materials consist, for the most part, of scattered fragments, gleaned from various records, and their combination will leave much of the following sketch to be filled in by the help of the reader's imagination. Imperfect as may be the result, it will at least serve to indicate the material and social progress that was made during the eighteenth century, and to render its annals more interesting and intelligible.

It may be observed in the first place that between the Middle-Age picture sighed for by Mr. Dallaway, and that of which the outlines are about to be drawn, the difference in substance must have been practically trivial. Town life in England marked a slight progress at the darkest periods of history; but it is certain that the Bristol of 1700 bore a far closer resemblance to the Bristol of the Plantagenets than it did to the city of the p esent day. A few great monastic edifices had disappeared, and the massive Norman castle that long frowned over the town had been, like the feudal institutions it represented, swept away. But in other outward respects there was little changed. The city was still surrounded by walls, and entrance could be effected only through the ancient gates of Redcliff, Temple, Newgate, and the rest. The High Cross, one of the most striking local erections of the Middle Ages, held its original place at the junction of the four leading thoroughfares, and had just

B

been repaired, gilded, and painted, at an expense denoting the honour in which it was held. The obscurity, narrowness, and intricacy of the streets, many of which are now fairly represented by the unaltered part of Maryleport Street, had undergone no improvement. The picturesque old bridge, with its double row of houses, between which the stream of traffic struggled painfully, was still one of the sights of the city. The muddy tide surged backwards and forwards twice a day in the Avon and the Froom, upon which rivers the local government, supremely indifferent to sanitary details down to the close of the seventeenth century, threw the functions of common sewers. "Washing places," such as may still be seen in continental towns, were maintained on the sides of the Froom for housewives of the labouring class, and were used at ebb-tide just as William Worcester described two centuries before. With the exception of the new streets that had recently sprung up on the site of the Castle, the extent of the town was almost unchanged. The increased population, whatever was its amount, had occasioned no proportionate increase of area. The circuit of the defences, with the ancient extensions around St. James's Church and the Cathedral, sufficed for the accommodation of the inhabitants. Saving half a dozen houses edging what is now called Park Row—then the only carriage road to Clifton Church—and a few cottages in Frog Lane, the slope of ground extending from the Royal Fort to the harbour was occupied by orchards, fields, and gardens. Stoke's Croft was a rural promenade, having fields on either side, and was sheltered from the summer sun by rows of trees. Kingsdown was literally a down, ramblers on which beheld a "grove" of church steeples on the one hand and stretches of pasture land and orchards on the other. More to the west, the city ended near St. Michael's Church and at College Green. Clifton "on the hill" was divided into about a dozen dairy farms, separated here and there by unenclosed common, gay with furze blossom. A single mansion, the Manor House, stood near the church, and another in Clifton Wood. Around them straggled a few cottages, the inmates of which earned a little money from the parish by killing the foxes, polecats, and hedgehogs that strayed from the downs into the cultivated fields. Even in the low-lying district, although a few lodging-houses had sprung up for the accommodation of visitors to the Hot Well, the road from College Green, until far into the century, ran between gardens, dotted at intervals by houses. Bedminster was even more isolated than Clifton. Ogilby, in his Road-book dated 1698, stated that a clear space of half a mile separated the city from the village. As may be seen from Buck's view of the city, Redcliff and Temple Gates looked upon open country so late as 1730. In fact, Bristol had only one real suburb—the district lying beyond Lawford's Gate, inhabited by a few hundred weavers, colliers, and market gardeners.

The streets of the old city had been laid out at a period when the inland traffic of the country was exclusively carried on by means of pack horses, and when the wealthiest travellers moved from place to place on horseback. The average breadth between the base of the houses in the busiest thoroughfares was under twenty feet, while, owing to the practice of constructing the upper storeys so as to overhang the lower, the width was often greatly diminished towards the roofs. The central portion of Wine Street was of exceptional breadth, but upon this spot the Corporation had placed a market house, which, with the pump, a whipping post, and the frequent erection of a pillory, left the locality little better off than its neighbours. Building stone being expensive, owing to the cost of transport, and bricks being rarely made in the district, houses had been almost exclusively constructed of timber, with an outer covering of plaster. An order of the Common Council in 1703 forbade the use of thatch for roofs; but it is certain that slates and tiles were then in general use. The leading streets were paved with rough blocks of stone, but there were no footpaths for pedestrians; and owing to the ceaseless passage of trucks and sledges, called geehoes (the only vehicles permitted for moving goods in the centre of the city), the roadways were so slippery in wet weather as to be a fertile cause of accidents. The channel for carrying off water was in the middle of the street, and was often filled with mud. (Two generations after this date, two woollen drapers' apprentices, one of whom, Matthew Brickdale, was to be many years Member of Parliament for the city, were accustomed to play a nocturnal joke on their neighbours by sweeping the filth of the High Street gutter under the dark and narrow pass of St. Nicholas's Gate, with results to unwary pedestrians that may be imagined.) The shops had massive projecting heads, called penthouses or bulks, which were often very low and inconvenient to passengers. The shops themselves, with few exceptions, were without the protection of windows, and quite open, like butchers' shambles of the present day. Occasionally they were furnished with "lattices," of chequered willow or laths, which must have increased the gloom caused by the penthouse and the overhanging roof. In many of those places of business articles were not merely sold, but made, for the simple retailer was still uncommon. In every thoroughfare, therefore, prevailed the discordant noises of smiths', coopers', braziers', and joiners' hammers, the click of looms, and the burr of lathes; while wayfarers were regaled with the penetrating fumes of the soap boiler, the tallow chandler, and the dyer. Every Saturday, Wine Street, Broad Street, and High Street were blocked by the markets for butchers' meat, butter, fowls, vegetables, and other produce, that were held in those thoroughfares; and fruit women screamed, porters fought, and garbage accumulated in heaps under the shadow of the Council House. The streets were resonant at all times with the bawlings of hawkers and petty dealers. Crowds of boys, who knew as little of school as of a palace, pursued their rough sport in the most crowded localities. There was no protection against the brutality of truck and sledge drivers, the manœuvres of pickpockets, or the knavery of ring-droppers. The laws against vagrancy were severe; so late as 1729 the magistrates sentenced an incorrigible vagrant to three years' hard labour in the house of correction; but the number and the importunacy of professional beggars were ceaseless nuisances. One other difficulty in the way of locomotion remains to be noticed. In spite of the authorities, the streets could not be kept clear of the numerous pigs belonging to careless housekeepers. On one occasion the Corporation paid a fee to an officer "for cutting off the tails" of these wandering scavengers; but neither the maiming of the animals nor the fining of their owners was of much avail; and irrepressible porkers are heard of from time to time to the very end of the century.

A more picturesque feature of the time was due rather to necessity than to a desire to please the eye. In an age when not only the working classes, but practically the whole of the rural population and no small number of petty traders, were unable to read, a conspicuous shop sign was indispensable as a guide to customers. These ensigns, suspended over the roadway, were of varied designs, and, as enterprising shopkeepers declined to be eclipsed by their neighbours, there was often a rivalry as to size. From numberless advertisements dating from 1700 to 1750, when the practice began to lose favour, an idea may be formed of the curious medley of figures which sought to catch the eye of spectators. Lions, spread-eagles, griffins, elephants and tigers were to be seen of every tint. Suns, moons, and stars were equally popular. Wheat-sheaves, bee-hives, horses, blackbirds, grasshoppers, dogs, hares, and various agricultural implements courted the attention of country patrons. A mercer sported an entire " Turkish Bashaw "; a jeweller rejoiced in a Golden Boy; and a calendar displayed a Watering Roll, whatever that may have been. A great number of tradesmen flaunted a double device, such as the Tye Wig and Griffin of a barber; the Hand and Pen of a schoolmaster; the Half Moon and Wheat-sheaf of a draper; and the Sword and Crown of a cutler. Booksellers frequently adopted the Bible and Sun; and at least one undertaker set up the lugubrious representation of a Coffin and Shroud. Even the business of the stamp office was conducted " at the sign of the King's Arms." Wood carvers and painters must have reaped a good harvest in carrying out the eccentric conceptions of their patrons, for it appears that some of the signs cost from £20 to £40 each. Whatever may have been the artistic results of their labours, the swinging designs, which from morn till eve threw moving shadows over the pavement, must have presented a quaint attractiveness and variety now entirely lost. A serious inconvenience, however, was occasioned by the display. Only a scanty supply of lamps was provided for the public, and the lights were frequently so eclipsed by the overhanging signs as to be practically useless.

Bristol in 1700 was on the point of attaining the position of second city in the kingdom. Until the Restoration she had been surpassed by York and Norwich; but the subsequent development of commerce with America and the West Indies gradually secured her an unquestioned supremacy. Even in 1700, however, the wealth of Norwich appears to have equalled that of Bristol. In the previous year, the House of Commons, in granting a vote of money for the navy, fixed the amount to be contributed by each county and important town; and the figures, which were doubtless based on the best statistics then available, are of considerable interest. It is scarcely necessary to say that Liverpool, Manchester, Leeds, Sheffield, and Birmingham do not appear in the return, being included, like other small towns, in their respective counties. The four chief cities assessed were:—Norwich, for £4,259; Bristol, £3,695; Exeter, £2,354; and York, £2,319. Other western towns were:—Gloucester,

£695; Wells, £241; Bath, £221; Bridgwater, £183. The population of the 42 parishes of Norwich, from an actual enumeration, was about 29,000. Lord Macaulay estimated the inhabitants of Bristol in 1685 at the same number; but it will be shown further on that the calculation was excessive. The actual population in 1700 was about 25,000.

In point of commerce the superiority of Bristol over all her provincial rivals was beyond dispute. Some statistics published by a Government official, Captain Grenville Collins, based on the Custom House returns for 1701-2, give the following details respecting the principal outports:—

	Ships.	Average Tonnage.
Bristol	165	105
Newcastle	163	73
Hull	115	66
Liverpool	102	85
Yarmouth	148	69

Glasgow, in 1700, had no ships, and its exports—confined to a few barrels of herrings and a few pieces of coarse woollens—were shipped in vessels belonging to Whitehaven. According to contemporary statements of good authority, Bristol was the only port which could pretend to enter into competition with London, and was able to trade with entire independence of the capital. In part this was due to the remarkable energy and enterprise of the trading classes of the city, who, not content with supplying the demands of the district, competed with their London rivals in the provinces, and conducted an inland trade in the southern and midland counties, from Southampton to the Trent, by means of their own carriers. They did not, moreover, confine themselves to domestic enterprise. Roger North, who, as Recorder of Bristol, had means of obtaining good information, observed twenty years before this date that petty local shopkeepers, selling candles and the like, would venture a bale of stockings or a piece of stuff in a cargo bound for Nevis or Virginia. It will be seen later on that Savage, in his rancorous satire of 1743, alleged that Bristol freights were owned, not by merchants, but by mechanics. A keener observer, in a "Journey through England," published in 1724, remarked that "The very Parsons of Bristol talk of nothing but Trade, and how to turn the Penny." To a certain extent, the speculations of persons outside the mercantile class must have added to the aggregate commercial returns of the port, and may have extended that taste for display to be referred to presently. In other directions Bristolians were keenly attentive to the progress of industry and manufactures, and so seldom let slip a new chance of profitable enterprise that some envious observer attributed to them the power of sleeping with one eye open. The importation of French brandy having been stopped during the war of 1689-96, the cheapness of coal (2s. to 2s. 6d. per ton) encouraged the erection of numerous local distilleries. In the manufacture of glass, which was then in its infancy in this country, the city soon took a leading position. Somewhat later, a few Bristol merchants, having discovered that copper ore was thrown aside as worthless by the Cornish tin miners, set up the manufacture of brass and the refining of copper on the Froom and Avon, securing great profits for themselves, and opening out a new field of labour to the working classes. More than one effort was made to establish manufactories of cotton fabrics. Several notices occur of salt refiners, carpet weavers, silt and velvet weavers, drugget makers. A pottery for making imitation Delft ware was opened about 1703, and was one of the earliest in England. These and other similar adventures were but supplements to the old industries of the city—the weaving of cloths, friezes, and fustians, the building of ships, the refining of sugar, and the manufacture of soap, tobacco, tobacco pipes, and pins; but they added sensibly to the general activity of commerce and the prosperity of the inhabitants. The development of the port would have been even more rapid than it was but for the erroneous views of political economy which then prevailed. For many years importations of Irish cattle, meat, butter, and cheese were absolutely prohibited as a "publick and common nuisance." In times of scarcity the restriction was relaxed, but in 1696, during a severe dearth, when the Corporation petitioned the Government for leave to import 5,000 bushels of Irish grain duty free, for the relief of the distressed poor, the appeal met with an emphatic negative. The entry of even lean cattle, prohibited about the same date, put an end to a profitable local trade; and in 1699 the import of Irish woollen goods was interdicted under a penalty of £500 and forfeiture of the vessel.

Gregory King, whose statistics were compiled with care, and were generally accepted as trustworthy, estimated that in 1688 the profits of "eminent" English merchants averaged £400, those of the lesser merchants £200, and those of shopkeepers £45 per annum. As trade made rapid strides after the peace of Ryswick, it is probable that King's figures ought to be increased by a fourth to represent the average returns of 1700. Even after making this correction the estimated incomes seem small; but it must be remembered that the rate of wages (about 1s. a day) and the price of the necessaries of life were correspondingly moderate. Whatever may have been their incomes, the Bristol merchants of the time were famous for their love of display. In spite of the narrowness of the streets, many of the upper classes paraded in private carriages, which were then a great luxury. (It is somewhat surprising to find from the records of the Society of Friends that in 1699 wealthy Quakers were accustomed on Sundays to proceed to chapel in their own coaches.) The baptism of children was an especial occasion for feasting and ostentation. According to a custom of the city, the religious ceremony took place at the house of the parents, in the presence of as many friends and relatives as could be accommodated, and was followed by a copious distribution of caudle. Every family which respected itself had a large silver caudle cup, and many had two or three. The practice of entertaining large parties to dinner in private houses had not yet become fashionable; but strangers, as Mr. Pepys' diary shows, were sometimes offered generous hospitality, and made agreeable acquaintance with the far-famed Bristol milk. Other visitors, it is true, refer to the manners of the citizens in less complimentary terms. Thus Mr. Marmaduke Rawdon, a York merchant, who made a tour in the West about the same time as Pepys, remarks of Bristol :—" In this city are many proper men, but very few handsome women, and most of them ill-bred, being generally, men and women, very proud, not affable to strangers, but rather much admiring themselves, so that an ordinary fellow who is but a freeman of Bristol conceits himself to be as grave as a senator of Rome, and very sparing of his hat; insomuch that their preachers have told them of it in the pulpit."

But it was especially at funerals that wealthy families were prone to indulge in costly parade. Roger North, who seems to have taken a grudge against the citizens during his judicial connection with them, and who never lacked acrimony in criticising those whom he disliked, alleged that the vanity of Bristolians incited them to an extravagance "beyond imagination." "A man," he wrote, "who dies worth £300 will order £200 to be laid out on his funeral procession." Unfortunately for the censor's credit for accuracy, the wills of the Bristolians of his time may still be read, and as a matter of fact his assertion is not verified by a single testament. In the majority of cases, traders in easy circumstances directed that their burial should be conducted "decently," at the discretion of their executors, who, being generally relatives and legatees, had no temptation to act wastefully. Many others stipulated that their funeral expenses should not exceed £20 or £30. Women were more disposed than the ruder sex to follow the pompous customs of the wealthy. A lady, who does not appear to have been rich, directed that "at least" £50 should be spent on her burial, exclusive of £18 for a collation for six bearers, £9 to be distributed to the poor, and £10 to two women who were to accompany the hearse. Other instances of feminine vanity in the same rank of life indicate the outlay that took place amongst the leading mercantile grandees. All the friends of a deceased merchant were invited to his interment, and were often provided with gold rings and mourning; a great number of poor people received money and food, and were furnished with hats and cloaks for taking part in the procession. The consumption of "funeral baked meats," as well as of wine and other liquors, was profuse on such occasions; and from a deprecatory minute in the records of the Society of Friends at Frenchay, smoking seems to have been an ordinary incident in the proceedings. The great funerals took place at or about midnight, the coffin being borne along the streets with all the pomp of escutcheons, sconces, waxlights, flambeaux, plumes, pennons, and mutes. The tolling of the parish bell before the ceremony must have been a dreary infliction on the neighbourhood, for an economical mercer, desirous of avoiding display, ordered in his will that the bell at his interment should not toll "above six hours." The funeral service was followed by a sermon, for which testators left from one to six guineas to a favourite clergyman, frequently stipulating that he should preach on a text selected by themselves. Another item of expense may be mentioned. To gratify the clothing interest, an Act of Parliament was passed in 1678 requiring every dead body to be buried in a woollen shroud. But, as Pope's well known verses show, ladies thought the enactment fit to "provoke a saint," and some of them in Bristol ordered their executors to pay the fine of £5, and bury them "honourably." The unseemly show and dissipation of funeral ceremonies was then common to all wealthy communities, but it certainly seems to have been abnormal in Bristol. As an illustration, it may be stated that in 1699 a gentleman named Taylor, the owner of about thirty houses in various parts of the city, ordered that half a year's rent of all his property should be applied to the discharge of his funeral expenses. His contemporary, Alderman Lawford, left instructions that eighty poor men should be provided with gowns, hats, and shoes in order to attend his burial, and that the grocers of the city who took part in the ceremony should be furnished with a dinner. In another will, of 1706, there is a curious conflict between personal economy and family conceit. Thomas Ivy, "gentleman," also a considerable owner of house property, began his testament by ordering £50 to be spent on his burial in St. Nicholas's Church. Before the will was finished, however, his vanity got the uppermost, and he determined, "for-as-much as I have a desire to be buried in such manner as my father was," to increase the outlay to £100. Many undertakers' bills of that period having been preserved, it may be safely asserted that an outlay of £100 in 1706 was equivalent to nearly thrice that sum in a funeral account of the present day.

The entertainment of friends at baptisms and burials being so generally practised, one might suppose that the comforts and luxuries of the citizens' dwellings would be commensurate with the feasting which took place in them. But such was certainly not the case. With the exception of large displays of silver plate, to be referred to presently, the furniture of a tradesman's house was generally as rude in quality as it was meagre in quantity. Many contemporary wills show the extreme simplicity of the arrangements, and the description of Bath dwellings given by John Wood, in his account of that city in 1727, applied with equal truth to those of Bristol a quarter of a century earlier. The floors of dining rooms, says Wood, were destitute of carpets, and were stained, to hide the dirt, with soot and small beer; the walls were of mean wainscot, never painted; the fireplaces and hearths were daily daubed with whitewash. Cane or rush chairs, oaken tables, coarse woollen or linen hangings, and a small mirror constituted the chief garniture of the apartment. The equipment of the bedrooms was equally common and scanty; the best chambers for gentlemen, according to Wood, being no better than the servants' garrets of the middle of the century. Allusion having been made to servants, it may be amusing to note the advice given by Mr. Cary, a Bristol merchant who wrote an "Essay on Trade" in 1695, in reference to menials. "As for maid servants," he said, "let them be restricted from excess in apparel, and not permitted to leave their services without consent, nor be entertained by others without testimonials: this will make them more orderly and governable than they now are." While as to men, "no servant should be permitted to wear a sword, except when travelling; and if all people of mean qualities were prohibited the same, 'twould be of good consequence."

Taking a more comprehensive view of the social and domestic peculiarities of Bristol, so far as they can be gathered from contemporary documents, it will be found that what has been said of the material aspect of the city applies also to the moral and intellectual condition of the inhabitants, and that the society of 1700 more closely resembled that of the Middle Ages than that of our own times. In the first place, although the energy and enterprise of the citizens were noted by every visitor, and although a knowledge of what was passing in the world must have been of great interest to the mercantile classes, the town, like every other provincial town in the kingdom, was without a newspaper. It is true that, if a local chronicle had existed, its circulation must have been limited; for a vast majority of Bristolians were "as illiterate as the back of a tombstone." There were two or three bookshops in the city, or, rather, shops at which stationers undertook to obtain books if they were ordered; and John Dunton, the garrulous London bookseller, states in his curious autobiography that he regularly opened a stall at Bristol fair. But local purchasers generally contented themselves with almanacks, sermons, pamphlets, and other fugitive publications. Clergymen, ministers, and medical practitioners refer in their wills to their "closet of books"; but literary property is conspicuous from its absence in the testaments of well-to-do traders. A few thoughtful merchants may have amused their leisure with the poems of Milton or Dryden, the "Mariner's Magazine," or Purchas's collection of voyages; but many artisans of the present day possess a wider range of literature than could be found on the best furnished local book shelves of 1700. In only one of the wills in the Bristol Prerogative Office dated before that year, that of a Quaker grocer, is there a bequest of a book (it was Rushworth's Collections). For many later years, the only volume that testators seemed to have owned was a Bible, with perhaps a Book of Common Prayer. The lack of literature is sufficiently accounted for by the general deficiency of education. In Queen Elizabeth's hospital thirty-six boys received the barest elements of schooling. In the Red Maids' institution forty poor girls were taught to read, but not to write, by two mistresses, one of whom could not sign her own name, and the other appended an unsightly blotch, to the quarterly receipts for their salaries of £5 each. It is possible that about a dozen children were received in Redcliff Grammar School, and a school maintained by Cole's trustees on St. James's Back may have benefitted as many more. The records of both institutions are lost; it is only known that the former was not always open, and that the latter was closed about 1700. Saving this provision, the many thousand children of artisans and labourers were destitute of the means of instruction. The first bequest towards the foundation of a parish school (there were only two such institutions in London in 1697) appears in the will of a Miss Mary Gray, of Temple, who, in 1699, left £50 for the purchase of land, the rent of which, after deducting 6s. 8d. for a yearly sermon, was to be devoted to teaching seven poor orphans of that parish to read. For the boys of tradesmen and others, there was the Grammar School, with three or four private " writing schools," but the first mention of a school for girls does not occur until several years later. It is not surprising, therefore, to find that many men in prosperous circumstances, purchasing leases from, or lending money to, the Corporation, and disposing of large sums in their wills—some of them being styled gentlemen, merchants, tobacconists, and soapboilers—were unable to write their own names. Churchwardens have always been selected from the "substantial" class of parishioners. Yet one of the churchwardens of St. Stephen's in 1702 was unable to write, and the civic records show that so late as 1718 one of those officials for St. James's parish attached his "mark" to a receipt, and that both the churchwardens for St. Philip's displayed the same illiteracy in 1725. Some of the men who conducted private schools would not a century later have been deemed fit to take the management of a charity school, for their extant letters and petitions abound with grammatical errors. Their pupils could not be expected to surpass them. It may be assumed that the clerks of the Corporation were selected from the best-instructed candidates that offered themselves on a vacancy; yet the civic records literally swarm with blunders in syntax and orthography. Turning to the other sex, there is abundant evidence that, even amongst the widows of mayors and the sisters and daughters of knightly aldermen, an ability to write was, in 1700, unusual. As a safeguard against fraud, those incapable of subscribing their signatures possessed signet rings, or seals bearing their arms, and often learnt to form two rudely shaped Roman letters, the initials of their name, which were appended to documents as their "mark." Wealthy testators of this class almost invariably disposed of gold coins, jewellery, and silver plate to an extent which at the first glance seems astounding. The explanation, however, is not hard to find. No facilities then existed for the profitable investment of the savings of a household; many cautious people declined to entrust their spare money to the goldsmiths and other traders who carried on theybusiness of bankers; and, as the most convenient resource, purchases were made from time to time of substantial gold coins or articles of plate, which could be relied upon to fetch their value in an emergency. In this way tradesmen and owners of house property often hoarded a surprising quantity of old "broad pieces," "sceptre guineas," "Jacobuses" and "Caroluses," that had ceased to circulate as current coin, together with a rich store of silver beakers, bowls, cups, tankards, salvers and salt cellars, which were distributed by will amongst their surviving relatives. The profusion of gold rings, which also formed part of the "portable property" of the period, was due to a less excusable custom. Amongst the indispensable features of a pompous funeral was the gift of rings to those invited to the ceremony. On the occasion of an interment in 1704, Luttrell noted in his diary that 1,500 rings were presented to the deceased's friends and acquaintances. And as in the case of an eminent Bristol alderman of far later date, when the fashion was nearly extinct, 91 gentlemen's and 67 ladies' rings were distributed by his executors, it is easy to understand how elderly citizens of 1700, outliving many acquaintances, became possessed of more rings than they could have displayed on their fingers.

The Will Office furnishes other curious information respecting the habits of the community. Tea and coffee in 1700 were expensive novelties beyond the reach of ordinary households, even had a taste for them been developed. Their place at the breakfast table and at the afternoon meal was supplied by beer, the reported consumption of which would seem incredible but for the testimony of official documents. The price of malt was so low, and the duty so trifling, that good household beer was produced in 1690 at a cost of under twopence per gallon. The common-brewers' charge for strong beer in 1700, when the duty had been increased, was only sixpence per gallon. The best ale, by an order of the Corporation in 1703, was to be sold by brewers at 3s. 4d. per dozen gallons, being less than a penny per quart; and common qualities were to be vended at the "accustomed rates," which probably meant about one-half less. Indeed, by an Act of James I., which was still in force, the price of "the smaller sort of beer" was not to exceed one halfpenny per quart. The cost of home-brewed liquor being, of course, much below the price charged by retailers, every economical upper-class family, and the bulk of the trading community, in Bristol as elsewhere, brewed for home consumption, and quite one-half of the enormous annual total was produced by private persons. For this purpose nearly every household boasted of "great brass pots," "great brass kettles," "great bell-metal crocks," and other utensils, the cost of which must have been considerable from the figure they make in testamentary bequests. (A brass kettle holding "about 16 or 18 gallons" was stolen from Long Ashton Court in 1726.) Smaller articles of brass are also frequently mentioned; indeed, as the art of casting iron vessels for kitchen purposes was unknown in England, and as tin plates were also a foreign import, the brazier had a practical monopoly of this branch of trade. Equally flourishing was the pewterer. English earthenware makers had not advanced beyond the manufacture of coarse dairy pans, loaf sugar moulds, and other rude utensils. A few Dutch plates and dishes were imported from Delft, but were too costly and fragile to be popular. The first Bristol will bequeathing dinner crockery was made in 1715, and it is also the first to mention table glass. The earliest bequest of china occurs in a will of 1703, but the articles were probably mere chimney ornaments. The dinner services of merchants and shopkeepers, in fact, were universally of pewter, of which some families could exhibit copious stores. Pewter platters of six different sizes are distributed by one testatrix. Yeomen and artisans, on the other hand, unwilling or unable to buy metal plates and dishes, continued to eat their food on the wooden trenchers that had served their fathers, and perhaps their grandfathers, and in their wills divided these homely articles amongst their children. In their anxiety to avoid the cost of a sale by auction, indeed, testators condescended to a minuteness of detail which may seem amusing to a later age, but which is of great service for the light it throws, negative as well as positive, on the habits of the time. All the furniture in a house is sometimes described by its departing owner. Some men leave their best periwig to one relative, and their second best to another. Others particularly mention their various hats, great coats, shirts and leather breeches. Ladies recount all their gowns, good, bad, and indifferent, and there is sometimes a precise bequest of "my best silk petticoat," "my best head cloth" (a prodigious structure a foot in height and costing about £20), "my green say apron," "my worst little bed," down to "my third best under-petticoat." As an illustration of this custom, and also as affording some evidence of the personal effects of a wealthy widow, the following extract is taken from the will of Sarah Deane, who in 1696 left to a favourite god-daughter "my black flowered silk gowne and petticoat, my broadcloth petticoat with a gold fringe thereon, my under serge petticoat with a gold galoome thereon," another petticoat, a silver great tankard, some other plate, a "brass kettle pot," other brass utensils, and several pewter platters and plates; while to this legatee's brother there is a bequest—evidently intended as a compliment—of "a scarlett petticoat to make him a waistcoat." This lady appended a fine armorial seal to her will, but was unable to write her name. A more remarkable legacy appears in the will of a ship captain named Nightingale, who, in 1715, devised "the proceeds of his two boys and girls, then on board his ship." Again, a merchant, named Becher Fleming, in October, 1718, left to Mrs. Mary Becher "my negro boy, named Tallow." But it will subsequently be shown that negro slaves were numerous in Bristol until far into the century.

The economical instincts of the age come into prominence in divers social arrangements. The only source of artificial light ordinarily available was the tallow candle, the feeble gleam of which was hardly worth its cost. Evening reading was out of the question when there were no local journals or circulating libraries, and when most households were without books. Music had not yet become an item of a young lady's accomplishments, and the only musical instrument mentioned in contemporary wills is a solitary violin. Gossiping over the fire being the chief amusement of an evening circle, staid and thrifty heads of families, abhorring late hours, were naturally fervent believers in the old dictum of "early to bed and early to rise." In Hippisley's farce of "A Journey to Bristol," printed in 1731, and played too often before the citizens to have been a mere caricature, Mr. Doubtful, the local merchant, referring to his wife's frivolity and his own good nature, observes, " Though I go to bed at eight o'clock, I let you sit up with your maid till ten." If this was held to be a faithful picture of life in 1731, it is certain that the hours of 1700 were earlier still. Probably the nine o'clock curfew of St. Nicholas was the signal for the most belated Bristolians to retire to rest. On the other hand, the citizens were as wakeful as the " bright chanticleer " of the hunting song. In the parochial books of St. Thomas is a note made by the vicar in 1710, for the guidance of his successors in the then united livings of Bedminster, St. Mary Redcliff, St. Thomas and Leigh, in which it is stated that he "did not scruple " to marry couples bringing a licence at any hour " after four or five in the morning." The ordinances of the Joiners' Company required journeymen to begin work " between five and six." An advertisement of a quack doctor, of 1704, notifies that he receives patients every morning between six and nine o'clock. By order of the Corporation, the boys in Queen Elizabeth's Hospital rose at five o'clock even in winter, and the Grammar School boys assembled during the summer months at six o'clock. The courts of quarter session were opened at seven o'clock. The Common Council assembled at nine o'clock. The first meal of the day must therefore have been disposed of in what a degenerate posterity may term the middle of the night. The elements of a modern breakfast being unknown, the meal was chiefly composed, as it had been composed for centuries, of cold meat or skimmed-milk cheese, according to the position of the household, and bread, accompanied with milk for the younger members, and beer for the adults. The food of the working population was of the rudest character. A petition of the Corporation to the House of Commons, dated 1699, stated that the bread eaten by labourers was chiefly made from barley, whilst Gregory King about the same time estimated that half the working classes ate animal food only twice a week, while the other half scarcely ate it at all. One cannot, therefore, be surprised at the great consumption of malt liquor, which was exceedingly cheap and to a large extent nourishing. According to the official statistics of 1695, the quantity of beer brewed in England was upwards of 408 million gallons. Taking the grown-up population at 2,700,000, the production averaged over a quart and a half daily per head, for women as well as men, irrespective of a vast consumption of cider.

By about eight o'clock in the morning business affairs

were in full swing. The Merchants' Tolzey, a mean and narrow penthouse adjoining All Saints' Church, was thronged with shipowners, manufacturers, and traders; and Defoe found that, "just as in London," the surrounding taverns and coffee houses were crowded with bargainers, and "Bristol milk, which is Spanish sherry, nowhere so good as here, plentifully drunk." The narrowness of house accommodation was doubtless one of the causes of the popularity of these places of resort. Medical men and lawyers in good practice, being without convenient consulting rooms at home, were to be conferred with at their favourite taverns, and the habits of each important practitioner were generally known. Merchants, whose only office was a room in their dwellings, found the coffee houses convenient for the transaction of business. Every alternate day, at irregular hours, depending upon the state of the weather and the roads, the accidents of the journey, and the caprices of the postboys and the sorry nags that carried them, there arrived a mail from London, with a handful of letters and newspapers, the contents of which gave an additional spur to the prevailing animation. The newspapers, about the size of a sheet of letter paper, went chiefly to the coffee houses, where any one found admittance by the payment of a penny for a tiny cup of Mocha. If the intelligence of the day was exceptionally interesting, it was read aloud for the benefit of the company. In times of peace, however, as in 1700, the humble chronicles offered nothing more exciting to their subscribers than the rates of exchange, a list of bankrupts, the price of stocks, an account of a robbery, or the execution of a highwayman. By midday every citizen was ready for dinner (the Grammar School boys dispersed for this meal at 11 o'clock), and great was the clatter of pewter plates in the hands of youthful apprentices, who were required to serve their masters' tables. Business was afterwards resumed, and continued until six o'clock, when a supper, of the same character as the morning meal, wound up the day. For an hour or two in the evening the taverns and ale-houses were filled with habitual customers, who, furnished with pipes and tankards, discussed the current topics of the day with their friends. As was natural enough, politicians selected a tavern where they were certain to meet with acquaintances of kindred principles. From an early period, the White Lion inn, in Broad Street, was the favourite rendezvous of the leading Tory merchants. The nightly potations were not generally prolonged, but, taking into consideration the liquor consumed

c

during the day, they were often too deep. Dr. Johnson, when once referring to the customs of this period in his native town, asserted that all the decent people of Lichfield got drunk every night, and were not thought the worse of. And it may be doubted whether Bristol, which had about 240 inns, taverns, and ale-houses in 1700, or one for every twenty families, could boast of much more sobriety than the sleepy little Staffordshire city. Revellers, however, had good reasons for separating at an early hour, even if an order of the Corporation had not required the closing of public-houses at nine o'clock in winter and ten in summer. Locomotion after nightfall in the dirty, dark, and virtually unguarded thoroughfares, in which all the public lamps, or, rather, candle lanthorns, were extinguished at nine o'clock, was always disagreeable and sometimes perilous. The citizens, then, hastened home ; the night constables, numbering twelve all told, and farcically called watchmen, slunk off to smoke or sleep; and night prowlers had free course for their drunken outrages.

The united energy of the community in affairs of commerce and trade disguised a very different state of feeling as regarded political and religious controversies. Nearly a hundred years after the period under review, Southey complained of the impassable barriers which hostile parties and sects in Bristol had set up against each other, to the almost total destruction of social intercourse. But the ill-feeling caused by the French Revolution was but a feeble reflex of the passions that had been aroused by our own political conflicts of the previous century. Cavaliers and Roundheads, Tories and Whigs, had by turns enjoyed a temporary domination, and each, in abusing power, had inflicted wounds on their adversaries which still rankled in 1700. Bristolians yet lived whose fathers had lost their lives in defence of the Crown and the Church, and who had been oppressed, and sometimes ruined, in subsequent persecutions. The clergy of the city parishes had been banished from their livings and reduced to beggary, and their flocks had seen the pulpits filled with ignorant fanatics. Then the tide had turned, and the exultant Royalists had hastened to better the worst instruction of their opponents. Obstinate nonconformity was punished with transportation, and even with death. The dissenting community—and it was locally numerous—suffered under every ignominy at the hands of the Government and its supporters in Bristol. The closing of meeting-houses and the persecution of dissenting ministers did not satisfy the victors. In 1682 there were 120 god-fearing Quakers in the city gaol, where many of them died of pestilential diseases, for the so-called crime of non-attendance at church. The fines imposed upon local Friends in the following year for the same delinquency amounted to nearly £16,500. One of these culprits, condemned to death for incorrigible nonconformity, was saved from the gallows only by the exertions of his wife in London. Baptists and Independents had not been more mildly dealt with. During the High Church persecution upwards of 4,000 Dissenters died in the prisons into which they had been flung for infractions of the Conformity Acts. William Penn estimated the number of families ruined during this intolerant crusade at 15,000. And it is beyond question that Bristol produced a large contingent of these martyrs for conscience sake. The men who distinguished themselves in the local oppression were rewarded and honoured by the Government, being introduced by its orders into the Corporation, which was "purified" by the ejection of more moderate men. Later on, under James II., the Common Council was in the first place cleansed of every trace of Whiggery, and was subsequently stuffed with supporters of the memorable Indulgence, the bitterest feelings being stirred up amongst the persons successively degraded. The Revolution which followed only aggravated the animosities of politicians. Walter Hart, one of the prebendaries of the Cathedral, and three Bristol clergymen, Elisha Sage,—Burges, and—Edwards, followed the example of Bishop Frampton, of Gloucester, and Bishop Ken, of Wells, in refusing to swear fealty to William and Mary. It was notorious that many others were at heart disloyal, some of them refusing to allow the bells to be rung for the new king's successes in Ireland. A powerful section of the laity was equally Jacobitical, and scarcely disguised its aspirations for the overthrow of the "usurper." Two illustrations will suffice to show the intense animosity of the factions into which the city was divided. On the death of Queen Mary the Bristol Jacobites, says a contemporary news-letter, "caused the bells to be rung out, and went dancing through the streets, with music playing 'The King shall enjoy his own again.'" The fanatical admirers of the Commonwealth, on the other hand, though they did not dare to rejoice in public, held a feast in every populous town on the anniversary of the death of Charles I. The standing dish at those festivals was a calf's head, the appearance of which was always greeted by a song, of which one verse will suffice,—

"Now let's sing, carouse, and roar,
The happy day is come once more,
For to revel
Is but civil,
Thus our fathers did before,
When the tyrant would enslave us,
Chopt his calf's head off to save us."

For more than forty years after this date the fiercest passions were aroused by the Jacobite jubilations on the birthdays of the two Pretenders on the one hand, and by the holidays in honour of the reigning monarch on the other. On more than one occasion the mutual exasperation led to violent riots in the city, and once to loss of life. General elections, which then took place every three years, afforded the rival factions especially favourable opportunities for displaying their mutual passions. It seems unquestionable that in these contests a free expression of public opinion was frequently prevented by fraud or force. A popular candidate, with a majority of votes, if not defeated at the poll by riots and open violence, or defrauded of his votes by the partiality of the returning officers or the factious manœuvres of his opponents, was all but ruined by the extravagant cost of his victory. The poll could be kept open for forty days, entailing an enormous expense upon the candidates, and prolific of bribery, treating, and disorder. During this period the public-houses were thrown open, and drunkenness and violence prevailed in the streets and at the hustings. Bands of hired ruffians, armed with bludgeons and inflamed by liquor, paraded the thoroughfares, intimidating voters, and resisting their access to the polling place. Candidates, often assailed with filth and missiles, braved the penalties of the pillory; their supporters were exposed to the fury of drunken mobs; while an outrage incited by one camp forthwith provoked a revengeful retort by the other. How little such chronic antagonism was compatible with social communion, courtesy, and good feeling between the hostile parties may be left to the reader's consideration.

On one point, however, all ranks and parties seem to have been thoroughly in unison—namely, in the exclusion from the trade and industry of the city of those not born within its boundaries. Every one coming from outside those limits —even from Clifton or Redland, or the out-parishes of St. James or St. Philip—was stigmatised as a "foreigner," and often treated as an enemy deserving extermination. In 1696 the Corporation passed a by-law, prohibiting every person not a freeman from exercising a trade or opening a shop in the city, "whether with or without latesses or glass windows; botchers, coblers, and hoxters alone excepted." The penalty upon an interloper was £5 a day. In 1703 the fine was raised to £20 on each conviction. The authorities, it is true, acted capriciously in the matter, sometimes shutting their eyes to incursions from outside, and sometimes encouraging informers to prosecute, and convicting all and sundry. Minutes exist of several foreigners' shops being "shut down," and the goods therein seized to defray the penalties; while the dealings of "one foreigner with another" in the city were presented by one grand jury as a great grievance to legitimate traders. In 1695 William Bonny, a printer, was permitted to set up business, the Chamber believing that a printing house "might be useful"; but he was forbidden to sell books. In 1700 a watchmaker was allowed to open a shop on presenting a "curious watch and dyall to be set up in the Tolzey," and undertaking "to keep the same in repair during his life." In the same year the Council empowered the mayor, "there being a confederacy among the cooks now in the city," to confer the freedom on any "able cooks" that might come down from London; the freedom being also granted to an interloping brushmaker, because there was no other in Bristol. The applications of other strangers were rejected, or such heavy fines were imposed for admission to the burgess roll as to be practically prohibitive. Many other restraints on business, mostly imposed by the incorporated trades of the city, affected the citizens themselves, and must have operated grievously. Before commencing business on his own account, a man was required to serve seven years' apprenticeship in Bristol to a member of his trading company. No shopkeeper not being a tailor was allowed to make or sell linen or woollen stockings. A skinner was forbidden to buy skins used by the trades of whitetawers and glovers. No glover was to make points, and no pointmaker was to make gloves. No carpenter was to meddle with the work of a joiner, and vice versâ. Neither joiners nor carpenters were to furnish customers with locks, bolts, hinges, etc., or to make use of any tools, save those made by the Smiths' Company. No one except a member of the Cutlers' Company was permitted to sell a knife. Articles produced by suburban joiners and carpenters, including rough boards and planks, were forbidden to enter the city. A similar law interdicted the admission of casks and washing pails. No butcher was to cook meat for sale. No victualler was allowed to buy country bread, or even to bake in his own house. Tilers were forbidden to lend a ladder to a carpenter or mason. No baker or barber was to open two shops. Interloping artisans from the neighbouring districts, and enterprising country youths seeking to raise themselves by exchanging a rural for a town life, but unable to pay an apprentice fee, were hounded out of the city as soon as they were discovered, and people harbouring such "inmates" were prosecuted. The law which prevented a trader or an artisan from changing his occupation for a more eligible one was common to the whole kingdom, but was not the less onerous. Under an Act of Elizabeth such a change could not be made without passing through a second apprenticeship of seven years, and the members of the trading companies were always on the alert to maintain this preposterous restriction on individual energy.

The exclusive monopolies which the trading community, in a short-sighted and erroneous view of its true interests, sought to establish for its own profit, do not appear more reasonable when one considers the difficulties which then existed in travelling from place to place, and the consequent immobility of the poorer classes of Englishmen. An account book of the Gore family, of Flax Bourton, shows that a public coach, one of the earliest known, was running between Bristol and London in 1663. The journey occupied three days in summer, and probably four or five in winter. The fare was 25s. Soon after 1700, "flying" coaches, in the summer months only, made the journey in two days by starting at two o'clock in the morning. No greater speed was attempted for upwards of half a century, for in 1754, the Bristol flying machine, setting off at the same hour, did not reach London until the night of the following day. There were then three of those vehicles weekly, and they were the only coaches on the road. As they carried no more than six passengers each, the aggregate conveyed in the summer half-year, supposing them to have been always full, did not exceed the number often transported in an ordinary railway train. A few additional persons of the poorer class were conveyed by wagons, one of which, with a load of two tons, required seven or eight draught horses; while the maximum distance covered in a day was twenty miles. In many districts the rate of travelling was somewhat slower.

Bristolians were thus in 1700 practically as far from the county towns of Somerset and Gloucestershire as they now are from Paris, and as far from Edinburgh as they are now from California. And the perils to life and property were certainly greater on the short journeys than they now are on the long ones. As robbers swarmed on every highway, travellers armed themselves on setting out as if they were going to battle, and a blunderbuss was as indispensable to a coachman as his whip. Taking all these facts into account, one cannot be amazed at the stay-at-home propensities of Bristolians. But why should they have dreaded greater restlessness on the part of their neighbours, whose movements were restrained by the same causes? The state of the highroads, even in the richest parts of the kingdom, cannot be fully realised at the present day. Their extreme narrowness is brought to light by an Act of 1691, which required local surveyors to make highways between market towns "eight foot wide at the least," the minimum breadth for "causeways for horses" being fixed at "three foot." Narrowness, however, was not their worst fault. Nothing was more common than for a coach to stick fast in its journey, and for a dozen horses or oxen to be called in for its rescue. The writer of "A Step to the Bath," published in 1700, stated that a portion of the London road between Marlborough and Chippenham was got over in winter by the coaches at the rate of two miles in three hours. The risk of breakdowns on all the highways may be inferred from the fact that a box of wheelwright's tools was carried by every coach. In 1702, when Queen Anne visited Bristol, the chief road from Bath was in so founderous a condition that the royal carriages had to make a detour to Kingswood by way of Newton St. Loe. A few months later, when the Queen's husband travelled from Windsor to Petworth, one of his attendants recorded that "the last nine miles of the way cost us six hours to conquer them," nearly every carriage in the procession being overturned at least twice. The road from Bristol to Brislington was frequently represented to the Common Council as dangerous to life. It was only seven feet wide at Temple Gate, and on one occasion Sir Abraham Elton narrowly escaped drowning near Totterdown, through his carriage encountering a coach at a point where two vehicles could not pass each other. Other instances of the difficulty of locomotion will be given in the course of these annals.

From what has been already said, the reader will find an

explanation of the undoubted fact that the Bristolians of
1700 never dreamt of travelling merely for recreation or
amusement. A large majority of the citizens lived and
died without having lost sight for even half a dozen times of
their familiar church towers. Nobody then went to bathe
in the Bristol Channel, unless he was under the apprehension of having been bitten by a mad dog. A taste for the
grander beauties of Nature, or for the architectural masterpieces of the Middle Ages, had not arisen even amongst the
educated and wealthy; and if a tradesman had been invited
to visit the Wye at Tintern, the rocks at Cheddar, or the
ruins of Glastonbury, he would have regarded the proposal
as that of a lunatic or a Papist. (Even so late as 1752 a
writer in the *Gentleman's Magazine* observed that a Londoner
would no more think of travelling in the West of England
for pleasure than of going to Nubia.) Resolutely confining
themselves within the city walls, the inhabitants consequently sought their amusements during the summer
evenings in the neighbourhood of their dwellings. The
Corporation had stated festivities at this period, in which
the public may have taken a certain share. The mayor and
his colleagues paid a yearly visit to Earl's Mead, for what
would now seem the preposterous purpose of fishing in the
Froom; and mighty was the feasting that took place over
the captured perch and eels. On another autumn day, the
worshipful body, headed by the city trumpeters, and greeted
by the bells of Redcliff, proceeded gravely to Treen Mills,
to witness the sport of duck-hunting on the pool now
covered by Bathurst Basin. From the copious potations
which took place in honour of this pastime it may be conjectured that the civic magnates returned in scarcely so
dignified a manner as they set out. The duck-hunting was
followed by the perambulation of the city bounds, when those
allured by invitations to partake in the carousal had often
to pay for their rashness by being ingloriously "bumped"
against the boundary stones. The inspection of the water
limits, a rarer ceremony, was, if the weather proved favourable, an event never to be forgotten by the junior members
of the Council, who saw the Holmes and the half score of
hovels composing Weston-super-Mare for the first time in
their lives. If "rude Boreas" was wicked enough to mingle
in the festivity, their recollection of the "voyage" was
doubtless acuter still. Although precise evidence is wanting
until a later period, it is probable that previous to 1700 a
horse race took place yearly on Durdham Down, then almost

covered with furze, and shunned by the citizens at ordinary times owing to the frequency of robberies and outrages. A more common amusement was cock-fighting, which was patronised and chiefly supported by the county gentry, but was popular with all classes. In 1656 Parson Allambrigge, of Monkton Farleigh, fought a main of cocks with a neighbour, and was so delighted by his victory that he recorded it in the parish register; while in 1700 a gentleman named Richards noted in his diary that he visited Wimborne School to see the cock-fight annually held by the boys with the approval of their masters. The city cockpit, according to Mr. Richard Smith, was in a court in Back Street; but there was one in the Pithay, another in Redcliff, a fourth in Temple, and a fashionable one at the Ostrich Inn, Durdham Down. The stakes at the last-named were generally about five guineas a fight, and from 30 to 50 guineas for the concluding battle. Returning to every-day life, the City Marsh, planted with numerous rows of trees, and made cheerful at high tides by the movements of the shipping, had long been the favourite promenade, and at least one deceased lover of the spot had bequeathed a yearly rent-charge for keeping it in order. It had also the attraction of a bowling-green and tavern, constructed by public subscription after the fall of Puritanism, where grave and reverend fathers of the city were wont to take their pleasure. But in the spring of 1700 masons and bricklayers had invaded the quiet meadow, and the first steps were taken towards constructing a handsome square of mansions, worthy of the growing wealth of Bristol merchants. The closing of the bowling-green, necessitated by the operations, largely profited other places of the same character, of which there were several. There was a bowling-green in the Pithay, near the City Assembly Room, which was also placed in that oddly chosen nook. There was another bowling-green in St. James's Barton, another (then or soon after) at Redcliff Hill, another at Wapping, another, chiefly for visitors, at the Hot Well, and many more at the suburban taverns. A tennis-court, established in Broad Street, seems to have completed the list of public resorts. But many citizens had private greens adjacent to their dwellings. For although the original builders of the city had been so parsimonious in setting out the public thoroughfares, they had generally allowed ample space for gardens in the rear of dwellings. In 1700 some houses on the north side of Wine Street had gardens extending to the bank of the Froom.

Mr. W. H. Wills informs me that there was a bowling-green behind the old mansion in Redcliff Street in which his father was born, now covered by one of the manufactories of the firm. The mansions on the west side of Small Street possessed large plots of garden ground at the back. The orchards and gardens pertaining to houses in Lewin's Mead are mentioned in many legal documents. Reference will afterwards be made to a summer house and garden at the rear of Baldwin Street, and old maps show that the same conditions prevailed in many quarters now gorged with warehouses and offices. Indeed, a little before this date, one of the corporate books speaks of a mow of hay standing at the back of a house in Halliers' Lane (Nelson Street), and of another haystack near Old Market Street, which affords striking evidence of the semi-rural condition of those neighbourhoods. As regards indoor amusements for the winter months, the city had little to boast of. At some period between the Restoration and the Revolution, a theatre was erected on the south side of the bridge, on ground now occupied by Bath Street; and a company of comedians made its appearance from time to time. But the immorality of the dramas then popular in London scandalized soberminded Bristolians, and shortly before the Revolution the play-house was converted into a dissenting chapel. Performances were still permitted in St. James's parish during the great fair, but the Corporation, after compensating the sheriffs for the loss of fees derived from this source, notified in the *London Gazette* for July 2nd, 1702, that "acting plays, interludes, or exposing poppets" was for the future forbidden. Billiard tables were sometimes introduced; but the magistrates promptly ordered their suppression, and imposed fines on their owners. Evening concerts were the invention of a later age; and although the Corporation maintained a band of musicians, or waits, their only recorded performances were at public ceremonies, which may have been supplemented by some nocturnal fantasias at Christmas. Thus the only source of gaiety in the monotonous winter season lay in occasional reunions in the Assembly Room, where the young danced jigs and minuets, while their elders relaxed in "whisk" and card games now forgotten. The entertainment began before the modern hour of dinner, and the dissipation was over before a modern ball has commenced.

The diversions of the lower classes, if diversions they should be called, were more varied than those of their betters. The poor witnessed the horse-racing; they had their own cock-fighting, cock-throwing, and duck-hunting; and at the revels which took place yearly in all the suburban districts they rejoiced in backsword fighting, cudgel playing, climbing greased poles for legs of mutton, and hunting pigs with soaped tails; while young women ran races for smocks, or boxed for money. For their especial pleasure, it may be presumed, the Corporation provided an occasional bull-bait. The civic audit for 1697 records a payment for a bull rope, and that of the following year contains an item, "Paid for a collar to bait bulls in the Marsh, 6s." Prize-fighting, in which Bristolians took a deep interest, and often displayed exceptional skill and endurance, also had the patronage of wealthy citizens, and was always in season. But it was to the local courts of justice that the labouring community were indebted for the most frequent interludes in the dulness of a life of toil. In 1703 the Corporation, renewing an old by-law, ordered that the authorities of each ward should "take care" that the stocks of each parish were kept in good order. Those instruments did not rust from want of work. Men and women convicted of drunkenness, or of profane swearing, and barbers caught shaving customers on a Sunday, were condemned to detention in the stocks, sometimes for as long as six hours at a stretch. Being wholly defenceless while thus entrammelled, the culprits were often the victims of the hard-hearted crowd which assembled to pelt them. After a quarter sessions court, again, prisoners convicted of cheating or petty thieving were—females as well as males—stripped naked to the waist and whipped at the cart's tail through several streets, or lashed at the whipping-post in Wine Street, or set up in the pillory in the same thoroughfare, in which latter case, if the mob was malevolent, a luckless wretch was in danger of being killed outright by missiles. Persons convicted of lewdness were, "by the ancient custom of the city," say the records, set backwards upon a horse, and paraded about for the delectation of the multitude. Women found guilty of "common scolding" were punished by being dragged to the Wear, thrust into the city ducking-stool, and plunged into the Froom amidst jeering acclamations. Finally, as the result of a giol delivery, murderers and the worst class of thieves were compelled to walk to the gallows on St. Michael's Hill to suffer death. These executions were frightfully numerous; on two occasions within the space of twenty years five unhappy creatures were hanged in a batch. For various crimes, the punishment of women was death by burning. On the 15th of June, 1695, according to a local calendar, a woman, a shopkeeper in Temple Street, was burnt for coin clipping; but Mr. Seyer alleges, on the authority of another manuscript, that she escaped from Newgate before the day fixed for her execution. A girl of fourteen years, for murdering her mistress, was burnt in London in 1712. A woman, who had murdered her husband, suffered at Gloucester in 1753; another for the same crime perished in Somerset in 1765; and a girl, eighteen years old, for murdering her mistress, underwent the same fate at Monmouth in 1764. The witches remain to be mentioned. In 1700 there were few Bristolians who were not in dread of them, and such apprehensions were common amongst cultivated Englishmen. The contemporary Bishop of Gloucester, according to Bishop Kennet (Lansdowne MSS., British Museum), avowed his belief not merely in witches, but in fairies; and John Wesley, long after this date, declared that non-believers in witchcraft were little better than infidels. In 1683 three women were hanged at Exeter for witchcraft. A wizard was tried about the same date at Taunton, and was rescued from death only by the sceptical ingenuity of the judge, Lord Guilford. In 1701 Luttrell records in his diary that a woman narrowly escaped conviction as a witch in London, the prosecutor's perjury being discovered, apparently, in court. In 1702 a so-called witch perished at Edinburgh, then the seat of a Parliament, and the chief centre of Scotch learning and science. And two more women were executed at Northampton in 1705. In or about the latter year a man named Silvester, in Bristol, fell under such deep suspicion of unholy arts that he prudently disappeared before his neighbours could take action (Stewart's MS. Annals, Bodleian Lib.). So late as 1730, at Frome, a poor old woman, suspected of being a witch, was, by the advice of a "cunning man," thrown into a pool and drowned by twenty of her neighbours, in the presence of 200 persons, who made no attempt to save her life. To sum up what has been said respecting the punishments of the age, it seems certain that the frequency and brutalising character of the legal spectacles aggravated the vicious instincts of the ignorant population, and exasperated the evils they were devised to correct.

A brief account of the corporate body and of the Cathedral dignitaries may bring this review to a close. The evident intention of the early charters of the city, and especially of that of Edward III., was to place the power of electing the local government in the hands of the free burgesses, or community at large. But by later grants solicited from the Crown the Corporation had gradually acquired the right of self-election and become wholly irresponsible. As was natural, its pride grew in proportion with its power. In the manuscripts of Archbishop Sancroft, preserved at the Bodleian Library, is some curious information respecting the arrogance of the city authorities. About 1679 they quarrelled with the dean and chapter of the Cathedral, because that body refused to give the Corporation precedence in the "bidding prayer" over the Church and the bishops. In 1681 the dispute was still raging, the Corporation claiming a right to have the state sword placed erect in the choir, while the Cathedral authorities wished it to be laid on a cushion—as was done at York, through a compromise effected by Charles I. Bishop Goulston, who sends this information to the Primate, adds that the mayor had just set off for London, and begged the archbishop's interest in support of various requests he was about to make to the Government, one of them being that Bristol should in future have a Lord Mayor. (The civic petitions were all rejected; but, to soften the disappointment, the mayor, Thomas Earle, and one of the sheriffs, John Knight, were presented to the king, and received the honour of knighthood.) At the assizes in the following year a violent struggle between the city and capitular authorities was about to take place in the Cathedral respecting the state sword, when Chief Justice North, urged by the bishop, induced the mayor and his retinue to retire sulkily into the palace until the conclusion of the service. The dispute was at last settled by the interposition of the bishop and the two judges of assize; it being arranged that the sword might be borne erect into the choir, but was there to be "turned down upon a cushion, and not erected or set up." But it will be seen hereafter that the Corporation, taking fresh offence with the dean and chapter, and hankering after increased ostentation, treated themselves to a private chapel, where they could fix their own ceremonial. The arbitrary dismissals and nominations of civic functionaries by the last two kings of the house of Stewart have been already mentioned. At the Revolution the Corporation was emancipated from regal control, and the system of self-election was revived. Nevertheless, a remarkable and now inexplicable change soon took place in the political composition of the chamber. In 1690 the Council

was described by Sir Thomas Earle as "a nest of Jacobites," which is not surprising when one remembers that the Whig element had been nearly eliminated in the reign of Charles II. Sir Thomas Earle had just been expelled from the Council by a great majority of his colleagues, professedly for having written offensively of the mayor and reflected injuriously on the Corporation, but really because he had drawn the attention of the Government to the disloyal designs of the chief magistrate and his Jacobite colleagues. Sir Thomas regained his seat by appealing to the Court of King's Bench; and after this defeat the high Tories lost ground in the Chamber, perhaps from inability to find eligible recruits. New members being generally drawn from the supporters of the Revolution settlement, the Jacobite party was in a few years reduced to insignificance. It cannot be said, however, that the ascendancy of the Whigs brought about any improvement in the government of the city. As before, the Corporation, which was mainly comprised of a narrow oligarchy of mercantile families, though drawing what was then considered the large average income of about £2,700 from the civic estates, practically repudiated its duties whilst tenaciously asserting its rights. The work of paving, scavenging, lighting, and watching the streets was thrown upon the inhabitants. (The efficiency of the cleansing operations may be judged by the fact that St. Stephen's Vestry paid 4s. a week for scavenging in 1690, whilst St. Leonard's parish got the work performed for £6 a year.) Now and then, when a thoroughfare like the Old Market was reported to be almost impassable, owing to the inefficacy of the by-law requiring house-owners to pave half the width of the street in front of their property, no matter whether that width was 15 feet or 100, the Chamber doled out a few pounds towards the repairs. Similar donations were made towards mending the roads leading from the city gates, the state of which was almost continually complained of as perilous to life and limb. But the Council held large trust funds specifically bequeathed to afford help in such contingencies. With respect to lighting, the Corporation was less liberal. Its contribution towards the protection of the streets is recorded in 1700 under the following item:—
"Paid for repairing the city lanthorn, 3s." (This instrument, furnished with a candle, served for "enlightening the Tolzey.") Watching devolved upon the inhabitants of the twelve wards, who until 1700, when a new Act was obtained for improving the service, had paid a small rate to provide

wages for a solitary old man in their respective districts. Scavenging was delegated to the parochial officers, who, as far as possible, delegated it to the elements. The repair of the quays of the port devolved upon the Merchants' Company, to whom the wharfage dues had been transferred for that purpose. The city gaol was rebuilt in 1691 by the Chamber, but a rate was levied on the citizens to defray the expense. The corporate revenue being thus relieved of. every important public burden, the Chamber applied it, as was the custom of similar bodies in other towns, to the maintenance of civic magnificence and revelry. A large staff of marshals, sergeants, yeomen, and clubmen, armed with maces, swords, and partisans, and finely apparelled, preceded and followed the mayor on public occasions, when he was always arrayed in a stately robe, gold chain, and gauntlets, and accompanied by his sword-bearer. The etiquette of the Corporation was as fastidious as that of a Court. On the great Church festivals, during the assizes, and on certain political anniversaries, the mayor and aldermen blazed out in scarlet attire; at other seasons they appeared in black robes trimmed with fur; at others again in black gowns trimmed with satin. The Great Sword, the Pearl Sword, the Mourning Sword were each paraded on certain special days; but there were other days when they were all out of place. The business of getting a new mayor into office, and an old mayor out of it, involved a prodigious complication of minute courtesies and ceremonies. It is almost needless to add that every civic incident was the occasion of more or less conviviality. Whatever was going on, much progress could not be made without a festive lubrication. Once a year the mayor and aldermen held a manor court at Portishead, and a supply of claret and sack (with sometimes "half a groce" of tobacco pipes) was sent down for their entertainment; yet a "refresher" was needed at Failand Inn both on setting out and returning, and a final booze took place at Rownham before the party re-entered the city. The Chamber was entitled to a banquet after every meeting; the aldermen had a feast after every quarter session. If a committee were appointed, creature comforts were essential to its deliberations. An important document could not be signed, or a contract entered into, without the assistance of "refreshments." When an address was drawn up in 1702, to congratulate Queen Anne on her accession, the mayor and aldermen incontinently adjourned to drink wine at the Raven tavern in High Street. When the same dignitaries assembled a few weeks later to proclaim war against France, visits were paid to six different taverns in various parts of the city, about two gallons of sherry being drunk at each. And a few weeks later still, when they accompanied Mr. Colston in an inspection of Queen's Elizabeth's School, a supply of liquor was at once commanded. On the proclamation and coronation of a new sovereign, the juice of the grape flowed in copious streams; and every royal birthday was similarly celebrated. The entertainment of the judges and of distinguished visitors, which was worthy of the city's fame for hospitality, was almost the only other item of expenditure in ordinary years. The salaries of the civic officials were trivial, the town clerk receiving £20, the recorder £20, the sword-bearer £40, the chamberlain £100, the coroners £6 13s. 4d. each, the vice-chamberlain £14, and the keeper of Bridewell £20 yearly, some other officers being chiefly paid by fees. But it repeatedly happened—notably between 1690 and 1700— that the corporate income did not suffice to defray the prodigal expenditure of the city magnates. Although no evidence of public feeling on the subject has come down to us, it is scarcely possible that the inhabitants can have looked with affection and respect on a body which, through love of parade and feasting, had become indifferent to the duties for which it was created. At a later period the indignation of the citizens became manifest enough.

Side by side with this exclusive corporation had recently been established an institution of a representative character —namely, the Incorporation of the Poor, for which the city was mainly indebted to the exertions of an able and thoughtful Bristol merchant, John Cary. Though not strictly within the limits of this work, a sketch of its foundation will be useful to elucidate subsequent events. During the war with France the local clothing trade had been much depressed, and many weavers, through want of work, had been reduced to pauperism, causing a serious increase in the rates. Much litigation, moreover, arose respecting the "settlements" of many of the people seeking relief, for as each parish administered its own poor rates, each was anxious to evade additional burdens. Whilst the subject was occupying public attention, Cary issued a pamphlet— one of the first published in Bristol since the civil war— suggesting the erection of a central workhouse, in which able-bodied paupers might be provided with and be compelled to work, the infirm economically maintained, and the young trained to fit them for a life of honest labour, "and not be bred up in all manner of vice as they now are." To effect these ends the projector, propounding an idea which was to bear fruit over the whole kingdom nearly a century and a half later, urged that "the rates of the city being all united in a common fund" would be "enough to carry on the good work." Mr. Cary's scheme having been approved by the Corporation as well as by a public meeting of the citizens (the earliest recorded), a petition was presented to the House of Commons in February, 1696, and an Act passed in the course of the session. Under its provisions four "guardians" were soon after elected by the ratepayers of each ward, and these representatives, with the mayor and aldermen, who were *ex-officio* guardians, held their first meeting in May, in St. George's Chapel, in the Guildhall, when Samuel Wallis, mayor, a warm supporter of Cary, was elected governor, and Alderman William Swymmer deputy governor. Preliminary discussions and inquiries occupied the following months. The yearly amount to be raised by rates was fixed at £2,370 under the terms of the Act, being the alleged average outlay of the previous three years. Several parishes had maintained poorhouses, but none of the buildings were found eligible for a general workhouse. The Corporation, however, granted the loan of a house called Whitehall, adjoining Bridewell, which was ordered to be fitted up for the reception of 100 girls, to be employed in carding and spinning wool. The guardians were thus quietly proceeding with the work devolving upon them when they were smitten with sudden and somewhat ridiculous impotence by an unforeseen incident. The mayor's term of office having expired, he was succeeded in the chief magistracy by one John Hine, who was as antagonistic to the guardians as his predecessor had been helpful. Under the Act, the mayor's signature was indispensable to certain formal documents required for putting the new machinery in motion; but Hine flatly refused to sign them; and nothing remained for the guardians but to fold their hands for a twelvemonth. When the obstructive's term of office had expired, operations were resumed with renewed vigour; several prominent citizens offered loans to furnish Whitehall; a master of that workhouse was elected at a salary of £10, and a committee was appointed to treat for the purchase of "the Mint"—in other words, the mansion built by the Norton family in St. Peter Street, which, after having been many years a sugar

D

house, had been hired by the Government in 1696 and 1697 for carrying out in this district the great work of restoring the silver currency. In June, 1698, the Government having consented to surrender its occupancy, the house was purchased for £800 from its owners, Edward Colston, Richard Beecham, Sir Thomas Day and Nathaniel Day, and the guardians held their first court in the building on the 30th October. In the meantime another difficulty had arisen in the working of the new system; the overseers of the city parishes, annoyed at the loss of their former prestige as dispensers of relief, having refused to collect the rates assessed by the guardians. A singular expedient was adopted to defeat this manœuvre. A Bill was then before Parliament for establishing a workhouse at Tiverton on the Bristol model. Into this Bill the guardians contrived to obtain the insertion of a clause (at a cost of £7 9s. 4d.) which dispensed with the signature of a reactionary mayor like Hine, and enabled distresses to be levied on recalcitrant overseers. The hospital, as the new workhouse was styled, now rapidly progressed. A hundred boys were received, and the making of fustians and cantaloons began; "a pair of stocks and a whipping post" being set up in the yard, and a place of detention, called "purgatory," garnished with chains and locks, being provided in the house, for the encouragement of the inmates. As the outlay was considerable, a subscription, headed by the Members of Parliament for the city, was started to reduce the burden on the ratepayers, and in two years about £1,700 were received. In 1700 was published a pamphlet, dedicated to both Houses of Parliament, briefly recording the progress of the Bristol experiment. From a copy of this rare tract, now in the British Museum, and fairly attributable to Cary, it appears that the boys were earning £6 weekly, besides being fitted for an honest life; while the aged and impotent were decently maintained. "The success," adds the writer, "hath answered our expectation; and the face of our city is changed already." (Some years later, the guardians asserted in a memorial to the Council that the amount of the new poor rate did not much exceed the sum previously extorted from the citizens by strolling beggars.) Presently, the master of the workhouse reported that he had "kept the fair" with the cantaloons made by the boys, who had produced more than could be sold. The manufactory was not a pecuniary success, however, and the guardians will presently be found discussing other projects for dealing with young paupers. The spinning of woollen by the girls at Whitehall was also unprofitable, and in June, 1700, it was resolved to employ half the inmates in spinning cotton yarn. In the same month the guardians bethought them that a little education might not be amiss, whereupon a house adjoining St. Peter's Hospital was bought for £160 and ordered to be converted into a school; but the number of boys taught to write was for several years limited to 20. That Cary's project as a whole excited much attention and was widely approved is sufficiently attested by the fact of its being speedily adopted at Norwich, Exeter, and other industrial centres.

There is not much to be said respecting the ecclesiastical dignitaries of the city. They came, indeed, but little under the notice of the inhabitants, for they were rarely in residence. The estates originally destined for the endowment of the bishopric having been for the most part appropriated by rapacious courtiers, the income of the see was less than that of many country rectories. Amongst the voluminous papers of Archbishop Sancroft, already referred to, is a scheme for augmenting the revenue, from which it appears that the fixed receipts of the bishop were about £360, from which had to be deducted £150 for certain charges, leaving a net receipt of 200 guineas. (So late as 1750 the clear income was only about £350.) In a letter in the archives of St. Paul's Cathedral, dated 1677, Bishop Carlton declares that his see was so beggarly as to make him a beggar likewise, and that unless the king would render him some additional support " the dignity must fall to the ground, and I with it." The bishopric, in fact, was generally accepted by an ambitious clergyman only because he hoped, by courtly arts, to make it a stepping-stone to one of the prizes of the Church. In the meantime, such occupants pressed for sinecures and preferments that could be held with the see. At the time when Carlton was lamenting his poverty (and also harrying local Dissenters) he held a rich prebend at Durham, and a valuable rectory which he never visited. After his intolerance had won him the well-endowed see of Chichester from Charles II., he set up a pack of hounds, and hunted foxes instead of Nonconformists. Bishop Lake, who held Bristol shortly afterwards, had a prebend at York, and a well-endowed rectory in Lancashire. Bishop Trelawny, whose elevation, according to contemporary critics, was due to his military exploits during the Monmouth rebellion, who continually "swore like a trooper," and who in later life was a zealous canvasser at county elections, held many preferments *in commendum*, and often asked for more. Bishop Hall, who held the see in 1700, was Master of Pembroke College, Oxford, where he, of course, resided. His successor, John Robinson, enjoying also the deanery of Windsor, was a member of the Government as Lord Privy Seal, and acted as principal English diplomatist in arranging the Peace of Utrecht. As a natural consequence, the episcopal residence, which ought to have been a refuge of literature set in a wilderness of counting-houses, was generally deserted. Besides the scantiness of the income, there seems to have been another reason why Bristolians saw so little of the prelates who followed each other in bewildering succession. In Bishop Tanner's MSS, at Oxford, is a petition from Bishop Goulston to Charles II., written about 1683, complaining that the dean and chapter had lately disposed of the "Canon's Little Marsh" (the ground extending from the back of the Cathedral to the Froom) for the building and repairing of ships, and, the workshops being contiguous to the episcopal palace, "the noise and stench is (*sic*) such an intolerable nuisance that your petitioner is not able to live in any part of his house with any health or comfort." The king appears to have treated the grievance with his customary indifference. Perhaps he knew that the bishops and the capitular body of Bristol lived habitually at variance. The members of the chapter had each a substantial mansion near the Cathedral, but another of Tanner's papers, of about 1684, states that not one of them was in residence. The incomes, it is true, were not large. The fixed capitular revenue in 1700 was about £700, out of which the dean received £100, and each of the six prebendaries £20; but this did not include the fines for the renewal of leases, which were sometimes considerable. In 1700 the deanery was held by a man named George Royse, Provost of Oriel College, Oxford, whose non-residence cannot have been a misfortune. Bishop Kennet states that this worthy, "in his latter days, sank much into drinking, and kept an ill woman, who came to Windsor and waited with him when he attended at chapel to Queen Anne" (Lansdowne MSS., British Museum). The extreme poverty of the city incumbencies at this period will be noticed hereafter.

On the 1st January, 1701, in pursuance of an ancient yearly custom, the sheriffs of Bristol waited upon the mayor, and presented him with a new scabbard for the state sword usually borne before him. The "scafford," as it is called by Peter Mugleworth, sword-bearer, was always of silver gilt, and appears to have cost the sheriffs about £80. It is supposed that each mayor, on his retirement, retained this ornament as a souvenir of his civic grandeur. The sheriffs, in return for the gift, were each entitled to a pair of gold-fringed gloves, costing about £20. On the Sunday after the presentation, the "scafford" was carried to the mayor's parish church, and on the two following Sundays to the parish churches of the sheriffs, to rejoice the eyes of the respective congregations.

The opening of the century was marked in Bristol by the introduction of an improved system of lighting the streets. For the previous forty years this service had been imposed by the Corporation upon such of the inhabitants as it thought fit to select. The householders so burdened, between 500 and 600 in number, were severally required to hang a lanthorn and lighted candle at their doors from 6 until 9 o'clock at night "during the winter season," artificial light during the remainder of the night and throughout the summer months being deemed a superfluous luxury. Although defaulters had been threatened with a fine of 3s. 4d. for each infraction of this order, its end had never been satisfactorily attained, and in some districts there were practically no lights at all. In 1700, when the Corporation was seeking legislative powers to suppress nuisances in the Avon and Froom, which, said the preamble of the Bill, were the receptacles of most of the ashes and filth of the city, it occurred to some one that the opportunity should be seized to institute a better lighting system, and three clauses were tacked to the scheme whilst it was passing through Parliament. They enacted that every householder paying 2d. per week towards the relief of the poor should, from Michaelmas to Lady Day, hang out a lighted lanthorn at his street door from dusk to midnight; but it was provided that if any parish agreed to pay a lighting rate, and erected as many lamps as were approved by the justices, the parishioners should be relieved of the personal burden. It was characteristic of the Corporation that while lights were required to be maintained before churches, and buildings like the Merchants' Hall, the Act was silent respecting the Guildhall and the Council House. A little time was needed to put the parochial machinery in operation, but the new arrangement was at work in January, 1701. On the 23rd of that month the Common Council confirmed the following report from the mayor and aldermen: " The parishioners of Christ Church having at their charges set upp a larg fair double glass lamp at the corner of their church for enlightening the streets there, and applying for some contribution towards the same, which request the maior and aldermen thought reasonable, for that the chamber, which used to be at the charge of a lanthorn and candle at the end of High Street for enlightening the Tolzey is by means of that lamp eased of that charge, the said lamp affording far greater light than can be expected from many candles in lanthorns, and being of great credit and reputacōn to the city, Do think proper that the yearly sum of 50s. should be allowed." An early arrangement for parochial lighting under the Act further illustrates the corporate idea of what was needful for the public convenience. The parishioners of St. Stephen's escaped the personal burden on consenting to pay collectively for twelve lamps in that extensive parish, Prince's Street, Queen Square, and the Quay being allotted two each. The arrangement made for St. Peter's parish is shown by the following invoice, preserved in the Jefferies' collection:—"April ye 1st 1704. Mr. Charles Bearpacker for St. Peter's parish is to Daniel Fry and Wm. Curd Dr. ffor maintaining with Oyl, Lighters, &c., five Lamps, also ½ of one more Lamp and ¾ of another from Xmas last to our Lady Day £6 8s. 4d." It will be observed that lighting was wholly discontinued from the 25th March to the 29th September. The above Act also required householders to sweep the streets twice a week in front of their respective doors; a rate was to be levied for the hiring of scavengers to remove the refuse; and the Corporation was to fix certain places where it should be deposited, the pollution of the rivers being prohibited under penalties.

In the closing months of 1700, the Post Office authorities in London, after being earnestly petitioned by local merchants, counselled the Government to establish a "cross post" from this city to Chester. Up to that time, Bristol letters to Chester, Shrewsbury, Worcester, and apparently Gloucester, had been carried round by London, involving double postage and great delay. The effect of this system had been to throw nearly all the letters into the hands of public carriers, by whose wagons they were conveyed more quickly than by the post-boys and at a cheaper rate. Moved by the success of the cross post from Bristol to Exeter, established in 1697, and producing a "neat profit" of £350 yearly, the Treasury consented to the starting of a similar service to Chester, commencing at Michaelmas, 1700. The people of Cirencester and Exeter, hearing of this concession, hastened to complain of shortcomings affecting themselves. The Devon clothiers had a considerable trade with the wool dealers of Cirencester, which town was served by post-boys riding between Gloucester and London, with a branch mail to Wotton-under-Edge. But there being no postal service of any kind between Bristol and Wotton, correspondence betwixt Exeter and Cirencester had to be sent *viâ* London, and a fortnight elapsed between the despatch of a letter and the receipt of an answer, the result being that not one letter in twenty was sent through the post. All that was needed to shorten the transit from fourteen days to four was to put Bristol in communication with Wotton, the expense being estimated at £30 a year. But the Government declined to comply, and nothing was done. (As a further illustration of the embarrassments of the time, it may be stated that in January, 1701, when some deeds had to be conveyed for execution to Leicester, the Corporation of Bristol was obliged to send its agent, with a servant *and guides*, all on horseback, to the midland town, the journey occupying nearly a fortnight, and costing £10.) Returning to the Chester post, the Post Office reported to the Treasury in March, 1702, that the profit for the first eighteen months had been only £156. The additional expense in future would be about £80 a year, and as the double postages earned when letters went round by London were lost, they apprehended a net diminution in the revenue. The accounts of Henry Pyne, the Bristol postmaster, appended to the report in the State Papers, show that he had received £168 for letters by this post, whilst his expenses had been £60.

This mention of the Bristol postal official appropriately introduces a document describing the humble dimensions of the establishment under his control. In the bargain books of the Corporation is the following memorandum :—" 22 June, 1700. Then agreed by the surveyors of the city lands with Henry Pine, Deputy Postmaster, that he the said Henry Pine shall have hold and enjoy the ground whereon now stands a shedd having therein four severall shopps scituate in All Saints Lane, and as much more ground at the lower end of the same shedd as that the whole ground shall contain in length twenty seven foot, and to contain in breadth from the outside of the churchyard wall five foot and a half outward into the lane, with liberty to build upon the same for conveniency of a post office, (viz.) the first story to come forth into the said lane to the extent of that ground and no farther, and the second story to have a truss of 18 inches over the lane, or more, as the said surveyors shall think fitt, that persons coming to the post office may have shelter from the rain and stand in the dry. To hold the same from Michaelmas next for 50 years absolute under the yearly rent of 30s. clear of taxes." This agreement must have been afterwards modified. Perhaps possession could not be obtained of one of the "shopps," the frontage of which, including the doorway, measured, it will be seen, only about six feet each. (Attorneys' offices were of an equally humble character. By a will dated in May, 1708, an attorney named Martyn Nelme bequeathed to his wife his "office, shed, or penthouse in All Saints' Lane," held by lease from the Corporation.) At all events Pyne paid no rent until Michaelmas, 1705, when 25s. were received by the chamberlain, and "the Posthouse" produced the same yearly sum until 1742, when the rent was raised to £3, for reasons that do not appear.

It will be impossible to notice the innumerable discussions on the badness of the roads which are recorded in the civic records. The first of the century may serve as an example. In February, 1701, the churchwardens of Temple drew attention to the lamentable state of the great road leading "from Temple Gate to the bottom of the hill near Totterdown Castle." (The latter spot probably owed its name to some remains of the defences raised during the Civil War.) The Common Council contributed £20 towards the repairs, and shortly after voted £30 more, owing to the heaviness of the outlay.

In July, 1701, the vestry of St. Nicholas' parish resolved upon demising, upon a lease for three lives, an estate called the Forlorn Hope, near Baptist Mills, purchased by the vestry in 1693, mainly from charity funds, for £590. The estate, which comprised a house and fourteen acres of land, was let in the following month to James Bush, linen dyer, for 40s. a year, in consideration of a payment of £360, and of two guineas (to be spent at a tavern) on the sealing of the lease. A renewal of the term took place on the dropping of a life in 1720, when a fine of £240 was demanded. The land has been in our own time converted into building sites, and the annual ground rents of the property must far exceed the sum which was originally given for the feesimple. With reference to the above provision for a drinking bout, it may be added that no lease was signed or any other parochial business transacted by the vestries of that age without an adjournment to a wine shop. In the St. Nicholas' accounts for 1746-7 is the following entry:— " Paid for wine, and spent with the vestry of St. Leonards, and signing leases £11 17s."—a sum then sufficient to purchase an enormous quantity of liquor.

Attention will be directed at a later period to the capricious treatment of condemned felons by the magistracy of the city. At the gaol delivery in September, 1701, one John Rudge was convicted and sentenced to be hanged for horse-stealing. As he was a lusty young fellow, however, he was shortly afterwards pardoned, on condition of his entering the army! This system of dealing with thieves, which was common during the greater part of the century, accounts for the frequency of violent crimes committed by soldiers quartered in the city.

Amongst the devices for raising money attempted by the impecunious Government of William III. was a tax on births, marriages, and deaths. The birth of a child was taxed upon a sliding scale; the son of a duke brought in £25, and the impost gradually fell to 12s. on each child of persons worth £600 in personal estate, and to 2s. on the infants of labourers. A marriage amongst the commonalty incurred a duty of 2s. 6d., and the charge rose to £50 for the nuptials of a duke. Similarly, the tax on burials varied from £50 to 4s. Paupers were exempt from the impost on births, but not from that on burials. The two last-named burdens were repealed in 1700, but that on marriages continued until 1706. In 1701 the Corporation was applied to by a Government official for the arrears of the burial tax due on account of several Bristol paupers; but the Common Council repudiated its liability, and ordered payment to be made by the poor law guardians.

Another curious Act of Parliament came into operation on the 29th September, 1701, and caused much discontent amongst the fair sex. Since trade with France had reopened in 1696, the use of woollen cloth for female attire, previously universal, had been diminished by a growing taste for foreign silk, and other light material. Bitter complaints of the change in fashion were raised by the clothiers of Bristol and the western counties, who represented to the House of Commons that the popularity of French and Indian tissues threatened ruin to their industry. The clamour forced the Government to take legislative action, and the use of foreign-made silks and calicoes was absolutely prohibited after the above date. Ladies' tastes, however, were not to be changed by Act of Parliament. The smuggling of French silks enormously increased, and it is said that some Bristol mercers, playing on feminine weakness, were adroit enough to pass off large quantities of home-made silks as contraband imports from across the Channel.

A dissolution of Parliament took place in November, when the country was in a flame at the intelligence that Louis XIV. had just acknowledged the son of James II. as rightful King of England. No information can be discovered respecting the election for Bristol, saving that the members returned were Whigs—Sir William Daines, whose mayoralty had ended a few weeks previous, and Colonel Robert Yate, also a former mayor, and a wealthy and public-spirited alderman. The contest for Gloucestershire on this occasion excited intense interest in the political world, and readers of Lord Macaulay's History are aware that his work stops short in the midst of a brilliant account of the struggle. It may be useful, therefore, to state that John Howe, one of the former members, whom Lord Stanhope describes as an insolent and unscrupulous defamer of William III., was defeated by a majority of nearly a thousand. The Parliament had a brief career, the death of the king in the following March necessitating another dissolution. The members for Bristol were re-elected, probably without opposition. Howe again came forward for Gloucestershire, and, although at the bottom of the poll, he was declared duly elected by a sheriff of kindred principles.

Down to this date the Society of Merchant Venturers were content to assemble in what had once been the chapel of St. Clement, at the end of Marsh Street, but which was desecrated in the reign of Edward VI. Having become dissatisfied with this building, the Company, in 1701, erected a new hall of much larger dimensions upon the site and some adjoining vacant ground. In 1721 there was, says Tucker's MS., "a further addition to the grandeur of the hall by pulling down several old tenements and erecting a sett of steps there." A view of this hall, which may have been commodious, but was certainly not ornamental, will be found in Barrett's History. The present front was added in 1790, when the building underwent extensive alterations.

The first house erected in the Marsh (afterwards Queen

Square) was finished during the year 1701. The builder was the Rev. John Reade, D.D., Vicar of St. Nicholas, who, by an agreement with the Corporation dated October 27th, 1699, obtained a lease of the site for five lives, at a rental of 40s., "being 1s. per foot in front," on his undertaking to build a house 40 feet high, with a brick front and stone groins, within two years. This was probably one of the first brick dwellings constructed within the city walls. It is somewhat incomprehensibly described in a later deed as standing at "the east (north?) corner of the east row." Other sites were leased on the same terms, but as the lives fell in pressure was put upon the Corporation for a relaxation of the conditions, and renewals were granted, first for a term of fifty-three years, and afterwards for one of forty years, renewable every fourteen years on payment of a year's rent.

The Merchant Tailors' Almshouse in Merchant Street (then called Marshall Street) was also built in 1701, when the inmates removed from the old hospital of the Company in Marsh Street.

The Quakers of Bristol and the neighbourhood established, in 1699, a boarding school at Sidcot, Somerset, which had a long and prosperous career. The fee for teaching was 20s. annually, 10s. extra being charged for classics. The cost of boarding was £9, but in 1701 complaints were raised that this was excessive, and it appears from the records of the Society of Friends that the charge at their boarding school at Skipton in 1728 was only £8 a year, teaching included.

The accession of Queen Anne was proclaimed early in March, 1702, with the ceremonies customary on such occasions. The disbursements of the Corporation amounted to £21 5s., about £7 of which was "for wine drunk at the Raven"; £2 for "wine at the Bull," and £6 for "wine that the constables drunk." Her Majesty was crowned on the 23rd April, amidst much popular rejoicing; for the late King's excessive attachment to the Dutchmen who had come over with him had caused much discontent, while the devotion to English interests adroitly expressed by Anne in her first speech to her subjects had naturally kindled their enthusiasm. There was a grand corporate procession to the Cathedral, a novel feature amongst the inevitable civic functionaries, city companies, school children, and bands of music, being "twenty four young maidens, dressed in night rails and white hoods, with fans in their hands, being led, as their captain, by a comely young woman, clad in a close white dress, wearing on her head a perriwig and plumed hat, carrying in her hand a half-pike," to the admiration of all spectators. Moreover, there were "twenty four young damsels in sarsnet hoods," armed with gilded bows and arrows; also "the principal citizens' daughters wearing branches of laurel," two of them supporting a gorgeous crown; and finally "Madame Mayoress," and the wives of the aldermen and common councillors, "splendidly apparelled, with the city music sweetly playing before them." The streets, churches, houses, and ships were plentifully decorated. The great guns in the Marsh fired numberless salutes. And for a certain time the conduits, decorated with garlands, ran wine for the delectation of such of the mob as could get at them. In the evening a party of young men, wearing "furbelo'd" white shirts over their clothes, led into the streets an equal number of young women in white waistcoats, red petticoats, night headdresses, and laced hats. These strangely accoutred revellers were followed by other men, bearing an effigy of the Pope, arrayed in glaring robes and gilded tiara, and surrounded by unsaintly counsellors with masks and croziers. Having paraded this mockery to their hearts' content, the populace flung it into one of the numerous bonfires amidst loud acclamations. The Corporation spent £53 2s. 10d. over the day's rejoicings, of which more than three-fifths went for wine, £7 19s. for gunpowder, 2s. for a pound of tobacco, and 7s. 6d. for "hanging the High Cross." Even this demonstration of loyalty seems colourless when compared with the great local event of the year. In August the Queen, who was a constant sufferer from gout, paid a visit to Bath for the purpose of trying the efficacy of the waters. The Corporation lost no time in appointing a committee to wait upon her, with an earnest prayer to visit the city. Her Majesty had had previous experience of the good feeling of the civic body. Some years before, whilst sojourning at Bath, the Common Council had forwarded to the Princess of Denmark a gift of sixty dozen of wine, besides a hogshead of sack sent on to London. Moved, perhaps, by this reminiscence, she received the deputation cordially, and responded to its wishes by graciously consenting to spend a few hours in Bristol. The royal party, occupying thirteen coaches, each with six horses, set out from Bath on the morning of the 3rd September. The only practicable coach-road between the two cities was on the north bank of the Avon; but as the portion between Bath and Kelston was then founderous, while the narrow track by Keynsham was in a still worse condition, the carriages proceeded as far as Newton St. Loe, forded the river at Swinford, and then traversed the usual course through Kingswood. Her Majesty was received at Lawford's Gate by the mayor (John Hawkins) and the rest of the civic functionaries, arrayed in their scarlet paraphernalia. The corporators on this great occasion had mounted on horseback, to the no small tribulation and alarm, we may feel assured, of those unaccustomed to that mode of travelling. Mr. Seyer has copied from a contemporary chronicle so lengthy a description of the subsequent proceedings that it is unnecessary to repeat the details. Her Majesty was conducted into the city amidst the cheering of the multitude lining the way, passed under a gaily ornamented triumphal arch at St. Nicholas' Gate, and descended from her carriage at the " great house " of Sir Thomas Day, at the south end of the bridge. There she dined, having first knighted the mayor, and permitted the mayoress and other ladies and gentlemen to kiss her hand. From a curious note in the minute book of the Gloucestershire Society, it appears that that body postponed its annual feast, and " at the request of the city spared the provision " made for it, in order that her Majesty might be the better entertained. During dinner a salute was fired by 100 guns planted in the Marsh, the cannon of the numerous ships in the harbour adding their tribute to the din. As soon as the repast was over, at five o'clock, the Queen re-entered her carriage, and the royal party set off again by the same route for Bath, which was not reached until long after nightfall. This visit cost the Corporation £466; out of which a firm of vintners got £110, while the baker's bill amounted only to 10s. 6d.—facts which remind one of Falstaff's famous little account. The loan of pewter plates and cups—indicating the furniture of the dinner table—cost £12 12s. The sum of £6 14s. was paid for glasses; " beer from the mayor's brewery " ran up to £11 15s., but only 24s. were spent in " decorating the banqueting hall with flowers." Sir Thomas Day received £22 19s. for the use of his mansion. The oddest item enumerated in the long account is:— " Apothecary, 2s. 4d." What he furnished remains a mystery. To perpetuate the memory of this auspicious day, the mayor and aldermen resolved, on the 10th December, " that the square now building in the Marsh shall be called Queen Square "; and soon afterwards Sir Godfrey Kneller received a commission to paint her Majesty's portrait, for which he was paid £20 in the following summer. In connection with this royal visit, a legend has become attached to an old mansion at Barton Hill, now popularly called "Queen Anne's house," where her Majesty is alleged to have rested previous to entering the city. Such an incident, had it occurred, would scarcely have been omitted in the chronicles of the day. The house is known to have belonged to the mayor, and it is probable that it was selected as a convenient rendezvous for the members of the Corporation whilst awaiting the Queen's arrival.

In the spring of 1702 the dilapidated condition of Foster's Almshouse being reported to the Common Council, it was ordered that the building be taken down and reconstructed, at an expenditure "not to exceed £400." The meanness and narrow accommodation of the new structure were the unavoidable consequences of this resolution. It was wholly swept away in 1883, when the present building was completed.

During the summer of 1702, whilst the great philanthropist, Edward Colston, was temporarily residing in the city (he had been drawn from his house near London in the closing months of the previous year by the fatal illness of his mother), he appears to have acquainted the Corporation with his desire to make a large endowment for local educational purposes. The details are unfortunately lost, for the civic records throw no light upon the precise nature of his communication. That it was deemed of considerable importance seems proved by the fact that he was requested to sit for his portrait to a London artist, who executed the picture still in the Council House. (The cost, including the frame and the case in which it was forwarded, was £17 11s.). Queen Elizabeth's Hospital boys, increased in 1701 to forty, were lodged and taught in the crumbling monastic buildings formerly belonging to the fraternity of "the Gaunts." At a meeting of the Common Council on the 8th August, a resolution was passed setting forth "that Mr. Edward Colston, a very great benefactor to this city by several charities and bounties," had that day proposed to add a further number of boys to those settled in the hospital, and ordering that a deputation should wait upon him with the thanks of the Council. The biographer of Colston has hastily inferred that the "proposal" here spoken of related to an addition of four boys which was temporarily made to the school soon after this time at the cost of the philanthropist. But this supposition seems irreconcilable with the terms of a document which was signed by Colston and several leading citizens on the 26th August, only a few days later. The paper in question contains an undertaking on the part of the signatories to subscribe "towards the pulling down the hospital and rebuilding it convenient for the accommodation of one hundred and twenty poor boys"; and the name of Edward Colston heads the list, with a written promise to give £500. The names of twenty members of the Corporation follow, their donations amounting to £1,400. (The paper was probably drawn up and signed at the school, for an item in the civic accounts, already referred to, shows that the civic body visited the hospital in company with Colston.) It would be absurd to suppose that the parties to this agreement proposed to contribute large sums towards accommodating 120 boys without having reasons for believing that the existing forty scholars were likely to be largely increased. And as Colston certainly made some overture to the Council to furnish funds for the maintenance of fifty or sixty more lads, it seems reasonable to suppose that his "proposal" was then under consideration. Much contempt has been thrown upon the city authorities for the ignorance and indifference to education they are said to have betrayed in declining Colston's offer. But their conduct admits of a worthier interpretation. A body of men who had subscribed £1,400 (which, considering the commercial incomes of the age, would now be equivalent to nearly £5,000) towards enlarged school buildings cannot have been so selfish, churlish, and sordid as has been gratuitously asserted. And when it is remembered that Colston afterwards deliberately excluded from his school the children of Dissenters, and strictly forbade the use, in Temple charity school, of books containing any "tincture of Whiggism," one may not unreasonably assume that, when he proposed to make a munificent addition to the funds of Queen Elizabeth's Hospital, he sought to impose conditions as to the future management of the institution which its governors were justified in rejecting. (To deepen the discredit of the Common Council it has been alleged by the same critic that "their autographs were crosses and unsightly blotches," and that they could see no utility in a school, because "they could not write" themselves. These assertions, when tested by the corporate minute books, which every councillor signed on his admission, only afford another, and unfortunately a needless, proof of the prejudices and blundering that disfigure the censor's work.) The rebuilding of the hospital began in the early months of 1703, when a house was taken for the temporary accommodation of the scholars. In 1705 the Corporation made another arrangement, by which the boys were boarded and educated in St. Peter's Hospital, a weekly allowance of 2*s.* 6*d.* per head being paid for victuals, firing, washing, and lodging. The new and stately buildings adjoining St. Mark's Chapel were finished in the following year, at a cost of about £2,500, of which nearly £500 were drawn from the funds of the hospital, and the boys took possession in September, 1706.

At the summer assizes in 1702 Mr. Justice Powell was entertained at the house of Mr. Alderman Lane, who remitted to the city chamberlain a detailed account of his expenditure during the visit. The items for food show the remarkable cheapness of provisions. For two turkeys, six ducks, four capons, and twelve pullets, the outlay was only £2 3*s.* (Five turkeys and six geese cost 12*s.* 3*d.* in 1708.) A buck cost £2 2*s.* 6*d.*; and fruit, vegetables, and "hartichoaks" £1 4*s.* 3*d.* His lordship's wine-bill amounted to £10 8*s.*, although sherry was then only 7*s.* a gallon; and he required two pounds of tobacco, and two gross (288) pipes. Lemons were 6*s.* a dozen, and 4*s.* 6*d.* were paid for a pound of "choclat." Neither tea nor coffee appears in the bill, which amounted to £28 5*s* 1*d.* The chief justices travelled the circuit in coaches with six horses, but the puisne judges seem to have progressed on horseback, accompanied by a large staff of servants. In 1710 Chief Justice Parker had twenty-one "saddle horses." Food and stabling for the animals were provided by the Corporation, which also paid the farrier for shoeing them and the coachmaker for repairing the carriages, which were always dilapidated, owing to the badness of the roads.

As Bristol was at this time the second city in the kingdom as regarded manufactures and commerce, it was fitting that she should be the first to follow the example of London in the establishment of a newspaper. Such of the local annalists as have not deemed journalism unworthy of the dignity of history have denied the city a newspaper until 1715. As a matter of fact the *Bristol Post-Boy* was published in Corn Street by William Bonny in 1702. A copy of the first number not having been preserved, the precise date of its publication is uncertain. The earliest copy known to be in existence was issued on the 12th August, 1704, and is numbered 91, from which it might be inferred that Bonny started his enterprise in November, 1702. The early printers, however, were singularly careless in numeration. As an example, the *Post-Boy* issued on the 20th March, 1708, was numbered 281, and that published on Sept. 10th, 1709, nearly eighteen months later, bears the number 287. All that can be positively affirmed, therefore, is that the paper was in existence in 1702, or four years before the appearance of the Norwich *Postman*, which historians of the press have hitherto asserted to be the earliest provincial English journal. The publisher of the *Bristol Post-Boy*, William Bonny, has been already briefly mentioned. Having been unfortunate as a London printer, he seems to have thought that a busy port like Bristol presented favourable ground for setting up a press, and his petition for leave to do so was laid before the Common Council in April, 1695. The Chamber, being of opinion that " a printing house would be useful in several respects," conferred the freedom of the city upon him, on condition that he became an inhabitant; but for the protection of the existing booksellers he was restrained from exercising " any other trade but that of a printer." He lost no time in removing from London, but cannot at that time have contemplated the starting of a newspaper; for until May, 1695, when the censorship of the press came unexpectedly to an end, there was no newspaper even in the capital save the official *Gazette*. Bonny's first known production in his new home was a pamphlet on English trade, written by John Cary, to whom the city owes the Incorporation of the Poor. This is dated on the title-page " November, 1695." In the session of Parliament which opened in the same month a Bill was introduced to " regulate printing," whereupon Cary, dreading the revival of restrictions, addressed a letter to the members for the city, desiring them to take measures for safeguarding the only press in Bristol. Mr. Yate, replying for Sir Thomas Day and himself on the 5th December, explained that the object of the Bill was to secure the privilege of printing for towns like York, Bristol, and Exeter. (This correspondence is in the British Museum.) The Bill was fortunately dropped, and the success of the London *Post-Boy* and other papers encouraged Bonny to make a similar adventure here; though he must have proceeded under painful difficulties, for John Dunton, the London bookseller, states that in 1705 he had wholly lost his sight. The *Bristol Post-Boy* was printed on both sides of a coarse and dingy leaf, somewhat less in size than half a sheet of ordinary letter paper. The contents of a number would not suffice to fill three-quarters of a column of a daily journal of our time. No. 91 contains no reference to local events, and only one advertisement. Another extant copy shows that the restriction placed on Bonny by the Corporation had been relaxed or forgotten, for the publisher announces that he buys old rope and "paper stuff," and sells Welsh Prayer-Books, Bibles, paper-hangings, music "with the monthly songs," maps, blank ale licenses, and blank commissions for private men-of-war. On another occasion (May 31st, 1712) he informs the public that he has some "very good Bridgwater peas and large brown paper" for sale, and in 1716 he frequently supplied the Council House with charcoal. The number of May, 1712, is the latest known copy of the *Post-Boy*. If it long survived that date, which is improbable, its printer had to sustain the competition of a more enterprising rival—the *Bristol Postman*, the only known copy of which is dated July 15th, 1713, and numbered 24. The *Postman* was published by Samuel Farley, the earliest of a numerous and puzzling family of printers, "at the house in St. Nicholas' Street, near the church." It marked a great improvement upon Bonny's tiny journal, containing twelve small quarto pages, with pictorial initial letters, and two woodcuts—a postboy and a full-rigged ship—on the title-page. The price was three-halfpence in the city, and twopence when delivered in the country. The deliverers, it may be added, hawked the books, quack medicines, mustard, snuff, etc., advertised in the paper, thus turning an honest penny for their employer. The third local journal, the *Bristol Weekly Mercury*, printed by Henry Greep, made its appearance on the 1st October, 1715. The price was three-halfpence "in town," and the title declares that in point of news it far excels all other papers; but as the latest issue preserved is No. 61, it probably died in infancy. In April, 1725, a new stamp duty of one penny per sheet on newspapers came into force, in consequence of which Farley discontinued the twelve-paged *Postman*, and produced in its place a four-paged journal, entitled *Farley's Bristol Newspaper*, price twopence, "printed at my house near Newgate, in Wine Street." The title of this paper, of which various copies have survived, is accompanied by a view of the city, including old Bristol Bridge. In April, 1727, either the *Mercury* or some other unknown journal ceased to appear, for Farley announced that, "after all ignorant and fruitless attempts of pretenders," his was the only newspaper published in the city.

The printer, as is proved by a handbill in the Record Office, had taken two sons into partnership in or before 1718, but seems to have managed the paper himself. The issue of July 9th, 1737, is styled *Sam. Farley's Bristol Newspaper*. In 1743 the *Bristol Newspaper* had disappeared, the sons had separated, and a curious arrangement appears to have been entered into between them. On the 24th March, 1743–4, for example, was issued *F. Farley's Bristol Journal*, No. 17; and a week later appeared *Farley's Bristol Advertiser*, No. 18. The former was printed by Felix Farley in Castle Green; the latter by "Felix Farley & Co." This alternation of titles continued until the summer of 1746, the last *Advertiser* being issued on the 23rd August, and *F. Farley's Journal* was alone published until the close of 1747. On the 9th January, 1748, the title was changed through some freak to *F. Farley's Advertiser*, but in the following week the printer altered it to *Farley's Bristol Journal*, which was stated to be published by S. and F. Farley, at the Shakespeare's Head in Castle Green, denoting a brief family reconciliation. Soon afterwards the word *Farley* was removed from the title, the paper being styled simply the *Bristol Journal*. (The final separation of the brothers will be recorded under 1752.) The numbering of the journal issued by Felix Farley is bewildering. For about four years it proceeded pretty regularly, though the printer on more than thirty occasions neglected to alter the figures. But on the 14th March, 1747, the issue, which was really the 171st, was called "No. 1"; whilst that of the 18th April following, actually the 176th, bears the astounding number "1560"—upon which all the subsequent numeration was based, with the effect of increasing the apparent age of the paper by nearly twenty-seven years. Though no explanation of this leap is offered by the printer, some light as to the motive is found in his previous asseverations that the figures appended to the title were no index, as some readers had fancied, to the number of copies issued weekly. "No. 1" seems to have been tried as a *reductio ad absurdum*. Probably from its failure, for the editor indignantly asserted a month later that he sold more than his two local rivals put together, a jump was made in the opposite direction. Farley's competitors, just referred to, may be dismissed briefly. The first was the *Oracle*, edited by "Andrew Hooke, Esq.," a descendant of an eminent Bristol family in the previous century, but reduced in circumstances. (He was actually a prisoner for debt in Newgate when he started the paper.)

The first number was issued on the 3rd February, 1742, and the last about September, 1749. The title underwent constant changes, and the numbering seems to have been left to chance, for it never reached 70 in an existence of nearly eight years. (Since the above was written, some documents have been found in the Record Office from which it appears that Hooke was prosecuted by the Attorney-General for seeking to evade the advertisement duty on weekly newspapers by systematically altering the title of his journal. The result does not appear. At this period the advertisements in any of the local papers rarely exceeded ten, and sometimes fell to half that number. The earnings of the publishers were so meagre that they eked out a living in odd ways. Thus Felix Farley announced that he was the sole retailer of "the Bristol Tooth-water, made out of the noblest ingredients in the whole materia medica." He also vended quack medicines, Durham mustard, and writing ink, lent Acts of Parliament to read at the rate of 3*d*. for two hours, and gave ready money for old books and paintings.) The other journal was a revived *Bristol Mercury.* The only copy known to exist is dated October 20th, 1748; and was printed by Edward Ward in Castle Street. Being numbered "24" one might assume that the paper had first appeared in the spring of 1748, but the *Mercury* is mentioned by name in the *Bristol Journal* of October 10th, 1747. It expired before the *Oracle*; and Ward, its printer, produced the first number of the *Bristol Intelligencer* on the 23rd September, 1749, stating that he had come into the field in consequence of there being only one journal "exhibited" in the city—the *Journal* of S. and F. Farley. Ward removed to Broad Street in 1750, and subsequently published his paper "at the King's Arms [the Stamp Office] in the Tolzey." The latest extant copy of the *Intelligencer* is dated August 12th, 1758.

The practice of tobacco smoking was exceedingly popular amongst the upper classes of society at this period. The tobacco and pipes purchased for Mr. Justice Powell in 1702 have been already mentioned. The recorder was allowed 5*s*. for pipes and tobacco at the gaol delivery of the same year. The members of the Corporation were also ardent smokers, but therewithal economical, sending their foul pipes back to the kiln to be purified by burning. The vice-chamberlain was paid the following little account at the audit in 1704 :—"December 22, 1703, paid for pipes, 5*s*. May 15, a gross of pipes and for burning pipes, 2*s*.

July 2, pipes at Muster, and burning of pipes, 1s. August 8, more pipes, and for burning fowle pipes, 1s. August 22, a gross of pipes and burning fowle ones, 2s." Another half-gross of pipes was bought in September at the celebration of the victory of Blenheim. The expenditure under this head increased in subsequent years, no less than nine gross of new pipes being bought in 1716, while several gross of old ones were reburned. At the yearly celebration of the King's coronation in 1723, the civic body, after ordering in 216 pipes, consumed 2½ lb. of tobacco, with "6 jugs of ale, 10 quarts each," and upwards of 60 gallons of wine. In the petty payments for 1738 there are small payments for tobacco on every day on which the Council assembled.

An outbreak of fire in a city mainly constructed of wood and wholly uninsured was naturally regarded with terror; but to modern eyes the measures taken in Bristol to meet an emergency seem ludicrously inefficient. Some disaster having happened during the autumn of 1702, the Common Council revived an old order in November, requiring every alderman and councillor to keep six leather buckets in his house for the use of his neighbours in the event of a fire. This was an ancient duty of each corporator, but it had been evaded or overlooked. The churchwardens were at the same time requested to provide a "sufficient" number of buckets and ladders, according to the extent of their parishes. St. Nicholas' vestry added an "engine" to this provision. The Corporation also had two "engines," similar to the garden utensil of later times, consisting of a vessel on low wheels, containing about twenty gallons of water, with a force-pump and nozzle. Fortunately for the citizens no serious fire occurred for several years. But on the 26th December, 1716, a calamitous outbreak took place in Wine Street, near the High Cross, when the deficiency of the apparatus was made manifest by the total destruction of three houses; and the Council, in a panic, appointed a committee to consider what should be done. In July, 1717, this body recommended that the two engines should be made serviceable, or replaced by better ones, and that a "fireman" should be appointed for each of the twelve wards, to be provided with two buckets, a pickhook, and an axe, and to be paid 1s. an hour during a fire. It was also suggested that four dozen buckets should be kept at the Council House, and that hose should be provided to feed the engines, and to convey the water from them to the burning premises. The city accounts shortly afterwards show that a new brass engine was purchased at a cost of £8 15s., which affords the reader an idea of the efficiency of the apparatus. Six dozen buckets, costing £10 16s., were doubtless for supplying the instrument with water. In 1720, however, another engine was made out of the materials of two old ones at an expense of £17 11s.; and a few weeks later, after the destruction of a large sugar house and several adjoining dwellings, about £5 were spent in "mending and painting the city buckets." The Wine Street disaster occasioned the first local movement for securing protection from losses by fire. In 1718 a number of leading merchants guaranteed a fund of £40,000, and thereupon founded the Crown Insurance Fire Office. The directors' meetings were held for some years in the court-room of St. Peter's Hospital, £4 per annum being paid for the accommodation. The charge for the insurance of house property was sixpence per pound on the rental.

A violent but now obscure controversy raged about this time between the Corporation and John Sansom, jun., who was the son-in-law of the town clerk, John Romsey, and had been appointed Collector of Customs in 1700. In June, 1703, the Council complained to the Government respecting the Collector's conduct, particularly for "notorious violations of her Majesty's peace upon private persons, indecently contemning the authority of the magistrates by words and writing, and exciting a challenge to a principal officer of the city for what he did by order of the Court of Quarter Sessions, and other unwarrantable actions." The Sessions grand jury had already made a presentment accusing the Collector of "endeavouring the ruin" of the trade of the city by imposing illegal oaths on persons sending goods coastwise. The Government appears to have taken no action. In January, 1706, an instrument was read to the Council, signed by the town clerk, intimating that he was imprisoned in London "at the suit and eager prosecution" of his only daughter and her husband Sansom, and constituting Nathaniel Wade, an ex-town clerk, his deputy. In 1707 Sansom came to grief, the Government discovering that he was in arrears in the sum of £30,351, the larger part of which, however, was recovered. Romsey subsequently resumed his office, which he held until his death in 1721.

A resolution discussed by the Incorporation of the Poor at a meeting on the 3rd August, 1703, shows that Cary's scheme of united parochial management was passing

through another crisis in its career. The question put
before the board was whether it was for the interest of the
city that the incorporation should be continued, or the old
system revived. After a debate, the former alternative
was unanimously approved. The institution had doubtless
encountered much opposition in certain circles. The mere
fact that it was a novelty was sufficient for its condemnation in many prejudiced eyes; the training of young paupers
so as to fit them for future self-support was offensive to
artisans whose privileges were attacked ; and the guardians
themselves, so far from conscientiously performing the duties
of their office, frequently thwarted Cary's design in a spirit
of short-sighted parsimony. A casual minute dated Sept.
27th, 1701, shows that a number of the boy paupers were no
longer being trained as weavers, but were engaged in
"heading pins," a juvenile occupation that could be of no
service to them in later life. The court ordered the lads to
be sent back to the looms, but changed its mind a fortnight
later, and quashed its resolution. A few months afterwards
it was determined to purchase a farm in order to teach the
boys to labour in the fields, whereupon Hungroad manor-
house and 112 acres of land near Shirehampton were bought
for £1,600, all of which was borrowed, chiefly from the
Corporation. Before the guardians got possession of the
farm, however, they had repented of their action, and no
steps were ever taken to remove the young paupers into the
country. Further subscriptions in support of the hospital,
amounting to about £1,200, were received about the same
time, but the money was applied to meet current expenses,
and the gifts were of no lasting benefit. Cary's idea, again,
was to maintain the aged poor in a central institution where
they could be economically overlooked. But the guardians,
having accepted a number of small almshouses from the
parish officials, filled them with paupers left to their own
devices, and the old evils of mendicity and dissipation
naturally reappeared. An amusing illustration of the intelligence of the age remains to be given. On the 21st September, 1703, when the Queen was again residing at Bath,
the board resolved " that the several poor persons under the
care of this corporation now afflicted with the King's Evil,
not exceeding the number of twelve, be sent to Bath at the
charge of this corporation, to have a touch from the Queen,
for a cure." (Her Majesty was exceedingly fond of dis-
pensing her healing influence. During the year ending
May, 1707, she " touched " upwards of 3,600 people at about

seventy religious services held for the purpose.) Unfortunately the local records are silent as to the results of the anticipated miracle. It will be shown later on that a robust faith in the magical powers of a "king by divine right" survived long after this date. The poor sought for superhuman influence at the other end of the social scale—amongst robbers and murderers. Mr. Johnson, an ex-governor of the Incorporation of the Poor, in some historical notes on that body published in 1826, observed that old superstitions were still far from extinct. "I believe," he said, "that few executions take place without persons touching the dying malefactor, in order, as they hope, to obtain a cure for the King's Evil."

Queen Anne's second visit to Bath, just referred to, afforded the Common Council a fresh opportunity for displaying its loyalty. The mayor and aldermen were sent off with a congratulatory address, and were directed "to wait upon the Prince (of Denmark) with a compliment from the city"—which probably took the shape of "Bristol milk." The party was graciously received, and the mayor (William Lewis) received the honour of knighthood.

Many of the ancient ordinances of the Corporation having become obsolete through various causes, the Corporation appointed a committee to revise the "Red Book of Orders" in which they were contained, or rather to produce a new code embodying such orders as ought to continue in force. The committee completed its task in September; and the revised code was ratified and confirmed by the Chamber. Several of the regulations have been already noticed in referring to restraints on trade. Amongst the others it is significant to find a prohibition of kidnapping. Complaint having been made, says the book, that certain persons had been in the habit of stealing maids, boys, or others, and of transporting them beyond the seas, and there selling them without the knowledge of their parents or others, it was ordered that no such young people should be removed unless their indentures of service were enrolled in the Tolzey Book. Masters of ships transporting such people contrary to this order were to forfeit £20. Another order deals with Sunday idlers. The deputies of each ward were ordered to perambulate it on the Lord's Day, to see that the constables cleared and quieted the streets, to close the conduits, and to prevent drinking in public-houses. The city gates were closed on Sunday mornings, apparently to prevent country excursions. In 1703 the Society of Friends, as had been their custom for thirty years, paid 20s. to the porter of Newgate "for his pains in opening the gate," so as to enable them to attend their chapel.

During the autumn the board of guardians forwarded a memorial to the Corporation, expressing their opinion that the exorbitant number of ale-houses in the city was one great cause of the increase of pauperism, and suggesting a diminution of licenses. In October the mayor and aldermen resolved that the number of these houses should be fixed at 220, the proportion of licenses to population being thus about one to twenty-two families. The guardians addressed another complaint to the authorities on the same subject in 1707, but their representations were disregarded, and in 1712 the magistrates increased the number of licenses to 253.

The "great storm" of November, 1703, has been so fully dealt with by Mr. Seyer and others that it seems unnecessary to narrate its local ravages. A few facts not hitherto published have been found in James Stewart's MS. Annals in the Bodleian Library. "My father," he writes, "was at that time usher to the Boys of the Gaunts' [Queen Elizabeth's] Hospital, and was called out of his bed to attend the children to the Chapter House in the Cloisters, where they remained and sung psalms all the night." A part of the cloisters, he adds, was blown down during this strange nocturnal concert, and the great [north transept] window of the Cathedral was demolished, no doubt to the increased terror of the quavering little vocalists. Owing to the force of the wind, the tide was driven up the Avon to an unprecedented height, aud boats are said to have been rowed in Thomas and Temple Streets. The damage sustained by the flooding of cellars was estimated—perhaps somewhat wildly—at £100,000. The vestry minutes of St. Stephen's parish record that the floor of the church was six feet under water, and that through the fall of three of the four pinnacles, with the battlements and the clock, the edifice was seriously damaged. (Mr. Colston forwarded £50 to the fund for its reparation.) One chronicler asserts that Sir John Duddleston, Bart., respecting whom a silly legend is to be found in some histories of Bristol, lost £20,000 in this storm, and was thereby ruined. But more than a year later Sir John made a donation to the city poor "in remembrance of his deceased daughter"; and in 1715 he was elected master of the Merchant Venturers' Society, in which office he died in 1716.

The first medical dissertation on the virtues of the Hot Well was published in 1703 under the whimsical title:—

"Johannis Subtermontani Thermalogia Bristoliensis, or Underhill's short Account of the Bristol Hot Well water. Printed and sold by William Bonny, at his house in Small Street." The author was a medical practitioner residing in College Green, where most of the visitors to the spring then lodged, owing to the scantiness of the accommodation at Clifton. Underhill cites a great number of cases in which sufferers from various maladies had been restored to health by drinking the water. Amongst the persons named is William Beckford, Esq., His Majesty's Slopster, who was cured of diabetes in thirteen weeks. The author adds that many persons of the first quality had ordered certificates bearing their names and the nature of their former diseases to be exposed in print, and to be exhibited at the Well, for the benefit of the public, the list including Viscount Stafford, the Earl of Meath, Viscount Devereux, Lady Spencer, and Lady Porter. For himself, the writer took the Hot Well water "to be the most certain and cheapest cure (yet known) of most diseases." Underhill dedicated his pamphlet to the mayor and Corporation. The style of the work is fairly illustrated by a single sentence:—"Providence having cast me under your care and umbrage, I wholly submit it to your censure and promulgation." The well was held, at this time, under a lease granted in 1695, by Sir Thomas Day, Robert Yate, Thomas Edwards, Thomas Callowhill, and other wealthy citizens, who had spent considerable sums in protecting it against the tide, and erecting the Hot Well House, to which the water was raised by pumps. The neighbouring rocks almost overhung the pump-room, and the narrow footway along the bank of the Avon passed through the house.

For the last fifteen years of the previous century, the Corporation, owing to the prodigalities of a previous age, was in great pecuniary embarrassment. A debt of about £16,000 having accumulated, and the yearly income being insufficient to meet the charges upon it, the Council, between 1690 and 1700, was compelled to effect retrenchments. The Members of Parliament for the city had hitherto been paid 6s. 8d. per day each whilst attending to their duties. This allowance was ordered to be withdrawn. The judges were politely informed that the hospitality usually offered them would be discontinued, "not from want of respect, but pure necessity." By another resolution, entertainments and presents of wine to distinguished visitors were suspended "until the city debts were paid." The mayor's allowance was reduced by fifty guineas, the salaries of various officers were cut down, gifts to some of the parishes were retrenched; in fact, economy was for a season in the ascendant. In 1700 the Council even resolved to dispose of the silver trumpets used on state occasions, together with the trumpeters' laced coats, and these articles were actually sold; but as the payments to trumpeters soon reappear in the accounts it is probable that the civic dignitaries could not reconcile themselves to the loss of their sonorous heralds. By that time, indeed, the fines for renewing leases of the new property in the Castle precincts and King Street were becoming fruitful, and the distress of the civic treasury was consequently relieved. Signs soon became manifest of a turn in the financial tide. In 1700 the Council ordered that the judges should be again entertained at Sir Thomas Day's house at the charge of the city. In 1701 the Corporation paid £10 for three days' keep of Mr. Justice Powell's horses, of which he had no less than twenty-two, and also furnished him with six gallons of sherry, costing £2 2s.; six gallons of claret, £2; eighteen quarts of sherry, 21s.; and twelve quarts of claret, 20s. The return to ancient custom became definitive in 1702, a house of a leading corporator being annually selected for the reception of the judges. How munificently the Queen was entertained has just been shown. Though the city debt was still heavy, the improving prospects of the Chamber caused it speedily to ignore its former pledges of economy. The Council House in Corn Street, with the adjoining Mayor's Tolzey, had been constructed in the reign of Elizabeth, and meanly repaired after a fire which occurred soon after the Restoration. The building was no longer deemed worthy of the wealth and dignity of the city, and in January, 1704, the Common Council resolved to pull it down, and to erect a Council House that would be "honourable and useful." St. Ewen's Church, however, was not interfered with, and the new edifice, though presenting a decorous semi-classical front, offered very meagre accommodation. Amongst the items of expense incurred during the reconstruction were:— " Wainscotting the great room £50; Chimney-piece £7; drawing, painting, and gilding the four coats of arms upon the new cloth £14; gilding and painting the carved coat of arms and two figures of Prudence and Justice, and the frame for the Sword £4 10s.; Frontispiece for Council House £12." Bricks were then 16s. per thousand. The wages of masons and carpenters were 1s. 8d. and of labourers 1s. 2d. by day. The building was probably the first in the central streets which was furnished with sashed windows. The timberwork and stone pillars of the Tolzey, being no longer required, were presented to the parishioners of St. Nicholas, "to the intent they be used in making a walk in the nature of a Tolzey, near the Custom House," which then stood on the Welsh Back, and also had a covered "walk" attached to it. The Corporation granted £25 and the vestry of St. Nicholas £20 towards erecting the new penthouse, which was completed in 1707. Owing to the scanty accommodation which offices and shops then offered for business consultations, the "walk" was much frequented before the opening of the Exchange. It was removed in 1775, but the parish vestry, loath to part with it, erected it afresh in the churchyard on the Back.

An association styling itself the Society for the Reformation of Manners was established in London about the beginning of the century, and found active and influential supporters in Bristol. Apparently at their instance, the Common Council, in July, 1704, requested the mayor and aldermen that "by regard to the ill consequences by the introduction of lewdness and debauchery by the acting of stage plays," players should not be allowed to act within the city. The magistrates must have held a deaf ear to this demand, for at the quarter sessions in the following December the grand jury delivered a lengthy presentment, in which, after acknowledging the exertions of the justices in suppressing music rooms, limiting the number of ale-houses, and "punishing idle walking on the Lord's Day," they express their dread of an outbreak of immorality and profaneness from the increase of unlicensed ale-houses, where "the Lord's Day is much profaned by tippling, and also by the great concourse of people in public places under pretence of hearing news on that day. But that which puts us more especially under these sad apprehensions is the late permission given to the public stage within the liberties of this city." The jury went on to predict that if play-acting were permitted, it would "corrupt and debauch our youth, and utterly ruin many apprentices and servants, already so unruly and licentious that they are with great difficulty kept under any reasonable order or government by their masters." The magistrates, nevertheless, refused to take alarm. In the summer of 1705 the players again made their appearance, led by a popular actor named Power, and the pious horror of their opponents has preserved the information that they performed "Love for Love" on the 23rd July, and "The Provoked Husband" on the 13th August. Their theatre was probably situated in Stoke's Croft, a few yards beyond the city boundaries. They met, moreover, with so large a measure of support that they not only returned in the summer of 1706, but audaciously entered the city, and built themselves a playhouse on St. Augustine's Back. Their enemies were, of course, intensely indignant. At the August quarter sessions the grand jury presented the offences of Power and his company; five days later the grand jury at the annual assizes appealed to the magistrates to "crush the newly-erected playhouse, that school of debauchery and nursery of profaneness," which the Bishop of Bristol had been "seasonably" denouncing from the pulpit; and the Common Council, on the same day, appointed a committee to take steps for the punishment of the delinquents and the suppression of the house. The Rev. Arthur Bedford, Vicar of Temple, also entered the field with a pamphlet, entitled "The Evil and Danger of Stage Plays," one of the rarest of the productions of Bonny, the only Bristol printer in 1706. "The Enemy," says the author, "lay sometime without our Gates, and is now come into the City in Defiance of the Magistrates." The hands of the unwilling justices were evidently forced by the rash adventure of Power, and the playhouse was closed. Even the playing-booths which had been winked at during the fair were suppressed by the sheriffs, the Council granting them £12 in compensation for lost fees. Encouraged by public support, however, the poor players still ventured to return occasionally to the house in Stoke's Croft or the neighbourhood of the Hot Well. In December, 1709, according to the minutes of the Council, " players and other roving persons having been driven out of the city, and found shelter in Gloucestershire near it, and the justices of Gloucestershire being willing to assist that they may have no reception within five miles of the city," a committee was appointed to co-operate with the county authorities. There is no evidence that this arrangement was ever carried out. At all events, the comedians returned from time to time, and in 1717 their manager accepted as a recruit a young Irishman named Macklin, who remained with the Bristol companies for about fifteen years, and afterwards attained great fame both as an actor and an author. (It appears from a note in Macklin's memoirs that the only playbills at this period consisted of two or three written notices, posted up at public resorts. Mr. Seyer's MSS. state that he was informed by an aged citizen that the plays were announced in the leading streets by beat of drum, one of the principal actors accompanying the drummer.) Aroused by the continuance of what he deemed an evil, the Rev. A. Bedford produced a more elaborate work in 1719, "Against the horrid Blasphemies and Impieties which are still used in English Playhouses." The book proved the extraordinary industry of the author, for no less than 7,000 passages were quoted from acting dramas, Mr. Bedford contending that they offended 1,400 texts of the Bible. Amongst the plays especially condemned as blasphemous were "Macbeth" and "The Tempest"; the same sin was even discovered in Addison's "Cato." The reverend gentleman's efforts can have had little effect on public opinion, which was setting in the opposite direction. From Stewart's manuscript annals of the city, it appears that some players from Drury Lane had been permitted to reopen the theatre at St. Augustine's in the autumn of 1726, "Cato" being one of the plays performed. July 16th, 1728, the *Gloucester Journal* announced that a band of comedians, after having played the "Beggars' Opera" at Bath, under the supervision of its author, Mr. Gay, with great success, were then "playing of it at their great booth in Bridewell Lane, Bristol, and have been sent for by the quality to play it at their houses, and to the Long Room near the Hot Well several times." *Farley's Newspaper* stated that one of the representations at the Hot Well was "attended by 200 persons of the first rank," that the dresses of the actors had been presented by the nobility at Bath, and that Mr. Gay would be present at the next representation. It is a remarkable fact that the play was performed here no less than fifty times. (From the Tyson MSS. in Alderman Fox's collection it would seem that playbills were introduced at this date.) From another paragraph it appears that the company obtained leave from the mayor for the erection of their booth. Moreover, the playhouse in St. Augustine's was open at the same time (*Farley's Newspaper*, July 30th, 1728). In September the grand jury at the assizes, much incensed, presented "the *two* playhouses frequently acted in here as public nuisances and nurseries of idleness and vice"; and the new mayor, holding different views from his predecessor, issued warrants against the St. Augustine's company, and ordered the actors to be arrested in the midst of a performance. The natural result was a disturbance, during which the players seem to have escaped; whereupon the Corporation ordered proceedings to be taken against Joseph Earle, Esq., a member of an influential Bristol family, for abusing and assaulting the officers. Earle died, however, before judgment was obtained, and the Council made nothing out of the affair, except a lawyer's bill for about £35, which was paid in 1731, when another prosecution was ordered against "Thomas Lewis and company, common players at St. Augustine's Back." Before that date, however, some of the players, harassed by constant persecution, had effectually baffled their opponents, and gratified the lovers of the drama both in Bristol and at the Hot Well, by building another theatre beyond the city boundaries. About the close of 1728 one George Martin, who held from the Society of Merchants a public-house called the Horse and Groom, and some adjoining land at Jacob's Wells, under a lease granted in June, 1723, transferred the vacant ground to John Hippisley, a native of Wookey, Somerset, who was a popular actor in London, and had played for several seasons in Bristol, his success as a comedian being largely due to a distorted face caused by a burn received in early life, when he fulfilled the humble functions of a stage candle-snuffer. Hippisley was supported by several prominent Bristolians—amongst whom were Abraham Isaac Elton, John Brickdale, John Peach, William Vick, the Clifton Bridge projector, and Stephen Nash—who lent him £300; and he forthwith erected a theatre, which was opened on the 23rd June, 1729, with the comedy of "Love for Love" (*London Weekly Journal*, June 28th). The new place of amusement, "being convenient," as the reporter said, "for coaches, as well as for the Ropewalks leading to the Hot Well," was largely patronised, and in June, 1736, Hippisley prudently obtained from Martin a transfer of his entire lease, and subsequently occupied the Horse and Groom as a dwelling. Finally, in June, 1746, Thomas Longman, John Blackwell and Joseph Brown, on behalf of the Merchants Company, granted to Hippisley the Horse and Groom, and also "the piece of ground called the Margaretts," on which the theatre was erected, during the lifetime of his two children, on payment of two rents of 5s. each. Mrs. Green, one of those children, and long a celebrated actress, resided in the old inn until her death, in 1791. Hippisley himself died in 1748. (Much of the above information respecting Jacob's Wells has been obtained from the MSS. of Mr. Tyson, now in the possession of Alderman Fox.) The theatre might well be described by Chatterton as "a hut." The accommodation for the players was so

contracted that an actor who left the stage on one side and
re-entered on the other had to walk round the outside of the
house. Adjoining it was another ale-house, the Malt Shovel,
and a hole was made in the party wall, through which
liquors could be handed in to the players, as well as to the
upper class spectators who in those days crowded the stage.
Instead of footlights, the stage was illuminated by tallow
candles, stuck in four hoops, and suspended over the actors'
heads. And it is recorded that on one occasion a personator
of Richard III. wielded his sword so recklessly that he cut
the rope of one of the primitive chandeliers, and had to be
rescued from the hoop by the laughing spectators. The
drama nevertheless flourished in this humble abode, and
Mr. Smith (MSS. Museum and Library) states that Hippisley, and afterwards his daughter, Mrs. Green, paid his
friends £41 a year for the above loan. An advertisement of
July, 1759, announces that for the greater convenience of the
public "an amphitheatre will be erected after the manner
practised at the Theatres Royal in London, where servants
will be permitted to keep places." In the following year
" ladies and gentlemen are desired to send their servants by
five o'clock," to secure seats. The great drawback of the
establishment was the total absence of lights in the neighbouring roads. Sometimes the manager announced that
men would be placed with torches from the theatre to College
Green. One playbill informs the public that "the night
will be illuminated with the Silver Rays of Cynthia." Less
poetically, some conclude with a prominent note:—"A
Moon Light Night." In 1763 Mr. Winstone, a popular
comedian, added to the announcement of his benefit:—"It is
presumed Madame Cynthia will appear in her utmost splendour." But his wit nearly caused a riot, for the occupants
of the gallery, complaining that "the foreign lady" was
not forthcoming, became noisy and unruly, and were with
difficulty appeased. The St. Augustine's theatre was converted into an Assembly Room previous to 1742, but the
theatre in Stoke's Croft continued to be occasionally occupied. Advertisements of the " seasons " of 1744 and 1745
appeared in the *Bristol Oracle*, and the same paper of
August 5th, 1749, announced the performance of "Scapen's
Metamorphoses," at Lloyd's Great Room, at the end of the
Horse Fair, a place frequently used by strolling players
during the annual saturnalia of the fair. Temple fair had
also its patrons, and the *Oracle* of January 15th, 1743, stated
that amongst "the many elegant divertisements to be ex-

hibited" at the forthcoming holiday, "something new and curious" would be given "at the large Theatrical Room, near the Counterslip." Mr. Smith asserts that a theatre also existed about this time in Orchard Street, but this is unquestionably erroneous. The advertisements which led him into the mistake refer to the old theatre in Orchard Street, Bath, projected by Hippisley, in concert with Roger Watts, of Bristol, in 1747.

News of the great victory at Blenheim on the 13th August, 1704, was received in the city a fortnight later with every token of enthusiasm. The streets, says a contemporary chronicler, "were in a flame with bonfires," and the enormous pile set on fire at the newly decorated High Cross so "tarnished and blistered it that it was grievous to behold." The illumination of the houses, he adds, could not be surpassed in brilliancy, but the absence of coloured lamps at the residence of the mayor (Peter Saunders) gave offence to the populace. His worship was suspected of having made money out of his office, "giving no hospitality; moreover, he had a sour and lofty look, which made him much disliked." Wherefore the mob called for the exhibition of more candles; and the demand not being complied with, they smashed the windows, and committed other mischief, giving the constables "sore discomfort."

Previous to this time the road from Bristol to Kingsweston and Shirehampton was extremely narrow and inconvenient, having been originally designed only for horse traffic. By a subscription amongst the neighbouring landowners, the present road was laid out in the autumn of 1704, and the Corporation, "to encourage so good and useful a work," contributed £20. The new road passed close to Stoke and Kingsweston Houses, so that visitors might alight at the doors of those mansions. Some years later, at the expense of the respective owners, the highway was slightly diverted, and assumed its present lines.

Allusion has already been made to the barbarous treatment of women convicted of petty offences. At the sessions in March, 1705, Mary James, "for a cheat," was sentenced to stand *in* the pillory half an hour and *on* the pillory one hour for six successive market days. She probably suffered severely from the missiles of the mob, for about seven weeks later another woman, convicted of a small felony, "prayed transportation," which was granted. A third female, found guilty of obtaining three yards of dowlais by fraudulent pretences, was sentenced to be stripped naked to the waist, and whipped down one side of High Street and up the other. In the same year a man, for stealing a cheese, was ordered to be flogged from All Saints' Church to the White Horse inn, Redcliff Street, and thence back to Newgate, the cheese to be carried by his side.

A general election took place about the end of April, 1705. Unusual excitement prevailed throughout the country, and there was a "mighty stir" in Bristol on behalf of "Mr. Edward Colston's nephew" (name not given); but the former members, Sir William Daines and Colonel Robert Yate, appear to have been returned without opposition.

Mr. Evans, in his "Chronological Outline," noted under the year 1705, "The first brass made in England at Baptist Mills"; and the statement has been accepted and republished by Mr. Pryce, Mr. Nicholls, and others. The truth is that brass was manufactured in this country from a very early period. The Parliaments of Henry VIII. and Edward VI. passed statutes to prevent the exportation of the metal, "lest there should not be enough left for making guns and household utensils." During the reign of Elizabeth the monopoly of making brass was granted to two men, who sold their patent rights to a London "Mineral and Battery Society"; and this company, as appears from an Exchequer Commission in the Record Office, had permitted certain lessees to erect wire works at Tintern before 1604. Another Exchequer Commission refers to a "furnace of battery" seized by "the searcher of the port of Bristol" before 1638. The English copper mines, however, were so neglected in the reign of Charles II. that the Government had to obtain foreign supplies of that metal, and the manufacture of brass may have been cramped from the same cause; but from the multitude of "great brass pots" that has been shown to exist in Bristol households, the trade of the brass founder evidently continued a prosperous one. It is true that it underwent a great local development in 1705, when a company of Bristol merchants, having made arrangements for obtaining a cheap supply of copper ore from Cornwall, and of calamine from the hills around their own city, established a "brass battery works" at Baptist Mills. The copper, it is said, did not cost the undertakers more than from £2 10s. to £4 per ton for several years, and the profits of the brass works were consequently very great. Mr. Thomas Coster, of Bristol, who was largely concerned in the enterprise, invented a hydraulic engine, and introduced it into Cornwall, for the purpose of draining the mines, and made a large fortune by working some of them himself. The water power of the Froom being insufficient for the growing business in Bristol, more extensive mills were erected by the company at Keynsham, where, at the end of the century, fully one half of the brass wire made in the kingdom was produced, besides an immense quantity of other goods. The same company (the principal partners of which in 1749 were Walter Hawksworth, Edward Harford, Harford Lloyd, Nehemiah Chapman, Trueman Harford, Henry Swymmer, Richard Champion, Andrew Lloyd, and Joseph Loscombe, but which was known for many years as Harford's and Bristol Brass and Copper Company) had smaller mills on the Avon at Weston, Saltford, and Kelston, and on the Wye at Redbrook. (The works at Baptist Mills were not removed to Keynsham until after 1814.) Competitors were naturally tempted into the field by the success of the first enterprise. Messrs. Elton and Waynes had extensive copper and brass works at Crewe's Hole and Hanham about 1750. A still larger concern was that of Messrs. Freeman and Bristol Copper Company, of Small Street, who had works at Swinford, Woollard, Publow, and elsewhere, and did not relinquish business until 1860. In *Bonner and Middleton's Bristol Journal* of March 3rd, 1787, it is stated that the works, mills, etc. of the United Brass Battery, Wire and Copper Company of Bristol had been sold on the previous Monday for £16,000. A very large spelter (zinc) manufactory, the ruins of which extend over some acres, was established at Warmley by William Champion, who had also a " commodious brass foundry " on St. Augustine's Back. Bishop Watson, who states that spelter was first made in Bristol in 1743, personally visited Champion's works in 1766 to see the process of making zinc, which was at that time kept rigidly secret. Champion, though a man of conspicuous skill and ingenuity, was unsuccessful in business, and his works at Warmley, described as " the most complete in the kingdom," with smelting furnaces at Kingswood and forges at Kelston, were offered for sale in March, 1769, and were soon afterwards purchased by Harford's Copper Company. According to a story in Ellacombe's History of Bitton, the new owners acquired great riches from working Champion's processes, and having subsequently sought him out (he was found in Liverpool working as a mason), they offered him an annuity, which he declined. John Champion, Bristol, merchant, became bankrupt in 1798, and his brass and copper wire works, together with his copper and lead mills in Lewin's Mead, were offered for sale in the *Bristol Journal* of December 1st in that year. Owing to the local demand for copper when the above brass works were in vigour, a large proportion of the metal consumed yearly was smelted around Bristol. The refuse ore, cast into square blocks of almost impenetrable hardness, were largely employed to form copings of walls. The well-known Black Castle at Arno's Vale, built by a copper smelter named Reeve, about 1760, is chiefly constructed of this material.

On the 12th December, 1705, Sir William Lewis represented to the Common Council " that the great noise made by trucks in this city by means of the iron materials about them is a great annoyance to the inhabitants thereof." Whereupon it was resolved that no trucks should be permitted in the streets unless they were made wholly of wood (excepting the banding of the wheels). And the bellman was ordered to proclaim that offenders against this order would be fined 3s. 4d. for every offence. At a subsequent meeting, also on the motion of Sir William Lewis, a committee was appointed to take measures for preventing heavy carts, having wheels banded with iron, from traversing the streets. The obnoxious carts, it may be observed, were not the property of outsiders. The corn brought to the city by farmers, and the coal supply from Kingswood, were alike transported by pack-horses. The terms of the resolution show that the old interdiction of carts was frequently infringed, and Sir William's attempt to renew its vigour seems to have been abortive. Nevertheless, at the March quarter session in 1708, two tradesmen were presented by the grand jury for making use of carts with iron-bound wheels, when the bench gave orders that, " unless they took off their bandages by the 1st April," they should be prosecuted at the next session.

The misfortunes of the family of a deceased member of the Corporation came before the Council about this time, and furnish an early instance of what afterwards became a regular custom. The case was somewhat peculiar. In the reign of James II., a mercer named John Bubb, who also held the office of Collector of Customs, was elected a common councillor, but refused to accept the honour on the plea that he was a servant of the Crown. The matter led to a correspondence between the Corporation and the Government, the former insisting on its right to elect any free burgess. Mr. Bubb's collectorship, it was urged, did not "disturb him in his trade of shopkeeping, which he follows very considerably." The King, however, sent positive commands that Bubb should be excused, and the royal word was at that time law. But when regal intermeddling came to an end with the Revolution, Mr. Bubb was again elected a councillor, and in due course sustained the offices of sheriff and mayor. Dying about 1699 in embarrassed circumstances, his widow petitioned the Chamber for relief, and on the 12th December, 1705, she was granted a yearly annuity of £30 for life.

The war with France, although singularly glorious, was attended with the usual difficulty in raising reinforcements for the army and navy. In 1703 the court of quarter sessions ordered a number of the debtors imprisoned in Newgate to be liberated, on condition that they "listed as soldiers" or found substitutes, and some of them found means to adopt the latter course. In August, 1706, one Edward Taunton, sentenced to death for burglary in 1704, but repeatedly reprieved, obtained the Queen's pardon on condition that he entered the navy, and was thereupon released. A few months later a half-witted man named Stockman was brought before the magistrates charged with shouting "God save James III.," and causing a riot in the streets. Evidence having been given that the culprit was of unsound mind, the bench consented to dismiss him if he would serve in the Marines; but as he was not only mentally but bodily infirm, he was granted leave to find a substitute, which he did, and was discharged! Early in 1706 an Act of Parliament was passed under which every imprisoned debtor owing less than £60 was permitted to volunteer into the navy, or, on his failing to do so, could be forced into the fleet by a magisterial order. The supply of men was nevertheless insufficient, and in May, 1706, a ship of war having been obtained "to take care of the vessels belonging to this port," the Council resolved to advance £150, and the Merchants' Company £200, to promote the enlistment of a crew. Two months later there was a general muster of the militia forces of the district, when the entertainment of the Earl of Berkeley, Lord Lieutenant, cost the city £68.

One of the barbarous customs of the age was the branding upon the cheek of persons convicted of petty thefts. The practice, which was performed in open court, was so repugnant to the feelings of sensitive officials as to lead to evasions of the law. In one case the Bristol sheriffs were fined 40s. for not causing two women to be "well burnt"; in another instance the same functionaries were fined £5 for a like offence. At the sessions at which the felon Taunton was transformed into a defender of his country, the keeper of Newgate was fined £5 " for not having his irons for burning ready," but ultimately escaped with a reprimand. It would appear that prisoners frequently gave bribes to get the branding-iron applied cold, but that wily old magistrates, to defeat such shifts, insisted on seeing the smoke arise from the singed skin of each offender.

The Corporation had a windfall in 1706, upon the death of Queen Catherine, widow of Charles II. During the transports of the Restoration, the Council handed over to the king, for life, certain fee-farm rents that the Corporation had purchased of the Commonwealth in 1650, and these were transferred to the Queen as part of her dowry. On Sept. 30th, 1706, the chamberlain records :—" Received of Morgan Smith and Nathaniel Webb, sheriffs, being a year's fee-farm rents formerly paid to Queen Dowager but now faln to the city's hands by her death, £142 10s."

The West of England weavers were probably the first artisans in the district to form what later generations have called a trade union. On the 25th February, 1707, a petition was presented to the House of Commons from the clothiers and serge and stuff makers of Bristol, complaining that their journeymen, having combined together, not only prevented youths being taken as apprentices without leave of the confederacy, but required the dismissal of such weavers as would not join in their combination. These demands, with others, had been urged with threats of leaving work, and with riotous conduct, attended with destruction of goods. A similar petition from Taunton stated that the weavers had provided themselves with a common fund, a common seal, colours and tipstaffs, and that the gaol had been broken open by them and several prisoners rescued. The Government soon after undertook to suppress disturbances and prosecute offenders. It appears from contemporary documents that there were many weavers at this time in the parishes of Westbury and Clifton, and in the out-parish of St. Philip. The complaint as to the workmen's combinations was renewed in 1726, when the corporations of Bristol and Taunton, in petitions to the House of Commons, stated that unlawful clubs of weavers and woolcombers had attempted to fix the rate of wages, assaulted workmen who refused to join them, and insulted the magistrates. The House ordered an inquiry, in the course of which some of the employers admitted that the insubordination of the artisans was often due to the payment of wages in goods instead of in money.

The scanty demand of the rural population for books was supplied early in the century by hawkers and pedlars, whose packs contained a very miscellaneous assortment of wares. Dealers of this class attended Bristol fair in great numbers for the purpose of replenishing their stores, and the wholesale traders with whom they dealt found it convenient to address them through the London newspapers. The following example of these advertisements is extracted from the London *Post Man* of July 19th, 1707:—"This is to give notice to all chapmen keeping Bristol Fair, that Benj. Harris, bookseller, in Gracechurch Street, will (as usual) keep the said fair this year at his shop under Christ Church, in Wine Street, where they may be furnished with Bibles, Common Prayers, shop books, pocket books, as also all other chapman's books in divinity or history."

On the 22nd July, 1707, Abraham Darby, blacksmith, was admitted a freeman of the city without paying a fine, on the nomination of the ex-mayor, Nathaniel Day, who exercised the right by an ancient custom. Darby, born in Dudley, had commenced business as a malt-mill maker at Baptist Mills in 1700. Being joined by three partners, Quakers like himself, he added brass and iron founding to his original business. At that time the art of casting iron pots for cooking purposes had scarcely been attempted in England, and Darby was as unsuccessful as had been many others in producing pots equal to those made in Holland. Resolved on overcoming the difficulty, he made a tour in the Netherlands, and engaged some Dutch workmen; but his experiments still continued to fail until a Bristol boy in his service, John Thomas, made a suggestion which brought about complete success. To prevent piracy, Darby applied for a patent, asserting that he had discovered and perfected "a way of casting iron bellied pots and other ware in sand only, without loam or clay," by which such vessels could be sold cheaply, to the advantage of the poor and the benefit of commerce. A monopoly of the process was granted to him for fourteen years. Thomas was well rewarded for his ingenuity, and his descendants, agents of the Darby family for about a century, ultimately attained a high position in the city. Darby proposed to carry on his new manufacture on a great scale at Baptist Mills, but his partners having refused to advance the required capital, he removed in 1709 to Coalbrookdale, Staffordshire, where he established works that acquired a European reputation whilst under the management of Richard Reynolds, who has been styled by Mr. Pryce the greatest of Bristol's great philanthropists. Darby died in 1717, and was succeeded by a son, also named Abraham. Reynolds, born in Corn Street in 1735, married in 1757 the only daughter of the second Darby, and assumed the management at Coalbrookdale on the death of his father-in-law, in 1762. During the first half of the century scarcely any iron was manufactured in England, the woods having been mostly cut down, and the attempts to use coal for smelting having proved unsuccessful. It was chiefly under Reynolds's supervision that the difficulty was overcome, and that coal was employed, not only to smelt the ore, but to convert the cast metal into malleable iron. The latter improvement, known as puddling, due to the sagacity of two workmen, was communicated in April, 1766, to Thomas Goldney, a Bristol Quaker who held a share in the works, with Reynolds's strong recommendation that a patent should be obtained for the discovery. The patent was secured in the following June, and produced enormous profits to the firm. Reynolds, who returned to Bristol in 1804, is said to have given upwards of £200,000 towards philanthropic and charitable objects.

Some notable regulations bearing upon infant labour and the education of the young were made by the Incorporation of the Poor on the 13th February, 1707. A committee reported that one Seth Shute had offered to employ sixty girls and boys, of about seven years of age, in spinning, the guardians granting him suitable accommodation for eight or ten looms for weaving linen in St. Peter's Hospital. Each child was to work six weeks without pay; afterwards the guardians were to receive 1s. per head per week. The hours of labour, it was recommended, should be "the accustomed hours of the house"—namely, from 6 a.m. to 7 p.m. in winter, and from 5 a.m. to 7 p.m. in summer; half an hour being allowed for breakfast, one hour for dinner, and one hour for schooling. As the guardians had determined that twenty of the boy inmates should be taught writing and arithmetic, it was further proposed that this favoured handful should have two hours' schooling upon three days a week, but should "make good" the time thus lost by working from 5 a.m. to 8 o'clock at night in summer! The report was confirmed, but it will cause the reader no sorrow to learn that the scheme afterwards proved unworkable. The clerk to the board, who had a salary of £30, from which

£7 were deducted for rent, petitioned the guardians that, as his time was mostly taken up by its work, and as he had to instruct about twenty boys in writing, they would permit him to live rent free. This was granted; but in October, 1709, the guardians changed their minds, and reduced the clerk's income to £23. At the last-mentioned meeting the most valuable gift ever made to the incorporation was reported to the board—namely, the bequest, by John Knight, Esq., of London, deceased (supposed to be a son of the John Knight who was mayor of Bristol in 1670-1), of a house then known as the George, in High Street, occupied by a linendraper.

At the quarter sessions in May, 1707, the justices, under their statutable powers, made a new table of rates for the carriage of goods by wagons and pack-horses between London and Bristol. The charges, which would be deemed onerous by modern tradesmen, were as follows:—By horse carriage: packages above 28 lb. at 5s. per cwt. in summer, and at 6s. per cwt. in winter; packages between 14 lb. and 28 lb., 1d. per lb.; above 5-lb. and under 14 lb., 1½d. per lb.; small parcels, 6d. each. By wagons: heavy goods, 3s. per cwt. in summer, and 4s. in winter; light goods, 5s. and 6s. per cwt. in the respective seasons.

The bellman was an important institution in an age in which newspapers and advertising were still in their infancy. In the civic accounts for 1707 is a payment to John Packer, founder, who charged 14s. for "a bell for ye bellman, for ye yous of the sitty, made of newe mettell," and 8s. for "new casting and turning the bellman's bell"; but allowed 4s. 6d. for "a ould bell waying 6 lb." The account, for some unexplained reason, had been outstanding for eleven years.

The Thanksgiving Day ordered by the Crown to celebrate the Union between England and Scotland evoked but little enthusiasm in Bristol. The corporate disbursements on the occasion amounted only to about £13. It may be worth recording that the postage of a congratulatory address, forwarded to the Queen on the occasion, amounted to no less than 11s. 6d., half a crown of the amount being "ye charge for delivering early." The postage of a petition to Parliament, soon afterwards, cost 10s.

The church of St. Mary Redcliff was at this time in a state of great dilapidation through long-continued neglect, and the parochial authorities found it necessary to resort to extraordinary means for procuring funds. Probably encouraged by the support of William Whitehead, then mayor ("the first mayor that past his mayoralty in Redcliff since the memory of man in this present age," says a contemporary annalist), at the adjourned session in May, 1708, they represented to the justices that the estimated cost of repairing the edifice was upwards of £4,400. As the money could not be raised in the parish, they prayed the magistrates to certify the petition about to be sent to the Lord Chancellor for a brief, and their request was approved. A brief, it may be explained, was a royal mandate, ordering a collection to be made in every parish in England on behalf of a certain designated object. The document was obtained in due course, but distant congregations naturally displayed no great liberality in responding to the appeal, and the gross amount collected was only £1,400. Owing to the heavy fees extorted by officials in London, the net produce of the brief was reduced to about £700. In consequence of this disappointment only about £2,000 were spent on the church, the Corporation giving £200. "Nevertheless," says the above annalist, "the inside was beautified and accommodated with abundance of rare things which it had not before, and in particular the chancell enlarged, and a new alter piece." The reparations were effected with much less damage to the fabric than might have been expected from the barbarous architectural taste of the time.

During the many wars of the eighteenth century, privateering was a favourite pursuit of speculative Bristolians, some of whom profited largely by their enterprises, whilst others sustained heavy losses. The most successful and interesting of those adventures was that started in 1708 by a confederation of merchants, embracing Christopher Shuter (mayor, 1711), Sir John Hawkins (mayor, 1701), James Holledge (mayor, 1709), John Romsey (town clerk), Philip Freke (sheriff, 1708), Thomas Clement (sheriff, 1709), John Batchelor, Francis Rogers, Thomas Goldney, Thomas Dover, M.D., Richard Hawksworth, and others—several of the company, strange to say, being Quakers. With the joint capital subscribed, two vessels, called the Duke and the Duchess, were carefully fitted out for the purpose of preying upon the Spanish and French ships, laden with precious metal and goods, which were frequently passing from South America and the West Indies to Europe. The Duke, of 320 tons and 30 guns, was placed under the command of Captain Woodes Rogers, the second officer being one of the adventurers, Dr. Dover (afterwards a famous physician, and the inventor of

Dover's Powder). The Duchess, of slightly inferior size and armament, was commanded by Captain Stephen Courtney and Captain Edward Cooke. The pilot for both ships was William Dampier, a Somerset man, who had joined the South Seas buccaneers in early life, and had gained wide repute by two filibustering cruises round the globe. On the 2nd August, 1708, the sister vessels sailed from Kingroad, and convoyed several small ships to Ireland. The original complement of men, says Capt. Rogers in his account of the voyage, was 225. Only about forty of these were sailors; above one-third were foreigners; of the rest, "several were tinkers, tailors, haymakers, pedlars, fiddlers, etc." A portion of this "mixed gang" ran away at Cork; others were got rid of, and the vacancies filled by a better class; the total number being raised to 334, so that the ships "were very much crowded and pestered." With the exception of the capture of a small Spanish barque, nothing of interest occured until the 31st January, 1709, when, on approaching the island of Juan Fernandez, reported as uninhabited, they were surprised at the sight of a fire, and feared that it was a token of a French or Spanish fleet. The signal had been raised, however, by Alexander Selkirk, a Scotchman, who had been an officer in one of the ships led by Dampier on a former voyage, and had voluntarily separated from the party owing to a quarrel with his captain. Selkirk, who had lived alone on the island for nearly four years and a half, was offered the post of mate by Capt. Rogers, and proved himself an able seaman. Filibustering now began in earnest. After capturing six vessels, one of which was a Frenchman of over 400 tons burden, an attack was made upon the city of Guayquil with complete success, the inhabitants flying after a brief resistance. A portion of the town was burnt; the rest was plundered; and a party sent up the river despoiled some fugitive ladies of about a thousand pounds worth of jewels. Selkirk, who led this foray, was complimented by Rogers for his "modest" treatment of the victims. Finally, the privateers extorted 30,000 "pieces of eight" (about £7,000) for the ransom of the city, exclusive of their previous plunder. Four more vessels were next taken at sea, some of which were ransomed. The largest of the former prizes was now converted into a sister privateer, which was named the Marquis. Whilst she was being fitted out, there were found in the hold "500 bales of Pope's Bulls [indulgences], 16 reams in each bale," so that there must have been nearly four millions of those documents, which the Spanish colonists were accustomed to purchase of the clergy at high rates. "We should have made something of them," said Rogers, "if we had taken the bishop" (who escaped). Making the best of the matter, "part were used to burn the pitch off the ships' bottoms when we careened 'em"; and the rest were thrown overboard. After sailing about some time in search of a Spanish treasure-ship expected from Manilla, the vessel in question, or rather the smaller of two ships which had departed together, hove in sight. A brisk engagement ensued, and although the Spaniards had twenty guns and twenty "pateraroes" (small breech-loaders), they were compelled to surrender. Capt. Rogers was severely wounded in the battle, but lost none of his crew. Learning from the prisoners that a still richer prize was not far distant, the privateers went in search, but were destined to "catch a Tartar." The other Spaniard had forty guns and forty pateraroes, and defended himself so stoutly during a running battle of two days that his assailants found it prudent to sheer off. The captured ship was re-named the Batchelor, in honour of one of the Bristol adventurers, and was put under the command of Dr. Dover, Selkirk being appointed master. The Marquis was afterwards sold at one of the Dutch settlements. The remainder of the voyage presented few incidents. As was almost always the case in privateering expeditions, the chief officers had several violent quarrels respecting the best course to pursue. Finally, the ships made for the Cape of Good Hope, whence, under the convoy of some Dutch men-of-war, they sailed for Europe, and arrived in the Texel in July, 1711. Some of the lucky owners repaired to Holland to feast their eyes on the booty, the gross value of which was reported to be £170,000. On the 14th October the three privateers anchored in the Thames. The story of Selkirk, who had not been heard of for eight years, excited much interest. Some details of his singular career were given in 1712 by Woodes Rogers in his well-written account of the voyage, as well as in the rival publication of Capt. Cooke, and a fuller narrative was published in 1713 by Steele in the *Englishman* Magazine. Selkirk informed Steele that he had received £800 as his share of the prize money, but that he was happier when he had not a farthing. He spent some time in Bristol, doubtless to obtain his money, but the local tradition that Defoe obtained his "papers," and was thus enabled to produce "Robinson Crusoe," is an idle fiction. It is known that Selkirk had no manuscripts, and the immortal story of Defoe was not published until nearly eight years after the return of the wanderer. Captain Woodes Rogers (who had built two houses in Queen Square before his privateering days) commanded an expedition sent out by the Government in 1717 for the purpose of crushing the formidable band of pirates that harboured in the Bahama Islands, and committed great ravages on passing vessels. His efforts were speedily successful, 200 of the sea brigands being forced to surrender at discretion. A curious paper written by Rogers to some one connected with the Government is amongst the State Papers for 1717. It states that the writer, out of his own money and on his credit with his friends, had raised £17,500, "to be employed towards making a settlement in the islands." The Government appear to have rendered him the support he appealed for; as he established himself at Providence, and was appointed Governor of the Bahamas in 1728. He died at his post in July, 1732. The embarrassments of John Romsey, the town clerk, seem to have been removed by the profits of his privateering adventure. In August, 1712, he presented to the Cathedral a pair of massive silver candlesticks, which cost him £114. One chronicler states that these articles were actually captured from the Spaniards by the Duke and Duchess in 1709. After standing for a century on the Communion Table, they were removed by a Low Church dean and chapter, but were restored to their old position in 1891, soon after the death of Dean Elliot.

It has been already mentioned that the Corporation, owing to financial difficulties, had felt compelled to suspend its yearly payment to the city members for their services in Parliament. The last "wages" were paid in 1695, when Sir John Knight received £95 13s. 4d. for 287 days' service, and Sir Richard Hart £101 13s. 4d. The civic treasury being once more prosperous, the Chamber, on the 5th July, 1708, initiated a less costly method of recognising the services of the city's representatives. It was ordered that a present of wine be made to them, one hogshead for each. One may feel certain that the quality of the gift would not be unworthy of the Corporation, but the wine (130 gallons) cost only 8s. per gallon. It afterwards became the custom to offer this honorarium annually, the quantity of wine being doubled later on, and it was not discontinued until within living memory.

During the year 1708, when William Penn was in great pecuniary straits owing to frauds practised upon him in Pennsylvania by a rogue named Philip Ford, a Bristol

Quaker whom he had sent out as his agent, he applied for pecuniary help to his wife's relatives and other friends in this city (which he had left in 1699, after residing here about two years). The Callowhills, Goldneys, and others advanced him £6,800, taking as security a mortgage upon the entire province of Pennsylvania. The formal " lease for a year," which formed part of the conveyance to them, is still amongst the archives of the Bristol Friends.

In February, 1709, the guardians of the poor, putting in force an Act passed in the previous century, resolved that all persons receiving weekly relief in the city should bear sewed upon the sleeve of their outer garment the letters .*. cut out in red cloth. The poor were reluctant to wear this degrading badge, which placed the lazy drunkard and the honest but unfortunate workman on the same level ; but in 1714 the guardians issued a warning that those who did not obey the order would be deprived of relief ; and it continued in force for many years.

In the spring of 1709 it was resolved to dispose of part of the civic plate, which was regarded as old and unfashionable, and to purchase several new articles of a more ornamental character. The London tradesman employed accordingly furnished " a large tankard, newest fashion," costing £17 5s. 2d. ; " a large salver, newest fashion," £11 7s. 7d. ; " a large monteth," £34 4s. 6d. ; and " two paire of candlesticks, snuffers, and pan," £33 10s. The plate, 300 ounces in weight, cost about 6s. 6d. per ounce. The silversmith allowed 5s. 4d. per ounce for the 214 ounces of old plate transferred to him.

Owing to a disastrous harvest in the preceding year, the price of corn in the early months of 1709 advanced to rates which placed the commonest bread almost beyond the reach of the poor, wheat rising to nearly 90s. per quarter. To add to the suffering, a terrible frost, " which rent and destroyed vast large trees," continued without intermission from Christmas Eve until the middle of April. As an inevitable consequence of dearth in those days, the labouring classes had recourse to violence and rioting ; and, as was usually the case in Bristol, the Kingswood colliers, perhaps the most neglected, degraded, and reckless community in the kingdom, took the lead in outraging the law. On the 21st May a body of about 400 miners, armed with cudgels, burst into the city demanding food, and speedily found sympathisers amongst the lower class of labourers, who had been intensely irritated by some shipments of wheat to

France and Spain. Warned by some previous disturbances, the authorities ("our maggotty governours," as Tucker irreverently terms them) had a party of militia in readiness, of which Major Wade took the command. But previous to resorting to extremities, the magistrates acquainted the rioters that wheat should be sold on the following Monday at 6s. 8d. per bushel, and the mob forthwith dispersed. A few of the colliers remained in the streets, using threatening language, whereupon they were caught, after a sharp scuffle, and imprisoned in the Council House. This came to the ears of the party that had left the city, who returned to rescue them; but a sanguinary conflict was avoided by the escape (said to have been winked at by the justices) of those in durance, who broke the new sash windows of the municipal building and went off with their companions. The crisis was costly to the Corporation. Besides having to compensate several constables for the loss of "cimeters," "fuzeys," halberts, hats and wigs, and to pay for a huge supply of beer for the militia and for extra assistance, the authorities found it necessary to make arrangements for selling corn at a reduced price; and Alderman Batchelor was paid £275 13s. "for corn had of Mr. Hort, occasioned by the mob." The corn, however, was resold, and produced £216. The sales to the poor exasperated the bakers, who "shutt up their ovens" on the mayor insisting that they should lower their prices; but they were compelled to submit on the magistrates giving the country bakers "free tolleration to come every day in the week to our citty and serve us with bread, tho' contrary to the citty libertys" (Tucker's MS.).

The Dean and Chapter and the neighbouring inhabitants having undertaken about this time to "level and beautify" College Green, which had long lain neglected and unfenced, the Corporation, in June, 1709, subscribed £40 towards the improvements, which included the planting of a double row of young trees (most of the old ones having been destroyed in the great storm of 1703).

Except under extraordinary circumstances, the yearly exercise of the train bands, or local militia, was confined to one day during the summer. The rural parishes seem to have been represented by a single man each, and the Corporation provided for only six. The arms and ammunition were furnished by the local authorities, and the charge for St. Philip's out-parish generally appears as "for serving in arms, and cleaning and mending them, and powder and shot," the total amounting to about 12s. In 1709, however, the parish was called upon for only 1s. for cleaning the musket, and 6d. for powder. In 1716 a new musket and bayonet cost 20s. 6d.

A movement started in London for spreading knowledge amongst the poor by the establishment of parochial charity schools extended about this time to Bristol, whose destitution in regard to education has been already noticed. The first to take action in the city was the Rev. Arthur Bedford, vicar of Temple, who, in a letter to the Christian Knowledge Society, stated that out of 232 poor children in his parish, only three were being instructed by the board of guardians, "whose pretence of their teaching the children has hitherto hindered all endeavours of this nature in Bristol." The parishioners having promised to subscribe £35 yearly, to which Mr. Colston added £10 per annum, a school for thirty boys was opened in August, 1709. Shortly afterwards Colston undertook to clothe the scholars, and followed this up by transferring an annuity of £80 to certain trustees "for clothing and educating forty poor boys for ever," also promising a site for adequate buildings "as soon as your parish is in cash to build a school." The money required, to which Colston largely contributed, was soon forthcoming, and the new institution was opened in December, 1711. The first local charity school for girls, also in Temple parish, was founded in 1713. The next parish school was opened in 1714 by the combined exertions of the inhabitants of St. Michael's and St. Augustine's.

The Government were much embarrassed in 1709 by the arrival of about eight thousand German Protestants, who, ruined by the French excesses in the Palatinate, fled to England for refuge. In a letter to the mayor of Bristol, dated the 29th June, the Privy Council, using the old Tudor formula, "after our hearty commendations," acquainted his worship with the Queen's order for a general collection on behalf of the unhappy fugitives, and went on to "earnestly recommend" the magistrates to find employment for some of the exiles in any local trade for which they might be fitted. Although the city had greatly profited by its reception of the industrious and skilful Huguenots and other foreign Protestants some twenty years earlier, the Corporation viewed the new appeal with extreme disfavour. Replying to the Government on the 9th July, the mayor had the effrontery to assert that "we have no manufactures save the making of cantaloons and woollen stuffs, which trade is so far decayed and lost that the great number of French refugees and of our own people who were employed therein are grown so poor that many hundreds have lately become chargeable"; adding that "the trade of this city consisting wholely in merchandize, shopkeeping, and navigation, we are not able of making any provision for these poor sufferers." Upwards of £15,000 were subscribed in London for relieving the immigrants, a number of whom were sent to the North of Ireland, and most of the others to Carolina and New York.

It was certainly true that the woollen manufactures of the city had shown signs of rapid decline. In October, 1709, the poor law authorities, unable to meet the cost of relief out of the amount of rates fixed by the Act of 1696, petitioned the Common Council to assist them in procuring further powers. The increased pauperism was alleged to be due to the general decay of the clothing trade, the high price of food during the previous three years, the draughts into the army and navy of men whose families were left destitute, and "the continual increase of buildings and inhabitants in the city, which increases the poor." The Corporation at first imagined that the difficulty could be overcome by temporary expedients. It had already advanced the guardians £1,000, chiefly from charitable funds, free of interest. In 1710 further loans were made to the extent of £550, on which no interest was to be paid for seven years. In 1712 the guardians applied for, and received, £300, and in 1713 they obtained £300 more, promising interest on the two latter sums. How the guardians succeeded in establishing an equilibrium will afterwards be seen. In the meantime it may be recorded that their embarrassments furnished arms to their opponents, in the front of whom were the churchwardens, still indignant at being deprived of their ancient privilege of distributing the poor rates. In Alderman Fox's collection is an exceedingly rare pamphlet, dated 1711, entitled "Some Considerations offered to the citizens of Bristol relating to the Corporation of the Poor." The writer, who denounces the institution as a "Whig device," states that all the plans attempted for employing the paupers had proved costly failures. The sum of £5,000 [really £4,360] had been raised by gifts to relieve the corporation, "but all is unaccountably sunk," while the workhouse is "crowded with idle, lazy, and lewd people."

The police arrangements of the city continued to be very defective. At the quarter sessions in October, 1709, the grand jury presented the officers of the rich parish of St. Stephen's, who, though they had only twelve public lamps to maintain, persistently neglected that duty. The scavengers were also presented for leaving the streets uncleansed—a neglect that remained chronic throughout the century.

In despite of the distress caused by war and bad harvests, the commerce of the port was making rapid strides. In 1710, the Custom House near Bristol Bridge being insufficient and inconvenient, the Commissioners suggested that the Corporation should erect a fitting building in Queen Square, for which they undertook to pay a rental of £120. On the 20th May the Chamber agreed to this proposal, and determined that the house should be built under its own supervision. The cost far exceeded expectation, being £2,725, exclusive of the value of the extensive site. The building, the basement storey of which was ornamented with pillars, was destroyed during the riots of 1831.

Although tea was extremely dear from 1707 to 1710, the cheapest being 16$s.$, and the dearest 43$s.$ per pound, tea-drinking was gradually increasing amongst the wealthier class of citizens. The first silver teapot mentioned in local wills was bequeathed by Robert Bound, whose testament was made during his mayoralty, in June, 1710. The next, accompanied with a silver milk-jug, occurs under 1719, in the will of Edith Morgan, whose daughter was married to a tea-dealer; and the third, to which a "tea table, with all the furniture of it, and my china ware," are added, is found in the will of Lady Cann, in 1722. Earthenware continued a great rarity. Amidst a quantity of household goods left by a Mrs. Turford in 1715, the testatrix proudly bequeathed "my fine earthen basin, and three fine earthen platters, a white cup with two handles, and a glass mug." There is no similar bequest until 1719, when half a dozen earthen plates are mentioned in a lady's will. No early record is found of coffee-pots. In 1708 the price of coffee rose, in consequence of the war, to 11$s.$ 6$d.$ per pound, and beer naturally maintained its supremacy.

The Common Council being of opinion, in June, 1710, that certain leaks in the wooden pipes laid by the Water Company on Bristol Bridge would gradually destroy the structure, ordered the managers to substitute leaden pipes. This is one of the rare references made in the Corporation minutes to the existence of the company in question, which never met with civic encouragement. From the "Act for supplying the City of Bristol with Fresh Water," passed in 1695, it appears that the promoters were Richard Bury, Bristol, silkman, Sam. Sandford, Bristol, wine cooper, and three London merchants. The capital was only £6,175, divided into 95 shares. Having purchased of the Corporation the right to take water from the Avon, for which they agreed to pay £166 13s. 4d. every seven years, the promoters erected some works at Hanham, whence the water was conveyed by gravitation to near Crewe's Hole, where it was driven by an "ingenious machine"—probably one of Savery's steam engines—to the higher level, and finally reached a small reservoir at Lawrence Hill. The supply pipes into the city were constructed of trunks of elms. The works were completed in 1698, for in October, 1699, a vote of thanks was passed to the company for having furnished, gratis, a twelve-month's supply to St. Peter's Hospital. The bulk of the citizens were dependent for water upon private wells (which in a town swarming with burial grounds and rank with surface impurities must have been often contaminated), or upon peripatetic vendors, who filled their buckets at the public conduits. But the yearly charge fixed by the company—40s. per family—deterred many people from resorting to the improved supply. From some expenses incurred by the Corporation in 1739, it appears that the company had then ten customers in High Street, and that the cost of 100 feet of new elm pipes was £7 10s. After an unprosperous career, the company abandoned the works at Hanham and Conham about 1783.

Luttrell's Diary briefly notes an incident in July, 1710, which must have occasioned great rejoicing in Bristol. Intelligence, it says, had reached this city that two ships belonging to the port, whilst on their way to the West Indies, were attacked by two French privateers of 110 men and 90 men respectively, but that the Bristol crews successfully defended themselves, and actually captured their assailants, whom they triumphantly carried to Antigua.

Reference has been made under 1702 to the abortive proposal of Edward Colston to make an extensive addition to the endowments of Queen Elizabeth's Hospital. After long meditation, Colston, in March, 1706, addressed a letter to the Merchants' Society, stating that although his offer to provide for fifty boys had been "hardly censured, even by some of the magistrates," yet he had not abandoned his design. Some thoughts had occurred to him of bestowing the gift upon London, where "I have had my education and spent good part of my days;" but as he had drawn his first breath in Bristol, he inclined to benefit its poor, and if the Merchants' Company would undertake the trust, he besought their consideration of the conditions appended to his letter. His intended endowment, he added, would amount to £600 per annum, to provide food, clothing, and education for fifty boys, at the rate of £10 each, and apprentice fees of £5, averaging £35 yearly; the salary of the master, etc., absorbing the balance. The company thankfully accepted the proposed trust, and soon afterwards recommended the purchase, for £1,500, of the "great house" on St. Augustine's Back, which had fallen from its ancient high estate, and been converted into a sugar refinery. Colston, by dint of higgling, obtained the mansion for £1,300, and the conversion to its new purpose was begun in August, 1707. In the following April, however, the founder informed the company that he had extended his design, and that accommodation must be provided for one hundred boys. He had been already told that the yearly outlay necessary for carrying on the school would not be less than £850, and estates valued at £18,000 had been secured to meet the charge. Further property was placed in the hands of the trustees to defray the additional expense, involving an outlay of, probably, nearly £10,000, the gross income being increased to £1,319. To complete his munificent purpose, Colston acquainted the Merchants' Society in April, 1710, that he should furnish the first hundred boys "each with a suit of clothes, cap, band, shirt, stockings, shoes, buckles, and porringer—one of each. Also brewing utensils, barrels, bedding, sheets, towels, tablecloths, notwithstanding the Hall was bound to provide the same" under the deed of settlement. Amongst other stipulations of that document it was provided that any scholar who should be taken to a dissenting chapel by his parents should be expelled, and that no boy should be apprenticed to a Dissenter. Colston nominated the first batch of scholars, but, as he was residing at Mortlake, the selection must have been made by his friends. The school was opened in July, 1710, when a special service took place in the cathedral. From an entry in St. Werburgh's parish accounts about this time, of a payment to the ringers when "Mr. Colston came to Bristol," he was probably present on the occasion. Amongst the Treasury Papers in the Record Office is a memorial from Colston, presented soon after this date, stating that he had formerly [in 1691] endowed a hospital [on St. Michael's Hill] for 24 poor persons, and now had provided for the training of 100 poor boys, and praying that the two charities might be exempted in the Land Tax Bill from the duty of 4s. in the pound. The answer is not recorded.

The following order was addressed to the civic chamberlain by the mayor and aldermen on the 5th July, 1710:— "The use of piques in the citty train-band being laid aside, you are hereby directed to provide three new musquets with suitable accoutrement for the [six] men appointed for the citty." The muskets cost £1 14s. 6d., and the "catouch boxes, &c.," 10s. 6d. The annual militia muster took place soon afterwards, when the six men who "appeared in arms" for the Corporation were paid 12s. for their day's work, and wine was drunk to the value of £3 12s. 6d.

The fit of High Church enthusiasm provoked by Dr. Sacheverell had at this time reached fever point, and the Government seized the opportunity to dissolve Parliament. The Bristol Tories, turning to advantage the great popularity of Colston, appealed to him to come forward as their candidate, and though he declined the honour on account of his age (74 years), it was nevertheless determined to nominate him in conjunction with Captain Joseph Earle, who was supposed to entertain kindred opinions. The result was disastrous to the previous members, Sir William Daines and Colonel Yate, who offered themselves for re-election. After a four days' poll in October, says the *Bristol Post Boy*, Mr. Colston was returned by a majority of "near a thousand voices, and Captain Earle by six hundred." [The actual numbers, according to the local record of Edmund Tucker, a High Church apothecary, were as follows:—Colston, 1785; Earle, 1527; Daines, 940; Yate, 744. Tucker adds that the Quaker electors were excluded, because they refused to take the oath of abjuration, and that the mayor, aldermen and councillors, "to their shame, stiffly opposed" the philanthropist.] The hazy newspaper reporter goes on to speak of the joy manifested "when they carried their member that was present along the city with the miter and streamers before him, the whole city being illuminated." Earle was a resident in Bristol, and Mr. Colston had apparently not arrived in time to take part in the celebration. He reached the city, however, on or before the 2nd November, his birthday, when a dinner was held to commemorate the triumph, at which he presided. His leading supporters seized the opportunity to found an association styled the Loyal Society, and the birthday dinners were continued by them (at Colston's School) until the death of Queen Anne, the Duke of Beaufort presiding in 1711 and 1713; but there is no evidence that Mr. Colston ever revisited the city. An unpleasant feature of his character was brought into prominence by this election. Having assisted in founding a school in Temple parish, he appears to have thought himself entitled to the political subserviency of the vicar. Mr. Bedford, however, was a Whig, and a Low Churchman. He had supported Whig candidates for Gloucestershire at a previous contest; he supported them again in 1710; and, what was worse, he did not vote for the High Church candidates in Bristol. Although the vicar had previously acquainted Colston with his intentions, the latter was deeply offended, and wrote to the trustees of Temple school to denounce Mr. Bedford's conduct as a "scandal" on the part of "no true son of the Church," adding that he should decline all further correspondence with this "favourer of fanaticism." Colston's biographer is driven to confess that "his antipathy to dissent approached the confines of bigotry," but it would appear that Low Churchmen were as obnoxious to him as Nonconformists. In 1712 the Corporation forwarded him a present of sherry, 15 gallons of which cost 7s. 4d., and 21 gallons more 8s., per gallon.

It was probably to the extreme bitterness of party feeling in Queen Anne's reign that the unwillingness of Bristolians to accept or retain municipal honours must be attributed. In the summer of 1707 four common councillors prayed liberty to resign their offices, while it was officially reported that several other members never attended, and that some who had been elected had never taken their seats. A few weeks later it was announced that Richard Leversedge, elected in 1706, and Thomas Hungerford, more recently chosen, had refused either to enter the Council or to pay the accustomed fine of £200. Some irregularity in the previous proceedings having been detected, the Chamber, in May, 1708, re-elected them, with just as little success. A committee was next appointed to devise a remedy, and upon its recommendation the Council resolved to apply for a new Charter, giving new and stringent powers for dealing with refractory citizens. After much secret negotiation between the Corporation and the Government, the sanction of the Queen to the coveted document was granted in July, 1710. The charter confirmed all the privileges conceded in previous reigns, ordered that the seven seats then vacant in the Chamber, through the "contumacious refusal" of certain burgesses to take the oaths, should be filled by fresh elections, and gave further powers to enforce penalties from defaulters. Up to this time the mayors of Bristol had been required, soon after election, to proceed to London to take the customary oaths before the judges. This irksome condition was now abolished, and the Crown surrendered its power to remove any member of the Corporation. The Common Council, after expressing its gratitude for the "great grace of her Majesty," bestowed ample largesses on the intermediary agents concerned in the transaction. Fifty guineas were voted for the purchase of a pair of coach horses for Sir Robert Eyre, the recorder (but preferring "your excellent sherry" he received a present of about sixty dozen); twelve dozen of the "very best sherry" were ordered to be sent to the Marquis of Dorchester, an equal quantity of "the best" to the Lord Chancellor (Cowper), and as much more (but not "best") to the Attorney General. A butt of the same liquor was forwarded to the Duke of Ormond, Lord High Steward of the city; while Mr. Town Clerk Romsey and Henry Yate, a lawyer, received upwards of £450 between them for their fees, expenses, and trouble. The fines for non-acceptance of the office of mayor, sheriff, or councillor were fixed at £400, £300, and £200 respectively, but with an exemption for any person making oath of being worth less than £2,000. Elections to fill the vacant seats followed, and Messrs. Leversedge and Hungerford were for a third time chosen. Urging conscientious scruples in reference to the oaths, they remained as impracticable as before. In September, 1711, the mayor acquainted the Chamber that he had caused them to be arrested, "of which the House approved," but their temporary detention was fruitless. A lengthy litigation followed, and in July, 1717, after judgment had been obtained against Hungerford, and execution levied, he paid £240, the fine and costs. Leversedge held out until 1721, when he paid the fine of £200, but prayed for a reduction of the penalty, asserting that his refusal to be sworn had arisen from "a rash vow." The Council, satisfied with its victory, returned him £60, "as a gift," towards paying his expenses.

Sir Robert Atkyns, whilst compiling his History of Gloucestershire, obtained statistics from Clifton in reference to the population. He was informed that the number of births in 1710 was 12, and that the inhabitants were estimated at 450. Probably about five-sixths of the parishioners resided on the low ground near the Avon.

The poor being again plunged in deep distress by the scarcity of food and the severity of the weather, the Council, in February, 1711, voted £100, and forthwith privately subscribed £2,500 more, towards the relief of the sufferers—an extraordinary act of munificence, having regard to the average mercantile incomes of that generation.

The following curious account was paid by the city chamberlain on the 17th February, 1711:—"John Carter, Dr. to Joseph Bates. For two months and three weeks meat, drink, washing and lodging at 2s. 4d. per week, £1 5s. 8d." Why the note was paid by the Corporation does not appear. Bates was keeper of Bridewell, and his cheaply provided guest may have been maintained to give evidence in some case tried at the quarter sessions. Other items in the civic accounts show the then low cost of living. On one occasion a man, his wife, and a child, having arrived with a magisterial "pass" on their way to Ireland, and being detained for seven weeks by contrary winds, were lodged and boarded for 5s. 8d. per week at the expense of the Corporation.

Owing to the narrowness of the streets, the civic officials kept a sharp eye on attempted encroachments. In May, 1711, a man who had built a house in Broad Street was found to have appropriated twenty-two inches of the roadway, and a similar offence had been committed in Corn Street. The Council gave orders that the "purprestures" should be removed and the offenders indicted. In February, 1716, the nuisance created by the vegetable markets in the central streets having become intolerable, the dealers in "garden stuff" were directed to migrate to Temple Street and Broadmead, a peremptory order being issued against the sale of such commodities in the principal thoroughfares. Another step in the same direction was taken in 1717, when the fish market, held in the middle of High Street, was removed to the Quay, near St. Stephen's Church. To make way for it, "the old Conduit was taken down, and a new one of a lesser bulk erected, somewhat nearer to the Aven" (Tucker's Annals).

The death of Dr. John Hall, bishop of Bristol, in 1711, enabled the Government to provide in an odd way for a retiring diplomatist, John Robinson, D.D., who had been the English envoy in Sweden for twenty-six years, being appointed to the vacancy. The new head of the diocese entered the city on the 15th June, "being accompanied from Wells with severall hundred horse, near thirty clergymen, and many coaches with the great men of our citty therein" (Tucker's MS.). The new bishop forthwith gave orders for a series of confirmation services, but was soon recalled to his old profession, and despatched to the continent to negotiate peace with France. A curious Runic inscription, placed in the Cathedral by Bishop Robinson, is the only local souvenir of his brief episcopate.

The importance of the trade between Bristol and the West Indies has been already indicated. It had largely increased since the beginning of the century, through the abolition, in 1698, of the monopoly previously enjoyed by the African Company—a handful of London capitalists—of the trade with Africa. Bristol merchants, who had long complained of the restrictions imposed upon the slave trade, lost no time in taking advantage of this new opening for commerce. Cargoes of goods suitable for bartering with the native slave dealers were made up in Bristol, where many of the articles soon began to be manufactured; the laden ships sailed direct to Africa, where the merchandise was exchanged for human beings; the latter were transported to the West India Islands; and the vessels finally returned with a cargo of tropical commodities. In 1709 the number of Bristol ships engaged in this trade was no less than fifty-seven. The impulse given to local trade was proportionate to the vast profits earned by the adventurers; and the discovery, in 1711, that the African Company were insidiously striving to secure a revival of their old monopoly excited dismay and wrath in local circles. The Corporation and the Merchants' Society took immediate steps to defend the interests of the city. Deputations were sent to Westminster to urge the advantages of freedom of trade, and the obnoxious scheme was defeated. Its baffled promoters renewed their efforts in the two following sessions, but were as pertinaciously opposed by Bristol and the other provincial ports. A petition to the House of Commons, forwarded by the Council in 1713, is now amusing for the frankness of its statements, and for the contrast they present with the Chamber's untruthful excuses for refusing to succour the German refugees in 1709. The Corporation alleged that the subsistence of Bristolians chiefly depended on their West India and African trade, which employed great numbers in shipyards and in "manufactures of wool, iron, tin, copper, brass, &c., a considerable part whereof is exported to Africa for buying of negroes." Commerce with Africa and America being thus "the great support of our people at home, and foundation of our trade abroad," the Chamber prayed that no favoured company should be allowed to exclude the rest of her Majesty's subjects from the African coast. A similar petition was forwarded by the Merchant Venturers, who declared that they had many ships suitable only for the African trade, and would be ruined if excluded from it. The would-be monopolists, after three rebuffs, temporarily abandoned the field. The Council subscribed £100 towards the expenses of the first year's opposition, and Mr. John Day, who had remained on guard in London during the two following sessions, received £293 from the Corporation and others for his services. In 1720 the South Sea Company, when at the height of its popularity, made a fresh attempt to secure a monopoly of the African trade, much to the exasperation of Bristol merchants. The Council alone spent £140 in baffling this attack, and on the bursting of the gigantic bubble, the Chamber addressed the House of Commons, praising its diligence "in bringing to condign punishment those voracious robbers, the mismanagers of South Sea stock," and praying that its rigour might not be slackened until they had met with their deserts. In 1725, and in successive sessions until 1731, the African Company made renewed but fruitless efforts to deprive the provincial ports of their share in a profitable trade. The cost incurred by Bristol in defeating the selfish manœuvrers was little short of £2,000, nearly £900 of which amount (including the cost of about 200 gallons of wine sent up to the civic delegates) were defrayed by the Corporation. In a pecuniary point of view the money was profitably laid out. The African Company abandoned the transport of slaves, contenting itself with a traffic in ivory and gold dust, and the triangular voyages of the Bristol ships greatly increased in number and yielded rich returns.

An illustration of the peculiar customs of the age in reference to criminals occurs in the minutes of the Council in September, 1711. A woman had been condemned to death for a felony in the previous year; but the under-sheriff, at the instance of the magistrates, had obtained the grant of a pardon, at a cost of six guineas, and applied to the Chamber to be refunded. The demand was conceded with reluctance, a resolution being passed "that no pardons be sued out for the future at the city's charge without the previous direction of this House." The order, like many other civic orders, soon became obsolete. On the 15th September, 1721, the Council resolved as follows:—"There being now four prisoners in Newgate who have layne under sentence of death for several years, being reprieved by the magistrates, and they having by the mediation of the Recorder been inserted in the Western Circuit Pardon, for the doing whereof the Clerk of Assize claymed an expense of four guineas per head, it is ordered that sixteen guineas be paid." In the following year the same official was granted fifteen guineas for the pardons (obtained "without the order of this House") of "eight or more" prisoners lying under sentence of death. This order was followed by a resolution indicating that ladies occasionally interested themselves in the fate of criminals:—" Several condemned persons having been begged off from execution by some persons of this body or their wives or relations, and afterwards the burthen of the expense in procuring the pardon has been upon the city: it is ordered that for the future such person who shall sue for any criminal's pardon shall at his own expense sue out the same." Nevertheless, in 1727, the clerk of assize was paid £33 for "incerting the condemned prisoners in the Western Circuit Pardon;" and in 1740, it being intimated that Henry Fane, Esq., had taken trouble to obtain several pardons, but had received no acknowledgment, he was voted "a present of a gross of sherry as a compliment." What seems still more strange to modern eyes, there is a record in the minutes that on one occasion the friends of a condemned criminal, being willing to purchase a pardon, were ordered to give security for £100 that they would transport the culprit; while in another case (April, 1711) a man charged with felony, but whose indictment had been rejected by the grand jury, was sentenced by the magistrates to be kept in gaol unless and until his father should give security to transport him to the plantations!

At a meeting of the Merchants' Society in December, 1711, a petition was read from Charles Harford, merchant, praying to be admitted a member of the body on payment of a fine. High Churchmen being then overflowing with intolerance, a resolution was passed rejecting the appeal, on the ground that Mr. Harford was a Quaker, and a further resolution was passed that "in future no professed Quaker should be admitted by fine into the freedom of the Hall."

The churchwardens of All Saints' became dissatisfied about this period with the low Norman tower of the church, and resolved to substitute it by something more "graceful." The old tower was therefore destroyed; but a bitter controversy arose amongst the admirers of "jarring schemes" of rival architects, and the hideous design carried out was not completed until 1717. The expenditure was about £600, of which Mr. Colston gave £250. Subsequently other "renovations" were proposed, and, the churchwardens having stated that £800 would be needed, the Corporation gave £100. The dome surmounting the new tower happily became ruinous in less than a century, and was replaced by the existing anomaly.

A considerable extension of the eastern suburb of the city took place about this time by the construction of Wade Street, Great George and Great Anne Streets, etc. The owners of the ground, Nathaniel Wade and Abraham Hooke, built a bridge in 1711 over the Froom, at Wade Street, for the development of the estate; and as Wade, though holding an important office under the Corporation, was generally unpopular from his abject confessions to James II., after being a leader in the Monmouth rebellion, the construction was universally known as Traitor's Bridge, and is even so designated in the minutes of the Common Council.

Early in 1712, the incumbents of the city parishes, encouraged by the exuberant High Church principles of the House of Commons, resolved on seeking the help of Parliament for the improvement of their incomes. Before narrating the issue, it may be interesting to show how pitiful those incomes were. Amongst Archbishop Sancroft's MSS. is a paper in the prelate's handwriting, from which it appears that the state of the Bristol clergy just before the Revolution had given him some concern. As his account of the livings has never been printed, and as little had occurred between Sancroft's deprivation and 1712 to improve the stipends, the document is here introduced, omitting the names of the incumbents, four of whom held two livings each:—

The parish Churches in Bristol with their present certain Endowments.
R. of S. Werburg. A House worth £10 per ann. Gift sermons £10 p. a.
R. of S. Stephens. A House worth £10 per ann. Gift sermons £10 p. a.
V. of All Saints. A House worth £10 per ann. Gift sermons £12 p. a.
V. of St. Augustins. A House worth £4 per an. Gift sermons 00.
V. of St. Nicolas. No House. [Gift sermons about £18.]
V. of St. Leonards. House worth £2 per ann. Tithe...
V. of St. Philip and Jacob. House worth £5 per. an.
R. of St. Peters. House worth
V. of H. Cross als. Temple. House worth £6 per an. Gift sermons £10 per an.
R. of S. Jo. Baptist w. } Gift sermons £5 per an.
S. Lawrence.
R. of Xt. Church. No House. Gift sermons...
R. of St. Michael. House worth £6 per an. Tithe...

Impr. of S. James. House worth £8 per an. Gift sermons £2 10s. per an.
R. of S. Ewens. No House.
Capella S. Marie Redcliff. A House. Gift sermons...
Capella S. Thomæ. Gift sermons £8 per an.
R. of S. Mary port. A House.

  The parish Churches nigh Bristol in Gloucestershire.
Curacy of Clifton. Ye Impropriator (Major Hodges) allows £10 per an.
—— Westbury. Sr. Fr. Fane Impr. allows £10 per an. }
V. of Almondbury. Ye Bp. Patron and Impr. }
 worth together £50 p. a.
V. of Henbury, w. Cap. Northwick and Aust. Val. £100.
Curacy of Stapleton. Impr. Mr. Walker. Val. £15.
Curacy of Horvill. Bp. Impropr. Val. £4.
Curacy of Abbots Leigh. Impr. Mr. Horton, Canon of Sarum. Val. £14.

  The clergy, in their published "Apology" for taking action, alleged that, by the confession of their opponents, they "had no legal claim to anything, and that their subsistence depended entirely upon the voluntary contributions of the people," which were collected in some parishes by the ministers and churchwardens, and in others by the ministers alone, who went "from house to house in order to provoke the people's bounty." That "bounty" seems to have been grudgingly bestowed. A physician or a barrister, says the writer, is not considered overpaid by a guinea for a single consultation; "but five shillings, by some who esteem themselves no common parishioners, shall be thought reward great enough not only for a single visit of a divine, but his sermons, his attendance, advise, throughout the whole year." It was further asserted that the income of some livings did not reach "above £30 a year, if that;" the medium value being set down at from £70 to £80, while that of "the largest and best parishes, where two sermons were preached every Sunday," did not exceed £100. During the Commonwealth, the Presbyterian clergy obtained a local Act for their better maintenance, by which a rate of 1s. 6d. in the pound was assessed on houses and warehouses, besides 5s. in the pound levied on tradesmen's stocks. Taking advantage of a precedent which many Dissenters would gladly have forgotten, the Bill produced by the clergy proposed to levy £1,500 a year on personal estates, to be collected by the parish officers. The sum intended to be raised in St. James's, St. Stephen's, St. Nicholas's, St. Philip's, and St. Michael's, where curates were kept, was £150 per parish, in Temple £110, and in All Saints' £100; smaller amounts being fixed for the ten remaining parishes, where only one sermon was preached on Sundays. The scheme was received with disapprobation, and the Common Council lost no time in declaring that it would strenuously oppose the Bill in Parliament. The clergy, disheartened by the storm aroused in the city, abandoned the field.

The enactment of the Occasional Conformity Act by the High Church majority in Parliament added fresh fuel to the excitement of the citizens in the early months of 1712. The statute, which inflicted a fine of £40 on any member of a Corporation who attended service in a "conventicle," rendered it impossible for conscientious Dissenters to accept or retain civic distinctions, and three leading members of the Council, Morgan Smith, Abraham Hooke, and Onesiphorus Tyndall (all ex-sheriffs) petitioned that they might be relieved of the office of counsellor without payment of a fine. Their request was complied with on the 22nd March by a unanimous vote. Mr. Tyndall was treasurer of Lewins Mead congregation in 1704. The Act which caused this secession was repealed a few years later.

Whilst the Corporation was deliberating on the case of the above aggrieved Dissenters, an extraordinary scene was taking place in the Cathedral. The records of the Consistory Court show that Ann Roberts, of St. Augustine's, had been convicted of having committed incest with her father, and that by the sentence of the chancellor she was ordered to repair to the cathedral at the hour of morning prayer on the 22nd March, and to stand in the choir before the minister and congregation, clad in a white sheet and bearing a white wand, during the whole of the service, and was further, after the second lesson, to make humble confession of, and profess penitence for, her crime. A certificate that the sentence had been carried out was signed by one of the minor canons.

In the session of 1699-1700 a petition was presented to Parliament by the corporation of Bath praying for powers to make the Avon navigable to that city, one of the chief advantages of which work, it was urged, would be to "bring down the dearness of provisions complained of by all persons who frequent the Bath." Vehement petitions against the scheme were addressed to the House of Commons by the Quarter Sessions Court of Somerset and the gentry, farmers, and traders of the neighbourhood, who pleaded that they would be impoverished by the competition of commodities brought in by cheap water carriage. The opposition became so formidable that the Bill was withdrawn. Early in 1712 the corporation of Bath renewed their application, when it was opposed with as much obstinacy as before. Some of the petitioners declared that the carrying trade of the district was threatened by the Bill with utter ruin; others, chiefly landed gentry, affirmed that the import of food "from Wales and other parts where the value of lands *are* low" would be so disastrous that they would be unable to pay their taxes. The grand jury at Wilts Assizes were amongst the most urgent suitors for the rejection of the Bill, as were the inhabitants of Marshfield, who affirmed that their malt trade would be destroyed if it had to compete with distant rivals. The measure, nevertheless, became law, but it remained a dead letter for several years. In March, 1725, a scheme for carrying out the work having been suggested by Mr. John Hobbs, a Bristol timber merchant, the corporation of Bath transferred the powers of the Act to thirty-two individuals, who undertook to open the navigation "at the equal cost of each copartner." The thirty-two shareholders included the Duke of Beaufort, General Wade, John Codrington, of Wraxall, Ralph Allen, of Bath, and Dr. John Lane, Thomas Tyndale, James Hardwick, and John Hobbs, of Bristol. The navigation extended only from Bath to Hanham, so that the remainder of the route was practicable only when the course of the Avon was filled by the tide. The works were finished in December, 1727, and on the 3rd January Lord Falmouth proceeded from Bristol to Bath by water, "being the first noble person who used that passage." The barges were towed by men, power to construct a towing path for horses being wanting until a much later period. A Bath correspondent of the *Gloucester Journal*, writing on the 3rd November, 1729, recorded that "Mr. Hobbes, merchant, of Bristol, who was the chief instrument of making the river Avon navigable to this place," had just been admitted a free burgess of Bath. The above facts dispose of the current story that all the credit of carrying out the undertaking was due to the Duke of Beaufort. The navigation was long obnoxious to the Kingswood colliers, owing to the quantity of Shropshire coal conveyed to Bath. In consequence of their violence, an Act of Parliament was passed, enacting that the destruction of weirs or locks should be punished with death. Nevertheless, in November, 1738, a disguised mob almost totally demolished the lock at Saltford, and escaped with impunity. The cost of the navigation works is not given in any local work, but in 1825, when the first proposal was started for a railway to London, a correspondent of a Bristol journal asserted that less than £150 each was contributed by the thirty-two original proprietors, and that one share had recently sold for £4.000.

The narrow-minded trading theories of the age are illustrated by a petition presented to the House of Commons in 1712 by Abraham Elton, Benjamin Coole, and Edward Lloyd, three Bristol merchants, and others representing the brass manufactories of the kingdom. The applicants, after pointing out that their goods were made by English workmen, and composed of English copper and calamine, complained that their foreign rivals were "encouraged" by the existing laws, and prayed relief. From the subsequent report of a committee, it appears that the encouragement of the foreigner consisted in his being mulcted with a protective import duty varying from £9 10s. to £30 per ton; and that the petitioners wanted this tax largely increased or foreign entries prohibited. It was stated that 21,000 men were employed in the home trade, and that at Bristol the two copper works consumed 2,000 tons of coal weekly, besides 400 tons of fuel used at the brass works. In opposition to the petitioners, a crowd of witnesses was brought forward by persons interested in the Dutch brass trade, who represented that the English-made goods were of an inferior quality, and that an increased duty on foreign brass would ruin many home industries depending on Dutch markets. To rebut this evidence a certificate was produced from the braziers of Bristol, asserting that the local manufacturers had brought their products to such perfection that satisfactory brass was now offered £20 per ton below former prices. A proposal to considerably increase the foreign duties was finally rejected.

Another local petition of the same year deserves a record. It proceeded from Nicholas Churchman, master of the Bristol Company of Tanners, and others, and set forth that the Irish people, having taken to purchasing bark in England, refused to ship their raw hides, preferring to make their leather at home, to the great loss and discouragement of English tanners. As the sale of bark caused all the mischief, the petitioners prayed that further exports should be prohibited. A committee was appointed, but without result.

The Rev. William Goldwin, M.A., master of the Grammar School, believing himself a poet, favoured the city in 1712 with what he was pleased to call "A Poetical Description of Bristol," which was published by "Joseph Penn, bookseller, against the Corn Market in Wine Street." Although Mr. Goldwin's verses can be qualified only as lamentably prosaic, they afford some interesting hints as to the appearance of the city at the time they were written. High Street, which during the Civil War had been noted by a traveller as a chief centre of mercers, silkmen and linen drapers, was still the favourite resort of fashionable customers:—

> Bedeckt with gawdy Shops on both its Lines.

And its shops had glass windows:—

> . . . Piles of Plate refined with Art,
> Refulgent Rays through glassy Barriers dart.
> Here the whole Wardrobe of the female Dress
> In wealthy Folds a standing Camp possess.

Temple Street also in fair time could boast of its splendours:—

> The spacious (!) Street, where London Wares
> Display the tawdry Pageantry of Fairs,
> Temptations offered to the Virgins there
> To choose a Marriage-dress of modish Air.
> Observe the flippant Sparks in Smartness nurs'd,
> With Fleet Street style and Ludgate Language vers'd, &c.

Mr. Goldwin is severe upon the wares of the Coffee Houses:—

> Here wise Remarkers on the Church and State
> O'er Turkish Lap and smoaky Whiffs debate.
> Here half shut Authors in Confusion lye,
> And kindling Stuffs for Party Heats supply.
> Pernicious Scribblers, &c.

The charms of Clifton were still undiscovered. When merchants had grown rich with trafficking in the chief imports of the city:—

> Florentia's Wines and Sherry's flavour'd Must,
> Jamaica's Growth and Guinea's Golden-dust,

they retired to the healthful slopes of St. Michael's Hill:—

> Here wealthy Cits discharged from worldly Cares
> Conclude the downward Race of falling Years.
> Here sickly Souls with broken Health repair
> To suck the wholesome Drafts of healing Air.

In other parts of the city the glass-houses were a nuisance:—

> Whose sootty Stench the Earth and Sky annoys,
> And Nature's blooming Verdure half destroys.

Mr. Goldwin's rambling pen carries him to Newgate, where he sees "mournful debtors weep in ghastly hue" in company, with felons, both inhaling unwholesome air in dungeons, and both eking out existence by the help of a begging box at the gaol door. He goes to the Back, and sees "cackling dames and feathered cacklers" in the Welsh Market. He passes on to Queen Square, and finds "grandeur and neatness shine" in the newly built Custom House, and the "Praetorian dignity" well supported in the dwelling of the mayor. Perhaps his most surprising discovery, to modern readers at least, was "Florio's happy spot," the Great Gardens, in Temple parish, now black, dismal, and sordid, but then, he said, fragrant with jasmin, roses, and orange flowers, and beauteous with fantastically cut yew and holly trees.

In 1712 a company of adventurous Bristolians, of whom the most prominent was Joshua Franklyn, a merchant, resolved upon constructing a dock for the accommodation of shipping at Sea Mills. The vanity of human aspirations was exemplified in the terms of the lease of the required land, which (by virtue of a special Act of Parliament) was transferred to the undertakers by Edward Southwell, of Kingsweston, for a term of 999 years, at an annual rent of £81. The site adjoined a Roman station, of which some vestiges still remain, and in the course of excavating the dock the workmen came across an ancient gateway, and a quantity of coins of Nero, Constantine, and Constantius. With the exception of a dock at Liverpool, commenced in 1709, but not finished until 1717, the Sea Mills dock was the first mercantile basin constructed in England. The adventure was divided into thirty-two shares, on which upwards of £300 each are said to have been called. Franklyn sank a large part of his fortune in the undertaking. There is no record of the opening of the dock. In a financial point of view, the place was a failure from the outset, the necessity of transhipping cargoes into barges overriding the advantage it possessed of keeping vessels afloat at low water. The dock was found useful, however, for the fitting out of privateers, and the discharging of whaling ships. Rudder, in his History of Gloucestershire, published in 1779, stated that the dock had then been "utterly abandoned for several years," and that the shares had only "an ideal value." One of the latest attempts to turn the property to account was made in January, 1798, when the dock, with its "spacious warehouses" and some adjoining tenements, was offered to be let.

Two ropewalks with some appended "tar houses" in close proximity to Queen Square having been much complained of, the Corporation, in August, 1712, agreed with the owners for the purchase of the ground, so as to remove the nuisances. One of the roperies belonged to the Merchants' Society, who refused to sell unless a term of 23 years was added to the 58 years' lease of the Wharfage Dues then in their hands. To soften the rigour of this condition, they promised that "any member of the Council should have liberty to make any publick feast or entertainment in the Merchants' Hall." The Chamber agreed to the conditions, but seems to have had a somewhat low opinion of the good faith of the Company, for a strict order was given to the town clerk to retain the new lease until the Merchants had delivered the conveyance of the ropewalk. Oddly enough, no complaint was raised against the receptacle for scavengers' sweepings, collected from all the central parishes, which was situated in the rear of the eastern side of the square; and it was not until many years afterwards that this nuisance was removed.

The members of the Corporation appear to have had a predilection for occasional sermons, but placed a low pecuniary value upon them. Perhaps in consequence of a remonstrance, the Council, on the 15th September, ordered "that the several ministers who have preached the publick sermons att the Quarter Sessions and gaole delivery for this year past shall have added to their usual allowances soe much as shall make itt upp one guinea for every sermon, and this order to continue till further order."

Up to this time, the only means of communication between the central parts of the city and College Green lay through Christmas Street and Horse (now Host) Street. In October, 1712, in compliance with a numerously signed petition, the Chamber ordered the erection of a "movable bridge" over the Froom, from St. Augustine's Back to the opposite Quay. The work must have proceeded with great deliberation, for the structure figures in the corporate accounts until 1718. The cost was £1,044. A lanthorn, costing 20s., was placed upon the bridge in May, 1718, doubtless to protect it against shipping collisions. In April, 1722, it was ordered that no laden cart should cross the bridge, under a penalty of £1. In 1738 the Corporation bought another lanthorn, perhaps for the same place. The article must have been of unusual size, for the glass sides cost 45s., and the framework £6 11s.

A scarce book entitled "An Account of Charity Schools in Great Britain," published in 1712, states that there was a school upon the Quay at Bristol, "endowed by Lady [Susanna] Holworthy, wherein eight persons are instructed in the art of navigation." This statement, although unnoticed by any local historian, is confirmed by the records of the Merchants' Society, a subscription of £2 having been yearly paid by them to the school, which in 1722 was removed to the Merchants' Hall, an old kitchen having been fitted up for its accommodation. In 1738, Lady Holworthy's bequest, then amounting to £260, and a gift of £100 made by Capt. John Price, R.N., were handed over by the Corporation to the Merchants' Company, upon the latter undertaking to pay £20 a year for ever to a master capable of teaching navigation.

Amongst the swords of state possessed by the Corporation is a handsome weapon presented to the city by John de Wells, lord mayor of London in 1431, and styled in civic records the Pearl Sword. As no traces of pearls are visible on the scabbard, a fiction has of course been invented to explain their disappearance, and the tradition of the Council House is that the jewels were pilfered by a succession of covetous mayoresses. A search into a quantity of old accounts, by the kind permission of the treasurer, has exploded this fable. In May, 1713, the sword was repaired by a silversmith named Cossley, who, after charging £17 for embroidering the scabbard, and £10 17s. 3d. for gilding and reparations, acknowledges the possession of "279 perls of noe use, neither could they be put on." The Corporation assessed the value of the pearls at £3 12s., which Cossley allowed.

Peace with France, arranged at Utrecht by Dr. Robinson, Bishop of Bristol, and others, was proclaimed on May 12th, 1713, at the High Cross, St. Peter's Cross, Temple Cross, and other places, amidst formal demonstrations of joy. The treaty, although far from popular at the time, contained provisions which tended largely to the development of local commerce. France ceded to this country Newfoundland, Nova Scotia, Hudson's Bay, and part of the island of St. Christopher; but to Bristol merchants the most popular feature of the treaty was the "Assiento clause," by which England was granted the monopoly of supplying the Spanish colonies with slaves. Bishop Robinson was rewarded for his labours by being translated to the see of London.

The expenditure for corporate festivities in connection with the Peace denotes a change of taste in reference to wine. The civic dignitaries had long regaled themselves exclusively on sherry and claret; and although in 1703, soon after the outbreak of war with France, a treaty was made with Portugal admitting her wines at an exceptionally low rate of duty, the Corporation at first forsook claret for Florence wine, which figures largely in the accounts. At the above rejoicings, however, the civic body consumed 21 gallons of claret, 11 of sherry, and small quantities of Canary and "Rhenish," while, instead of Florence, there was a purchase of 17 gallons of "red Alicant," costing 6s. a gallon. In the following year, on the accession of George I., Alicant gave place to Port, which is mentioned for the first time, and met with an enthusiastic reception, the wine bill on the proclamation day embracing 53 gallons of the liquor at 5s. 4d., 15 gallons of sherry at 7s. 6d., 15 gallons of claret at 10s., and other red wine to the value of £4 15s. 6d. The relish of the corporate body for the Portuguese import subsequently became proverbial.

It was the intention of the Government to follow up the Peace with a treaty of commerce, by which a system of free trade would have been established between England and France. Such a scheme, however, was opposed to the commercial ideas of the age, and many interests promptly raised an agitation. The distilling trade in Bristol was especially loud in its protests. During the war, the lack of brandy was supplied by distillation from domestic produce, cider and perry being made largely available. It being certain that "apple brandy" would be rapidly supplanted by the genuine French article, upwards of twenty Bristol distillers petitioned the House of Commons for protection. They produced, they said, a "good wholesome fine brandy" which answered every needful purpose, and, if only kept long enough, was hardly distinguishable from grape spirit; but if the latter came into the field local distillation would be stopped, the petitioners impoverished, and good crops of English fruit left rotting on the ground. Distillers from malt and sugar, raising a similar outcry, were supported by the West India interest. The silk manufacturers petitioned earnestly against the admission of French goods, while the clothiers prayed for the "discouragement" (meaning interdiction) of Spanish and Portuguese fabrics. The agitation was fatal to the Government Bill. It was found impracticable, however, to prohibit the importation of French brandy, which soon recovered its old supremacy. In the *Bristol Newspaper* of January 27th, 1728, John King, merchant, Queen Square, the ancestor of a still eminent mercantile family, announced that he had "fine Nance Brandy" on sale at 7s. per gallon by the butt, or 7s. 6d. retail; also good rum at 6s. 6d. by the hogshead, or 7s. by the single gallon.

A general election took place in September. Mr. Colston having retired, the Tory party nominated Thomas Edwards, jun., who married Mary Hayman, the philanthropist's niece; Colonel Joseph Earle solicited re-election; and Sir William Daines endeavoured to recover his former seat. The polling went on for two days amidst perpetual tumult and bloodshed; rival mobs, stimulated by unstinted supplies of liquor, assailing not only each other, but peaceful electors. Ultimately the sheriffs, dreading loss of life, closed the poll, although less than a fourth of the citizens had voted. The numbers recorded for the candidates (communicated by the Rev. A. B. Beaven) were:—Colonel Earle, who was supported by both parties, 656; Mr. Edwards, 474; Sir William Daines, 189. The unsuccessful candidate petitioned against Edwards in the following session, alleging that his return (which was made only by one sheriff, the other admitting the illegality of the proceedings) was due to rioting and intimidation on the part of a hired multitude " who were not inhabitants," meaning, doubtless, mercenaries from " outside the Gate." The committee of privileges had not reported on this petition when the Parliament came to an end through the death of the Queen. A few months later, the Tory party, which had been instrumental in returning Mr. Earle, had a violent quarrel with that gentleman. In the British Museum is a very rare pamphlet, printed in 1714, and entitled " A few short and true Reasons why a late Member was expelled from the Loyal Society." The writer alleges that the person in question—who could be no one but Earle—was scandalously loose in his principles, of so little reputation that he could not gain a handful of votes on his own account, so shabby that when president of the society (which Earle was in 1712) he starved the company at the annual dinner, and afterwards refused to pay the cook, so mean as to plead his privilege of Parliament to avoid payment of dues to his parish church, and so false that " though he solemnly promised Mr. Colston to stand by the Society and the Church, he keeps no correspondence with the city except with " Dissenters.

Flushed with the success of the election, the High Church party resolved on pursuing their victory into the Corporation of the Poor, where a revolutionary change was accomplished. As has been already shown, the guardians were staggering under a constantly increasing load of debt arising from the growth of population. It was at length resolved to apply to Parliament for power to increase the total yearly rates from £2,370 to £3,500. A Bill for that purpose was introduced in 1714, but was bitterly opposed by the Tory party, who alleged that the Corporation of the Poor was a Whig device, and that the guardians had been guilty of mismanagement. The latter retorted that their difficulties had arisen through the deliberate misstatement by the churchwardens of the actual amount spent on the poor in 1695, which was £500 in excess of the sum reported. They showed, moreover, that the rates outside the city, still administered by the churchwardens, had increased 150 per cent. In the result, the guardians obtained increased rating powers only by submitting to be swamped. The High Church party having obtained the assistance of the Government, which was bent on persecuting Dissenters, provisions were introduced into the Bill by which the thirty-four churchwardens of the city parishes became members of the incorporation by virtue of their office. A clause was also introduced into the Act requiring every guardian to take the sacrament in a parish church, thus disqualifying Dissenters. (By another Act, passed simultaneously, though urgently petitioned against by Bristol Dissenters, every schoolmaster and private teacher was subjected to the same test.) The violence of the Tories, however, brought about a reaction. The exclusion of many experienced guardians, and the irruption of a crowd of men experienced only in party intrigues, were found to be disastrous to the working of the poor law machinery, and four years later, by another Act, the junior moiety of the churchwardens was excluded from the board and the sacramental test repealed. Some curious documents relating to the latter statute are in the British Museum. In one of these it is alleged that the Church party promoted the reform, having perceived "their mistake in encumbering themselves with offices unattended with profit, honour, or interest," and being now desirous of forcing Dissenters to bear such offices, "and in some measure to ease churchmen." But the Bishop of Bristol (Smalridge) offered a strenuous resistance to the Bill in the House of Lords, and signed an indignant protest against "letting in" Nonconformists and "shutting out" churchwardens. One may divine the political character of the guardians from the fact that they passed a vote of thanks to Dr. Smalridge for his opposition to the measure.

A murder that caused a great sensation was committed about this time, on Durdham Down, by one Captain Maccartny on a person named Beechy, who had lodged with him in Bristol on the night before the crime. The facts are briefly summarised in the Common Council minutes dated April 12th, 1714. It seems that upon the murder being discovered the mayor despatched officers on the track of the culprit, who fled into West Somerset, and subsequently crossed the Channel, but was finally run down in Glamorganshire. The mayor further bestirred himself to procure evidence against the prisoner, despatching witnesses to Gloucester Assizes at his own expense. Being convicted, Maccartny was hanged and gibbeted near the great ravine on Durdham Down. The Council ordered the payment of £25 11s. 11d., the amount expended by the mayor, who received a vote of thanks for his exertions. The murder was long remembered with horror. From an official document dated November, 1787, the ravine appears to have been even then generally known as "Maccartny's Gully."

The civic authorities displayed great liberality at this period in their presents of wine, but it may be suspected, from the position of the recipients, that an adequate equivalent was expected from them sooner or later. At a meeting of the Chamber in February, 1714, a letter was read from Mr. Southwell, of Kingsweston, who was Secretary of State for Ireland under a grant not only for his own life but afterwards for his son, acknowledging the receipt of 12 dozen bottles of sherry, and promising "on all occasions to be serviceable to the city." He also intimated the arrival of 36 dozen forwarded to the Duke of Ormond, who "very highly approved" of the liquor. The Duke, who was Lord High Steward of the city and many years Viceroy of Ireland, had received numerous presents of the same kind; some of them for his "great services" to Bristol interests in the sister island. Another gift of wine is somewhat mysteriously recorded on the 7th July, 1714:—" Ordered that Mr. Chamberlayne pay for the 20 dozen of sherry sent to London to Collonell Earle, by him disposed of for the service of the city." It ought to be added that Bristol sherry had at this date an unrivalled reputation. Mr. Ashton in his "Social Life of the reign of Queen Anne" states that the most eminent London merchants "brought wine by road from Bristol" (i. p. 200).

In the Bodleian Library is a curious and probably unique

pamphlet, entitled "An Account of the Lead Mines producing Callamie, &c., on Durdham Downe, near Bristol, with a Proposal for the Disposing of a small Part thereof." It is undated, but a contemporary hand has written, "17 June, 1714." The writer sets off by stating that Sir John Smith, of Long Ashton, Richard Orlebar, of Poddington, Beds., and Arabella Astry, of Henbury, owners of the manor of Durdham Down, had granted a lease for twenty-one years, from Michaelmas, 1712, of two thousand acres of the down, with leave to dig, sink, and mine thereon for iron ore, lead ore, manganese, and "callamie," to John Glover, of London, gentleman, he paying yearly 1s. per ton for iron ore, 2s. for every 20s. worth of lead ore and callamie, and 4s. for the same value of manganese ore. The lessee, having discovered valuable deposits, had divided the undertaking into 400 shares, and transferred the lease, with 240 shares, to John Martin, of Hatton Garden. Martin had since sunk above twenty pits, whereby several hundred small veins of lead and callamie had been discovered, and the profit of three pits only, worked by six men, was equal to £4 19s. per share per annum. In order to carry on the concern more vigorously, Martin proposed to sell forty shares at £50 each; and it was estimated that, if thirty men were employed, the weekly output would be worth £240, from which would be deducted £24 for lords' dues, and £25 for expenses, leaving a profit equivalent to £24 16s. 6d. yearly on each share. What the profit would be if "300, nay 600 men were employed, as we despair not of doing in a little time," the wily prospectus maker left "the reader to consider." He added that a smelting furnace was about to be constructed "at the end of a large storehouse we lately built on the spot, together with another oven for burning the callamie." Seven persons were then concerned in the enterprise, one of whom had given £350 for ten shares. Before engaging in the affair, Martin had sent down a mining expert, who had found lead veins in all the pits, while the head miner, who had accepted 25 shares in lieu of salary, declared that there was then "£1,000 worth of oar in view." Persons desiring further information were directed to apply to Mr. Glover, "who is here in town . . . at Tom's Coffee House." Nothing more has been discovered respecting this enterprise, which was doubtless a product of the speculative mania of the time. From the promoter's assertion that Durdham Down was 2,000 acres in extent, whilst its actual area is only 212 (though possibly as much more was subsequently enclosed), he clearly could have been taught little by modern bubble blowers. In October, 1721, complaint was made to the Bristol Council of the numerous and dangerous holes and pits on Durdham Down, "near the common ways." The cost of levelling the ground was estimated at £100, and a vote of half that amount was agreed to, the Merchants' Society having undertaken to pay the other moiety. The wealthy owners of the manor, who in their pursuit of profit had permitted the down to become perilous to the lives and limbs of the public, characteristically stood aloof.

On the arrival, on the 2nd of August, 1714, of intelligence of the death of the Queen, the authorities ordered the immediate proclamation of her successor at the High Cross and other public places. A grand entertainment was given at the Council House, and the conduits ran wine for the populace. [Whilst the friends of the House of Hanover were celebrating its advent, hundreds of superstitious Bristolians were profoundly agitated by a discovery made that day. A cooper living in Baldwin Street had invited some friends to spend the afternoon with him, and proposed that they should smoke in the summer-house of the "pretty large garden" attached to his house. The pavilion was said to have been a rendezvous of the Bristolians concerned in the Rye House plot, and to commemorate the circumstance, a wooden crown surmounting a globe had been suspended from the roof. On entering the building, the revellers were horrified by observing that the ornament was completely hidden by an enormous black cobweb, measuring 3¼ feet in length. The cooper averred that the place had been swept during the previous week. The phenomenon was regarded by many as an awful portent, and multitudes flocked to witness it. The web was destroyed by curiosity hunters, but some portions were long preserved. A drawing of the marvel is amongst the Catcott MSS. in the Museum and Library.] When George I. made a state entry into London in September, the Common Council resolved that his arrival should be observed "with the utmost pomp, splendour, and solemnity that this city is capable of." A general holiday was ordered, the streets were ablaze with bonfires and tallow candles, and about £84 were disbursed by the Corporation in the customary festivities.

The new king's coronation, in October, afforded the Whig party another opportunity for rejoicing. Possibly the repeated demonstrations had irritated the Tories, the bulk of whom were Jacobites, and they resolved to manifest their discontent. The alarming riot which marked the day has been described by Seyer and Pryce, and it seems unnecessary to reproduce their narratives. It will suffice to say that whilst the citizens were preparing to illuminate their houses, and the upper classes were assembling to take part in a grand ball at the new Custom House, a horde of colliers and labourers, hired for the purpose and primed with liquor by some fanatical Tories, burst into the city, where they were joined by great numbers of the lowest class, and soon worked serious havoc to the cry of "Sacheverell and Ormond, and damn all foreigners." A report had been spread that the Dissenters had prepared effigies of Sacheverell, with the intention of burning them at the bonfires; and this malicious fiction provoked the populace to attack the dissenting meeting-house in Tucker Street, and several private houses. The dwelling of a baker, named Stevens, in Tucker Street, was three times assailed, and eventually plundered, but the mob were at last driven off by the occupant's son, captain of a West Indiaman, who shot at and mortally wounded a rioter. A well-meaning Quaker, named Thomas, who entreated the mob to retire, was trampled under foot and fatally injured. After committing much destruction in the same neighbourhood, the sufferers being invariably Dissenters or prominent Hanoverians, the rabble adjourned to Queen Square, where they smashed the windows of the Custom House, and forced the terrified ladies within to seek safety in flight. Upon being charged by a number of gentlemen and livery servants, the rioters scattered; but the disturbance was not quelled until midnight. The Corporation, angry and indignant, requested the Government to issue a special commission for the trial of such of the rioters as had been captured, and three judges were accordingly sent down in November. The Jacobites, who were not without audacity, rivalled the Whigs in their greeting of the ministers of justice. A great crowd assembled on the arrival of the judges, and their entry into the city was converted into a political demonstration, in which seditious cries were not wanting. An ultra-Tory merchant, named Hart, even ventured to exhibit his Jacobite sympathies in court, but was suppressed by Colonel Earle, M.P., who charged him to his face with being an instigator of the riot. The prisoners were of the lowest class, the ringleaders having absconded; and, to the exuberant joy of the Jacobites, the culprits were dealt with very leniently. Stevens's son, impudently charged with murder at the instance of the Tories, was acquitted. Riots of a similar character to the above occurred at Bath, Gloucester, Bridgwater, and Taunton.

The general election caused by the death of the Queen occurred early in 1715, whilst the city was still seething with faction and disorder. The Whig candidates were Colonel Joseph Earle (the former nominee of the Tories) and Sir William Daines, who were opposed by Mr. Thomas Edwards, jun., and Mr. Philip Freke. Confused and contradictory accounts of the proceedings are given by contemporary annalists. The most amusing is that of Edmund Tucker, apothecary, whose manuscript is in the Council House. The writer, an enthusiastic Tory, states that the election began on the 9th February, and continued until the 16th. "During which election the mayor, aldermen, and com. councill (not so much for keeping the Kings peace as was pretended, but chiefly to cast an odium on the Loyal Society in order that they might be for ever dispersed, and so be baffled and dashed out of countenance, in order to raise a fresh mutiny for shutting up the poll) constituted and swore near 80 fresh constables of the most vile poor and scurrilous wretches of the citty, both free beggars and foreign ruffians." But the "noble behaviour of the Church party frustrated their designed villainy," the poll being as follows:—Freke, 1991; Edwards, 1976; Daines, 1936; Earle, 1899. The defeated candidates, however, demanded a scrutiny, "which thô never known in this citty yett was granted." The sheriffs next spent two days "in bantering and caffleing with the Loyall freeholders" as to how the scrutiny should be conducted, proposing amongst other "bugbears" to strike off the votes of all who had children in the public schools; but as the Low party would have lost more by this operation than their opponents, it was abandoned. Finally, the sheriffs adjourned the scrutiny from the Guildhall to the Council House, "refusing the land owners attendance as much as possible, and in private signed a returne for Daines and Earle." To please the other side, indeed, "that scrutinising tool, Dick Taylor" [sheriff] offered to sign "a double returne, althô like a villain he well knew it would never be sent up," and so "the libertys and properties of this citty" were betrayed by men "with foreheads of brass, who could not blush, their crime being so hellish." Messrs. Edwards and Freke petitioned for the seats in 1715, 1717, and 1718, contending that they were duly returned, but the committee of elections never reported on their case. The expenses of the Whig candidates amounted to £2,257, about two-thirds of the money being spent in entertaining the electors in the various parishes. Amongst the items were:—" Woman's note under the Guildhall for beer," doubtless drunk at the polling, "£47 17s.," equivalent to about 1,000 gallons; and " Knots " (ribands), £78 18s. 10d.

The extreme poverty of many of the ecclesiastical livings in Bristol has been already noticed. In 1714 an Act of Parliament was passed for facilitating grants from Queen Anne's Bounty to places in need of help, and inquiries were soon afterwards made in local parishes in accordance with the provisions of the statute. Amongst the records in the Consistory Court at the cathedral is a certificate signed by the bishop's commissioners, Dean Booth and two of the prebendaries (who held their sittings at the White Lion inn, Broad Street), recording the results in St. James's, and the suburban parishes in Gloucestershire. Two of the principal inhabitants had been required to make an affidavit as to the "clear yearly profits demandable by law" by each incumbent. The account rendered was as follows:—

		£	s.	d.
St. James's.	Gift sermons	3	12	0
Westbury.	Mr. Henry Fane pays yearly	10	0	0
"	Gift sermons	8	6	8
Clifton.	One gift sermon	1	0	0
"	The impropriator of tithes pays yearly	5	0	0
Stapleton.	Small tithes	14	10	0
"	Vicarage house (lets for)	0	10	0
Horfield.	Gift sermon	0	10	0
"	Interest on Bishop Hall's gift	2	10	0
Mangotsfield		13	0	0

The certificates relating to the rest of the city parishes are unfortunately missing. In 1718 Horfield, Westbury, Mangotsfield, and Stapleton obtained grants of £200 each from Queen Anne's Bounty, in consequence of donations of £100 each made in their favour by Edward Colston.

A tailor's bill, dated May, 1715, records the cost of a rich suit of clothes furnished to a Bristolian named Lane Hollister, who is believed to have been a Quaker. The garments were embroidered with 13¾ yards of silk, which cost £3 19s., and were lined with "sattin," costing £1. The total was £12 11s. The tailor was unable to sign his name to the receipt.

The imminence of a Jacobite rebellion, and the probability of the overthrow of the new dynasty, seem to have weighed at this period over the whole community. In the preparations made for a revolt, the hopes of the Pretender's friends in Gloucestershire and Somerset rested chiefly on the young Duke of Beaufort, Lord Lieutenant of Bristol, who, though he had renounced the Roman Catholic faith of his ancestors, was an enthusiastic supporter of the exiled family. Happily, perhaps, for his house, the Duke fell ill, and died a few weeks before the Queen, leaving as heir to his vast estates a boy of seven years. The Western Jacobites then accepted for leader the Duke of Ormond, Lord Lieutenant of Somerset, much being also expected from Sir William Wyndham, M.P. for that county. Owing to Ormond's popularity and reputation for energy, the leading Jacobites anticipated greater results from his action in the West than from the revolt already concerted in the North. "Before leaving London," says Lord Stanhope, he "had concerted measures for seizing Bristol, Exeter, and Plymouth, had assigned stations for a great number of discharged officers in his interest, and had even provided relays of horses on the road to secure his rapid progress. But though personally a brave man, at the last moment his heart failed him. He slunk away, and crossed over to France." He was impeached in June, 1715, and was thenceforth politically dead. In the meantime the rival parties in Bristol, as elsewhere, scented the approach of an outbreak, and fanatics on each side lost self-control. At the quarter sessions in June, an indictment was found against a clothier named Clisile, charged with "justifying the murder of King Charles I.," and he was committed for trial. (He was afterwards convicted and fined two marks.) At the September Sessions, Francis Colston, merchant, a nephew of the philanthropist, charged with dispersing a seditious Jacobite pamphlet, entered into recognisances to appear for trial at the next gaol delivery (when the grand jury ignored the indictment). Other indications of party passion were visible in the streets. The 28th May was King George's birthday, and whilst loyal citizens hung out their banners, Jacobites carried thyme and rue in their coat breasts to denote their grief. On the following day, however, the tables were turned, the Tories jauntily ornamenting their houses with branches of oak, and their persons with oak leaves, in honour of the Stewarts, and humming, "The King shall enjoy his own again"—a strain still more in vogue on the 10th June, the birthday of the

Pretender, whose admirers, male and female, bedecked themselves with white ribbons. In September, in concert, as was supposed, with the northern rebels, the leading Jacobites of the West assembled at Bath, under pretence of drinking the waters, bringing with them a number of horses and a quantity of arms; while the situation in Bristol became so serious that the Government ordered the Earl of Berkeley, Lord Lieutenant, to take measures for the security of the city, which he forthwith did, calling up the militia, and putting them under arms. His Lordship was appointed Lord High Steward on the 23rd September—a fact overlooked by Barrett, while Pryce states that the office was vacant for 54 years. On Sunday, October 2nd, the authorities got wind of a plot, hatched by the Somerset Jacobites, to seize the city, whereupon the militia were mustered, and the gates shut, cannon being mounted at Redcliff and Temple. Several prominent members of the "Loyal Society"—patronised by the second Duke of Beaufort and Edward Colston, but described by their opponents as "a set of rakehells, who kept up a drunken club to carry on treasonable designs"—were arrested; amongst them, according to Oldmixon's History, being "Mr. Hart, a merchant, who was charged with having gathered a great quantity of warlike stores for the use of the disaffected." The prisoners were confined in "the Marshalsea" (in Narrow Wine Street), which Tucker in his annals calls "the old Olliverian prison house," adding that "the puritans" continued to search the dwellings and take away the arms of the real Churchmen of the city, "till they had even depopulated the city of its best members"; but the evidence against them was insufficient, and they were soon afterwards liberated. (The annual dinner of the Loyal Society on Colston's birthday was henceforth abandoned.) Oldmixon adds that in despite of the activity of the authorities, the Jacobites proclaimed the accession of "James III." in Bristol on the 27th October. But the arrival of a large body of troops, coupled with the tragic failure of the Northern rebels, dashed the hopes of the disaffected. The Bath conspirators dispersed upon the arrival of General Wade, who was despatched with two regiments to secure against a surprise. Wade's troops seized 200 horses, eleven chests of fire-arms, two hogsheads filled with cartridges and swords, three small cannon, and a mortar. [So confident were the Western Jacobites in the success of the conspiracy that a report, founded on their boastings, spread through

Paris on the 29th October, that Bristol had actually fallen into their hands. This curious fact came to light only in 1889, on the publication of some letters of the celebrated Duchess of Orleans.] As Sir William Wyndham was suspected of being a ringleader in the plot, he was arrested, when compromising papers were found in his pockets. He subsequently escaped, but finding it impossible to leave the country, he gave himself up, and eventually was pardoned. The alarm cost the Corporation several hundred pounds, chiefly for the entertainment of the troops. Amongst the items are £114 12s. for two entertainments to Lord Berkeley (who also was presented with a butt of sherry), £107 10s. "paid the ten captains of the ten companies of the militia, for what they paid their serjants and drumers;" £11 6s. 6d. " paid for making batteries and persons to attend them;" £20 3s. 10d. for entertaining General Wade (including 1s. 8.l. for a barrel of oysters and 38s. 5d. for a Westphalian ham), and £42 8s. for " candles for Guildhall guard and main guard." (The gates of the city for some weeks were locked nightly at 8 o'clock, and remained closed until 7 o'clock in the morning.) A copy of a popular Whig song, denouncing the disaffected faction, has been preserved in the British Museum. The following are extracts:—

> See now they pull down meetings
> To plunder, rob, and steal,
> To raise the mob in riots,
> And teach them to rebel.
> At Oxford, Bath, and Bristol
> The rogues designed to rise,
> But George's care and vigilance
> There's nothing can surprise.
> Base Ormond's fled and left them,
> And Perkin dare not come,
> And gibbets are preparing
> For those we've caught at home.

Owing to the increasing population of the out-parish of St. Philip's and of Kingswood, the " cage " maintained near Lawford's Gate by the county magistrates was found no longer adequate, and an application was made to the Common Council for a site on which to construct a " Bridewell." The Chamber, on the 23rd September, accordingly granted in fee, at a yearly ground rent of 10s., a small plot of ground in Well Close, on which a house of correction was soon after erected.

A curious windfall benefited the poor of St. Stephen's during a remarkably inclement winter. Butter being unusually dear, some one connected with an Irish trading vessel attempted to smuggle into Bristol four casks of butter from the sister country, where the article was worth only twopence a pound. The casks were, however, detected by the Custom House searchers, and the forbidden import was seized, half the value being handed over to the officers of the parish where it was found, for distribution amongst the poor.

In spite of the failure of the Northern insurrection, the Jacobites continued to conspire. In January, 1716, a manifesto of the Pretender was audaciously flung about the city, and the Government spies having reported that another plot for seizing Bristol was in preparation, some infantry reoccupied the city, and two troops of horse were voluntarily formed by the inhabitants. The precautions were justified, for on the morning of the 16th a wagon, ostensibly laden with goods for Bristol fair, took fire at Hounslow, when great quantities of arms and ammunition were found concealed amongst the packages. On the 10th of June, to the exasperation of the civic authorities, an enormous bonfire blazed on Brandon Hill in honour of the Pretender's birthday. About the same time a spy living in the city forwarded to the Government a list of disaffected persons into whose society he had insinuated himself. His letter is amongst the State Papers. The spy stated that he had dined with the Jacobites on several occasions at the King David's Head, at a house on the Back, at the Blue Posts in Thomas Street, at Penworth (*sic*), and at " the camp on the Down," and that King James's health was always drunk, the company sometimes toasting their idol " on their bare knees." On the 10th June, 1718, the rebel bonfire was again raised on Brandon Hill, while so many white roses were displayed by Jacobites of both sexes that the Corporation issued two placards denouncing the seditious manifestations. In the following October, doubtless in consequence of private information, a descent was made by the county authorities upon Badminton, the seat of the Duke of Beaufort, where were seized three concealed field pieces, a " pateire " (a small breech-loading cannon), two blunderbusses, 84 muskets, 12 matchlocks, eight carbines, 12 swords, a barrel of gunpowder, a barrel of musket balls, and 18 bandeliers, (cartridge cases) with shoulder belts (Berkeley Castle MSS.). No prosecution followed, the Duke being a mere child. In March, 1719, a still more serious affair came to the ears of the Government, doubtless through the treachery of some Jacobite agent. Amongst the documents relating to the subject in the State Papers is a letter from the Commissioners of Customs, reporting that their officers had captured, at the King's Head, Holborn, two cases of arms consigned to Bristol, one of which was directed to "Mr. James Bernard, at Mr. Deane's, in Balance (Baldwin) Street." Immediately afterwards, the magistrates of Wilts at Chippenham acquainted Secretary Stanhope that "a considerable quantity of gunpowder (an enclosed paper says 30 bales of one cwt. each) had been stopped at Calne, directed to John Darkin, of Bristol." This formidable store had been sent off from the Holborn inn before the Customs officers made their seizure. These discoveries put an end to the conspiracy.

With reference to the volunteer movement referred to above, the Council, to mark its approval of the loyal zeal of the citizens, resolved that "two banners, two trumpets, and two standards, and two new coats for the trumpeters be provided at the city charges, and that the said trumpeters be added to the city musick, with salaries." The banners and standards, embroidered in gold and silver, with gold "torsells," cost £79, the trumpets £21 17s. 6d., and "four" trumpeters' coats £34 10s. Several pounds were also spent on a " pad saddle with cloth hoosing and bays embroidered with gold," which may have been provided to display the martial capacities of the mayor. As a further mark of its loyalty, the Chamber gave an order for a portrait of the King, for which it paid 30 guineas.

It is a remarkable scientific fact that the *aurora borealis* was so completely unknown in England at this period that its appearance on the 6th March, 1716, excited great alarm amongst the superstitious in all parts of the island. "Mighty dismall apparitions," says E. Tucker's MS., "appeared in the Element at about 8 o'clock at night, to the great amazement of the spectators, it being so terrible to behold; it held to 2 or 3 o'clock the next morning, and returned a few nights after, but not in so dismall a manner."

The increasing population of the city was indicated at this time by building operations in the northern and western outskirts. St. James's Square, begun about 1707, and containing some fine examples of the genuine Queen Anne's style, was finished in 1716, and forthwith occupied by wealthy families. The space between what is now Park Row and St. Augustine's Parade, consisting chiefly of fields and gardens, began also to be converted into building sites. Especial earnestness was exhibited to appropriate the orchard of the old hospital of "the Gaunts," adjacent to St. Mark's

Chapel, owing to the amenity of the site. The Council, in March, 1716, resolved that this ground should be offered in building plots, many of which were quickly disposed of, and Orchard Street soon became a fashionable locality, although it could be reached by carriages only through Frogmore Street. For the improvement of the estate, the Corporation, as trustees, leased some property from the dean and chapter, "to make a way from St. Augustine's Back to Frogg Lane," which was followed later on by the conversion of Gaunt's Lane into Denmark Street. Hanover Street was built about the same time by the Combe family, on a plot of ground leased for 1,000 years by the Corporation so early as 1593, at a yearly rent of 28s. 8d.

At this period the celebration of divine worship according to the rites of the Church of Rome was forbidden by law. It was equally illegal for a Romish priest to dwell in any English city. The statute was, however, often transgressed. M. Jouvin, a Frenchman who travelled in England in the reign of Charles II., states that the Fleming with whom he lodged in Bristol had "long entertained a priest who said mass secretly in his house" for the benefit of the many foreign sailors frequenting the port. A few years later, the House of Commons received information that Henry Carew, a friar, had for several years executed the office of surveyor in the Bristol Custom House, and secretly acted as a priest About 1710, there is reason to believe, a few of the perse cuted faith were accustomed to assemble for worship in th upper room of a house at Hooke's Mills, outside the civic boundaries. The authorities were nevertheless vigilant. In April, 1716, one Ward, a gunsmith, "suspected for a popish priest," was brought up at the quarter sessions, but was liberated on offering recognisances for his good behaviour. About the same time, a list of Roman Catholics living in the city was forwarded to the Government by the town clerk. They were all workmen, and consisted of two tailors, a shipwright, a weaver, a cordwainer, a gardener, and "a stranger" (State Papers). During the rebellion in 1745 all the "professed Papists" in the kingdom were required to take the oath of allegiance. Only nineteen such persons were found in Bristol. They had, however, a small chapel on St. James's Back, where a priest named John Scudamore began to officiate about 1738. The chapel accommodated only about 80 persons, and many of the congregation are said to have been Flemings, employed in the local spelter works.

The cost of a parochial feast at this period is shown by

the records of St. John's parish for April, 1716. The following are the chief items :—" 3 dozen Pidgings, 10s; 2 pigs, 5s; a loin of veal and side of lamb, 8s. 6d; a rump and middle cutt beefe, 17s; 1 gallon Rhenish, 7s; 2 gallons port, 12s; 3½ gallons sherry, £1 6s. 3d."

At the midsummer quarter sessions the constables of the wards received special instructions to suppress "all gaming houses, bileard tables, and other unlawful games." The proscription of billiards was maintained for many years. In 1732 a man who had ventured on importing a table escaped prosecution only by promising to remove it and not offend again. The magistrates had also a strong antipathy to fencing. A peripatetic teacher of the art was sent to prison for some weeks in 1730 as a rogue and vagabond.

The Council, in 1716, appointed a committee to settle terms for the sale of two houses in Temple Street to the trustees of Alderman Stevens, "for the purpose of building an almshouse." The minute illustrates the peculiar manner in which corporate business was transacted, for it is an unquestionable fact, as the conveyance sealed soon after bears witness, that the hospital was built before the negotiations for purchasing the site appear to have been opened. As a gross error respecting the founder of this charity appears in a local work, it may be stated that Thomas Stevens (mayor, 1668) devised estates in 1679 for the erection and maintenance of two almshouses (for twenty-four poor persons), one in St. Philip's and the other in Temple parish. The former was erected in 1686 in the Old Market. Funds having accumulated, the trustees, in 1715, ordered the construction of the other.

Clifton parish church, which in its original form accommodated a very limited number of worshippers, was enlarged in 1716 by the addition of an aisle.

The incursion of "foreigners" within the corporate boundaries for trading purposes roused the indignation of the Council in December, 1716. A number of those audacious intruders had been already brought before the justices, and fined £5 each, and the chamberlain was ordered to proceed rigorously against every "unfreeman keeping shoppe." At a subsequent meeting he was charged with remissness, but contended in his defence that through his numerous prosecutions many of the "usurping foreigners" had left the city. Further legal proceedings probably followed, as an unusual number of persons applied for the freedom, and were admitted on paying fines varying from £100 to £30. One of the men taxed at the latter amount was a "gingerbread-baker."

Nearly all the houses in Queen Square having been erected, the Common Council gave directions for ornamenting the quadrangle with trees, of which no less than 240 were planted; fifty loads of fresh earth being brought from Stokes Croft to improve the soil. The improvement cost only £20.

At the quarter sessions in December, a man named Plumley, who may possibly have been one of the "usurping foreigners" just referred to, was solemnly indicted for the scandalous offence of having publicly "cursed the late mayor." In dread of exasperating the indignation of his aldermanic judges, the culprit pleaded guilty, and escaped with a fine of "five nobles" (£1 13s. 4d.) and costs.

At the same sessions, the grand jury presented, as a great danger to the navigation of the Avon, a ship named the Delaval, which had stranded on the side of the river near Pill, and threatened to fall into the stream. Nothing being done, the wreck fell as was anticipated, and the Corporation was then forced to employ men for its removal. The cost exceeded £114, but £58 were recovered by the sale "by beat of drum" of the ship and materials to John Hobbs, a merchant whom the reader has already encountered. The owner of the Delaval could not be discovered. But fourteen years later, after the ship had made twenty-eight voyages for Mr. Hobbs, a man named Martin, claiming to be the original owner, commenced an action for the recovery of the ship and the entire profits made since her sale! In this he was of course defeated, but as he had carried on his suit *in formâ pauperis*, Hobbs was unable to recover his costs. The Corporation, in 1731, voted the latter £50 towards his expenses.

In January, 1717, a great sensation was produced in the city by the return—apparently in good health—of a labourer named Christopher Lovell, who had been sent to Avignon at the expense of a number of local Jacobites, to be "touched" by "James III." for the king's evil, a disease from which he had long suffered. The assertions of his patrons that he had been miraculously relieved were enthusiastically accepted by the ignorant and disaffected, and even some educated people expressed themselves convinced that the royal finger had effected a cure beyond the power of medical science. The man was visited, says a believer, by "infinite numbers," who deemed their examination completely satisfactory, and the joy of the Jacobities as the marvel spread through the kingdom was unconcealed. Unfortunately the so-called cure of Lovell was of brief duration. He was again frightfully attacked by his old malady, and those who had paid the expenses of his pilgrimage, and gloried in its results, could find no decent pretext for declining the cost of a second experiment. The poor man was again smuggled to France, but succumbed under the ravages of the disease before he could reach the Pretender. It was now the turn of the Whigs to rejoice over the chapfallen Jacobites. The incident would probably have been lost to posterity but for the credulity of a man of learning and culture, Thomas Carte, a non-juring clergyman. In his History of England, published in 1747, under the patronage of the Duke of Beaufort, the Corporation of London, and many of the leading Jacobites at Oxford, Carte, who was ignorant of the ultimate fate of Lovell, spoke of the regal unction as of infallible efficacy in healing scrofulous diseases, and narrated the cure of the Bristolian as one which he was able to attest personally, having visited Lovell at his home "in the week preceding St. Paul's fair, 1717," and found him "without any remains of his complaint." Intelligence, however, had made some progress in 1747, and the author's superstition, which was triumphantly exposed in the London *Evening Post* (by Josiah Tucker, afterwards Dean of Gloucester), was fatal to the success of an otherwise valuable work. Tucker was subsequently styled "Josiah ben Tucker ben Judas Iscariot" by the exasperated Jacobites.

The leisurely manner in which the Corporation habitually dealt with public improvements is impressively shown in the story of the Exchange. The civic minutes of the 16th January, 1717, contain the following entry:—"Several members of the House took occasion to mention many inconveniencyes, that there was not a more convenient place than the Tolzey for the assembling of Merchants, and that there had been discourse of building a place in nature of an Exchange for that purpose. Whereupon the Mayor [and several others] are appointed a committee to receive any proposall that shall be made for that purpose." The subject was then allowed to sleep for over four years. In October, 1721, a petition of merchants and shipowners prayed the Council to take action, and the Chamber resolved to obtain an Act to authorise the necessary works, undertaking to bear half the expense of the building. The corporate petition to the House of Commons stated that the Tolzey was insufficient to accommodate those attending it, and that many persons suffered seriously in health there, owing to being unprotected from the weather. The Act was obtained without difficulty early in 1722, and a committee was appointed to exercise its powers; but, in consequence of the persistent obstruction of " a senior gentleman " (*Mist's Journal*, December 25th, 1725), the vigour of the Corporation was again exhausted. As will afterwards be seen, the Tolzey remained the only rendezvous for mercantile men for more than a quarter of a century after it had been condemned by the Chamber.

The Rev. William Goldwin, whose " poetical description " of the city has been already mentioned, resigned the headmastership of the Grammar School in July, 1717, under peculiar circumstances. In the previous year, the Rev. Benjamin Howell, rector of St. Nicholas, refused to take the oath of allegiance to George I., and was consequently deprived of his living. The dean and chapter, the patrons, immediately presented a clergyman to the vacancy; but the Crown intervened, claiming the right of presentation to all the incumbencies forfeited by non-jurors. Mr. Goldwin, having been recommended to the Government by the Corporation, was soon afterwards presented to the living; whereupon Bishop Smalridge opposed the royal nomination, and excited so much ill-feeling towards Goldwin amongst High Churchmen that one-third of the boys in the Grammar School were withdrawn. (Smalridge's sympathy for High Church principles threw suspicion on his own loyalty, and he was dismissed from the office of Lord High Almoner.) After some delay, the episcopal obstruction was overcome, and Goldwin, on entering upon the preferment, relinquished his previous post. In a letter to the Council he gave an account of his mastership. " In 1710," he wrote, " I found 47 boys. Since that time to the present I have disposed of the youth as follows, viz :—To Oxford, 12; to law, 7; to physick, 1; to the army, 1; to shop trades, 56; to merchants and the sea, 53," which with 25 others variously distributed or dead made a total of 155. The number attending the school had nearly doubled while it was in his hands, but owing to the bishop's hostility it had fallen to 56. After his departure there was a further decline, the scholars numbering only 20 in 1722; but eighteen months later, under the Rev. A. S. Catcott, the institution was again flourishing, the youths having increased to seventy.

The Council, in August, 1717, resolved upon the purchase of the " Great Tower on the Quay," a huge structure originally built for the defence of the western side of Bristol, about the time of the excavation of the modern course of the Froom. The tower, which was about 100 feet in circumference, and stood on the Quay near the site of the late drawbridge, had long been an inconvenience to traffic. It was secured for £250, and was removed in 1722.

Mr. Edmund Tucker, the amusing Tory annalist, was greatly incensed about this time by the resolve of his Whig fellow citizens to celebrate the coronation-day of George I. He records the matter as follows:—" This year on the 21st 8ber (October) a poor ragged society of fellows, terming themselves the Hannoverian Society, mett and walked up to Redclift Church with the fidlers before them, where was a sermon preached before them by Mr. Arthur Bedford, in opposition to the Loyall Society's commemoration of the 2nd 9ber yearly in the late raigne. The said fellows were treated by the   at a paltry alehouse on St. Austin's Back." The blank in this angry note ought doubtless to be filled by the word Corporation. Mr. Bedford was the vicar of Temple denounced by Mr. Colston in 1710.

Readers of Lord Macaulay's History will remember his severe condemnation of Sir John Knight, M.P. for the city in 1693, who made a virulent attack on William III. in the House of Commons, and whose speech, printed by tens of thousands at the Jacobite presses, was burnt at Westminster by the hangman. (Mr. Nicholls commits the extraordinary blunder of fixing the latter event in 1744, fifty years after the actual date.) Sir John subsequently gave much offence in Bristol by extorting from the Corporation, under a threat of legal proceedings, his " wages as a Parliament man," and, falling into poverty, he retired to Congresbury, where he had a small estate. In October, 1713, his daughter Anne set forth her " deplorable state " in a petition to the Council, and was granted £20. In December, 1717, Sir John himself made a similar appeal, asserting that he was reduced to great necessity and want by the unnatural treatment of his son, and praying for the charitable assistance of the Chamber. Little sympathy seems to have been felt for the old persecutor of Dissenters, for the sum accorded was only £20. The Merchants' Society, a few weeks previously, had granted him an annuity of £20; but Sir John died in the following February. In June, 1722, his daughter presented her "very poor and mean condition," and her inability to support herself owing to failing sight, whereupon the Council granted her a life annuity of £12.

A beautifully engraved view of the city, drawn by an

artist named Blundel, was published in 1717. The sketch was taken from Totterdown, and shows that only five buildings, clustered against the city wall, stood outside Temple Gate. The road to Keynsham, as well as that to Bedminster from Redcliff Gate, was a mere track through unenclosed land.

On the 31st March, 1718, John Bracegirdle, a tide surveyor, appeared before the mayor to give information of a seditious sermon. The officer had attended service at St. George's church, near Pill, a few days before, when the Rev. Edward Bisse, incumbent of that parish and of Portbury, had delivered a scurrilous Jacobite tirade, denouncing William III and George I. as usurpers, denying the validity of laws to which "the rightful king" had given no assent, and declaring that the country was doomed to misfortune until James III., whom he called "his master," was restored. The mayor hastened to forward this information to the Government, and the latter was equally alert in ordering the arrest of the culprit. It appeared that Bisse, who had taken the oath of allegiance to George I., had repented of his submission, and had sought to appease his conscience by venting seditious opinions in various parts of the country. Five treasonable discourses were reported against him, and for these he was arraigned and convicted at the following assizes for Bucks, Wilts, and Somerset. In November he was brought up for judgment, and was ordered to be imprisoned for four years, to be exposed twice in the pillory, and to be fined £600. As he had taken the oath, he could not be deprived of his livings, which he held for several years.

The evils of mendicancy were a chronic source of trouble to the Incorporation of the Poor. In their earlier days the guardians, taking the law into their own hands, sentenced incorrigible vagrants to three years' hard labour in Bridewell. Having abandoned this course, the board, in 1718, requested the churchwardens and elected guardians to meet at 8 o'clock in the morning, seize all beggars they could lay their hands upon, and carry them before a magistrate. This practice also became obsolete, and in 1726 the court ordered its two beadles to arrest all vagrants, and "bring them to this house; and that they do not go to the Tolzey or Council House any more." The magistrates could scarcely have been complained of for excessive lenity. In March, 1729, Mary Edwards, an incorrigible vagrant, was sentenced to three years' hard labour in Bridewell.

Mr. John Day, mayor, died suddenly from apoplexy on

the 20th June, 1718. His funeral, which was attended by nearly every person of note in the city, took place about midnight, and was the most imposing ever witnessed. The growing wealth of the mercantile class was displayed in the long procession of private coaches, a luxury which had become fashionable amongst wealthy merchants. It is recorded that upwards of fifty carriages followed the remains from Queen Square to St. Werburgh's church, and that nearly 500 persons were presented with gloves. On the 26th the Council assembled to fill the civic chair, and the minutes record the ceremonial, stating that it was dictated by the "president" of 1607. The sheriffs having obtained from Mrs. Day the deceased's insignia of office, " the Mayor's Sword, with the Scabbard presented to him by the present Sheriffs the Sword of State, the Sunday's Sword, and the Mourning Sword, the two Charters and boxes, the Red Book of Ordinances, both parts of the Seal of the Statute Merchant, the Mayor's Pocket Seal of office, the Keys belonging to the Mayor as Clavinger or otherwise (*sic*) of the great Chest at the Tolzey wherein the City Seals and the Iron Caskett are kept," were laid upon the table. Thomas Clement was then elected chief magistrate for the remainder of the civic year; whereupon, " the whole House, being all in their black Gownes, removed from St. George's Chappell into the Guildhall, where Nicholas Hickes Esq., the last Mayor living, was by the House called to the Chair." The usual oaths were then taken. " After which all the Insignia were in the usual manner delivered to Mr. Mayor, whereupon the attending Company were ordered to withdraw. And the new Mayor with the Sword before him was attended in the same form in Black Gownes to the Tolzey, where they all separated."

The Historical Register for 1718 records, under the 19th August, the death of Sir Edward Longueville, Bart., " killed by a fall from his horse, as he was riding a horse-race near Bristol." This appears to be the first printed record of the annual gathering on Durdham Down. *Farley's Bristol Newspaper* of October 9th, 1725, announces that a velvet saddle, value £5, would be run for on the following Friday, " the best of three heats, two miles each," after which a laced Holland smock would be run for by maidens, " on the same Down, near the Ostridge."

Amongst the fashionable company which visited the Hot Well in the autumn of 1718 was Joseph Addison, who had just resigned a high office in the Ministry, but is now better known as the most distinguished of English essayists. The locality may have been familiar to him in early life, for his mother was a sister of Dr. Goulston, Bishop of Bristol, and, according to Mr. Seyers's MSS., he offered during this visit to promote the interests of two youths, sons of a near relative named Addison, a merchant in the city. In a letter to Swift, dated "Bristol, Oct. 1, 1718," Addison wrote :—"The greatest pleasure I have met with for some months is in the conversation of my old friend Dr. Smalridge" (Bishop of Bristol), " who is to me the most candid and agreeable of all bishops. . . . We have often talked of you." The two friends were in declining health, and both died in the following year. Owing to the inadequate income of the see, the bishop's wife and three children were left in penury, but they found a zealous patron in the Princess of Wales, afterwards Queen Caroline, who obtained a pension for the widow and preferments for the sons.

The Recorder, Sir Robert Eyre, one of the justices of the King's Bench, having scrupled to receive the small yearly salary attached to his civic office, the Council, in November, 1718, forwarded one hundred guineas to Sir William Daines, M.P., to "make a present" to Lady Eyre. The gift was renewed three years later, when Sir William was repaid 10s. 6d. for a purse he had purchased "to make the city's present more acceptable to ye lady."

The existence of a local cotton manufactory seems attested by a corporate minute of December, 1718, noting the admission to the freedom of a "calico printer." Another man admitted the same day is styled a "translator," which Lord Macaulay, in replying to a local inquirer, supposed to mean a foreign interpreter, but who was really a cobbler who converted old boots into shoes. Amongst other trades recorded in the freemen's admission-book about this time are found whisk-binders, stuff makers, lace weavers, wool combers, drugget weavers, bellows makers, steel-mill makers, needle makers, clog makers, framework knitters, scribes, a fan maker, corn badgers (travelling dealers), velvet weavers, and a vice maker. The last named, in consequence of the utility of his trade, was charged only 40s. on becoming a burgess. In 1722 Mr. John Jones was admitted to the freedom gratis, on account of his skill as a teacher of writing, and his ability as an author of treatises on arithmetic and book-keeping.

The bitterness of party feeling at this period is indicated by the minute books of the poor law guardians. When the board was first formed, the Council granted it the use, rent free, of Whitehall, for the purpose of employing children in spinning. This industry, proving unprofitable, was given up, but in February, 1719, when the Corporation demanded re-possession of the building, the guardians impudently required the Council to prove its right to the property. The Chamber, again, had paid the expense of obtaining two Acts of Parliament for the board, and had lent it large sums of money free from interest. At this date upwards of £2,100 were due on these loans, most of which had been outstanding for over ten years. But when the Council requested two years' interest on the Shirehampton mortgage, according to the bargain made in 1710, the guardians, or at least the Tory majority, flatly repudiated the liability. Legal measures were taken for the recovery of Whitehall, and the guardians sulkily came to terms respecting the loans. In 1723, when a mortgage of £600 on St. Peter's Hospital was paid off, the civic body generously remitted the heavy arrears of interest.

A letter dated the 6th April, 1719, illustrative of the system of political patronage in the Georgian era, is amongst the Treasury Papers. Sir William Daines, addressing the board, asserts that he had represented Bristol in Parliament for about twenty years, at a cost of above £10,000. As a trifling compensation, he prays that his sister's son, Thomas Cary, may be appointed a landing-waiter in the Custom House. The application was ordered to be acceded to "upon a vacancy."

In 1719 the woollen manufacturers of the kingdom, dissatisfied with the restrictions already placed on lighter textile materials, raised a strong agitation against the use of printed calicoes and linen, the popularity of which, they asserted, threatened them with ruin. In December the weavers of Bristol petitioned Parliament for relief on "behalf of many thousands" locally employed in woollen manufactures, alleging that most of them were destitute owing to the growing taste for lighter fabrics. Similar appeals were made by the Corporation, the merchants of the city, the weavers of Bedminster, Barton Regis, Keynsham, and Chew Magna. Being in consonance with the ideas of the age, the cry of the clothiers met with sympathy in the House of Commons, and a Bill to prohibit the obnoxious foreign imports was passed, in despite of the protests of the linen interest. The measure was rejected by the Lords, but in 1720 the peers also yielded to the pressure, and an identical scheme became law. It enacted that, after a delay of two years, any person wearing a garment of printed calico, foreign linen, or coloured linen mixed with cotton, should be liable to a fine of £5. The use of coloured calico or mixed goods for bed curtains rendered the offender liable to a fine of £20. An attempt to exempt home-made calico of which the raw material was grown in our colonies was defeated, but by special favour the Act exempted such calicoes as were dyed "all blue." The Bristol weavers attempted to put this statute into operation by means of brute force. On the 8th July an exciseman and his wife, whilst walking through the city, were set upon by a party of weavers, who tore the woman's calico gown off her person. As they were continuing to insult her, the husband stabbed one of the ruffians, who died soon afterwards. A gentleman's daughter was treated with similar indignity, and was left nearly naked in the streets (*London Journal*, July 16th, 1720). There is good reason to believe that the above legislation prevented Bristol from becoming the chief seat of English cotton factories, for which the city then possessed unrivalled advantages. The cotton produced in the West Indies was mainly brought here. It was not until 1758 that any Jamaica cotton was imported into Liverpool.—To appease the discontent of the local makers of needle-worked buttons, another Act was passed in 1720, imposing a penalty of 40s. a dozen on any person wearing clothes of which the buttons were made of cloth!

The Company of Weavers and Dyers petitioned the Corporation in December, 1719, representing "the serious inconvenience to their woollen manufacture by the foulness of the water at the Horse poole, near the Wear Bridge, by the frequent washing of horses there—the only place the petitioners have to wash their goods." In spite of the latter remarkable statement, the Chamber seems to have taken no action.

Owing to a great inundation of the Froom on the 17th and 18th May, 1720, Earl's Mead was several feet under water, which "rose as high as the wall at the Ducking Stool." Broadmead and Merchant Street were flooded for some hours.

At a meeting of the Council in August, 1720, it was resolved that Bridewell, a mean and inconvenient edifice, should be demolished and rebuilt. The new prison, which was no great improvement upon its predecessor, was finished in the following year, at a cost of about £1,040. It was destroyed in the riots of 1831. The condition of the prisoners in Newgate came also before the Chamber, "a raging distemper" having caused many deaths. Nothing was done to improve the sanitary state of the gaol, but Dr. Chauncey, who had voluntarily attended several of the victims, was presented with a piece of plate, which cost £21, and an apothecary received £26 for supplying drugs.

For many previous generations it had been the custom of the Corporation to attend divine service at the Cathedral, except on stated festivals when visits were paid to certain parish churches. No inconvenience had therefore resulted from the grant of St. Mark's Chapel to the Huguenot refugees in the reign of James II. The growing wealth and love of display of the Corporation, however, brought about new arrangements. In September, 1720, the Chamber gave orders that "the Gaunts Chapel" should be repaired and beautified. For some reason this resolution led to no immediate action. But in October, 1721, the mayor, addressing the Council, "mentioned the affront the city had lately received from the dean and chapter, and recommended the repairing, new pewing, beautifying, and adorning" of St. Mark's, with a view to its constant use as a civic place of worship. Fresh orders were thereupon given and rapidly carried out. Happily for the fabric, the beautifying and adorning involved less destruction than was then common. The worst deformity was an ugly gallery, erected against the great west window. In April, 1722, when the alterations were nearly finished, the mayor suggested to the Chamber that if the four bells in the tower were recast and the number increased to six, " it would be for the grandeur of the city," and his hint was at once adopted. The renovated building, henceforth called the Mayor's Chapel, was probably opened for service in the following September, when the Council empowered the mayor for the time being to appoint a clergyman to preach on such Sundays as his worship should think proper; the chamberlain receiving instructions to pay 10s. for each sermon. (This fee was raised to 20s. in 1725, and to 21s. in 1738, the latter advance being made because 20s. was "not so genteel a satisfaction as a guinea.") The Rev. A. S. Catcott read prayers, for which he received 5s. a week until 1729, when his salary was fixed at £20 per annum. A deplorable act of vandalism was ordered in February, 1725. The mayor having alleged that the "altar piece" of the chapel needed "beautifying," the Chamber permitted him to display his taste, and the result was the mutilation of the ancient reredos in order to introduce a huge oaken screen carved in the Dutch Corinthian style. The "adornment" seems to have been finished in 1729, when a marble "altar piece," costing £80, was added. The total cost of the alterations was about £650, exclusive of £190 for bells.

The great South Sea "bubble" burst in 1720, scattering desolation and ruin throughout the kingdom. Amongst the victims was Dr. Boulter, Bishop of Bristol, who in a letter to a member of the Government, dated October 11th, writes, "In the general ruin I have lost the little imaginary wealth I took myself to be master of" (State Papers). Many prosperous Bristolians were reduced to bankruptcy, amongst them the mayor, Abraham Elton, jun., who "submitted to the fate, and withdrew into France as soon as out of office." (Tucker's MS.).

Some documents in the State Paper Office under the year 1721 bring to light the existence of a trade carried on by Bristol merchants of which no inkling can be obtained from ordinary sources of information. The vessels which left the Avon to transport slaves to the West Indies were all ostensibly bound to the west coast of Africa. As a matter of fact, many of them secretly proceeded to Madagascar, then a great resort of smugglers trafficking with India, where slaves could be obtained at much cheaper rates than prevailed in the Gulf of Guinea. The clandestine traffic was by some means discovered by George Benyon, a landing-waiter in the Custom House at Bristol, who acquainted the East India Company of the infringement of its monopoly in the Indian Ocean; and the company, in great wrath, appealed to the Government. Compassion for the unfortunate beings torn from their families and country had of course nothing to do with the company's indignation. What aroused its ire was the conveyance of arms and stores to Madagascar, whence they were brought into competition, by so called "pirates," with the goods forwarded from London direct to India. The Government responded to the company's demand for the protection of its privileges by issuing an Order in Council on the 2nd October, 1721, forbidding any interference by private merchants in the trade with Madagascar, and probably measures were taken at the Custom Houses for checking clandestine adventures. Amongst the Treasury Papers for 1725 is a memorial from the East India Company praying that Benyon might be promoted, and also protected from the resentment of the merchants whose profits had been curtailed. The first avowal of the illicit traffic was made about thirty years later by William Beckford, one of the slave kings of Jamaica, whose brother Richard was shortly afterwards elected one of the members of Parliament for Bristol. Speaking in the House of Commons in 1752, Beckford said, "Many gentlemen here know that formerly the sugar colonies were supplied with negroes from Madagascar, a vast island abounding with slaves, from whence the colonies drew large quantities till the East India Company interfered and prevented private traders from carrying on a commerce which they despised."

John Oliffe, vintner, a former member of the Corporation, petitioned the Council in August, 1721, to grant him some relief, having been "reduced by losses to great necessity." An annuity of £20 was granted, £5 being paid in advance owing to the extreme distress of the applicant. Oliffe was probably a descendant of Ralph Oliffe, a mayor who gained an infamous notoriety for harrying Dissenters in Charles the Second's reign. (The granting of money to impoverished aldermen or councillors was a common practice of English corporations. In 1712 one Alderman Hoar, of Hull, being greatly embarrassed, the Common Council "supplied him with money for the payment of his creditors" (Tickell's History of Hull, p. 597).

Another death of a mayor (Henry Watts) occurred on the 19th September, and owing to peculiar circumstances caused much embarrassment. A commission of gaol delivery had issued, and the assize was fixed for the 20th September; but the proceedings would be informal unless "the mayor" were present. A new mayor had been elected on the 15th, but by the charter of Queen Anne the next chief magistrate could not enter upon his functions until Michaelmas Day. The Council was therefore hurriedly summoned to meet on the 20th, when Sir Abraham Elton was elected to fill the chair for the intervening nine days. The ceremonies attending the transfer of the regalia (see p. 122) were again scrupulously performed.

Reference has been already made to the civic sport of duck-hunting. which was for many generations an incident of the annual perambulation of the city boundaries. About 1710 the chief members of the Corporation seem to have thought a regular attendance at this function beneath their dignity, and when the mayor was not present the duck-hunt was omitted. After a purchase of ducks in 1721, the item does not occur again until 1738. Six birds were usually sacrificed, but in 1742, the latest hunt recorded, nineteen unfortunate ducks were purchased for the amusement of the worshipful spectators.

The salaries of the two civic coroners had been fixed at the paltry sum of £6 13s. 4d. each many years before this date. As a natural result, the duties had been often unsatisfactorily performed, and in 1715, when both coronerships were vacant, the Council minutes state that the office had "become contemptible." More efficient persons were secured, but the new functionaries soon became discontented with their stipends, and in October, 1721, they prayed for an advance, owing to the "great enlargement of the city." The Council thought they would be fairly remunerated if the payment were raised to £10. One of the coroners died about six months afterwards, when the candidates who offered themselves for the vacancy consisted of two "marriners," a brewer, a linen draper, and a "gentleman," the last of whom was elected. So late as 1765, one of the coroners held the mean office of keeper of the city scales, at St. Peter's Pump.

Edward Colston, whose munificent gifts for educational purposes have been already recorded, died at his residence, Mortlake, near London, on the 11th October, 1721, in his 85th year. In pursuance of his instructions, his remains were removed to Bristol for interment in the ancestral vault at All Saints' Church. The funeral procession, which was a week or ten days upon the road, consisted of a hearse with six horses, covered with plumes and velvet, and attended by eight horsemen in black cloaks, bearing banners; and three mourning coaches with six horses to each. At the resting places on the way, a room was hung with black, garnished with silver shields and escutcheons, while upwards of fifty wax candles in silver candlesticks and sconces were placed around the coffin, covered with a silver-edged velvet pall. The gloomy cavalcade reached Lawford's Gate on the night of the 27th October, where it was met by the boys of deceased's schools in St. Augustine's and Temple, the almspeople in the hospital on St. Michael's Hill, and the old sailors maintained at Colston's charge in the Merchants' Almshouse. (The thirty old people received new clothes for the occasion.) The procession, accompanied by torches, with the schoolboys singing psalms, made its way to the church amidst continuous torrents of rain, and the interment took place about midnight, in the presence of as many persons as could crush into the building. The bells of the various parish churches tolled for sixteen hours on the day appointed for the funeral.

K

A portrait of Mr. Colston, engraved by Virtue, was published in London in 1722.

The precept to set a thief to catch a thief was literally adopted at this period by the local authorities. The London *Daily Journal* of November 2nd, 1721, says:—" They write from Bath and Bristol that their roads are much infested with robbers, and that application having been made to Jonathan Wild, that gentleman (!) has resolved to take a tour towards those cities as soon as his equipages can be got ready." It will be seen presently that the following assizes at Gloucester brought several robbers to the scaffold.

The first notice of the existence of hackney coaches in the city occurs in the minutes of the Court of Quarter Sessions for January, 1722, when a hackney coachman was charged with assaulting Alderman Mountjoy. The carriages did not stand in the streets, but were kept in the yards of some of the principal inns. Glass being expensive, the windows of London hackney coaches were filled with tin plates "pricked like a cullender," and it is unlikely that the Bristol vehicles were better supplied. In December, 1741, the Common Council directed the chamberlain to provide great coats and laced hats for three hackney coachmen, "to attend this Corporation on publick days or occasions." In 1749 the Chamber obtained Parliamentary authority to regulate hackney coaches. With characteristic supineness, the Council allowed more than a quarter of a century to pass away before putting its powers into execution. Ignorant of these facts, some local histories assert that hackney coaches were not established here until 1784.

Four local malefactors—three convicted of robberies in St. Philip's out-parish and one of a similar crime near Redland— were executed at Gloucester on the 21st March, 1722. Previous to their trials these men, with other desperate felons, having resolved to murder the turnkey of the prison and escape, requested a confederate outside to bring to the gaol a large pie, as if from some charitable persons in the city, within which he was to conceal pocket pistols, ammunition, chisels, etc. The conspiracy was, however, exposed by one of the prisoners.

The first septennial Parliament expired in the spring of 1722, and the election of members for Bristol opened on the 28th March. Sir William Daines retired, owing to failing health, but Mr. Joseph Earle solicited re-election, and Sir Abraham Elton came forward on similar principles. The Tory candidate was Mr. William Hart, who scarcely attempted to conceal his Jacobite sympathies. At the close of the poll, on the 3rd April, the numbers were: Mr. Earle, 2,141; Sir Abraham Elton, 1,869; Mr. Hart, 1,743. This was the first occasion on which a "poll-book" was published, showing the votes given by each burgess. This exceedingly rare pamphlet was printed by "Joseph Penn, bookseller, in Wine Street." There were only 22 electors living in the parish of Clifton, all of whom were artisans except John Baskerville, gentleman, Thomas Garland, mercer, Thomas Hungerford, draper, Edward Jones, merchant, Charles Jones jun., merchant, and John Williams, grocer. Mr. Hart petitioned against the return, alleging that he had more legal votes than Sir A. Elton, who, being an alderman, deterred many from voting by using violent threats, bribed others, and brought up many to poll who had no right to the franchise. The petitioner apparently produced no evidence, and his claim fell to the ground. Sir William Daines died in the autumn of 1724, and a London news letter of September 19th mentions a report that the prosperous Bristolian had left his son-in-law, Lord Barrington, £50,000—an enormous sum in those days. But unless the statement refers to landed estates settled on the viscount's marriage, it is incorrect. By his will Sir William bequeathed £10,000 each to the families of his two daughters.

The extreme narrowness of the streets occasioned frequent minutes in the municipal records. On the 1st May, 1722, an agreement was made with Abraham Harris, "search maker," who was about to rebuild his house in Nicholas Street, whereby he agreed to set back the premises, so that the street in front might be 14 feet 8½ inches, and at the corner facing the church 13 feet 3 inches, in width. The breadth previous to this improvement is unfortunately not recorded. Thirty years later is a corporate minute referring to the width of the other end of the same street; the Council ordering, in May, 1754, that when a lease should be granted of a house at the corner of Corn Street, the entrance into Nicholas Street should be made not less than 16 feet in width.

Amongst the strangest engines of punishment devised by our ancestors was the trebuchet or ducking stool, an instrument which, with its companion the pillory, was required by law to be maintained in hundreds of manors in England. The ducking stool was originally devised for the castigation of brewers and bakers who used false weights and measures, or sold an adulterated article, and also for punishing common scolds, convicted by a jury of being public nuisances. In course of time, roguish traders contrived to escape by paying fines, but the stool was still maintained for the correction of vixenish females. The Bristol instrument was probably somewhat similar to that still preserved at Warwick. A strong wooden chair was fastened upon the end of a long beam, which worked like a see-saw on a post fixed at the edge of a pool in the Froom, near Castle Ditch. A scold was strapped into the chair, which was then whirled over the river, and on the shaft being tilted up the culprit was plunged into the stream. Three duckings were administered to each culprit. When the Stewarts came to "their own again" in 1660, the Corporation ordered a new ducking stool—which cost £2 12s. 6d.—to do honour to the event, and a few years later there is a record of four women being ducked within a twelvemonth. In 1692 the engine was renewed and "coloured," at an outlay of 30s. Unfortunately many of the sessions books about that period have been lost, and the fate of contemporary scolds is unknown. In 1716 an indictment was found against one Susannah Morgan as a common scold, and she was committed for trial, but the volume recording her fate has disappeared. In August, 1722, Maria Lamb was convicted before the mayor, Sir William Daines, Sir Abraham Elton, and other aldermen, who ordered "that she be ducked to-morrow at twelve of the clock in the common Ducking Stool, and remain in custody till the same be done." No details as to her ducking have been preserved, every copy of the local newspaper of the week having perished. In March, 1723, one Susannah Tyler was found guilty of the same offence, but judgment was respited until the next court, and the culprit liberated on bail. Susannah was no sooner free than she fled from the city, and her sureties were ordered to be prosecuted. Eventually the scold surrendered, and then all trace of her case mysteriously disappears. In 1730, and again in 1731, a woman was brought up and solemnly tried for objurgating propensities, but in both cases the jury returned a verdict of not guilty. Although these appear to be the last local instances of judicial proceedings, the authorities continued to keep the instrument of punishment in good order. So late as September, 1754, Daniel Millard, carpenter, was paid £9 8s. "for making the Ducking Stool." At that time the Westminster ducking stool stood in the Green Park; and Blackstone's Commentaries, published in 1765, contain nothing to indicate that the engine was then regarded as obsolete. Mr. Bellamy, clerk of assize on the Oxford Circuit, who attended the assizes at Gloucester for sixty years, and who died in 1846, told a friend (Wiltshire Magazine, i. 74) that the remains of ducking stools were to be seen at the sides of many village ponds when he first practised on the circuit. (The story recorded in Evans's Chronological History, under 1718, is apocryphal.)

An extreme dearth of copper coin existed at this date in Ireland, where employers were often obliged to pay their workmen with card tokens, or in counterfeit halfpence worth less than half a farthing. The Scotch, at the Union, had insisted on the maintenance of a mint at Edinburgh, but no similar institution existed in Ireland, and such issues of coin as had taken place there were made by private persons, to whom patents were granted rather for their private profit than the public good. Following these precedents, the urgent needs of the Irish were in 1722 made the basis of a job. The privilege of supplying a new coinage was granted to the Duchess of Kendal, one of the King's mistresses, who sold the patent to William Wood, an iron and copper manufacturer at Wolverhampton. A Treasury warrant of the 31st August authorised Wood to establish "his office" at or near Bristol. By the terms of the grant, a pound of copper, worth 13d., was to be coined into halfpence and farthings of the nominal value of 2s. 6d. The English coinage value of a pound of copper was 1s. 11d. To make the profits still greater, the patentee was allowed to coin to the value of £100,000, though the highest Irish estimate of the amount required was only £15,000. The nominal value of the coins minted by Wood in Bristol was £13,480, exclusive of £1,086 in farthings. But meanwhile the action of the Government had been denounced by Swift with characteristic unscrupulousness, and his "Drapier's Letters" lashed Ireland into fury. It was in vain that Sir Isaac Newton, after sending down a competent person to Bristol to assay the halfpence, demonstrated that the new coinage was greatly superior to any previously circulated in the island. It was equally in vain that the total amount allowed to be coined was reduced to £40,000. The Government were forced to withdraw the patent, and had to compensate Wood for his lost profits by a grant of £3,000 per annum for eight years. Wood had another patent for coining "halfpence, pence, and twopences for all his Majesty's dominions in America," and the *London Post*, of January 18th, 1723, stated that he was about to mint those pieces at Bristol. They were actually coined, however, in London.

At a meeting of the Council in June, 1722, a committee strongly condemned the training received by the girls in the Red Maids' School, the mistresses of which were declared to be incapable to fulfil the duties confided to them. The only work on which the children were employed was the "mean and unserviceable" task of spinning wool, which unfitted them to become good domestic servants. The report recommended that the mistresses should be discharged, and, as the existing allowance to them (of £4 per girl per annum) would not suffice to procure others of better capacity, that the yearly grant for each scholar (for food, clothing, and education) should be raised to £7; the new mistresses to have the profit of the children's work, as before. In a second report, three months later, it was suggested that the forty girls should thenceforth dwell in one house under a single head mistress, and be furnished with new clothing every two years. The committee's recommendations were adopted, but the extent of the improvement effected was insignificant. Down to the end of the century, the instruction of the girls was confined to reading, and some of the mistresses could scarcely scrawl their own names.

A desire for increased pomp and display frequently crops out in the corporate records. At the meeting in June, 1722, mentioned in the last paragraph, "Mr. Mayor represented that the maces born by the sergeants to him and the sherrives were much less and meaner than what were made use of in lesser corporations, and moved that hee thought twould be for the honour of the city to have them made larger and of a better fashion." This suggestion was approved, and eight elegant silver maces, weighing 216 oz., were purchased in August, at a cost of £91 8s. 5d.

Two new charities were founded about this date. Abraham Hooke, merchant, and other wealthy members of Lewin's Mead meeting, erected in 1722 a school house in Stoke's Croft, to which was attached an almshouse for twelve poor women. The buildings and school endowment involved an outlay of £4,200. "Mrs." Elizabeth Blanchard, an unmarried lady, who died in 1722, established an almshouse in her dwelling house in Milk Street for five poor spinsters, Baptists, "whose labour is done;" ordering in her will that her clock and furniture should be left in the house for the benefit of the inmates.

The first "umbrello" mentioned in our local records was purchased by the city treasurer in August, 1722, for £1 5s. His cash book states that it was "for the Guildhall," that is, for the protection of the judges and magistrates on wet days when they quitted and returned to their carriages—the only purpose for which umbrellas were then used in England. A fashionable youth, who about this date borrowed the umbrella of a London coffee house during a shower, found himself advertised in the newspapers, and made "welcome to the maid's pattens."

The Corporation, in September, 1722, subscribed £50 towards a movement to obtain Parliamentary relief for the local tobacco trade, alleged to be in a state of "great decay." The true motive of the agitation was far from creditable. Glasgow, hitherto despised by Bristol and Liverpool, had opened a considerable import trade with the American colonies, especially in tobacco, and offered that article in the English market at a great reduction in price. The undersold dealers, greatly irritated, raised a cry that the Scotch traders were evading the Customs duties, and clamorous demands were made to Parliament to suppress the alleged frauds. Owing to the influence of the English mercantile interest, the Government raised a number of vexatious actions against Scotch importers, and though in every case the charges of fraud proved to be groundless, the persecution reduced the northern tobacco trade to insignificance for many years, to the great joy and profit of southern competitors. A letter written by Mr. Isaac Hobhouse, an eminent Bristol merchant, admitting that the charges against the Glasgow firms were untruthful, is amongst the Newcastle MSS. in the British Museum.

The inscription placed in 1872 under the statue of Neptune, in Temple Street, asserting that the figure was set up in the reign of Elizabeth to commemorate the defeat of the Spanish Armada, is a remarkable illustration of the rapid development of local legends. The fiction is not mentioned by Mr. Barrett, or by any of the earlier historians of the city, and in Mr. Seyer's MSS. the erection of the figure is recorded to have taken place in 1723. John Evans, however, gave credit to the Armada story in his Chronological History, and that book being the *vade mecum* of many dabblers in archæology, the fable is now recorded on granite for the edification of posterity. The true facts respecting the figure were known to Mr. Tyson, whose notes are preserved in the Jefferies MSS. From these it appears that in 1723 the old reservoir of Temple Conduit was taken down, and a new one constructed, chiefly of the old materials. Mr. Tyson adds that the statue of Neptune, cast by a person named Randall, made its first appearance on the renovated structure. Two dates were upon the "front stone" of the reservoir when Tyson's note was written—1586 and 1723—the first denoting when the old conduit was erected, and the second when it was rebuilt. 1586 was two years anterior to the Armada, but legend makers do not stick at trifles, and the figures served to lay the basis of a now popular figment. The statement that one Randall produced the figure is confirmed by a paragraph to the same effect in *Sarah Farley's Bristol Journal* for December 22nd, 1787, when the Armada myth was clearly unborn. The name of "Joseph Rendall, founder," appears in the Bristol Poll-book for 1734. It is not improbable that he turned out other similar works. Amongst a list of miscellaneous articles advertised for sale in Thomas Street in July, 1752, was "a large lead statue known by the name of the Gladiator, or Roman Prize Fighter." The earliest printed mention of Neptune occurs in *Farley's Bristol Newspaper* for January 27th, 1728, a dealer in looking glasses announcing that at the approaching fair his goods would be exposed for sale "at the Barber's Pole and Sign of the Looking Glass, a little below the Neptune in Temple Street."

The records of the local gaol deliveries previous to 1742 having been lost, while the files of newspapers are imperfect, it is impossible to state with accuracy the number of executions that took place in the early years of the century. At the Assizes of 1723, five men are known to have been sentenced to death, for Mr. Stewart, in his MS. annals, states that he witnessed their execution on St. Michael's Hill, and he expresses no surprise at the number of the victims. This was the first occasion, he says, on which convicts were carried from Newgate in a cart, they having previously been forced to walk to the scaffold. One of the five sufferers, convicted of coining, then styled petty treason, was dragged on a sledge, in pursuance of his sentence. In Mr. Pryce's list of local executions—the only one published by a Bristol historian—only five deaths are recorded previous to 1751. The following mournful catalogue, unquestionably incomplete as it is, gives a more adequate idea of the sanguinary jurisprudence of the age, the convicts numbering no less than seventy-seven. The cases in which the crime of the malefactor is unknown have been kindly furnished by Mr. William George, who obtained them from the burial registers of St. Michael's parish. Felons interred in that churchyard were persons destitute of friends, and the fact that the five sufferers in 1723 were buried elsewhere shows that the register affords little evidence as to the total number of executions. Crimes committed in Clifton, Cotham, Redland, and the out-parishes of St. James and St. Philip were then dealt with at Gloucester, while Bedminster and Knowle prisoners were tried in Somerset, but there is no reason for excluding such cases from the following list:—

1705. September 12, John Roberts.
1711. Aug. 17, William Holland.
1713. Sept., John Shrimpton—murder.
1714. April, Capt. Maccartny (gibbeted on the Down)—murder.
1714. September 8, Daniel Roberts.
    „ „ Ann Pugh.
1716. Aug. 29, Henry Pearson.
    „ „ Roger Wall.
1718. Oct. 8, Elizabeth Cowley.
1720. April, Two men—robbing the mail.
    Sept. 5, A blacksmith—murder of a girl.
1721. October, A sailor—rape.
1722—Mar. 21 (at Gloucester) Geo. Harver—burglaries, St. Philip's.
  „   „   John Bampton—do.
  „   „   John Smith— do.   [par.
  „   „   Richard Bayton—burglary in Westbury
July 29   „   Isaac Linnet—housebreaking, Clifton.
1723. (no date). Five men—one for coining.
1724. Sept. 10, Constant Smith.
    „ James Williams.
    „ John Phillips—robbery.
    „ Richard Roberts—robbery.
1725. Sept. 8, William Morgan—robbery.
    „ Mary Tedman—robbery.
1728. June 15, Thomas Bell, soldier (shot on Downs)—desertion.
1729. Sept. 12, George Bennett—housebreaking.
    „ William Taylor—murder.
1730. July 23, George Bidgood, weaver—rioting.
    (no date, at Glouc.). Another weaver—rioting, St. Philip's.
1731. Mar. 22 (at Glouc.), Wm. Crown—robberies on the Downs.
    Sept. 24, Thomas Sleep—horsestealing.
1733. Sept. 21, William Bussell—unrecorded.
    „ James Jones—unrecorded.
1734. Sept. 16, Thomas Kitchenman—murder.
    „ Martha Morgan—child murder.
1737. Aug. 26 (Glouc.), John Willis—burglary, St. Philip's.
    „   „ John Gibbs—burglary, suburbs.
    Sept. 8, John Vernon—burglary.
    „ Joshua Harding—shoplifting.
1738. April 14, Thomas Boone—rioting?
    September, John Hobbs—coining.
1739. May 4, John Kimberley—murder.
    „ John Philips—robbery.
1740. April 1, A so dier (shot)—desertion.
    April 14 (Glouc.), Benj. Fletcher } robberies on Durdham Down.
    „   „ Wm. Lewis
    Sept. 4 (Bedminster), J. Millard (gibbeted)
    „ (Brislington), Corn. York (gibbeted) } robberies in Bed-
    „ (Ilchester), Wm. Derrick   minster, &c.
    „   „   — Masters

1740. Sept. 19, William Roe—shoplifting.
1741. April 17, Samuel Goodere }
　　　　 ,,　　Charles White　　　　} murder of Sir John Dineley.
　　　　 ,,　　M. Mahony (gibbeted) }
　　　　 ,,　　Jane Williams—child murder.
1742. April 8, Wm. Curtis—returning from transportation.
1743. May 13, Sarah Barret, *alias* Dodd—theft.
　　　　 June 6, John Woods—forgery.
　　　　 July 11, John Partington (shot)—desertion.
1744. March 22 (on Downs), Andrew Burnett (gibbeted) } murder　near
　　　　 ,,　　　　 ,,　　　 Henry Payne (gibbeted)　　} Downs.
1746. April, John Barry—forgery.
　　　　 Sept., Matthew Daly—murder.
1747. August 17 (Glouc.), Robert Hine } robberies in suburbs.
　　　　 ,,　　　　 ,,　　　 Samuel Baxter }
1748. April 22, Wm. Nicholas, a boy (gibbeted)—poisoning his mistress.
　　　　 ,, Eleanor Connor—stealing from person.
　　　　 Sept. 21 (Ilchester), J. Mundoso—murder, Knowle.
1749. Aug. 25, Jeremiah Hayes—murder.
　　　　 ,, Joseph Abseny (gibbeted)—murder.
1750. April 19 (Somerset), J. Perryman } destroying a house, Bed-
　　　　 ,,　　　　 ,, Thos. Roach } minster.

The *Gloucester Journal* for March 4th, 1723, contains the following account of a custom which has hitherto escaped notice:—" We have advices from Bristol that on the 27th past, being Ash Wednesday, [really on Shrove Tuesday], the blacksmiths of the city assembled in a body in St. Thomas Street, in order to engage their annual combatants, the coopers, carpenters, and sailors there; which last bore so hard upon the weather quarter of the smiths' anvils (notwithstanding the furious discharge of their wooden thunderbolts) that they drove every Vulcan into his fiery mansion. The noise of this defeat alarmed the whole posse of weavers, who joined the smiths, and made a general attack on the wrong wing of their enemies, for they then totally routed them, sending 'em home in the utmost disorder to show their wives, &c., a parcel of broken loggerheads. However, we understand the smiths and weavers are resolved to form another campaign next year, and try their success at arms on the same day therein." The custom was not extinct in 1757, when *Felix Farley's Journal* of the 26th February says:—" Tuesday last, being Shrove Tuesday, the apprentices of coopers and ship-carpenters, with their respective colours and ensigns, made the usual procession through the streets. In the evening, happening to meet on the Quay, and contending for the upper hand, a fight ensued, in which several were wounded, and one of the carpenters had the misfortune to have his skull fractured." At a later period the procession was postponed to Whit Monday, *Sarah Farley's Journal* recording its occurrence in May, 1780.

The Whit Monday "revel" held at Bedminster was at that time very popular.

Jacobitism continued to give anxiety to the Government. In the State Papers is the following letter to Sir Robert Walpole, dated Bristol, June 25th, 1723, from "a lover of his Majesty," one John Eblass:—"There is a very dangerous person at Bristol, carrying on a design for to secure the Prince and young Princess, and so raise a rebellion while his Majesty's abroad. If you send a messenger ye minute you receive this, ye may have several letters on him to several people who are not yet come to Bristol and Bath, where they meet on pretence of drinking the waters. His name is Peter Hammond," (lodging at a sugar baker's, near St. Philip's Church). The man was arrested, but no information of importance was obtained. On the 26th August the *Gloucester Journal* recorded that a Bristol Jacobite, Peter Cumberbatch, had just got his head broken by the dragoons encamped at Maisemore for having, with some fellow fanatics, raised a disturbance, crying "Down with the camp; down with the Roundheads; the King shall enjoy his own again."

The popularity of the Hot Well at this period is proved by a scarce book of poems, entitled "Characters at the Hot Well, Bristol, in September, 1723," published in London the same year. Amongst the personages mentioned by the writer are the famous Duchess of Marlborough, the Duchess of Kent, Lady Diana Spencer, Lady A. Grey, "Ld. R——y (late Sir R. M.)," and "Sir D——y B——y." [The two last named personages were Lord Romney and Sir D. Bulkeley.] Unfortunately, the writer throws no light on the amusements of the visitors, for whose convenience a "Publick Room" had been opened in the previous year (*Weekly Journal*, August 4th, 1722). Edward Strother, M.D., forwarded, in 1723, a paper to the President of the Royal Society, describing his experiments for ascertaining the constituents of the Hot Well water. The result of his researches, he said, showed that the spring was "Æqueo-salino-alcalino-cretaceo-aluminoso-cupreo-vitriolick"—which merely proves that the doctor was a skilful practitioner in the art of using scientific jargon to conceal profound ignorance. So far as concerned Clifton "on the hill," the only important advance made since 1700 was the erection of a mansion by Thomas Goldney, a Quaker grocer in Castle Street, and one of the lucky owners of the Duke and Duchess privateers. (Following a taste made fashionable by Pope, Mr. Goldney constructed in his grounds an extensive grotto, the walls of which were elaborately ornamented with Bristol diamonds, shells, and other curiosities. John Wesley, who visited this sparkling retreat, notes with a groan that Mr. Goldney spent twenty years and large sums of money in amassing its decorations. The grotto, which still exists, was an object of great attraction to visitors at the Hot Well.) Mr. Goldwin, the " poetical delineator " of Bristol, is reported to have said that in his time there was just sufficient society in Clifton to establish a whist table (Seyer's MSS). That the farmers who held parochial offices were determined enemies of " sport " will be seen from the following extracts (slightly curtailed) from the churchwarden's accounts :—

	s.	d.
1723—For 2 foxes, 8 hedgehogs, and a polecat	5	0
1726—For a fox	1	0
1730—For 7 hedgehogs	1	8
1731—For a polecat and 2 hedgehogs	0	10
1731—For 2 foxes, 18 hedgehogs, and a kyte	6	6
1731—For 2 ,, and 10 ,,	5	4
1733—For 85 hedgehogs in the year	11	8
1734—For 84 ,, ,,	12	4
1735—For 6 foxes and 15 hedgehogs	12	0

Similar items occur in the accounts for many subsequent years. (What seems still more strange in our day, premiums for killing vermin were also yearly paid by the churchwardens of St. Philip's, who disbursed 4s. 10d. for the destruction of 28 hedgehogs and 4 polecats in 1723). The local instruments for maintaining law and order were kept in a state of efficiency. In 1730 the stocks and whipping post were repaired at a cost of £1 4s. 4d.; and they were renewed four years later, when £2 1s. 10d. was expended upon them.

Reference has been already made to the popularity of cock-fighting. In March, 1724, a great match took place at the White Lion inn, Bath, between the gentlemen of that city and those of Bristol, the stakes being six guineas on each battle, and sixty guineas on the concluding fight. As the tournament extended over three days, a great number of birds must have been sacrificed.

The *Gloucester Journal* of April 27th, 1724, announced that the coaches to Bristol and Bath had begun to " fly " on the 22nd of that month, and would continue for the season to perform the journey " in ONE day (God permitting)." The return journey from Bath *vid* Bristol occupied two days, and the above rate of speed southwards was found too great in the following summer, when passengers for Bath had to spend the night in Bristol—an arrangement which continued until 1753, and probably later. It does not appear that any coach travelled between Gloucester and this city during the winter months, when the traffic was abandoned to the wagons, occupying two days in the transit. The *London Evening Post* of May 23rd, 1724, announced that the flying, or two days' coaches from London to Bristol, and also the three days' coaches to the same destination, started from " the Sarazen's Head, Friday Street—the Flyers every Monday, Wednesday and Friday, and the others every Monday and Thursday." The two days' coaches ran only during the summer half year, and the slower vehicles appear to have occupied four days in their journeys during the winter months. Even though their progress was so deliberate, a contemporary writer complains that the passengers "after being brought into their inns by torchlight, when it is too late to get a supper, are forced so early into their coach next morning that they can get no breakfast." Pennant, the well-known antiquary, states in one of his works that in March, 1739, the coach from Chester to London, drawn by six good horses (helped by two extra ones where there were sloughs), was six days on a journey of 190 miles. "We were constantly out two hours before day, and late at night."

The Corporation, in August, 1724, voted £40 to the vestry of St. Nicholas, which had undertaken to renovate the ancient conduit on the Back, at an outlay of £100. The " fair castellet " mentioned by Leland as surmounting the fountain in his time had probably already disappeared.

The manner in which the estates of the dean and chapter of Bristol were managed at this period was that adopted by ecclesiastical corporations generally. The property was leased, generally for three lives, at a nominal rental, but heavy fines were levied on renewals. Thus, in ordinary years, the dean's income was only £100, and that of each prebendary £20; while in exceptional years the receipts were multiplied six or eight fold. One of those golden periods occurred in 1724, when the chapter exacted the sum of £2,000 for renewing the lease of the rectorial tithes of Halberton, Devon, while Sir Abraham Elton was charged £300 for adding a life to his lease of the manor of Blacksworth (in St. Philip's and Clifton), and other lessors' fines amounted to over £700. The dean reaped one-fourth of these occasional harvests, and each of the six prebendaries received an eighth.

An action at law, apparently for the recovery of tithes on

fruit, was pending at this time between John Hodges, impropriator of the parish of Clifton, and Edward Jones, Esq., who possessed a garden attached to his house there, valued at £4 a year. A commission to receive the evidence of local witnesses held a sitting on the 25th September at the " Blackmoore's Head, Clifton." Almost the only point of interest in the depositions, preserved at the Record Office, is the statement of a witness to the effect that he had rented a farm of 26 acres in the parish for forty years, at a rental of £33, and paid two shillings in the pound additional for tithes. The result of the action does not appear.

The Jefferies collection contains a document, dated the 24th October, 1724, fixing the tares to be allowed to purchasers of sugar landed at this port. The paper is now interesting only for the proof it affords of the vast extent of the West India trade then enjoyed by Bristol. No less than 99 local firms appended their signatures to the arrangement. It may be doubted whether the West India merchants in London were much more numerous. In March, 1789, when another regulation concerning tares was agreed to at a meeting of planters and merchants at the Bush Hotel, the number of firms represented was only 35.

In the month of October, 1725, the Bristol ship Dispatch, the property of three influential merchants, Isaac Hobhouse, Noblet Ruddock, and William Baker, left the port for the coast of Africa, on a slaving voyage. The instructions of the owners to the captain and the manifest of the cargo having luckily been preserved (they are in the Jefferies collection), a summary of their contents will give the reader an insight into the manner in which the slave traffic was carried on. It may be well, however, to premise that the eighteenth century merchants who pursued this trade ought not to be judged by the higher moral code of the present day. Many of them were regarded in their generation not merely as honest and honourable, but as benevolent and kind-hearted men. John Cary, for instance, the founder of the Incorporation of the Poor, was conspicuous for his integrity and humanity; yet in his " Essay on Trade," a work applauded by statesmen, he spoke of the commerce with Africa as "of the most advantage to this kingdom of any we drive, and as it were all profit, the first cost being little more than small manufactures, for which we have in return gold, teeth (ivory), wax and negroes, the last whereof is much better than the first, being the best traffic the kingdom hath, as it doth give so vast an employment to our people both by sea and land." When it is remembered that more than half a century after Cary's book was published, the Rev. John Newton, the friend of Cowper, was studying for the ministry when in command of a slave ship, one cannot refuse to make a liberal allowance for contemporary mercantile habits and ideas. It is, indeed, a melancholy but incontestable fact that although the most hideous cruelties were practised to procure slaves, many earnest professors of Christianity in Bristol and elsewhere felt no scruple in engaging in the traffic, and even in seeking divine sanction for their enterprises. The bill of lading of a slave cargo described the miserable captives as "shipped by the grace of God"; the captain (generally a ruthless brute) was declared to hold his office "under God"; the vessel was said to be bound "under God's grace" with so many slaves; and the document ended with the pious prayer, "God send the ship to her desired port in safety." Turning to the documents relating to the Dispatch, the first important paper is the manifest of the cargo destined to be exchanged for human beings. The following is a summary:—

	£	s.	d.
4,000 copper rods	251	12	0
A quantity of cotton goods, called Niccanees, Bejutas, Chints, Romalls, &c.	455	9	6
A cask Cowries	13	12	4½
2,000 Rangoes (?)	12	0	0
206 cwt. iron bars, @ £19 per ton	196	1	8½
10 barrels gunpowder	40	17	6
180 musquets @ 10/6 and chests	96	19	0
4 casks Monelas (?)	51	11	9
4¼ cwt. Neptunes (copper pans)	88	0	9¾
207 gals. brandy @ 2/6 and casks	28	1	4½
87 gals. cordial (gin) @ 2/9	5	3	1½
12 cwt. bugles (glass beads?)	76	2	10
18 fine hats edged with gold and silver, and 8 doz. felts edged with copper	21	4	0

With a few miscellaneous items the total value of the cargo amounted to £1,330 8s. 9¾d. The vessel also carried a quantity of provisions for the voyage from Africa to the West Indies, including 40 cwt. of bread, 6 cwt. of flour, 66½ cwt. of beef and pork, 190 bushels of beans and peas, 6 bushels of "grutts," 12 tierces and 4 hhds. of ship beer. In the owners' letter of instructions to the captain, William Barry, he is ordered to make the best of his way to Andony, on the African coast, and there traffic with the cargo for "240 choice slaves" and a good quantity of elephants' teeth, "seeing in that commodity there is no mortality to be feared." The slaves must be healthy and strong, and between the ages of 10 and 25—males to be preferred as more valuable. Attention must be paid to their feeding, and to prevent their being ill-used by the crew, "which has often been done to the prejudice of the voyage." When loaded, the ship is to sail for "Princess," where the unsold goods are to be disposed of, and the slaves sold if they will bring "10 moidores (£13 10s.) per head all round." If this cannot be done, the vessel is to sail for Antigua to await orders, failing which the slaves are to be sold at Nevis or South Carolina. The captain is to have four per cent. commission on the net proceeds of the live cargo, and is allowed to buy two slaves on his own account. The chief mate may also have two slaves, but is to pay for their food. As another ship was ready to sail on the same enterprise, Capt. Barry was to endeavour to outsail her, and to "see that he is not outdone in slaving by other commanders." Finally he is "recommended to the Good God Almighty's protection." Captain Barry's signature is appended, acknowledging the above to be a true copy of his orders, which he promises "to perform (God willing)." The results of the voyage are not preserved. In 1727 another Bristol ship, the Castle, proceeded to Andony, and took in a cargo of 271 slaves, for which iron, copper, etc., were exchanged, according to the ship's day-book, now in the possession of Miss Fry, to the value of about £2 15s. per head. Notwithstanding the lowness of the cost, and the increasing popularity of the trade, by which at least 30,000 Africans were yearly conveyed to America, the price of slaves was steadily rising across the Atlantic. In a letter to Mr. Isaac Hobhouse, from John Jones (his nephew and agent), of the firm of Tyndall, Assheton and Co., dated Jamaica, March 2nd, 1728, the arrival is reported "of the Virgin, from the Gold Coast, with 262 slaves to our address, and they comes at £30 17s. 6d. per head round, which is a good price considering there was so many small among them. . . . The demand for negroes continues; there is now 500 in harbour and all bought up." In a letter of February, 1730, R. Assheton, a member of the same firm, reports to Hobhouse:—"Surely negroes were never so much wanted, nor can that want be supplied for two years to come, which the Days [a great Bristol firm] are very sensible of, and push all they can. The general terms Pratten buys at is £30 to £32 per head for men, women, boys, and girls." Another letter from Assheton to Hobhouse reports that a Bristol cargo of 234 slaves had sold for £35 all round. It would therefore appear that in a fortunate voyage the profit on a cargo of about 270 slaves must have reached £7,000 or £8,000, exclusive of the returns from ivory, and it is not surprising to learn that Mr. Hobhouse, like some other local adventurers, acquired "a very large fortune" (*Felix Farley's Journal*, Feb. 26th, 1763). Amongst the Jefferies MSS. is an account from Barbadoes, dated 1730, showing the produce of "Merchandize, being 329 negroes, per the Freke Galley, from Guinea, for account of William Freke, Esq., and Company, merchants, in Bristol." The cargo consisted of 141 men, 75 women, 65 boys, and 48 girls, but was not in good condition. Most of the men brought from £22 to £29, but a few sold at from £2 10s. to £7. The women averaged about £23, but two brought only 15s. each. The boys and girls produced about £14 a head. Altogether the "merchandise" realised £6,207. The agents' commission (including an import duty of 5s. per head, and £25 9s. "paid for treating customers during the sale") amounted to £460 6s. 9d., leaving a net return on an indifferent cargo of £5,746 18s. 3d. Some adventures turned out more unluckily. Mr. Assheton informs Hobhouse, in 1729, that a cargo had sold for only £19 10s. a head, owing to the slaves being nearly all "children or grey headed." (More than one-third of them died a few weeks after being disposed of, but this loss fell upon the purchasers.) The captain of the Greyhound galley, writing to Hobhouse, one of the owners, reports that out of a cargo of 339 "jolly, likely" slaves shipped at Bonny, he had landed only 214 at Barbadoes. Most of the survivors were sold at £40 a pair, "a very poor story after such a loss." In another case Jamaica agents inform Isaac Hobhouse and his partner, Onesiphorus Tyndall, that two-fifths of the slaves on board one of their ships had died on the passage, many more had died after landing, and several were almost valueless. But the writers conclude with the encouraging intelligence that there was an immediate demand for 1,000 good negroes, "and fine cargoes will make agreeable sales." Besides the losses incurred by the outbreak of pestilence during a voyage, the slave traders had occasionally to deplore a revolt amongst their unhappy victims. The *Gloucester Journal* of January 28th, 1729, has a letter from Bristol containing "the melancholy news that Captain Holliday, with all his crew except the cabin boy, have been murdered on the coast of Africa by the negroes" he was about to carry off. (As showing the slow circulation of news at that time, it may be stated that the disaster occurred in May, 1728.) *Read's* (London) *Jour-*

nal of June 18th, 1737, published an extract of a letter from the Bristol ship Princess of Orange, stating that whilst proceeding to the West Indies " a hundred of the men slaves jumped overboard, and it was with great difficulty we saved as many as we did. We lost 33 . . . who were resolved to die. Some others have died since, but not to the owner's loss, they being sold before any discovery was made of the injury the salt water had done them. The captain has lost two of his own slaves." It was possibly in the hope of cheering the poor captives that musicians were engaged in some slaving vessels. It is incidentally stated in August, 1729, that the ship Castle of Bristol had a piper, a fiddler, and a drummer on board.

It will be seen from the above extracts that the commanders of slaving vessels were allowed to transport a few slaves in each cargo for their personal profit. It was doubtless through this custom that so many negro slaves were brought to England, and lived and died here in servitude. The post of captain in a slaving ship was a lucrative one, and those who gained it were prone to make a display of their good fortune. Their gaudily-laced coats and cocked hats are often mentioned by contemporary writers. As their wills bear witness, they were accustomed to flaunt large silver, and sometimes gold, buttons on their apparel, and their shoes were decorated with buckles of the precious metals. But the most distinguishing mark of a captain in the streets was the black slave who obsequiously attended him, and who was often sold to a wealthy family when the owner again embarked for Africa. Sometimes, as has been already shown, a black servant was bequeathed to a friend by will. Female negroes reached this country in the same manner, and were purchased for domestic service. The House of Commons Journals for March 16th, 1702, in reporting evidence given before a committee, described a witness as a slave to a Jew merchant in Holborn. "She had lived with him," she deposed, "14 years as a slave." The newspapers of the first seventy years of the century contain scores of advertisements concerning the sale or elopement of blacks held in slavery. A few examples may be interesting. In the *London Gazette* of January 17th, 1713, Captain Foye, of Bristol, offers £5 for the capture of " a negro called Scipio, aged about 24," who had escaped. In the same journal for July 5th, 1715, Mr. Pyne, the Bristol postmaster, undertakes to pay two guineas and expenses for the recovery of Captain Stephen Courtney's negro, aged about 20, " having three or four marks on each temple and the same on each cheek "—which were presumably testimonies of the affection of his master. (Captain Courtney, it will be remembered, was one of the commanders of the fortunate Duchess privateer.) Nothing, perhaps, better indicates the distance which separates us from the reign of George I. than the fact that the postmaster of Bristol was the agent employed to recapture a slave living in Bristol, and that this fact was published in the official organ of the Government. In *Farley's Bristol Newspaper* for August 31st, 1728, Captain John Gwythen offers for sale "a Negro man about 20 years old, well limb'd, fit to serve a gentleman or to be instructed in a trade." In the *Journal* of November 15th, 1746, Captain Eaton announces the evasion of his negro Mingo, whom he had owned for eight years, for whose recovery he promised a guinea. "All persons are hereby forbid entertaining the said Black at their peril." Josiah Rose, of Redcliff Street, advertised the elopement of his negro boy, aged 13, in the London *General Advertiser* of April 8th, 1748. In the *Bristol Journal* of June 23rd, 1750, appears:—" To be sold, a negro Boy of about 12 years of age. . . . Inquire of the printers." The *Bristol Intelligencer* of January 12th, 1754, offers for sale, to "any gentleman or lady who wants a Negro Boy," a lad of 14 years, recently landed. The *Bristol Journal* of March 12th, 1757, publishes the elopement of a young negro called Starling, who " blows the French horn very well." His owner, a publican in Prince's Street, offers a guinea for his capture. A week later it is announced that the negro of Captain Bouchier, of Keynsham, has escaped; while on the 22nd September the evasion is published of the negro servant of Captain Ezekiel Nash, who offers to reward the person giving him up, and threatens to prosecute any one secreting him. On the 15th April, 1758, the same paper offers £5 for the recapture of a "Malotta Boy," absconded from one McNeal, of St. Philip's Plain, who also menaces legal proceedings against a detainer of his property; and on the 14th April, 1759, Captain Holbrook advertises a "handsome reward" for the recovery of his "Negro man named Thomas." *Felix Farley's Journal* of August 2nd, 1760, contains a pithy advertisement:—" To be sold, a Negroe Boy about ten years old. He has had the small pox." A Liverpool paper of 1766 has an announcement of the sale by auction in that town, on the 12th September, of " Eleven Negro Slaves." In the *Bristol Journal* of June 20th, 1767, we have:—" To be sold, a Black Boy, about 15 years of age; capable of waiting at table;" and the same paper of January 9th, 1768, offers for sale "a healthy Negro Slave named Prince, 17 years of age; extremely well grown." Some of the fugitive slaves are described as wearing silver collars round the neck, engraved with the owner's name.

The only mode of travelling available to the poor at this period was by stage wagons, progressing at the rate of about twenty miles a day. No early advertisement of a Bristol wagon having been found, the following is extracted from the *Whitehall Evening Post* of April 24th, 1725 :—" For the benefit of the distressed. In a few days (if God permit) will set out for the Bath, a large commodious waggon, which will conveniently hold 36 persons. Such weak persons as are willing to take the advantage of this conveyance are desired speedily to send in their names to Robert Knight, waggoner, at the Three Crowns in Arlington Street."

Owing to the brutality with which persons exposed on the pillory were often treated by the mob, it was not unusual for the victims or their friends to hire a number of ruffians, who undertook to drive off the assailing rabble. The exhibitions in Wine Street thus occasionally produced "free fights" of a violent character. A paragraph in the *Gloucester Journal* dated August 25th, 1725, states that one John Millard, convicted at the Bristol assizes of forgery, by which he obtained large sums of money, was sentenced to a year's imprisonment, to pay a heavy fine, and to stand in the pillory on two market days. The latter part of the sentence had taken place during the week. (If the forgery affected real estate, Millard must have had his ears cut off and his nose slit.) "The last day he was severely pelted with rotten oranges and eggs by a common mob, after they had overcome the mob which stood up in his defence, though not 'till some of their leaders were taken up and carried to Bridewell." Stewart records another case, of seven years later date, in his manuscript annals. Richard Baggs, who will be heard of again, had been sentenced to the pillory for a filthy offence. "Fearing the exasperation of the populace, he hired 100 colliers to protect him, and provided himself with an iron skull cap, and thickly covered his body with brown paper. The rioting was so violent that the magistrates permitted him to be removed before the time fixed by his sentence." *Felix Farley's Journal* of June 21st, 1766, states that a lady who was looking at a pillory exhibition from a window in Wine Street, "had her eye cut entirely out of her head by a piece of glass," the window having been smashed by a cabbage stump. Returning to the first mentioned case, the quarter sessions records show that Millard was still in Newgate in December, 1737, twelve years after his conviction, being an insolvent debtor. The magistrates ordered his discharge, as concerned his private debts. "But as he stands indebted to the Crown for £103, a fine inflicted upon him at the gaol delivery in 1725, he is ordered to remain in custody." As nothing more is heard of him, he was probably released only by death.

At the quarter sessions in October, 1725, Sir John Duddleston, grandson and heir of the first baronet, prayed for his discharge from Newgate as an insolvent debtor, under an Act of the previous session, and was liberated accordingly. The young man was regarded as a discredit to his family by his widowed grandmother, who "cut him off with a shilling" by her will, dated 1718. He afterwards obtained a humble office in the Custom House, but fell into such obscurity that his ultimate fate is unknown.

The upper portion of Prince's Street was constructed in the closing years of Queen Anne's reign, and the name of the thoroughfare was intended as a compliment to Prince George of Denmark. The mansions in the lower part of the street were not commenced until 1725, when the Corporation leased several plots of land to John Becher, Henry Combe, and other wealthy merchants, who undertook to build houses on the sites. One or two of these stately dwellings still bear the crests of their builders.

Owing to the increasing trade of the port, which rendered it difficult to find accommodation for the numerous market boats bringing provisions, the Corporation ordered the building of two new quays—one on the Avon near the east end of King Street, the other on the Froom at St. Augustine's Back. The quays, which were together about 160 yards long, were completed in December, 1725.

At a meeting of the Council in January, 1726, "the petition of Mr. John Legg, keeper of Newgate, was read, setting forth that he had within a year past been at very great charge in removing sundry prisoners to distant places out of the common way, and had executed two severall persons at the last Gaol Delivery who might have been tried in the adjacent counties, and had buried them at his own expense; and therefore prayed some allowance." After an inquiry, he was voted £8 0s. 10d. The remarkable statements of the gaoler throw a little more light on the capricious treatment of criminals in that age. The reader has been already shown that prisoners sentenced to death were frequently pardoned, when they or their friends could excite the sympathy of members of the Corporation. The above minute proves that civic officials sometimes went out of their way to bring convicts to the scaffold. The " removing of prisoners to distant places," of which the gaoler boasts, was doubtless effected by transportation, a form of punishment which judges were first authorised to inflict on common felons in 1718, but which had been long adopted for saving the lives of convicts sentenced to death. The system was conducted with the looseness characteristic of the time. The Government standing wholly aloof—except when it accepted felons to recruit the army and navy—local authorities had to make their own arrangements for shipping off prisoners, who sometimes lay for years in gaol before being embarked. Occasionally, an enterprising shipowner, or a ship captain about to sail for America, offered to take a batch of convicts at a low price, intending to sell them as temporary slaves at New York or Baltimore; and a bargain was thereupon struck by the authorities. In 1727 Mr. W. Jefferis (mayor, 1738) received twelve guineas for transporting four felons, and the same gentleman, in several succeeding years, performed similar services at the same rate. In a few cases, during war with France, convicts were shipped in "letters of marque," and may have had to fight. On several occasions, the off-scourings of the gaols were embarked in vessels carrying honest emigrants, as to whose general treatment revelations will be made presently. In these transactions the speculative shipper naturally demurred to accept aged or weakly felons, who were unlikely to find purchasers. Thus, in August, 1723, the Common Council voted a sum of ten guineas, "paid for obtaining pardons for seven prisoners (being mostly women who have laine long in Newgate under sentence of transportation, and no person would take them)." In the State Papers of 1733 is a letter from Mr. William Cann, town clerk, to Mr. Scrope, M.P. for Bristol and Secretary of the Treasury, expressing the desire of the mayor and aldermen that one Phillips, condemned to death for horse stealing, should be transported for fourteen years, and that the necessary warrant should be issued at once, as "two lusty young fellows" were about to be shipped, and if Phillips did not accompany them "it would be difficult to prevail on any one to take him singly, by reason of his being in years." In January, 1745, Alderman Lyde applied to the Council for the usual sum of three guineas each for "eight convicts transported by him," which was ordered to be paid, but the minute adds that four female convicts were still in Newgate, where they had lain "a considerable time," so that the alderman had selected only the marketable prisoners.

The Dean and Chapter always studied economy in the arrangements of the Cathedral. According to the deed of incorporation there should have been six lay vicars, or singing men; but it was resolved on the 25th February, 1726, that the verger should be paid £9 a quarter, "including his salary as verger and the salaries of two singing men's places." The lay vicars were paid only £12 each yearly. The then organist, Nathaniel Priest, was also organist at All Saints' and Christ Church, though it is difficult to imagine how he fulfilled those united charges.

The following curious advertisement in the *London Weekly Journal* of April 30th, 1726, indicates the popularity of Hot Well water. The trade of the vendor and the average rate of transit from Bristol are alike remarkable:—"Bristol Hot Well water. Fresh from the wells, will be sold and delivered to any part of the town at six shillings per dozen, with the bottles, from Mr. Richard Bristow's, goldsmith, at the Three Bells near Bride Lane, Fleet Street." The advertiser offers to prove the genuineness of the water, and proceeds:—"These bottles are of the largest size, and by the extraordinary favour of the winds arrived but the last week in eight days from Bristol, the common passage being a month or six weeks."

John Jayne, captain of a Bristol merchant ship, was hanged and gibbeted on the banks of the Thames on the 13th May, 1726, having been convicted in the Admiralty Court of the atrocious murder of a cabin boy at sea. In June, 1733, Rice Harris, commander of a Bristol slaving ship, underwent the same punishment for the murder of a seaman under circumstances of horrible barbarity. The trials in the Admiralty Court were so imperfectly reported in the London papers that other local cases have probably escaped attention.

The inconvenience to traffic caused by the "corn market house," standing in the middle of Wine Street, having been much complained of, the Corporation, in July, 1726, resolved that the building should be cleared away. (It was demolished in June, 1727.) A house in Wine Street was purchased for £700, and the Swan Inn in Maryleport Street and some adjoining tenements were acquired from the trustees of Trinity Hospital. These premises were removed in 1727, and a new market house of two storeys was erected on the site, at a cost of about £1,900. The building, which some sixty years later was converted into a cheese market, was demolished about 1885, by Messrs. Baker, Baker & Co., the site being absorbed in their extended warehouses.

The emigration to America early in the century was extremely limited. Those who quitted England, moreover, were generally so poor that they were obliged to sell themselves on disembarking to pay for their passage. Many were offered a free transit by speculative shipowners, on condition of their signing indentures binding them to work as "servants," which really meant slaves, for a certain number of years. On the arrival of each vessel a sort of public market was held on board, the emigrants being sold to the highest bidder, and large profits were realized by this traffic in human flesh. The young emigrants brought the best prices, and it was not uncommon for parents to sell their children in order to avoid personal servitude. If a family lost a member on the voyage, the term of engagement of the survivors was lengthened, so as to recoup the shipowner. The traffic flourished in Bristol from an early period. The historian of Jamaica (1774) states that the Assembly of the island in 1703 relieved a ship from port charges if it imported thirty white servants, and that these emigrants, who were purchased at a minimum price of £18 in time of war, and £14 in time of peace, were required to serve—adults for four years, and youths for seven years—being treated as "little better than slaves." Many of them, he adds, were known to have been kidnapped, yet the colonial law inflicted the penalty of death on a ship captain who removed an indentured servant from the island. From Jamaica letters of 1729, to Isaac Hobhouse and Co., of Bristol, in the Jefferies collection, it appears that the firm had just shipped thirteen "servants" at London for the colony. One of the emigrants escaped at Cork. The rest were sold in Jamaica at from £13 to £30 a head. Stewart, in his MS. annals, writes under January 9th, 1725, "Twenty four persons were put on board the Raphannah frigate bound for Virginia, who had bound themselves as servants for four years according to the custom of the colony. Another ship was then lying in the river bound for Philadelphia on the same account." The captains of vessels of this kind were frequently suspected of securing passengers by force or fraud. The *Gloucester Journal* of March 25th, 1729, contains a Bristol paragraph stating that the water bailiff had been sent down to Hung Road, with the mayor's warrant, to bring from a vessel bound to Jamaica a young man who was forced on board against his will by some relations, but that the people in the ship beat off the officer and threatened to drown him. The prisoner, who was secured in irons, had been shortly before left a legacy of £800. At the quarter sessions in August, 1736, an indictment was found against John Dryland, mariner, for kidnapping a girl "and spiriting her beyond the seas," but his surety having come forward to assert that the accused was abroad and that the girl's friends declined to prosecute, the complaisant magistrates allowed the recognisances to be discharged! From a curious account, in the *Gentleman's Magazine* for 1744, of a girl who, dressed as a lad, shipped on board a Bristol vessel bound for Virginia, it would appear that the emigrants, after signing indentures, were sometimes kept three weeks in Bridewell until their ship was ready to sail. In an advertisement in the *Bristol Journal* of April 5th, 1755, inviting "handicraft tradesmen, husbandmen and boys to go over to the most flourishing city of Philadelphia" in a ship of 200 tons burthen, lying at the Quay, the captain held out the usual bait of "a new suit of clothes" to each passenger. A similar announcement appeared in the *Bristol Intelligencer* of May 7th, 1757. The vessel in this case was a privateer, and the emigrants were accompanied by "40 transports," the dregs of the neighbouring gaols. The contaminating effects of herding thieves and cutthroats with honest workmen excited no remark, and the practice was common. To give one more example, *Felix Farley's Journal* of October 26th, 1754, pleasantly announced that "Captain Davis is arrived at Annapolis, in Maryland, from this port, having 50 indentured servants, and 69 of the King's seven year passengers." The cargo was doubtless sold off indiscriminately to the neighbouring planters.

A revival of the movement for doing honour to Edward Colston's birthday took place in 1724, when a sum of £20 was raised by subscription in the parish of Redcliff, and handed to the vestry, "the profits thereof to be paid for ringing the bells on the 2nd day of November yearly, for ever." In 1726 a society styled "The Colston" was established, and held its first dinner on the philanthropist's birthday, when £34 4s. were subscribed by twenty-three gentlemen, and ordered to be invested, part of the interest to be paid for an annual sermon at Redcliff church, and the balance to Temple school. In 1729 the society raised £50

18s., "the profits to be given to the poor (of Redcliff) in bread on the 2nd November for ever." No further subscriptions are recorded, but it became the custom to fine such members as declined the office of president, and sums varying from £5 to £50 were occasionally received in this way. It may be as well, perhaps, to complete the story of this association, which eventually became known as the "Parent Society." In 1801 its funds had accumulated to £1,100, when it was resolved that the interest should be given to poor lying-in churchwomen, the wives of freemen in Redcliff parish, and the surplus to other charitable purposes. The fine for declining the presidency was raised soon after to thirty guineas, and so many of these payments were made that the funds had increased to £2,300 in 1840, the interest continuing to be distributed as before. An odd blunder remains to be mentioned. In 1752, on the reformation of the calendar, the date of the annual gathering was altered from November 2nd to November 13th, with the intention of adhering to the actual date of Colston's birth; but as that gentleman was born in the seventeenth century, when there was only ten days' difference in the "styles," the feasts should have been held on the 12th.

The churchwardens of St. James's parish petitioned the Council in November, 1726, representing the incapacity of the church to accommodate the greatly increased population, and seeking approval of a scheme for building a chapel of ease, for which a site was offered free of cost. The petition was referred to a committee, which never reported, and the subject remained dormant for sixty years.

The Council, on the 7th November, voted a sum of £20 to Walter Hawkins, common brewer, "on account of his poverty and pressing necessities." A further gift of £10 was made to him in the following year. It is probable that the recipient was a son of John Hawkins, brewer and mayor, who was knighted by Queen Anne.

Instigated by the trading companies, the Corporation occasionally undertook to punish roguish tradesmen. At the above meeting the Chamber ordered that 276 pairs of shoes "made of insufficient leather," seized on the premises of a tanner named Weaver, should be appraised, and then purchased by the city treasurer. In the following May the Council was informed that the shoes had been valued at £9 4s. (eightpence a pair!), and that the appraisers had given up their right to one-third of that amount out of consideration for the poor. The chamberlain was thereupon ordered to pay the money to the poor-law guardians. What he did with the shoes does not appear. Another seizure of a like character was dealt with in a different manner. In a Bristol paragraph dated November 29th, 1726, which appeared in the London *Weekly Journal*, the writer says:— "Yesterday was the general meeting of our shoemakers in this city, and at the High Cross, in presence of our magistrates, they burnt a great number of shoes made of seal and horse skins, which they lately seized at several places." Another seizure, dealt with in the same manner, was reported in the *Gloucester Journal* of March 11th, 1729. The destruction of bad shoes was long in favour. A Bristol paragraph in the London *Morning Post* of October 2nd, 1751, states that a parcel of shoes brought from Scotland had been just burned in the market, having been "judged by a jury of six worthy men to be made of unlawful leather."

The French Protestants, who had been deprived of the use of St. Mark's church by its conversion into a corporate place of worship, petitioned the Chamber in 1726 for a lease of a plot of land in Orchard Street on which to erect a chapel. A site was granted on a forty years' lease, at a yearly rent of £1 17s. 6d. The Corporation moreover subscribed £50 towards the building fund. The chapel was opened in 1727. In 1748 wine was advertised as on sale "in a vault under the French Chapel."

The establishment of turnpike tolls, with a view to improve the wretched roads of the country, came into favour during the reign of George I. According to the ancient law of the realm, every farmer paying £50 rent was required to give the service of a wagon and team for six days yearly, to work on the roads in his parish, and the poorest country labourer or artisan was under the same obligation as regarded his own labour. These provisions, however, were often evaded, and in many districts were inadequate, and with the increase of coaching the state of the roads fell from bad to worse. In 1726, when a report was made to the Council that the roads leading to the city were " extremely ruinous," a vote of £100 was made for their repair. But it was seen that more effectual measures were necessary, and a petition was presented to Parliament in the following session praying for power to erect turnpike gates. Evidence was given before a committee of the Commons as to the urgency of the case. It was deposed that all the roads near the city were dangerous to passengers, and that part of the London road, and several of the highways near Sodbury and

Wotton-under-Edge, were not wide enough to allow two horses, going in opposite directions, to pass each other. A witness swore that one of his horses had been suffocated in the mud, and another that his team had been saved from a slough only by being pulled out by ropes. The road to Bath from Temple Gate to Totterdown was still only seven feet wide. The Bill received the Royal assent in April, 1727. It enacted that the members of Parliament for Bristol, Gloucestershire, and Somerset, the justices of the two shires, the members of the Corporation, and a great number of local gentry should be appointed trustees for the reparation of the roads, with power to levy tolls. Wagons, etc., with six horses or oxen were to pay 1s., with four 8d., with two 4d., and with one 2d.; a pack horse 1d., if with coals ½d; there were also tolls for cattle and sheep. The limits of the trust extended from about ten to twelve miles on the chief roads out of Bristol, and the tolls were to continue for twenty-one years only. In accordance with the terms of the Act, turnpike gates were set up in order that tolls might be first collected on the 26th June. But the trustees forgot that they would have to reckon with the lawless mining population of Kingswood, roused to wrath by the charge imposed on the horses and donkeys which brought coal into the city. The colliers assembled in great numbers and pulled down all the gates, burning some, and throwing one barrier into the Avon. The mayor's letter to the Government, dated the 28th, and detailing the proceedings, is amongst the State Papers. His worship wrote:—"They are a set of ungovernable people, regardless of consequences. They extort money of people as they pass along the road, and treat them very rudely unless they give them some. They have passed through this city with clubs and staves in a noisy manner, but committed no violence here. I am persuaded, had any opposition been made, the consequences would have been fatal." Some of the gates were again erected, only to be demolished in a few hours, and the colliers would suffer no coal to enter the city. The price of fuel, ordinarily sold at 1s. a horseload, having risen to 2s. 3d., the Council, on the 28th, ordered off messengers to "Swazey, [Swansea], to buy cole on account of the Chamber" for the use of the citizens—which turned out a somewhat costly procedure, for the Kingswood men returned to work, and the Welsh coal, when it arrived, had to be sold at a loss of £215, exclusive of £4 5s. worth of wine sent to the Customs Collector at "Swanzy" for his services. The turnpike trustees, supposing the disturbances at an end, had the toll-gates reconstructed; but the colliers again rose, and burnt the gate " near Durdham Down." Further outrages were prevented by a body of soldiers, who captured four of the rioters, and the gate was restored. But on the night after the troops had embarked for Ireland, all the gates were again demolished by men disguised in women's clothes and wearing high-crowned hats. To complete the joy of the mischief makers, the four men committed to prison had to be released, Parliament having omitted to impose any penalty upon assailants of turnpikes. After vainly struggling to perform their functions, the trustees asked for further legislative powers in 1730, stating that through their inability to borrow money, the roads remained wholly unimproved. It was hoped that by allowing animals carrying coal to pass toll free, no further difficulty would be encountered, but the remission had little effect. In the State Papers is a letter from Sir W. Codrington to the Duke of Newcastle, dated July 14th, 1731, stating that the house of Mr. Blathwaite, of Dyrham, who had made himself obnoxious by attempting to defend the turnpikes, had been attacked by 400 colliers, who threatened to demolish it. The writer rode to the spot with twenty of his tenants and servants; but he was forced to release four of the rioters previously captured, and to give the rest a hogshead of ale, before they would depart. Nearly all the gates were then down. The following is highly significant: —" I am afraid, my lord, these wretches would never have been so impudent if they had not been prompted by men of some fortune and figure; and we have been informed that two or three bailiffs, as we call them, to some gentlemen, were seen to be a-drinking with the colliers the evening before they were at Mr. Blathwaite's." A week later, in a letter dated from Bristol, Sir William reports that " the insolencies of the rioters are greater than ever, they having cut down some of the gates even at noon day, and are now collecting money of travellers where the gates stood. . . . The remaining part of the inhabited turnpike house at Yate was burnt down last night." Troops were sent to Bristol, but inspired no terror amongst the rioters, who continued to defy the law. The destructive spirit of the Kingswood men was singularly manifested in the following year, when a large body marched to Chippenham, and demolished the turnpike gate at Ford, near that town (*London Journal*, Sept. 23rd). Two years later, June, 1734, every gate between Bristol and Gloucester was destroyed by armed bands. In

August, 1735, Sir William Codrington informed the Duke of Newcastle that the colliers still held the roads, sometimes extorting 50s. in a single day, and that if the Government would not render more help, "God knows how it may end." He added that a bailiff named Prichet, at Westerleigh, was "at the bottom of the whole affair." To complete the chaos, the rural trustees quarrelled with those representing Bristol; and Oldmixon, writing in 1735, asserted that "the roads, as bad as most in England, remain unrepaired to this day." Four years later, Ralph Allen, of Bath, in giving evidence on behalf of a local turnpike Bill, deposed that the Bristol Acts were still inoperative, "by reason the colliers have pulled down, and do constantly pull down, the turnpikes."

The *Bristol Newspaper* of February 4th, 1727, contains the first reference yet discovered to a locality destined to enjoy a season of great favour, but now long fallen from its high estate. The paper announces as to be let, "a large new built house, with coach-houses, stables, &c., situate in the New Square in Dowry," near the Hot Well. The square was not completed until many years afterwards.

The universality of wig wearing by the male sex at this date is amusingly testified by an advertisement in the *Bristol Newspaper* of February 25th, 1727, noting the elopement of one of the choristers of the Cathedral, 14 years of age, wearing "a peruke and a light drab coat." (In school play-grounds, according to the first Lord Thurlow, the boys were accustomed to stuff their wigs into their breeches pockets.)

At the quarter sessions in May, 1727, John Boroston, a barber, was charged with pretending to be in holy orders, whereby he had defrauded various persons of their money after professing to have clandestinely married them. No prosecutor presenting himself, and the man having lain long in gaol, he was discharged on paying the usual fees. The *Bristol Newspaper* records that the accused had "made it a practice to marry people for so small a price as eighteen pence." Prior to 1754, a valid marriage could be celebrated by a person in holy orders at any time or place, without notice, consent of parents, or record of any kind. The celebration of such marriages naturally fell into the hands of disreputable clergymen, who found competitors in rogues like Boroston. The scandal of these unions was nowhere greater than in the great seaports when a fleet of merchantmen arrived, and when drunken sailors were sometimes married by scores together at a low public-house. In the suburbs of

London at least one publican kept a priest on the premises, and married couples gratis provided they held their wedding feast at his house. At Bedminster, shortly after this date, the Duke of Marlborough inn was kept by a clergyman, the Rev. Emanuel Collins, and, if tradition is to be trusted, the shameless extent to which he carried on a similar traffic contributed to bring about the amendment of the Marriage Law in 1753.

Two prize fights took place at the Full Moon inn, Stokes Croft, during the month of June, 1727, one of the competitors in both battles being "Mr. Shiney, the champion of the West."

The accession of George II. was proclaimed with the customary ceremonies on the 17th June, 1727. The High Cross having been hung with black cloth, as a mark of respect for the deceased monarch, the mayor and corporate body, clothed in funereal robes, marched round it, preceded by the "mourning sword." The civic officials then returned to the Council House to array themselves in scarlet, and drink a bumper to the health of the new king; and the High Cross having in the meantime exchanged its gloomy gear for a blaze of coloured decorations, the sheriffs made proclamation amidst a flourish of trumpets. St. Peter's Cross, Temple Cross, and other places were afterwards visited for the same purpose, and the conduits ran wine for the populace. Further festivities took place on the occasion of the coronation, October 11th. The Corporation resolved in January, 1732, to obtain a permanent memorial of the new sovereign, directions being given by the Chamber for the purchase of a portrait. As no payment was ever made to the painter of the two handsome pictures of George II. and Queen Caroline, now in the Council Chamber, their history has hitherto been a mystery. It appears, however, from the diary of Peter Mugleworth, city swordbearer, of which Mr. Wm. George possesses a copy, that the portraits were presented by the King, and that they were set up on the 12th June, 1732, when the military officers in the city, the clergy, and many prominent citizens were entertained at the Council House, the soldiers firing salutes in Corn Street in honour of the loyal toasts drunk within. No reference to the gifts is to be found in the civic minute books, but the chamberlain paid the carriage of the pictures from London, and also "Alderman Day's disbursements, £11 4s," chiefly fees to the Lord Chamberlain's staff.

An election was, in those days, an indispensable consequence of a demise of the Crown. The writ was received early in September, 1727, when a vigorous contest took place. From some unexplained cause, Colonel Earle, who sought reelection, had lost his former popularity. Sir Abraham Elton retired in favour of his son Abraham, and the new Whig candidate was John Scrope, M.P. for Ripon in the previous Parliament, who may fairly be styled one of Fortune's favourites. The son of a merchant dwelling in Small Street, Scrope, when very young, took part with several other Bristolians in Monmouth's rebellion, and subsequently acted as an agent between the Whigs and the Prince of Orange, making one voyage to Holland in woman's clothes. After the Revolution he adopted the law as a profession, and in 1708 he was appointed one of the Barons of the Scotch Court of Exchequer, practically a sinecure office, for which he received £500 a year, while Queen Anne subsequently granted him a pension of £1,000, in consideration of his having given up his practice at the English bar. Having resigned his judgeship in 1724 (though he continued to enjoy its title by courtesy), he was now Secretary to the Treasury, and a trusted lieutenant of Walpole. The Tory aspirant was William Hart. The Bristol correspondent of the *Gloucester Journal*, writing on September 9th, gives the following account of the proceedings:—" The poll on Thursday stood thus: Baron Scroope, 765; Mr. Elton, 411; Mr. Hart, 386; Col. Earle, 4. Yesterday morning the poll was given up by Mr. Hart (as is generally said, for 1100 guineas), when he had, as his managers say, above 1500 men to go to the poll that could not have been corrupted, which so provoked his friends that the mob part of them would not let him go home [to Clifton] but under a strong guard of constables attended by the mayor and sheriffs, and threatened to pull down his house at night. Some of his managers threaten to hiss him wherever they see him, and some, instead of the [gilt] hearts they wore in their hats before, wore knaves of hearts to express their abhorrence of his action. But on the other hand Mr. Hart alleges . . . the treachery of the common people occasioned by the uncommon bribes given and offered by the opposite party, . . . and the satisfaction of seeing the corrupted part of the commonalty justly disappointed in their mercenary expectations." Stewart, in his MS. Annals, says that some thought the election was "sold" by one of Hart's managers, who feared the contest would ruin him.

It has been already mentioned that the works for rendering the Avon navigable to Bath were finished in 1728. Even before their completion an enterprising person sought to make use of the water way for the transit of passengers, for *Farley's Newspaper* of September 2nd, 1727, records an accident to "the new Passage Boat between Bristol and Twerton." As travellers by land were then liable to be pillaged by turnpike rioters and highwaymen, whilst the roads themselves were almost impassable, the boat had many patrons. "Samuel Tonkins, the first and only waterman on Bath and Bristol river," announced in the *Gloucester Journal* for April 15th, 1740, that he had added three new boats to his previous stock, "with a house on each, with sash windows," and that two boats plied daily. The journey occupied "about" four hours, and the fare was one shilling.

A musical festival, probably the first held in Bristol, took place in the Cathedral on the 22nd November, 1727. The programme consisted of "a fine Te Deum, Jubilate, and Anthem, composed by the great Mr. Handell, in which above 30 voices and instruments were concerned." In the evening of the same day two "consorts," conducted by musical rivals, took place in the Merchants' Hall and the Theatre on St. Augustine's Back, "the gentlemen of the Musick Society" taking part in the former. The festival in the Cathedral was repeated a year later.

In 1727 a topographical work of an elaborate character, in six quarto volumes, was published in London under the title of "Magna Britannia, or a New Survey of Great Britain." A few extracts from the description of Bristol, which appeared in the fourth volume, may be worth reproduction. The city, says the writer, "is very populous, but the people give up themselves to trade so entirely that nothing of the gaiety and politeness of Bath is to be seen here; all are in a hurry, running up and down with cloudy looks and busy faces, loading, carrying and unloading goods and merchandizes of all sorts from place to place, for the trade of many nations is drawn hither by the industry and opulency of the people. This makes them remarkably insolent to strangers, as well as ungrateful to benefactors, both naturally arising from being bred and become rich by trade as (to use their own phrase) to care for nobody but whom they can gain by; but yet this ill-bred temper hath produced one good effect, which our laws have not yet been able to do, and that is the utter extirpation of beggars." The author goes on to refer to the large importations of Spanish sherry, which "is therefore (*sic*) called Bristol Milk, not only because it is as common here as milk in other places, but because they esteem it as pleasant, wholesome and nourishing. . . . The Exchange is situate in the heart of the city. It consisteth only of a Piazza on one side of the street, but hath something surprising in it, being planted round with stone pillars, which have broad boss [brass?] plates on them, like sundials, and coats of arms, with certain inscriptions on every plate. They were erected by some eminent merchants, for the benefit of writing and despatching their affairs on them, and at Change time the merchants every one taking up their standing about one or other of these pillars, that masters of ships and owners may know where to find them."

Sir Abraham Elton, Bart., one of the greatest magnates of the city, died on the 9th February, 1728, probably at his house in Small Street. The announcement of his death in the local newspaper credited him with what was then considered the stupendous fortune of £100,000, "which he acquired by his own industry, raising himself and wife from a state of meanness and obscurity into wealth and notice." Stewart, the contemporary annalist, in copying this notice, explains :—" His father was a scavenger and his wife a milkmaid." (Jacob Elton, the father, was in fact a market gardener in St. Philip's out-parish, but may have collected the town refuse for the improvement of his land.) Sir Abraham was treasurer of Lewin's Mead Chapel in 1693-4. By his will, after bequeathing the manor of Clevedon to his eldest, and the manors of Whitestaunton and Winford to his other surviving son, and leaving large legacies to his widow and grandchildren, he made bequests to the Merchants' Almshouse, Trinity Hospital, the poor of St. John's, St. Werburgh's and St. Philip's parishes, and all the workmen in his extensive copper works at Conham, where he had founded a chapel. He also left a piece of land in St. Philip's for the endowment of a school in the out-parish, and ordered small yearly payments to schools at Clevedon and Winford.

On the 28th March, 1728, an unfortunate Bristol bookseller, J. Wilson, appeared at the bar of the House of Commons, in company with Robert Raikes, printer of the *Gloucester Journal*, charged with breach of privilege. Raikes, it appeared, had ventured to print part of a news-letter (forwarded by the celebrated Edward Cave), giving a brief account of a debate in the Lower House. As Wilson had merely sold a few copies of the *Journal*, and pleaded ignorance, he was discharged ; but Raikes was kept in custody nearly a fortnight, had to make an apology on his knees to the Speaker, and was mulcted £40 in fees. In Raikes's copy of the *Journal*, the words, " The woful paragraph," are written over the few lines which cost him so dearly.

A fiscal interference with the glass trade, exciting much local irritation, was resolved upon by the Government during the session. With the object of preventing smuggling, the importation of wine in bottles and small casks was absolutely prohibited. The Bristol glassmakers petitioned against the proposal, asserting that many thousand persons were employed in making bottles for exportation, which were reimported filled with wine, and that the stoppage of this business would cause the entire destruction of the bottle trade ; but the protest was ineffectual.

The first circulating library in Bristol was announced in *Farley's Newspaper* of March 30th, 1728. The proprietor, Thomas Sendall, bookseller, "at the sign of the Lock's Head in Wine Street," stated that he had begun " a method of furnishing curious lovers of reading with a great variety of books to read by the year at a very easy rate." Mr. Sendall boasted in a later advertisement that his library contained no less than 200 volumes.

The pompous and costly funeral of Mr. John Day has been recorded under 1718. In April, 1728, Mr. Thomas Day, eldest son of Sir Thomas, died at Brentford, leaving instructions as to his interment which shocked the sentiments of the age. His executors were directed to bury his remains by daylight, in the churchyard of any parish in which he might die, permitting no hearse or coach to attend, and giving the parson a guinea for doing his duty, the clerk ten shillings "for doing nothing," and the sexton as much for " making my bed." No monument was to be erected, and his coffin was to be " without any gimcracks, or what some people call ornaments." Nothing was to be given at the funeral, " no, not wine " (which was always given), but six labouring men were each to have a guinea and a bottle of wine for bearing him to the grave. The deceased left considerable property to his kindred, but excepted two of his nephews in Bristol, Nathaniel and Thomas, who had only 5*s*. each, " for reasons which to them are not unknown." (Their grandmother, Lady Day, had " cut them off" in similar terms in 1721.) To Mary Blackwell, a grand-niece, he left £200, " with all the furniture in the Great House at the Bridge End," so often referred to in local history. Thomas

Day is stated by a contemporary London journal to have taken an active part in the Revolution, and to have enjoyed a pension of £400 a year for his services to the House of Hanover.

One of the perennial outbreaks of disease having occurred in Newgate, the authorities, who dispensed with a regular medical officer, frugally availed themselves of the help of a surgeon or apothecary who was incarcerated for debt. In March, 1728, he was paid £10 "as a free gift for his medicines and services to the sick."

The Princess Amelia, daughter of George II., paid a visit to the city on the 9th May, 1728, in compliance with an invitation forwarded by the Council during her sojourn at Bath. The Avon having just been made navigable from Bath to Hanham, her Royal Highness, who detested bad roads, and had travelled from London to Bath in a sedan chair, resolved on making the journey by water, and a roomy wherry was gaily decorated for the occasion. The reader shall be spared a lengthy account of the reception. The Princess landed at Temple Back, where she was complimented by the mayor, and, having been handed to a sedan chair, she was conveyed by way of Thomas Street, High Street, Small Street, and the Quay to Alderman Day's mansion in Queen Square, where an address of welcome was presented. After an entertainment in the Merchants' Hall, the royal visitor was driven to interesting points in the city, then partook of dinner privately at Alderman Day's, and finally departed as she had come. The entertainment of the Princess cost the Corporation £242 14s. 11½d., of which about £50 were for wine, £8 6s. for "14 black velvet capps" (for the rowers?), £5 3s. 10d. for the use of knives, forks, and pewter plates, and 1s. 6d. for Hot Well water.

The first celebration of Royal Oak Day after the death of George I. was marked by the Jacobites all over England with unusual rejoicing, and the display in this district was doubtless intensified by the royal visit just recorded. A paragraph in the following week's *Gloucester Journal*, dated Bath, May 29th, states that "this morning the whole city was as a green wood, and all the people like walking boughs." The oak trees around Bristol were seriously mutilated to make a similar display. For the following thirty years the 10th June, the Pretender's birthday, and the 11th June, the date of George II.'s accession, invariably gave rise to rival demonstrations.

In proportion as the civic treasury increased in wealth,

the love of the city magnates for feasting and ostentation correspondingly developed. Down to 1714 the entertainment of the judges was considered to be satisfactorily accomplished at a cost of from £25 to £30, the money being paid to the alderman or councillor who lent his house for the occasion. The outlay then gradually increased, and in 1721 Mr. Jacob Elton received £105, while £32 10s. were paid for keeping the judges' horses. In 1728 the Chamber resolved that, as Alderman Shuter, who occupied one of the finest houses in Queen Square, had been "at great trouble and expense in providing pewter, linen, and other necessaries for the maintenance of the judges for so many [four] years past," the sum of £315 should be granted him. Next year Mr. Peter Day was voted £134 for entertaining the judges and the recorder. About this time the practice began of giving "suppers," or in modern speech dinners, to the judicial functionaries at the conclusion of their daily labours. In 1731 the expenditure included suppers to the judges £46 3s. 3d., and similar treats to the recorder £40 5s., besides the usual sums for lodgings, servants, and horses.

Farley's Bristol Newspaper for July 20th, 1728, contains an account of a remarkably gallant combat sustained by a Bristol captain and crew against heavy odds. The writer states that the Kirtlington galley of 280 tons, 12 guns, and 17 men, under the command of Samuel Pitts, was on her way from Jamaica on the 8th June, when she was attacked by a Spanish rover, with about 100 men, armed with two swivels and abundance of blunderbusses. The Englishmen, urged by Pitts, struggled bravely, but after an hour's fight within pistol shot, the overpowering fire of the enemy forced the little band to take shelter, and about fifty of the Spaniards boarded the galley. The crew then rallied, shot the man who was about to strike the English flag, and fell so furiously on the assailants that "in about an hour's time they despatched all the rest but two," who were severely wounded, and finally killed. Hereupon the pirate sheered off, pursued by the galley, which fired three broadsides in the hope of sinking her, but night fell, and her fate was unknown. It was believed that the Spaniard had lost between sixty and seventy men. Captain Pitts "had only four or five men wounded, and brought home his ship and cargo in honour and safety." His triumph occasioned a lively feeling of pride and joy amongst the citizens, and the Merchants' Society presented him with a splendid piece of plate, weighing 266½ ounces, bearing an appropriate record of his bravery. (This testimonial was purchased by the Corporation in 1821 for £148 16s., and now forms part of the civic plate.) Through some unaccountable blundering, Pitts's brilliant feat is recorded in Evans's history under 1628, and by Mr. Nicholls under 1629–30.

The new representative of the city, "Baron" Scrope, received a new honour in July, 1728, being appointed Recorder of Bristol upon the resignation of Chief Justice Eyre, who had held the office for twenty-four years. The new functionary, as a member of the Government, rendered local merchants great service in Parliament by opposing the attempts of the African Company to monopolise the slave trade. In 1730, when he came down to deliver the gaol, he was met some miles outside the city "by a great number of gentlemen on horseback, and forty or fifty coaches," as a demonstration of respect.

The rural character of Stoke's Croft is illustrated by an announcement in *Farley's Newspaper* for July 27th, 1728, of a house and five acres of garden ground to be let there. The same paper, about six months previously, offered "four good pasture grounds to be let on St. Michael's Hill." Another Stoke's Croft garden, of eleven acres, is mentioned in 1730.

An advertisement in *Farley's Newspaper* of December 21st, 1728, notifies that the fair previously held at "Points Pool" every New Year's Day would in future be held in West Street. "For encouragement, the inhabitants will give the use of their bulks and standings gratis, and a very good ox to be roasted whole in the said street." This fair continued throughout the Georgian era, and was often the scene of great disorder, the city authorities having no power to interfere.

The years 1728 and 1729 were marked by bad harvests, high prices of food, and much consequent misery and discontent. Robberies from the person in the public streets at night were of frequent occurrence. Owing to the dearth, no less than 199 shiploads of grain were imported, the duties on which amounted to over £26,000. The arrival of nine cargoes of wheat from New York and Philadelphia was an unprecedented feature of this traffic. The clothing trade being much depressed, the employers combined to effect a reduction of wages, with the result of irritating the weavers into acts of violence. A Bristol paragraph in the *Gloucester Journal* of October 8th, 1728, stated that on the previous Thursday about 500 of the workmen living without Lawford's Gate, after seizing and burning thirty looms there, set off in a body for Chew Magna, Pensford, and Keynsham, where they destroyed a quantity of machinery, pulling down a house in the course of the raid. On the 1st and 2nd September, 1729, there was another violent outbreak "outside the Gate," in which many looms were torn out of the employers' houses and burnt in the streets. A much more serious affair occurred on the 29th September. The weavers met at Kingswood, and, after marshalling their forces, marched to the house of Stephen Fecham, in Castle Ditch, where they threatened to pull down the dwelling and murder the occupier on the ground that he paid his workmen 1s. per piece less than was given by other masters. (They had demolished another house on the Saturday before, says a contemporary reporter, and beaten off a body of soldiers.) Fecham had made preparations for resistance, and fired "several musquetoons" into the crowd, whereby five of the rioters were killed and two mortally wounded. The regiment brought to the spot also fired several volleys, though only, it was believed, of blank cartridge. One of the sergeants was killed by an accidental shot from Fecham's house. The affair excited great popular indignation, and a coroner's jury in the out-parish of St. Philip returned a verdict of wilful murder against Fecham, who, to escape the consequences, appealed for the protection of the Government. In the State Papers is a letter from him stating:—"The coroner of the county of Gloucester intends to endite the officers of the out-parish for not taking me up, so I should be glad if any way can be found to move it out of his power." Mr. Scrope obtained for him the King's pardon, which he pleaded at the assize, and was liberated. One of the rioters was sentenced to death, and afterwards hanged. At the summer assizes at Gloucester four weavers were convicted and sentenced to death for destroying looms and cloth in the eastern suburbs of the city. (These outrages, as well as a serious riot in Temple Street, occurred after the Castle Ditch tragedy.) One culprit only was executed. He declared that the riots were solely due to the masters having reduced wages at a time when the weavers were starving. Soon afterwards Fecham absconded under disgraceful circumstances, when the weavers (13th March, 1731) carried his effigy in a cart to the city gallows, hanged it there amidst loud acclamations, and afterwards gibbeted it at Lawford's Gate (Stewart's MS.). Three days later some of Fecham's friends attempted to cut the gibbet down, "but the weavers immediately beat to arms with a frying-pan, and collected money on purpose to pay a watch, and guard at night-time" (*London Journal*, March 25th). In the following May the magistrates, by virtue of their statutable powers, established "a table of rates of wages payable to weavers for divers sorts of goods," and all masters and men were required to abide by the same "under the pains inflicted by law." It would appear that the men could not earn more than about a shilling a day, which was inadequate, in seasons of dearth, to supply an average family with bread.

Although the country was at peace, the Government found it impossible to obtain the few men required for the navy except by impressment. *Read's Journal* contains a paragraph from Bristol, dated April 19th, 1729, stating that the press-gangs systematically seized the crews of vessels entering Kingroad, and that the captains of outward bound ships, to avoid similar losses, allowed the pilots to conduct the barques as far as the "Holmbs," while their men stole down the country, and were taken up by boats.

The excessive prevalence of duelling amongst the upper classes at this period occasionally led to its adoption by hotheaded young tradesmen. In a letter dated May 3rd, 1729, a Bristol correspondent of the (London) *Weekly Journal* gives the following amusing account of a local "affair of honour":—
"There happening lately a quarrel between a young gentleman and a tradesman of this city, the latter gave the former a challenge to fight him at sword and pistol, which he accepted, and accordingly went this morning to the Nine Trees (the place appointed to decide the dispute, near the city) with one friend with him, where he was prepared with a sword and a brace of pistols, expecting his antagonist equipped with the like utensils; but to his no little surprise the tradesman brought up his mother, &c., for seconds, with a rusty pistol without a flint, and instead of performing his challenge declined fighting with pistols, and would have boxed the said gentleman, his mother offering ten guineas upon his head, which the gentleman declined, as not being according to the challenge given him."

Prize fighting by women was also common at this date. *Farley's Newspaper* of May 31st contains the following:—
"Monday next, at the Green Dragon, upon St. Michael's Hill, is to be a compleat Boxing Bout by Moll Buck, of this city, and Mary Barker, from London, for seven guineas. The latter has fought many prizes at Sword and Staff, and

she designs to perform the same at Bedminster one day next week."

The city gaol was practically cleared of insolvent debtors about this time, by virtue of one of the haphazard "Acts of Grace" which Parliament was accustomed to pass when the complaints of the unhappy people wrung temporary attention to their sufferings. All this class of prisoners was released, save those owing more than £500. According to a London news letter of May 31st, the almost incredible number of 97,248 debtors applied for the benefit of the statute.

A costly local funeral is recorded in the (London) *Weekly Journal* of July 26th. "Cornelius Stevens, Esq., of Queen Square, the noted beau," having died about the beginning of the month, his remains were placed in a coffin covered with crimson velvet, and lay in state for nearly a week. Twelve carriages with six horses each carried the mourners to St. James's Church, preceded by a hearse covered with heraldic escutcheons; but the mob, as was its custom, tore off the glittering panoply, "and acted so violently that the ceremony, for which the deceased had left £300, was shorn of its grandeur."

The extraordinary looseness of the police of the streets is illustrated by the following minute of the vestry of St. Stephen's, dated September 4th:—"Inasmuch as many annoyances have been done to the church by many, by throwing grains, street dirt, ashes, rubbish, and likewise by putting tanners' bark, hides, bricks, hopps, hay, &c. against the church, as well as by putting boards and boxes against the walls and before the door," orders were given to prosecute the persons committing such nuisances. The resolution proceeds:—"And we have also agreed that a turnpike shall be erected and set opposite to the vestry room." A fortnight later, the vestry resolved that "whereas there hath been for time out of mind a turnpike in the lane near St. Stephen's Church which is now decayed," a new one should be erected at the same place. The "turnpikes" were doubtless turnstiles.

A movement for the suppression of drunkenness and profanity sprang up about this time in Bristol and other towns. The remedy propounded for these offences was the stocks, which were in great favour amongst local aldermen during the last six months of 1729. Incorrigible drunkards were incarcerated for four hours. Persons convicted of cursing or swearing were held in durance for from one to four hours according to the number of their offences. One man, who had been not only "prophane," but drunk, was ordered to be exhibited no less than six hours. Females were frequently subjected to the punishment, and to the same painful extent as men. All these offenders, however, were rather pitied than tormented by the populace, and the magisterial severity was ineffectual. In December the last instance is recorded of another unavailing chastisement. A woman and two men having been convicted of lewdness, the aldermen (no less than nine of whom attached their signatures to the judgment) ordered "that they all three be put on horseback and ride" through the streets "according to the ancient custom of this city."

A record of an unusually heavy rainfall in November, 1729, incidentally acquaints us with the state of the roads around Bristol. Several travellers, says a local newspaper, were obliged to swim their horses in order to reach the city, "as did the Bath coach for a considerable way."

On the death, in 1730, of Robert Booth, who had been dean of Bristol for twenty-two years, the office was conferred on Samuel Creswicke, a descendant of an eminent local family in the previous century, and, by the gift of the Corporation, incumbent of St. James's. Dr. Creswicke seems to have held clerical conventionalities in slight esteem. In the British Museum is a letter of Berkeley Seymour, a Bitton squire (murdered in 1742 by his brother William, who was hanged for the crime), to a neighbour, whose name does not appear. The missive, which is dated August, 1730, states that in default of a satisfactory answer by the bearer about the repayment of money arbitrarily taken from the writer's tenants, "I will demand justice of you this afternoon at your door with my sword. If your neighbour, Mr. Justice Creswicke, has a mind to divert himself that way, my cousin Bowles, who has come from Bristoll on purpose, has a sword at his servis; and if the tall learned divine, Dr. Creswicke, the present worthy dean of Bristoll, has any inclination to be of the party, the habit of a dragoon *which he generally wears* will be proper for the occasion : a young fellow of King's Collegde shall throw more Greek and Latin in his teeth than he will be able to digest in twelve months." In 1739 Dr. Creswicke was promoted to the deanery of Wells, but continued to hold his Bristol parish. At his residence, Haydon, near Wells, he ordered a cockpit to be constructed, so that he and his guests could witness the "sport" from his dining-room, the window of which was enlarged for the purpose. The death of Dean Booth put an end to a long standing quarrel between the cathedral authorities and the Corporation.

The year 1730 was made memorable in England by the outbreak of a previously unknown species of crime, invented by a few miscreants in Bristol, but which rapidly spread in all directions. The trick conceived by the knaves was of the simplest character. A letter was thrown into a warehouse or shop, threatening that if a certain sum of money—generally eight or ten guineas—was not deposited in a certain secluded place, the building would be burnt down or the owner murdered. It was not discovered when this practice commenced, for the villains at first exacted secrecy, and probably many persons submitted in silence to the extortion. About the end of September, however, a Mr. Packer, whose house adjoined the shipbuilding yard of Mr. Clement, near Trinity Street, received several letters with demands for money, with which he refused to comply; and the conspirators, resolving to strike general terror, set fire to his house on the night of Saturday, the 3rd October. The building was burnt to the ground, but the premises of Clement, from whom money had also been demanded, escaped uninjured. On the following day, a letter was flung into a Mr. Boltby's shop, stating that Packer could have prevented the fire if he had placed ten guineas in the place assigned, and that the writers would pursue him if he went into twenty houses, and murder him at the first opportunity. Another paper threatened to set the whole city in flames. Packer that day took refuge at a house in Canons' Marsh, adjoining the warehouse of Messrs. Teague and Farr, in which cordage and hemp to the value of £10,000 were stored. During the night fire-balls were flung into this warehouse, but the flames were extinguished. The whole city was aroused by the malignity of the criminals, the watch was doubled, and voluntary aid was plentifully offered to the authorities. In a few days several persons were arrested on suspicion, some being sent for security to Bath and Ilchester gaols; but the real culprits remained at liberty. Letters were still thrown about threatening to burn various buildings, as well as the shipping at Sea Mills dock, and a reward of £500 offered for the detection of the gang was without effect. Owing to repeated threats to destroy Mr. Clement's shipyard, it was guarded by soldiers for several weeks. The terrorism which had been so profitable to its original inventors speedily found imitators amongst the criminals of neighbouring towns, and "threatening letters" were soon disseminated in every county in the kingdom, exciting universal alarm. The Bristol malefactors were doubtless ruffians of the lowest class, but many ruined gamblers and unscrupulous knaves in other localities had recourse to a proceeding by which money could be so easily gained.

The story of the panic gives us also a glimpse into the treatment of suspected but innocent persons awaiting trial in Newgate. A man named Power, son of a Dublin attorney, happened to be in Bristol on the day when Packer's house was destroyed. Being a stranger and in poor circumstances, he fell under suspicion, and upon a little girl declaring that she had seen him throw the letter into Boltby's shop he was arrested. Two other children next asserted that he had given them letters to throw into Packer's house, whereupon he was committed for trial and thrown into the "Pit" at Newgate—an underground dungeon generally reserved for condemned convicts. There, as he told the jury at his trial, he was "chained down to a staple, and was kept fourteen weeks and three days, in the winter weather, without pen, ink, paper, fire or candle, far distant from my relatives and destitute of money, and have now suffered almost twelve months' imprisonment." The evidence against him being quite untrustworthy, he was acquitted, but he was compelled to pay the gaoler's fees before his liberation. The marvel is that he escaped with his life. During the spring assizes of 1730, at Taunton, the Lord Chief Baron, the sheriff of Somerset, a serjeant-at-law, and several judicial officers died from gaol fever, owing to the horrible condition of some of the prisoners brought from Ilchester gaol.

During the alarm caused by the incendiaries, the Common Council was inspired by the happy thought that it would be useful to the citizens to know where they could find a constable in an emergency. It was therefore ordered that a "painted staff" should be affixed at the door of each constable. Those officials, however, disliked a regulation which, in times of riot, exposed their dwellings to the vengeance of the rabble, and the symbol of law and order seems to have often disappeared when it was most sought for. Another order, issued by the magistrates, required the twelve watchmen who guarded the city during the night to remain on duty from 10 p.m. to 6 a.m. during the winter months, each man to receive 9d. per night for his pains.

A coach undertaking to perform the journey between Bristol and Salisbury in one day, during the summer season only, started for the first time on the 25th March, 1730.

The Elizabethan mansion called Redland Court was demolished in or about 1730 by order of Mr. John Cossins, the owner, who commissioned John Strahan, a Bristol architect, to erect the handsome building in the Italian style now standing on the same site. Mr. Cossins afterwards built and endowed a chapel on Redland Green, for the use of his household and of the handful of families then dwelling in the neighbourhood. It was opened for public worship on the 5th October, 1743.

A paper war in the local press between rival practitioners affords a glimpse of the costume of the medical profession at this time. One of the antagonists sneers at the other's "monstrous wig, ornamental sword, velvet sleeves, and fashionable great cloak." We learn from other sources that the cloak then worn by the middle and upper classes was always of blazing scarlet.

In consequence of numerous representations of the citizens, a committee of the Council reported in February, 1731, that the times fixed for holding the two great local fairs were inconvenient and prejudicial to traders, for whose relief it was recommended that the summer, or St. James's, fair should in future commence on the 1st September, and the winter, or St. Paul's, fair on the 1st March. The report was adopted, and there is nothing in the minutes to show that the alterations did not forthwith take place. As a matter of fact, the Corporation had no power to change the dates except under legislative authority, and an Act for that purpose was not even applied for until 37 years afterwards. The committee also reported that the standings set up in Wine Street during St. James's fair were a common nuisance, and should be suppressed, but as the sheriffs were entitled to exact fees from the stall-holders, it was suggested that similar standings might be erected in Broadmead. These recommendations were also approved, and the Council further resolved that the stalls annually set up about the High Cross should be thenceforth prohibited. The sheriffs subsequently complained that their income had been reduced by the removal of the Wine Street standings, and they were voted a yearly compensation of £20. It is to be regretted that no description of the city during fair time has been preserved. From casual references in newspapers and letters, the scene, especially during the summer fair, must have been one of remarkable animation and gaiety. Lengthy preparations were made for the great local event of the year. The corporate records show that other business was frequently thrust aside until "after the fair," in order that the civic mind might not be disturbed in maturing its arrangements. When the day at length arrived, gentry, farmers, and well-to-do tradesmen, with their families, arrived from the neighbouring counties and South Wales, and the citizens offered generous hospitality to their country friends. Home manufactures of every description poured in by means of wagons and pack-horses, and London mercers and milliners eagerly hired shops in the oddest localities—the Pithay was one of their favourite nooks—in order to dazzle provincial eyes with their fashionable wares. What seems still stranger to modern ideas, the fair was extensively attended by wholesale purchasers of foreign merchandise. A London journal of July, 1729, contains a report from Bristol lamenting that "sugars are very scarce here for want of the Jamaica fleet, which is a great disappointment to our fair." How extensive was the business transacted may be imagined from a petition presented to the House of Commons by the Corporation in 1697, in which it is estimated that at least £150,000 in old silver coin would be brought to the next fair from Wales and other districts. Goldsmiths, the bankers of the time, arrived from distant places and set up standings for carrying on their business in the Meal Market (afterwards the Guard House) in Wine Street. The week was as notable for its amusements as for business. A company of play-actors was rarely wanting, and all the peripatetic conjurors and showmen of the midland counties and the south of England flocked in to compete for the smiles, and pence, of a public eager to be entertained. The grossest impostures were practised with impunity. Southey records, as a youthful reminiscence, that he once saw a shaved monkey exhibited as a veritable fairy; while a shaved bear, in a checked coat and trousers, was sitting in a great chair, and styled an Ethiopian savage.

On the 16th February, 1731, a petition was presented to the House of Commons from the merchants of Bristol trading with America, complaining of harassing interruptions to trade, caused for several years by Spanish ships of war. Several Bristol ships having been plundered and captured, the petitioners prayed for relief. A committee having been appointed to investigate the case, a number of Bristol captains and sailors gave evidence as to the cruel treatment they had undergone. The committee reported that the petitioners had fully proved their allegations. A message was soon afterwards read to the House, declaring that the

King would take steps to prevent depredations, and to procure satisfaction for the damages already sustained. The truth was that the English merchants were carrying on an extensive smuggling trade with the Spanish colonies, for which their vessels were often seized by the Spanish coastguards. The matter, as will be seen later on, brought about a war between the two countries. The Bristol merchants appear to have suffered severely before appealing to the House of Commons. In a memorandum book once belonging to Edward Southwell, M.P. for Bristol in 1750, now in the British Museum, is a brief jotting to the effect that a Mr. Hawksworth and other Bristolians claimed £60,000 as compensation for losses between 1718 and 1721.

Although the growing traffic caused by increased population gave rise to complaints as to the inconvenience of the gateways into the city, the Corporation was in no humour to remove those ancient defences. Lawford's Gate was "repaired and beautified" in 1721, although it was so narrow as to cause a daily block of traffic. A petition of the inhabitants of Temple parish, in 1730, asserting that Temple Gate was so low and narrow as to be highly incommodious and dangerous, met with no response. The people of Redcliff having complained of the Gate in that parish, and being more influential, the Council resolved, in 1731, not to remove the obstruction, but to rebuild it, and £250 were spent in rearing a very ugly and inconvenient structure. In 1734 it was found indispensable to improve Temple Gate also. It was consequently rebuilt in a "rustic classic" style, with an extremely narrow roadway for carriages, and two passages for pedestrians. The expenditure was £476. As the gates could not accommodate the traffic, the Chamber persisted in accommodating the traffic to the gates. An influential committee, in February, 1731, asserted that the entry into the city of wains and carts having iron-bound wheels was a public nuisance, and recommended that all such vehicles, except the London wagons unloading at St. Peter's Pump, and a few others, should be forbidden to pass along the streets. The Chamber adopted this advice, and the fine for infringing the regulation was fixed at 6s. 8d. The "nuisance" nevertheless was not abated; for in January, 1736, a committee was fruitlessly appointed to suppress "the growing evil" of heavy cart traffic. A misdated note amongst Mr. Seyer's MSS., founded on the remembrance of an old citizen, must belong to about this time. The statement is to the effect that the Corporation prohibited carts and wagons from crossing Bristol bridge, compelling the drivers to unload hay, etc., on sledges, but that "about 1720," Mr. Smyth, of Long Ashton, denying the right of the authorities to do this, one day took the whip from one of his carters and personally drove a loaded wagon over the bridge, " since which time the passage of wagons has been permitted." Another civic report, presented in 1731, was inspired by the old prejudice against "foreigners." A committee reported that they had obtained evidence that a freeman named John Clark, a mercer in Wine Street, had been secretly in partnership with one John Steward, a foreigner, whose merchandise he had "covered" from town dues, contrary to his oath. Clark, who was Steward's brother-in-law, was disfranchised by the Chamber. In December, 1736, it was reported to the House that Clark continued to carry on business in Wine Street. After being persistently worried, he at length begged for readmission as a free burgess, and paid a fine of £30.

In the meantime, a number of unfortunate people were arrested for following a trade to which they had not served an apprenticeship of seven years. They were generally committed for trial, and, if unable to find bail, they often lay several weeks in the unhealthy gaol. The absurdity of the law was admitted by all except the selfish interests that put its powers in force, and on only one occasion did the prosecutors obtain a conviction, with a fine of 40s.

Although the early newspapers were remiss in chronicling local disasters caused by the flooding of the Froom, there can be no question that that river was a frequent terror to the inhabitants of Broadmead and the adjacent district. In the summer of 1731 the Corporation spent the large sum of £337 12s. 6d. in "making new sluices at St. James's Mills for the better venting of the water in great freshes."

The Council, in September, 1731, ordered that markets for the sale of hay should be established in Broadmead for Gloucestershire produce, and in Temple Street for that of Somerset. Hay arriving by water was to be sold on the Quays. The chief intention of the arrangement was to prevent the passage of heavy carts through the central streets. A machine for weighing loaded carts, the first introduced into the city, was purchased for the Broadmead market in 1738.

The year 1731 is notable for the definite establishment in Bristol of a manufacture for which the city continues to be famous. *Farley's Bristol Newspaper* of August 21st contains the following advertisement :—"His Majesty having been pleased to grant to Walter Churchman, of Bristol, Letters Patent for the sole use of an Engine by him invented for the expeditious, fine, and clean making of Chocolate to greater perfection than by any other method in use, the patentee purposes to sell his Chocolate at the common prices. . . . N.B. Buyers of shells may be furnished with any quantities of them at a low price at his house in Broadmead." After the death of the inventor, the business was carried on by his son Charles, a solicitor, who lived at the premises in Broadmead. The latter died in May, 1761, and in the following month the *Bristol Journal* announced for sale "the Castle Mills of Bristol, with all the buildings adjoining, late the estate of Mr. Charles Churchman. . . . And also the said Mr. Churchman's Chocolate Mills and works there, which being a Secret cannot be exposed to view." Another local chocolate manufacturer had entered the field before Churchman's demise. Joseph Fry, born in 1728, settled in Bristol as an apothecary about twenty years later, and was admitted a freeman in 1753, on payment of a fine of fifteen guineas. The *Bristol Journal* of March 24th, 1759, announced that "Joseph Fry, Apothecary, is removed from Small Street to a house opposite Chequer Lane in Narrow Wine Street, where he makes and sells Chocolate as usual." Mr. Fry forthwith negotiated for Churchman's premises, and in November, 1761, an advertisement in the same paper announced that "Churchman's Patent Chocolate is now made by Joseph Fry and John Vaughan, jun., the said Churchman's executor, the present sole proprietors of the famous Water Engine at the Castle Mills." In 1763, Fry, still styled an apothecary, had a house and shop in Wine Street "next door to the Crispin inn;" but in 1777, soon after the construction of Union Street, he announced his removal there, "opposite the upper gate of St. James's Market, where he keeps his shop for the sale of Churchman's Patent and other sorts of Chocolate, nibs, and Cocoa." The fame of Churchman's preparation was so widely spread that the name was and still is retained by the Frys for some of their productions. The founder of their house appears to have been a man of great ingenuity and enterprise. In conjunction with a printer named Pine he established a type foundry in Bristol, which was removed in 1770 to London, where "Fry and Son" were type-founders to the Prince of Wales in 1786. In a handbill announcing the publication of the *Bristol Mercury*, January, 1790, it is stated that the paper would be "printed in a new and most beautiful type by the ingenious Fry." We shall subsequently find him connected with Champion in the celebrated Bristol China works. In 1771, in conjunction with Samuel Fripp, he purchased the soap and candle manufactory of Farell, Vaughan, and Co. in Christmas Street. The works were removed to Castle Gate, and developed into the extensive manufactory carried on in later days by Messrs. Thomas Brothers. And besides these businesses, he had chemical works at Battersea. By his brethren of the Society of Friends Joseph Fry was greatly respected for his earnest efforts to raise the moral tone of the denomination, which in his youth had degenerated from its pristine purity and simplicity. Extravagance of dress was common amongst youthful Quakers, who flashed to chapel in gay clothes and powdered wigs. Drunkenness and gambling were not unknown. Many wealthy Quakers were engaged in privateering. These annals will record a challenge to mortal conflict proffered by a Bristol Quaker to a lawyer. In August, 1722, at Gloucester, an Irish Quaker exhibited his skill with broadsword and dagger, falchion and quarterstaff, in combats with a Bristol gladiator. The minutes of the Bristol Friends refer with grief to the dealings of some of the members in smuggled goods. And in the Jefferies Collection is a singular document showing that a family of Quakers at Alveston bought, and enjoyed for many years, under the name of an attorney, half the tithes of the lordship of Tockington. Against the various backslidings Fry urgently remonstrated, and his efforts, with those of others, eventually succeeded in accomplishing a complete regeneration in the Society.

In the autumn of 1731 a movement was started by the Whig party in London for the erection of a statue of William III. A large sum was soon raised by subscription, but when a site for the monument was requested, the Common Council, in which the Tories had gained predominance, refused even to receive the petition. The incident caused much comment throughout the country, and notably amongst the merchants of Bristol, a great majority of whom were Whigs, and steps were forthwith taken to prove the loyalty of the city to the Revolution settlement. On the 8th December, say the minutes of the Council, "a memorial, inscribed by a great number of gentlemen, setting forth that the memorialists, with many other inhabitants, were willing at their own charge to erect a public statue to the memory of our great and glorious Deliverer, William III., was produced." The document, which prayed for a suitable site for the monument, was cordially received. The Chamber fixed upon Queen Square as an appropriate site, and unanimously voted £500 towards the expense, adding that the subscription might be increased if "occasion required." The Merchants' Society, equally enthusiastic, voted £300 (having previously negatived a proposal, insidiously made by the Tories, to erect a statue to George II.). A few weeks later a committee of nine gentlemen—three appointed by the Corporation, three by the Merchants' Company, and three by the subscribers—proceeded to carry out the undertaking. Two designs were received in July, 1732, one by the celebrated Rysbraek, the other by a Mr. Schymaker, the former of which was selected. In September, 1733, the ground was broken in the centre of Queen Square for the purpose of laying the foundation of the monument, when, says a mocking paragraph in the *Gloucester Journal*, Alderman John Becher " uttered this pious ejaculation, 'My shepherd is the living God, in whom is my defence,' and out of his abundant generosity gave the workmen two shillings and sixpence to drink his worship's good health." (Becher had shortly before been paid £413 by the Corporation for his exertions in defending the interests of the local slave traders against the African Company.) From some unexplained cause, there was a long delay between the casting of the statue and its erection. In December, 1734, the Hull monument, by Schymaker, was uncovered with great ceremony, when the mayor and corporation "drank prosperity to the friends of the Revolution, particularly in the city of Bristol." But it was not until September, 1736, that the work in Queen Square was reported to the Council to be " handsomely finished." Rysbraek received £1,800 for one of his finest productions. Schymaker had £50 for his model. The subscriptions being insufficient, the Council voted a further gift of £500 in December, 1736.

Another of the great cockfighting "entertainments" of the time was announced in the *Gloucester Journal* of the 9th November. The match was between "the gentlemen of Bristol and the gentlemen of Bath," who were to produce forty-one birds each, "for four guineas a battle and sixty guineas the odd battle."

A Latin inscription in the old church of St. Nicholas recorded that in the year 1731, when the building threatened to fall to ruins, four new columns were erected by the churchwardens, serving both for strength and ornament. It appears from the vestry records that one of the piers was three times rebuilt, and that John Podmore—styled "the ingenious" for his erection of a great crane on the quay—vainly contrived a cast iron machine to screw up the neighbouring pillars to their capitals. John Wood, of Bath, was at length engaged, and the danger of a complete collapse was averted. The total outlay was very great, and crippled the vestry for several years.

Whilst the above reconstruction was proceeding, the dean and chapter evinced their culture and sense of beauty by ordering the destruction of the original Romanesque windows in the Chapter House of the Cathedral, including the graceful ornamentation surrounding them. Four ugly sash windows were inserted in their place.

After having taken breath for ten years, the Corporation, on the 5th January, 1732, resolved to resume operations for the building of an Exchange, and a committee was appointed to negotiate for a site. This body reported in July that it had contracted for the acquirement of the Guilders tavern (rental £46), the Guilders inn (rental £80), and other premises for the sum of £2,500, and also for the possession of the Three Tuns tavern (rental £89), and other buildings for £2,000. The contracts were confirmed by the Council. The owner of the Guilders estate resided in London, and some difficulty was encountered in remitting the purchase money. Eventually ten bills of exchange and two promissory notes were bought up from various mercantile firms, and the balance was forwarded in Bank of England notes. As all the money had to be borrowed, the Chamber again shelved the matter for some years.

A shocking illustration of the barbarous military punishments of the age is recorded in a Bristol paragraph, dated March 18th, 1732, in *Read's Weekly Journal*. The writer states that a soldier, convicted of drinking the Pretender's health, had just received a thousand lashes with a cat of nine tails in Queen Square, and was afterwards drummed out of the regiment. (*Mist's Journal* of June 22nd, 1728, contains a report that an Irish Roman Catholic soldier had been whipped at Bristol two days in succession with a cat of nine tails for persevering in his religion and refusing to go to church, the punishment being so severe that he begged to be shot or hanged.) In another case, about the same date, a sergeant in the Fusiliers, for desertion and fraud, was sentenced to receive 2,000 lashes; but at the intercession of several ladies the frightful punishment was remitted. The prisoner, stripped to the waist and with a halter round his neck, was drummed through the streets, and finally driven out of the city.

The church and tower of St. Stephen being reported in a state of great decay, and the cost of restoration being estimated at £1,000, the Common Council, in May, 1732, voted £100 towards the renovation.

The Chamber, at the above meeting, appointed a committee to consider the charges imposed by the trade companies of the city upon the admission of new members, it being alleged that these demands were in many cases "exorbitant." The committee never reported, and as it does not appear that the Corporation took any further action in the matter, the companies seem to have been allowed to persist in a system which gradually brought about self destruction. In 1719 there were twenty-three of these fraternities, which embraced nearly every mechanical trade in the city, seniority being claimed by the merchant tailors. To all of them the Corporation had delegated powers for regulating their respective trades. Thus, so late as 1730, the Common Council approved of new ordinances for the Carpenters' Company, by which no person save a member of that society was allowed to exercise the trade of a carpenter in the city, either as a master or a journeyman, under a penalty of 10s. a day, while no employer was to take an apprentice without the leave of the company. As population and business developed, however, it was found impossible to coerce young tradesmen into entering societies which demanded large fees on admission and offered nothing in return. Moreover, as local goldsmiths, drapers, grocers, and stationers were never incorporated, the Bristol companies had neither the wealth nor the prestige of the similar associations in London. As a natural consequence, the societies gradually faded out of existence as the old members dropped off. Of only one or two have we any record. The annual meetings of the richest of the companies, the Tailors, were generally attended by some 50 to 70 members about the beginning of the century. But in 1757 the attendance sank to 27; in 1767 to 24; in 1777 to 20; in 1787 to 7; and in 1797 to 6; the members being soon after reduced to 2, who alternately elected each other master until 1815, when a Mr. Amos elected himself, and continued to do so until his death (Minutes of the Company, Jefferies Collection). The Mercers numbered about forty in the first decade of the century, but the last mention of their hall occurs in 1718.

At the Gloucestershire quarter sessions in April, 1732, the justices made an order respecting the wages of labour throughout the county, which affords an insight into working-class life in Clifton, Westbury, and the out-parishes of St. James and St. Philip. The magistrates seem to have considered every labourer entitled to consume a quart of beer daily. The daily wages of every carpenter, wheelwright and mason, as well as a mower in hay harvest, were to be 1s. 2d. "without drink," or 1s. "with drink." [The same rates for artisans had been fixed by the justices of Somerset some years earlier.] An ordinary labourer, without diet or drink, was to be paid 10d., with drink 8d., and with diet 4d. A head maid-servant or cook was to have £2 10s. a year; a second maid-servant £2. On farms, a driving boy under 14 years was allowed £1 yearly, a head labourer £5, and a second labourer £4, with food. The magisterial scale was accompanied by a notice that any master presuming to give higher wages than those fixed would on conviction be imprisoned for ten days and fined £5, while servants accepting higher earnings would be imprisoned for three weeks. Any servant who, after concluding his term of service, should remove from one parish to another, without a certificate from the constable and two householders, was declared incapable of being hired, was to be imprisoned until the certificate was forthcoming, and was "to be whipped and used as a vagabond" if he failed to obtain it. Any person hiring such a servant was to be fined £5. Artificers and labourers were to work, from the middle of March to the middle of September, from five in the morning until between seven and eight o'clock at night, two hours and a half being allowed for breakfast, dinner, and "drinking." In the winter half year, they were to labour from dawn to night.

A minute of a meeting of St. Stephen's vestry, dated July 18th, deals in a characteristic manner with one of the most shocking customs then prevalent throughout England—the practise of burying deceased parishioners in the interior of churches. The vestry had discovered that their fabric had been much injured by the frequent interments within it, "which is wholly owing," says the minute, "to the low price fixed for burying there." It was resolved that the fee for breaking the ground should be increased to three guineas, a charge which may have brought in some additional revenue, but which could have had little effect in improving the sanitary condition of the church. In despite of this order, moreover, the vestry, in 1740, permitted an ordinary grave to be dug within the building on payment of a fee of 13*s.* 4*d.* It was not until 1763 that burial in the church was forbidden unless the grave was lined with bricks.

The wholesale price of wine at this period was exceedingly moderate. In the local Prerogative Court is an inventory of the estate of John Duval, a Bristol merchant, dated 1729, whose stock comprised upwards of ninety pipes of "new Port," appraised as of the value of £26 10*s.* each; and one pipe of "old Port," valued at £30, equal to 4*s.* 9*d.* per gallon. In the Jefferies Collection, amongst some accounts of James Cadell, a prosperous Bristol merchant, is the following:— "Aug. 2, 1732, Received of J. Cadell, Esq., £11 for half a pipe of wine, spared him. B. Webb." The wine remained in the wood nearly six years, when Mr. Webb received £3 16*s.* for "bottles, corkes and botteling." The total cost of the well-matured liquor was therefore equal to about 9*s.* 6*d.* a dozen.

The Corporation, in August, 1732, paid £6 to one John Mason, for "turning six large posts for the brass heads to be put on at the Tolzey, near All Saints Church." These articles were similar to the brazen pillars now standing in front of the Exchange.

One of the kindly habits of the time was the annual gathering of prosperous Bristolians, born in one or other of the neighbouring shires, for the purpose of assisting other natives of the respective counties who had been less fortunate in the battle of life. A Bristol paragraph in a London newspaper of September 2nd records that the yearly feast of the Wiltshire Society had just taken place. The members walked in procession to Christ Church to hear a sermon. "There was a fine appearance, and a shepherd, with his habit, crook, bottle and dog attended them." The proceedings of course concluded with a dinner, which took place in the Merchants' Hall. The subscriptions were generally appropriated to the apprenticing of boys. Herefordshire, Gloucestershire and Somerset men held similar festivities at the same period, whilst the families of poor Welshmen were relieved by the Society of Ancient Britons.

On the 10th January, 1733, the Common Council drew up a representation to the members of Parliament for the city, desiring them to strenuously oppose any project of an Excise "on customable merchandise or home manufactured goods." The instruction, like a similar memorial of the Merchant

Venturers, was drawn up in consequence of a rumour that the Government was maturing such a proposal; and in fact Sir Robert Walpole, two months later, introduced a scheme for placing the tobacco trade under the supervision of the Excise authorities. The chief reason offered for the change was that enormous frauds were perpetrated under the existing system, with the effect of reducing the produce of the tobacco duty from a gross receipt of £750,000 to a net sum of £160,000. The arguments of the Minister, though unanswerable, had no effect in calming the popular clamour, and, after a vehement struggle in the House of Commons, the measure was dropped on the 11th April. As Bristol enjoyed a large share of the tobacco trade, the joy of those concerned in it was naturally exuberant. (The Corporation and the Merchants' Company each spent £81 5s. 6d. in furthering the agitation against the Bill.) An express announcing the failure of the scheme was forwarded from London by Sir Abraham Elton, M.P., and reached the city at eleven o'clock in the evening of the following day. Whereupon, says the only local newspaper, the merchants and traders (at the mayor's invitation) assembled at the Council House to drink the health of Walpole's opponents. Thirty-six gallons of port and sherry and 42 bottles of claret were consumed by the revellers, while 108 gallons of strong beer were distributed to the populace at the High Cross, all at the expense of the Corporation. The London *Daily Courant* stated a few days later, on the authority of a Bristol letter, that the mayor sent orders " to have the bells tuned; all the schoolmasters in town were ordered to keep holiday; the boys were employed in making squibs; and the mayor erected a battery of seven great guns behind his house, to the great annoyance of the small beer in the Square. Fagots and tar barrels were erected into monstrous bonfire piles [one of them blazed before the Excise Office in Broad Street] and some ships showed their dirty colours: few of the fires were without some instruments of execution" (by which, as we learn from Stewart's MS., it was meant that the unpopular Minister was hanged and burnt in effigy). This account, which concluded with some caustic remarks on the mayor's sympathy with the mob, caused great irritation in corporate circles, and after being stigmatised by the grand jury at the next sessions as a scandalous libel, the newspaper was ordered to be publicly burnt. In the following June, when Sir Abraham Elton returned to Bristol, his warm opposition to the Excise Bill was rewarded by a popular demonstration. He was met, on his approach, and ushered into the city by 500 horsemen, many of whom wore knots of gilded tobacco in their hats, and the procession was wound up with coaches and sedan chairs; Temple Street was dressed with boughs, and the towers of the churches were adorned with scarlet cloth (Stewart's MS.). (After Walpole's fall, the unpopular features of his Excise scheme were enacted by his opponents.)

Trinity Street, which for many years commonly bore the odd name of the Masonry, was in course of erection at this time. The minutes of the dean and chapter, dated the 17th January, 1733, record the renewal to Mr. Jarrit Smith of his lease of "the Masonry and Covent Garden," on payment of a fine of £73 14s. The lease was again renewed in 1746, when the chapter accepted a fine of £750. A larger extent of ground may have been included in this document, for in September, 1743, an exchange of lands took place between the bishop and the capitular body, the former surrendering the Bishop's Orchard, for which he accepted certain "gardens in Dean's Marsh." In 1761, when Jarrit Smith's lease again crops up in the chapter minutes, the place is styled "the late Masonry, now Trinity Street." The fine for renewal, including "the Bishop's Orchard, lately improved by buildings," was £1,075, as it was again in 1774.

A discreditable exposure was made at the meeting of the poor-law guardians on the 8th February, 1733. It was discovered that Richard Baggs, of Temple Street, a member of the board (who in the previous year had been convicted of an abominable offence, for which he was sentenced to stand in the pillory for an hour, to pay a fine of £200, and to be imprisoned for six months), had obtained sums of charity money from several of the churchwardens, undertaking to distribute the amount amongst "sundry poor people," but that he had defrauded the intended recipients, and put the money into his own pocket. His prosecution was ordered, but at the next meeting, in consequence, no doubt, of the supplications of the knave, still in prison, it was ordered "that Mr. Matthew Purnell do wait on Mr. Richard Baggs and receive of him the sum of £200, for which he hath given bond this day, for his having defrauded the poor, and that the same be paid to Mr. Nehemiah Champion, treasurer to this corporation, and that he [meaning Baggs] shall have a general release from this corporation, and that he shall make a resignation of his guardianship." The guardians thought the scandal deserving of a permanent record, and a board was set up in the court-room narrating the offence and the punishment as a memorial and a warning. The inscription still remains.

At a meeting of the Council on the 21st July, 1733, a "representation" of several of the inhabitants of High Street and the neighbourhood was read, suggesting the removal of the High Cross. A portion of this document is worthy of record :—" It hath been insinuated by some that this Cross, on account of its antiquity ought to be lookt upon as something sacred. But when we consider that we are Protestants, and that Popery ought effectually to be guarded against in this nation, we make this our request to you to consider, If the opening of a passage to four of the principal streets in this city ought not to outweigh anything that can be said for the keeping up a ruinous and superstitious Relick, which is at present a public nuisance." After a discussion, the question as to the removal of the Cross was put to the Chamber. "It was voted in the affirmative by a great majority, and Mr. Chamberlain is ordered to cause the same to be forthwith pulled down, and to dispose of the images and materials as shall be thought fit." According to tradition, the chief agitator for the destruction of the Cross was John Vaughan, a wealthy goldsmith and banker, whose shop and dwelling were in the curious wooden house still standing at the corner of Wine and High Streets, and who, it is said, offered to swear that his life and property were endangered in every high wind by the shaking of the weather-worn "relick" before his door. But Mr. Vaughan's name was not appended to the memorial. The Cross was removed in the following month, the stones being deposited in the Guildhall. Its dishonoured condition, however, gave pain to many citizens, and Alderman Price, with a few other gentlemen, provided funds for its re-erection in College Green. It is characteristic of the loose business habits of public bodies in that age that there is no record, either of the Council's permission to remove the materials, or of the dean and chapter's grant of the new site. The Cross was, however, reconstructed in the spring of 1736, and somewhat garishly ornamented with gold and colours.

A resolution passed by the Common Council in August, 1733, proves that the old dislike of "foreigners" was still an active force. On the motion of Alderman Becher, it was determined "that no person residing without the liberties of the city shall henceforth, upon any consideration whatever, be admitted into the freedom of this city." Honorary freedoms were of course excepted from the regulation, which was carried by 16 votes to 13. The order, which soon became obsolete, may possibly have been intended to discourage the residence of merchants in Clifton and other suburban districts.

The Council, on the 12th December, voted a pension of £10 yearly to Elizabeth Joy, grand-daughter of Edward Morgan (mayor, 1667), and niece to Sir Robert Yeamans, Bart. (mayor, 1669), she being "reduced to very great straights for the necessaries of life."

The accounts of the parochial vestries about this time contain references to an instrument called an umbrella, which, as the St. Nicholas' books explain, was used for the purpose of protecting clergymen in wet weather whilst reading the burial service in churchyards. The earliest discovered mention of the article occurs in the St. Philip's accounts for 1723, when 5s. was paid for "mending the umbrella." In 1733 the same parish paid for "5 yards oil'd cloth for ye umbrella, 12s. 6d.," from which it would seem that the apparatus was something in the nature of a portable canopy. Christ Church vestry, in 1740, ordered the purchase of "another umbrelloe for the use of this church," in 1744 St. Nicholas' vestry laid out £2 16s. for the same purpose; an umbrella "for the use of the rector" was ordered for St. Stephen's in 1761, and in 1765 a new umbrella cost the St. Philip's authorities £3 3s. As evidence that these instruments were not adapted for locomotion, the corporate accounts for 1750 show a payment of £5 17s. "for saile cloth used in the umbrelloes for the market," and four similar items, amounting to over £30, occur between 1757 and 1762. The portable umbrella of the present day was, in fact, then unknown in England.

The Prince of Orange, who was about to marry the Princess Royal of England, being on a visit to Bath, the Corporation resolved, in January, 1734, "in regard of his illustrious descent and firm attachment to the Protestant religion," to invite him to Bristol. His Highness, in response to the request, came to the city on the 21st February, and was entertained to dinner at the Merchants' Hall, conducted to the Hot Well and the Quays, and treated to a sumptuous supper and ball. Having slept at the house of Alderman Day, the Prince next morning received the city clergy, and shortly afterwards departed. The cost of the entertainment was £297 1s. 3d., exclusive of £52 10s. spent upon the visitor's servants. From one item in the accounts,

26s. " paid for the use of Cheny," it would appear that pewter platters were for the first time deemed unworthy of the guest's table.

The piratical vessels sent out by the barbarous States of Morocco and Algiers were at this period the terror of the seas. The *London Journal* of February 16th, 1734, published a letter from Philip Graves, master of the Bristol ship Ferdinand (of only eighty tons and seven men) to Thomas Pennington, a local merchant, announcing that his vessel with three other English ships bound for the Peninsula, had been captured by the Admiral of Sallee, and himself and the other men thrown into prison. Captain Graves craves Christian assistance for the redemption of the party, and unconsciously reveals the strange conditions then permitted to exist. Relief in money, he says, could be sent to a certain mercantile house at Gibraltar, one of the partners of which, " a worthy countryman of ours," carried on business at Sallee, and would faithfully apply the sums forwarded. The affair appears to have stirred up the English Government, not to suppress the pirates, but to buy off their victims. In the following November the same journal announced that 135 persons, redeemed from slavery in Morocco, had been brought to George II., who presented them with £100 for their relief.

A plot of ground at the west end of Milk Street was sold by the Corporation in March, 1734, for the erection of an almshouse for the maintenance of five old bachelors and five old maids, in conformity with the will of " Mrs." Sarah Ridley, an aged spinster, who died in 1726. The site cost £150. The building was finished in 1739.

A dissolution of Parliament occurred in the spring of 1734, and the election of new members for Bristol commenced on the 14th May. Sir Abraham Elton, who was generally popular, solicited re-election, as did his colleague, Mr. Scrope. The energetic support which the latter had rendered to Walpole, in the Excise struggle, had raised him many enemies, and the Tory party brought forward, in opposition to him, Mr. Thomas Coster, who was largely interested in the local copper trade and a hearty opponent of the Excise scheme. At the close of the poll on the 24th May, the figures stood: for Sir A. Elton, 2420; for Mr. Coster, 2071; for Mr. Scrope, 1866. The issue excited great irritation amongst the Whigs. Upon the opening of Parliament, a petition was presented from the mayor and Corporation asserting that the return of Mr. Coster was due to invalid votes, and paying for relief. The Commons resolved on taking evidence at the bar, and a large part of one sitting was occupied in hearing counsel and witnesses. Before the case came on again the petition was withdrawn. In the British Museum is a printed poll book of the election, with manuscript notes describing the disqualifications of many of the voters, according to which about one-sixth of the votes polled were bad. The writer appends to the names of some of the dubious electors such observations as "stood in the pillory," "burnt in the hand for felony," and "a common beggar," but in most of the cases the voters are described as paupers, receiving relief. (To the name, in Redcliff parish, of John Chatterton, weaver, grandfather of the poet, is added, "Sexton; received a loaf every 14 days.") The result given by the writer is that 362 bad votes were recorded for Coster, and 91 for Scrope, leaving the latter a majority of 66 good votes on the entire poll. But the hasty withdrawal of the petition shows that this assertion could not be sustained. The Corporation paid the whole of the expenses incurred in prosecuting the case, amounting to £563. On comparing the poll book with a list of members of the Merchants' Society, printed in 1732, it appears that 55 members voted for Scrope and 18 for his opponent. Out of about 3,800 Bristolians who took part in the election only four had two Christian names. Only 25 voters, apparently artisans, lived in Clifton. At the gaol delivery in the autumn the friends of the recorder manifested their regret at his defeat by offering him a magnificent reception. The local newspaper says, "The gentlemen on horseback, coaches, &c., were very numerous, and the weavers and combers, dressed in their customary habits, made the cavalcade extend a great length." What seems still more strange, the grand jury presented the recorder with an address regretting the late "incident," and hoping that the "reproach lying upon the city" would be removed by the parliamentary inquiry.

At a meeting of the Council in August, 1734, a petition was produced from the Innholders' Company, representing their "inability to preserve their ancient rights and customs from want of good laws, orders and customs." A committee was appointed with power to draw up ordinances, but it never reported, and the Company gradually died away.

"In 1734," writes David Hume, in his autobiography, "I went to Bristol with some recommendations to eminent merchants, but in a few months found that scene totally unsuitable to me." The future historian was then twenty-one years of age. His employer was Mr. Michael Miller, a merchant, residing at 15, Queen Square, who had made a fortune by his enterprise, but whose education, in the opinion of his new clerk, left much to be desired. It is said, and the story is practically confirmed in a letter of Dean Tucker to Lord Hailes, that Mr. Miller, exasperated at the criticisms passed on the style of his business letters, told Hume that he had made £20,000 with his English, and would not have it improved. The offended Scot, who hated all Englishmen, many years later took an odd opportunity of displaying his scornful opinion of Bristolians. Describing in his history the progress of Naylor, the Quaker fanatic, Hume says:—" He entered Bristol riding on a horse; I suppose from the difficulty in that place of finding an ass." There is a tradition, nevertheless, that he kept up friendly relations with Mr. John Peach, of Maryleport Street, to whom he sent the manuscript of the first volumes of his history, desiring him to remove any dialectical barbarisms. The story, if true, does not redound to Mr. Peach's credit, for the first edition abounded with Scotticisms.

The first Clifton boarding school appears to have been established in this year. The *Gloucester Journal* for April 30th, 1734, contains the following advertisement:—" This is to give notice that on the 25th March was opened (to be continued), at a pleasant part of Clifton, a boarding school for the education of young ladies : where in the best manner they will be taught Dancing, by Mr. Lewis, dancing master, and by his wife Needlework and genteel Behaviour; and by the best masters will also be taught (at the parents' pleasure) the French language, Musick, Writing, and Arithmetic, or any of them. The known healthful situation of Clifton has occasioned this boarding school to be fixed there, but Mr. Lewis will continue to teach dancing at the Coopers' Hall in Bristol."

A Bristol paragraph in the *Gloucester Journal* of November 26th announces that " Mr. Onesiphorus Tyndall, jun., an eminent drysalter of this city, is appointed by his Majesty Verderer and Chief Ranger of the forest of Kingswood, with a grant or feoffment for letting the coal mines, &c., as soon as the lease is expired held by Thomas Chester, Esq., Thomas Player, Esq., and several other gentlemen ever since the reign of King Charles II. The said coal mines chiefly supply this great city and the neighbouring country with their production, and bring in a great revenue." On a reference to the State Papers it appears that the lease was granted for thirty-one years, on condition of the payment of 40s. yearly, and on the lessee trying the title of the Crown to the estate, any composition with persons pretending to possess portions of the premises being forbidden. Tyndall was also demised, for the same term, all the coal pits and mineral mines within the forest, on rendering one-tenth of the yearly profits. This appears to have been the last of the many fruitless attempts made by the Crown to recover those rights over the ancient forest which had been gradually undermined by the acquisitive artifices of the neighbouring landowners, and were totally lost during the troubles of the Civil War, when the royal deer were eaten up and the woods utterly destroyed. The forest originally comprised, under the name of Fillwood, a large tract of land in Brislington and Bedminster, but through the negligence of the Crown officials the royal rights over that district had been usurped and lost before the death of Elizabeth. Verderers were appointed for Kingswood after the Restoration, but some made no effort to perform their duty, and others reaped nothing from their action but interminable and ruinous law suits. Mr. Tyndall's appointment seems to have been wholly resultless either to himself or the Government.

The low price of animal food during the year 1734 seems almost incredible to modern readers. Cary, in his Essay on Trade, stated that the average cost of beef in Bristol in his time was $2\frac{1}{2}d.$ per lb. But the *Weekly Journal* of November 16th, 1734, recorded that at the cattle market of that week, "the best beef sold at 10d. per stone [of 8lb.] alive, and the best mutton at 9d."

In the closing years of the previous century, the corporation of Newcastle, then the wealthiest of provincial municipalities, erected an imposing Mansion House for civic receptions and entertainments. A similar building was erected at York in 1728, and about seven years later the Common Council of London resolved to follow the example. An impulse being thus given to the local weakness for display, Mr. William Jefferis, at a meeting of the Chamber in June, 1735, "represented that it would tend to the Honour and Grandness of this city if some convenient Mansion House was purchased by this Corporation for the mayor of the city for the time being to reside in during their respective mayoralties; and signified that the late dwelling house of Peter Day, Esq., one of the aldermen of this city [who died about six months previously], together with its furniture was to be disposed of, and was very fit for the purpose in his judgment . . . and thereupon the House being called over the question was carried in the affirmative by a great majority." The project was soon afterwards abandoned, and fifty years elapsed before Mr. Jefferis's proposal was carried out. The above minute, however, has led several local writers into error as to the history of the subsequent Mansion House.

At a meeting of the Council in August, 1735, a letter was read from Mr. Scrope resigning the recordership on the ground of age and infirmity. The learned gentleman, whose laborious services at the Treasury had led to a perfunctory performance of his duties in his native city, had refused to receive any salary from the time of his appointment. He had already been complimented with a present of plate, which cost £119, and it was resolved to forward him another gift of the same kind, value £150, together with a butt of sherry. The precious articles selected were a basin and ewer, which the recipient, in a graceful letter of thanks, described as "the most curious that ever was seen." Having been requested to recommend a fitting person for the vacant office, Mr. Scrope, observing that more frequent gaol deliveries were desirable, and that it would be convenient to have a recorder living in the neighbourhood, suggested Mr. Michael Foster, then clerk of the peace for Wiltshire. Mr. Foster, who was unanimously elected, relinquished his previous office, took up his residence at Ashley, and, until his elevation to the judicial bench, was an active and useful member of the Chamber by right of the aldermanic office then attached to the recordership. Mr. Scrope, who continued to hold the secretaryship of the Treasury, died in 1753, aged upwards of ninety years.

Bristol was visited in September by a traveller from the East, apparently in pecuniary difficulties. The Council gave directions to the chamberlain to pay five guineas "to Scheck Schidit, one of the nobility of the city of Beritus, to help support him in his travels." Beritus was probably the modern Beyrouth, the seaport of Damascus.

A horrible incident, only recorded because of the light that it throws on the barbarity of the age, occurred in September. A ship captain, named James Newton, was convicted of the murder of his wife, by trampling upon her in a fit of passion, and was sentenced to be hanged. Two days after the trial, however, he succeeded in committing suicide in Newgate, by means of poison, whereupon the coroner's jury returned a verdict of self murder, and the body, according to custom, was buried at four cross roads, with a stake through the middle. Newton had long borne an evil character. He had been previously tried for piracy, and it was believed that his brutality had, at various times, caused the death of four of his sailors. The populace were so exasperated at his escape from the halter that they dug up his body, which was literally torn to fragments, and scattered about the highway. There is little doubt that, if this revolting scene had not occurred, the wretch's remains would have been appropriated by others. *Farley's Bristol Newspaper* for January 27th, 1728, says:—" The shoo-maker that hang'd himself last week without Lawford's Gate, was bury'd in the Cross Road called Dungen's Cross, but we hear some young Surgeons have since caused it to be taken up again to anatomise."

Jacobitism had still many devotees in the city, who, by a liberal distribution of beer, could easily excite the passions of the lower classes. A local correspondent of a London journal, writing on October 30th, the King's birthday, says:—" Party violence is grown to such a height here that as the magistrates and other gentlemen were met at the Council House to celebrate the evening, and had made a fine illumination representing his Majesty's name in cypher, and under it an Orange, from which issued a spear wounding a dragon [hieroglyphics understood with no great difficulty], the mob arose, and pelted out the lights with dirt and stones." To about the same period may be attributed a printed pasquinade on the statue of William III.—a monument which was naturally the object of Jacobite spleen. The writer represents the magnates of the city " gathered together unto the dedication of the image which Nebuchadnezzar the king had set up."

The extreme inconvenience caused by holding the public markets twice a week in High Street and Broad Street at last induced the Corporation to deal with them. In December, 1735, a committee was appointed to treat for the purchase of property, and to build a fitting market house. This step ultimately led to the inclusion of markets in the Exchange scheme. In the meantime a curious regulation was enforced in the existing markets. The civic Fine-book records that in December, 1744, nine butchers were mulcted 10s. each " for staying in Broad Street market after six o'clock in the evening," and there were many subsequent convictions for this offence.

In Evans's Chronological History is an entry under 1736, alleging that a survey of the city and suburbs made in that year showed the number of the houses to be 1,300, with 80,000 inhabitants. The writer does not seem to have observed that his figures represented an average population of sixty-one in each house. A more trustworthy record of this census is amongst the Cole MSS. in the British Museum, in the handwriting of Browne Willis, the eminent antiquary, who resided here for some time, and had many influential local friends. From Mr. Willis's notes it would appear that an enumeration had also taken place in 1712; and as in January, 1713, the Corporation of the Poor drew up a petition to Parliament for power to levy a larger rate, owing to "the city being considerably enlarged, and its inhabitants increased," it is probable that the survey was made under its authority. As Willis's paper is very brief, it may be given entire:—

```
                                         1712      1735
"Houses in Bristol      ...   ...   ...  4811      5701
"Encrease in 23 years, 1390. Besides what are in the suburbs.
"N.B.—Lawford's Gate not reckoned, nor what are out of the
     city liberties, wherein may be computed upwards of a 1000.
"In 1752 1 was at Bristol [which had] increased above 2000
     since 1735. Burials in St. James's parish, 400 a year."
```

Estimating the average number of inhabitants at a fraction over five per house, the population of 1712 must have been about 23,000, and that of 1735 about 30,000, or, with the suburbs, 35,000.

A belief became prevalent amongst the local merchants about this time that the so-called mayor's due of 40s. on each vessel of sixty tons burden entering the port was an illegal exaction, and several firms consequently refused to pay the charge. In order to insure the receipt of the due, the Corporation had frequently issued orders forbidding vessels above the taxable tonnage from coming to the quays without obtaining a warrant from the mayor—the license being granted only on receipt of the impost. This arrangement being set at defiance by the recalcitrant firms, the Chamber resolved, in January, 1736, to prosecute the pilots who brought up ships without a warrant; but subsequently a bolder course was adopted, and actions at law were instituted by the mayor against Messrs. W. Hart and Sons, and others, who had repudiated the civic claim. On the 14th July, 1737, one of the actions, taken as a test case, was tried at the King's Bench sittings in the Guildhall, London, before a special jury, and the *Weekly Journal* of the 16th has, for those days, an unusually full report of the proceedings. " The Plaintiff," it says, "pleaded custom immemorial by very antient men and much antienter writings ; that the property was vested in the mayor for the time being by a bye-law of the Corporation, and proved that the mayor, burgesses and commonalty had power to make such a law vested in them by Act of Parliament. He further assigned the reason for it—the great expence of keeping in repair the quay, the use of which saved the trader twice the sum demanded in lighterage only. . . . For the defendant it was urged that the demand was an imposition and of no older date than 1711 . . . that he was not the only person that denied the payment, and produced evidence thereof, who upon their examination declared their dislike and denial of it, but that nevertheless they had paid it. . . . After a trial of several hours, in the course whereof . . . half the archives relating to the city of Bristol were read by order of counsel on one side or the other, the jury gave a verdict for 40s. damages [the amount claimed] for the plaintiff, and confirmed the custom, which brings in upwards of £1000 per annum." The last observation is of interest, as it throws some light on the business of the port. Until many years after this date, no information as to the receipts from the due is to be found in the civic accounts, the money being paid directly to the mayor. In the course of this dispute, the Chamber ordered the publication of several of the charters of the city, translated from the Latin originals. The Rev. Charles Goodwyn is supposed to have been employed as translator. The book is now extremely scarce.

The Merchants' Society having solicited the Corporation to concur with them in opposing Bills about to be laid before Parliament for permitting the exportation of sugar from the West Indies to various continental ports without being first landed in England, and for allowing the Irish people to export their wool to foreign countries, the Chamber unanimously agreed in March, 1736, to petition against these "dangerous" proposals. The Government, however, persisted with the Bill allowing British ships to carry sugar from the colonies to the continent direct, and the scheme became law in 1739, amidst the wails of local merchants. The scheme for permitting the export of Irish wool was dropped, to soothe the English clothing trade, to which the interests of Ireland were deliberately sacrificed.

A change in the habits of the age is denoted by the resolution of the Council, at the meeting just mentioned, to alter the time of assembling for civic business from nine o'clock in the morning until two hours later. A fine of twelvepence was imposed on members who neglected to appear in their robes. A few weeks later, leave of absence for three weeks was granted to the mayor, in order that he might take a tour " on horseback " for the benefit of his health. Up to this time the mayors had been required to remain uninterruptedly at their post during their year of office, a fine of £100 being imposed on any one absent for more than three successive days. But the above concession became a precedent for a summer holiday, which was at first limited to a month, but during the last half of the century was extended to six weeks. By another regulation, made in June, 1736, the mayor and his successors were granted the privilege of nominating such keepers of game on the corporate manors —then numerous and extensive—as they might deem necessary. The right of shooting was of course reserved to the members of the Corporation.

Reference will be found in a previous note to the restraints imposed upon English cotton manufactures by an Act of 1719, and to the depressing effects of that law on a rising local industry. By 1736 the production of cotton fabrics had much increased in England, and the restrictions of the statute became irksome. The Merchants' Society, amongst other bodies, petitioned Parliament for relief, alleging that the cotton mills employed vast numbers of people, that large quantities of the raw material were imported into Bristol to the profit of the West India trade, and that the goods made therefrom were " very essential in purchasing negroes on the coast of Africa." In spite of the opposition of the clothiers, the restrictions of the Act were abolished as regarded fabrics of which the weft was cotton and the warp linen. This may have given a temporary stimulus to the industry in Bristol. In October, 1737, the poor law guardians empowered a committee " to treat with Mr. Alker concerning the employing of the poor of this house for the cotton manufactory," but no result is recorded.

The marriage of Frederick, Prince of Wales, in April, 1736, was celebrated in Bristol with the customary tokens of rejoicing. A grand corporate entertainment was given in Merchants' Hall at a cost of £110, while bell ringing, salutes, bonfires, and 500 gallons of beer, distributed at Merchants' Hall and Brandon Hill, entailed a further charge of £28. The Jacobites, to console themselves, made an unusually ostentatious display of white roses on the following 10th of June.

The magistrates still attempted to suppress the trickery of knavish tradesmen. On the 17th June a butcher was convicted of " exposing for sale in Broad Street an old ewe, dressed up in the same manner as a lamb," for which he was fined 40s. The hand of the law, however, fell most heavily on " foreigners." In the same month, a poor non-freeman, convicted of trading as a hawker, and exposing goods for sale, was condemned to pay £12 for his " offence."

It has been already stated that the protection of the streets was confided at night to twelve constables, one being appointed for each ward. On the 5th July, 1736, the magistrates ordered that in addition to this force, a body of fifty-one " able men " should be enrolled as watchmen, and distributed amongst the wards for the better security of the city. As the justices had no power to levy a rate, and the Corporation offered no pecuniary assistance, this order soon became a dead letter.

At a Council meeting on the 25th August, it having been reported that the recorder, Mr. Serjeant Foster, had delivered the gaol three times since his appointment in the previous year, and had also resigned his post of clerk of the peace for Wiltshire " in honour of this city," it was unanimously resolved to present him with 200 guineas. Subsequently, a present of 50 guineas was usually made after each gaol delivery.

During the gaol delivery in August a prisoner named John Vernham, charged with a burglary on St. Michael's Hill, obstinately refused to plead to his indictment. The recorder warned him of the terrible consequences of his persistence in "standing mute," but though told that he would be pressed to death according to the ancient custom of the realm, he continued stubbornly silent. Orders were therefore given for carrying out the *peine forte et dure* in Newgate. As a man had been pressed to death at Lewes assizes in the previous summer, the case excited intense interest. At the last moment, however, the horrible nature of the punishment overcame Vernham's resolution, and he was forthwith tried, convicted, and sentenced to death. Another man, named Harding, convicted of shoplifting, was also left for execution ; and both convicts were taken to the gallows field at St. Michael's Hill on the 3rd September. The careless manner in which executions were then conducted, frequently noticed in contemporary newspapers, was strikingly manifested on this occasion. After the two men had hung for the usual time, the bodies were taken down, but whilst being placed in coffins both showed signs of life. Surgical assistance having been rendered, Vernham recovered consciousness, and was able to speak to several of the bystanders, but died during the following night. Harding, who also revived after being bled, was removed to Bridewell, where great numbers of persons were allowed to visit him. A local newspaper afterwards announced that as he had been " always defective in his intellects," he was not to be hanged again, but " to be taken care of in a Charity House "—meaning, apparently, an almshouse! His strange story can be traced no further.

To what extent the "gin madness" of London affected Bristol contemporary records are silent. In consequence of the delirium of the capital, where, in some streets, one house in every six was converted into a ginshop, a Bill was brought into Parliament imposing a license of £50 on each retailer, and a duty of 20s. per gallon on all spirits (the duty previously had been 5¾d. per gallon); and although the Bristol Merchants' Society represented that the tax on rum would be "destructive to them and to many thousands in the colonies," the measure became law. On the 29th September, when it came into operation, the lower classes in Bristol, says a local paper, made merry on the death of Madam Gin, and "got soundly drunk at her funeral, for which the mob made a solemn procession." The Act, however, had no practical effect. Amongst many liquors concocted to evade the law, "Mr. Thomas Andrews, distiller, in Back Street, Bristol," produced a compound which was called " A New Invention found out in Time," and alleged to be a substitute for all spirituous liquors. " The price too is upon a par with geneva, &c. Sold at 4s. a gallon or three halfpence the quartern or nogin " (*The Weekly Journal*, December 18th, 1736).

In October, 1736, the vestry of St. Mary Redcliff addressed a petition to the bishop, stating that they had recently erected a "fair organ" in the church, for which they had neglected to obtain the necessary faculty. The petition further set forth that a charity school for forty boys had been maintained for some time at Redcliff Back by voluntary subscriptions in St. Mary's and St. Thomas's parishes, but that the owner of the schoolroom had demanded an additional rent of £6 yearly, which could not be paid without injury to the charity. The petitioners went on to allege that the east end of the Lady's Chapel in St. Mary's was a convenient place in which to make a schoolroom, and as no other suitable place could be found, they prayed for a faculty to remove the school there. The bishop's reply has not been preserved. No difficulty was probably raised respecting the organ, but the chancellor issued an order requiring dissentients to the school scheme to show cause against it. The design must have been abandoned, for in 1739 a school-house for the education of forty boys of the two parishes was erected in Pyle Street, to which Thomas Malpas, who had made a fortune as a pinmaker, added a dwelling for the schoolmaster in 1749. (Chatterton's father became subsequently master of the school, and the poet was probably born in this house.) About the period when the school changed its quarters, the trustees of Edward Colston, under powers conferred upon them by his will, endowed it with a sum of £20 a year, originally bequeathed for an annual series of lectures.

The court of mayor and aldermen, in November, 1736, fixed the number of alehouses in the city at 331, exclusive of inns, wine-shops, and coffee houses. It has been shown that the number of houses in 1735 was 5701, so that there was one alehouse for every sixteen private dwellings. St. James's parish had sixty of those places, St. Stephen's and St. Nicholas' ninety between them, and St. Michael's, forty-five.

At this date the roadway from St. Augustine's Back to College Green was a dark and narrow alley, very difficult of ascent owing to the steepness of the hill. In December, 1736, the Council directed a committee to improve the thoroughfare, the traffic having greatly increased since the opening of the Drawbridge. The committee did not venture to widen the lane, but the gradient was improved by an outlay of £359.

In the closing months of 1736 Mr. John Elbridge, deputy comptroller of the Customs, with other philanthropic gentlemen, started a movement for the establishment of an Infirmary in Bristol. The proposal being favourably received, a meeting of citizens was held on the 30th December, when, says a local reporter, "persons of all persuasions appeared and subscribed. . . . Among several other good laws, it was resolved that no person be admitted who has not been resident in the city or the out-parishes of St. James and St. Philip for the space of six months, except mariners or in the case of casualties in the city or out-parishes." The promoters soon afterwards obtained, on a lease of 1,000 years, a plot of ground in Jobbin's Leaze, adjoining Magdalen Lane, and it was resolved to at once erect the central portion of the design adopted, leaving two wings to be added at a future time. The building arose under the unwearied superintendence of Mr. Elbridge, who subsequently equipped it with furniture, linen, and surgical appliances, at a personal cost of £1,500. The Infirmary was opened for in-patients on the 13th December, 1737. In the following year, Mr. Elbridge added an additional ward, and just before his death, a few months later, he bequeathed £5,000 to an institution of which he may be fairly termed the founder. The example of Bristol occasioned similar movements at Bath, Edinburgh, York, and Exeter.

Owing to the want of a lighthouse at the Holmes, disasters to Bristol ships were of frequent occurrence in foggy weather. During the later months of 1736 the wreck of a vessel having sixty soldiers on board, all of whom were drowned, caused a great sensation, and the Society of Merchants, supported by the mercantile body, memorialised the Trinity House authorities in London for the erection of a lighthouse on the Flat Holme. The building was finished in November, 1737. The lamps of the time being useless for such a purpose, the beacon consisted of a large brazier, fed with wood or coal. Strange to say, this primitive arrangement continued without improvement until 1820, although many fatal disasters had occurred in rough weather owing to the inefficiency of the light and the carelessness of the warders, who sometimes fell asleep and allowed it to disappear. An agitation on the subject having arisen in Bristol, it was discovered that the corporation of the Trinity House had at the outset permitted the owner of the island to erect and maintain the beacon, guaranteeing him, by lease, a passing toll on the vessels supposed to be benefitted by it. The representative of the lessee was alleged to be enjoying a clear income of nearly £4,000 a year from the lighthouse, and to have refused to incur an additional outlay of £100 annually for its improvement. Owing to the indignation aroused by the affair, the outlying interest in the lease was purchased by the Trinity House for £14,000 in December, 1823.

The introduction of Methodism into Bristol by the Rev. George Whitefield took place in January, 1737. Whitefield may be almost claimed as a Bristolian, his father, Thomas, having been a wine merchant in the city before his removal to the Bell inn at Gloucester, whilst his mother, originally

Elizabeth Edwards, was of Bristol birth, and related to the reputable civic families of the Blackwells and the Dinmours. Their son was ordained at Gloucester in June, 1736, and had just completed his twenty-second year when he paid this memorable visit to his Bristol friends. Being already famous as a preacher, the pulpits of several churches were placed at his disposal, and he stated in a letter that the attendance on week-days forthwith became as great as it was previously on Sundays, and that Dissenters of all sects flocked to hear him. Amongst other marks of respect, he was requested to preach at the Mayor's Chapel. Occasionally he preached four times a day, yet his admirers continued so numerous that the churches were sometimes filled to overflowing. Whitefield's primary object in visiting the city was to take leave of his relatives previous to sailing to the new colony of Georgia, to which he was called by his friends, John and Charles Wesley, then about to return to England. The vessel in which he was to sail being detained for many months, he was again in Bristol in May and June, when the multitude of his hearers largely increased, all ranks, sects, and classes falling under the spell of his eloquence. Some people, he wrote, unable to gain admission into the churches, " climbed up to the leads " in the hope of hearing him. After his farewell sermon " multitudes followed me home weeping." At the close of 1738, when he returned from Georgia to receive priest's orders and to raise funds for his new orphanage near Savannah, he found that the Wesleys' evangelising efforts in London and Oxford had given great offence to the clergy, and he was himself refused admission to many pulpits. In Bristol, where he stayed with friends in Baldwin Street, he was allowed to preach a few times, but met with a rebuff at St. Mary Redcliff, and was threatened with similar treatment at other churches. On appealing to the Dean of Bristol against the proscription, Dr. Creswicke (whose love of cockfighting has been already mentioned) replied:—" We would rather not say yea or nay to you; but we mean nay, and greatly wish you would understand us so." Whitefield thereupon took a step which he had often meditated. The moral and spiritual destitution of the Kingswood colliery district at that period seems almost incredible to a later generation. Many hundreds of families were scattered over what had anciently been a royal forest, grovelling in wretched hovels, utterly uncared for by the half dozen " lords " who had usurped possession of the soil, and dreaded far and near from their barbarous ignorance and brutality.

A large tract of the "chase" was in the parish of St. Philip, but it contained no place of worship, and of course no school, while the area in the parish of Bitton was, if possible, still more uncivilized On this race of domestic heathens Whitefield resolved to exert the powers which he was forbidden to employ in the city; and one Saturday in February, 1739, the day after his interview with Dean Creswicke, he repaired to a place called Hanham Mount, and addressed about a hundred men who gathered round from curiosity. On the following day he preached to overflowing congregations in St. Werburgh's and St. Mary Redcliff, and on Monday there was an immense attendance at his lecture in St. Philip's. This was too much for the patience of the authorities, who summoned him before them. On Tuesday he attended the chancellor of the diocese, a worldly cleric named Reynell, afterwards an Irish bishop, who asked him why he presumed to preach without permission, in defiance of the canons. Whitefield replied that licenses had become obsolete, and observing that there was another canon, forbidding clergymen to haunt taverns and to play at cards, he inquired why greater offences than his were practised without rebuke. The chancellor, exasperated at the reply, declared that if Whitefield repeated his illegal conduct, he should be first suspended and then excommunicated. A license was then formally refused—probably against the wishes of the estimable Bishop Butler, who seems to have expressed sympathy with Whitefield, and afterwards made a donation to the funds of his orphanage. Next day, undismayed, the obnoxious "Methodist" went again to Kingswood, where he had 2,000 eager listeners, and the audience was more than doubled two days later, when he preached at the same place. "The first discovery of their being affected," he wrote afterwards, "was by seeing the white gutters made by their tears, which plentifully fell down their black cheeks as they came out of the coal-pits." At subsequent services the number assembled was computed at 20,000, Bristolians of all ranks being attracted in crowds. The desire of the citizens to listen to the fervent missionary soon afterwards brought about an invitation that he should preach in "a large bowling green" within the walls. The green was situated in the Pithay, and 5,000 persons were present at an early morning service in this novel place of worship. Receiving an appeal from Wales, Whitefield records that, whilst on his way to respond to it, he was temporarily delayed at the New Passage, where he encountered a clergyman who refused to enter the passage boat "because I was in it. . . . He charged me with being a Dissenter. I saw him soon after shaking his elbows over a gaming table." On returning to Bristol, he found that the mayor (William Jefferis), following up the action of the clergy, had forbidden him to preach to the neglected prisoners in Newgate. He consequently held services in the yard of one of the glass-houses, which was filled by the neighbouring poor. Georgia, however, could not be neglected, and Whitefield, before leaving for America, appealed to the Wesleys to continue the work he had begun in Bristol. The brothers were strongly indisposed to accede, but John, after frequently resorting to his practice of biblomancy, believed that the passages he hit upon conveyed approval of the undertaking, and on the 31st of March, 1739, the founder of Wesleyanism reached Bristol, and was introduced to Whitefield's friends. Wesley, who had hitherto stickled for "decency and order," recorded that he could scarce reconcile himself to the "strange way of preaching in the fields"—an example of which was given him on the following day, Sunday, when Whitefield held three open-air services, and preached a farewell sermon in a private room, the way to which was so thronged that to gain admittance he had to mount a ladder, and climb over the roof of an adjoining house. The orator departed next morning, passing through excited crowds, and laying the foundation stone of a school on his way through Kingswood. [A more convenient site having been afterwards obtained, the foundation stone of the school actually built was laid by John Wesley in the following June. It was opened about a twelvemonth later.] Wesley's first service had been held on the previous evening, "to a little society in Nicholas Street." Next day, whilst Whitefield was bidding adieu to the Kingswood colliers, "I submitted," says Wesley, "to be more vile . . . speaking from a little eminence in a ground adjoining to the city to about 3,000 people." Two days later he preached again at Baptist Mills, to an audience of 1,500. This distinct repudiation of the custom of the Established Church was a turning point in the career of Wesley, and led to unforeseen results. Little "societies" had been already formed in Nicholas Street, Baldwin Street, Castle Street, Gloucester Lane, Back Lane, and Temple Street, where frequent services were held, and within a few weeks Wesley records many of those scenes of agonised " conversion " which afterwards marked the movement. He was also allowed to preach in Clifton Church, and at Newgate. But a building suitable for regular services was needed, and on the 9th May "we took possession of a piece of ground in the Horse Fair, where it was designed to build a room large enough to contain both the societies of Nicholas and Baldwin Streets, and on Saturday, 12th, the first stone was laid." This " New Room," the first chapel of the denomination, which Wesley built without knowing how to defray the cost, was first used on the 1st July, for evening service. (It was not, however, certified by the magistrates as a place of worship until the 17th October, 1748, on which day "the house of Joseph Matson, glass-maker, Great Gardens," also obtained a certificate.) Two apartments were added, in which Wesley and the early preachers lodged—described by the former as " a little room, where I speak to the persons who come to me, and a garret, in which a bed is placed for me." Services were afterwards held at six o'clock in the morning, "by which means many more attend the College [cathedral] prayers, which immediately follow, than ever before." But in despite of his respect for the Establishment, Wesley was excluded from all the pulpits in the city. Some felons under sentence of death earnestly desired to speak with him, but Alderman Becher gave orders that he should not be admitted into Newgate. The new chapel was soon afterwards attacked by a raging mob, and one of the rabble subsequently admitted that they were hired for the purpose, while another, a ringleader, committed suicide in a fit of remorse. About the same date— one of great Methodistic development—Wesley began to employ lay preachers, the first of whom was John Cennick, who laboured at Kingswood, and the second Thomas Maxfield, a Bristolian, who was sent to London. Wesley's divergence from Whitefield, which occurred soon after, belongs to the general history of Methodism; but it is painful to read that, in 1741, the former expelled two of his followers because they had gone to hear Whitefield preach. Intolerance, however, was then deemed a virtue. Whitefield himself denounced the Wesleys, and in the Broadmead Records, under September, 1742, it is noted that three Baptists, after being reproved for frequenting the Wesleyan services, were repelled from communion for having lapsed into Methodistic heresies. The second Wesleyan Conference (the first was in London) was held in the New Room, in August, 1745; and the Bristol Conferences were very numerous during the following thirty years. In 1749 Charles Wesley, on his marriage, became a resident in Bristol, occupying a house in Stoke's Croft, at a rental of £11 a year. He resided there until 1771, and his brother often lodged at the house during his numerous visits.

The estate known as the Montagues, on Kingsdown, having been purchased by Giles Greville, a prosperous apothecary, from the representatives of the four daughters of Henry Dighton, Esq., the new owner, in February, 1737, laid out the land for building, and commenced by erecting the Montague Tavern. (R. Smith's MSS.) The intended new suburb made little progress for many years. A house with a turret, or gazebo, on the roof, known as Wint's Folly, was advertised to be let in March, 1750; and a house "in the Parade" was for sale in March, 1756. In the *Bristol Chronicle* of July 5th, 1760, is the announcement of a sale, at the sign of the Duke of Montague, of "two new built houses situated on Kingsdown." In another contemporary advertisement the inn is styled the Montague's Head. One or two houses were built in Southwell Street about 1740.

From an early period in the century, the industry and enterprise of the American colonists had excited the jealousy of home manufacturers and traders. Hats, for example, were naturally produced at a cheap rate in regions where fur was plentiful; but, on the appeal of English hatters, an Act was passed in 1732 forbidding colonial makers to export their hats, or even to transport them from one settlement to another. In 1719 a Bill passed the House of Commons forbidding the manufacture in the colonies of "any ironwares whatsoever," but the measure was dropped in the Upper House, and the American iron works slowly developed. At length, in March, 1737, the ironmasters and ironmongers of Bristol petitioned the House of Commons, alleging that the people of New England were producing much bar iron, and not only supplying themselves with nails and other iron ware, but were exporting large quantities to neighbouring colonies, to the great prejudice of the English iron trade, which, if not relieved from this competition, must certainly be ruined. Other petitions to the same effect being presented, a committee of inquiry was appointed, which soon after reported that, upon trials at the dockyards, the American iron had been found equal to the best Swedish, and that if the import of pigs were encouraged by removing the customs duty, this country would be rendered independent of the continent, while the colonists would be no longer encouraged to work up their raw material to the prejudice of English manufacturers. A great difference of opinion arose amongst the domestic interests affected, one party urging that the colonial iron should be permitted to enter in bars, while another wished to restrict the imports to pigs. On behalf of the latter, Mr. William Donne, ironmonger, of Bristol, the owner of two furnaces in Virginia, represented to the committee that if the New Englanders were allowed to make bars, they would infallibly compete with home manufactures in the production of iron ware. Some Gloucestershire landowners next alleged that if colonial bar iron was allowed to enter, their woods would be rendered valueless, and a large population impoverished. The subject was shelved; but in 1738 was brought again before the House by the iron merchants of Bristol, who represented that the home trade was in a state of manifest decay, and prayed for the "discouragement" (meaning prohibition) of American imports. The Commons passed a resolution affirming the advisability of prohibiting the extension of the colonial works; but nothing further was done. In 1750, however, an Act was passed for encouraging the import of American pigs and bars, and for prohibiting the erection of rolling mills or steel furnaces in the colonies. How trumpery were the grounds of English jealousy may be judged by the fact that the colonists even then possessed only two slitting mills, one plating forge, and one steel furnace. The measure excited the customary resistance of domestic monopolists; the Gloucestershire iron interest vehemently protesting that the success of the Bill would lead to their "entire ruin." Probably in consequence of these and other appeals, the American imports were confined to London, whence the iron was not to be removed either by land or sea—a restriction repealed in 1757 on the petition of the Bristol Merchants' Society and others, amidst renewed clamour from the protected industries.

At a meeting of the Council in May, 1737, a petition was presented from Rachel Day, widow of Alderman Peter Day, stating that by reason of heavy debts contracted by her late husband's partners in Jamaica, his creditors had seized his personal estate, whereby she was reduced to the greatest necessity. The Chamber granted her an annuity of £30. The Days, in the previous generation, had been one of the richest families in the city.

In the spring of 1737, Dr. Thomas Secker, who had held the bishopric of Bristol for three years, in conjunction with a prebend at Durham and a rectory in Westminster, was translated to Oxford. He was subsequently advanced to London, and ultimately to the Primacy. Like Bishop Butler, Dr. Secker was the son of dissenting parents, and was educated at a Presbyterian school at Tewkesbury. His successor at Bristol was Thomas Gooch, who was granted permission to hold with his bishopric the rectory of St. Clement's, London, a prebend at Canterbury, another at Chichester, the office of residentiary at Chichester, and the mastership of St. Mary's hospital in that city. Only fourteen months later—July, 1738—the well-endowed prelate was translated to Norwich, and was succeeded here by Joseph Butler, the most distinguished bishop that Bristol has ever possessed.

What is called by the contemporary press "a merry accident" occurred at the Michaelmas quarter sessions. Some days previously, a man, intending to inform against a woman who clandestinely sold spirituous liquors, went to her house and asked for a quartern of gin for his alleged sick wife. The woman, suspecting his design, put a measure of vinegar into his bottle, which he at once carried to a magistrate, but the latter, declining to take action, told the informer he might bring the matter before the sessions. This the man did, with the effect of being sentenced to the stocks for affronting the court by the production of his vinegar. Being incontinently placed in the instrument of punishment, he was pelted almost to death by the mob, who finally "brought a pitch kettle, pitched him all over, and afterwards rolled him in feathers, by which means he made a grotesque figure."—The pillory was also popular with the justices this year. Sarah Elliott, convicted of " discolouring the face of an infant and endeavouring to impose the same on a negro as his child," was sentenced to stand in the pillory an hour, and to undergo three months' imprisonment. Two knaves were sentenced to be twice exposed on the pillory, but at their first exhibition in Wine Street, according to the Sessions' Book, " the mob grew outrageous, broke down the iron bar of the pillory, threw down the malefactors, and treated them in so cruel a manner as that one of them was near expiring at the place." The magistrates thereupon ordered the second exposure to be remitted. In February, 1738, a surgeon was paid two guineas for attending two men grievously injured in the same manner. The humours of the populace in reference to the pillory are amusingly illustrated by a Bath paragraph in the London *Weekly Journal* of June 16th, 1739, in which it is gravely stated that a local culprit was pelted so vigorously during his exposure "that eggs sold for two a penny"—about three times the ordinary price.

One of the great funerals for which the city was famous took place on Sunday, the 30th October, 1737. About 8 o'clock in the evening, the body of Alderman Robert Yate, colonel of the militia, and father of the city, was carried from his mansion, the Red Lodge, in a magnificently apparelled hearse, to Christ Church, followed by the officers of the Corporation, the boys of Queen Elizabeth's school chanting a dirge, and thirty-one coaches, containing the mayor, aldermen, and other gentlemen. The way was lighted at intervals with large flambeaux, and the streets were thronged with spectators, but, says a London journal, "according to a rude unmannerly custom, the hearse was dismantled of the escutcheons, streamers, &c., before the procession was half over."

A prodigious flood occurred in the Avon and Froom on the 10th January, 1738, owing to protracted rains. A high tide aiding in the inundation, many low-lying streets were submerged, and the destruction of goods on the quays and in cellars was enormous. A local correspondent, who communicated a few details to a London newspaper, estimated the loss at £100,000. Another great flood took place in January, 1739, when two houses in the Shambles (Bridge Street) were undermined by the water, and became a heap of ruins.

The migration of many of the leading families to Queen Square led to the abandonment of the old Assembly Rooms in the Pithay. About 1737, according to the memory of an aged citizen (noted in Mr. Seyer's MSS.), Messrs. John Wallis, John Summers, and Roger Elletson succeeded in establishing winter assemblies at the Merchants' Hall. An incidental notice in a London paper of December, 1738, states that the Bristol Assemblies were held in Coopers' Hall—then near Corn Street; and balls were probably given in one or the other of these buildings until the conversion into an Assembly Room of the theatre in St. Augustine's. Mr. Seyer's informant added that ladies used to be lighted home from the balls by their maid servants, who attended with lanthorns.

A remarkable disaster to the Bristol ship Charming Sally occurred on the 8th March, 1738. While the vessel was on a voyage from Jamaica it struck during the night upon a whale, by which it received so violent a shock that it almost immediately foundered. The crew were luckily picked up by a passing vessel.

Owing to the difficulty experienced by the sheriffs in

prevailing upon a clergyman to attend condemned felons in Newgate, the Council, in April, resolved that a sum not exceeding £5 yearly should be granted to any clergyman who would undertake to visit the gaol and accompany convicts to the gallows. A few months later a physician to the prison was appointed at a salary of fifteen guineas.

Upon the death of the third Earl of Berkeley, the Council, in June, elected Lord Hardwicke, who had been appointed Lord Chancellor in 1737, to the office of Lord High Steward. In December, 1739, his lordship received the first of the numerous butts of sherry with which he was complimented by the Chamber.

The low rate of wages prevailing in the clothing trade—doubtless due to its declining prosperity—has been already recorded (see p. 168). As a natural consequence in those days, the workmen broke into disorders whenever there was an advance in the price of food. Great distress existed in the spring of 1738, and there were numerous disturbances. A Bristol paragraph in the London *Country Journal* of May 20th states that the weavers had been suffering for years under inexpressible hardships. They complained that their masters had " engrossed into their hands the most necessary commodities of life, such as corn, butter, cheese, eggs, salt, milk, mutton, pork, &c.," and that when they carried home their work, they received only a tenth of their earnings in money, and were forced to take the rest in provisions at twenty per cent above market price. "At this time of the year eggs may be bought of the country people hereabouts six for a penny, but no more than four is allowed by their masters." Moreover, " those who will not take provisions are obliged to take goods fifty per cent dearer than the shopkeepers will sell for, which they are obliged to vend at any rate, to get a little money to support their poor distressed families." The writer alleges that the riotous conduct of the workmen had been occasioned by these practices (which were common in the western clothing districts).

The abortive attempt of Mr. Jefferis to extend the fame of the city by setting up a mansion house is noted at page 191. In June, 1738, the same admirer of display moved in the Council that " for the honour and grandeur of the city, a public coach should be provided at the expense of the Chamber, for the use of mayors for the time being." As Mr. Jefferis was already designated as mayor for the following year, the lack of modesty shown by his proposal seems to have provoked opposition, and the motion was negatived.

For nearly three-quarters of a century previous to this date, scarcely any mention occurs in the corporate records of the Library House given to the city by Robert Redwood in 1613, or of the books presented to it by that eminent native of Bristol, Tobias Mathew, Archbishop of York. Entries, indeed, are made from time to time of the election of librarians, but the office held by those worthies (who had £2 a year and a residence) was practically a sinecure. On the 8th December, 1725, a petition was presented from the Rev. Robert Clarke, vicar of St. Leonard's, and styling himself "librarian by will of the donor," setting forth that the building was ruinous and unsafe, while the books were in danger of being spoiled, whereupon a committee of inquiry was appointed. The interest taken in the institution may be judged by the fact that nothing more is recorded about it for thirteen years. In September, 1738, however, the recorder (still taking an active part in corporate affairs) drew attention to the forlorn state of the Library, and obtained the appointment of another committee, which soon after reported that the books were in so much danger in the ruinous building that they had been removed to the Council House. It was recommended that the house in King Street should be forthwith rebuilt, some old hovels in front of it removed, and an adjoining piece of ground purchased. The Council having adopted those suggestions, the Library as it now stands (excepting the western wing of later date) was completed in 1740. An interesting feature in the principal room—the beautifully carved chimney-piece by Grinling Gibbons—is said to have been given by Alderman Michael Becher. In 1743, when the librarianship became vacant, the Chamber appointed the Rev. W. Williams, much to the wrath of the vicar of St. Leonard's, the Rev. Wm. Pritchard, who claimed it by right of his incumbency, contending that several of his predecessors had so held the office, "or at least," he ingenuously added, "received the rent of the librarian's house." His threat to seek relief in the law courts was never, however, carried out.

A robbery of the postboy carrying the mails between London and Bristol was so common an occurrence in the early part of the century as to be unworthy of record. To give an illustration, two men were executed in April, 1720, for having twice committed this crime, yet the letter bags were again stolen seven times during the following twelve months, the *London Journal* of August 27th remarking, "It is computed that the traders of Bristol have received £60,000 damages by the late robberies of the mail." In 1722 the postboys were pillaged twice in a single week, and three men were executed in London for the robberies. The only other incident of this kind worth mentioning occurred in September, 1738. The bag then carried off by three highwaymen contained a reprieve for a man lying under sentence of death in Newgate, and a second reprieve, despatched after the robbery became known, would have arrived too late to save the man's life, had not the magistrates postponed the execution for a day or two, in order that it might not clash with the festivities of a new mayor's inauguration.

A singular entry occurs in the minutes of a Council meeting on the 23rd September. "Alderman Becher complained that this city had been reflected on, in that the Butchers' Company here was by their ordinances restrained from killing any fresh meat on Mondays for the accommodation of strangers and others, an inconvenience attending no other town in England." A committee was appointed to consider the matter, but it never reported. Mr. Becher's statement is not corroborated by the Butchers' ordinances, which had been confirmed by the Council in 1714. According to these regulations, no animal was to be killed on Thursday for sale on Friday, nor on Saturday for sale on Sunday or Monday. Any citizen, not a free butcher, who killed an animal for sale in the city was liable to a penalty of 20s.

A breach in the ancient fortifications, with a view to accommodate the increasing traffic of the streets, was resolved upon by a reluctant Council in the autumn of 1738. The first of the old gateways ordered to be removed was the Back Gate, which had long been a great inconvenience to carriages proceeding to and from Queen Square. The strongly conservative instincts of the Chamber in reference to the defences of the city were shown three years later (May, 1741), when orders were given that the porter's lodge at Redcliff Gate should be taken down and rebuilt. In 1753 a sum of £1 18s. was paid "for making three city locks for the city gates." The porters at Redcliff and Temple Gates received a salary of 37s. per annum each from the sheriffs, and probably eked out a living by imposing a toll on persons passing the barriers during the night.

A violent rising of the Kingswood colliers occurred early in October, 1738. It was occasioned by some of the petty coalowners having undersold the other proprietors in the fuel used by the glass and sugar houses, whereupon the injured firms reduced the miners' wages from 1s. 4d. to 1s.

per day to meet the competition. Refusing to work at this rate, the colliers rose in a body, filled up the shafts of several pits, cut off communication with the city by carts and packhorses, stopped the coaches, demanded money from travellers on the London road, sacked Totterdown House (an inn), and forced the Brislington miners—called by a local paper the "civilised colliers"—to join them. Rioting continued for several days, many suburban public-houses being sacked. The justices sent off an express to the Government asking for troops, the watch was doubled, and the city gates were guarded. The arrival of a regiment struck the Kingswood colliers with a panic. Upwards of sixty were arrested, and the corporate accounts of the following year contain the following unique item:—"Recovered from the colliers who was prosecuted for a riot, Oct., 1738, £51."

Responding to an invitation from the Common Council, the Prince and Princess of Wales, then sojourning at Bath, paid a visit to this city on the 10th November. As the accounts hitherto published of the proceedings are very meagre, it may be amusing to read some additional details from contemporary documents, especially from a lengthy narrative which the civic scribes, for some inexplicable reason, inserted in the midst of the Council minutes for 1744· As soon as the royal journey was determined upon, the parochial officers along the intended route summoned the inhabitants to perform their statutable duty in mending the roads, which had become almost impassable since the turnpike riots. Fortunately, says the London *Evening Post*, Colonel Brydges, of Keynsham, invited their royal highnesses to proceed through his park, which extended almost to Brislington Common, and one of the worst portions of the miry highway was thus avoided. The civic chronicler states that the sheriffs met the distinguished party at Totterdown, where a procession was formed, headed by " the wool-combers in their shirts, with wigs and other emblems of their trade in wool; the weavers in the same manner, with a loom, and a boy in it making a piece of stuff." (The boy had a gift of five guineas from the Prince.) Then came a long file of citizens on horseback, the sheriffs with an imposing retinue, a band of music, and a great number of coaches, followed by "the glassmen in white shirts, on horseback, with glass swords and other devices." At Temple Gate, where the corporate dignitaries were assembled in a booth covered with scarlet cloth, the cavalcade received a salute from 200 cannon, and the recorder made a "most excellent speech" to the Prince, concluding with a humble desire that he would accept the freedom of the city. The Prince assenting, the certificate of freedom in a gold box was presented by the mayor. The procession was then reformed. "The throng grew now exceeding thick. The citizens seemed to vie with one another in adorning their houses; some hung out velvet, others silk tapestry, carpets, and cloth of gold; so that the streets appeared to be covered with the richest furniture of the inhabitants. The city companies contributed a great share to the grandeur of the solemnity. The church steeples and towers made a splendid show, and the ships in their marine gaiety and glory." The royal guests having reached the house of Mr. Henry Combe, in Queen Square, which had been specially prepared for their reception, they were met on the stairs " by Mrs. Mayoress and Mrs. Recorderess; and then they showed themselves to the populace from the windows." The mayor and recorder next came forward to pay their compliments; the master of the Merchants' Society presented the Prince with the freedom of the company in a gold box; the clergy offered a loyal address; and every one who took part in these ceremonies kissed the princely hands. At 4 o'clock the visitors and their hosts adjourned to the Merchants' Hall, where the wives of the civic notables were assembled, and there was much more hand-kissing for their satisfaction. At length the party sat down to dinner. "As there was no limitation to the expense of the entertainment, it was immensely grand, and no livery permitted to be in the hall, but the tables of their Royal Highnesses were served by gentlemen's sons, and the others by officers of the Corporation." After dinner, " the Prince began the healths of his Majesty and Prosperity to the City of Bristol in sherry and sugar in the city Gilt Cup, and delivered it to the mayor, and so each gentleman drank it, and the cup being replenished was by the mayor presented to the Princess, who drank of it with the usual healths, as did the rest of the ladies." On rising from the table, the visitors went for a short time to their lodgings, while the hall was rapidly converted into a ball room, two chairs of state being placed at the upper end. At 9 o'clock the Prince opened the ball with the mayor's daughter, and afterwards danced with "the recorderess" and other ladies. During the evening " the Princess diverted herself with a short pool at Quadrille, and the Prince did the company much honour in talking with many of them till about 12 o'clock. Then being mightily fatigued (they) withdrew to their lodgings, attended by the mayor as before." (The royal suite were accommodated at the mansions of Sir Abraham Elton, Alderman Elton, and Mr. Calwell.) Fireworks forthwith began to play around the statue of William III., "and lasted till 2 in the morning, and thus ended that glorious day." Next morning the Prince, after visiting the Hot Well, partook of a grand breakfast with the Corporation. His Royal Highness gave the mayor £200 for releasing poor prisoners for debt in Newgate, whilst the Princess presented the mayoress with a bloodstone repeating watch, and finally the Prince gave Mr. Combe's son a snuff-box set with diamonds. The visitors then returned to Bath, where a deputation afterwards waited upon them to return thanks for the honour they had been pleased to confer on Bristol. Such is the record of the civic scribe, much shorn of uninteresting details. The chamberlain's accounts show that the entertainment entailed an outlay of what was then considered the enormous sum of £955. Amongst the payments are £6 0s. 6d. for "Shampeighn" (probably drunk for the first time in Bristol), 12s. for about 800 tobacco pipes, £78 10s. for gunpowder, £14 10s. for the hire of pewter plates and dishes, and thirty guineas to the weavers and woolcombers for their display. The London *Evening Post* stated that upwards of 500 partook of the great dinner, for which some tickets had been eagerly purchased at five guineas each.

The reader will have observed that the road out of Bath was put in order on the occasion of the Prince's progress. Nevertheless, early in the following January, after heavy rains, access to Bath became almost wholly impracticable owing to the state of the highways. The farmers seized the opportunity not merely to raise the price of butter to four times its usual price in Bristol, but "to bring a great deal to market several ounces under weight."

The temper of the authorities was much exercised at this time by an impracticable baker. On the 2nd December, 1738, the mayor reported to the Council that he had lately sent a warrant to Thomas Tawman, ordering his attendance, and that the man, on appearing, had behaved insolently, and stood in open defiance of his worship's orders and of the Bakers' Company. The Chamber ordered that he be summoned to show cause why he should not be disfranchised. The baker continuing rebellious, he was deprived of the freedom in May, and the bellman announced the fact in the streets. Tawman, however, coolly took no notice, and went on selling his bread. The Council next ordered that the culprit should be prosecuted for obstinately keeping open his shop, and the opportunity was seized to make a raid on all "foreigners" carrying on business in the city. As non-freemen were wholly defenceless, many of those threatened paid fines for admission to the freedom. Tawman and the rest were doubtless expelled.

The minutes of the Dean and Chapter record, under the 6th January, 1739, that the capitular body had that day sealed a lease to the "Mayor or Burgesses and Commonalty" of Bristol for liberty to make a way or passage, nine feet wide, through the croud or crypt of St. Nicholas's church. Soon afterwards, a "faculty," authorising this strange design, was issued by Carew Reynell, chancellor of the diocese. This document, preserved in the Consistory Court, recites that owing to the narrowness of St. Nicholas's Gate and the increase of carriages and carts, traffic was frequently interrupted, and foot passengers could not proceed without peril of their lives, to the great impediment of trade. The Corporation having obtained permission to make a passage through the croud, the chancellor granted this faculty, enabling the civic body to open out the proposed footway. Strange to say, although a yearly way-leave of £5 had been promised to the vestry of St. Nicholas by the civic body, the minutes of the Council contain no reference to the subject, and the footway was never constructed.

The exasperation of the English merchants at their losses in carrying on a vast illicit trade with the Spanish American colonies has been already noticed. As they persisted in pursuing that trade, while the Spanish Government was equally obstinate in maintaining its monopoly, British ships were frequently captured, and Walpole's policy of peace became gradually unpopular. In 1738 the nation was roused to madness by a ship captain named Jenkins detailing to the House of Commons his alleged sufferings at the hands of the Spaniards, and producing one of his ears, which he said they had cut off with taunts at the English king. (Jenkins seems to have been a knave; Alderman Beckford afterwards assured Lord Shelburne that if the House had caused the fellow's wig to be removed they would have found his ears as whole as their own; and it is satisfactory to add that Mr. Nicholls' assertion that the man was a Bristolian is erroneous.) Cases of alleged ill-treatment continued to pour in. Amongst the Newcastle MSS. is a letter to the Duke signed by R. Farr, Thomas Roach, and two other Bristol merchants, dated January, 1739, complaining " of a flagrant instance of cruelty and injustice " offered to British subjects by the Spaniards, and trusting that effectual measures would be taken for relieving the sufferers and obtaining compensation for the writers' loss. It appears from an enclosed document that the Bristol ship Sarah, whilst on a voyage home, was stopped and searched by a Spanish man of war, which, finding " one stick of logwood " (smuggled goods) on board, made prize of the vessel, carried her into Havanna " ignominiously, with the Union Jack turned downwards," sold the cargo for one-tenth of its value, set the crew adrift, appropriated 1,800 pieces-of-eight, which the captain had hid in a cask, and then sent him to prison, where he still remained. The ship and cargo were valued at £9,000. The Ministry replied to complaints of this kind by pointing out that the English laws against smuggling were as harsh as those of Spain, but the plea, though true, did not mitigate mercantile discontent. The Cabinet negotiated a convention with the Court of Madrid with a view to obviating disputes; but the English shipowners denounced the arrangement as a sacrifice of British rights, and petitions against it having been forwarded to Parliament from Bristol and other leading ports, Walpole's opponents, taking advantage of the general clamour, joined in a violent attack on the policy of peace. After a vain struggle, Walpole submitted to the popular will, and war was proclaimed in Bristol on the 29th October amidst demonstrations of joy. Preparations for the struggle had been going on for some time. The London *Weekly Journal* of August 4th contained intelligence that, in pursuance of orders from the Government to impress landsmen as well as seamen for the king's service, the magistrates of Bristol had remained sitting at the Council House until between two and three o'clock on Sunday morning, whilst the constables were scouring the city and throwing their captures into Bridewell; similar scenes being repeated on the two following nights. Permission having been granted to fit out privateers, a correspondent of the London *Country Journal* stated that the breast of almost every Bristol citizen " was fired with martial ardour and an ambition of plucking off as many Spanish ears as would serve to nail on every gate throughout Great Britain." A few weeks later the *Gloucester Journal* announced that " some eminent merchants of Bristol had subscribed £5,000 for the glorious purpose of fitting out privateers to go upon an expedition in quest of the Spanish villains who insulted and robbed British subjects, and especially those belonging to the port. It was expected that £5,000 more would be raised at the next meeting." A number of such vessels, in fact, were sent to sea in the following year, one of which, the Vernon, captured a prize valued at £18,000.

A craving for news, excited by the war, led to curious innovations in the Council House. The members of the Corporation had hitherto sought for intelligence of public events at the coffee houses; but it was now determined to subscribe for two of the London daily newspapers for the use of the civic body, who lost no time in converting the municipal building into a sort of free club house. The arrangement soon became very popular amongst the aldermen and councillors, and almost daily charges are recorded for bread, oysters, cheese, wine, ale, porter, cider and tobacco, consumed by them at the expense of the city. In the quarter ending June, 1742, the items include 132 bottles of wine, 4lb. tobacco, 288 pipes, and 1lb. of "smoaking candles," with a great quantity of ale and cider. Another daily newspaper and the *London Gazette* were shortly afterwards ordered, and the items for "refreshments" became larger than ever. The system gave rise to abuses that brought about its suppression. On the return of peace the newspapers were discontinued.

The watching and lighting arrangements of the city being much complained of, the justices requested the parochial waywardens to report on the number of lights and lamps in each district. No return was made for the parishes of St. Nicholas and Redcliff, or for Castle Precincts. In St. James's and St. Michael's it was stated that there were few lights (lanthorns) and no lamps at all. In the rest of the city, including the out-parish of St. Philip's, the total number of glimmering oil lamps was 128. Three of the central parishes had four each, and the populous district of Temple only six. On the 10th February, 1739, the Council adopted a petition to Parliament praying for further powers. The document alleged that in several parishes the number of persons paying 2*d*. weekly in poor rate (who alone were liable to the lighting rate) was so small that an adequate number of lamps could not be maintained, while the nightly watch was equally defective. The Chamber desired to take the two matters into its own hands, and to be enabled to levy a general rate to meet the future outlay. It also sought for power to make regulations for paving and cleansing the s'reets, and for preventing the erection of houses with wooden fronts and over-hanging storeys. The design, however, became known to the inhabitants, and excited so many threats of resistance that the Bill was summarily dropped. The measure was again proposed in 1740, with a similar result.

Mr. John Elbridge, whose zeal and munificence in promoting the establishment of the Infirmary have been already noticed, died on the 22nd February, 1739, at Cote House, Durdham Down, a mansion which he had erected. Descended from the Bristol family of the Aldworths, from whom he inherited a large estate, Elbridge obtained the deputy comptrollership of the Custom-house in the reign of William III., and held it for many years. During his residence in the Royal Fort he erected a school house on part of the garden, adjoining St. Michael's Hill, and bequeathed £3,000 to trustees for the clothing and education therein of twenty-four girls.

After another long slumber, the Corporation, urged by the practical and energetic recorder, again took up the question of the proposed Exchange. In May a committee reported that the most convenient site for the building, and also for the proposed market-house, was the area stretching from All Saints' Lane to Cock Lane in Corn Street, and extending backwards to Nicholas Street. The proposal was adopted, and the committee were empowered to purchase such additional property as might be required. (The project is said to have been condemned by the citizens generally as too costly to be practicable.) Amongst the payments soon after made on this account was "The feoffees of All Saints for the Old Maids' Alms-house, £420;" but Mr. Nicholls' statement that this building occupied the whole site of the present Exchange is absurdly incorrect. A new almshouse was built by the trustees in 1741, in St. John's Lane.

Much dismay was created in the municipal body in May, 1739, by the discovery that the chamberlain, Mr. Holledge, had not accounted for several thousand pounds of the money entrusted to him. He was, however, possessed of valuable property in Prince's Street and elsewhere, and the loss was reduced by its sale to £2,400. His sureties were answerable for the remainder, but they pleaded inability to pay, and only £500 appear to have been obtained from one of them, Richard Hart. Holledge, who had been mayor in 1708-9, petitioned the Council for relief in September, alleging that he had been ruined by his son's recklessness, and other misfortunes. The Chamber granted him an annuity of £50. Upon his death, in 1742, his widow obtained a pension of £25; in 1751 one of his daughters was granted an annuity of the same amount; and in 1759 another daughter was voted £15 a year for life.

The old difficulty of inducing prominent citizens to enter the Corporation revived about this date. John Tyndall and David Dehany had been elected councillors, but both refused to accept the office, and actions at law were commenced to recover the penalties. Dehany soon after surrendered, and, after paying the fine of £200, was re-elected, and the money refunded. After a further struggle, Tyndall adopted the same course; but he soon wearied of his new dignity, and relieved himself of it in 1741 by paying the penalty of £200.

The combination in the same trading company of educated and prosperous surgeons with humble barbers and wig-makers was a medieval anomaly certain to become mutually disagreeable as society progressed. In May, 1739, a number of peruke makers and barbers, freemen of the Barbers' Company, presented a petition to the Council, complaining of "diverse impositions and grievances" inflicted by their surgical brethren. A petition of the masters and wardens of the company was also produced, in which surprise was expressed that some "uneasie members" should importune the Chamber with unfounded discontents. The documents were referred to a committee, and were heard of no more. In later years many surgeons refused to become members of the company, which gradually died out. Its hall was in or near Shannon Court.

The London *Weekly Journal* of July 21st, 1739, contains a brief paragraph illustrative of the effects of the Methodist crusade in Kingswood. The astonished writer states that a sheriff's officer with two assistants had ventured into that barbarous district, and had even levied an execution upon the chattels of an inhabitant, "without meeting with the least obstruction. No officer within the memory of the oldest man living has been able to effect an undertaking of this nature in so peaceable a manner."

About the end of July, 1739, Richard Savage, a poet of some genius, but whose extraordinary career as narrated by his friend Dr. Johnson has secured for the man an undeserved rank in English literature, was induced by Pope and other well wishers to remove from London, where his health had been shattered by alternate plunges into debauchery and misery, and to take up his abode in Wales, where they undertook to provide him with the then sufficient yearly income of £50 for life. He set off provided with fifteen guineas for travelling expenses, but the money carried him only a few miles, and another remittance was needed to enable him to reach Bristol. Here, as he alleged, he found an embargo laid upon shipping, and was compelled to remain for some time; but as the Welsh mail by the New Passage was never interrupted, the pretext alleged for delay was merely one of Savage's habitual shifts. The truth is that the poet, to use Johnson's words, "ingratiated himself with many of the principal merchants, was invited to their houses, distinguished at their public feasts, and treated with a regard that gratified his vanity." At last he sailed for Swansea, where he remained a year, eking out his income by a trick not then uncommon—soliciting subscriptions in cash for a new edition of his works which he made no effort to produce. In the meantime, having offended many of his London friends by insolent importunities, they withdrew their support, and, after denouncing their inhumanity, he resolved to return to England. On reappearing in Bristol, says Johnson, " a repetition of the kindness which he had formerly found invited him to stay. He was not only caressed and treated, but had a collection made for him of about £30." To offer help to Savage, however, was only to provoke further demands; he asked for assistance as if it were legitimately due to him; and instead of being grateful for what was offered, he became insulting when further importunities were unsuccessful. The hospitality he continued to meet with was recklessly abused. He could not brook the trammel of stated hours; he treated all family regulations with scorn; and could neither be induced to retire to bed at night nor to leave it next day for dinner. As was natural, every door gradually closed upon him, and he was driven, with empty pockets, to seek for sustenance at the taverns. The debts incurred in this way becoming troublesome, he took refuge in the garret of an obscure inn, from which he sallied by night to beg from his former admirers. At this crisis a remittance of £5 arrived from London, to enable him to return, but the money was forthwith squandered in a debauch. Help and shelter were nevertheless still extended to him by a surviving friend, in despite of his perverse habits. At length, on the 15th January, 1743, he was lodged in Newgate for nonpayment of a debt of £8, due to a coffee-house keeper, and was treated, as Johnson admits, with great humanity by Mr. Dagg, the gaoler, who provided him with food, and even accompanied him in country walks. Some Bristolians suggested a subscription to pay his debts, but as he was to reap no personal gain by the operation, " he treated," to use his own expression, " the proposal with disdain." The occasional gifts sent to the prison were accepted in the poet's characteristic fashion. He took the money and impudently asked for more ; and, as he deemed the response illiberal, he snatched up a pen to revile his benefactors. While engaged in this congenial task, he was smitten with fever—never long absent from the unhealthy prisons of the age—and died on the 1st August, 1743. He was buried in St. Peter's churchyard, about six feet from the entrance to the south porch, at the expense of Mr. Dagg. The vigour of Dr. Johnson's sympathetic memoir long protected Savage's greediness, dissipation, and ferocity from general discredit. Since the publication of Mr. Moy Thomas's researches, there has been practically no question that the poet's account of his noble birth and subsequent persecution by a cruel mother was as gross an imposture as the story concocted in our own time by the Tichborne claimant. A few lines of the unfinished satire on Bristol, entitled " London and Bristol delineated," are subjoined.

>In a dark bottom sunk, O Bristol now
>With native malice lift thy lowering brow!
>*   *   *   *   *
>Present we meet thy sneaking, treacherous smiles;
>The harmless absent still thy sneer reviles,
>Such as in thee all parts superior find,
>The sneer that makes the fool and knave combined;
>When melting pity would afford relief,
>The ruthless sneer that insult adds to grief.
>What friendship canst thou boast ? what honours claim ?
>To thee each stranger adds an injured name.
>What smiles thy sons must in their foes excite!
>Thy sons, to whom all discord is delight;
>Thy sons, though crafty, deaf to wisdom's call,
>Despising all men and despised by all;
>Sons, while thy cliffs a ditch-like river laves,
>Rude as thy rocks, and muddy as thy waves,
>Of thoughts as narrow as of words immense,
>As full of turbulence as void of sense.
>*   *   *   *   *
>Boast swarming vessels, whose plebeian state,
>Owns not to merchants but mechanics freight.
>Boast nought but pedlars' fleets . . .
>Boast thy base Tolsey, and thy turn-spit dogs,
>Thy halliers' horses, and thy human hogs.
>Upstarts and mushrooms, proud, relentless hearts,
>Thou blank of sciences, thou dearth of arts.
>Such foes as learning once was doomed to see,
>Huns, Goths, and Vandals, were but types of thee.

In November, 1739, another and more celebrated poet, Alexander Pope, paid a visit to the Hot Well for the purpose of drinking the water. In two letters to Martha Blount he gives a description of Bristol which, amidst some amusing cockneyisms, is not without vivid touches. After describing the journey from Bath, Pope states that the first view of Bristol presented him with " twenty odd pyramids smoking over the town (which are glasshouses)." Then " you come first to old walls [Temple Gate], and over a bridge built on both sides like London bridge, and as much crowded, with a strange mixture of seamen, women, children, loaded horses, asses, and sledges with goods, dragging along altogether, without posts to separate them. From thence you come to a key along the old wall, with houses on both sides, and in the middle of the street as far as you can see, hundreds of ships, their masts as thick as they can stand by one another, which is the oddest and most surprising sight imaginable. This street is fuller of them than the Thames from London bridge to Deptford." When the tide was out, the ships grounded, and then " a long street full of ships in the middle, with houses on each side, looks like a dream." The picturesque road to the Hot Well is next described. " Passing still along by the river, you come to a rocky way on one side, overlooking green hills on the other; on that rocky way rise several white houses, and over them red rocks, and as you go further more rocks above rocks, mixed with green bushes and of different coloured stone. This at a mile's end terminates in the house of the Hot Well." Here the wondering writer found " several pretty lodging houses, open to the river, with walls of trees. When you have seen the hills which seem to shut in upon you, and to stop any further way, you go into the house [pump-room], and looking out at the back-door a vast rock of an hundred feet of red, white, green, blue and yellowish marble, all blotched and variegated, strikes you quite in the face; and turning on the left there opens the river at a vast depth below, winding in and out, and accompanied on both sides with a continued range of rocks up into the clouds, of a hundred colours, one behind another . . . very much like the broken scenes in a play-house (!) Upon the top of those high rocks there runs a large down of fine turf for about three miles. It looks too frightful to approach the brink, and look down upon the river. . . . There is a little village upon this down called Clifton, where are very pretty lodging houses, and steep cliffs and very green valleys. . . . I am told that one may ride ten miles further on an even turf, on a ridge that on one side views the river Severn." Turning to Bristol again, Pope writes:—"The city itself is very unpleasant, and no civilised company in it: only the collector of the customs would have brought me acquainted with merchants, of whom I hear no great character. The streets are as crowded as London; but the best image I can give you of it is, 'tis as if Wapping and Southwark were ten times as big, or all their people ran into London. Nothing is fine in it but the square, which is larger than Grosvenor Square, and well builded . . . and the key, which is full of ships, and goes half-way round the square. The College Green is pretty, and (like the square) is set with trees, with a very fine old cross of Gothic curious work in the middle, but spoiled with the folly of new gilding it, that takes away all the venerable antiquity." The poet thinks of returning to Bath, and of drinking there the Bath and Bristol waters mixed. "Not but that I am satisfied the water at the Well is very different from what it is anywhere else; for it is full as warm as new milk from the cow; but there is no living at the Wells without more conveniences in the winter." From a letter written by Martha Blount, addressed "To be left with Mr. Pyne, the postmaster, Bristol," and bearing internal evidence as to its date, it is certain that Pope paid a second visit to the Hot Well in 1743. It must have been on this occasion that, as an aged citizen informed Mr. Seyer, the poet once attended service at Redland Chapel (Seyer MSS.).

The *Gloucester Journal* of August 29th, 1739, reports "an outrage against immemorial custom which had excited great resentment" in Bristol. A few days before the opening of the assizes, a regiment of infantry was marched into the city, and, in spite of the protests of the mayor, the troops continued in quarters after the commission was opened. The judge (Aland) summoned the commanding officer before him, and demanded the removal of the soldiery, but it was not until his lordship threatened to despatch a messenger to the Government that his order was complied with.

A civil action was tried at the above assizes between a baker and a butcher, both of Lawford's Gate, the former claiming £30 as won during a single sitting at "the favourite game of Hussle Cap." He obtained a verdict, with 40s. damages.

The prevalence of superstition amongst the wealthier class

of the city is illustrated by a Bristol paragraph in the London *Weekly Miscellany* of September 1st, stating that only one prisoner received sentence of death at the local gaol delivery just concluded, " namely Halley Price, convicted of stealing (under the guise of a fortune teller) twenty guineas. This is the creature who stole (under the same delusion) a gold chain and several gold rings from a creditable inhabitant of this city lately." Price escaped the gallows. When the victims of the fortune tellers were of low degree the knaves got off lightly. The *Bristol Journal*, of September 15th, 1752, states that six of those impostors had just been "handsomely" whipped at the whipping post, outside Lawford's Gate.

Banking in provincial towns being still in its infancy, the Corporation of Bristol was sometimes much inconvenienced in remitting Sir Thomas White's yearly gift of £104 to the distant civic bodies which were, as they still are, entitled to it in rotation. The case of Cambridge, in 1739, indicates how the matter was arranged. The corporation in question sent an acquittance and a power of attorney to one Samuel Herring, " woollen draper, at the Artichoke, Lombard Street, London." The Bristol authorities on their side handed the money to John Vaughan, a local goldsmith, whose agents, Spindler and Co., of Gutter Lane, were ordered to pay the money to Herring. The chamberlain, in acquainting the latter where the money was lying, writes:—" Bills are very scarce with us. I was obliged to pay ½ per cent. for negotiating this affair."

Mr. Thomas Coster, M.P., of College Green, died on the 30th September, to the great regret of his friends. A contemporary notemaker recorded that the great bell of every parish church in the city tolled an entire day by order of the family. An election to fill the vacant seat commenced in the following November. The candidates were Mr. Edward Southwell, of Kingsweston, nominated by the Tory party, and Mr. Henry Combe, merchant, a Whig. (Mr. Serjeant Foster, the recorder, also offered himself, but retired in favour of Mr. Combe.) The *Gloucester Journal* of November 27th says :—" The Hon. Mr. Southwell has kept open house at Shirehampton ever since he has declared. There are constantly employed a baker, a butcher, and two brewers to provide for the reception of all comers and goers." The singular coalition of Jacobites, Tories, and " Patriots " then raging against Walpole in the House of Commons was not without influence in the provinces, and Mr. Combe's support of the Excise scheme told heavily against him. The contest closed on the 12th December, when Mr. Southwell had polled 2,651 votes, and Mr. Combe 2,203. In singular contrast to a modern election, only about one twenty-fifth part of the voters refrained from polling, the total number of abstentions being 214. Only thirty-seven electors resided in Clifton. The Tory party rejoiced greatly over their success, and a local poet produced an enthusiastic ode, commencing :—

O glorious victory, divine defeat!
Hail mighty Southwell, eminently great!

Various improvements were resolved upon by the Council during the closing months of 1739. The ascent in High Street being very abrupt, some alteration was made in the gradient at a cost of about £150. The scheme for making a footpath through St. Nicholas's crypt having been abandoned, it was determined to remove two houses on the east side of St. Nicholas's Gate, so as to make a footway from High Street to the Bridge, thus protecting pedestrians from the peril of struggling through the always crowded gate. Works were ordered at Bridewell for the purpose of making the prison more secure, and for enlarging it by the incorporation of Whitehall. The provisions against fires being again found insufficient, a new fire engine was purchased at a cost of £51. Finally, the mayor having stated that there was a considerable sum of money in the Council House, the lower windows of which were unprotected, a motion was made that substantial shutters should be provided. The civic scribe omits to note the result. The following winter was one of great severity, and owing to the sufferings of the poor the Chamber voted £200 for their relief; while twelve starving insolvents were liberated from Newgate, their creditors consenting to accept 6s. 8d. in the pound on their debts, which on the average amounted to only £6 each.

One of the most curious items in the civic account books of this period is as follows :—" Oct. 16. Entertaining Captain Rais Condela, Admiral of Salle, £39 17s. 3d." This is followed by :—" Paid to his passage to Milford, 5s. A sack for him, 5s." The mystery hanging over those items has been cleared up by the discovery of the detailed accounts, the innkeeper's bill describing the visitor as the " Embaseter of Murroker." The Admiral being a Mahometan, and consequently an abstainer from intoxicating liquors, the civic dignitaries were unable to entertain him in a manner congenial with their own tastes. They however appreciated his own, by presenting him with a handsome scarlet cloak fringed with gold, and other apparel, including shirts and "Morocco pumps," conducted him to the Hot Well and Sea Mills dock, paid for his modest entertainment at an inn, at the rate of 7s. 6d. per day, and defrayed his passage from Milford to Bristol (5s.), and from Bristol to London (three guineas.) A treaty of commerce with Moroccco, by which British ships were protected from the raids of "Sallee rovers," was concluded soon afterwards.

At a meeting of the Council in February, 1740, the mayor explained to the House the cause of a grave infraction of ancient customs. It was the time-honoured duty of one of the sheriffs to give a dinner to the Corporation soon after his appointment, and Mr. Dehany had intended to comply with the usage, but owing to the bustle caused by the election and the severity of the weather he had been prevented from doing so "in so handsome a manner as the nature of the thing required." He therefore proposed that, in lieu of the dinner, he should give 100 guineas to the Corporation, to be distributed amongst the poor. The Chamber, after passing a solemn resolution that this proceeding was not "to be drawn into a president," accepted the money.

The Exchange scheme was now making substantial progress. At the Council meeting in March a committee reported extensive purchases of property with a view to clearing the site for the Exchange and markets, and for opening approaches. The total amounted to £19,343. As showing the intricate net of lanes and alleys swept away by the improvement, it may be stated that one of the new purchases comprised certain "premises in King's Head Court and Thorough Lane, in or near Foster Lane, otherwise St. Martin's Lane," in St. Nicholas' parish. The vendors were the right honourable Giles Earle, one of the Lords of the Treasury, and William Earle Benson, son and great grandson of Sir Thomas Earle. A large portion of the site having been cleared, the foundation stone of the Exchange was laid by the mayor on the 10th March, 1741, amidst much rejoicing, to which a bountiful distribution of ale to the populace may have contributed. A few weeks before the ceremony, Mr. John Wood, one of the creators of modern Bath, had been appointed architect of the new building, which made rapid progress under his supervision.

Having just referred to a local work which was in hand nearly thirty years, the opportunity may be taken to note the deliberation with which a much more important public improvement was carried out. On the 9th August, 1740, the Council granted to Alderman Nathaniel Day, on payment of £20 a year, the reversion of certain land near the Boar's Head inn, to enable him to open a street forty feet wide in Bullock's Park, "to lead from College Green up into the road towards Jacob's Well." The project thus oldly described was the first sketch of what was to become Park Street, but more than twenty years elapsed before a house was built, and some sites remained vacant at the beginning of the present century.

The suburbs of the city were infested about this time by a number of ruffians who seem to have had no qualms in supplementing robbery by murder. In April, 1740, two men were executed at Gloucester for two violent highway crimes on Durdham Down. In the following July a servant of Mr. Thomas Knight, of Southmead, Westbury, was found, nearly dead, on the Down, with twenty cuts on his skull, and his pockets rifled. "The young man's horse was found near the gallows." A week or two later two soldiers, named Millard and Masters, were charged with the crime by a comrade named York, who confessed that he had been their companion in the perpetration of two atrocious robberies at Brislington and Bedminster, in a burglary in Wine Street, and in stealing twenty-one sheep at various times in the southern suburbs. York was thereupon arrested, and, at the following Somerset assizes, the three men were sentenced to death and afterwards hanged, together with a fourth culprit, convicted of a robbery at Brislington. Millard and York spent the night previous to their execution in "Bedminster Bridewell," a prison maintained by the county of Somerset. The former was hung in chains on Bedminster Down, and the latter on Brislington Common, in the presence of thousands of spectators. A few days later Millard's father-in-law, a cobbler in Thomas Street, strongly suspected of being concerned in the above crimes, was executed in Bristol for a shop robbery.

Much trouble and expense being caused by the influx of paupers from Ireland, the court of quarter sessions, in August, 1740, by virtue of an Act passed in the spring, fixed the rates to be paid to masters of ships for the reconveyance of vagrants to their native country. In this matter, at all events, the aldermanic body studied economy. The amount fixed for each adult was 6s. 6d., including food; for children half price. As the voyage frequently lasted a week, and occasionally a month, shipowners must have found the business far from profitable.

The minutes of Christ Church vestry contain the following record, dated December 1st, 1740:—" It was ordered that Mr. John Berrow do erect another butcher's standing on the porter's walk adjoining on to this church." It will be shown at a later date that, in consequence of the excrescences that had been permitted to grow around the church, the width of Wine Street at this point was only seventeen feet.

One of the most audacious and cold-blooded fratricides ever recorded was committed at Kingroad on the 19th January, 1741, on Sir John Dineley, Bart., by his brother, Samuel Goodere, captain of H.M.S. Ruby, then stationed in the port. Sir John, who had dropped his family name on succeeding to a maternal estate in Worcestershire, married the grand-daughter and heiress of Alderman John Lawford, of Bristol, in whose right he possessed a mansion at Stapleton and another at Tockington, near Thornbury. For many years the baronet and his brother had been on unfriendly terms, and the former, whose conduct was described as scarcely consistent with sanity, took advantage of circumstances that will be hereafter mentioned to cut off the entail of the family estates, with the intention of leaving them to two nephews named Foote, and thus impoverishing the captain, his heir presumptive. The ill-feeling of the latter was inflamed by this proceeding to deadly hatred, and soon after his appointment to the command of the Ruby (through the suicide of the previous captain at Kingroad, in October, 1740), he resolved on the murder of his brother, and devised a plan for carrying it out. Knowing that Sir John had business relations with Mr. Jarrit Smith, a solicitor, in College Green, the captain urged that gentleman to endeavour to bring about a reconciliation, stating that it might be effected in an interview at Mr. Smith's house. The solicitor assented, and prevailed upon Sir John to promise a meeting on the first day he should visit Bristol. Subsequently, upon Mr. Smith being informed that the baronet would call upon him on the 13th January, he acquainted the captain, who lodged in Prince's Street, of the fact : whereupon the latter. in pursuance of his deadly project, brought up a number of sailors from the Ruby, and hired some ruffians belonging to the Vernon privateer, giving them orders to seize Sir John when he quitted Mr. Smith's. (The site of his house is now occupied by the Royal Hotel.) The baronet, who was then negotiating a mortgage for £5,000 with the attorney to clear off some of his debts, kept his appointment, but declined to see his brother until his next visit to Bristol, fixed for the following Sunday, the 19th January; and as both he and his servant were well mounted and armed with pistols, the intended attack was postponed. A day or two later, Captain Goodere made elaborate preparations for the coming tragedy. Nearly opposite to Mr. Smith's residence stood the White Hart alehouse, which on the first floor had a room projecting over the porch, affording an outlook over the traffic to and from the quays. Captain Goodere having again assembled his mercenaries, directed them to take up their quarters in this room on Sunday afternoon, adding further instructions which they faithfully followed. The ambuscade being laid, the captain called upon Mr. Smith at the hour appointed, and met his intended victim, whom he kissed, and then congratulated on his apparent better health. Mr. Smith, pouring out a glass of wine, drank to "love and friendship," to which Sir John responded, "With all my heart." The captain also drank to the toast, and Mr. Smith believed that the reconciliation was complete. After an amicable conversation the party broke up, the solicitor accompanying his guests to the door, whence he saw Sir John walk down towards the quay, while the captain was joined by several sailors from the alehouse, and was heard to say, "Is he ready?" adding an order to make haste. Mr. Smith, supposing that the captain was giving orders for returning to Kingroad, thought no more of the matter, and closed his door. Only a few seconds afterwards, Mahony, the leader of the captain's gang, seized the unfortunate baronet under the wall of the churchyard, and, with the assistance of others, partly carried and partly dragged him along the Ropewalk towards the Ruby's barge, which was moored near Mardyke. Captain Goodere followed a few steps behind his myrmidons, who were about sixteen in number, and who, in reply to the questions of timid wayfarers, stated that their prisoner was a murderer, about to be tried on shipboard. Acts of brutal violence by press gangs were then of constant occurrence, and this fact, joined to the ferocious ruffianism of the privateer's men, who threatened to throw a bystander into the river, accounts for the apathy of the spectators. The captive shouted "Murder. I am Sir John Dineley," several times, but his red cloak was thrown over his head, and he was soon thrust into the barge, of which Captain Goodere took the command, and which was rapidly rowed to Kingroad, the captive protesting all the way against the barbarity of his treatment. On boarding the Ruby, the captain told the officers that the prisoner was insane, and ordered him to be placed in the purser's cabin, which had been specially cleansed for his reception some days before; a sentinel was directed to keep guard over him; and two large bolts were fastened upon the door. Suspicions as to the captain's purpose were excited amongst the officers by the repeated cries of the unhappy man, but habits of discipline prevented interference, and they retired to rest at the usual hour. "Between 2 and 3 o'clock" (in the morning), said Captain Goodere in his confession, "I ordered Mahony to call Charles White—for Elisha Cole, who was intended to assist Mahony in the murder, was dead drunk—and to bring him into my cabin. White came presently, and I believe I made him drink a quart of rum out of gill glasses. When he was near drunk, I asked him if he would kill a Spaniard. The poor fellow seemed surprised, but Mahony and myself worked him up to a proper pitch, so that he was ready enough to assist. All the night long Mahony was to and fro in deceased's cabin, and the sentry thought he was sent by me to assist Sir John. . . . I gave him a handkerchief and a piece of half-inch rope about ten foot long, bidding him and White follow me. The rope was to strangle him, and the handkerchief to thrust into his mouth to stop his making a noise. . . . I ordered the sentry to give me his sword, and to go up on deck, which he did." Mahony and White then went into the cabin and finished their work, the victim's cries of "Murder" nevertheless awakening several persons in the ship. "I stood at the cabin door," added the captain, "with my sword drawn, and gave them the lanthorn, which hung up in the cabin [gunroom], just as they had got the rope about his neck. The sentry, seeing me without a candle, brought one to the cabin door, but I held my sword to his breast and ordered him away." On the murderers reappearing, the captain went in and felt his brother's corpse, observing:—"'Tis done, and well done." Thereupon locking the door, he took the two miscreants to his own cabin, where Mahony gave him his brother's gold watch, and received the captain's silver one in return. The gold found in the dead man's pockets, about £28, was shared by the assassins, who immediately left the ship. The horrible nature of the crime soon after excited some of the petty officers to a daring breach of discipline. Early in the morning, the cooper, who lay in an adjoining cabin, having related that he had seen the closing scenes of the tragedy through chinks in a partition, the carpenter broke in the cabin door, when the state of the body left no doubt as to the crime; whereupon the cooper, finding that the lieutenant was too timid to take action, boldly arrested the captain with the help of eight or ten of the crew. After an unaccountable delay on the part of the Bristol magistrates, the water-bailiff was sent down, and took charge of the prisoner. The other culprits were apprehended in the city by four sailors, and with their tempter were brought before the justices, when Mahony and White made voluntary confessions, each throwing the guilt upon his companions in the dock. Previous to the trial the Government made an attempt to remove the case into the Admiralty Court, alleging that the city authorities had no jurisdiction; but the recorder clearly demonstrated that the scene of the murder was within the boundaries conceded to Bristol by ancient charters. The gaol delivery took place in March, when Captain Goodere boldly denied his guilt, alleging that his brother was really insane, and that, being heir to the family estates, it would have been folly in him to commit an act certain to deprive him of £40,000. If his counsel had been sharp-sighted, he might have availed himself of a more successful line of defence. At that period, if the slightest inaccuracy in names or descriptions occurred in an indictment, the charge against a prisoner was vitiated, and he was entitled to be discharged. Now the chief prisoner was indicted under the name of Samuel Goodere, "Esquire," though he had unquestionably succeeded to the baronetcy on the death of his brother, whilst the latter was styled John Dineley Goodere, though he had for some years dropped the latter surname, and is said to have obtained the royal license to do so. The prisoners having been convicted, Goodere insisted upon walking through the streets to Newgate, arrayed in the red cloak then generally worn by the upper classes. Still professing innocence, he forwarded a petition to the Crown, as did his wife and daughter. Finding this step hopeless, according to an early edition of the Newgate Calendar "he got some person to hire a great number of colliers to rescue him while going to the place of execution; but some notice of his design having transpired, the sheriff raised all the people in the city that were able, in order to frustrate any attempt of that nature." The authorities certainly feared an attack on Newgate, for a new door, plated with iron, was set up, and watched by a guard. At last Goodere fully admitted his guilt in the written "confession" quoted above. Mahony and White made a joint confession, alleging that they were made almost insensible with liquor before they consented to commit the deed. The three murderers, accompanied by a wretched woman convicted of killing her child, were executed on the 15th April. The body of Mahony was gibbeted on Dunball Island, near the scene of the murder. Goodere's body was removed to the Infirmary, where, in the presence of as many spectators as could crush into the hall, a surgeon stuck a scalpel into the breast. In this state it was exposed to the popular gaze until the evening, and then despatched to Herefordshire and buried in the family vault. It was reported at the time that both the brothers had been subject to fits of insanity. One of the murderer's sons, who succeeded to the baronetcy, died in a lunatic asylum.

Some additional curious facts, hitherto unpublished, respecting the Dineley family, have been kindly furnished by Mr. William George, from his extensive collection of local manuscripts. The most amusing is a letter from Lady Dineley, the widow of the murdered man, to a cousin, Miss Bubb, written a few days after the tragedy. This missive, indicating the education acquired by the heiress of a wealthy Bristol alderman, is as follows :—

> Dr Cosen: Whatt your hard in the new [news] of poor Sr Jon is to trow and itt have all mostt ben my Dath for I am frit outt of my wits. So horrid a murder I never hard of, I can nott till you how but refure you to the newpaper which is very il ritt. I have a greatt deall to say butt my Hartt is to full Dr Mis bubb I mustt still be troblesume to you. to by me moung [mourning] I wood have itt in the very pink of ye mode & very sollom a weed of Silk as is made on this a Kaons [occasions?] & everthing as be Long to a Wedw butt no Shou or Stokin thett I can have here I have sentt my says [size] butt lett itt be to big and Long thatt [it] may be alltud [alter:d.] I have a blak nightt goond & Dr Cosn pray lett it be sentt the beginn of nextt weeke for Mr Smith and I am abligd to be in wostershere the Latta Inn [latter end] of the week in greatt bisness I live itt to you, if I could a till how to sentt ye money up wood butt belive if you go to Mr Howard he will lett yu have money. or yu lett me know how to remitt itt to you.

On the back of the leaf containing the above, in the same hand, is the following note, addressed to "Mr. Howard, Inner Temple":—

> Sr, I bag you will lett Miss bubb have wit money she sholl whantt to by me some things, and will pay you itt as soon as I see you which I hope will be in may nixtt after I have dun with ye egstt [executors] I hope yu had my letter in hastt Sr your humbll Sertt M Dineley.

Miss Bubb's acknowledgment of the receipt of £15 follows. Lady Dineley, whose "hartt was to full," but who required a mourning dress in the pink of the fashion, does not improve on further acquaintance. In May, 1732, the *Gentleman's Magazine* recorded that "Dingley Goodere, Esq., son of Sir Edward Goodere, Bart., recovered of Sir Robert Jason, Bart., in the Court of Common Pleas, £1000 for *crim. con.* with his wife." A subsequent suit for a divorce was not prosecuted, probably from the pecuniary embarrassments of the husband. Sir Edward, the father of the two brothers, survived until March, 1739. At that time Sir John had an only son, Edward Dineley, who had reached manhood, but was evidently another sufferer from the mental weakness of the family. Owing to his dissipated habits as a boy, his father apprenticed him to a saddler, and he appears to have been afterwards wholly discarded. According to an affidavit of an attorney's clerk, dated the 22nd January, 1740, in Mr. George's possession, this Edward, in the previous month, was lodging at a low alehouse in Southwark, when he expressed his willingness to serve his father, and spite his uncle, "who had used him very ill," by destroying the entail of the family estate. By order of Sir John, the young man, who was in the last stage of illness, was removed to the house of an attorney in Fetter Lane, where, in consideration of being promised £200 a year, he executed, only two days before his death, the necessary deed for effecting what was called a "common recovery" of the property. Captain Goodere attempted to defeat the proceeding, and alleged in court that Edward Dineley was dead when the deed was executed, and that the signature was the forgery of Sir John, who had put a pen in the hand of the corpse. This charge, which was disproved by the witnesses and rejected by the judges, increased the exasperation of the baronet, who was himself so ill as to apprehend death, and he made a will before the end of the same month, leaving his Worcestershire estates to his sister's son, John Foote, and his Gloucestershire property to another nephew, the afterwards celebrated Samuel Foote. The testator appears to have forgotten the existence of his wife, who was entitled to enjoy the latter estates (her father's) for life, and had also a jointure on the former. Shortly after the murder, however, she asserted herself in a remarkable manner, by producing a boy, aged about eleven years, to whom she alleged she gave birth about two months before flying from her husband's house owing to his ill usage. In the case drawn up under her directions for the opinion of counsel, it was stated that all the witnesses of the birth were dead, that the boy's existence had been concealed from his father, and that the proof of his rights would mainly rest on the mother's testimony. Her legal adviser—the Mr. Howard already referred to—endorsed the document as follows:— " This was the fictitious case Lady Dineley made me draw and take opinion on when she wanted to set up and pretend she had a son by Sir John then living, and which was all false." The adventurous lady afterwards married one William Rayner, a printer, in London, who disposed of her rights to the Tockington and Worcestershire properties. She died in 1757, at Stapleton.

A successful battle against heavy odds was fought by a Bristol privateer on the 8th February, 1741. The Princess Augusta, a vessel of 14 guns and 25 men, commanded by Captain Gwynn, was attacked to the West of Scilly by a Spanish privateer with 24 guns and 78 men. The Bristol ship delivered the first broadside, which was of so effective a character that the enemy's vessel blew up, and all her crew, save five men, were drowned. A still more adventurous affair was soon afterwards announced. The Boyd privateer, Captain Colt, with 60 men, had made prize of two Spanish merchantmen in West Indian waters, when one of the enemy's men of war hove in sight. Desirous of securing the prizes, Colt drafted into them 48 of his crew, with orders to make all sail for Jamaica, while he remained to fight the Spaniard. After a long engagement, the Boyd was, of course, captured, and the captain and crew were sent prisoners to Carthagena. On the night after being landed they broke out of prison, seized a yawl in the harbour, and escaped, subsequently plundering houses on the coast for provisions. On arriving safely at Jamaica they rejoined their comrades, with the prizes. Jamaica was raised to a state of great prosperity by the war, which largely increased the prices of colonial produce. In a letter from a planter to a Bristol merchant, published in the *London Journal* of July 21st, 1741, the writer asserts that he has longed for many years to return to England, and " especially Bristol, the place of my birth;" but that he would have been condemned to perpetual exile or to beggary but for " the happy change in public circumstances. 'Twas ' poor Jamaica,' before the war broke out, but 'tis now rich Jamaica I assure you." He is selling his three plantations on his own terms, and hopes to embark with others in an early ship. " We have some of us got enough, thank God."

A dissolution of Parliament took place in 1741, but led to no change in the representation of the city, Sir Abraham

Elton and Mr. Edward Southwell being reelected without opposition.

The growth of trade and population at this period encouraged the citizens to appeal to the Ministry for an improvement in the postal communication with London, which was still limited to three days per week. Yielding to the pressure, the post office authorities established three additional mails in June, 1741, so that letters might pass to and fro every working day.

During the discussion on the Mutiny Bill in the House of Commons this year, the Ministry stated that to allay many complaints respecting the relations betwixt innkeepers and marching regiments, they proposed to allow fourpence for each man billeted, in return for which the victualler would provide bedding, candle, fire, cooking utensils, and three quarts of cider or small beer. Some West of England members protested against the quantity of cider allowed, declaring that the excess would lead to drunkenness; but it was retorted that the average quantity of liquor daily consumed by gentlemen's servants was at least three quarts. Eventually the allowance to the troops was reduced to five pints. It was estimated that this quantity of light beer would cost the innkeeper $1\frac{1}{4}d$. The working class consumption of beer was still prodigious. In December, 1742, the Bristol magistrates increased the number of alehouses in the city to 384, exclusive of 28 inns and many vintners' shops, being nearly double the number granted in 1700. Yet 30 more alehouse licenses were granted in 1744, and the number was raised to 500 in 1747, and to 625 in 1754, although the entire city, at the latter date, did not contain more than about 6,250 houses.

A four sheet plan of the city, from a survey made in 1741 by John Rocque, was published soon afterwards by Benjamin Hickey, an enterprising Bristol bookseller. The Council, in 1744, voted Hickey £20 for the "great pains, trouble, and expense" he had bestowed on the production. The price of this finely engraved plan was only half a guinea. Chatterton incidentally states in one of his poems that Hickey was ruined by this adventure.

An extraordinary but well authenticated story, illustrative of the state of the marriage laws, was published in the *Bristol Oracle* of January 8th, 1742. One Edgar, a stuff maker, of Bristol, left about £3,000 to the only daughter of his son Thomas, to be paid when she married or came of age. Thomas having died, and his widow having promptly married a second husband, named Allen, the trustees under the will sent the child to a boarding school; but the mother, having determined on making money out of her daughter, succeeded in abducting her by stratagem, and refused to give her up. Mrs. Allen next opened negotiations with a clerk, nineteen years old, offering to sell the child in marriage for the sum of £500. The terms being agreed upon, the parties requested an attorney to draw up the necessary deed, but the lawyer warned the mother that the youth's proposed bond would be valueless, as he was under age. Mrs. Allen thereupon dismissed the clerk, and made a fresh bargain of a similar character with a sheriff's officer named Taylor, who secretly conveyed the child (under thirteen years of age) to Bath, and there clandestinely married her.

The prediction of Walpole, on the declaration of the Spanish war, that bell-ringing would soon give place to hand wringing, was only too soon realised. The conflict proved very calamitous to the English mercantile marine. Spanish privateers hovered near every port, and Bristol was an especial sufferer from their raids. In January, 1742, a petition of the Merchants' Society was presented to the House of Commons, representing that trade was becoming daily more precarious owing to the ravages of the enemy's cruisers, and praying that adequate provision might be made for the protection of commerce. It was found impossible, however, to prevent disasters, which were far from being counterbalanced by the occasional captures of Spanish vessels. The local clothing trade suffered a check, from which it never recovered, and there was a marked increase of pauperism. A loan of £1,000, free of interest for three years, was made by the Common Council to the guardians. It was stated in May, 1742, that the poor rate in Frome had been raised to 12s. in the pound, and that although 1,000 weavers there had been driven by starvation to enter the army, yet that many of the remaining workmen were destitute of the necessaries of life.

An odd occasion for rejoicing notwithstanding presented itself. From the beginning of the reign, George II. and his eldest son, the Prince of Wales, had lived on exceedingly bad terms, and the heir to the throne, through hatred of his father, eventually made his little court the focus of opposition against the Ministers of the Crown, even Jacobites receiving a cordial welcome. The quarrel having threatened such grave results as to cause disquiet throughout the country, the patching up of a reconciliation assumed the aspect of a great political event. Its announcement in Bristol on the 19th February, says a London journal, "occasioned a general joy on all faces. The churches of Temple and St. Stephen were adorned with colours, and large bonfires were made in each parish. The mayor, aldermen, common council, clergy, and gentlemen met in the evening at the Council House, and unanimously expressed their great satisfaction at this happy event."

It is probable that the above incident was intended to be commemorated by the name of "Unity" given to the street leading from College Green to Orchard Street, which the Corporation laid open at this date.

At a meeting of the Council on the 1st March, an account sent in by Abel Dagg, the keeper of Newgate, was refused payment, on the ground that the charges were "unprecedented." It is impossible to identify the items objected to. About two-thirds of the claim were for "allowance of 2*d.* a day for felons under sentence of transportation," who were required to find food for themselves out of this pittance. The other items were "three quarters rent of the New Water," £1 10*s.*, showing that the Corporation patronised the Water Company to this meagre extent, and three coffins for White, Mahony, and Williams (executed with Captain Goodere), 15*s.*

At the same meeting a committee was appointed to consider how the by-law imposing fines on members for nonattendance could be more stringently enforced, many defaulters having omitted to pay. The committee was also to consider the case of "such members of the House as reside altogether out of the city, and neglect their duty and attendance." Some notable instances of irregularities of this kind occur in the minute books. A gentleman named Noblet Ruddock, having become bankrupt and taken up his residence in the West Indies, was "dismissed" from the Corporation in 1734, when he had been absent seven years. In several other cases absenteeism was condoned, however long might be its duration, and insolvent councillors were not uncommon.

A man named William Curtis was hanged on the 8th April for having returned to England before his term of transportation had expired. The case was somewhat peculiar. In 1739 Curtis had acted as hangman at an execution in Bristol. A few months later he was sentenced to death at Gloucester for robbing a Scotch pedlar, but was transported for fourteen years. In October, 1741, the Scotchman was an insolvent debtor in Newgate prison, and Curtis, having returned to Bristol from America, and seeing his former victim at the debtors' gate, loaded him with insults. Having returned to Newgate day after day to continue his abuse, Curtis was at length denounced by the pedlar, on whose information he was arrested, and in due course brought to the scaffold.

Mr. Richard Bayley, then serving the office of mayor, died on the 17th May, 1742, when, according to precedent, the aldermen temporarily undertook "the government of the city." On the 26th the Council elected John Bartlett as chief magistrate for the remainder of the municipal year. The elaborate ceremony of installation on such occasions has been already described.

An event probably more painful to the civic body than the death of a member was announced in the same month. Alderman Henry Nash (mayor, 1727) forwarded his resignation, accompanied by a petition for relief, having "through a series of misfortunes" been reduced to beggary. An annuity of £50 was voted. Mr. Nash was unable to bear his misfortunes with dignity. In 1744 the Council found that he was making "an ill use of its benevolence," and he was warned that further misconduct would cause the stoppage of his pension. Debasement of this character is, however, rarely curable, and the annuity was actually suspended for three years, when it was formally revoked, and a payment of £3 a month substituted. The unhappy man lived on for several years.

Some matters connected with the Exchange came before the Council during the summer of 1742. The most interesting incident was a discovery, in excavating the site, of 174 ounces of silver plate, including a salver, six cups, a beaker, two tankards, four salts, twenty-three spoons, and an earthen flask with a silver top and cover. The civic cash-book contains the following entry:—"Received of John Vaughan, silversmith, for several pieces of old silver plate that was found in digging the foundation of the Exchange, £49 2s. 9d." On the other side of the account is a payment of £1 17s. 3d. made to Vaughan for "what he lost in purchasing" the plate in question. The relics seem to have been committed to the melting-pot. The Rev. Josiah Tucker, incumbent of All Saints, petitioned the Chamber for relief, stating that one-fourth of the annual collection from the parish towards his support had been lost by the removal of inhabitants whose dwellings had been destroyed to clear the site. His appeal was laid on the table. In another case the corporators met with their match. They wished to purchase and demolish the hall of the Hoopers' (Coopers') Company, in order to widen the passage on the western side of the Exchange. Mr. Wood describes it as a "shattered old building," but after some negotiation the Chamber offered £1,400 for it, and £100 more for the company's interest in a house in Corn Street. The Hoopers, however, refused to part with their hall unless they were granted four houses in King Street, together with £900 in cash; and the Council was forced to submit to the terms. The new Coopers' Hall appears to have been forthwith erected, as its architect, William Halfpenny, published a view of the building in 1744.

Salt refining was a considerable local industry at this date. The *Gloucester Journal* announced in June that one John Purnell had opened a warehouse in St. Peter's Street, Bristol, for the sale of salt, "refined from the rock, being the same sorts as are made in the city."

A vacancy having occurred in the band of civic musicians, the mayor and aldermen, on the 8th July, elected David Hughes, and ordered "that he enter into the usual bond for the re-delivery of the silver chain and badge usually worn by the said waitplayers, and pay £10 to the widow" of his predecessor. The badges continued in use until the great municipal "revolution" in 1835. Mr. T. D. Taylor kindly informs me:—"The waits after making night hideous, the week before Christmas, with their 'sackbut, dulcimer,' &c., used to come round on boxing day to receive gratuities, and the badge was shown as a guarantee that they were the genuine tormentors. I remember, when I was a tiny youngster, being deputed to tip them, and I was then shown the badge, and had it in my hand." The chains, of ancient workmanship, are preserved at the Council House.

Owing to the death of Sir Abraham Elton, Bart., an election of a member for the city took place in November, 1742. Only one candidate came forward—Mr. Robert Hoblyn, a Cornish gentleman of literary tastes, who had in 1741 married the heiress of Mr. Thomas Coster, of College Green, M.P., deceased, "an agreeable lady," says the marriage announcement, "of fine accomplishments, and reputed a fortune of £40,000!" The new member being a Tory, the Whigs lost their share in the representation.

Numerous references to coffee-houses occur about this time, and the opportunity may be taken to note the most prominent of those institutions. A manuscript note by Mr. Tyson (Jefferies Collection) states that the earliest was the Elephant coffee-house near the Merchants' Tolzey, adjoining All Saints Church, which house, says our authority, was in existence in 1677. But according to a book in the Council House, four men were presented by the jury of All Saints and St. Nicholas for selling "coffey" and ale without a license in 1666, from which it may be inferred that the establishment of coffee-houses in London, about 1657, had soon given birth to similar licensed places of entertainment in Bristol. They soon became so numerous as to excite the suspicion of the arbitrary faction then predominant, and in 1681 the grand jury, alleging that they were frequented on Sundays by seditious sectaries and disloyal persons, recommended that no newsletter or pamphlet should be suffered to be read in them unless it had first received the approval of the mayor or the aldermen of the wards in which the houses were situated! Even so late as 1712 the author of "Bristol Delineated" has been seen denouncing the "pernicious scribblers" whose writings were read by those who indulged in "Turkish Lap." By a will dated in 1713, a lady disposed of her interest in "a corner messuage in the Tolzey in All Saints parish, occupied by John Cooke as a coffee-house;" and in 1718 the feoffees of All Saints granted to Cooke, "the great roomth called the old vestry, lying over the northward isle of the church," reserving a right of passage "up and down the stairs coming through a messuage called Cooke's Coffee House." This house, probably the most popular in the city, was in 1723 known as the London Coffee-house. It was closed about 1769, when the American Coffee-house was established. The Elephant, mentioned by Tyson, was in All Saints Lane. In 1730 there was a coffee-house in College Green—probably identical with that sometimes called "Will's" in advertisements. In 1740 mention occurs of Little John's Coffee-house in Temple Street. In June, 1742, soon after the *Oracle* was started by Andrew Hooke, his wife set up St. Michael's Coffee-house in Maudlin Street, where Hooke, after being liberated from a debtors' prison, used to enliven the dulness of his editorial labours by teaching geography and the use of the globes three days a week. Encouraged by the patronage afforded him, Hooke soon afterwards rented the Barber Surgeons' Hall, near the

Exchange, which was first called Hooke's, and subsequently the West Indian Coffee-house. The Hot Well Coffee-house, adjoining the spring, and the Castle Coffee-house in Castle Street are also mentioned in the journals of 1743. The Exchange Coffee-house was opened in that year. The Custom House Coffee-house, in Queen Square, occurs in 1744, the African Coffee-house, in Prince's Street, in 1749, the Marine Coffee-house, in Queen Square, in 1750, the Gibb Coffee-house, in Prince's Street, in 1751, and the Green Coffee-house, in Denmark Street, in 1755. In 1760 the *Bristol Chronicle* incidentally mentions, in addition to several of the above, the coffee-houses known as Foster's, the New Assembly Room's, and St. Augustine's. The Somerset on Redcliff Hill, the London and Bath in All Saints' Lane, and the house at Rennison's Baths are mentioned in or before 1767. The American Coffee-house stood in 1770 between the White Lion and the White Hart hotels in Broad Street, but was afterwards united with the former, and had its name altered to "British" about 1785; it remained a part of the premises until they were destroyed in 1865. About 1789 Jack's Coffee-house, opposite the Exchange, kept by John Weeks, of the adjoining Bush hotel, began to be much used as a sale room, as the Exchange Coffee-house had been from an early date. Before the close of the century the practice of drinking coffee in public places had gone out of fashion, and as it had become customary for hotel keepers to reserve an apartment for newspaper readers under the name of "coffee room"— a misnomer still retained—the coffee-houses proper fell out of favour and gradually disappeared. Only four survived in 1798.

Admiral Vernon, one of the popular idols of the day, landed at Bristol on the 6th of January, 1743, after one of his West India cruises. He was greeted with great acclamations in proceeding to Small Street to partake of the hospitality of the mayor, Sir Abraham Elton. A week later, thirty chests of silver bullion, containing about 900,000 pieces-of-eight, "a large portion being the glorious trophies of the admiral's conquests," were taken out of his ship and despatched to London. By dint of much exertion, the journey was completed in five days.

One of the earliest Bristol boarding schools for young ladies was announced by the local *Journal* of March 31st, 1743, as having been just opened in College Green by Mrs. Becher, widow of a clergyman. The best boarding school for boys was then kept in Small Street by Mr. John Jones. The school premises are described in an advertisement of September, 1742, as "over the Post House." (The site of the little Post-office in All Saints Court had been required for the Exchange.) Mr. Jones, who began teaching here in 1713, published a work entitled "A Step towards an English Education," from which it appears that he had shocked contemporary prejudices by teaching his pupils geography. In defence of this innovation he produced a laudatory testimonial from "the celebrated Whiston." At a later date his school was located in Maryleport Street. In 1730 Thomas Jones, a brother of John, had a boarding school in Wine Street, to which he annexed an "Intelligence Office for Apprentices"—and doubtless also for servants—the first established in the city. A few years later Thomas is found to have betaken himself and his boarders to the salubrious Pithay, but he removed in 1747 to Nicholas Street, and in 1752 to Castle Green, which, he says in an announcement, "is reckoned one of the airiest parts of the city." In April, 1747, Mr. James Stewart, writing master (the author of the MS. annals so often quoted), advertised that he should continue to carry on the boarding school established in Christmas Street by his late father. Stewart was a skilful draughtsman, and made sketches of every ancient edifice in the city, one of which—a view of Redcliff Church—was engraved, and a few others are in the Bodleian Library. He subsequently removed his school to Maudlin Street, where he died in March, 1759. A boarding school that attained great repute was that of the Rev. William Foot, a classical scholar, who opened his first seminary in Redcross Street in 1748, but soon removed to a large mansion on St. Michael's Hill, the site of which occupied the whole of the ground now covered by St. Michael's Terrace. In 1758 there were two schools in Tower Lane, and others in Bell Lane, Christmas Street, and Milk Street. The charge for boarding was extremely moderate. A Yorkshire schoolmaster announced in the *Bristol Journal* for June 9th, 1759, that boys of between six and ten years were "comfortably boarded, decently clothed, and carefully educated" in his establishment at £10 per head per annum. The Rev. James Rouquet, a Bristol clergyman, opened a high-class boarding school at Kingswood in 1752, at which the charge was £14 a year. It appears from the Gore Papers in the Jefferies Collection that Nathaniel Ainsworth, a famous teacher, who removed his boarding school from Yatton to Long Ashton in

1755, demanded only 30s. a year for teaching gentlemen's sons who were out-door pupils. Coming down a little later, one Nathaniel Cope, in 1771, opened a boarding school for young gentlemen in Cathay, "a very delectable and healthy situation;" and allowed them the use of his extensive library "at so small a gratuity as half a crown per quarter." A more popular school was that of John Jones, who occupied Cotham House in 1771, but removed two years later to the Royal Fort. His pupils were boarded "in the most genteel manner" for £16 yearly, but extra fees were charged for any instruction exceeding "the three R's." Jones was succeeded in this school by the Rev. Samuel Seyer, the historian. It may be noticed that in 1771 the Christmas holiday generally concluded with the first week in January.

The Common Council received a memorial in May, 1743, from Martha Creswick, daughter of Joseph Creswick (mayor, 1679), by Martha, daughter of Sir John Knight (mayor, 1663), setting forth her extreme distress through misfortunes. A pension of £20 a year was granted to the aged petitioner. The Creswick family, one of the wealthiest in the city during the previous century, was at this time declining, chiefly owing to its inveterate fondness for litigation. Within living memory, the lineal representative of Sir Henry Creswick, of Bristol and Hanham, is said to have worked as a common labourer on the lands owned by his ancestors.

For some inscrutable reason, the feast of the Ascension, or Holy Thursday, was selected all over England during the Middle Ages as the fittest day for the perambulation of manorial and parochial boundaries, and the custom, which still survives, was in full vigour in Bristol at the period now under review. From the following items extracted from the accounts of St. Nicholas's parish for 1743, it would appear that disputes as to boundaries between adjoining districts sometimes brought about personal collisions, but that they were on this occasion avoided by a modest outlay for liquor :—" Wine, when it was agreed between the gentlemen of All Saints parish to perambulate peaceably, 3s. 8d. Paid for a barrell of ale (36 gallons) £1 4s. Thomas Neast for dinner &c. £6 7s. 6d. Paid for a quarter of mutton for the almswomen, 4s. 4½d. One hundred and a quarter of twigs 3s. 9d. Paid ringers 12s." (The twigs were applied during the proceedings upon the tender parts of boys and meek-minded spectators, to impress their memories with the precise limits of the vestry's jurisdiction.) At a later period the authorities increased the jollification of the day, £17 13s. being spent in 1759; but this brought about a reaction, and a resolution was passed that the outlay should not in future exceed £8. The vestry of St. Stephen's, the adjoining parish, being less richly endowed, confined its expenses on such occasions to £3 or £4. It appears, however, that it engaged the parish mason to attend the perambulations " to move any [boundary] stones that shall be false arreckted " (Minutes, 1727).

An interesting, but unfortunately obscure, entry occurs in the minutes of a Common Council meeting held in June, 1743. A letter, it appears, was read from Mr. William Champion [see page 67], stating that some years previously he had acquired possession of Baber's Tower (standing near St. Philip's Church) and had erected large " fire works " on the premises at a great expense. Finding that the works had become a nuisance to the neighbourhood, he had destroyed them, and now undertook to make improvements on the property if he were granted a renewal of the lease. His request was acceded to, provided that he " erased certain air furnaces" and built a dwelling house. A steam engine being then called a fire engine, a conjecture is permissible that the " fire works " included the first labour-saving machine erected in Bristol. Champion removed his works to Warmley, taking with him, according to Ellacombe's History of Bitton, the Baber's Tower referred to above, which eventually was called Babel's Tower, and gave birth to idle legends. In the *Bristol Journal* of September 30th, 1749, is an account of a " fire engine " just constructed near Birmingham, for William Champion and Co.'s brass works at Warmley. " The machine is the most noblest of the kind in the world; it discharges upwards of 3000 hhds. of water in an hour. The water is buoyed up by the several tubes in a hemispher of a conical form, and falls into a pool as a cascade, and affords a grand and beautiful scene." The water raised by the engine was used to turn a large waterwheel, by which rotary power was obtained for driving the machinery of the factory.

The Hot Well was at this period in great repute among people of fashion. The *Oracle* of June 11th, 1743, states that on the previous Wednesday the Earl of Jersey gave a breakfast at the Long Room to 150 persons of high life, and that the Hon. Mr. Ponsonby offered a similar entertainment two days later. Public breakfasts, followed by a dance, were given once or twice weekly during the season at the Long

Room, and there were also evening balls. To provide additional accommodation, a number of extensive lodging-houses were built in Dowry Square about 1746. Further amusements being demanded, a piece of ground near the Long Room was opened for evening dances, under the name of the New Vauxhall Gardens, the place being gaily illuminated. This met with so much approval that the proprietor, in July, 1751, announced that public breakfasts, with music, would be given twice a week. "Admission 2s. each, including breakfast. The evening entertainments as usual." In 1757 four concerts weekly were given in these Gardens; "admission one shilling." Some facilities were also offered for reading and conversation. The *Bath Journal* of January 7th, 1754, contains an announcement by a fan maker that he has opened a shop at Bath for ladies to read the newspapers, "as at the Ladies' Tea Room at the Hotwells, at half a crown the season." One Robert Goadsby, a bookseller, had, in 1743, a shop at the Hotwells and another at Bath, which were alternately opened for the respective seasons. Later on, a firm of London lace dealers brought down their wares to tempt the fashionable throng in Dowry Square. "Lappet heads from 6 gs. a pair, to 100. Ruffles for gentlemen from 2 to 16 guineas." The great charm of Hot Well life seems to have been its cheapness and simplicity. A Mr. Owen, who published "Observations on the Earths, &c., for some miles about Bristol," in 1754, states that riding on Durdham Down was very popular, and that "the best lady attending the Hot Well will not refuse riding behind a man, for such is the custom of the country. Numbers of what they call double horses are kept for that purpose." Many gentlemen repaired to the well on horseback, and paid a penny for the accommodation of their nags in a stable near to the spring. Several small private baths were then open for the use of the visitors. "No price," adds Mr. Owen, "is paid for the water: all the expense is that every one when he goes away makes a present to the master, and a trifle to be divided amongst the servants." It is somewhat remarkable that the popularity of Clifton in fashionable circles deterred rather than encouraged the migration of Bristolians. Amongst Mr. Seyer's MSS. (Jefferies Collection) is a note stating that "About 1750, out of about twenty houses of which Clifton [on the hill] then consisted, eleven were to be let or sold at one time." Even about 1780, according to the reminiscences of Mr. Richard Smith, the eminent surgeon, the upper class dwellings scarcely exceeded thirty.

Desertions were at this time very common in the army. Probably to strike terror in the ranks, a youth named John Partington, nineteen years of age, was shot on Clifton Down on the 11th July, 1743, for this offence. The firing party on the occasion was entirely composed of men who had been deserters.

The mind of the Corporation was much exercised about this time by the attempt of two obscure persons to establish a ferry between Temple Back and the opposite bank of the Avon, in rivalry with the ancient ferry there, known as Bathavon, from which the civic body derived the large yearly rental of £137. The intruders persisting in their enterprise, an action at law was raised against them, which was brought to trial at Salisbury in July, 1743. An imposing procession of corporate functionaries, in four coaches, guarded by seven horses, some of which bore two men, set off for the capital of Wiltshire. The party, twenty-one in number, accomplished a journey of about fifty-five miles in two days, making many halts for refreshment. Having proved the corporate rights, and obtained a verdict against the interlopers, the civic agents returned in triumph, but in the same deliberate fashion that had marked their outset, and doubtless congratulated themselves that only one of the coaches broke down during the journey. The travelling expenses incurred, including a guinea to a Salisbury barber for shaving and powdering, amounted to about £80. The coach hire was 25s. a day for each vehicle, and 2s. a day (the customary charge of the time) was paid for the hire of each horse.

The harvest of 1743 was one of the finest ever known in the district. In a letter of Mr. George Knight, of Cannington, to Mr. Gore, of Bourton (Jefferies Collection), it is stated that wheat was selling in September for 2s. 6d. and barley for 1s. 6d. per bushel in his local market, and that most people thought it would be cheaper. The effects on local enterprise will be noticed presently. The writer also mentions a fact in connection with his family which, though not bearing on Bristol history, is amusingly illustrative of the time:—" My cousin Steare have a living about eight miles from here, called Lympson (otherwise Kill Priest), worth £120 or £140 a yeare, given to him by the late Ld. Pawlett for voting for a Mare at Bridgwater." (The parliamentary elections in that borough, one of the most corrupt in England, were powerfully influenced by the corporation.)

The completion of the Exchange—delayed until nearly all

the original promoters of the building had found a more durable shelter from temporal discomforts—was at length accomplished in the autumn of 1743, and the structure was opened with great civic pomp on the 21st September. A grand procession was formed at the Guildhall, in which a new functionary, styled the Exchange Keeper, "in a very handsome dress with a noble Staff in his hand," made a conspicuous figure. (The "silver head and ferrel" of the noble instrument had cost £9 15s.) Then came the city officers, the mayor and the mayor elect, followed by the rest of the Corporation, the members of the Society of Merchants, and forty-eight private carriages. The pageant, which was three-quarters of a mile in length, made its way by High Street and the Back to Queen Square and the Quays, where it was cheered by the sight of what Mr. Wood, the architect, terms "a glorious object"—the Princess Augusta privateer (some of whose exploits have been already recorded), then undergoing repair after four victorious engagements with the Spaniards. After a couple of hours' perambulation, the procession reached the Exchange, where speeches were made extolling the munificent public spirit of the Corporation, and the Exchange was then formally opened amidst the salutes of cannon and popular acclamations. As the gunpowder burnt on the occasion cost £20 18s. 6d. there can have been no lack of uproar, but the "scramble for money," liberally strewn about by many gentlemen at the conclusion of the ceremony, was much more attractive to the assembled multitude. To commemorate the day, the poor debtors in Newgate were liberated by a corporate subscription, the leading trade companies and the citizens generally were regaled with wine, the inmates of the almshouses were not forgotten, and the mayor gave a mighty banquet to his civic colleagues and the Merchants' Society. Mr. Wood, from whose elaborate report these leading incidents have been culled, concludes by observing that if further "pageantry had been thought necessary the public had certainly been gratified with it: But what pageantry could illustrate a sober procession of the magistrates and whole collective trading body of a city that pays the Government a Custom for their goods of above £150,000 a year?" The building involved an outlay of nearly £50,000. In view of alterations made in it in our own time, it should be stated that Wood's original design contemplated a large "Egyptian Hall" in the centre of the Exchange, capable of receiving 600 persons; but some influential citizens disapproved of the novelty of a covered building for mercantile gatherings, and the hall was consequently "turned into a peristyle, with very wide inter-columniations," and made capable of holding 1,440 persons. Hotels then being the favourite resort of merchants and traders (there were more than twenty clustered around the Royal Exchange in London), the front of the Bristol structure was fitted up for two such places of accommodation, respectively styled the Exchange Tavern and the Exchange Coffee House.

On the night of the 27th October, 1743, a murder which created great local excitement was committed near Redland Court, on the road leading from Stoke's Croft to Durdham Down. A farmer, named Winter, of Charlton, had gone to Bristol market that morning with some cattle, and two men, named Andrew Burnet and Henry Payne, who had been comrades in a cavalry regiment, anticipating that he would return with the price of the animals in his pocket, resolved on his murder and robbery. Through some circumstance, the farmer remained in the city for the night, but Richard Ruddle, coachman to Sir Robert Cann, Bart., of Stoke Bishop, who also had been in Bristol, was mistaken for Winter by the two ruffians, who attacked him with such brutality that he died shortly afterwards. The only fruits of the crime were a watch and a few trifling articles. Some time elapsed before a clue to the murderers could be obtained. At length one day a man entered the shop of a watchmaker in Castle Street, produced the missing watch, and requested the tradesman (said to have been the maker of the article) to repair it. Being questioned, he stated that he had just bought it from two men in a public-house; and whilst he was being taken by a constable to the tavern in question, he recognised Burnet and Payne in Stoke's Croft, and assisted in their arrest. The murderers were tried at the ensuing county assizes, and sentenced to be hanged and gibbeted on Durdham Down. As an additional punishment, it is presumed, they were first taken to Cirencester, to witness the execution of another murderer, condemned at the same assizes. On the 22nd March, 1744, they were conveyed through the city to the place where the crime was committed, and their sentence was afterwards carried out, says the *Oracle*, "in the presence of the most numerous assembly of people of all ranks that ever were seen together on such an occasion." They were hung in chains at what is now called the Sea Walls, so that their bodies might be seen from passing vessels. In the following April, the two bodies were removed by (it was supposed) a party of Irishmen, but were found amongst the rocks, and replaced.

The *Gloucester Journal* of November 8th, 1743, contains a lengthy account, by a Bristol correspondent, of what he clearly believed to be an abominable case of witchcraft. A poor cobbler living in Horse (Host) Street, he says, had imprudently called a woman in the neighbourhood "an old witch," whereupon she sent a cat to his house, which seized his finger while he was attempting to drive it out, and would not loosen its hold until it was squeezed to death. The man was dipped nine times in salt water at Sea Mills, but the counter-charm was not successful, and he died in great agony.

A brief extract from the minutes of Temple vestry, dated the 30th December, evidently refers to some recent proceeding of the incumbent. The clerk is requested to inform the reverend gentleman that, "as we allow him £4 a year for the use of the churchyard, he shall have no right or leave to feed horses, sheep, or cattle of any sort in that place."

A terrible fire at Crediton, Devon, which destroyed a great part of the town, occurred at this time, and excited much sympathy in Bristol for the unfortunate sufferers. A public subscription, started for their relief, produced the large sum of £887 13s. 7d.

War was proclaimed against France in April, 1744, with the usual ceremonies. The copious harvest of the preceding year had partially revived the clothing trade as well as other industries of the city, and vigorous measures were taken to repulse the expected attacks of "our national enemies." The Corporation forwarded a petition to the King, praying for the protection of the African slave trade, described in the memorial as the most valuable branch of local commerce, and appealing for an additional naval force to safeguard local ships from the insults of foreign privateers, which swarmed in and near the Bristol Channel. The mercantile interest, having lost many vessels, thought it advisable to take active steps for self-defence, and started a subscription for fitting out an additional fleet of armed cruisers. Ninety Bristolians at once offered £100 each. Other privateers were built or purchased by r ate co-partnerships. Amongst the finest and largest of the Bristol ships were the Southwell, of 400 tons, carrying 24 guns and 200 men; the Bristol, 550 tons, with 38 guns and a crew of 300; the Leviathan, 28 guns, 250 men; the Rover, 24 guns, 210 men; and the Townshend, 22 guns and 180 men.

Many others were quickly equipped. (Liverpool fitted out only three.) Most of the privateers that put to sea immediately after the declaration of war were very successful, and from time to time the harbour was the scene of tumultuous enthusiasm. The Southwell captured eight prizes during the first four months of her career. The Constantine made three prizes in as many weeks, the last being valued at £14,000. The Queen of Hungary took a ship with a cargo worth £20,000; the Prince Charles snapped up two French Greenlanders, with seven whales; and the King William returned again and again with valuable booty. Large sums were thus distributed amongst the privateering crews (who generally had no regular pay), and as the money was scattered as lightly as it came, scenes of dissipation were of every-day occurrence. "Nothing is to be seen here," says a Bristol paragraph in the *Gloucester Journal* of September 4th, "but rejoicings for the great number of French prizes brought in. Our sailors are in the highest spirits, full of money, and spend their whole time in carousing . . . dressed out with Laced Hats, Tassels, Swords with Sword Knots, and in short all things that can give them an opportunity to spend their money." In the meantime, many hundreds of French prisoners were thrust into Bedminster Bridewell. As the privateersmen were exempt from empressment, many adventurous landsmen enrolled themselves, and the Government were driven to strange shifts to secure men for the regular forces. All the able-bodied felons were swept out of the gaols, more than a thousand being caught up in London alone; while crimps and press gangs scoured the country, especially the fairs, and dealt ruthlessly with the lower class of labourers. A Bristol paper of April 28th states that at Witney fair a quack doctor's Merry Andrew, a then popular buffoon, was impressed from off the stage, whilst the quack himself escaped only by flight. Returning to the Bristol privateers, one or two instances of their dashing bravery deserve to be recorded. In May, 1744, the Vulture, of 14 guns and 130 men, when cruising off the Spanish coast, captured an English merchantman, which had been taken a few days before by a Spanish privateer. One of the sailors left by the captors in their prize informed the captain of the Vulture that two other large vessels belonging to Bristol had been taken by the same Spaniards, who had put both cargoes on board one of the ships—the Dursley—and had sent the latter into a little harbour near Finisterre. The Vulture forthwith sailed for that place, which was entered by a boat's crew during the night, and whilst the Spaniards were carousing in the Dursley, the vessel was attacked and captured, and finally carried into Kinsale, with many of the Spanish crew still on board. The double cargo, consisting of African and West Indian produce, was of great value. Unfortunately, the Vulture, whilst returning to Bristol, was herself captured by a French privateer of greatly superior armament, after a long and desperate struggle. The following paragraph referring to the Tryall privateer, which will be heard of again, occurs in a local journal of November 3rd. "This week the Tryall privateer sent in the Prime Minister privateer of London, of 22 ninepounders, which had been taken by five French men of war, but which the Tryall afterwards retook, in the sight of the said men of war." The Tryall had only 16 guns, and a crew of 120 men. The greatest local disaster of the year occurred in July to the privateer Somerset, of 12 guns and 96 men. The ship, which had just been fitted out, capsized off the Holmes, and only ten of the crew were saved.

Down to the year 1744, the "town dues" payable upon goods imported into Bristol were not paid into the city treasury, but were received by the sheriffs, and expended, for the most part, in a round of entertainments given by those functionaries during their year of office. As the trade of the port, and consequently the income from the dues, steadily increased, the necessity of altering this arrangement became urgent; and on the 22nd August, 1744, the Common Council resolved that the dues should thenceforth be received by the chamberlain, whilst the sheriffs should be allowed a fixed sum of £665 15s. 3d. yearly. As it was notorious that the average expenditure had greatly exceeded the proposed allowance, the Chamber further determined that the "great dinner," "the count (account?) dinner," and the supper "between election and swearing day" should be abolished. Two dinners to the judges of assize, two to the recorder, and two to the Corporation were retained. The new arrangement was distasteful to the younger members of the Council, who refused to accept the shrievalty on the new terms. Two gentlemen were induced, however, to serve a second time, and the opposition afterwards died away.

At a Council meeting in November, a document signed by the town clerk, William Cann, was read, intimating that in consequence of indisposition he had deputed his clerk, John Michel, to perform certain acts, and requesting the Chamber to appoint a permanent deputy, which was done. The town clerk, in fact, was insane, and by a strange coincidence Michel also became deranged a few months later. Mr. Cann, who was probably the first member of the civic body who took up a permanent residence at Clifton, became a baronet on the death of his elder brother in 1748. He died at his suburban residence in March, 1753.

A somewhat puzzling item appears in one of the corporate " bargain books," under the date, 6th November, 1744. It is as follows:—"Agreed between the Mayor and the Surveyors of the City Lands, and John Blackwell, of the city of Bristol, gentleman, that in consideration of paying the yearly rent and performing the covenants following He shall hold and enjoy the profits arising from the Income of Wheelage within this city according to the antient usage and custome, for one whole year, to commence the 29th September last, at and under the yearly rent of Fifteen Pounds *de claro.*" The following note is appended:—" Not to be made in a lease." The peculiarity of the matter is that no receipts from wheelage have been found recorded before the date of this agreement, and no payments appear in later years. Presumably, the object of the municipality was to revive a long obsolete toll of threepence per cart or wagon passing the city gates. But in a description of Bristol published in the *London Magazine* of May, 1749, the writer speaks of the narrowness of the thoroughfares, "through which the goods are conveyed on sledges, no carts being permitted to come into the city."

" The Red Book of Orders " was again revised by a committee of the Chamber in the closing months of 1744. On the 19th December this body recommended the omission of some obsolete regulations, and the insertion of others adopted since the revision of 1703. Their report was adopted, and a new Red Book, on vellum, was ordered to be made for the use of the mayor for the time being, with another copy, on paper, for the town clerk's office.

Through the growth of population and the increase of pauperism caused by the war, the maximum amount of poor rates granted under the Act of 1714 no longer sufficed to meet the expenditure. The guardians, who were heavily indebted to the Corporation and to their treasurer, resolved on applying to Parliament for additional powers, and besought the help of the Council. The latter body appears to have suspected improper practices on the part of the Tory majority at St. Peter's Hospital. A committee reported to the

Chamber on the 16th January, 1745, that in consequence of the constitution of the poor law board "there is too much room left for oppression and partiality, and for an undue application of the great sums yearly raised." It was therefore suggested that a clause should be introduced into the intended Bill, empowering ratepayers to make inquiries as to how the poor rates were applied, and also authorising the magistrates to hear complaints of the poor, and to order relief irrespective of the guardians. The latter opposed this inroad on their rights, which was ultimately abandoned, and an Act was soon afterwards obtained, raising the maximum yearly rate from £3,500 to £4,500, the board being permitted to levy £500 extra for four years to clear off its debts. The Common Council defrayed the cost of the statute (£167 10s.). A few years later—in 1758—the absurdity of fixing a maximum rate in a constantly increasing community being at length recognised, another Act was obtained, empowering the collection of such a sum yearly as would meet the expenditure of the guardians.

New ordinances respecting the meetings of the Common Council were made by that body on the 2nd March, 1745. Any member failing to attend was ordered to forfeit 5s.; those who did not appear at 11 o'clock in the morning, or came into the chamber without gowns, to pay 1s. The fines were to be applied to the relief of indigent vagrants. The fine of £100 on a mayor absent from the city for more than three days and three nights was retained, but the words were added, "without leave of the Common Council." By a subsequent ordinance a fine of £10 was imposed on any member divulging the nature of a debate when secrecy had been enjoined during the sitting.

On the 28th March, 1745, the new market-house erected behind the Exchange for the sale of meat and vegetables was opened for business, and gave much satisfaction, a local journalist declaring that the building "for its commodiousness and beauty exceeds all the market places in England." In December, 1746, the open markets hitherto held in Broad Street, High Street, and Wine Street were suppressed, and the building known as the New Market, situated in an alley between Broad Street and Tower Lane, was converted to other purposes. In the corporate regulations for the new building it was ordered that retailers of meat and vegetables should not resort there until after 11 o'clock in the morning, in order that housekeepers might provide themselves at first hand and at a cheap rate. It was also decreed that farmers and others should not hawk meat, bacon, butter, or cheese from door to door (but this order caused so much discontent that it was rescinded in 1750). A third regulation forbade butchers from exposing or selling meat after 8 o'clock on Saturday evenings. A penalty of 10s. was enforced against many tradesmen for disobeying this order, the Butchers' Company being active in bringing up offenders. In 1756 a man was fined 10s. for exposing poultry in the market before 8 o'clock in the morning.

That industrious chronicler of English maritime events, *Lloyd's List*, published the following news from Bristol on the 9th April, 1745:—" The Falcon privateer drove ashore the 5th inst. in Kingroad, and soon fill'd and overflowed even to the main top. She is since drove up Bristol River, where she now lyes across, so that no ship can get in or out." The Falcon was still lying a dangerous wreck on the 1st May, when the Common Council appointed a committee to secure the removal of the obstruction. The ultimate fate of the privateer is not recorded.

At a meeting of the Council in May, 1745, a committee, that had been previously appointed to inspect certain " nuisances "— apparently shoals — obstructing the course of the Avon at Hungroad, reported that it was absolutely necessary to take measures for their removal. The modesty of the provisions recommended for this purpose now seems somewhat ludicrous. " The cost of a vessel that will carry 35 tons " is estimated at £25; "a boat, with a pair of oars, second hand, £3 10s.; " . . . " If the sand &c. that shall be taken up be delivered in Kingroad then the vessel will want a mast and sail, which will cost £20." " One pair of iron tongs to take up large stones that are sunk," figure for 18s. 8d. The fitting up of the vessel, cables, etc., raised the total cost of the apparatus to £110. As to working expenses, an " engineer," engaged in London, was to receive 30s., a waterman 18s., and four labourers 12s. each weekly. The committee was empowered to carry out the improvement, which was effected without delay, for in the following July the chamberlain records the receipt of £73 7s. 10d. from the Merchants' Company, " one moiety of the expense of cleaning Hungroad." A further outlay of £155 in September, divided in the same manner, completed the work. Besides the tongs, afterwards called " skimmer tongs," which cost 26s. 6d., the charges include £10 12s. for " an engine," the real character of which it would be interesting to discover.

Allusion has been already made to the corporate jaunts into the country for the purpose of holding courts in the manors belonging to the city. It would be tedious to note the expenditure incurred on such occasions, but the items in June, 1745, when the deputy town clerk and the chamberlain visited Stockland Bristol, mention an unprecedented provision for sobriety. The officials provided themselves with a quart of rum and several gallons of wine, but their stock also included "six bottles of Hot Well water," which cost 1s. 6d. The carriage of water for festive purposes was probably afflicting to civic economists, for the item, after being reduced one half in a later year, at last disappeared. Another charge on this occasion was 5s. 10d. for "mending a male pillion," so that the excursionists must have travelled on horseback in a very sociable fashion.

Prodigious excitement was created in the city on the 8th September by the arrival of two London privateers in Kingroad, with treasure captured from two French merchantmen valued at upwards of £750,000. The two privateers, the Prince Frederick and the Duke, sailed from Cowes in June, in company with a consort named the Prince George, which soon afterwards foundered. A month later, near the American coast, they encountered three French ships, from Callao, and after a resolute fight, in which two of the French commanders were killed, the Englishmen captured two of their opponents, the other escaping by flight. The masts of the prizes being shot away, the conquerors had to tow them across the Atlantic. The cargoes consisted of 1,093 chests of silver bullion, weighing 2,644,922 oz., besides a quantity of gold and silver wrought plate, and other valuables. The treasure was conveyed to London in twenty-two wagons, each guarded by armed sailors on horseback. Its arrival in the capital and removal to the Mint caused a great sensation, and kindled a fresh passion for privateering enterprises. The shipowners raised to opulence by this lucky adventure begrudged the crews their share of the booty. Most of the men were kidnapped and sent to unhealthy countries or on board men of war, and many of their children, though entitled to large sums, were reduced to pauperism. A portion of the money to which they were entitled was paid into the Court of Chancery, where it probably now forms part of the unclaimed funds.

The landing of the "Young Pretender" in Scotland seems to have caused little excitement in the south and west of England. The defeat of Cope, at the close of September, however, gave a prodigious shock to the equanimity of the country, and the Government, in intense alarm, made appeals for assistance. On the 5th October, in compliance with a summons issued by the Earl of Berkeley, Lord Lieutenant, who had already hurried to the city, the principal merchants waited upon his lordship at the Merchants' Hall, to consider the best means of raising a body of troops for the defence of the Crown. On the 9th a general meeting was held in the Guildhall, the mayor presiding, when a letter was read from the Duke of Newcastle, expressing the satisfaction of the King at the zeal and loyalty displayed by the city, and enclosing a warrant authorising the mayor to enroll volunteer forces, and appoint officers to command them (State Papers). An "Association" was thereupon established for the support of the common cause, when the mayor (authorised by an informal meeting of the Council) subscribed £10,000 in the name of the Corporation, while £5,000 were offered by the Merchants' Society. The aldermen subscribed from £500 to £100 each, and many gentlemen and merchants from £300 to £100. The mayor, writing to the Duke on the 14th, announced that nearly £30,000 had been already promised, and that the fund was increasing daily (State Papers). The amount raised in Liverpool was only £6,000, and in Hull £1,800. An uncommon ardour, says the *Bristol Journal*, was shown by the common people in martialling themselves into companies to learn the art of war, and Lord Berkeley succeeded in forming a new regiment. In the meantime the magistrates bethought themselves of the peril arising from the vast quantity of gunpowder stored at Tower Harritz, and orders were given for the removal of the magazine to Portishead Creek. In the midst of the excitement, the Bristol privateer Tryall brought into Kingroad a Spanish prize of 12 guns, containing gold and silver coin to the value of £6,000, a quantity of muskets, bayonets, and cartridges, and 100 barrels of gunpowder. A box of papers was thrown overboard before the ship surrendered, but there was no doubt that the cargo was destined for the Pretender. On the 30th October, the King's birthday, the influential citizens were entertained at the Council House, where, says the Whig *Oracle*, "all the loyal toasts were drank under salvos of small arms, and the glass went round with an uncommon cheerfulness and gaiety; the populace being at the same time entertained by bonfires, illuminations, and liquor in great abundance." But in the following week the anniversary of the Gunpowder Plot gave the inhabitants a better opportunity of venting their enthusiasm. The effigies of the Pope and the Pretender were carried through the city amidst loud acclamations, and were finally burnt on a vast bonfire in College Green. Jacobitism, however, was by no means extinct. A tavern keeper in Broadmead was committed to Newgate for drinking the Young Pretender's health, and declaring him lawful heir to the throne. A more exciting case occurred on the 14th November, the facts of which, unknown to local chroniclers, are preserved amongst the State Papers. One Robert Burges, a Bristol baker, deposed before the magistrates that, about three weeks previously, being in want of about £35, and stating the fact to "Joseph Rendall, founder" (probably the Randall already mentioned in connection with the figure of Neptune), the latter told him he knew a person who would lend him £50 or £100, provided he would be a friend to the High Church Club, which met at the White Lion. Rendall promised, moreover, that the baker should have from 6s. to 10s. a week on the same condition, adding that he was frequently employed by Mr. "Gerard" [Jarrit] Smith in carrying weekly allowances to several persons. Rendall further stated that there was a stranger in Bristol who lodged at Mr. Smith's and at other houses for two months, and was then at Mr. "Cousins'" [Cossins, of Redland Court], and who as he believed was the Pretender's son. Rendall called this person his master, and said he expected every day to hear that 10,000 men were landed in Cornwall. The illustrious stranger wore sometimes a black and sometimes a fair wig, and disguised his face with paint. He had great plenty of money, having received several chests of English coin from Holland. After this it is not surprising to find that Mr. Rendall was soon in Newgate. In an extraordinary letter, addressed by him to James Erskine, Esq., of London, and dated the 6th December, he stated that he had been thrice examined by the justices, and had made certain discoveries respecting disaffected people in Bristol. He had been pressed to name the person who had fixed upon the Cathedral door a paper "cursing his Majesty" [and threatening to burn down the house of Mr. Richard Farr], and had given information respecting a man, who was consequently "kept in custody alone, out of 150 or upward that had been arrested." Other information that he had given as to people who were "true to their King and country" had, however, given offence, and as he was then kept in irons, under a charge of perjury, he solicited Mr. Erskine's assistance. There can be little question that the latter was a Jacobite; but before this letter reached London the back of the rebellion was broken, and he discreetly forwarded the letter to the Government, professing to know nothing of the writer. Rendall's fate is not recorded. (Randall, of Neptune fame, voted at the local election of 1754.) Only £2 15s. per cent. of the Bristol subscriptions were eventually required, the sum expended by the Corporation being £275. Notwithstanding the crushing defeat of the Pretender, Jacobite principles were still cherished in many influential families. Ladies were especially fond of displaying their sympathies, and so many white roses were flaunted in the city on the 10th June, 1750, as to provoke some satirical comments in the press. The irritated Whigs celebrated the next anniversary of the Revolution with great enthusiasm. A gay procession of the trading companies accompanied the Corporation to the Mayor's Chapel, fireworks were played off before the Exchange in the evening, and Corn Street was illuminated.

In the archives of the Bristol Consistory Court is a curious document, dated November 18th, 1745, signed by the Rev. William Cary, vicar-general of the bishopric, granting permission to John Coopey to practise medicine in the city, deanery, and diocese. The "faculty" professes to be granted in consequence of Coopey's lengthy knowledge of medicine, and of the proof of his skill offered in his tract on diabetes. The ecclesiastical authorities claimed the right of issuing licenses of this character, and in 1670 the Chancellor of this diocese attempted to force all the "chirurgeons" of the city to take out a license from him to practise; but the Corporation forbade their compliance, and undertook to defend them against the clerical aggressor, who discreetly abandoned his pretensions. (The Archbishop of Canterbury is still entitled to confer the degree of M.D. without examination.)

Early in the session of 1746, the Merchants' Society again petitioned the House of Commons for a more effective protection of English commerce, asserting that if measures were not taken for the suppression of the enemies' privateers, it would be impossible for Bristol merchants to carry on their trade. The previous year had been a very disastrous one for local shipowners, few prizes having been captured by the privateers, whilst some of the finest of those vessels had been caught by French and Spanish men of war. During the spring, however, the citizens were cheered by a brilliant achievement of the Alexander privateer. Whilst at sea the commander, Captain Philips, learned that H.M.S. Solebay, of 28 guns, captured by a French man of war, was being fitted out in St. Martin's Bay, near Bordeaux, to convoy a fleet of merchantmen to the West Indies. Philips having determined to cut out the ship, despatched his boats to the spot with fifty of his best men, who dashed on board during the night, overcame the Frenchmen on deck after a desperate struggle, cut the cables, and carried off their prize. Philips brought the ship safely into Kingroad, with 200 of the French crew prisoners. For his gallant action he received a present of 500 guineas and a medal of £100 value from the King. A less successful but still more heroic affair occurred in the following June. The Tryall, of Bristol, whose exploits have been already mentioned, encountered a French privateer carrying 24 guns and 370 men, whilst the former had only 16 guns and 130 men. After a fiercely fought battle of several hours, during which the Tryall had most of her officers killed or wounded, she was compelled to strike, but was recaptured soon afterwards by an English man of war. The greatest success of the year was that of "The Royal Family" privateers, belonging to a London copartnership, but fitted out at Bristol. These ships—the Prince Frederick and the Duke (whose immense booty in the previous year has just been recorded), the King George and the Princess Amelia—left Kingroad on the 28th April, and in an eight months' cruise captured prizes valued at £220,000. On this occasion also, the crews, about 826 in number, were basely defrauded by their employers. The men had been promised 15 guineas a head before sailing, but the amount was reduced to 5 guineas, which caused a riotous demonstration in the streets. On returning with their booty, great numbers of the crew, at the alleged instigation of the owners, were forced on board the royal navy, and never received their prize money. In 1749 some of the sailors (of whom many were Bristolians) filed a Bill in Chancery, demanding an account; and in 1752 the Master of the Rolls made a decree in their favour. The owners, however, raised dilatory pleas, and the plaintiffs through lack of means were unable to pursue their claims with vigour. Partial hearings took place in 1783, 1789, and 1799. Finally in 1810 Lord Chancellor Eldon said he was reluctantly obliged to allow the demurrers raised by the representatives of the owners, owing to some irregularities in the plaintiffs' Bill (Papers in the possession of Mr. F. G. Powell).

The punctiliousness of the civic authorities in reference to the admission of persons claiming the privileges of free-burgesses is exemplified in a petition laid before the Council in March, 1746. The applicant, Jeremiah Osborne, solicitor, represented that his father, Joseph Osborne, shipwright, was a freeman, but had removed, shortly before the petitioner's birth, to a house near the Limekilns (Hotwell Road). This house was partly in the city and partly in Gloucestershire, and the petitioner was "unfortunately born in that part of the house which lyes in the county, but the room in which he was born is but 18 inches or thereabouts out of the libertys of the city, and the chimney projecting from the wall is partly in the city." After a grave discussion, the Chamber relieved Mr. Osborne of his disqualification, and admitted him to the freedom on paying the ordinary fees. At the next meeting, in April, a fine of £52 10s. was imposed upon the freedom applied for by William Hulme, a retailer of tea. Hulme thought the charge exorbitant, and delayed payment, whereupon he was prosecuted for keeping a shop, "he being a foreigner," and was fined £5. He then availed himself of an expedient. Mr. John Berrow had served as mayor in 1743-4, but had not exercised his right to nominate a person to the freedom, and was since dead. Hulme entered into negotiations with the ex-mayor's executor, who, on receiving £40, claimed and was allowed the right of nominating the tea-dealer. The latter then petitioned for the return of his £5, in which he was also successful. At the quarter sessions in May a man was charged with "using the trade of a blacksmith" in the city, not having served an apprenticeship for seven years. He was found "guilty for a month," and was fined (amount unrecorded). A similar case and sentence, in reference to a tin-plate worker, occurred in 1748.

The *Bristol Journal* of April 26th announced that the summer flying coach to Gloucester would recommence running on the following Wednesday at 5 o'clock in the morning, and perform its journeys, "if God permit," in one day. From a similar advertisement in 1750 it appears that the fare was 8s. A summer coach between Bath and Oxford, less than sixty miles apart, spent two days on the journey in 1756.

Dowry Chapel, Hotwells, built for the accommodation of fashionable visitors, was in course of erection in May, 1746, when that indefatigable antiquary, the Rev. William Cole, visited the place, and, with his customary painstaking, jotted down the outlay that had been incurred (Ad. MSS. British Museum). The expenditure could scarcely have been more modest:—" To Mr. Tully, for the ground, £50. Agreed with the builder for what is already erected for £168. For ceiling and plaistering, £20. For glasing ye windows £9 15s." The conveyance, plans, and a few trifling items raised the total to £259 6s. 4d. "laid out in all."

In the early years of the century the Stamp Office for the city of Bristol and county of Gloucester was established at Gloucester, under the superintendence (from 1722) of Mr. Samuel Worrall, a proctor. The arrangement must have been inconvenient to Bristolians; and when Worrall's son, also named Samuel, removed to this city to assist in the management of the great business of Mr. Thomas Fane, attorney, Small Street, he probably acted as an agent in the sale of stamps. At all events, on the death of the elder Worrall, in 1746, the Government, consulting local convenience, appointed his son distributor for Bristol only, and stamps were sold at Mr. Fane's house until December, 1747, when the new official opened a regular Stamp Office, "at the sign of the King's Arms," being a shop on the Tolzey opposite to the Council House, where he occasionally sold pens and paper to the Corporation. Ten years later Mr. Fane, having become heir to the earldom of Westmoreland, resigned the post of clerk to the Society of Merchants, and Worrall, then styled "an eminent attorney," was appointed in his room. Mr. Fane's retirement from business, about the same time, threw a lucrative practice into the hands of his former servant, and Worrall acquired a fortune, and was the head of a banking firm in 1775. His son, who may be styled Samuel the Third, was educated as a barrister, and was appointed town clerk of the city in June, 1787. Notwithstanding the dignity of that position, he applied for and obtained the office of distributor of stamps on the death of his father; he further secured the patent place of printer of the Custom House presentment; and he also founded a bank. Some anecdotes of this worthy, who was rather proud of the nickname of "Devil Worrall," appear in the "Annals" of the present century.

John Barry was executed on the 16th May at St. Michael's Hill for forgery. The case, which excited much interest, illustrates the social habits of the time. Barry kept the Harp and Star public-house on the Quay, where many privateersmen and other sailors were accustomed to live whilst on shore. As the men generally ran into debt

to the publican before embarking, Barry required them to
append their signatures or "marks" to blank forms of wills,
which, in the event of death, he filled up in his own favour,
and secured the testators' wages or prize-money from the
shipowner. To facilitate these transactions, Barry maintained in his house a man named Peter Haynes, styled a
" hedge " attorney—that is, a person debarred from regular
practice owing to nonpayment of fees. About the end
of 1745 a sailor named James Barry, an officer of the Duke
privateer, who was said to be entitled to nearly £2,000 of
the immense booty captured in the Callao ships, took up his
quarters at the Harp and Star at the landlord's invitation,
and a few days afterwards he suddenly died there. The
publican forthwith announced that the deceased had made
a will in his favour, and took measures for having it proved.
But strong suspicions of foul play having been excited,
inquiries took place, when the hedge attorney and a servant
lad at the inn tendered such evidence against Barry that
he was brought to trial. Haynes deposed that after the
privateersman had expired, Barry's wife put a pen into
the dead man's hand, and thus made a "mark" upon a
blank form of will, which was at once filled up in Barry's
favour by Haynes himself, who admitted that several
hundreds of sailors' wills had been written by him at
Barry's dictation after the men had left the port. The boy
deposed that he had signed as a witness to the will through
the intimidation of his employer, who had forced him to
go before a master in Chancery and make oath with Haynes
as to the validity of the document. He received £11 for
these services when Haynes obtained the deceased's prize-
money. The malefactor, it is recorded, appeared on the
scaffold " as though he had been going to a wedding," and
affirmed that he was as innocent of the forgery as he was
of the murder which was very generally attributed to him.
Barry's gaiety on the occasion was not an unusual feature
of an execution. In May, 1743, Sarah Dodd, on her way
to the gallows, " pledged the hangman out of a bottle of
liquor about the middle of Wine Street."

One Robert Leat, announcing in the *Bristol Journal* of
June 28th, 1746, his òccupation of the Bear inn, Redcliff
Street, adds :—" All the post horses and post chaises that
belong to this city are kept at the said inn." Although the
charge for travelling post was then only about sixpence per
mile, the mercantile class generally preferred the stage
coach. Occasionally, however, an intending traveller adver-

tised in the local journals for "a companion in a post chaise for London."

The removal of the Post Office from All Saints' Lane to Small Street in consequence of the building of the Exchange has been already noticed. There seems to have been some informal understanding that, when the Exchange was finished, a suitable adjacent site should be provided by the Corporation for postal business; and in August, 1746, a committee reported to the Council that they had contracted for the erection of "a house intended to be made use of as a post office," certain workmen having "agreed to build and find all the materials at the rate of £60 per square" (*sic*), while Mr. Thomas Pyne (nephew to Henry, the former postmaster) had offered to become the tenant at "£40 a year, which he alleges is the highest rent he is able at present to pay." The Council approved of the proposal, recommending the committee to get as much rent as was practicable. The house, of which the scanty original dimensions may still be observed, cost £700, exclusive of a ground rent of £15 a year, given for the site. Only the ground floor was set apart for postal business, Mr. Pyne residing above. The first year's rent (£43) was paid in 1750. (The house now (1892) produces a rental of £250 yearly, and the shed in the rear, which the Corporation built, and from time to time extended, as postal business increased, brings in £200 per annum additional).

The following curious illustration of eighteenth century law and justice is extracted from the *Bristol Advertiser* of August 9th, 1746 :—" The beginning of this week a recruiting sergeant was made to pay 20*s*. for profane cursing and swearing, and order'd to sit in the stocks several hours. Examples of this kind are almost daily making of blasphemous delinquents by the worthy magistrates of this opulent city. It seems a person hearing anyone swear or curse may go privately to the clerk's office in the Council House, give in the name of the offender, with the number of oaths, upon oath, and never be known as to his person. On which a warrant is issued out, the offender seized thereon, and punish'd according to the tenour of the glorious new Act of Parliament in that case made and provided."

The Council, in August, voted a grant of £20 to Ann Mansfield, grand daughter of John Hine (mayor, 1696), owing to her "deplorable condition."

The insignia of office borne by the water bailiff being apparently deemed not sufficiently imposing, a Silver Oar was now purchased for the functionary in question, at a cost of £18 7s. 6d.

The overcrowded condition of the burial ground adjoining Christ Church at this date forced the vestry to apply a remedy. On the 8th October, 1746, it was resolved to close the place for fourteen years, a new cemetery in Duck Lane having been enclosed and consecrated. In August, 1764, another vestry minute orders that the old cemetery " be again solely used "—to the improvement, no doubt, of the neighbouring public well in Wine Street.

The national Thanksgiving for the suppression of the rebellion was celebrated on the 9th October with great fervour. Twenty pieces of cannon on Brandon Hill awakened sleepy citizens at 6 o'clock in the morning by a royal salute. Later on, the corporate body, the trade companies, and the boys of the City School repaired to the Cathedral, and were saluted after service with three volleys by the regiment stationed in the city. In the afternoon, an effigy of the Young Pretender, clothed in tartan, was carried through the streets and ignominiously burnt in Prince's Street. Bonfires, fireworks, and a ball concluded the festivities, which cost the Corporation about £135. Some Falstaffian items appear in the accounts:—" Wine, (70½ gallons of Lisbon and Port at 6s. per gallon) £21 3s.; Arrack, (6 gallons, the first time that this liquor is mentioned in the city accounts) £4 16s.; Ale (144 gallons) £4 8s.; Hot Well water, 1s." The revellers also disposed of 4lb. of tobacco and a vast number of pipes.

The first attempt to found a local Medical School appears to date from this time. The *Bristol Oracle* of October 24th, 1746, announced that a " Course of Anatomy " would begin on the 7th of November (without naming the locality), and referred intending subscribers to Mr. John Page, in St. James's Barton, or to Mr. James Ford, in Trinity Street. Page was the leading Bristol surgeon of the period. The enterprise appears to have been unsuccessful, as was a similar effort in 1777.

Shopkeepers, as a rule, were still content to carry on business in open booths. In the Bodleian Library is a drawing, dated November, 1746, representing nine houses in Wine Street, the gate of the Guard-house forming the centre of the group. Only three of the shops are provided with glass windows.

The existence on the shore of the Avon, near the mouth of the great ravine on Durdham Down, of a copious spring of water, as much entitled to be called " hot " as the ancient well at St. Vincent's Rocks, must have been always well known. The first record of its having been turned to profitable account does not occur, however, until 1743, when its owners, the Merchants' Society, ordered that the lessees (unnamed) should be sued for arrears of rent. In the *Bristol Journal* of December 20th, 1746, is the following advertisement:—" To be sold for a term of years, The New Hot Well, situate within the parish and manour of Clifton. Enquire of Mr. Fane " [the clerk to the company]. As there was no carriage road by the river side, and pedestrians had some difficulty in traversing the rocky pathway, the place offered little temptation to the speculative; but in October, 1750, the proprietors succeeded in leasing the well to — Newcomb and John Dolman, for a term of 21 years, at a rental of £24 per annum. One or two cottages were then erected for the accommodation of visitors, and it appears from John Wesley's diary that he took up his abode at this secluded spot in 1754 for the purpose of drinking the waters " free from noise and hurry." The visit of so prominent a personage was naturally made the most of by the lessees. In 1755 Dolman, who was a preacher at two dissenting chapels, and a basket maker, as well as a dispenser of spa water, published a dreary pamphlet entitled, " Contemplations amongst Vincent's Rocks," in which he stated that "when he (Wesley) first came . . . his countenance looked as if a greedy consumption had determined to put an end to his days. But in less than three weeks . . . he was enabled to set out on his Cornish circuit . . . preaching every day." The extreme solitude of the spring, however, proved fatal to its popularity. Dolman admitted that the nearest dwelling was a mile distant, and that the only human objects ordinarily visible were the gibbeted remains of two murderers (the assassins of Sir Robert Cann's coachman). In 1761 the lease was offered for sale, but failed to find a purchaser, and the premises were frequently but vainly advertised to be let. Dolman published a second edition of his " Contemplations " in 1772. He had then blossomed into " Vicar of Chalk, in Kent ;" but was better known in Bristol as " Parson Twigg," in allusion to his original calling. His book had no better effect than before on the repute of the spring. In September, 1778, the premises, then in bad repair, were offered to be let by auction ; but no bidder appeared, owing, it was believed, to the permission given to the public to carry off the water in their own bottles and baskets. Being unable to procure a tenant, the Merchant Venturers, in June, 1785, appointed a person to take care of the premises for five years, apparently as their manager. This seems to have been the last effort made to maintain the public character of the place. In 1792 a passing visitor noted that the pump room was falling in ruins, and that the adjoining cottages had been converted into dwellings for quarrymen.

During the year 1746, a wall was erected along the northern edge of the great ravine on Durdham Down, and continued thence to the point where the common touched the boundary of Sneyd Park, at the rocks overhanging the Avon. Many fatal accidents had occurred in the locality, owing to its unprotected condition, and the builder of the wall, Mr. John Wallis, was regarded as a public benefactor. In the *London Magazine* for 1746 is a poem on "Wallis's Wall on Durdham Down," beginning:—

> Let Cook and Norton tow'ring Follies raise,
> Thy wisdom, Wallis, will I sing and praise.
> Let heroes and Prime Ministers of State
> Smile when they're called, ironically, great;
> Superior merit shall my muse employ,
> Since better 'tis to save than to destroy.

The "Follies" on either bank of the Avon (Norton's is now in ruins) are styled in a note "two whimsical and useless buildings." The wall retained its original name for many years, but later generations have oddly transmuted the cognomen into Sea Walls.

The narrow pass known as St. Nicholas' Gate was the scene of many serious accidents. John Wesley notes in his diary that on the 22nd January, 1747, whilst riding through the gate, he and his horse were thrown down by the shaft of a cart; but, by what he clearly believed to be a miracle, the wheel merely grazed his head without doing him any injury.

Reference has been already made to the "briefs" issued by the Crown, requiring collections to be made in parish churches on behalf of some religious or charitable object. The appeal was generally made for the repair of some ruinous church, but local calamities arising from fire, lightning, floods, hailstorms, and hurricanes were often the occasion of briefs. In the year ending Easter, 1747, no less than sixteen of these documents entailed collections in the city churches. Possibly in consequence of the number, the offerings were very small. At St. Nicholas the total sum received was £3 2s. 9½d., one collection from the wealthy congregation amounting only to 1s. 3d. Occasionally, when the case excited some sympathy, a collection was made by the churchwardens from house to house. Thus £6 were obtained in St. Nicholas's parish in 1754 for the sufferers from a fire at

"Almesbury," and £4 7s. 9d. were collected there in 1760 for a similar calamity at Kingswood.

A general election took place in June, 1747. The local candidates were the retiring members, Edward Southwell and Robert Hoblyn, and Mr. Samuel Dicker. The last named gentleman retired, alleging that a contest would excite bitter animosity amongst the citizens; and the old representatives were consequently returned. Both gentlemen were opposed to the Whig Government. The King's Speech at the dissolution of the previous Parliament was given in the *Bristol Journal* of the 20th June, but soon after the printer was compelled to publish, for three weeks, a humble apology to the King's Printer for having infringed his patent, promising to refrain from further offences. In fulfilment of this pledge, the *Journal* declined to explain the nature of the local Acts passed in 1749, "they being the property of his Majesty's Printer."

Although local privateering appears to have been very unprofitable in 1746 and 1747, and though many of the Bristol war vessels fell into the hands of the enemy, additions continued to be made in order to keep up the previous strength. The following is a list of the vessels fitted out in the city during the war which was now drawing to a close, with such details as have been preserved. Those marked with an * were captured, and † denotes a recapture.

	Guns	Men		Guns	Men
Alexander	22		Leviathan	28	250
Blackjoke	10	70	*Lion	20	180
*Blandford	22	240	*Mediterranean		
*Bristol	30	300	Pearl	14	80
Constantine	18	180	Phœnix		
Despatch			Prince Charles	20	150
Dragon	22	180	Prince Frederick		
Duke of Bedford	26		Prince Harry	16	120
*Duke of Cumberland			*†Queen of Hungary	12	100
Duke of Marlborough	20		Resolution	16	160
			Ranger	12	100
*†Dursley			*Rover	24	210
Eagle			Royal Hunter (wrecked)	22	132
*Emperor			Salisbury		
*Farmer			*Secker		
Falcon (French prize)			Sheerness	26	
*Ferret	10	90	Somerset (lost)	15	96
*Fly			Southwell	24	200
*Fox (French prize)	16	150	*Spry		
Gallant			Tiger (French prize)	26	
*Hannibal	30		*†Tryall	16	120
Harlequin	20		Townshend	22	180
Hawk	16	160	*Tuscany	24	175
Jamaica	20		Vernon (lost)	14	180
King William	20	150	*Vulture	14	130

The Tiger took three of the enemies' privateers during the year, for which the commander, Captain Siex, was presented by the merchants of Bristol with a handsome testimonial. In September, Captain Philips, whose gallant recapture of a man of war has been recorded (see p. 259), returned to Bristol from Jamaica. His vessel was attacked during the voyage by a large French privateer, which he not only beat off but drove ashore on the coast of Cuba, where he rifled the enemy, and finally sank her. From some accounts of the Southwell privateer, preserved in the Jefferies Collection, it appears that an unsuccessful cruise of such a vessel cost the owners little short of £2,000. The cost of fitting out the Southwell for her fifth cruise, in 1746, was £1,888, though the crew was reduced to 187, but the value of the only prize taken was but £220. Amongst the owners were Michael Miller, Thomas Deane, James Laroche, W. Aleyn, and Cranfield Becher.

The power of granting licenses for the sale of liquor being vested in the aldermanic body, their worships naturally attended to their own interests. The following advertisement in the *Oracle* of July 25th, 1747, requires no comment:—" To be lett, by Alderman Nath. Day, The Royal Anne, at Wapping. N.B.—There will be no other public-house admitted at Wapping." From an advertisement relating to the same house, in the *London Gazette* of January 17th, 1713, from which we learn that a bowling-green was attached to the inn, it appears the monopoly of the Day family had been enjoyed for upwards of thirty years.

At a meeting of the Council in August, 1747, a petition was presented from the inhabitants of St. Philip's, complaining of "the great inconveniency and obstructions arising from the narrowness of Lawford's Gate;" but it received no attention. Another memorial to the same effect met with similar treatment in 1751. A "whipping post" was erected a short distance without the gate for the punishment of offenders in Gloucestershire, and was in frequent use.

The fine of £20 imposed by the Carpenters' Company on persons desirous of pursuing that trade in the city was condemned as exorbitant by the Council in September, 1747, and the company was ordered to content itself with £5 for the future. The corporate accounts for repairs show that the wages of journeymen carpenters were then 1s. 10d. a day.

The average speed of coaches being barely forty miles per day, the reader may easily divine that the poorer class of travellers, who journeyed by stage wagons, had no ground for complaining of the swiftness of their transit. An advertisement in the *Bristol Journal* of October 10th, 1747, states that a wagon set out from Basing Lane, London, every Thursday, and arrived at the Lamb inn, at Lawford's Gate, on the following Wednesday. The local agent was "Richard Giles, at the Lamb inn," who will be heard of again. The fare for passengers was about 10s. a head, but 1d. per lb. was also charged for their luggage. Tradesmen who did not require such "quick conveyance" for their goods were invited to send them (at the rate of 3s. per cwt. in summer and 3s. 6d. in winter) by a wagon leaving for Newbury, where they would be shipped in barges, and conveyed to London "commonly in 12 or 14 days." From another newspaper it appears that the Exeter wagon left St. Thomas Street on Friday, and completed its eighty miles journey on Tuesday. In October, 1758, a carrier named James boasted that his London wagons (three weekly) were the most expeditious on the road, only four nights being spent on the journey. "They are likewise made very commodious and warm for passengers."

A proposal was started about this time for the establishment of a hospital for the relief of merchant sailors and their families, and promised to be a great success. The Council, in December, 1747, voted £500 towards the fund, and granted a site on Brandon Hill for the proposed building. The Merchants' Society also subscribed £200. Afterwards, for reasons now unknown, the scheme was abandoned.

About this time a swimming bath was opened by one Thomas Rennison, a threadmaker, at a suburban place called Territt's Mills, "near the upper end of Stokes' Croft." The mill was used for grinding snuff, and there was a large pond on the premises, which was probably the original bath. The public being largely attracted to the spot, Rennison opened, in 1765, a new "grand swimming bath, 400 feet in circumference," to which a "ladies' swimming bath and coffee house" were added in 1767. A thread factory as well as the snuff mill still formed part of the premises. In 1774 Rennison, styling himself "Governor of the Colony of Newfoundland," solicited attention to his baths and coffee house, while in a somewhat later advertisement the place was called the Old England tea gardens, to which a tavern had been annexed. The spot, being quite in the country and beyond the civic jurisdiction, became a popular resort; and an annual bean feast was held, at which a mock mayor, sheriffs, and other dignitaries were elected, and various high jinks played by the not too abstemious revellers. In June, 1782, evening concerts, twice a week, were announced for the summer season; admission one shilling, including tea and coffee.

The chapel of the Society of Friends in the Black Friars was rebuilt in 1747, at a cost of £1,830. Having regard to the debased architectural taste of the time, the building is of remarkable purity of style.

The difficulty experienced in inducing youths to enter the army is indicated by an advertisement in the *Bristol Journal* of January 9th, 1748, offering two guineas, and a crown to drink the King's health, to every recruit measuring 5 feet 9 inches. "Whoever brings a good man shall have half a guinea reward. Excellent Punch and ale at the sergeant's quarters [the Boot, Maryleport Street], and the famous Corporal Francis Bird's agreeable and humourous Diversions. All for Nothing."

In despite of the Turnpike Acts, the roads of the neighbouring districts remained as bad as before. About this time, Miss Mary Champion, aunt of the celebrated Bristol potter, was travelling with her grandmother in their carriage to Bath, when the vehicle became embogged, and the two ladies had to climb over a wall by the side of the road, and make their way through the fields to "Kainson." About two years later, the *Gloucester Journal* reported the great road to the north to be so bad that a "sober, careful farmer" had fallen and been suffocated in one of the sloughs between that city and Cheltenham.

The story of the long struggle between the African Company and the merchants of Bristol, in which the latter successfully maintained their claim to participate in the slave traffic, has been recounted under the year 1711. In the early months of 1747, the London firms who sought to monopolise the trade made another attempt to induce Parliament to drive their rivals from the field. The chief argument advanced for their unconcealed selfishness was that the trade on the African coast could be protected from foreign aggression only by the erection of additional forts and castles, and that such defences could not be raised and maintained except by a joint stock company enjoying exclusive privileges. The truth was that the African Company was practically insolvent, and was unable to raise fresh capital without legislative help. The Corporation of Bristol lost no time in defending local interests. A petition was addressed to the House of Commons, setting forth that the trade from Bristol to the West Indies and North America, by way of Africa, was "the principal and most considerable branch belonging to the city; and that since such trade has been free and open, it has greatly increased, and his Majesty's plantations thereby much better supplied with negroes, and larger quantities of the manufactures of this kingdom exported." Defeated in the sessions of 1747 and 1748, the Londoners made another, and an equally unsuccessful, effort in 1749, when the Bristol Council passed a vote of thanks to the local merchants who had conducted the opposition at Westminster. At length, in 1750, the contending interests came to terms. The Act passed in that year recited that the African trade, being "very advantageous, and necessary for supplying the plantations with a sufficient number of negroes at reasonable rates, ought for that reason to be free and open to all his Majesty's subjects." It was therefore enacted that the Royal Company should be dissolved, that all British subjects should trade to Africa without restraint, and that such traders should be deemed a corporation, styled the Company of Merchants trading to Africa, in whom the old company's forts and stations were vested. The direction was confided to a body of nine persons, three of whom were to be elected by the members in London, Bristol, and Liverpool respectively. The qualification of an elector was the payment of £2, by which a merchant became a freeman of the company. This was the only capital possessed by the new concern, but the payments thus made throw some light on the extent of the African trade in the three leading ports. Williamson's "Liverpool Memorandum Book for 1753" states that there were in Liverpool 101, in London 135, and in Bristol 157 merchants who were members of the African Company. But by a Bristol list, dated June 23rd, 1755, giving the names of all the firms, it appears that 237 members resided in Bristol, 147 in London, and 89 in Liverpool. Some of the pamphlets published by the respective parties previous to the compromise are in the British Museum. From one of these, apparently written by a Bristolian in 1750, it appears that the enormous drain of human beings from the Slave Coast had brought about a great advance in prices. Instead of the £3 or £4 paid for a slave in Africa about 1725, the writer alleges that the price demanded by the native dealers was from £28 to £32 a head. It was admitted, he adds, that the Bristol and Liverpool shippers could "carry on the trade 10 or 15 per cent. cheaper than London," and he asserts, with much complacency, that in the first nine years of open trade, ending in 1706, they despatched no less than 160,950 slaves to the English colonies. Another writer quite unintentionally discloses the horrible destruction of life on the plantations by giving the aggregate import of slaves into Jamaica from 1700 to 1750. The number was 408,101, of whom about 108,000 were transferred to other islands, leaving 300,000 settled labourers. As it is known from other sources that the black population in 1750 was less than ought to have been naturally produced by the negroes living there in 1700, the treatment of the unhappy captives must have been simply murderous.

On the 20th March, 1748, a baker bearing the singular name of Peaceable Robert Matthews was convicted of selling bread deficient in weight, and was fined £6 12s. 6d., being at the rate of 5s. per ounce on the deficiency. The charge was brought by the Bakers' Company, which was then zealous in laying informations, and many of the fines were handed over to the prosecutors.

At the gaol delivery in April, Thomas Betterley was convicted of murder and sentenced to be hanged. Soldiers being scarce, however, the culprit was pardoned on condition of his continuing to serve as a dragoon.

A boarding school, erected under the auspices of John Wesley, was opened at Kingswood on the 24th July. It was chiefly designed for the education of the sons of Wesleyan ministers; and its original regulations, drawn up by Wesley himself, indicate the training that was thought suitable for such boys. The lads rose at four o'clock, winter and summer, and, excepting short periods allowed for breakfast, dinner, and supper, they prayed, learnt lessons, and worked in the garden or the house until eight o'clock at night. There were no holidays throughout the year, and on every day, except Sunday, a full day's work was to be done. "We do not," writes Wesley, "allow any time for play on any day." The food was of an equally Spartan character. It consisted of milk porridge and water porridge alternately for breakfast; bread and butter, and cheese and milk, by turns, for supper; and meat with apple puddings for dinner, except on Fridays, when the fare was "vegetables and dumplings." No relaxation of the code was granted to weakly boys, Wesley ordering that the rules should not be broken in favour of any person. The founder laid his hand upon a headmaster named Simpson, who, with his wife, the housekeeper, seems to have gloried in aggravating the severity of the regulations. Dr. Adam Clarke, who was one of the pupils, afterwards stated that the supply of food was deficient, and that even in the depth of winter, though coals could be obtained for a trifle within a few roods from the house, he was refused permission to warm himself at a fire. The teacher of English, Cornelius Bayley, afterwards D.D., was allowed by Wesley only £12 a year and his board. The school, which under more sensible rules acquired a high reputation, was removed to Lansdown in 1851.

Pugilism at this period enjoyed the patronage of all classes of society, from the royal family to the rabble. On the 15th October, 1748, a prize fight took place in College Green between a soldier and a sailor. Felix Farley, one of the printers of the *Bristol Journal*, was one of the most cherished local friends of John Wesley, but his paper contains an account of the battle. Though the sailor, it says, was short in stature and his antagonist a lusty man, the latter was fearfully beaten, and was saved from expiring only by an "application of palm oil and spirits." "The little sailor had a pretty deal of money given him by the gentlemen present." The same newspaper of February 4th, 1756, gives more minute details of another boxing match which had taken place in the suburbs, and offers unconscious evidence of the unfeelingness of the spectators. One of the combatants was allowed to fight until he had an eye beaten out, eight ribs broken, his shoulder blades smashed "in four quarters," and his jaw broken in three pieces. He was reported to be dead. The other man had his collar bone broken and one ear torn off.

The first mention of a steam engine in the local press occurs in the autumn of 1748, in an account of an assault committed by a negro on a person styled "the master of the fire engine, and one of the overseers of the cole-works in Kingswood." The engines of that period were serviceable only for pumping water, horses being employed to draw the coal from the workings.

In December, 1748, a novel spectacle took place at Oxford. A man and woman, Quakers, apparelled in "hair sackcloth," walked through the principal thoroughfares at separate times, as a penance for having had an illegitimate child. Three or four days later, the couple repeated the expiatory performance at Gloucester, amidst the derision of the populace; and the *Gentleman's Magazine* states that they also did penance in Bristol. Felix Farley being a member of the Society of Friends, all reference to the subject is suppressed in his journal.

T

The proclamation of peace with France and Spain was made in Bristol on the 6th February, 1749, with the usual ceremonies. Seven "scaffolds" were constructed for the use of the sheriffs, Mr. Stephen Nash being paid £5 16s. for the use of "bays." Thirteen French-horn players were engaged, and 34 coachmen were paid a crown each for conducting the carriages of the civic dignitaries and of some of the leading inhabitants, amongst whom were two physicians, Dr. Logan and Dr. Middleton—probably the first professional men who kept coaches in Bristol. "Ribbons" were extensively worn, for the mercer's bill amounted to £4 17s. 6d. The rest of the outlay, over £40, was chiefly expended in feasting. A national Thanksgiving for the peace took place in April, when a great quantity of ale was distributed to the populace at the bonfire on Brandon Hill, while the Corporation treated itself to a copious entertainment, the total expenditure being nearly £73.

In February, 1749, the Bristol turnpike trustees forwarded a petition to the House of Commons, setting forth that, notwithstanding the Act of 1727, the roads were still, owing to various causes, in as ruinous a condition as before the trust was created, and praying for a renewal of the powers about to expire. A petition was also presented on behalf of several of the neighbouring gentry, asking that certain "ruinous" roads, not included in the former Act, might be embraced in the new statute. The Bill, with extended powers, received the Royal Assent in May. In the hope of allaying discontent, carts laden with coal were exempted from toll. The farmers, however, had always detested the turnpikes, and the inclusion of additional roads in the trust irritated them into open revolt. During the month of July great bodies of rural labourers, styling themselves "Jack a Lents," some wearing shirts over their clothes, others naked to the waist, and all with blackened faces, twice destroyed the gates at Bedminster, Ashton and Don John's Cross, and threatened an attack on the city. On the 1st August, they came for the third time, with drums, colours, and arms, and demolished the toll houses on the Ashton and Dundry roads. Headed by a young gentleman-farmer of Nailsea carrying an improvised standard, they next proceeded to Bedminster, to be avenged on Stephen Durbin, the tything man, who had caused three rioters to be captured during the previous raids. After drinking freely they attacked Durbin's house, which by order of their leader was levelled with the ground. Subsequently the mob, finding Redcliff Gate closed, made its way to Totterdown, where it demolished the two gates and houses. The magistrates, aided by a number of constables and fifty sailors armed with cutlasses, at length appeared on the scene, and after severe fighting, in which one Farmer Barns. was conspicuous as a rioter, about thirty men, several of them severely wounded, were arrested on Knowle Hill. An affair so congenial with their habits would have excited the Kingswood colliers, even if the Somerset farmers had not prompted them with bribes. On the 3rd August they assembled in force, and almost all the remaining toll-gates were burnt or destroyed by gunpowder, money being demanded from every traveller as a reward for this patriotic service. On the arrival of a regiment of dragoons the disturbances ceased, but letters were sent to the Council House threatening to blockade and burn the city if the arrested rioters were not released. (Five of these prisoners died in Newgate from smallpox.) The judges of assize were on circuit during the tumults, and special precautions had to be taken for their safety. The recorder was stopped at Pensford by a turbulent mob, which demanded money, but his firmness awed the rabble, and he was allowed to proceed. The Kingswood colliers maintained a nightly guard for several weeks after the riots, in order to defeat any attempt of the authorities to capture the ringleaders. In the correspondence between the mayor and the Government, part of which is in the British Museum, the inactivity displayed by the county gentry throughout the tumults is said to have increased the difficulties of the magistrates. (In a private account book of Mr. Gore, of Barrow Court, is the following remarkable entry :—August 26, 1753. To Mr. Hardwick, on my account, for cutting down the turnpikes, £10.) The sympathy of the farmers with the rioters was so unconcealed that the trials of eighteen of the Somerset prisoners were removed to Wiltshire; but not a single conviction was obtained there, the juries acquitting the ringleaders in spite of the clearest evidence of their guilt. Two men, concerned in pulling down Mr. Durbin's house, were condemned in Somerset on the testimony of an accomplice, and were executed at Ilchester. Their fate caused a deep sensation; and the rural war against turnpikes, maintained obstinately for upwards of twenty years, was at length sullenly abandoned. The improved roads, however, were long disliked by persons of conservative instincts. Nearly thirty years after this date Mr. Windham recorded in his diary Dr. Johnson's strong hostility to them. "Formerly," said the sage, "there were cheap places and dear places. Now all refuges were destroyed for elegant or genteel poverty, and men had no longer a hope to support them in their struggle through life. The roads moreover caused disunion of families by furnishing a market to each man's abilities, and destroying the dependence of one man on another."

A violent dispute between Thomas Chamberlayne, dean of Bristol, and the prebendaries of the Cathedral broke out in the spring of 1749. The dean suddenly claimed the sole right to appoint the minor canons and all the inferior officers, and on the 27th January, in despite of the fact that his alleged prerogative had been referred to the arbitration of the Primate and the Bishop of London, he instituted the Rev. John Camplin as a minor canon, in the place of the Rev. John Culliford, who had been dismissed by the chapter for holding two cures in addition to that office. The action of the dean was denounced by the prebendaries, a few weeks later, as contrary to their privileges, and as highly indecent towards the two prelates to whom the matter had been referred; but the dean treated their proceedings with contemptuous indifference, and amicable relations were suspended. In June, 1750, another minor canonry became vacant, whereupon the dean, "in the presence of the choir," instituted the Rev. Benjamin Hancock, jun. Ten days later, a chapter meeting was held, when the reverend dignitaries came perilously near to fisticuffs. The dean's account of the affair, appended to the minutes, is that he had nominated a clergyman for a vacant rectory, and proposed that the chapter should proceed to the election, when the sub-dean (Castelman) seized the minute book out of the clerk's hands, "and held it from me by violence, and would not let me have it till they were going out of ye chapter." Next day, at another meeting, the dean proposed several gentlemen for the vacant livings of St. Leonard's, Bristol, and Sutton Bonnington, but the prebendaries rejected all of them. On the other hand the prebendaries were unanimous in the choice of a clergyman for St. Leonard's, but the dean refused to put the question. In July three of the prebendaries held a chapter in the dean's absence, and elected their protegé, Berjew, to St Leonard's, another person being instituted to Sutton. Berjew was also appointed precentor. But when the dean came back, in February, 1751, he protested against all that had been done whilst he was in waiting on the king, and denied the right of any prebendary to enjoy his stipend unless he resided in his prebendal house and came properly apparelled to church during his term of residence—which indicates the laxity then common amongst the dignitaries. After much more squabbling, the contending parties agreed to leave the great point in dispute to the bishops of London, St. David's, and St. Asaph, who in March, 1752, determined against the claim of the dean, declaring that the right of electing minor canons, schoolmaster, etc., lay in the dean and chapter. At the next chapter meeting the elections made by the dean were declared invalid, and it was resolved to fill certain vacancies at the next gathering; but, doubtless in dread of a scandal, matters were compromised. Berjew, promoted to All Saints, resigned his minor canonry, and two of the dean's former nominees were ordered to draw lots for it, the loser being given the next vacancy. Hancock was got rid of by being instituted to St. Leonard's. Harmony was thus temporarily restored.

A Bill was promoted by the Corporation in the session of 1749 to amend the existing statute "for cleansing, paving, and enlightening" the city. The witnesses examined at Westminster in support of the measure stated that the old lighting Act was defective, the magistrates having no power to compel the parishes to erect public lamps, or to fix the hours when they should be lighted. The overhanging signs, moreover, so obstructed the lights that in several streets there was not a lamp to be seen. The injustice of compelling the poor inhabitants of wide streets to maintain half the pavement before their houses, the injury done to the pavements by carts and wagons having "iron-bound" wheels, and the want of by-laws to enforce order amongst the hackney coachmen, said to have greatly increased in number, were also urged in support of the Bill; which received the Royal Assent in May. The Corporation spent nearly £650 in passing the scheme through Parliament—about five times the usual cost of a Bill at that period. The expenditure was doubtless caused by the opposition offered to the measure by a section of the inhabitants, supported, there is reason to believe, by the members of Parliament for the city, whose Tory principles were in antagonism to those of the majority of the Council. The new measure enacted, *inter alia*, that the magistrates should determine the number of lamps, and where they should be placed, and should require them to be lighted from sunset to sunrise from the 20th July to the 30th April—no provision being made for the rest of the year. The expense of lighting and paving was to be defrayed by rates. The justices were also authorised to order the removal of projecting signs, but this clause was so offensive to the trading community that the power remained dormant for nearly twenty years. The clause dealing with wagons and carts belonging to Bristolians forbade the use of iron tires of less than six inches in breadth. The lighting clauses were put in operation in 1750, and effected a striking improvement, the number of lamps being increased nearly fourfold. St. James's, which had not a single lamp in 1738, was allotted 104 out of a total of 560.

Amongst the perils of the streets which ladies had to encounter at this period was the violence of a base class of men styled "informers," who gained a living by enforcing the fiscal laws concerning apparel. In 1745, after the outbreak of war with France, an Act was passed prohibiting the sale of French cambric, and inflicting a penalty of £5 on persons wearing it, half the fine being allotted to those who put the law in motion. The "informers" were accustomed to stop ladies in the streets, though they often did so at their peril. On the 28th March, 1749, a man who had snatched off a woman's cap in one of the streets of London was so mercilessly whipped by the mob that he died soon afterwards. A writer in the *Bristol Journal* of the same week says:—" It is notorious that several ladies of this city have been so far insulted as to have the frils of their caps, aprons, &c., violently tore, cut, and rended from them with abusive language;" and the local populace is unlikely to have been more forbearing than that of the capital. A new Act, permitting ladies to wear cambrics purchased before 1748, put an end to the scandal.

The statue of William III. appears to have shown early signs of dilapidation. The civic chamberlain was directed, in April, 1749, to write to Mr. "Rysbrac" informing him "that it was in so ruinous a condition there was a danger of its total decay unless some speedy and effectual means were used to repair it." The sculptor seems to have repudiated his liability, for repairs to the statue and pedestal cost the Chamber £111 in the following year. The matter aroused the ire of the Jacobites, for a profuse display of white roses was made by the Tory ladies on the following 10th June.

Durdham Down races, rarely noticed in the early newspapers, were popular at this period. The *Oracle* of May 20th, 1749, stated that the sports, "for which great preparations had been making for a fortnight before," began on the previous Monday. "The course was enlarged, the ground levelled, and a great number of booths and scaffolds erected for the accommodation of spectators, who were vastly more numerous than had ever been seen there on any other occasion." For the prize of the day, a silver punchbowl, gold watch, &c., value £50, two horses, carrying ten stones, ran three heats of four miles each, and the affair was not decided until nearly nine o'clock in the evening. On Tuesday a race for £20 was run on the same course, "and on Wednesday began the foot races, when 3 gs. were run for by two men, naked; and a Holland smock and one guinea by five women, which was won by a Kingswood girl." Owing to the large attendance at these annual sports, another inn, called the New Ostrich, was opened on the edge of the Down in competition with the original Ostrich, which was largely patronised by people of fashion from the Hot Well.

Selina, Countess of Huntingdon, the patroness of the Whitefield sect of Methodists, was a frequent sojourner at the Hot Well about the middle of the century. During one of these visits, in July, 1749, she ransomed thirty-four poor insolvents in Newgate, whose debts were under £10 each. The captives included seven persons who, though acquitted of the crimes for which they had been arrested, were detained in gaol through their inability to pay the fees demanded by the prison authorities.

At a meeting of the Council in August, 1749, a pension of £30 a year was voted to Andrew Hooke, Esq., in reward for his services to the Corporation in furthering the erection of the Exchange. A further pension of £20 was granted by the Merchants' Society. Mr. Hooke, descended from a wealthy Bristol family, and himself a magistrate for Gloucestershire, was a man of literary attainments, but appears to have fallen from affluence to poverty through unfortunate speculations. His newspaper, the *Oracle*, has been already mentioned. A history of the city, entitled "Bristollia," was another of his many projects, but only two small parts were published. After his death, in 1753, his widow supported herself and family by keeping a coffee house at Jacob's Wells, where she p nte the playbills for the neighbouring theatre. In 1766,ron the opening of the new theatre in King Street, the unfortunate old lady removed her press to the Maiden Tavern in Baldwin Street, where she continued to print for several years.

On the 25th August, a foreign sailor named Abseny, who had lodged at a solitary publichouse called the White

Ladies, "on the footpath leading to Durdham Down" (the site is now covered by the eastern end of South Parade), was hanged and gibbeted on the Down, in company with the bodies of Burnet and Payne (see p. 248), for murdering a girl of thirteen years, who acted as servant at the inn. On the same day, Jeremiah Hill was hanged at St. Michael's gallows, for having, in conjunction with two confederates, who escaped, murdered a prostitute by tying her up in a sack, and throwing her into the harbour. The two crimes excited a profound sensation in the city. Abseny, in killing the girl, cut his hand so deeply that he was tracked by his own blood all the way to Hungroad, where he had taken a boat to an outward-bound vessel.

The institution of an annual dinner to commemorate the birth of Edward Colston has been noticed under 1726. As the gatherings in question were of a non-political character, the Tory party now resolved to hold a festival amongst themselves, and on the 2nd November, 1749, eighteen gentleman sat down to the first "Dolphin" banquet, Francis Woodward presiding. The first "collection" for charitable purposes was made two years later, and amounted to £4 17s. The contributions slowly increased as the society became more popular, and in the last year of the century reached £195 16s. 6d. Although somewhat anticipating dates, it may be as well to record at once the rise and progress of the two other societies still in existence. The "Grateful" was established in 1759, its promoters soliciting the support of those who had been educated at Colston's School, and recommending that the after-dinner collection, instead of being distributed in doles of bread and money, as was then the practice, should be devoted to apprenticing freemen's sons and relieving real distress. At the first dinner, held at the Ship inn, Small Street, at 2 o'clock p.m., twenty-two persons attended, the collection amounting to £16 11s. 6d. It had increased to £191 in 1800. The "Anchor" was founded by the Whigs in November, 1768, when it was resolved to hold an evening meeting once a month at the Three Tuns tavern in Corn Street, each member paying 10s. 6d. as an entrance fee to a fund for charitable purposes. The first dinner took place in the following year, when twenty-two citizens assembled under the presidency of Gilbert Davis, and £12 1s. 6d. were collected. The monthly suppers, costing 8d. a head until 1773, when the charge was increased to a shilling, seem to have been for some time more popular than the dinners, but were eventually dropped. For the last fifteen years of the century, in spite of the forlorn condition of the party in Parliament, the yearly benefactions averaged over £300. Presumably from their action in reference to the Lighting Act, the members of Parliament for the city were very unpopular in corporate circles. At a meeting of the Council in December, the usual vote of a pipe of wine to the members was evaded by a resort to "the previous question." This offended the representatives in their turn, and when the motion for the customary gift was passed a twelvemonth later, Mr. Southwell, in a letter from Kingsweston, expressed his obligations for the "usual compliment in lieu of the ancient wages of service in Parliament," but as "the ancient custom was discontinued last year," he declined the renewal of it, though he would continue his faithful services. A similar refusal was sent by Mr. Hoblyn, from Cornwall. The customary present was not again offered by the Council until after the general election of 1754.

The looseness of police in the suburban districts was a great encouragement to dissipation and crime. The *Bristol Intelligencer* of December 16th, 1749, " hears " from Westbury-on-Trym that crowds of "dissolute and disorderly persons have been entertained at about seven or eight unruly public houses near the Gallows on St. Michael's Hill, and many insults and robberies committed on the market people and others travelling thereabout. But the gentlemen of that parish having bravely prosecuted and caused several penalties to be levied on the keepers of the houses, they are all routed away."

St. Peter's church being in a state of great decay, a faculty was obtained in 1749 to repair and "beautify" the edifice, and upwards of £800 were spent on the renovation. Mr. Barrett states that £420 12s. of the outlay were raised by a rate of 4s. 3d. in the pound on the landowners; but the figures seem irreconcilable with the historian's subsequent assertion that there were 203 houses in the parish in 1749, paying £225 in poor rates at 11½d. in the pound.

On the 10th January, 1750, the Bristol vessel Phœnix, Captain Carbry, arrived at Kingroad after a remarkable adventure. The ship was off Lisbon on the 22nd December, with a cargo from Malaga, when she was boarded by an Algerine corsair of 30 guns. Carbry had one of the passes which European Powers then allowed their merchant-men to purchase from the Dey of Algiers, but under pretence that this document was a forgery, the Phœnix was seized as a prize by the pirates, who sent six Turks on board with instructions to make for Algiers. On the passage, however, Carbry, assisted by three of his crew, recovered his ship after flinging two of the pirates overboard. He was warmly praised for his bravery on his arrival in Bristol. The above account, which varies slightly from that in the local journals, is taken from Carbry's affidavit forwarded to the Government, and now in the Record Office.

The first banking company established in Bristol was formed early in March, 1750, and the proprietors opened their offices in Broad Street on the 1st August. The partners in the enterprise were Isaac Elton, Harford Lloyd, William Miller, Thomas Knox, and Matthew Hale. Some local annalists have asserted that when this institution was opened, the only banking house out of London was one at Derby, kept by a Jew. As a matter of fact, private bankers were then to be found in all the chief provincial towns, though banking was rarely their professed occupation. One of the earliest in Bristol was one Richard Bayly, who was employed by the Corporation to remit money to London in 1685. About twenty years later, banking business was transacted by a bookseller named Wall, in Corn Street, and after his death his widow carried on both branches of his trade for many years with great reputation. John Vaughan, a goldsmith living at the corner of Wine Street and High Street, was at the same time conducting financial transactions on a more extensive scale, and they were continued by his son, who will presently be found cooperating in the establishment of a second banking company. In the city of Gloucester, James Wood, a prosperous draper, began to be known as a banker in 1716. He was succeeded by his son and grandson, the latter of whom became famous for his vast wealth, eccentricity, and sordidness. The Woods had an early rival, the *Gloucester Journal* of May 17th, 1748, making mention of " T. Price, banker and jeweller in this city." Returning to the new (which soon acquired the title of the " Old ") Bristol bank, the company, in April, 1776, announced their removal from Broad Street to " the house erected for their business at the upper end of Clare Street, and adjoining to Corn Street." (Leonard's Lane then formed the point of division between the two thoroughfares.) The removal to the present site took place nearly half a century later.

After what has been already said respecting the manners and customs of the Kingswood colliers, one is not surprised to learn that the spiritual destitution of the district gave Bishop Butler much anxiety during the later years of his residence in Bristol. At his instigation, a committee of the Council was appointed to consider the advisability of separating Kingswood from the extensive and populous parish of St. Philip, the bishop offering to give £400 (more than a year's income of his see) towards the endowment of a new church. The committee reported in August, 1750, in favour of the scheme, and on their recommendation the Chamber subscribed £250 towards the building fund, on condition that the patronage of the new living should be vested in the Corporation. A further donation of £250 was made in 1755. (The advowson was sold about eighty years later for over £2,000.) An Act to authorise the division of the parish was obtained in 1751. A satirical comparison in a local paper between the open-handedness of Bristolians in rearing the new Assembly Room in Prince's Street and their apathy as regarded the edifice at Kingswood—the first local church erected for nearly 300 years—indicates the religious lethargy that then prevailed in the Establishment. The foundation stone of the church was laid by the mayor on the 3rd March, 1752, and the edifice was consecrated on the 6th September, 1756, by Bishop Hume. It had cost about £2,000. How little the spiritual welfare of the population was considered by some of the promoters of the scheme may be imagined from the fact that the first incumbent appointed—William Cary—was non-resident, being already rector of Winterbourne, rector of St. Philip's, and chancellor of the diocese.

The promotion of Kingswood Church was one of the latest incidents in the local episcopacy of Dr. Butler. In August, 1750, he was translated to Durham. During his twelve years' connection with Bristol he is said to have expended nearly £5,000 in the restoration of the palace and private chapel in Lower College Green. It is now amusing to read that the bishop fell under suspicion of being a Papist through his ordering a plain white marble cross to be placed at the back of the communion table in this chapel. (Lord Chancellor Hardwicke subsequently urged Bishop Yonge to remove this ornament. Coles' MSS., British Museum.) One of Butler's peculiarities was a fondness for walking for some hours in the palace garden at night, especially on dark nights. Dr. Tucker, then his chaplain, who was frequently his companion in these perambulations, states that one wild evening, while the wind was howling around the Cathedral, the bishop suddenly astounded him by inquiring whether he did not think it probable that nations, like men, were sometimes stricken with insanity. Nothing else, he added, could account for many striking facts in history. Dr. Butler's health having failed soon after his removal to Durham, he returned to the Hot Well, and subsequently went to Bath, where he died on the 16th June, 1752. At his request, his remains were interred in Bristol Cathedral, at the foot of the episcopal chair.

Dr. Tucker, referred to above, published in 1750 an "Essay on Trade," remarkable for its exposition of principles far in advance of the age. The writer, who had become rector of St. Stephen's a few months before, advocated the throwing open of English ports, the liberation of trade and industry from numberless oppressive restrictions, and the sweeping away of monopolies, duties, bounties, and prohibitions—in short, asserting those principles of free trade inculcated many years later by Adam Smith in the "Wealth of Nations." In 1752, under instructions from the Court, Dr. Tucker wrote a treatise on the "Elements of Commerce and Theory of Taxes" for the instruction of the young Prince of Wales, afterwards George III. He was appointed, in 1756, a prebendary of the Cathedral, a post which he relinquished in 1758 on being appointed dean of Gloucester. He retained, however, the rectory of St. Stephen's, and continued to be a prominent personage in Bristol until nearly the close of the century.

In August, 1750, the Common Council appointed John Wraxall to the office of swordbearer, a comfortably endowed post, often bestowed on fallen greatness. Mr. Wraxall, who had been an extensive linen draper and a master of the Merchants' Society, long occupied a house and shop on Bristol Bridge. In December, 1778, Nathaniel Wraxall, a member of the same family, and father of the once famous Sir Nathaniel William Wraxall, Bart., but who had been unfortunate in business as a merchant, was also appointed swordbearer. Southey states that the baronet's mother resided for many years in Terrill Street.

The value of agricultural land in the immediate vicinity of the city was still very low in 1750. An advertisement in the *Bristol Journal* of September 8th offers for sale a farm house and 45 acres of land at Redland. The farm, which was tithe free, let at £40 per annum.

Dr. Newton, Bishop of Bristol, relates in his memoirs a local anecdote of Robert Henley, many years leader of the western circuit, and afterwards known as Lord Chancellor

Northington, the date of which may be assigned to about 1750. During the Bristol Assizes, says the Bishop, in a cause of some consequence, Mr. [William] Reeve, a considerable Quaker merchant, was cross-examined by Henley with much raillery and ridicule. When the court had adjourned, and the lawyers were gathered at the White Lion, Mr. Henley was informed that a gentleman desired to see him in an adjoining room, and on the counsellor responding to the summons he found Mr. Reeve, who locked the door, put the key in his pocket, and forthwith demanded satisfaction for the scurrilous treatment he had received. "Thou might'st think, perhaps, that a Quaker might be insulted with impunity, but I am a man of spirit. Here are two swords, here are two pistols; choose thy weapons, or fight me at fisty cuffs if thou had'st rather; but fight me thou shalt, or beg my pardon." Henley pleaded the privileges of the bar, but was finally forced to say that if he had offended Mr. Reeve he was sorry for it, and was ready to beg his pardon. The resolute Quaker replied that as the affront was public the reparation must be so too, and Henley, after some resistance, apologised to Mr. Reeve before the barristers regaling themselves in the hotel. Some years afterwards, when Henley had become Lord Chancellor, he wrote to Mr. Reeve, stating that he had ordered two pipes of Madeira to be imported into Bristol, and begging the merchant to pay the charges on them, and to forward them to their destination. This was done as desired; and the winter following, when Mr. Reeve was in town, he dined at the Chancellor's with several of the nobility and gentry. After dinner, the Chancellor related the story of what had passed when he made Mr. Reeve's acquaintance, to the no little diversion of the company. Lord Campbell, in his customary anxiety to heighten the effect of his stories, dubs Mr. Reeve "Zephaniah," in his "Lives of the Chancellors." In July, 1757, William Reeve and three other leading merchants, on behalf of the Union (Whig) Club, invited the Duke of Newcastle to the anniversary dinner of the society at Merchants' Hall. Mr. Reeve built a large mansion at Arno's Vale, to which he added the stables and offices locally known as Black Castle. Horace Walpole, as will be seen later on, styled the place "the Devil's Cathedral." Whilst the buildings were in progress, some of the old gateways of the city were being removed, and Mr. Reeve obtained four figures and other carved stonework from the relics, which he inserted in the walls and entrance archway. Subsequently the disruption of commercial relations with America was disastrous to Mr. Reeve, and his property came into the market. It was then discovered that the unfortunate gentleman, although a Quaker, was the owner of the tithes of the parish of Brislington! (*Felix Farley's Journal*, Oct. 29th, 1785).

Mr. Hugh Owen, in his "Two Centuries of Ceramic Art in Bristol," and Mr. Llewellin Jewett, whose account of Bristol productions in his "Ceramic Art of Great Britain" is chiefly copied from Mr. Owen, concur in asserting that the first attempt to produce an imitation of Chinese porcelain in this city dates from 1765; the evidence relied upon being certain letters written by Richard Champion in the closing months of that year, in which a small factory is mentioned as having been just established, and again as having been closed. The discovery of a file of the *Bristol Intelligencer*, however, has brought to light some new and interesting facts bearing on the subject, proving that the above authors have post-dated the earliest Bristol China works by at least fifteen years. In the newspaper in question, dated December 12th, 1750, is an advertisement commencing as follows:— " Whereas for some time past attempts have been made in this city to introduce a manufacture in imitation of China ware, and the Proprietors, having brought the said undertaking to a considerable degree of perfection, have determined to extend their works." The announcement goes on to inform parents and guardians of lads above 14 years that, if lodgings and necessaries be provided during their apprenticeship, youths will be learnt the art of pottery as practised in Staffordshire, without charge. The manuscript travels of Dr. Pocock, Bishop of Meath, now in the British Museum, contain two interesting references to this manufactory. When in Cornwall in 1750, the tourist made the following note dated October 13th:—" Visited the Lizard Point to see the Soapy Rock. There are white patches in it, which is mostly valued for making porcelane, now carrying on at Bristol. They get £5 a ton for it." In a note dated Bristol, November 2nd, 1750, Dr. Pocock adds:—" I went to see a manufacture lately established here by one of the principals of the manufacture at Limehouse, which failed. It is at a glass-house, and is called Lowris (?) china-house. They have two sorts of ware, one called stone china, which has a yellow cast; that I suppose is made of pipe-clay and calcined flint. The other they call old China; this is whiter, and I suppose is made of calcined flint and the soapy rock at Lizard Point, which tis known they use. This is painted blue, and some is white like the old china of a yellowish cast. Another kind is white with a blueish cast, and both are called ornamental white china. They make very beautiful white sauce-boats, adorned with reliefs of festoons, which sell for 16s. a pair." In the *Intelligencer* of July 20th, 1751, is the following :—" This is to give notice, That the ware made in this city for some time past in imitation of foreign China is now sold at the Proprietors' warehouse in Castle Green, at the end near the Castle Gate. For the future no ware will be sold at the place where it is manufactured, nor will any person be admitted to enter there without leave from the Proprietors." The names of those concerned in the works have not been found, but it may be added that Champion was only seven years of age in 1750.

This reference to Bristol China may appropriately introduce a few facts bearing upon local potteries. The existence at the beginning of the century of a small Delft ware factory in Bristol has been already mentioned, but unfortunately little is known respecting the manufacturers. The initials on an existing specimen, dated 1703, are S. M. B. Another, of 1716, has no maker's name; a third, of 1722, is marked M. S. About the latter date, the pottery, which was situated at Redcliff Back, came into the hands of Richard Frank, commonly called a gallipot maker, son of Thomas Frank, who had also followed the same trade, and is supposed to have been the only potter in Bristol in 1697. Richard Frank produced a quantity of plates and dishes, as well as imitation Dutch tiles for fire places, dairies, etc. His finest work at present known is a slab, composed of twenty-four tiles, on which is painted a view of Redcliff Church. This is now in the Museum of Practical Geology. As the arms of Bishop Butler appear on one of the tiles, the slab (which for many years ornamented the window-bed of a Bristol bacon dealer) must have been produced between 1738 and 1750. Several specimens in the hands of private collectors range between the same years. Frank afterwards took his son Thomas into partnership, and the works were removed in 1776 to a factory in Water Lane, previously occupied by a stone-ware potter. In 1784 they were purchased by Joseph Ring, a son in law of Richard Frank, who in 1786 began to manufacture what was known as Queen's ware, and the making of Delft was abandoned two years later. A contemporary of Frank was John Townsend, of whom the little we know is derived from the corporate archives. Describing himself as a " muggmaker," Townsend petitioned the Council in 1739, representing that about four years previously he had built a mugg-kiln in Tucker Street at a cost of £130, and carried on business there until December, 1738, when the Corporation, as owners of the land, had ordered him to stop the works, for which he prayed compensation. His name does not appear again. Another local Delft potter was Joseph Flower, whose name first occurs in 1741. In 1775 he lived on the Quay, but removed in 1777 to Corn Street, "the shop adjoining the Post Office," where he remained until his death in 1785. Specimens of his work, says Mr. Jewett, are regarded as superior to most Bristol Delft, and are in fact equal to Dutch. Returning to Ring's production of Queen's, or Staffordshire, ware, a few extracts from an invoice accompanying two crates, " sent to Calis for a sample," in December, 1787, show the remarkable prices of that age :—" 6 ovil dishes, 1s. 8 doz. table plates, 12s. 6 sallad dishes, 11 inches, 3s. 6d. 3 3-pint coffee pots, 2s. 6d. 2 sugar dishes, with covers, 4d. 4 doz. coffee cups, 2s. 4 dozen coffee cups and saucers paynted, 4s. 4d. 1 doz. table plates paynted, 2s. 3d. 1 doz. quart mugs varigated, 5s. 1 doz. pint do. do., 2s. 6d."

An interesting list of Bristol carriers in a "Guide to Bath and Bristol," published in 1750, shows the great development attained by that branch of traffic. The number of carriers plying to and from the city was ninety-four, many of whom must have had several wagons, as some of the vehicles transported goods to Leeds, Nottingham, and other distant towns. The chief inns at which the carriers were stationed were the White Lion, Thomas Street, and the Three Queens, Thomas Street, which each harboured twelve. Eight stood at the Dolphin Inn, Dolphin Lane; seven at the Horse Shoe, Wine Street, and at the George, Temple Gate; nine at the George, Castle Street; and six at the Bell, Thomas Street. Four London wagons had warehouses in Peter Street.

In January, 1751, was published "An Hymn to the Nymph of Bristol Spring (with beautiful Cuts, price 1s. 6d.)," by William Whitehead, who a few years later was honoured with the office of Poet Laureate. Mr. Whitehead's so-called poem is a finished specimen of the bastard classicism in vogue at that drearily prosaic period. Avonia, dishonoured by Neptune, is endowed by him, as an atonement, with the power of healing diseases, especially those that have relation to Love, and is always attended by her handmaids, Mirth and Peace. The respective beauties of the other English spas are declared to be united in Avonia's retreat, which has. an attraction peculiar to itself in the "lurking" diamonds which "mimic those of Ind." An incomprehensible episode follows, in honour of a certain Leya, who is said to have given her name to the village of Leigh; and Avonia is finally petitioned to diffuse her healing influence over foreign nations, as her waters never lose their virtue by time or change of climate—a little puff for which the Bristol bottle makers were doubtless grateful. Mr. Whitehead's poem seems to have had some influence on the attendance at the Well during the following summer, the London *Morning Post* of August 2nd observing:—" We hear from Bristol that there is the fullest season ever known at the Hot Wells."

William Champion, of Bristol, merchant, who had obtained a patent in 1737 for manufacturing spelter (zinc) from English ores, petitioned the House of Commons in 1751 for a renewal of his privilege. He asserted that previous to his discovery spelter was obtained solely from the East Indies, the price being at one time raised by the combination of importers to £260 per ton. Having erected large works [at Warmley] in which many hundred men were employed, he had produced spelter of the best quality, whereupon his rivals, importing excessive supplies, had reduced the price per ton to £48, though at a heavy loss to themselves. Being a great sufferer from this proceeding, he prayed for an extension of his patent. The House ordered a Bill to be brought in for that purpose, but owing to an opposition organised in Lancashire the measure was dropped.

Early in the session of 1751, Mr. Nugent, a member of the Government, who subsequently represented Bristol in three Parliaments, brought forward a Bill for the naturalisation of foreign Protestants, refugees from the persecution of the Romanist powers of the continent. A similar Bill had become law in 1708, but was repealed under the Tory Ministry of 1711. Its revival excited alarm in many quarters, and several corporations petitioned against it, alleging that such an encouragement to immigration would flood the labour market, and throw English workmen out of employment. The Common Council and the Merchants' Society of Bristol supported the measure, which also found a warm advocate in the Rev. Josiah Tucker, rector of St. Stephen's, who published an able pamphlet on the subject. On the other hand a number of citizens memorialised the Commons against the scheme, disapproving of its provisions, and asserting that the two local petitions in its favour expressed the opinion of less than forty persons. (The Opposition in London seized the opportunity to reprint Sir John Knight's famous tirade of 1694 against foreign Protestants. The rancorous effusion of the old Bristol Jacobite appeared in *Read's Journal* of March 9th, 1751.) The Ministry, with characteristic timidity, withdrew the Bill just before the third reading, in April. The intelligence was received with rejoicing by the opposition in Bristol. The church bells rang merry peals, while the populace patrolled the streets with Tucker's effigy, which was ignominiously burnt.

Petitions to the House of Commons were forwarded during the session by the Corporation and the Merchants' Society, expressing great concern at the excessive drinking of gin and other spirits amongst the working classes, leading to frequent instances of sudden death, the general depravation of health and morals, and the increase of crime and poverty. In consequence of numerous petitions to the same effect, an Act was passed, the preamble of which asserted that the above evils arose in a great measure from the number of persons who vended liquors under pretence of being distillers. The statute absolutely prohibited the retailing of spirits by manufacturers, and imposed increased penalties on unlicensed vendors, an offender being liable to a public whipping upon a second conviction and to transportation for seven years upon a third!

At a meeting of the Council on the 23rd of February, a plan was produced for building a new bridge over the Froom at the head of the Quay, by which a carriage road would be opened from the bottom of Small Street to St. Augustine's Back. The matter was referred to a committee, which, after considering the matter for nearly three years, reported that the proposed bridge would prove an accommodation to the citizens. The dean and chapter having some property near the spot, an application for the sanction of that body was made in December, 1753, and the first response was an unreserved assent. In February, 1755, the chapter required, however, that the approaches should not be wider than would admit two carriages abreast, and in the following year it was mutually agreed that the road should not exceed twenty-five feet in width. The bridge, which was completed in 1755, cost the Corporation nearly £1,826.

The death of the Prince of Wales, in May, 1751, occasioned demonstrations of regret which were probably much more noisy than sincere. Amongst the items of civic expense were "Gunpowder, £20 18s. Paid John Simmons for painting two royal escution and plumb of feathers, placed in the mayor's chapel, hauling and firing guns £11 10s. 9d."

At a meeting of the Council, in December, 1751, on the motion of Alderman Dampier, it was resolved that a handsome state coach and harness, bearing only the arms of the city, should be provided by the Corporation for the use of the mayor for the time being, "and that this coach shall not on any pretence whatsoever be used out of the liberty of this city." It was further ordered, on the motion of the same gentleman, that a handsome scabbard of gilt plate, with arms and devices, should be bought at the expense of the Chamber, to be used by each mayor "instead of the scabbard which hath been usually presented by the sheriffs on New Year's Day;" future sheriffs undertaking to present each mayor "with such piece or pieces of plate as he himself shall choose, of a value of not less than 50 guineas, on New Year's Day, as usual." It was further resolved that the cost of the new scabbard should be repaid by future sheriffs at the rate of five guineas yearly. The coach resulting from the above resolution was a very gorgeous affair, the pattern being taken from the carriage of the Lord Mayor of London; and it is amusing to find that the first payment (£34 8s.) was made to Alderman Dampier himself, for "42¼ yards of crimson cassoy." The manufacture of the vehicle occupied eighteen months. The coachbuilder was paid £139, the carver £134, the brazier £136, the lace-dealer £77, the painter £100, and the glass-maker £22 10s. With other items for leather, smith's work, etc., the outlay was over £700. The coach was displayed in public for the first time in June, 1753, on the anniversary of the king's accession, and excited much admiration. The vehicle had a brief career. After only sixteen years' use, it was reported as greatly out of repair, and it was soon after sold to Mr. William Weare for £63. The resolution in reference to the mayor's scabbard must have been tacitly modified, for the result was the magnificent sword still carried on state occasions, with a blade nearly 3¼ feet in length, and a silver handle of great size and massive scroll work. The silver work on the sword and scabbard, weighing nearly 202 ounces, cost £176 13s. 3d., and the velvet, gold plate, and other items, raised the first outlay to £188 6s. 3d., exclusive of £3 3s. given to John Simmons, a painter of local repute, for "drawing the design." In 1756 it required repairs, costing £13, and the silversmith, Nath. Nangle, for " his extraordinary trouble and expenses about the sword," was paid £21 more in 1758.

An attempt to ascertain the population of the city at the end of the first half of the century was made by a gentleman named John Browning, of Barton Hill. Having forwarded his calculations to the Royal Society, they were printed in the Transactions of that body for 1753 (vol. x. p. 379). Mr. Browning founded the statistics upon the number of burials recorded in the ten years ending 1750, and also upon the number of houses. As the interments of persons dying in the out-parishes of St. James and St. Philip took place in the city, the population of those suburban districts was necessarily included. The burials in the above period were stated to have been 17,317; and as "the latest and most accurate observations demonstrate that in great cities a 25th part of the people die yearly," Mr. Browning estimated the population at 43,275. The number of houses rated to the land-tax at Michaelmas, 1751, was 4,866, to which the writer added 1,216 for small tenements, hospitals, etc., and 1,200 more for the out-parishes, making a total of 7,282. Reckoning the average number of inmates at six per house, the population was found to be 43,692, of whom about 36,500 lived within the city, and 7,200 in the suburbs. The calculations tend to confirm the accuracy of the statistics preserved by Browne Willis (p. 194).

An account of the local newspapers issued in the first half of the century was given under the year 1702. It is now proposed to deal briefly with their successors. In March, 1752, Samuel and Felix Farley, sons and successors of the Samuel Farley who started a paper about 1713, dissolved partnership, and became rivals in trade, the elder brother continuing to publish the old *Bristol Journal* in Castle Street, while Felix, on the 28th March, issued from Small Street the first number of a periodical bearing his own name, which was destined to live until within living memory. Felix Farley assured advertisers that his new *Journal* would extend further than any other yet published in the city, while purchasers were advised to preserve their copies, because, in addition to the news of the week, "we purpose to render our composition a kind of library of arts and sciences." The brothers did not long survive their separation. Felix's death was announced in his paper of the 28th April, 1753, when the public were informed that the business would be continued by his widow [Elizabeth] and son, who alleged that their stock of types consisted "of a large and curious collection compleated by the most ingenious artists in Europe." Samuel died in the autumn of the same year, and was succeeded by his niece, Sarah, who soon after announced that she would continue the *Journal*, and that to give greater publicity to advertisements they would be posted "in the most public places in the city, and especially the Exchange and Tolzey, in the market place, and on the several city gates, and by men who carry the *Journal* into the country by Monday (two days after publication) to fix them up in the cities of Bath and Wells, and all the market towns." Neither of the papers showed any lack of vigour whilst conducted by ladies. Elizabeth published a letter in *Felix Farley's Journal* of January 11th, 1755, referring to the remarks of a rival editor, already mentioned:—"Edward Ward, originally a haberdasher, and late a maltster, distiller, &c., &c., at present a bookseller, printer, and publisher of a virulent party paper"—the *Intelligencer*. A little later she twitted Sarah Farley with publishing articles a month old, and described the editor of the *Bristol Chronicle* as unauthentic and hasty. Sarah was a Quaker, and horrified that pacific body in 1769 by reproducing in her paper Junius's celebrated "Letter to a King," for which, according to the chapel minutes, she was severely reproached, and took "the monition kindly." She continued, however, to reproduce Junius's invectives as they appeared. On her death, in 1774, the *Journal* was continued by her administratrix, Hester Farley, "a near relative." As Hester was, in fact, a daughter of Felix, the chronic quarrels of the family seem to have been still unappeased. In the following year, however, Hester disposed of the paper to "Rouths and Company;" who in July, 1777, gave it the distinctive title of *Sarah Farley's Bristol Journal*. In the meantime a new rival had appeared. Sarah's former foreman and clerk, annoyed at not being chosen as her successors, set up *Bonner and Middleton's Bristol Journal* in August, 1774, so that there were three local papers of the same name. The inconvenience of this arrangement was obvious, but it was not until about the close of the century that *Sarah Farley's Journal* was acquired by new proprietors, who changed its title, but were unable to keep it alive. *Bonner and Middleton's Journal* became the *Mirror* in April, 1804, and was for some years the most popular paper in the city. The *Bristol Chronicle* was started by John Grabham, in Narrow Wine Street, on the 5th January, 1760, but had a brief career. The *Bristol Gazette* was begun in 1767 by William Pine, an able printer, who had been connected with the *Chronicle*, and his paper was throughout the remainder of the century the organ of the Corporation and of the Whig party. The *Bristol Mercury*, " a new and impartial weekly paper," was started on the 1st March, 1790, by Messrs. Bulgin and Rosser, of Broad Street and Wine Street. Rosser retired a few years later, when Bulgin became sole proprietor.

The cruel sport of cock-throwing was still popular on Shrove Tuesday. An order was issued by the magistrates in the spring of 1752, requiring the parish constables to apprehend persons assembling for this purpose; but as the populace could easily evade the threatened penalties by taking a stroll into the suburbs, the decree can have had little effect.

A remarkable scene at an execution of three criminals at St. Michael's gallows is recorded in *Felix Farley's Journal* of April 25th, 1752: "After the cart drove away," says the reporter, " the hangman very deservedly had his head broke for endeavouring to pull off Mooney's shoes, and a fellow had like to have been killed in mounting the gallows to take away the ropes that were left after the malefactors were cut down. A young woman came fifteen miles for the sake of the rope from Mooney's neck, which was given to her, it being by many apprehended that the halter of an executed person will charm away the ague, and perform many other cures." (Another superstition of the time was that children suffering from wens could be cured by having their necks stroked nine times by the hand of an executed criminal, and little patients were often brought to the gallows to undergo this operation.) Mooney's life was afterwards published in pamphlet form by Felix Farley, at the instance of the local Methodists, who claimed him as a convert. On his own confession he had led a life of crime from the age of sixteen, and had fought with the rebels at Culloden after deserting from the army. As showing the insecurity of the streets at that period, it may be added that Mooney's first victim in Bristol was Mr. Rich, son of an alderman, who was robbed near his father's house in Maudlin Lane. An hour or two later the rogue despoiled Mr. Shiercliff, a skilful portrait painter, of his watch and money in Queen Square. On the following day, accompanied by another thief, who suffered death with him, he attacked Mr. Wasborough, of Pen Park, on Durdham Down, but that gentleman beat off his assailants after receiving a pistol bullet in his hat. Mooney then went alone to College Green, where he robbed a gentleman of a ring and some money. In honour of his conversion, the Methodists buried the criminal's body with great ceremony, and afterwards attempted to hold services over his grave, which were suppressed by the magistrates. This opportunity may be taken to give a list of the local executions that occurred during the second half of the century. Mr. Pryce's roll for the period contains the names of 32 criminals. The number of death punishments recorded below is 61, of which only five were for murder. It is probable that many other executions for suburban offences occurred at Gloucester and Ilchester, the newspaper reports being often defective.

1752. April 24, Nicholas Mooney } highway robbery.
    " " John Jones
    " " W. Cudmore—return from transportation.
1753. May 7, W. Critchett } unnatural crime.
    " " Rich. Arnold
1754. Sept. 27, Thos. Lafey—highway robbery.
    " " Eliz. Hind—highway robbery.
1755. Aug. 18, Cath. Gardner—child murder.
    Oct. 8, Wm. Williams—forgery.
1758. Mar. 10 (at Gloucester), Thos. Roberts—murder, Cutler's Mills.
    Aug. 24, John Hobbs—murder.
    Sept. 8, John Price—stealing ribbon.
    " " Wm. Saunders—stealing cloth.
1761. June 1, Wm. D. Sheppard—unnatural crime.
    Oct. 22, Pat. Ward (gibbeted)—murder.
    Nov. 6, John Cope—return from transportation.
1763. June 24, James Rendall—burglary.
1764. April 16, Wm. Dawson—robbery.
    May 14, Thos. Usher—robbery of £1800.
    Aug. 24 (Gloucester), John Jordan—robbery on the Down.
1765. Apr. 12 (Glouc.), Wm. O'Brien } burglary, Durdham Down.
    " " James Wall
1769. June 9, Robt. Slack—horse stealing.
1771. Dec. 10, John Faulker, soldier, shot on Brandon hill—desertion.
1772. May 15, Jonathan Britain—forgery.
1774. Apr. 22, Isaac Barrett—street robbery.
1775. Sept. 22, Dan. Haynes—housebreaking.
1776. Apr. 19 (Glouc.), John Gilbert—burglary at Clifton.
    Sept. 16 (Ilchester), John Stock—robbery, Bedminster.
1778. May 15, Thos. Crewys—forgery.
1781. Oct. 12, Benj. Loveday } unnatural crime.
    " " John Burke
1783. Mar. 31, Jenkin Prothero (gibbeted)—murder.
    Apr. 16 (Ilchester), Jos. Elkins—coining, Bedminster.
    May 23, Wm. Morley—forgery.
    " " Wm. Shutler—housebreaking.
    Sept. 6 (Bedminster), Geo. Gaines (17)—stealing linen.
1784. Apr. 8 (Totterdown), Rich. Randall—highway robbery.
    Sept. 1 (Ilchester), Thos. Phillips—robbery, Totterdown.
1785. Apr. 8, John Collins—murder.
    Aug. 10 (Ilchester), Wm. Jones } robbery, Knowl.
    " " Bar. O'Neal
1786. Oct. 6, Ambrose Cook—highway robbery.

1788. Apr. 16 (Glouc.), Thos. Fox ⎫ burglary,
 " " " Chas. Frost ⎬ Cote House,
 " " " Jas. Thorp ⎪ Durdham Down.
 " " " Rob. Collings ⎭
1790. May 7, Edw. Macnamara—forgery.
 July 9, Wm. Hungerford—robbery.
1792. Apr. 14 (Glouc.), Chris. Rochfort ⎫ robberies, Durdham Down.
 " " " John Hughes ⎭
1793. Apr. 10 (Ilchester), Jenkin Jones—robbery, Bedminster.
 May 3, Robt. Hamilton—robbery.
1795. Apr. 24, Benj. Smith—forgery.
1798. Aug. 11 (Glou.), John Roberts ⎫
 " " " John Hawkins ⎬ robbery, St. George's.
 " " " Benj. Gullick ⎭
1799. Apr. 26, James Baber ⎫
 " " Charles Powell ⎬ forgery.
 " " John Duggan ⎭
1800. Apr. 25, Rich. Haynes—shooting at a constable.

An attempt was made about this time by a joint stock company of local merchants to establish a new branch of commerce—the whale fishery. The concern was divided into 99 shares, the whole of which were apparently taken up *Felix Farley's Journal* of July 18th, 1752, stated that the Bristol and Adventure, two ships fitted out by the company, had just arrived, " having had the good fortune to catch five whales, and 'tis said they are valued at £2000, which with the bounty money of 40s. per ton, make their voyage a very successful one." The odoriferous cargo was landed at Sea Mills dock. The enterprise was continued for some years with varying results; and a third ship, the St. Andrew, was sent out in 1755 and 1756, perhaps by the same adventurers. Some difficulty was found in securing crews, and an advertisement in March, 1757, assured sailors that " a Greenland voyage is found by experience to be the healthiest in the world," and that out of over ninety men engaged in the Bristol and Adventure, only one had died a natural death, and two been killed, in six successive voyages. The announcement did not add that the Adventure in the previous year had been frozen in the ice for upwards of ten weeks. Some unsuccessful voyages followed, and the *Bristol Journal* of March 22nd, 1761, contained a notification that the Whale Fishery Company had dissolved. Nevertheless, in January, 1765, the same paper published a report that several eminent local merchants were then " soliciting the grant of an island in the Gulph of Lawrence, which they propose to settle at their own expense, it having on a late survey been found extremely commodious for carrying on a Whale Fishery in those seas." The application appears to have been unsuccessful.

A corporate notice in *Felix Farley's Journal* of July 18th, 1752, forbids any person to buy or sell leather in any tanner's yard or shop in Bristol, " or within ten miles round," on penalty of the forfeiture of the goods. Leather was to be sold only at the fair, or at the leather market in the Back Hall—an extensive building, from which a large rental was received by the civic body. The above regulation was certainly illegal, and could be safely set at defiance by the population outside the city boundaries.

Cricket had few local votaries in the middle of the eighteenth century. It is never mentioned in the newspapers except as offering, like pugilism, racing, and cockfighting, an opportunity for gambling. A London journal of 1729 notified that a cricket match would take place on the town ham at Gloucester on the 22nd September "for upwards of 20 guineas," and it is probable that the players were imported for the purpose. *Felix Farley's Journal* of August 29th, 1752, contains the following advertisement: "On Monday next will be played a match of cricket between eleven men of London and eleven men of Bristol, on Durdham Down, for the sum of 20 guineas." The result is not recorded. The following still more significant paragraph occurs in the *Gloucester Journal* of May 29th, 1769:—" We hear from Cirencester that the young gentlemen of that place are introducing the manly exercise of cricket into this county, where it has been hitherto unknown." The writer adds that some matches had been already played for "considerable sums." It may be interesting to add that many early cricket matches mentioned in the London newspapers were played by five men on each side.

The great success of the first Bristol bank naturally led to the establishment of a second local institution. *Felix Farley's Journal* of September 16th says:—" We hear that a Bank is now opened in Corn Street by Thomas Goldney, Morgan Smith, Michael Miller, Richard Champion, James Reed, and John Vaughan." Mr. Miller was the wealthy merchant whom Hume exasperated by criticising his ungrammatical epistles. Though Vaughan's name stood last in the roll of proprietors, the business of the concern was chiefly derived from the old and extensive financial connection formed by his father as a private banker; and he was for some years the managing partner of the firm. The names of Goldney and Champion soon disappeared. In 1789 the proprietors consisted of Messrs. Vaughan, Baker,

Smith, Hale, and Davis; but previous to July, 1794, important changes had taken place, the firm then consisting of Messrs. Philip Miles, Richard Vaughan, Jeremy Baker, Philip John Miles, Benjamin Baugh, and Samuel New. "Miles's Bank," as it was popularly called, had a lengthy and prosperous career.

The Act for the reformation of the Calendar came into force in 1752, when the legal supputation by which the year began on the 25th March was abolished, and the common mode of reckoning from the 1st of January was universally established. This alteration was generally popular, but it was far otherwise with the next clause of the Act, by which the day following the 2nd September, 1752, was ordered to be called the 14th September, the eleven intermediate nominal days being omitted from the almanacs. The arrangement caused much temporary inconvenience to traders, farmers, and others accustomed to settlements at stated periods; but it was especially obnoxious to the uneducated classes, who held certain fixed festivals in special veneration, who could not understand why they should be deprived of nearly half a month, and who, many of them, believed that their lives would be shortened to a corresponding extent. As is shown by a well known picture of Hogarth's, the popular demand for the restoration of "our eleven days" became an election cry in 1754. In the meantime the opponents of the law sulkily submitted to it until Christmas gave them an opportunity for a manifestation. *Felix Farley's Journal* of January 6th, 1753, says:— "Yesterday being Old Christmas Day, the same was obstinately observed by our country people in general, so that (being market day according to the order of our magistrates) there were but few at market, who embraced the opportunity of raising their butter to 9d. or 10d. per pound"— about double the ordinary price. In some market towns the farmers were wholly absent; and to gratify the feelings of their parishioners, many rural clergymen preached "Nativity sermons" on the following Sunday. The flowering of the celebrated Glastonbury thorn was looked for with much anxiety. The first intelligence of its deportment gave satisfaction, the above newspaper affirming that the holy plant, after having contemptuously ignored the new style, burst into blossom on the 5th January, thus indicating that Old Christmas Day should alone be observed, in spite of an irreligious legislature. This story, strange to say, was printed at Hull for the use of the "flying stationers" who then traversed the country, and produced an immense effect in the rural districts. Eventually some one thought it worth while to write to the vicar of Glastonbury, and the emptiness of the report was at once made known, the reverend gentleman declaring that the thorn " blossomed the fullest and finest about Christmas Day, new style, or rather sooner." As farmers and labourers were not newspaper readers, however, their faith in the fable was transmitted to their descendants. Mr. Humphrey, in his " History of Wellington," published in 1889, states that many of the labouring classes in that neighbourhood still strictly observe Old Christmas Day, believing that it would be wicked to work on the ancient festival.

The error committed at this time by the local societies in fixing upon a day for commemorating Colston's birth has been noticed at page 154. The " Loyal " (Tory) Society assembled on the morning of the 13th November, and went in " grand " procession to the Cathedral, where they heard an appropriate sermon. Thence, says the *Journal*, they marched to St. Mary Redcliff, where another sermon was preached " to a prodigious audience by the Rev. Mr. Sawier" (Seyer, father of the historian). The duplicate religious service was repeated in 1753, when the *Journal* stated that about 500 citizens were present at the dinners of the various Colston societies.

In November, 1752, the Merchants' Society unanimously resolved to address the members of Parliament for the city, requesting their aid in procuring the repeal of an Act passed during the previous session permitting English-born Jews to enjoy the privileges of British citizens. Similar representations were made by public bodies in other towns, and the statute aroused a storm of indignation throughout the country. A general election was approaching, and the Duke of Newcastle, trembling for his majority, characteristically retreated in a panic. A Government Bill was introduced at the earliest moment to repeal the Ministerial measure of the previous year, and Mr. Nugent, soon to become member for Bristol, was deputed to pilot it through the Commons. Nugent cynically admitted that he believed the Naturalisation Act to be a wise and just measure, and that he was acting against his conviction in proposing its repeal. His excuse was that " the passions of the lower sort of people ought to be humoured; for such people, like children, sometimes take a fancy to a hobby horse, without which there is no keeping them quiet." In the provinces, he added, he was charged with being the author of the New Style Act as well as of the Jews Act; and an old woman had been heard to remark, that "It was no wonder he should be for naturalising the devil, since he was one of those who banished Old Christmas." The political opponents of the Whigs having resisted Jewish emancipation from the outset, the Bill passed through both Houses with almost perfect unanimity.

Reference has been already made to the fatal prevalence of gin drinking. From a curious correspondence between Dr. Tucker and Lord Townshend in 1752, disinterred by the Historical Manuscripts Commission (11th Report, part iv.), it appears that merchants engaged in the slave trade found it profitable to spread a taste for the liquor on the African coast. Large supplies were bartered in exchange for human beings, and Tucker states, on the authority of "an eminent merchant of this place (Bristol), that he can get any quantity from Worcester to be delivered here at from 14d. to 15d. per gallon, the duty being drawn back."

An account, in the local newspapers, of a robbery committed in the house of a fashionable silversmith, living in Orchard Street, in January, 1753, depicts the style of dress then worn by the upper class of citizens. Amongst the property stolen were the following articles:—"A new Mazareen blue coat, lined with white; a silk camblet coat, lined with green silk; a Mazareen blue silk waistcoat, embroidered with gold; and a pair of silk breeches with gold button holes and buttons." Adding a large powdered wig, a cocked hat laced with gold, lace sleeve ruffles, silk stockings, shoes ornamented with gold buckles, and a scarlet cloak—all indispensable articles at that period—with a small muff carried during winter, we have the complete habiliments of the despoiled tradesman. The clergy, who also wore three-cornered hats and cauliflower wigs, with winter muffs, perambulated the streets in their cassocks, a practice which did not wholly expire until the beginning of the present century.

The magnates of the Corporation, although standing much on their dignity, occasionally condescended to patronise the entertainments offered to the dull city by roving showmen. On the 29th January, "the famous fire-eater, Mr. Powell," was requested to display his skill at the Council House, before the mayor, aldermen, councillors, "and other persons of distinction," which probably meant the ex-mayoresses and other worshipful females. Mr. Powell's advertisements informed the world that "He eats red-hot coals out of the fire as natural as bread; he fills his mouth with red-hot charcoal, and broils a slice of beef upon his tongue, and any person may blow the fire with a pair of bellows; he melts a quantity of resin, bees-wax, sealing wax, brimstone, and lead in a chafing dish, and eats the said combustibles with a spoon." The performance was rewarded by the pitiful payment of 21s. out of the corporate funds; but the poor conjurer may have been satisfied, for, unless he obtained the mayor's leave, he was liable to six months' imprisonment as a rogue and vagabond if he exhibited his tricks to the public. A few days later, the corporate dignitaries enjoyed another little relaxation, dimly indicated as follows in the civic accounts:— "James Kington, showing a machine for cut heads, &c. to Mr. Mayor and the Aldermen, £1 1s." The instrument was probably for engraving seals or cameos.

Felix Farley's Journal of February 10th, 1753, contains details of a horrible tragedy arising out of the slave trade. It appears that the captain of the Bristol ship Marlborough, while on a voyage from Africa to the plantations "indulged 28 Gold Coast negroes with their liberty on deck, for the sake of their assistance in managing the ship"—in other words, they were compelled to conduct themselves into bondage. But three days after the vessel left Bonny, whilst the sailors were between decks, engaged in washing the filth from about 400 slaves chained down to the planks, the above negroes seized firearms from the captain and watch, whom they shot, and spent the day in butchering the white crew, numbering thirty-five. The boatswain and about seven others were spared on their undertaking to navigate the ship back to Bonny, which was done, an attempt of the Bristol slaver Hawk to recapture the vessel being defeated by the determined firing of the negroes. About 270 of the slaves had been shipped at Bonny, and were to have been landed there, but a furious quarrel arose between them and the Gold Coast blacks, and in the fight which ensued about a hundred were thrown overboard or killed. After disembarking the survivors, the Gold Coast men, numbering about 150, stood off, retaining six English sailors to navigate them to their homes. The fate of the Marlborough is not recorded.

Gardens were still common in the heart of the city. An advertisement in a local paper of the 24th February states that a house, garden, and summer-house, in Tower Lane, lately occupied by an attorney at a rent of £9, were to be let. In the following week was a similar announcement respecting two houses in Milk Street, with "large gardens."

The law forbidding the dressing of dead bodies in linen was still enforced by the magistrates. In March, Mr. Christopher Willoughby, merchant, was convicted of violating the Act, and was mulcted in the penalty of £5.

Marmaduke Bowdler (sheriff, 1693), who had withdrawn from the Council owing to mercantile disasters some years before this date, and was then appointed clerk of the markets, was in March, 1753, granted a pension of £30 on account of his age and indigence. At the same meeting Elizabeth Dobbins, granddaughter of Samuel Wallis (mayor, 1695), and great granddaughter of Ezekiel Wallis (mayor, 1638), was voted an annuity of £4 for life.

An urgent complaint was made to the House of Commons during this session by local sugar refiners respecting the conduct of the sugar planters in Jamaica, who, it was alleged, so greatly restricted the culture of canes that sugar sold in England at 35s. to 40s. per cwt., while in France and Holland the price was only 19s. A pamphleteer, advocating the views of the petitioners, gives an interesting estimate of the extent of the English refining trade. "It is the general opinion," he says, "that there are about eighty refining houses in and about London, and twenty at least at Bristol; there are likewise refining houses at Chester, Liverpool, Lancaster, Whitehaven, Newcastle, Hull, and Southampton, and some in Scotland. I think there can be hardly fewer than 120 in all." He estimates that each refinery employed nine men permanently. The petitions were without effect.

The local press reported on the 5th May that two young ladies had just been robbed by a highwayman whilst walking in the fields near the city, and that the thief had stripped them of 35s. and two silver snuff-boxes. Snuffing was then a practice common to all ranks of society, and had many ardent votaries amongst the fair sex. Defoe, in whose time fashionable snuffs sold at from 8s. to 32s. per pound, remarked in one of his essays that his servant-maid took her snuff with the airs of a duchess. From the accounts of the Gore family at Bourton, already referred to, it appears that at least a pound of snuff weekly was consumed on an average in that gentleman's family. The manufacture of the article rose to considerable local importance, and about this time many of the corn mills in the suburbs were converted into snuff mills. The business must have extended rapidly, for at the Christmas quarter sessions in 1756 the grand jury represented to the justices that "the converting of any grist mills belonging to this city to any other purpose than that of grinding corn may become very detrimental to the publick," and expressed pleasure that the aldermen had been animated by the same sentiment in giving "notice to the tenant of the only mill belonging to the Corporation speedily to quit the same." The mill in question was the City Mill, St. James's Back, which was shortly afterwards advertised to be let for the grinding of corn only. The previous occupiers, Messrs. Weare, who were turned out in a very arbitrary manner, asked for compensation, but it was not until twenty years later that they were voted £200. Other snuff mills mentioned about the same period were known as Territt's, Lock's, Clifton (site of the Observatory), Combe Dingle, Barrow, Frenchay, and one or two others on the Froom. In 1754 William Hulme, a Scotch-snuff maker in Maryleport Street, leased a windmill at Cotham, and transformed it into a snuff manufactory. When he became bankrupt three years later, the place was advertised for sale, "having eleven mills erected for that purpose." The stonework of this mill forms the foundation of the lofty tower now standing in Cotham Park. There is reason to believe that the sign over Hulme's shop was a parrot. At all events Parrot snuff, which had a great reputation, was long sold in Maryleport Street by Messrs. Ricketts, the predecessors of Messrs. W. and H. O. Wills, and the latter firm still possess the grotesque wooden bird that formerly decorated the premises.

Owing to a deficient harvest in the preceding year, and a destructive cattle plague, which swept away a large proportion of the herds of the district, the poor were plunged in great distress in the spring of 1753. In May, the intelligence that a quantity of wheat was about to be exported from Bristol excited the Kingswood colliers to open violence. On Monday, the 21st May, many hundred miners and labourers entered the city at Lawford's Gate, and made their way to the Council House, where they represented their misery to the mayor and aldermen, and urged that exportation should be stopped. The authorities promised such relief as was in their power, especially a reduction in the price of bread; and many of the colliers expressed themselves satisfied. Some of the more violent, however, proceeded to the quay to plunder a ship bound for Dublin, laden with corn; but being charged by the constables armed with staves, they dispersed after a brief struggle, a few being wounded and others made prisoners. The news of this scuffle caused the rest of the colliers to take part with the rioters, and the constables, encountered in Small Street with their captives, having found it prudent to decamp, the victorious rabble smashed the windows of the Council House, wounded several persons with missiles, and eventually went off, vowing further vengeance. The outlook being serious, the militia was raised, a number of citizens were enrolled as special constables, and the inhabitants were directed to supply themselves with arms and ammunition. On the 24th a mob again appeared outside Lawford's Gate, but was attacked and dispersed without difficulty. Next day, however, the colliers, joined by a horde of weavers and disorderly ruffians living "outside the Gate," and numbering altogether about 900, entered the city by way of Milk Street, and advanced to Bridewell, where one of Monday's rioters was detained. The gates of the prison were attacked, and although one of the assailants was shot dead by a warder, the defences were speedily breached, the prison rifled, and the captive rescued. But before the rioters left, a small party of dragoons (sent from Gloucester by the Government) reached the place, and fired upon them, occasioning a general rout. The fugitives, scattered in small parties, were followed up by the special constables, and numberless petty conflicts took place, in which the partisans of order were not always successful, for the colliers carried off five or six gentlemen as prisoners. Three of these, Messrs. Brickdale, Knox, and Miller, were recaptured near Lawford's Gate, but the others were imprisoned in a coalpit for several days, and with difficulty released. In the various encounters, four colliers were shot dead, upwards of fifty wounded, and between thirty and forty made prisoners. (Owing to the extreme destitution of the sufferers who reached their homes, food and surgical aid were sent out of the city for their relief.) A quantity of correspondence relating to this affair is in the State Paper Office and the British Museum. Amongst the facts reported by the mayor to the Government it was stated that, even after the punishment they had received, the miners threatened " to return with armed force into the city," and that " from the height to which the tumult has grown, and the inclination of the lower sort of citizens to join with the colliers, the task of repression may prove beyond our force." The advance of troops from Worcester and other towns had a reassuring effect, but the colliers continued to threaten vengeance, and roved about the country endeavouring to raise a revolt among the country labourers. They were especially exasperated against Mr. Brickdale, who found it prudent to depart for London. Anticipating his return, every coach was stopped and searched on its way from the capital, but the unlucky gentleman reached home under the protection of a large escort of Bristolians, who guarded his carriage for the last twenty miles. He was not safe even in the city. Edward West, one of the county coroners (whom Brickdale describes to the Premier as a man of very bad character), held an inquest in or near St. George's, on the body of a rioter who had died from his wounds, and a verdict of wilful murder having been returned against John Brickdale, woollen-draper, Michael Miller, jeweller, and others, warrants were issued for their arrest. A few days later, Brickdale informed the Duke of Newcastle that West had held two more inquests—presumably on additional victims—with similar results. The Government put a stop to those proceedings by getting the verdicts quashed in the Court of King's Bench, and by granting a general pardon to Brickdale and his companions. A special commission was also issued for the trial of the rioters. Indictments of high treason were preferred against two ringleaders, but they eluded apprehension. Eight of the prisoners were condemned to two years' imprisonment. Many others were discharged owing to the non-appearance of witnesses that could have given evidence against them. The affair was costly to the Corporation. The expense of maintaining fifty special constables for ten days reached £268 17s. 6d. The sum of £7 18s. 8d. was laid out in "repairing constables' staves of St. Nicholas's ward which were broken in defence of this city;" and new staves for St. Stephen's parish cost £8 15s. 6d. more. The expenses of entertaining the judges and recorder in September amounted to nearly £300. [One of the constables' staves broken during this riot, and thrown into the Froom, was recovered in 1888. The head is of brass, engraved with the royal arms and those of Bristol, and bearing the inscription, "St. Stephen's, 1748."]

The corporate accounts for September contain the following unintelligible item:—"Paid for making the scarlet cloth, and for the gold fringe thereto, for Mr. Mayor's use when he goes to church, £11 6s." Another entry of the same date reads:—"Paid the Chamber's contribution towards the charges of passing an Act of Parliament for enlarging and regulating the trade into the Levant seas,

£105." The Act in question abolished the monopoly of the Levant trade enjoyed by the Turkey Company, of London; but Bristol merchants took little advantage of the new opening for commerce.

The ravages of the cattle plague having caused a great advance in the price of meat, attempts were made by adventurous people to smuggle in Irish beef—then a prohibited article—and large profits were made when the "run" was successful. In October the Custom House officers seized 108 barrels of this meat, which was sold for exportation, and £66 17s., half the proceeds, were distributed amongst the poor of St. Stephen's, the parish in which the capture was made. In December there was a further extensive seizure of Irish beef, etc., and three more discoveries of smuggled provisions took place in 1754, a moiety of the value in each case being paid to St. Stephen's parish.

A puritanic observance of Sunday was still enforced by the magistracy. *Felix Farley's Journal* of October 20th recorded that on the previous Monday two barbers were placed in the stocks in Temple Street for having shaved some customers on the preceding day. A fortnight later two other unhappy tonsors sat in the stocks on the Back for the same offence.

Christ Church, Broad Street, was re-opened on the 18th November, after having been closed upwards of two years for repairs. The restoration, which cost £1,500, did not succeed in preserving the old edifice.

On the 25th November, George Whitefield, who was then as popular in the fashionable world as amongst the poor, opened a chapel in Bristol for the accommodation of his followers. His "Society" had previously worshipped in the Smiths' Hall, near Merchant Street. The new chapel, like its founder's great building in London, was called the Tabernacle. It was, Whitefield recorded, "large, but not large enough; would the place contain them, I believe near as many would attend as in London." The Earl of Chesterfield, the only too-celebrated letter writer, contributed £20 to the building fund, but requested that his name should not be published. From an account book of the chapel, in the possession of Mr. W. H. Wills, it appears that the congregation provided board and lodging for the ministers, who rarely remained more than a few weeks in one place. Stabling and food were also furnished for their horses. On the other hand, the remuneration of the itinerant preachers can hardly be deemed liberal, most of them previous to 1770 receiving less than a guinea per week. Owing to the housekeeping arrangement, which cost under 20s. weekly, many of the items in the accounts have a singular look in a chapel record. For example, there are payments for tea kettles, "sugar knippers," saucepans, bedding, warming pans, nightcaps, shoes, slippers, and cobbling; a barber was paid a shilling a week for shaving; a domestic servant received £3 18s. yearly; and on one occasion the chapel bought a horse, a saddle, and a bridle for £18 6s. The brewer's account, again, rose sometimes to over £5 yearly; but some of the ministers preferred stronger liquors, and six or eight quarts of brandy or rum were sometimes consumed in a month. As nearly two gallons of wine were required on each Communion day, the expense under this head was large. In December, 1776, there is an item—" To the Rev. Rowland Hill, for one-eighth of a pipe of port, 6 dozen and 5 bottles, £5 17s. 10½d." (Mr. Hill had resided two months at the chapel in the previous year, and was paid six guineas for his services.) Candles were another heavy charge, and a special collection was made at intervals to meet the outlay. The total income of the congregation was only £143 in 1766, but it gradually increased until 1775-6, when there was a notable influx of new subscribers; and in 1777 Abraham Elton, Esq., joined the society, and contributed £50 both in that and the following year. About the same period a system was adopted of selling tickets for seats in the galleries—one of which was reserved for men and the other for women. The largest collection made at this period was in September, 1776, when, after a sermon by Mr. Hill, £20 14s. were obtained "for Kingswood Tabernacle, towards enlarging him." It is somewhat remarkable that in a single twelvemonth the treasurer had to take credit for £2 1s. "bad halfpence and silver, at various collections."

In the closing months of 1753, Messrs. Cranfield Becher and John Heylyn applied to the civic authorities, on behalf of several leading citizens, for the demise of certain premises in Prince's Street, for the purpose of erecting a handsome Assembly Room on the site. At a Council meeting in December, it was resolved to grant the applicants a lease of the spot, on which four old tenements then stood, on payment of a fine of £400, and a yearly rent of £5; the lease to be renewable every 14 years on payment, after the first renewal, of a fine of £100. The Corporation reserved a right of occupying the hall for six days in every year, thus securing a convenient dining or ball-room, for which recourse had previously to be made to the Merchants' Society. The promoters raised the needful capital by issuing 120 shares of £30 each on the principle of a tontine, the property to devolve eventually upon the nominees of the three last surviving lives. (One of these survivors was probably the once celebrated Sir Nathaniel Wraxall, Bart., born in Queen Square in 1751, who died in his 81st year.) The shares were allotted previous to the 23rd June, 1754, when the proprietors assented to the suggested scheme by formal deeds, one of which is amongst the Jefferies MSS. The building was constructed with unusual promptitude. In the *Bristol Journal* of December 20th, 1755, is the following advertisement:—"On Wednesday, the 14th January, 1756, will be open'd The New Musick Room, with the oratorio of 'The Messiah.' The band will be compos'd of the principal performers, vocal and instrumental, from London, Oxford, Salisbury, Gloucester, Wells, Bath, &c. . . . A concerto on the organ by Mr. Broderip." The tickets were 5s. each. The *Journal* did not notice the performance, but a correspondent, in praising its excellence, observed, "'Twill be superfluous to mention the elegance of the room, chandeliers, &c." Another musical festival took place in the building on the 2nd and 3rd March, 1757, "at the opening of the new organ," when "Judas Maccabæus" and "The Messiah" were produced. In the following July the furniture of the old Assembly Room was advertised for sale by auction, leaving the field open to the new institution. But according to "A Tour through Great Britain" (1761), the old theatre at Stoke's Croft was converted into an assembly room, and dancing took place there once a week during the winter.

The following announcement in *Felix Farley's Journal*, of the 22nd December, 1753, reads like a sorry joke; but frequent notices of a similar character prove that it was in fact a grim reality :—" The miserable, poor, unhappy, and long-confined insolvent debtors in Newgate, being 36 in number, hereby return thanks for twopence each distributed to them." In another paragraph, nine colliers, imprisoned for rioting, acknowledge with gratitude the receipt of a gift of sixpence each.

Mr. William Vick, a wealthy wine merchant, residing in Queen Square (often of late years, but inaccurately, styled an alderman), died on the 3rd January, 1754. By his will, Mr. Vick, after sundry dispositions, left his residuary estate to his sister Rebecca and to Roger Watts, subject to the payment of £1,000 to the Merchants' Society, directing that this sum should be invested, together with the yearly interest, until it should have accumulated to £10,000. When that sum had been attained, the Society were directed to construct a stone bridge over the Avon from Clifton Down to the opposite height, the passage to be free from toll. In the event of this design proving impracticable, the fund was to be transferred to the Corporation, which was to devote £4,000 to granting temporary loans to young clothworkers of Minchinhampton or Bristol, while the remainder was to be bestowed in founding and maintaining a hospital for illegitimate children, which the testator described as a "useful and much needed charity." The terms of Mr. Vick's bequest appear to have excited as much amusement as surprise, and witless gibes at the old wine merchant's morality have been re-echoed in our own time. The results of his gift are recorded in the Annals of the present century (pp. 131, 375).

Felix Farley's Journal of February 9th announces:—"The Bristol Flying Machine, for London, in two days, sets out on Monday, the 25th inst., at two o'clock in the morning." The machines took wing three times a week during the summer, and had no competitors, the only other coaches out of Bristol being three plying to Bath, and one to Gloucester. It should be added that the Bristol coaches were amongst the swiftest in the kingdom. In this year, 1754, the flying coach from London to Edinburgh, "a genteel glass machine, exceedingly light," performed the journey in "ten days in summer and twelve in winter." A Manchester advertisement of the same date stated that, "however incredible it might appear," a coach reached London from that town (187 miles) in four days and a half. Liverpool was destitute of a London coach until 1760.

An amusing illustration of the drinking habits of the age is afforded by an advertisement in *Felix Farley's Journal* for March 9th, 1754:—"Henry Haines, barber, Redcliff Pit, shaves each person for twopence, cuts hair for three half-pence, and bleeds for sixpence. All customers who are bled he treats with two quarts of good ale, and those whom he shaves or cuts their hair with a pint each."

A general election took place in April. The Bristol Whigs, who had been unrepresented for twelve years, brought forward Mr. Robert Nugent, one of the Lords of the Treasury, and a prominent member of the dissolved House of Commons. (Mr. Nugent is said to have begun life as a teacher in a nobleman's family, but through three successive marriages to wealthy ladies, aided by skilful trimming as a courtier, he acquired great riches.) Mr. Southwell and Mr. Hoblyn having both retired, their friends introduced Sir John Philipps, a Welsh baronet with Jacobite sympathies, and Richard Beckford, an alderman of London, largely interested in the sugar plantations. Beckford being then at Jamaica, his interests were championed by his more celebrated brother, William, and it is recorded that in the heat of the contest the peppery slaveowner, irritated by the jeers of a Whig mob, compared Bristolians in unequivocal language to "a parcel of hogs." No fewer than 986 persons were admitted to the freedom during the month of April, the fees being paid by one or other of the candidates. The contest was prolific in squibs, in one of which Mr. Nugent, who was a convert from Romanism, was styled "a whitewashed Protestant," while Mr. Beckford was stigmatised in others as a "West India hog" and "a Negroe tyrant." Nugent's friends recommended him to the electors for having "prevented the introduction of French bottles, and by that means saved hundreds of families in the city from starving;" while they jeeringly commended the candidature of Sir J. Philipps, who had paraded the streets of Bristol soon after the Jacobite rebellion in a plaid waistcoat, as "acceptable to our *friends* in the Highlands by wearing their livery." The polling, which continued for a fortnight, closed on the 1st May, with the following result:—"Mr. Nugent, 2590; Mr. Beckford, 2248; Sir J. Philipps, 2163. According to the poll book, only about 110 resident electors refrained from voting. Amongst the members of the Council, 33 polled for Nugent, 3 for Beckford, and 2 for Philipps; and Emanuel Collins, who seems to have opposed Nugent, praised the civic body for "gloriously" refraining from exercising any pressure on the citizens ("Miscellanies," p. 21). A novelty in electioneering festivities was introduced at the close of the poll—a display of fireworks before the Merchants' Hall in honour of Mr. Nugent's return. *Felix Farley's Journal* (the Tory organ) chucklingly recorded, however, that heavy rain fell during the evening, and that, although the public lamps "had been conveyed to their summer repository," leaving the streets in darkness, the display was so unsatisfactory that the populace, in spite of a "large quantity of liquor given away," went off "cursing the Yellows' empty show." In some doggerel lines that follow, Mr. Nugent's election is alleged to have cost the Whigs £20,000. As the Beckfords spent their enormous fortunes with great prodigality, the expenditure is not likely to have been less on the other side. The new members were immediately presented with the freedom of the city, and the yearly compliment of a present of wine was revived and continued.

The increasing popularity of the Hot Well is attested by the following announcement, issued in May, 1754:— "Elizabeth Trinder, from the Lebeck's Head Tavern, Bath, has opened a house at the Hotwells for the reception of company as a tavern or eating-house. An ordinary every day at three o'clock, at half-a-crown a head . . . the house being the first of the kind attempted here." The tavern keeper, who named her premises "the Lebeck" after a celebrated cook, occupied the large house standing at the south-west corner of Dowry Square.

The aldermanic order of 1736, requiring the inhabitants to maintain a body of fifty-one watchmen for the protection of the city during the night, was perfunctorily obeyed from the outset, and in the course of a few years, as appears from the *Bristol Journal* of January 13th, 1753, it became wholly obsolete. The Corporation was doubtless sincere in its anxiety to apply a remedy, but its usual practice of disclaiming any pecuniary burden while demanding unrestricted control of the needful machinery repelled popular support, and the announcement of its intention to apply for Parliamentary powers to levy a rate revived the hostile feeling excited by the Lighting Act of 1749. At a meeting of the Council on the 22nd May, 1754, a committee was appointed to prepare a Bill, and was empowered "to make use of, direct, and prosecute all such legal and justifiable measures as they shall think proper for the better support of the authority and the vindication of the honour and reputation of the magistracy of this city." On the other hand, a powerful opposition was organised, in which many of the guardians of the poor took part, party passions aroused by the general election embittering the strife. The Bill was brought into the House of Commons by Mr. Nugent early in 1755, and was supported by petitions from the Merchants' Society and influential citizens, while a petition against the measure, declaring that the Corporation in no respect represented the inhabitants, was forwarded by persons styling themselves the principal merchants and traders. On the 14th February the scheme gave rise to a remarkable debate, Sir John Philipps, the rejected candidate of the previous year, who had found a seat elsewhere, moving that the powers sought by the Corporation should be conferred on "trustees" elected by the ratepayers. The want of protection under which the city had long suffered was, he said, due to the contentions existing between the inhabitants and the Council. He was supported by the two Beckfords and a Mr. W. Northey, who contended, like the mover, that the Council was a narrow oligarchy, which had already usurped nearly all the rights of the inhabitants, and that the real object of the scheme was to corrupt the poor freemen by engaging some 300 as watchmen at a salary of 7s. a week each, by which means the members for the city would be practically nominated by the Chamber. The Bill was supported by three members of the Government, Mr. Nugent, Lord Barrington (grandson and co-heir of Sir Wm. Daines, M.P.) and Mr. Pitt. On a division—which was really a party one—the amendment was rejected by 153 votes against 71. Another amendment, disqualifying watchmen as electors, was negatived by 185 against 55 votes. The Corporation of the Poor then petitioned the House of Lords to reject the Bill, alleging that the guardians alone represented the opinion of the ratepayers; but the opposition was fruitless, and the scheme received the Royal Assent. It enacted that the number of watchmen should be settled yearly in quarter sessions, and that the aldermen should appoint or remove the constables, who were to keep watch nightly for eight hours in winter, and seven in summer. Their maintenance was to be defrayed by a rate on houses valued at £7 a year or upwards, and the ratepayers were discharged from the statutable liability to keep watch and ward. The Act was so badly drawn as to be unworkable, and an amending Bill was surreptitiously presented in the following session. The opposition, which gained scent of the scheme only through the privately printed votes of the Commons, again petitioned, asserting that men of bad character, having been appointed watchmen, had committed great irregularities, and even "committed a most horrid murder." (Three watchmen had really ill-treated a woman so cruelly that they were afterwards convicted of manslaughter.) The opponents did not challenge a division, and the Bill passed. New clauses in this measure restricted the number of constables to 150 (which in practice was reduced to 115), while occupiers of grass lands—still numerous in the city—were exempted from the rate.

In August, 1754, a ship captain was brought before the local magistrates and fined for having some soap manufactured in Ireland on board his vessel. The prosecution was instigated by the Bristol soapmakers, who offered a reward in the *Bristol Journal* to any one giving information of infractions of the English monopoly.

The Council, on the 31st August, presented the freedom of the city to the Earl of Berkeley, Lord Lieutenant, and also to Viscount Barrington, in gratitude for his support of the Watching Bill. Lord Berkeley died in the following January, when Lord Ducie was appointed Lord Lieutenant, and, a few weeks later, was made a freeman.

A writer in the *Gentleman's Magazine* for August, 1754, stated that the great west road from London to Bristol, "through the ignorance of its constructors, errs and blunders in all the forms. . . . No outlets were made for the water that stagnates in the body of the road; it was never sufficiently widened. . . . 'Tis the worst public road in Europe, considering what vast sums have been collected from it."

Glass was at this time very costly. The Corporation, in September, was called upon to pay £4 16s. for "a glass put into Mr. Alderman Laroche's coach, in the place of one broken at the gaol delivery." About fifteen glass manufactories were then being carried on in the city, but many firms confined themselves to bottle making.

The vestry of Clifton parish resolved, in November, to impose a rate upon the inhabitants for the repair of the church tower and of the road near Jacob's Wells. The fact is now interesting only from the information it affords as to the rateable value of the parish, which amounted to no more than £5,030—about one-fortieth of the value in 1892.

The city had been up to this time chiefly supplied with coal from Kingswood and Brislington. An advertisement in a local newspaper of January, 1755, announced that a new road had just been made from Bedminster Bridewell "to the new coal work there, where coal is sold on as reasonable terms as at any other colliery."

Pugilism was so extremely popular with all classes of Bristolians that an occasional reference to the "sport" is required to illustrate social habits. *Felix Farley's Journal* of February 1st, 1755, contains the following advertisement:—
"The famous boxing match depending between John Harris and John Slack will be decided on Thursday next, at the Tennis Court at Barton Hundred. The doors to be opened at 10, and the champions to mount at 2. Tickets to be had at the Bush and Rummer Taverns. . . . Gallery, 2s. 6d.;

court, 1s. N.B.—There will be several bye battles." The victory of Slack (a Norwich man) is recorded in the following week's paper. The Bristolians were rash enough to bet 10 to 1 on their favourite Harris, but he was overthrown in six minutes. Another fight, for £150, between Slack and Cornelius Harris, of Brislington, took place on the 6th March at a yard in Guinea Street, when Harris was so dreadfully beaten that his recovery was considered improbable. "On this battle," says the *Journal*, "centered all the hopes of that family, who have now lost their boasted honour of never having been beat." In connection with this subject, a brief notice of the Whitsuntide sports announced at Long Ashton in the following May may not be out of place. A good beaver hat was promised to the best wrestler, and another to the skilfulest player at "Butt and Cudgel," "he that breaks the most heads and saves his own" to have the prize. "A good buckskin pair of breeches" were also to be played for at backsword. In 1756 the "lovers of the noble and manly exercise of backsword" were invited to a tournament at the Ostrich inn, Durdham Down, five guineas being promised to "the first best man who breaks most heads, saving his own," and smaller prizes to second and third best competitors. The advertisement ends with the significant note:— "Vinegar by J. W."

War with France being imminent, the local authorities received instructions to employ the brutal measures then in favour for reinforcing the navy. A local journal of March 8th says:—"Last night the constables searched all our public houses, &c., for sailors, and having picked up about 120, lodged them in the Guildhall, where they are guarded by a party of soldiers." From subsequent references to the subject, it appears that the pressgangs continued briskly employed for upwards of two months. On the arrival of several vessels from distant ports early in May, 170 men who had been long separated from their families were impressed in a single night.

The consumption of tea was still too limited to enable a tradesman to live by the sale of it alone. One of the best known local dealers in the article, Hannah James, of High Street, announced in April her new purchases in ornamental china, adding the following note:—"Her stock in the hosiery way is to be sold off very low. All sorts of chip hats of the newest fashion. Teas as usual." A fortnight later, a snuff dealer in Maryleport Street announced that he sold "all sorts of fine teas at the London prices."

A strike of journeymen tailors took place in May. A paragraph communicated to the local papers stated that the magistrates were determined to put the laws against workmen's combinations strictly in force, and pointed out, as a warning to the refractory, that for the first offence a man was liable to a fine of £10, or twenty days' imprisonment; for a second, to a penalty of £20, or exhibition in the pillory; and for a third, to a mulct of £40, or to be pilloried and lose an ear. In despite of this menace, the workmen refused to submit. The issue is not recorded. The current wages of tailors were then 1s. 9d. for a day of thirteen hours.

English iron, being manufactured by means of charcoal, was still a costly article. An advertisement of this period states that bar iron, "inferior to none," was made by Nicholas Pryce and Son, and sold by Mr. Jenkins, Baldwin Street, " at £17 7s. 6d. per ton, ready money."

The library in the chapter house of Bristol Cathedral dates from this year. The capitular minutes record that the Rev. Dr. Hamond had proposed to establish a library for the use of the residing " prebends and cannons," and had paid for that purpose ten guineas, in lieu of a treat usually given by a new prebendary, whereupon he was desired to lay out the money in the purchase of books. A number of private gifts must have followed, for on the 27th August, 1760, the minutes state that the library had been " brought to some perfection, and was likely to meet with a great increase." The Rev. John Camplin, precentor, was thereupon appointed the first librarian, with a salary of 40s. a year. Nearly the whole of this library was destroyed in the riots of 1831 (see "Annals," p. 162).

The *Bristol Journal* of July 19th records that a soldier, convicted of stealing a shirt (of which he was probably in urgent need), had been sentenced by court martial to receive 1,000 lashes! The unhappy wretch, on learning the sentence, nearly killed himself by cutting his throat; so the authorities, on his partial recovery, ordered him 200 lashes, and had him drummed out of the regiment. About the same time a man, for an offence on a child, was sentenced by the magistrates to be twice whipped from Broadmead to Stoke's Croft Gate (Cheltenham Road) and back again.

The earliest mention of a long-popular place of recreation occurs in the *Bristol Journal* of July 19th. "The Old Fox public house, at Broad Stoney, near Lower Easton," is offered to be sold or let, having " a bathing place in the river Froom, with commodious dressing houses."

Dr. John Conybeare, Dean of Christ Church, who succeeded Bishop Butler in the see of Bristol, died in July, 1755, and was buried in his cathedral, being the ninth prelate whose remains had been interred there. Dr. Conybeare was little known in Bristol, but his theological works have still a high reputation. Poor as was the bishopric, there were many eager applicants for the vacancy. Amongst the Cole MSS. in the British Museum is a letter to Cole from Dr. Lyttelton, afterwards Bishop of Carlisle, dated September 8th, 1755:—" I thank you," he writes, " for your good wishes to see me at Bristol, but I believe that mitre will be placed on another person's head. As to the revenue . . . I am very certain Dr. Conybeare made no more than £330 clear, and during the whole time he was a bishop, except one fine of six guineas, which was all he ever received. It would almost ruin me to take it; but, however, was it offered, I should hardly refuse it, being a step to better things." The fortunate candidate was John Hume, D.D., who, in 1758, was translated to Oxford.

Various strange natural phenomena, inexplicable at the moment, were noticed in the West of England on the 1st November. The ebbing tide in the Avon suddenly flowed back for a time, and the water in many deep wells became discoloured and undrinkable. Captain G. W. Manby, in his " Fugitive Sketches of Clifton," published in 1802, stated on the authority of a person who witnessed the marvel that the Hot Well water suddenly became as red as blood, whereupon " all flew to the churches, where prayers were offered to avert the apparent approach of their destruction," and that of the world. " The water ran foul for a length of time." An explanation of the phenomenon was found soon afterwards in the tidings of the calamitous earthquake at Lisbon.

A document laid before the Council in December, 1755, offers the first indication of a feeling amongst some of the leading citizens that the shipping accommodation of the port was becoming too limited for its requirements. A committee appointed to consider the duties of the quay warden and water bailiff presented a report, recommending certain new regulations touching those officers, but expressing their opinion that " No human prudence could prevent the growing danger to ships without provision were made for further room, the want whereof doth greatly endanger the safety of ships, and by which they daily sustain considerable damage." No action was taken by the Chamber. The need for improvement, however, became more urgent; and in August,

1757, a committee was appointed to consider what provision should be made for the better accommodation of vessels. As no report was presented, it must be assumed that the progressive party were in a minority. Nevertheless, in February, 1758, the town clerk was ordered to publish advertisements in the London papers "for persons to survey the rivers Avon and Froom, and consider of proper measures for making some convenient part thereof into a wet dock." If this invitation produced any plans, the estimated cost of the improvement probably alarmed the Corporation. At all events, it abandoned all thoughts of a dock, and fell back upon a device which cast deep discredit upon its authors. In December, 1758, a committee appointed to consider "of ways and means for the better accommodation of the navigation of the port" reported that they had consulted with a similar committee nominated by the Merchants' Society, when the latter committee informed them that the Society would enlarge the quays and wharves at their own expense, provided that their lease of the quays and wharfage dues, which had "only 34 years to come," were regranted for a longer number of years and for a greater extent of ground. It was recommended that such a lease should be conceded for the term of 99 years at a rental of £10, and that the Society should have the whole of the quays and wharves along the east side of the Froom, and also along the north bank of the Avon to a dung wharf near the Welsh Back, including all the houses, slips, and duties embraced in the lease then running. In consideration of this grant the Society would undertake to erect quay walls where none then existed on the demised ground, and would also build a little quay, 130 feet long, at St. Augustine's Back. The Common Council confirmed this extraordinary report, and ordered the proposed lease to be executed; but it was not sealed until September, 1764, when the Corporation surrendered its property in the quays and wharfage dues for nearly a century, receiving merely a nominal consideration. The expense of constructing the new quay on the Grove, finished about 1771, is said to have been only about £9,700. The other works were of comparatively trifling cost. No accounts of the wharfage dues were allowed to see the light, but Mr. Barrett, in his History, stated that the income in 1787 already reached upwards of £2,000 a year, and the subsequent increase must have been very large.

The population seems to have been increasing somewhat rapidly at this period, but the wealthier classes still shunned the attractions of Clifton. About the close of 1755 a square was laid out on the slope of Kingsdown. "The New Square," for it was seldom styled King Square until some years later, was one of John Wesley's favourite preaching stations. Several wealthy families then inhabited it. The house numbered 18, built by a merchant named Ash, cost £3,000. Contemporaneously with these upper-class erections, a number of dwellings were rising in the " Old Orchard " of the Dominican friary—an estate which fell to the Penn family through the marriage of the famous William Penn with Hannah, daughter of Thomas Callowhill, a Bristol Quaker. "New built" houses in Callowhill Street are mentioned in a local paper in 1755. In March, 1757, another new dwelling was offered " in a street named Penn Street, in the Old Orchard." Philadelphia Street was built a few years later.

An appeal entitled "The State of the Bristol Infirmary" was published in the local journals of February 14th, 1756. The writer stated that owing to the increased number of casualties, it had been necessary to lodge several patients in neighbouring houses. By the aid of donations the centre front had been raised a storey, and two new wards had just been completed, increasing the number of beds to 134. On the other hand the annual charge of the institution had risen to £2,200, while the 403 subscribers contributed only £926. The debt having increased in 1757, the position of the charity was forced on public attention, and for the first time collections were taken in all the parish churches, while a house to house requisition was made in each district. The movement, which brought in about £650, is now interesting as affording an indication of the localities inhabited by the wealthy classes. Clifton produced £33, and Redland £20. In the city proper, St. James's contributed £114, St. Nicholas' £82, St. Augustine's £57, St. Philip's £57, Castle Precincts £51, St. Stephen's £50, Christ Church £30, Redcliff £22, St. Michael's £21, St. John's £21. The other parishes produced amounts varying from £19 to £3.

The death of Mr. Richard Beckford, in January, caused a vacancy in the representation of the city, and an election took place in March. The Tory party brought forward Mr. Jarrit Smith, the eminent local attorney, while the Hon. John Spencer (afterwards Earl Spencer) offered himself as a Whig. The local press was singularly remiss in reporting the incidents of the contest. *Felix Farley's Journal* did not even take the trouble to record the number of votes polled.

After a close contest, continued for fourteen days, Mr. Smith was found to have received 2,426 votes, against 2,374 recorded for his opponent. A curious letter written by John Wesley at Marlborough, in the Duke of Newcastle's MSS., says:—"I am hastening to Bristol on account of the election," and he is said to have worked energetically on behalf of Mr. Smith. A petition was presented against the return, alleging that many good votes for Spencer were rejected, but the case was eventually abandoned. Another document in the British Museum—a letter from Mr. Nugent to the Union Committee at Bristol—shows that the Whigs sought the pecuniary help of the Government. A deputation had applied to Lord Granville, but his lordship, says Nugent, had referred them to Mr. Spencer, who would soon be in London. "At the same time that you apply to Mr. Spencer for the £3,000, I suppose you will think it right to lay open to him the expenses already incurred, the debt now due by you, and the impossibility of raising by subscription a sufficient sum to carry on a petition." Mr. Nugent strongly advised the Duke of Newcastle to help his Bristol friends out of their difficulties, which "would confirm them our's for ever." The result does not appear. Mr. Smith, after taking his seat, set off for Bristol, and was met some miles outside the city by a large body of friends, in coaches, whose escort through the streets formed an imposing procession. At College Green a triumphal arch had been erected, in which a carved representation of the royal arms of the Stewarts, borrowed from All Saints' Church, was a conspicuous ornament. It is a curious illustration of the passions of the time that this decoration, being without the heraldic blazon of the Hanoverian family, was held to be a token of sympathy for the Pretender, and caused so much excitement that it had to be removed. What is still more amusing is that Dr. Tucker informed Mr. Nugent:—"I have been pestered all day with a lot of Methodist preachers who insist upon it that they have started and are now hunting a strange kind of game called the Young Pretender, and have fairly tracked him to Mr. Jarrit Smith's house at Ashton, where he is at present under cover." Tucker, with considerable difficulty, prevented his informants from making a deposition before the judges of assize (Newcastle MSS., British Museum).

The occupier of the Exchange Tavern, who was also a wine merchant, issued an advertisement in April, 1756, stating the current prices of wine. Madeira was 7s. 6d., port and sherry 5s., and mountain and Lisbon, 4s. 6d. per gallon respectively. Two years later a London vintner offered to supply local innkeepers with choice Malaga, in half hogsheads, at 2s. 6d. per gallon.

War with France was declared in May, 1756. The usual proclamation was made on the 22nd in Bristol by the sheriffs, accompanied by "the grand band of City Musick, assisted by two French Horns from the Prince Edward man of war, who, together with the chimes of Christ Church parish, played 'Britons, Strike Home.'"

Immediate measures were taken by the leading merchants and shipowners for the fitting out of privateers. The zeal displayed on this occasion produced a fleet of cruisers far exceeding anything attempted in previous wars; for within little more than a twelvemonth nearly forty Bristol ships had been equipped and sent to sea, over twenty more being added in the two subsequent years. The following imperfect list, made up from various sources, offers notable testimony as to the ardour of the citizens and the resources of the port. The * denotes vessels captured by the enemy.

	Tons.	Men.	Guns.		Tons.	Men.	Guns.
*Tyger	570	280	36	Sampson	—	—	—
Britannia	500	300	36	Gallant	—	—	—
Duke of Cornwall	400	220	30	King George	—	200	32
Antient Briton	400	250	30	Virginian	—	—	—
Eagle	400	200	30	Duke of Cumberland	—	—	14
Revenge	350	180	26	Blakeney	—	—	—
Lyon	300	200	28	Mercury	—	90	14
Cæsar	320	—	—	Lottery	100	100	16
St. Andrew	300	180	30	Tartar's prize	100	80	12
Defiance	250	170	20	Fortune (prize)	100	100	14
*Hawke	250	160	20	St. George	—	80	14
*Tartar	250	180	22	Crab	—	—	12
Anson	180	150	20	Ranger	80	60	10
Constantine	220	180	18	Ferret	70	—	10
Phœnix	200	120	20	Scorpion	60	60	8
Hercules	180	140	20	Sterling	50	50	8
Halifax	150	100	20	Leopard	260	200	24
Marlborough	150	120	18	Charles	300	120	22
*Enterprise	150	140	24	Bristol	500	250	28
*Tryall	150	120	26	New Grace	300	—	18
Cromwell	—	120	16	Amazon	300	60	18
Hibernia	130	130	16	Bellona	—	—	16
Dreadnought	120	110	16	Grace	—	—	18
Vulture	120	—	16	Johnson	—	—	—
Lyne	120	100	16	Dragon	—	100	14
Fox	120	110	16	*Lockhart	—	—	—
Prussian Hero	120	110	16	*Dispatch	—	—	—
Hawke	100	—	—	Drake	120	—	—
*Hay	—	—	—	Rialto	300	—	20
Pitt	—	—	—	Severn	—	—	—

	Tons.	Men.	Guns.		Tons.	Men.	Guns.
Hornet	—	—	—	Duke of York	—	—	—
Invincible (prize)	500	—	86	Gloucestershire	—	—	—
Salisbury	—	—	—	Tygress	—	—	16
Prince Ferdinand	230	—	8	Patriot	—	—	20
Fame	—	—	—	True Patriot	—	—	22
Antelope	—	—	—	Nancy	—	—	—
Hector	—	—	—	Spotswood	—	—	—

Several of the privateers were very successful in the early months of the war. The owner of the Fortune (captured from the French) boasted that she had brought in seventeen prizes in about three months. Later on, the number of English cruisers was so great that few French ships dared put to sea, and ruinous losses were sustained by privateer owners. The marvel is that crews could be obtained to man so many vessels. Many privateersmen, however, were rough and lawless youths drawn from the country districts, partly from hope of gain and partly from love of a reckless and idle life. To amuse those "gentleman volunteers," the advertisements for hands frequently added that "French horns," or even "a band of music," would "find great encouragement." Whilst on shore the crews were a terror to the citizens, committing many outrages, and frequently rescuing by force such of their comrades as were arrested.

In June, 1756, John Pitman and Son, "proprietors of the Bristol (new erected) Lead Smelting Works," announced that they had begun operations, and solicited support. Their factory was situated on the Somerset side of the Avon, near to the Hot Well, and the clouds of poisonous smoke issuing from the furnaces proved highly offensive to fashionable visitors. The nuisance was long submitted to in silence, but in 1761 a complaint was raised in the *Gentleman's Magazine* by Dr. D. W. Linden, a metropolitan physician, who followed his patients to Clifton every summer (and who is scurrilously caricatured by Smollett in "Humphrey Clinker"). Dr. Linden asserted that the Well was "not only the second medicinal spring in Britain, but in all Europe," and expressed astonishment that the "necessary improvements to the place should have been so much neglected." As no further reference to the subject has been found, the works were probably discontinued.

In the summer of 1756 the vestry of St. Mary Rec'c'iff purchased of William Hogarth three large scriptural paintings, representing Christ and the Woman of Samaria, the Sealing of the Tomb, and the Resurrection. Hogarth's receipt for the stipulated price, "£525, in full of all demands," is dated the 14th August, and is in the archives of the church. Nearly £250 more were spent on frames and in placing the pictures (under the personal direction of the artist) upon the altar screen of the church, where they remained until 1857. Hogarth's true excellence—his intense realism—was of no service to him in work of a higher character; and the above paintings, now in the Fine Arts Academy, merely serve to prove his impotence in idealistic conception, his lack of a sense of beauty, and his poverty as a colourist.

The ferocity of the impressment system may be imagined from an incident that occurred in Kingroad on the 10th September. The Bristol ship Virginia Merchant, which had arrived from the West Indies on the previous day, was boarded by a naval tender, the commander of which intended to impress the crew; but as the men, who had been about a twelvemonth from home, made a firm resistance, the tender opened fire upon the ship. One man was killed and several others wounded, while the ship was so much damaged that, after "firing several guns of distress," she sank in the sight of the spectators. The timid newspapers shrank from recording the fate of the crew.

Bristolians, in common with the nation at large, were flung into transports of indignation by the alleged cowardice of Admiral Byng in retreating from Minorca. *Felix Farley's Journal* of September 4th says:—"On Monday last the effigy of a (now) high-spirited admiral was carried through most of the streets of the city, accompanied by three gentlemen-dealers in soot; after which he was hung upon a gallows on St. Philip's Plain, and under it was made a large bonfire, which entirely consumed it in the sight of a number of spectators." Party spirit, perhaps, inspired many of the popular manifestations. Letters of Dr. Tucker in the Newcastle MSS. show that the local Tories, at a very late hour one evening, announced a meeting next day to address the King in condemnation of the Government; whereupon Tucker got some printers out of their beds, and issued another placard, advising the meeting to promise hearty support to the King against the common enemy. His tactics threw the opposite party into confusion; the meeting was not held; and although the "red-hot" Tories sent about an address, soliciting signatures, Mr. Smith, M.P., waited upon the bishop "to purge himself from having had any hand" in the manœuvre. The Duke of Newcastle complained to

Nugent of the apathy of the Whigs, when the member forwarded one of Tucker's missives stating that a corporate address had been drawn up, but that " this is the Assizes and Feasting time : all business is at a stand till that important affair is over." Nugent is not complimentary to his supporters. " Their mouths," he writes to the Duke, " are full of Turtle, and if you come in for the second place it is as much as I can hope for you. Their address will, I dare flatter myself, partake of their diet, for Turtle is wont to inspire warm, kind and vigorous sensations. . . . Is not Tucker a fine fellow ? He deserves a Bishopric." (He was appointed a prebendary of Bristol a few weeks later, and dean of Gloucester in 1758.) Eventually two addresses, expressing confidence in the Government, were forwarded— one from the Corporation, and the other from the citizens, the latter being signed by " great property and numbers." (Many letters on the subject from local magnates are in the British Museum.)

The copper coinage was at this period in a state of extreme degradation. A large portion of the halfpence having been worn entirely smooth, some unprincipled people at Birmingham issued an enormous quantity of " blanks," worth less than a fourth of their nominal value, and equally knavish persons purchased the false coin wholesale at a trifling price and foisted it upon workmen in payment of wages. Emanuel Collins mentions in his " Miscellanies " another difficulty in relation to the coinage. He heard, he says, the Bristol bellman proclaiming that as many scrupulous people refused to accept the half-pence of William III., the public were to understand that they could take or leave them at their discretion. " Ungrateful city, are these your Revolution principles ? But ye are the sons of barter : your principles are interest, and interest is your principle." He adds that a Scotch agent was offering to buy up the halfpence at the rate of six a penny. " And I just now heard that some of our shopkeepers that are of the kirk will admit them again on one-fourth of their dignity curtailed ; so that for a commodity which you may purchase for a shilling, you must pay in those plain halfpence sixteen pence." The corporate rents of the market stands fell off largely from this cause. The loss in September, 1756, was £12 2s. 7½d., while in the month ending 19th March, 1757, out of a receipt of £138, the loss from " plain halfpence " was £19 17s. 4d.

The harvest of 1756 was greatly deficient, and owing to the war the imports of grain were scanty. The price of wheat consequently rose to 80s. per quarter, causing dire distress. In November the Corporation offered two bounties of £50 each to the two first grain cargoes imported, and four of £25 each to the next arrivals. £200 were also granted for relieving poor householders. Mr. Nugent, M.P., purchased a cargo of 650 quarters of foreign wheat, which was to have been distributed to the distressed at half-price, but the ship was unluckily captured by the French. Another vessel, laden with corn, was stopped and plundered by a mob on her passage down the Severn. The prosecution of the rioters cost the Chamber £123. During the winter many hundreds of families were dependent for food upon the relief committees established by their wealthier neighbours. In January, 1757, the Corporation petitioned Parliament, representing that the barges coming down the Severn and Wye with food for Bristol were systematically plundered by the country people, and praying for the admission of foreign corn duty free, a suggestion which was adopted. In the following year, owing to the continuance of the dearth, an Act was passed permitting the importation for a short period of butter, pork, and salted beef from Ireland, and a subsequent statute allowed Irish cattle to enter English ports for a term of five years only. These unwonted concessions gave much offence to English landlords.

At a meeting of the Council in December, 1756, it was ordered that an apartment in the vestry room (the Poyntz Chantry) of the Mayor's Chapel should be fitted up as a receptacle for such corporate records and papers as it might be thought proper to remove there. Iron doors were soon afterwards affixed to two recesses, but the projected removal of documents never took place.

During a panic created by the preparations of France to invade this country with a large army, an Act of Parliament was passed in 1757, for raising a militia for the protection of the country. The number of men to be furnished by Gloucestershire and Bristol was 960 out of a total of 32,000. The local force was exceeded only by those of Devonshire, Lincolnshire, Middlesex, and the West Riding of York.

A brief notice of the fashionable method of locomotion at this time occurs in a local newspaper of January, 1757. "Louthian and Lavendar, chairmen," announced that they had "two commodious Sedan Chairs and one Boot Chair, with able men," which stood for custom in Queen Square and College Green. The "boot chair," having a projection in front, was brought into popularity by, and possibly invented for, the great War Minister, Pitt, who was a chronic sufferer from gout.

The road from the city to Pill at this period was a mere horse track, traversing an extensive common from Rownham to Leigh. In March, 1757, the Common Council voted 20 guineas "towards making a road over Leigh Down." Traffic by wheeled vehicles between Bristol and the neighbouring villages was then almost unknown. Mr. Tyson had a conversation in December, 1826, with a resident at Clevedon, 78 years of age, and recorded on his informant's authority that, when the latter was young, not more than four carts went from Clevedon to Bristol in the course of a year; almost everything being carried by pack-horses.

The protection of the Dean and Chapter was supposed to have been obtained for the High Cross when it was re-erected in College Green (p. 186). The capitular body, however, was apathetic about everything save its pecuniary interests. The Green was neglected for many years, and fell at last into so discreditable a condition that in December, 1756, the neighbouring inhabitants memorialised the Corporation, praying for assistance in restoring the turf and walks, and forty guineas were voted for that purpose. Shamed into action, the chapter thereupon doled out 15 guineas, which Mr. Wallis, the builder, was ordered to make the best of. In April, 1757, the chapter, in the absence of the dean, approved of what had been done. "And as the said Mr. Wallis has offered a plan for removing the Cross and cutting off a small part of the Green," his proposal was sanctioned, subject to the approval of the dean. Dean Chamberlayne, however, systematically disapproved of the suggestions of the prebendaries, and the scheme of destruction was temporarily abandoned. Another quarrel amongst the cathedral dignitaries broke out immediately afterwards. The outlay of the chapter having exceeded the ordinary receipts for two or three years, a debt of £250 had accumulated, which the prebendaries proposed to wipe off by means of the next good fine received on the renewal of a lease. The dean having, of course, refused his sanction, the chapter resolved that, if he persisted in his resistance, all further renewals should be postponed. Three months later, in July, the dean having condescended to visit the city, he was urged to accede, but replied that "it would take a long time to consider the proposal, namely, till next winter." He gave way, however, in September, a few days before his death.

The scandalous system of shipping off convicted felons in company with honest emigrants was still practised in 1757. The *Intelligencer* of May 7th contains an advertisement inviting artisans, husbandmen, and boys to take their passage to Maryland as "indentured servants" in the ship Frisby; and a paragraph in the same paper states that forty convicts had just been sent on board the vessel in question, which was a "letter of marque." The Council had paid the keeper of Newgate £107 2s. in the previous year for transporting thirty-four convicts, indicating a remarkable prevalence of crime. Referring to the transportation system, a historian of Jamaica, writing about 1770, stated that above 2,000 abandoned felons were shipped yearly from England to Virginia and Maryland, and were "as useful as scavengers to a dirty town."

Felix Farley's Journal of the 11th June contains the following paragraph:—"We hear that the churchwardens of a considerable parish in this city intend (conformable to the obligations of their oath) to put the laws in force against all those within the said parish who commonly absent themselves from the publick worship on the Lord's Day; and also against common swearers, drunkards, &c., and its hoped and much to be wish'd that an example of this kind will be followed by all others who are well-wishers to the country." The fine imposable on every adult person who systematically neglected to attend his or her parish church was £20 a month, and 1s. for each casual default. No attempt, however, seems to have been made to put the law in operation.

In August, 1757, the Rev. John Castelman, vicar of St. Nicholas, revived a long-standing dispute between the incumbents of that parish and its select vestry. It appears from a letter addressed by Dean Towgood to the vestry shortly before his death, in 1682, that when he was instituted to St. Nicholas, in the reign of Charles I., he took possession of a house which from time immemorial had been used as a vicarage. He was, however, immediately deprived of it, and it was only after several years' entreaty that he obtained from the vestry a yearly compensation of £4, which was lost during the Commonwealth. At the Restoration he remained at his living at Tortworth until the vestry made a promise, apparently verbal, that he should be allowed £14 for house rent. When he came back to Bristol this promise was repudiated, and the dean concluded his letter by asking the vestry to consider whether he had not just cause to complain of hard dealing and wrong. The old vicarage house was in the Rackhay, a part of which was converted into a burial ground in 1698, and a further portion was consecrated to the same purpose in 1743. In consequence of the alterations made at those periods the vicarage could no longer be identified. Mr. Castelman having found a copy of Dean Towgood's letter in the cathedral archives, now renewed the claim of his predecessor. He admitted that the old house could not be found, but suggested that he should be compensated by a money payment of not less than £400, in which case he "would scorn to claim arrears." (The fixed income of the vicar, arising from bequests for sermons, was under £15.) The vestry appears to have treated his application with contemptuous silence, and the copies of the above letters inserted in the minute book were ordered to be expunged.

At a meeting of the Council, on the 5th September, orders were given for the construction of a new bridge over the Froom, in order to open a direct route from Christmas Street to Lewin's Mead. St. John's Bridge, as it was called, was of great convenience to the numerous members of the Corporation who attended Lewin's Mead Chapel.

At the same meeting it was "Ordered that Moses Cone," possibly a phonetical spelling of Cohen, "who keeps a shop, with glass windows before the same, on the Key, and therein sells gold and silver ware without being a free burgess, be prosecuted for the same." The fact that the Jew had placed glass windows in his shop front seems to have been considered by the conservative-minded Chamber as an aggravation of his offence. About four months later a local journal records that, on the previous Monday, "in the dusk, most of a loaf of sugar, a cheese, and a large knob of salt were taken out of the window of a shop in Baldwin Street, and carry'd off." Southey states that his father came to Bristol about 1760, and was apprenticed to Mr. William Britton, the leading linendraper, who had an open-windowed shop in Wine Street.

The oratorio of " Samson " was performed in the Cathedral on the 7th September, by a " large band of the best vocal and instrumental performers." The price of admission was 5s. " The Messiah " was given in 1758 and 1759, after which the performances, which were for the benefit of the families of poor clergymen, were discontinued.

The once celebrated William Warburton, D.D., was preferred by the Duke of Newcastle to the deanery of Bristol in October, 1757. The Newcastle MSS. show that if Warburton did not sooner reach high rank in the Church the delay was not attributable to his diffidence. So early as 1725 he is found "presuming to acquaint your grace of the dangerous illness" of a well-beneficed clergyman, and hinting his hopes that the living he had already obtained from the duke might be the shoeing-horn to another. In 1727 he declines an offered incumbency, presses his suit "for a living of better value," and regrets that while every district abounded with marks of his grace's goodness, "I should be the only one amongst your most devoted servants in which they do not appear." Incessant importunity and flattery were rewarded by many gifts, and his lucky marriage with a niece of Ralph Allen, of Bath, placed Warburton on the road to the prizes of his profession. A curious incident occurred at his first visit to Bristol Cathedral, when he had to "read himself in." According to the rubric, the Athanasian Creed should have formed part of the service of the day, but it was omitted by an oversight; and upon protest being made by some person present, Warburton ordered the creed to be sung on the following Sunday (when it ought not to have been performed), and read himself in a second time. As both services were irregular, it has been doubted whether Warburton was ever legally dean of Bristol. Little more than two years afterwards, through Allen's influence, Mr. Pitt, then M.P. for Bath, procured Warburton's promotion to the bishopric of Gloucester, and though the arrogant cleric had previously contemned the spiritual lords as a "wooden bench," he eagerly took his place amongst them. Bishop Newton records that while Warburton was at Bristol "Mr. Allen laid out a good deal of money in repairing and refronting the deanery, and had not quite completed it when the dean was made bishop. However, such was Allen's generosity that he was willing to finish what he had begun, but inquired first who was likely to succeed to the deanery. It was supposed to lie between Dr. (Samuel) Squire and Dr. Tucker (rector of St. Stephen's), and Mr. Allen asked the bishop (Warburton) what sort of men they were; and the bishop answered in his lively manner that the one (Squire) made religion his trade, and the other trade, his religion. Dr. Squire succeeded to the deanery of Bristol, where Mr. Allen completed his intended alterations." The writer goes on to defend Tucker from Warburton's malice, observing that while he wrote upon commercial topics "with more knowledge than any clergyman, and with as much, perhaps, as any merchant," he also ably handled subjects pertaining to his profession. " He was an exemplary parish priest and an exemplary dean . . . but it is to be lamented that he had not the respect for [Warburton] which was due to his personal character." The truth probably is that Tucker held the bishop's literary and theological works in the contempt they deserved, and made no effort to disguise his scorn for their self-seeking author. As to Squire, one of Warburton's letters contains the following :—" Have you seen the Dean of Bristol's (the quondam Clerk of the Closet's) sermon at St. Margaret's? He has fairly canonised our gracious sovereign by the name of George the Good." The courtly sycophant (who had already gained the king's favour by some act of peculiar baseness towards his patron, the Duke of Newcastle) was promptly rewarded, George III. conferring upon him the bishopric of St. David's in 1761.

Felix Farley's Journal of October 29th, 1757, published an announcement that the parish church of St. Werburgh had become so ruinous as to render it unsafe for public worship, and that the parishioners had resolved to take it down. Being unable of themselves to bear the charge of reconstruction, contributions were solicited from the charitable. In the following April, a " brief" was obtained for the collection of subscriptions throughout the kingdom, and in December, 1759, the Corporation voted £200 towards the works (raising the money by a loan). The most important alteration was the removal of the east end of the chancel, which projected so far into Small Street as to render carriage traffic dangerous. An altar-piece in the Corinthian style was introduced into the church, which was re-opened for service in February, 1761. The ancient edifice had been crowded with monuments, but it was not until 1765, when a subscription was started for the purpose, that some of those memorials were sought for and replaced. On the 1st March, 1766, *Felix Farley's Journal* recorded that " the real monumental stone of Mr. Nicholas Thorne, founder of the Grammar School, and a liberal benefactor of this city," had just been recovered and re-erected. " It was to have been put up to adorn a gentleman's Gothic stable in the neighbourhood." From numerous fragments embedded in the walls of " Black Castle," Mr. Reeve, who was an industrious picker-up of medieval trifles, must have retained the rest of his gleanings from St. Werburgh's.

The price of French wine advanced considerably at the outbreak of the war. Owing to the numerous captures of merchantmen, however, the supply soon exceeded the demand.

The *Intelligencer* of November 26th, 1757, contained the following:—"To be sold; a large quantity of prize wines, taken by the Lyon, Cæsar, Phœnix, and Tygress privateers. Any person wishing to purchase any quantity not less than 10 hogsheads may pick any of it at 45s. per hogshead"—less than 1s. per gallon!

An amusing style of announcing marriages was in favour about the middle of the century, and several good examples occur in the local journals of 1757. The following are specimens:—February 3, " Was married Mr. Thomas Linford, an eminent cabinet maker in Redcliff Street, to Miss Cook, of Pipe Lane, an agreeable young lady, with a handsome fortune." May 31, " Was married at Warminster, Mr. Henry Davis, in partnership with Mr. John Hooper, linen-draper in St. Maryleport Street, to Miss Hart, daughter of Richard Hart, Esq., late of Hanham; a young lady endowed with a plentiful fortune and every other qualification to render the married state at once happy and engaging." June 23, " Was married, at St. Werburgh's, Dr. Archibald Drummond to Miss Parsons, of Rudgeway, a young lady with a fortune of £30,000." In July, Mr. Deane Bayly, of Wine Street, married " a young lady of plentiful fortune and every other engaging accomplishment." September 1, " Was married John Smith, Esq., of Long Ashton (eldest son of Jarrit Smith, M.P.), to Miss Woolner, of this city, a handsome lady with £40,000 fortune, and endowed with every other desirable quality that may render the married state compleatly happy." December 17, " This week was married, Mr. Jackson, of Bath, to the daughter of Mr. Elisha Hellier, an eminent sope boiler in Redcliff Street, a lady of commanding beauty and £5000 fortune." It is perhaps significant that in some notices, where the writer is silent as to the fortune of the brides, he is eloquent on their beauty and accomplishments; while in others he is reserved about the ladies' charms, but is emphatic about their money. On one occasion, when a spinster of 63 summers was led to the altar, the adroit chronicler recorded that she brought her husband " her weight in gold, and a comfortable landed estate, also with composed and prudent abilities that excel any fortune." Another marriage (May, 1761) of the same character was that of " John Durbin, jun., Esq., to Miss Drax, sister to the Countess of Berkeley—a lady with a fortune of £10,000," but whose age is politely concealed. Nothing is generally said about the wealth or character of the husband. The following is exceptional:—June 14, 1761, " Was married at St. George's, the facetious Mr. Young, of Landogo, to the agreeable Mrs. Williams, late of Screws Hole, with a fortune of £10,000." Now and then the hymeneal announcement smells a little of the shop. April 19, 1755, " Was married at Bedminster, Samuel Baker, Esq., of Whitchurch, to Mrs. Hannah Bullock, sister to Mr. Thomas Broackes, who has lately contracted partnership with Mr. Bush, an eminent silk mercer in Wine Street." February 12, 1784, " Married, at the new Church (St. George's), Mr. William Fripp, son of Mr. Samuel Fripp, partners with an eminent soapmakers' company of this city, to Miss Martha Catley, niece of the two Miss James's, formerly milliners in Wine Street, an agreeable young lady, with a fortune of £3,000."

A Bill for the extension of local turnpikes having been brought into the House of Commons in 1758, some of the turnpike trustees petitioned for the inclusion in the measure of two more highways, namely, the road through Stoke Bishop to Shirehampton, and the road to Aust (the Welsh mail route), which " was up a very steep hill (Steep Street) going out of Bristol." To avoid the latter difficulty, the petitioners suggested that a new turnpike road should be made from Frog Lane "through certain grounds (the site of Park Street) to a gate on the Aust road called the White Lady's Gate." Clauses carrying out these proposals were introduced into the Bill, which became law. It was not until October, 1761, however, that the trustees resolved to proceed with the Whiteladies improvement. The Shirehampton turnpike opened out that district to the fashionable throng at the Hot Well, and excursions to Kingsweston inn and Penpole Hill became popular. For the accommodation of visitors to the latter, a building called the Breakfasting Room was erected, the patrons of which were permitted to ramble in the shrubberies of Kingsweston House.

The local journals of March 11th, 1758, contain the following announcement:—" At No. 6 in Trinity Street, near the College Green. On Monday after Easter will be opened a School for Young Ladies by Mary More and Sisters, where will be carefully taught French, Reading, Writing, Arithmetic, and Needlework. Young Ladies boarded on reasonable terms." A few weeks later an additional line appears: —" A Dancing Master will properly attend." A few little boys were admitted as day pupils. Hannah More was at this date under thirteen years of age, which disposes of the statement of some historians that she was the foundress of the school. The institution was prosperous from the outset, and when Park Street was laid out, one of the first houses erected was the property of the Misses More, who removed the school there about 1762.

The achievements of the Bristol privateers were frequently the occasion of popular rejoicing. Early in April, 1758, a clever feat was reported of the Phœnix, of 16 guns and 90 men, which carried into Dartmouth the French privateer Bellona, of 20 heavier guns and 120 men. The Phœnix had come within hail of the Frenchman about midnight, and so terrified him by assuming the name of the King's ship Tartar (the terror of French privateers) that he immediately surrendered. A more gallant action was accomplished three weeks later by the Bristol privateer Bellona, of 16 guns. Her captain, Richards, ran the ship into St. Martin's, near Rochelle, and cut from their moorings fourteen French vessels, two of which, of 100 tons each, laden with wine, were brought safely to Galway. This daring act, says the *London Chronicle*, was done at noonday, and within gunshot of 7 French men of war and 4 frigates. It is needless to say that the contrast between the conduct of the English and the French Bellona was the source of exultation in Bristol. In October a brilliant deed was reported on the part of the local ship, Duke of Cornwall, Capt. Jenkins. The King's ship Winchelsea had been captured by a French man of war, which placed a crew on board, with directions to sail for France. On the voyage the Duke of Cornwall engaged the Winchelsea and succeeded in re-taking the ship. This achievement was crowned in November by the capture of the French man of war Belliqueux, the vessel supposed to have caught the Winchelsea. On the 21st October a despatch arrived in Bristol stating that a foreign ship of 64 guns was lying off Lundy Island, having been driven there by stress of weather. Captain Saumarez, of H.M.S. Antelope, of 50 guns, lying in Kingroad, was that evening at a ball at the Hotwells. The news being reported to him, he repaired on board, accompanied by several volunteers, and beat down Channel. On reaching the foreigner she showed signs of resistance, but soon struck her colours, and was towed up to Kingroad. The Belliqueux had 470 men on board, 60 of whom were sick, and the rest suffering from want of provisions. During the same week Bristol privateers brought eight French merchantmen to Kingroad, some of the prizes being of great value. The Merchants' Society presented Captain Saumarez with 100 guineas.

Paper-hangings for rooms were an expensive luxury

during the first half of the century. In one of the Countess of Hertford's letters, written in 1741, it is stated that superior paper-hangings then cost from 12s. to 13s. a yard. The *Bristol Intelligencer* of April 15th, 1758, contains an announcement of the sale of a house in Queen Square, "with the paper-hangings thereto affixed."

An enterprising Bath innkeeper started, in May, a "new machine, on steel springs," for the accommodation of travellers to and from Bristol. Each journey occupied three hours, and the fare was half a crown.

The original proposal for laying out what was to be subsequently called Park Street was recorded at page 227. After a sleep of 18 years, the project was again brought before the Common Council in July, 1758, its promoters, Alderman Day and George Tyndale, seeking approval of an extended design. They now proposed, on condition of being granted a fresh lease, to lay out a road from the top of the new street to Whiteladies' Gate, where it would join the turnpike road leading from the city *viâ* St. Michael's Hill, and thus afford a new and better route for the Welsh mail and other vehicles proceeding to Aust. The Chamber granted a renewed lease, but required the lessees to keep the intended new street in repair. The Act authorising the Whiteladies' extension has been already mentioned. It was not until February, 1761, that builders were invited to apply for sites in Park Street.

A modest equestrian entertainment—the first of its kind recorded—took place on the 17th July on Durdham Down. "The famous Thomas Johnson" rode two horses at full speed round the race-course with a foot on each of their backs, and afterwards rode 100 yards standing on his head, and 300 yards more standing on one leg. The public "encouraged this extraordinary undertaking" so liberally that it was repeated two days afterwards. To add to the enjoyment on the second occasion, a "game pig" with a greased tail was let off to be hunted by the populace, and afforded so much sport that it reached Westbury before it was caught, the efforts of a howling crowd of Bristolians being ultimately defeated by a nimble youth of the village. Probably in consequence of this disappointment a "free fight" followed on the Down, "in which several persons were much hurt."

Felix Farley's Journal of July 27th announces the sale by auction of "the large commodious public-house known by the sign of the Duke of Marlborough, at Bedminster, in the occupation of the Reverend Emanuel Collins; let at £20 per annum." As has been already stated, Collins is reported to have made a shameless living by celebrating irregular marriages at his public-house. The Act rendering such unions illegal passed in 1753, and his abandonment of the tavern soon after lends support to the tradition. In 1762 Collins, who (falsely) styled himself M.A., of Oxford, published some poetical effusions under the title of "Miscellanies," in which the depravity of his mind is only too clearly revealed.

Giles Earle, Esq., son of a once influential Bristolian, Sir Thomas Earle, died at his seat near Malmesbury on the 20th August, 1758, in his 80th year. Mr. Earle devoted himself in early life to politics, and after holding various inferior offices, was appointed a lord of the Treasury in 1737. He is often referred to in Horace Walpole's letters, and appears to have been famous for a wit which was coarse even for that age.

The Common Council, in September, granted the renewal, for fourteen years, to Thomas Tyndall, of the lease of a house in the Royal Fort, on payment of a fine of £60, and a yearly rent of £6. In May, 1762, the Corporation conveyed the fee simple of the property to the lessee for £670. Mr. Tyndall, in August, 1753, had purchased of a lessee of the dean and chapter an interest in plots of land called "Cantock's Closes," and the lessors granted him fresh leases of the estate, in consideration of a fine of £58. Having acquired several other adjoining fields, Mr. Tyndall demolished the house in the Fort, and set about the construction of an imposing mansion, and the laying out of the meadows into a park, which received the name of its owner. His improvements excited admiration. In a poetical contribution, published in *Felix Farley's Journal* of June 27th, 1767, a writer says:—

> Long in neglect, an ancient dwelling stood,
> With tottering walls, worn roofs, and perish'd wood,
> 'Till gen'rous Tynd-l, fir'd with sense and taste,
> S iw here confusion—ruin there—and waste,
> Resolved at once to take the rubbish down,
> And raise a palace there to grace the town.

Owing to the constant increase of population and the growth of trade, the difficulty of communication between the districts north and south of the Avon, through the extreme narrowness of Bristol Bridge, had been long painfully felt. Accidents to passengers being of frequent occurrence, memorials urging the necessity of a new bridge were presented to the Common Council from time to time; but the expense of an improvement involving the demolition of some thirty houses standing on the old structure long paralysed the Chamber. At a meeting on the 28th October, 1758, however, a committee was appointed to consider the best means of providing funds for the improvement; and this body invited plans and suggestions. After prolonged deliberation the committee prepared a Bill, taking powers to remove the houses on the bridge and to widen the roadway; and the scheme was laid before a meeting of the inhabitants held in the Guildhall in February, 1759. Much difference of opinion having been elicited, a committee of twenty-four citizens, chosen out of the several wards, was formed to confer on the details with the corporate officials. The remainder of the year was spent in fruitless debates, and in December another public meeting was held in the Guildhall, when it was resolved that the approaches to the bridge should be enlarged, that a temporary bridge should be erected adjoining the old one pending its reconstruction, and that a new bridge of one arch should be thrown "from Temple side to the opposite shore." The Council, still desirous of improving the old structure, accepted the citizens' suggestions as to the subsidiary bridges, and proposed that the cost of the improvements should be defrayed by a duty on coal, a rate on houses, a wharfage charge on imports and exports, and a toll for five years on the temporary and reconstructed bridges. The citizens' committee protested against the wharfage tax, and as the Council, offended at the opposition, refused to proceed with the scheme, a private Bill was presented to Parliament empowering its promoters to carry out the works. This brought the Corporation to terms, and another Bill was framed giving powers to construct a temporary bridge, and also a permanent bridge in a line with Temple Street, on the completion of which the old bridge was to be taken down and rebuilt. The measure also included powers for the removal of St. Nicholas's Gate and of the south side of the Shambles (the site of what is now Bridge Street). The citizens submitted to the wharfage duty, and the Corporation withdrew the proposed tax on coal; the rate on houses was fixed at 6*d*. in the pound, and the bridge tolls were to continue until the cost of the improvements was discharged. An Act of Parliament having been obtained (at a cost to the Corporation of £396), the construction of the temporary bridge was begun, and it was sufficiently advanced to permit the members of the Gloucestershire Society to make use of it for their annual feast-day procession on the 3rd September, 1761. The designs proposed for the new Bristol Bridge were the subject of protracted debates amongst the trustees appointed by the Act, who, like the citizens, were divided into two camps, one party urging that the river should be spanned by a single arch, while the economists contended that the old piers should be again made available. No less than seventy-six meetings were held by the trustees, who were bombarded by angry pamphlets and letters in the newspapers, emanating from rival architects, their supporters, and miscellaneous critics. The controversy raged for two years. At length, in November, 1763, it was resolved by a large majority to build a bridge of three arches on the old piers, according to the design of Mr. James Bridges. The foundation stone was laid on the 28th March, 1764. The bridge was opened for foot passengers in September, 1768, and on Michaelmas Day the retiring mayor was the first to traverse it in a carriage. The opening for general traffic took place in November.

A singular business was carried on at this period by a midwife living in Maudlin Lane, who announced that she conveyed or sent children every Wednesday to the Foundling Hospital in London, her charge to parents desirous of ridding themselves of their offspring being $2\frac{1}{2}$ guineas for each child, or four guineas for a couple. As the advertisement was repeated for some months, the woman seems to have found the traffic profitable.

At the swearing-in of the Master of the Barbers' Company, says a journal of November 18th, 1758, "the mayor was pleased to take notice to them of the scandalous practice of shaving on the Lord's Day, desiring the same might be suppressed." The barbers were accordingly warned that infractions of the law would be punished. Several convictions were subsequently recorded.

Mary Darby, styled by some admirers the English Sappho, was born in the Minster House, adjoining the Cathedral, on the 27th November. Her father was a local merchant, who ruined himself a few years later by a whale fishery scheme, when his daughter was removed from the Misses More's school in Park Street, and the family left Bristol for London. While in her sixteenth year Mary Darby was married to a worthless attorney named Robinson, who soon abandoned her, and the girl-wife, who was possessed of remarkable personal charms, adopted the stage as a profession, and at once became celebrated as an actress. In 1780, whilst playing the character of Perdita, she captivated the fickle heart of George, Prince of Wales, then in his eighteenth year, and, having listened to his proposals, she was forthwith provided with a splendid establishment. The connection, however, was a short one. In August, 1781, George III. having learnt that the actress was in possession of many compromising love-letters, employed an agent to secure them for the sum of £5,000, which was insufficient to discharge the lady's debts. The king was not aware that his son had also given her, on her consenting to quit the stage for his gratification, a bond for £20,000; but this she surrendered to Mr. Fox on being promised an annuity of £500. She subsequently formed a connection with one Colonel Tarleton, whose rapacity, aided by her own extravagance, reduced her to penury. She also lost the use of her limbs through travelling during a wintry night to rescue Tarleton from a debtors' prison. In 1788 she betook herself to literature, and eventually published about twenty novels and books of poems, several of the latter being characterised by taste and feeling. In despite of her exertions, Mrs. Robinson sank in her later days into destitution, her appeals to her princely seducer being treated with characteristic callousness. She had, however, some devoted admirers, amongst whom were Coleridge, Dr. Walcott, and Sir R. K. Porter. The unhappy woman died at Englefield Green on the 26th December, 1800.

The following advertisement appeared in *Felix Farley's Journal* of March 31st, 1759:—"To be sold, a handsome dwelling house and garden, with a brickyard, situate in the parish of St. Philip and Jacob. The Jews' Burial Ground and some buildings are in the said yard."

The impressment of sailors for the navy brought about many desperate conflicts between the press-gangs and their victims. A local newspaper of the 12th May reports that upon information being received that a number of privateersmen were concealed in a public-house at Long Ashton, a press-gang was sent off to capture them; but the sailors made a successful resistance, and mortally wounded the leader of the gang. On the following day a public-house in Marsh Street, in which were five of the privateersmen, was surrounded by the impressment officers, when the sailors mounted upon the roof and exchanged several volleys with their assailants, in one of which the landlady was shot in the neck by one of the press-gang. The privateersmen at last killed one of their own party, when the rest surrendered. The probable consequences of such conflicts to ordinary wayfarers is left to the reader's imagination. A more desperate conflict took place at Cardiff in September, between about seventy of the crew of the Eagle privateer, of Bristol, and an impressment party who had surrounded the house in which the sailors were quartered. The latter drew up in battle array, their war-cry being "Liberty:" and after a sharp fire on both sides the press-gang retreated, and would have suffered severely but for the interposition of the magistrates. One man was killed and several wounded.

Whilst the crews of the privateers were threatened with life-long servitude on board the fleet, the owners of those vessels were menaced with ruinous actions at law for overstepping their rights. In the Duke of Newcastle's MSS. is a letter, dated May 22nd, 1759, addressed to Mr. Nugent, M.P., by John Noble, Robert Gordon, and other eminent Bristol merchants, soliciting the protection of the Government, "in our deplorable case of the Dutch captures." A petition drawn up for presentation to Parliament accompanied the letter. The petitioners alleged that at an expense of £300,000 they had equipped and sent out a great number of privateers, which had been instrumental in preserving the commerce of the country and in annoying the enemy. Many French privateers had been captured, as well as ships laden with provisions, ammunition, and goods for the enemy; and more would have been caught but for the wiliness of the French in shipping their foreign imports in neutral bottoms. The petitioners, encouraged by the declaration of the king that he would not suffer French trade to be carried on under other flags, had seized vessels under Dutch and other colours trading with the French colonies; and such vessels had been duly condemned, with the effect of causing the petitioners to send out more privateers at great expense, by which many more neutral ships had been captured. If such prizes were to be delivered up, as was demanded by the neutral Governments, many of the petitioners, "who have adventured all or a large part of their property on the faith of the king's declaration, if not totally ruined, will be greatly injured, and many thousand brave seamen, whose sole dependence is upon their prize money, will be reduced to the utmost distress." The matter nearly occasioned a war with Holland. Eventually one ship was given up to the Dutch, and owners of privateers were ordered to be more careful in their treatment of neutrals. Bristolians, however, had had enough of privateering, and, indeed, the

French mercantile marine had been swept off the ocean. *Felix Farley's Journal* of June 9th says:—" Of fifty-six privateers fitted out at this port, there is at this time but a single one remaining at sea."

On the 15th October John Wesley inspected the French prisoners of war confined at Knowle. He wrote in his Journal:—" About 1100 of them were confined in that little place without anything to lie upon but a little dirty straw, or anything to cover them but a few foul thin rags, either by day or night, so that they died like rotten sheep." After making this private memorandum, it is amazing to find Wesley writing to *Felix Farley's Journal*, a few days later, to contradict the common report that the prisoners were "dying in whole shoals." He declared that he had seen no sweeter or cleaner prison in England, and that even during a sickly season there were not thirty dangerously ill out of 1,100 or 1,200. He admitted, however, that many of the captives were almost naked, and commended their wants to public charity. Subsequently, having collected £24, he sent in a supply of shirts and stockings. A subscription was entered into by the citizens, by which £313 were raised, and as the Corporation provided the prison with mattresses and blankets, Wesley had the satisfaction of recording that the prisoners " were pretty well provided with all the necessaries of life." The captives had increased to about 1,800 at the peace in 1763.

The announcement of the capture of Quebec was received in Bristol on the 18th October with transports of enthusiasm. In the evening the city and the shipping in the harbour burst into a general illumination, " every person," says the imaginative newspaper chronicler, dazzled by the glare of tallow candles and oil, " seeming to vie with his neighbour how much they could exceed each other in making night itself as bright as midday. . . . The cloud-capt towers of St. James, St. Stephen, &c., were illuminated, and their tops to the distant eye appear'd as if crown'd with stars." On the invitation of the mayor, the influential citizens assembled at the Council House, where bumpers were drunk in honour of the victors, amidst volleys from the military drawn up in front of the building, and salutes from the cannon on the Grove. The French had threatened a descent on England by means of a vast flotilla of flat-bottomed boats, but the dread of invasion was forgotten in the general rejoicing, and the peril had, in fact, passed away. Another public celebration of a similar character took place on the

8th October, 1760, on the arrival of the news of the surrender of Montreal.

In an advertisement dated the 27th October, 1759, the Bristol turnpike trustees made the following generous proposal:—"Notice is hereby given that any Persons willing to take off the Dirt from any Part of the Turnpike Roads leading from the City of Bristol may do it at their own Expense between this and the 2nd February next." The advertisement was repeated in subsequent years.

Resuming an ancient practice, the corporate body attended service at the Cathedral on the anniversary of Gunpowder Plot. *Felix Farley's Journal* thereupon congratulated the city on "the pleasing prospect of future peace" between the Council and the dean and chapter, who had been "unhappily divided for many years past."

Mr. Nugent, M.P., having been appointed a Vice Treasurer of Ireland, his seat became vacant in December, when he was forthwith re-elected. No opposition having been offered, Mr. Nugent "generously gave £500 to be disposed of as the citizens should think proper;" and the money was handed over to the fund for rebuilding the Bridge.

Thanks to the extraordinary successes of the English arms in India, America, and Germany, the two leading Ministers, Mr. Pitt and the Duke of Newcastle, were pelted in 1760 with gold boxes by the civic corporations. The Common Council of Bristol was naturally one of the first to take action. On the 10th January the Chamber resolved that the freedom of the city should be presented in gold boxes to the Duke and his colleague "in the most respectful manner." Two elegantly chased caskets were accordingly obtained at a cost of £113. (One of the above boxes, offered for sale in 1890, is now in the possession of Sir Charles Wathen.)

By a fire on the 16th March, 1760, in a house in Charles Street, "part of the new buildings in the parish of St. James," a respected schoolmaster, named Jones, was burnt to death, in company with his wife. The disaster was attributed to the negligence of the city watchmen, and some doggrel lines in *Felix Farley's Journal* expressed the feeling of the inhabitants:—

> The Watch burn Tobacco while Houses are burning,
> And the *Glass*, not the *Watch*, goes its rounds.
> A burning shame this and sad subject of mourning,
> That our Guard's such a mute Pack of Hounds.

The same journal of July 11th, 1761, reporting an attempted burglary, said, "The mistress of the house alarmed the watch, who came near enough to see them run away, but being an old decrepit man could not follow them."

"The noted Mr. Slack," a Bristol butcher, had a pugilistic encounter on the 2nd June, 1760, at St. James's tennis court in London, with "William Stephens, the nailer." The odds were 5 to 1 upon Slack, but he was defeated in four minutes. Many noblemen were present, and upwards of £10,000 changed hands. A still more exciting battle was fought at the same place in March, 1761, between "the nailer" and George Maggs, of Pensford. "There were assembled," says the *Bristol Chronicle*, "the greatest concourse of nobility, gentry, &c., ever known on a like occasion." The prices of admission were 10s. 6d. and 5s. Three to one were betted upon "the nailer," owing to his former victory, but Maggs defeated his adversary in 17½ minutes. "A certain Royal Personage [the Duke of Cumberland] was present and won large sums. 'Tis said upwards of £50,000 depended on the issue." The London *Evening Post* adds:—"The Bristol people, it is supposed, have carried away above £10,000, and are so elate with their success that they offer to back their champion for 1000 guineas against any man in the world."

In consequence of the narrowness of the roadway through the city gate near Needless Bridge, by which the traffic from the Stone Bridge to Broadmead was much impeded, the Council, in August, 1760, ordered the demolition of the gate and the widening of the thoroughfare.

Owing to the pressure of his judicial duties and advancing years, Sir Michael Foster tendered his resignation of the recordership to the Council on the 23rd August. The Chamber, however, begged that he would retain his office, and he temporarily complied. He refused his fee for the gaol delivery in 1762; but the Corporation presented him with a piece of plate. On his final resignation, in February, 1763, a second gift of plate was forwarded in appreciation of his services. His successor was the Hon. Daines Barrington, a grandson of Sir William Daines, and a distinguished antiquary. Sir Michael Foster died November 7th, 1763, and was buried at Stanton Drew. Blackstone and other eminent judges, as well as Horace Walpole, have referred to his distinguished learning, integrity and independence, and Churchill noted the general impression as to his character:—

> Each judge was true, and steady to his trust,
> As Mansfield wise, and as old Foster just.

The military glory surrounding the closing years of the reign of George II. evoked a feeling of respect for that monarch which had been previously lacking, and his death excited some popular regret. A poet, whose genius shone in the *Bristol Chronicle*, burst out as follows:—

> Hark! hark! the Bells, how solemnly they rings
> The Funeral Knell of George, the Best of Kings!

The accession of George III. was proclaimed on the 30th October, 1760, on the site of the High Cross and the other usual places, with the customary formalities. A hundred private coaches took part in the procession. Festivities followed in the evening, but the total outlay was only £129. The marriage and coronation of the young king in the following year were celebrated with greater parade. In the coronation procession of the trading fraternities—many of which displayed their waning numbers for the last time —the Smiths' Company was preceded by a man in armour; but the most interesting object was a stage drawn by four horses, whereon were printers engaged in working off an appropriate poetical effusion, copies of which were scattered amongst the spectators. Such an exhibition of the printing-press, according to *Felix Farley's Journal*, had never been made before in England. Following the trade companies were the boys of Queen Elizabeth's Hospital "with their hair powdered." During the service at the Cathedral two coronation anthems were sung, "French horns, fiddles, drums, &c., playing with the organ." Subsequently a quantity of beer was distributed, and many families were provided with dinner, an ox having been roasted whole at Temple Meads for that purpose. In the evening a painted transparency, brilliantly illuminated, 73 feet high and of proportional breadth, retained vast crowds in Queen Square until 3 o'clock in the morning; whilst pyrotechnic displays took place on the tower of St. John's Church and at Lawford's Gate. Amongst the items of civic expense, which exceeded £400, were—A ball in Merchants' Hall, £119; fireworks, £46; music, £24; wine, £21; gunpowder, £27; the transparency (painted by an able local artist named Simmons), £40; and "expenses on account of a champion," £10.

A gallant action between the Constantine privateer of Bristol and a French privateer called the Victoire took place on the 23rd November, 1760. Captain Forsyth was attacked by the enemy, which he had taken for an English man of war; and the French rushed upon the Constantine's

[1760.] IN THE EIGHTEENTH CENTURY. 343

ws. " But my
e English lions,
d head, though
ngagement, the
sted all sail in
enabled him to
We made great
out of his scup-
a was perfectly
I had but two
n as they were
as won against
y 18 four-pound
20 six-pounders

the West Indies
rade, which was
rotective duties.
English vessels
nearly one-half.
l. In 1762 the
bar coast. The
the 460 slaves
St. Michael, of
he loss, through
en of the crew,

districts of the
owly developed.
he families who
uthern slope of
A correspondent
) laments that
f the pleasantest
lown, delightful
experience the
s." The writer
concluded by hoping that the threatened devastation would
be avoided by the purchase of the ground by public subscription. A few weeks later another, or perhaps the same,
writer, lamented in verse the degraded condition of the hill,
observing,—

> Each petty tradesman here must have his seat,
> And vainly thinks the heights will make him great;

adding that, whatever the place might be called in future,

its proper title was Pedlars' Hill. As a matter of fact, the extension of the new suburb was highly beneficial. Sea-side resorts being still neglected, the professional and mercantile class living in the close streets of the old city frequently sent their children during the summer holidays to Kingsdown for a change of air. It may be worth while to note the rental of various houses advertised to be let in this year. A house in Broad Street, occupied by a haberdasher, £21; house in High Street, £21; house on the Bridge, £30; another, £12; two houses in College Green, £21 and £18; house and warehouses, Thomas Street, £13 8s.

In consequence of frequent complaints as to the dilatoriness of the postal service, the authorities in London announced in 1760 that letters or packets would thenceforth be dispatched from the capital to the chief provincial towns "at any hour, without loss of time," at certain specified rates. An express to Bristol cost £2 3s. 6d.; to Plymouth, £4 8s. 9d. Leeds, Manchester, Birmingham and Liverpool are not mentioned.

The earliest recorded Bristol riding school was opened on the 2nd February, 1761, by " R. C. Carter, riding master from London." The school was held in an extensive building called the Circular Stables, in the Backfields, Stoke's Croft, which had just been erected on the tontine principle by 95 citizens contributing £30 each, it being agreed that the property should be divided when the nominated lives were reduced to two.

A general election took place in March, 1761, when the local political leaders resolved to avoid a contest. The *Bristol Chronicle* stated that the Union (Whig) Society met in the Guildhall and nominated Robert Nugent, while the Steadfast (Tory) Club assembled at Merchants' Hall and nominated Jarrit Smith, "our late worthy representatives, which compromise have delivered the city from a very oppressive weight it used to labour under on such occasions." The members were formally elected on the 27th March, and " carried round part of the city on chairs." In the evening they entertained the electors of each parish. Mr. Smith was created a baronet in 1763, and subsequently took the name of Smyth.

Evidence as to the low price of animal food is offered by a *Felix Farley's Journal* of May, 1761, in which it is stated that a contractor had undertaken to provide "good beef" for the prisoners of war confined at Knowle at the rate of 13s. 11d. per cwt.—less than 1½d. per pound.

Down to this period the ancient gateway of St. Augustine's Abbey, in College Green, was provided with gates, and the communication between the upper and lower greens was under the control of the dean and chapter. Probably to save the expense of a porter, the capitular body resolved in June, 1761, that the gates should be removed; and as no steps were taken to safeguard the rights of the chapter, the thoroughfare became a public way. In the following September it was determined that the service held at 7 in the morning should be suspended from November 1st to March 31st. Scandal having been caused by the manner in which some of the members shirked their duties, it was further ordered that each prebendary should be mulcted £12 and the dean £24 if he failed to be in residence for the stipulated yearly period. This regulation was of no effect. Complaint being also made that "numbers of loose and disorderly people meet to go in the church cloisters as soon as it is dark, to the great scandal of the neighbourhood," orders were given to close the cloisters' gate.

Philip Yonge, D.D., who had held the bishopric for three years, was translated to Norwich in August, 1761. Nothing is locally recorded of this prelate, who was Master of Jesus College, Cambridge, prebendary of Westminster, canon of St. Paul's, and rector of a Hertfordshire parish. In the Cole MSS., however, is the following minute of a conversation relating to Redcliff church, held in 1771, between Mr. Cole and the Rev. Dr. Lort. "Mr. Lort mentioned that, calling on the Bishop of Norwich [Yonge], and talking with his lordship on the great qualifications of Mr. Cannings, his merits to the town of Bristol and the kingdom in general, the bishop made answer that if he had not prevented it, the inhabitants of that grateful parish had thrown out the monument of its so worthy benefactor." Cole adds:—
"Bristol may be a good trading city, and skilled in those arts that will at last end in the destruction of this and every other great trading and luxurious nation, but the virtues of gratitude, decency, and generosity I think their historian will be much difficulted to point out in it."

Dr. Yonge was succeeded in Bristol by Thomas Newton, D.D., prebendary of Westminster, sub-almoner and precentor of York, and rector of a rich London parish. A canonry of St. Paul's was conferred with the bishopric, when the other preferments were resigned. Dr. Johnson's contemptuous opinion of "Tom," who like himself was the son of a Lichfield tradesman, is well known. But if Newton lacked learning, he possessed all the arts by which adroit clergymen attained worldly distinction. No speculator ever watched the rise and fall of the funds with more anxious vigilance than Newton displayed in noting vacancies in and appointments to the great prizes of the church. The MSS. of the Duke of Newcastle prove his indefatigable activity as a suitor, while his numerous preferments attest the success of his exertions. In September, 1757, he sends off a hurried despatch to the all-powerful minister, advising him that one of the canonries of Windsor had just become vacant by the death of its holder. Writing on August 7th, 1761, he informs the duke that the archbishop of York lies in a dying state, and cannot possibly live beyond the next morning. " Upon this occasion of two vacancies, I beg, I hope, I trust your grace's kindness and goodness will be shown to one who has long solicited your favour." The duke hastened to reassure him. Replying on the same day (before the archbishop was dead), the minister stated that he had recommended the bishop of Salisbury to the King to succeed at York. " I hope you will fill one of the vacant sees if there should be two, and I have not the least doubt of it." Two days later Newton writes:—" Sunday morning, 10 o'clock. The archbishop of York is just now dead. My particular thanks are due to your grace for the honour of your letter." While he was paying assiduous court to the duke, however, Newton confesses in his autobiography—an amusing picture of the author and his times—that he was ardently supplicating the patronage of Lord Bute, the king's favourite; and while roundly asserting that he owed his bishopric to the personal favour of George III., he loses no occasion to vilipend the Duke of Newcastle. Newton's elevation to the bench did not slacken his courtship of the powerful. He was offered the deanery of Westminster, but declined it, he says, "having something better in view." His refusal of the Primacy of Ireland was due to the same cause—his anxiety to obtain the see of London, which according to his own account he was promised on two successive vacancies, but which the King conferred on other competitors. Unsuccessful in securing the rich bishopric of Ely on a later occasion, he was at length, in 1768, gratified with the deanery of St. Paul's, then much better endowed than many episcopates. In his memoirs Newton states that the office was spontaneously conferred upon him by the King. It was really gained by urgent solicitation. Warburton, writing to Hurd while the place was still vacant, said:—" I wish success to the Bishop of Bristol, though he played the fool in the affair you mention. But that will not hinder his exchanging his rectory for a deanery." Writing to the Duke of Newcastle in October, 1768, the lucky suitor thanks his grace for his congratulations on this windfall, regarding his esteem " a very considerable addition to the value of the preferment." During the earlier part of his long tenure of the see of Bristol (twenty-one years), Dr. Newton resided three, and sometimes four or five, months yearly at the episcopal palace, though he states that the income of the bishopric was little more than £300, and never exceeded £400. " By living and residing there so much," he wrote about 1781, " he was in hopes that his example would have induced the other members of the church to perform also their part, and to discharge at least their statutable duties. The deanery is worth at least £500 a year, and each prebend about half that sum, and for these preferments the residence usually required is three months for the dean and half that time for each prebendary. But, alas! never was church more shamefully neglected. The bishop has several times been there for months together, without seeing the face of anything better than a minor canon. His example having no kind of effect, he remonstrated several times, . . . their want of residence was the general complaint not only of the city, but likewise of all the country. . . . But the bishop's remonstrances had no better effect than his example, and to do more was not in his power. . . . While the deans of Gloucester, &c., were beautifying their churches, poor Bristol lay utterly neglected, like a disconsolate widow." The dean of this period (1763–80) was Cutts Barton, who followed the example of another dignitary referred to by the bishop, and was simply in residence "the better part of the year"—namely, the week during which the yearly revenues were divided.

The cruelty of the penal code is illustrated by the fate of John Cope, who was executed at St. Michael's Hill on the 6th November, 1761. Cope had been tried for felony in 1760, when he was sentenced to seven years' transportation. He subsequently succeeded in escaping from Newgate, in company with other prisoners, and on being recaptured he was tried at the next assizes for the capital offence of " being found at large after having received sentence of transportation." He was of course convicted, and, perhaps with a view to deter others from attempting evasion, the extreme sentence of the law was carried out.

In December, 1761, much excitement was caused in the city by reports of alleged supernatural disturbances in the household of Richard Giles, landlord of the Lamb inn, near Lawford's Gate, who had just started certain "flying wagons" to London. Two of Giles's numerous family, "Molly" and "Dobby," aged thirteen and eight, were stated to be nightly tormented by some invisible power, which bit them on the neck and arms, and pricked them with pins; various articles of furniture being at the same time thrown about their bedroom by incomprehensible forces. Amongst the persons desirous of probing the mystery was Mr. Henry Durbin, a prosperous druggist in Redcliff Street (uncle of Sir John Durbin), whose narrative of the marvels must be briefly summarised. When the children were together in bed, Mr. Durbin was shown marks of bites and scratchings that had just been made under the bedclothes, and was at a loss to account for them naturally; though he notes that the girls were never tormented when asleep. He also saw a wine glass rise perpendicularly a foot in the air, and fling itself with a loud report against a nurse five feet distant. Then Molly's cap flew four feet off her head, and something beat the tattoo on the bed-ticking with the skill of a drummer. During the biting and pricking Mr. Durbin and others thumped the bed vigorously, when something squeaked like a rat, but the practices continued. After other experiences the evil spirit—for Mr. Durbin was now sure it was a spirit—condescended to reply to questions by giving as many knocks as the interrogator required for an affirmative reply. By this means it was discovered, as had been suspected, that the spirit was instigated by an old witch, living at Mangotsfield, who had been paid ten guineas by a rival carrier to bewitch Mr. Giles's family and wagons. This confession was confirmed by the fact that one of Mr. Giles's flying wagons had suddenly stuck fast in the road at Hanham, where eighteen horses had been required to move it; while another wagon had a trembling fit in Giles's own yard. By February the subject had become the talk of the city, and Mr. Durbin had been joined in his numberless visits to the inn by several clergymen, amongst them being the Rev. J. Camplin, precentor of the Cathedral, and vicar of St. Nicholas, the Rev. S. Seyer, head master of the Grammar School, the Rev. R. Symes, of St. Werburgh's, the Rev. J. Price, of Temple, the Rev. — Brown, and the Rev. — Shepherd. It was now thought desirable to interrogate the evil spirit in Latin, Greek, and Hebrew, and

Mr. Durbin asserts that it answered correctly by knocks to all the questions put in those tongues. What was still more marvellous, Mr. Camplin asked several questions mentally, and received truthful taps in reply. Mr. Symes, equally convinced that the agency was diabolical, asked in the pulpit for the prayers of his parishioners on behalf of the tormented children. Another believer addressed a letter to *Felix Farley's Journal*, declaring that scoffers of witchcraft cast a slur upon the Bible. Soon after, the children began to be thrown violently out of bed, and Major Drax, a relative of the Countess of Berkeley, and a powerful man, assured Mr. Durbin that his strength, together with that of his footman and coachman, was insufficient to prevent the girls from being thrown upon the floor. Indeed, "four stout men could scarce hold one child," who was borne towards the ceiling. Pins next began to fly about the room. The major marked several pins, and laid them in a distant corner, but they were forthwith thrown back into his hand. The gallant officer then "carry'd them up to London to Court, and shew'd them to several noblemen and bishops" —with results unrecorded. Meanwhile the wagons were as much persecuted as the children, one vehicle being sixteen hours in making its way from the Lamb inn to Bath, while another had its iron chain twisted into knots; but Giles seems to have had a shrewd suspicion that the evil agency was simply the trickery of his servants. The children were removed to the houses of various friends, but the phenomena continued so long as they remained together, while there was a notable diminution of the marvels when they were separated. On the 12th May Mr. Giles suddenly became ill. He had ridden to Bath in a gig, but on returning home, on reaching the spot where his wagons were usually "affected," the harness broke, and he saw an old woman standing by the wheel, to whom he had not the courage to speak. He died on the 16th, and Mr. Durbin clearly believed (and in fact the demon told him) that the carrier was a victim to witchcraft. The customary disturbances at the Lamb then ceased for about two months (the eldest girl had been sent to Swansea); but in July Dobby began to be again tormented, and at the following fair many old frequenters of the inn declined to lodge in the witchstricken hostel. Soon after, the children being together again, the old phenomena revived, and Mr. Durbin, on questioning the spirit, learnt that the witch had received another fee of ten guineas to continue the persecution. The necessity of taking energetic measures being now apparent, Mrs. Giles resolved on calling in the assistance of a "white witch," commonly known as the Cunning Woman of Bedminster. A visit being paid to this redoubtable female, the witch at once stated to her disguised clients that she knew all about the case, named the spirit that had worked the mischief, and propounded a remedy for his summary overthrow which modern delicacy will not permit to be described. Her prescription was immediately followed with triumphant success. The demon was routed, and never ventured to return. The prosaic John Evans concludes his notice of the affair by stating that the whole imposture was planned by "Mrs. Nelmes, and her daughter, Mrs. Giles, the grandmother and mother of Molly and Dobby, for the purpose of depreciating the value of the house, of which Mrs. Nelmes became the purchaser."

On the 28th December the Duke of York, brother of George III., and then heir-presumptive to the throne, paid a brief visit to Bristol. He was met at Temple Gate by the mayor, the members of the Corporation, and others, who escorted him to the mayor's residence in Queen Square. After being presented with the freedom of the city and of the Merchants' Society in gold boxes, the young prince was entertained to dinner at the Merchants' Hall, where the tables groaned under "400 dishes"; and a grand ball was held at a later hour in the Assembly Room. The duke next morning inspected some of the principal glass-houses, and then returned to Bath. Unusual preparations for this visit were made by the Common Council, who sent for a noted cook from Bath to dress the dinner, and ordered that the principal table, "for both courses," should be set out with china plates and dishes, and silver knives, forks, and spoons. The plate was obtained by a perquisition on the wealthier aldermen and councillors, Thomas Deane and James Hillhouse lending 3 dozen each; John Durbin and Alderman Smith each 2 dozen; and Alderman Laroche, Alderman Abraham Elton, Isaac Baugh, Henry Bright, Daniel Harson, Charles Hotchkin, and M. Mease each 1 dozen. The chamberlain collected 138 more knives and forks from other persons. No less than 86 silver candlesticks figure in the list of borrowed plate, together with two punch bowls. Altogether the entertainment cost the Corporation upwards of £520.

The corporate accounts contain the following item, dated December 22nd, 1761:—" Paid for the ironwork in Gibleting Pat. Ward below Hungroad, Gloucestershire side, £10."

There was a further outlay of £12 19s. 6d. for the gibbet. Ward was executed for having murdered "the warner"—a man appointed to notify to Bristol merchants the arrival of their vessels in Kingroad—and the gibbeting of the body at the mouth of the Avon was intended to strike terror in lawless sailors.

The outbreak of war with Spain, in January, 1762, was followed in Bristol by the usual preparations for harrying the enemy's merchantmen by privateers. A number of ships were fitted out, but without any striking success. In the following March seven sailors belonging to one of those vessels—the King George, of 32 guns and 200 men—were tried in London, charged with mutiny and carrying off the ship. It appeared that a majority of the crew, having determined to undertake a piratical excursion, seized and imprisoned Captain Reed and the officers, and placed the sailing master in command of the privateer, with orders to navigate her eastwards. He brought her, however, to a European port, where 100 of the mutineers escaped. Four of the prisoners were convicted, and two of them were afterwards hanged.

The first recorded "lock-out" of workmen by employers took place in April, when the journeymen tailors demanded a reduction in the hours of labour—then 14 per day, less an hour for dinner. The masters refused to make any concession, and unanimously agreed to close their workshops until the men withdrew their request. A strike occurred at Bath at the same time, the men demanding that their daily labour should be "only from six in the morning till seven in the evening, which is usual throughout the kingdom." The issue is unknown.

Felix Farley's Journal of April 24th recorded the death, a week previously, of a wealthy pluralist, "the Rev. Mr. Thomas Taylor, minister or proprietor of Clifton," also rector of Congresbury, curate of Wick, and rector of St. Ewen's, Bristol. Consequent upon his demise, "the great and small tithes of the parish of Clifton, of the yearly value of £110," were offered for sale in October, 1763. They were again offered for sale by auction in April, 1778, when they were stated to produce £150 yearly, and were then or soon afterwards purchased by Mr. Samuel Worrall, whose descendants have reaped enormous profits from the investment.

The Council, at a meeting in May, gave orders for the demolition of Queen Street Gate, Castle precincts. Castle Street Gate was demolished in 1766. The two portals were erected at the close of the Commonwealth, when the locality was laid out for building sites.

Norborne Berkeley, Esq., of Stoke Park, Stapleton, having been appointed Lord Lieutenant of the city, the Council, in July, presented him with the freedom. Mr. Berkeley had shortly before rebuilt the ancient mansion of his family, to which his only sister, the wife of the fourth Duke of Beaufort, succeeded, the estate thus obtaining the vulgar name of "the Duchess's." Mr. Berkeley, who was stigmatised by Junius as one of the obsequious "King's friends," was gratified in 1764 by having the barony of Botetourt revived in his favour. In 1768 he was appointed Governor of Virginia, where he was so popular that the colonists, soon after his death, erected a statue to his memory at Richmond.

It has been already stated that the Act for rebuilding Bristol Bridge empowered the trustees to make improvements in its approaches, one of the most important of which was the throwing open of High Street by the removal of St. Nicholas's Gate. The work was beset with considerable difficulty, as the chancel of St. Nicholas's church, approached from the nave by about twenty steps, extended over the archway, and any interference with the crumbling old fabric threatened to bring the whole to the ground. The trustees long hesitated to take action; and the vestry was equally embarrassed as to the means they should take to supply the threatened loss of area in a church already too small. Early in 1762 the parochial authorities resolved to obtain estimates for building a new church in King Street, but this project was abandoned as too expensive. Negotiations were then opened with the Bridge trustees, and it was agreed in February that, in consideration of a grant of £1,400 and of certain small plots of ground, the vestry would remove the nave and chancel, including the gateway, and build a larger church on nearly the original site. A design, in what the architect (James Bridges) facetiously called the "gothic" style, was accepted in May; the last services in the old edifice took place on the 29th August, and in November certain contractors undertook to remove the gateway and church and rebuild the latter for the sum of £2,733. Saving a small part forming the eastern end, the ancient crypt was preserved intact. The work of demolition was forthwith commenced; but, although the removal of the Gate was a great public convenience, the date of its disappearance is not recorded. The vestry proposed to retain the ancient tower; but, as the wooden spire was decayed, a design was obtained for substituting a "cupola" similar to the All Saints' anomaly. When the spire was taken down, however, in 1763 (the leaden covering produced £245 17s.), the authorities learnt with dismay that the tower itself was ruinous, and they felt compelled to order its removal, and to accept a plan (by Thomas Patey) for a new one. In their tribulation to find funds for this and other charges the vestry hit upon a novel expedient. The only communication between Nicholas and Baldwin Streets was a dark and inconvenient flight of steps. The sub-structure of the spire offered space for another thoroughfare, and, an appeal having been made to the Corporation and the Society of Merchants, a grant of £210 was voted by the former and £105 by the latter towards making "an easy and convenient public passage under the new intended tower" from Nicholas Street to the Back. (Traces of this footway are still visible on the southern wall of the tower.) The deficit being still large, the vestry resolved to levy a yearly church-rate of 2s. in the pound on rack rentals; but the tax was stoutly resisted, the parishioners contending that the authorities should apply to the building fund the £1,241 received for church property on the old Bridge, or that the Bridge trustees should be compelled to pay the whole cost of the reconstruction. Secret negotiations followed between the vestry and the trustees, and the latter body, by what was subsequently denounced as a gross malfeasance, voted an additional sum of £1,000 towards the building fund. The vestry thereupon discarded the plan of a "cupola." An Act to legalise the trustees' grant and to empower the levying of church rates was successfully applied for in November, 1768. The statute stated that the church and tower, then completed, had cost £6,549 5s., and that the spire would entail a further outlay of £1,075. The capstone of the spire, 205 feet from the ground, was laid in December, 1769, by George Catcott, who was ridiculed by Chatterton for the eccentric freak. St. Nicholas's Conduit was removed by the Bridge trustees in 1762, and was rebuilt at their expense on the Back, the vestry requiring them also to construct two cisterns holding eighty tons of water.

Felix Farley's Journal of August 21st, 1762, announced that "several workmen are now employed in raising the walks in College Green, and in taking down the High Cross." No order for this demolition, subsequent to that of 1757, is to be found in the minutes of the dean and chapter; but it would appear that the Cathedral authorities were memorialised by several leading residents to remove the Cross, the chief grievance being that from its intersecting the walks it prevented parties of promenaders from walking abreast, and was often defiled by nuisances. (Mr. Richard Champion, the china-maker, is said, in a local work, to have been an earnest agitator for the removal, and to have raised a subscription for that purpose; but he was then a youth of 18 years, living in London.) The newspaper scribe added that the Cross, "when beautified," would be re-erected "in the middle of the grass plot near the Lower Green," near its former position; but if such a design was ever contemplated it was soon abandoned. The stonework and statues were deposited in the Cathedral, where they remained for two years. In the meantime the Rev. Cutts Barton became the head of the Cathedral, and that practical-minded worldling, dreading an appeal for the reconstruction of the Cross, which would have involved the chapter in some expense, resolved to get rid of the relics (of which he was not the owner) by presenting them to Mr. Henry Hoare, of Stourhead, a zealous collector of antiquities, who cordially accepted the gift. In October, 1764, the materials, excepting the much-worn lower columns, were despatched in six wagons to their final resting place in Wiltshire. Almost the only comment on this transaction published in the local press was the following epigram in *F. Farley's Journal* of October 28th:—

> Ye people of Bristol, deplore the sad loss
> Of the kings and the queens that once reigned in your Cross;
> Your great men's great wisdom you surely must pity,
> Who've banished what all men admired from the city.

By the death, on the 26th August, of the seventh Earl of Westmoreland, that title devolved upon Mr. Thomas Fane, long an eminent legal practitioner in Bristol, nephew and heir of John Scrope, M.P., and son-in-law of Alderman William Swymmer, a wealthy Bristolian. Mr. Fane, who lived many years in the Scrope mansion in Small Street, was appointed, through his uncle's influence, Customer of the port—a valuable sinecure—and was also steward of several royal manors, and clerk to the Merchants' Society. Having acquired a fortune, he retired from business about 1758, when his Bristol-born son and heir married a grand-daughter of the Duke of Ancaster, and he himself became M.P. for Lyme Regis. The statement in a local history that he was a low-class attorney, and succeeded to the earldom only through the rapid death of twelve intervening heirs, is a ridiculous fiction. After his death, in 1771, his widow returned to Bristol, and resided in her ancestral house on St. Augustine's Back until her demise in 1782.

A Government notification in the local newspapers of the 4th September, 1762, announced an acceleration of the mails between the southern counties and Bristol. In future the postboy was to leave Salisbury on Mondays at six o'clock in the morning, to arrive at Bath (a distance of about 39 miles) at 8 or 9 at night, and to leave Bath for Bristol at six next morning. On Wednesdays and Fridays the departure from Salisbury was in the evening, the journey occupying about nineteen hours. By this arrangement letters from Portsmouth were received two days earlier than before.

Owing to the increasing population of the out-parish of St. Philip's, a private cemetery, styled the Universal Burial Ground, was opened about this time. It is described as "behind Eugene Street, near the Poor House, without Lawford's Gate." The charge for an interment was 4s.

A local journal of the 30th October gave notice that an "Expert Tapster" was wanted for Newgate prison. "He will be under the protection of the Keeper from all harms and insults, and shall keep a genteel apartment free from disturbance. The Tap-house to be locked every night at half an hour after ten o'clock." The place was a profitable one, for prisoners and visitors were allowed to drink as much as they could pay for, and previous to the execution of an interesting criminal the gaol was crowded with bibulous sympathisers. In October, 1764, two felons under sentence of death had a quarrel whilst drinking in the "genteel apartment," when one of them drew the knife he was permitted to carry, and nearly killed his companion. Insolvent debtors mingled with criminals in this drinking den, and were physically and morally infected by them. Dr. Johnson, in a contemporary essay, computed that out of the 20,000 debtors in English prisons one-fourth perished yearly from the corruption of the air, want of exercise and food, the contagion of diseases, and the "severity of tyrants."

The civic arrangements for preserving order in the streets being inefficient, drunken quarrels were of everyday occurrence. On the 23rd October a desperate affray, arising out of a pothouse dispute, occurred near St. Nicholas's church between the butchers in the market and a number of Glamorganshire militiamen then quartered in the city. One butcher was mortally injured, and several on both sides were grievously wounded. No steps were taken for the punishment of the rioters, but on the 2nd November two of the militiamen, convicted of having taken money from French prisoners at Knowle to favour their escape, were drummed out of the regiment, "after receiving 1000 lashes each at three several times." About the same date, a correspondent of the *Bristol Journal* complained of the foulness of the public thoroughfares, which he declared to be a scandal to the city. "Your lanes and alleys," he said, "smell aloud," and filth lay in every direction.

In consequence of a fire which took place on the 16th November in a house on St. Philip's Plain, by which eight of the inmates lost their lives, attention was again called to the inadequate provisions existing for the prevention of such disasters. The Corporation took no action, and shortly afterwards, when a sugar-house was burnt to the ground, the only apparatus in working order was the engine of the Crown Fire Office, which is shown by a contemporary engraving to have contained about forty gallons of water, and to have been worked by two men.

The increased taxation rendered necessary by the Seven Years' War caused a notable rise in the price of beer. In November, 1762, the following advertisement appeared in the local press:—"The publicans of Bristol...greatly oppressed by the late Act of advancing 3s. per barrel, and now malt being at 4s. per bushel...ale cannot be afforded at 3d. per quart, and therefore give notice that from and after the 29th November, all ale will be sold at 4d. per quart." The announcement raised a storm of indignation, and three weeks later the trade notified that the price would be fixed at $3\frac{1}{2}d.$, "as in London, which we hope will be agreeable to the public." The retail charge for wine continued low. At the fashionable Ostrich inn, on Durdham Down, the price of half a pint of wine was sixpence in November, 1764.

The wrath of the Common Council was aroused in December by the discovery that several "foreigners" had opened places of business in the city. The town-clerk was ordered to prosecute the intruders, many of whom made their peace by purchasing the freedom. The persecution was renewed in 1765, when a draper was required to pay no less than fifty guineas. On his petition, however, a moiety of the fine was remitted. After this period the old detestation of intruders gradually died out. In a brief account of the city prefixed to "The New Bristol Directory for the year 1792," the compiler remarks:—"All kinds of persons are free to exercise their trades and callings here, without molestation from the Corporation."

The fee for "breaking the ground" for a funeral in the Cathedral was £10 for a grave in the choir, and £5 in the nave or cloisters, irrespective of heavy fees for the funeral service. The dean and chapter condemned these charges as "exorbitant" in December, 1762, and ordered them to be reduced to £5, £3, and £2 respectively. In 1776, however, the authorities again raised the fee to £10 for interment in the Cathedral, and in 1802 the charge was increased to £15, a grave in the chancel costing £5 extra.

The proclamation of peace with France and Spain was made on the 30th March, 1763, with the usual formalities. The peace, effected by the king's favourite, the Earl of Bute, was exceedingly unpopular, and although the Corporation ordered "a rundlet of wine to be let run at the several conduits of All Saints, St. Thomas, and the Key," for the gratification of the populace, enthusiasm was conspicuously absent. *F. Farley's Journal* indicated the prevalent feeling:—

> The Peace is good—who dare dispute the fact?
> See the first *fruits* thereof—the Cyder Act!

The Government had just kindled the wrath of the western counties by imposing an excise duty on the popular beverage of the district, and the hatred of the Scotch Minister was deep and widespread. In some neighbouring towns the peace proclamation was made amidst the funereal tolling of bells and the mocking salutes of "sowgelders' horns." Another Bristol poet may be quoted :—

> Our strong Beer is tax'd, and we're tax'd in our Lights,
> And more would they tax of our national Rights;
> But sooner than yield to a tax on our Fruit,
> The trees, though in blossom, shall fall to the root.
> May those who persist in enforcing the deed
> For evermore dwell on the north side the Tweed.

A week or two later there was a sale, on the Quay, of a quantity of Gloucestershire "S der," which, says the reporter, "sold for three-farthings a gallon ; so great is the aversion to the intended duty and the *agreeable* visits of the exciseman." The Thanksgiving Day to celebrate the Peace excited renewed manifestations of discontent. In spite of the corporate outlay for gunpowder, bonfires, and hogsheads of beer, the people stood sulkily aloof. In another western city, the church porches were decked with crape and apples; the mayor walked alone to the cathedral; while in the evening the mob, provided with a jack-boot, a punning symbol of the Scotch favourite's name and title, paraded an effigy wrapped in a plaid, which they hanged and burnt. When the Cider Act came into operation, in the autumn, a county meeting was held in Gloucestershire, at which it was declared that the tax had "spread a universal face of sorrow over the cider counties," while in the market towns apple boughs and empty barrels pranked with mourning were carried in procession, followed by "a number of poor objects with crape-covered apples in their bosoms." In the Forest of Dean an exciseman was seized by the colliers, who imprisoned him for more than a month in the workings of a mine. Two young Bristolians, engaged by the excise authorities to survey the orchards in this neighbourhood, relinquished their duties after one day's experience. They had been permitted to return home only after solemnly swearing that they would never adventure again on a similar errand. The tax was abolished in 1766.

An ancient chapel, dedicated to the Holy Spirit, but which in the reign of Elizabeth was converted into a grammar school, stood at this period in the cemetery of St. Mary Redcliff. Having become dilapidated, and being an obstruction to the south-western view of the church, it was taken down in March, 1763. No relic was preserved save the tombstone of a medieval chaplain, John Lavington, now in St. Mary's. The school was removed to the Lady Chapel in the church, where it remained for many years. The ancient Cross of Redcliff, standing in the churchyard, was demolished about the same time. The destructive mania provoked no comment. About the close of the year, however, *Felix Farley's Journal* stated that one of the churchwardens, styled "Joe" [Thomas], who had caused the removal of the Cross, had been carting away a quantity of earth from the churchyard to his brickfield, and was making bricks of the material. This story attracted attention, and "Joe" was the object of some violent attacks both in prose and verse. One satire (January, 1764), describing the apparition of Conscience to the culprit, was absurdly attributed by Mr. Tyson to Chatterton, then eleven years old, and complaisant editors have since inserted the verses in the poet's works. (The lines were doubtless written by the under-master of Colston's School, Thomas Phillips, a frequent contributor of rhymes to the *Bristol Journal*, who was eulogised by his friend and pupil, Chatterton, as one of the first of living poets.) A twelvemonth later the officers of the parish are recorded to have held their annual Easter feast in a "Banquetting Room lately erected at a very considerable expense," when the health of "Saint Joe, the founder of the edifice," was duly honoured.

The newspapers of the 9th April announced the starting of a "Flying Machine," which undertook the astounding feat of making the journey to London during the summer in "one day"—meaning twenty-four hours. The fare was 30s., or 3s. more than was charged by the two days' machine, which retained the favour of sober-minded travellers.

An advertisement in the local press of May shows that the White Hart inn, Lower Easton, "commonly called Barton Hundred," was a favourite haunt of Bristolians bent on a holiday. The landlady announced that she prepared an ordinary every Sunday at half-past one o'clock. For upper class visitors "Barbacues, Turtles, and dinners of all kinds" were "dressed in a genteel manner," while the best of tea and coffee were served in pleasant arbours in a spacious garden. Another advertisement shows that the large tennis-court attached to the inn was the scene of prize fights patronised by the upper classes. In July, 1763, "a public house known as Arno's Vale," another popular resort for the discussion of "politics and ale," according to one of Chatterton's poems, was advertised to be let. The derivation of the name is unknown. A publican named Arno occupied an inn in High Street in 1773. The Swan inn at Almondsbury was also much patronised by excursionists. The landlord, in May, 1773, announced that it had been greatly enlarged. There was an ordinary on Sundays; but turtles and dinners were dressed daily on the shortest notice, and a large bowling-green was open free every day except Friday.

One of the minor city gates, that of the Pithay, was ordered to be demolished in December, 1763.

The ducking stool for the punishment of scolds having gone out of fashion, a victim of female malice bethought herself about this time of another ancient piece of machinery —now equally obsolete—for castigating the evil-tongued. Eleanor Collins, a married woman, of St. Stephen's parish, commenced an action for slander in the Ecclesiastical Court of Bristol against a neighbour named Sarah Slack, wife of a butcher. The nature of the slander does not appear, but may be easily conjectured. After a solemn hearing before the chancellor of the diocese in the Consistory Court, a quaint old chamber adjoining the Cathedral, still to be seen, the defendant was convicted, and sentenced to undergo penance in her parish church. Mrs. Slack, however, was contumacious, and also refused to pay the prosecutrix's costs (£4 11s. 1d.). Having been vainly summoned three times to submit, she was solemnly excommunicated by the bishop. This also proving ineffectual, a writ *de excommunicato capiendo* was issued by the Crown, setting forth the defendant's enormities, and "forasmuch as the Royal power ought not to be wanting to the Holy Church in its complaint," the sheriffs were commanded "to attach the said Sarah by her body, according to the custom of England, until she shall have made satisfaction to the Holy Church." The writ came in due course into the hands of the under-sheriff, the afterwards famous Alderman Bengough, who, being a Unitarian, was so tickled by the duties it imposed upon him that he left a note of the case amongst his papers, now in the Jefferies Collection. Unfortunately he failed to record the issue. Ecclesiastical suits for slander were not uncommon down to the close of the Georgian era, but as reporters did not penetrate into the Consistory Court, the only record of its transactions exists in the books of the registrar, and in the loose papers remaining in the audience chamber. The slander was invariably a slur on the chastity of the complainant. In one case an offender, during a drinking bout at the Blackamoor's Head, Redland, styled a companion a "poor cuckold dog," whereupon a sharp attorney raised a suit on the part of the husband and his incriminated wife, and the culprit was mulcted in heavy costs. In another local case, that of a slanderous woman named Robinson, excommunicated in Bristol, the victim was by some legal trickery committed to Gloucester county gaol, and remained there three years and a half, only then obtaining her liberty on paying £11 12s. costs (Parl. Debates, xxi. 299). In 1808 one Mary Ann Dix, 18 years of age, of Redcliff parish, was cited to the Consistory Court for slandering an exciseman's wife, named Ruffy, who kept a house of ill-fame. In November, 1809, the defendant was adjudged guilty, and was enjoined in her absence to do penance and to pay the costs, £12 7s. 11d. Later on she was excommunicated during divine service in Redcliff church for not conforming to the sentence, although she was ignorant of its purport, while her father, who had a large family, was unable to pay the costs, now £30. She was attached under a writ *de excom. cap.*, and conveyed to Newgate, from which, in January, 1812, she petitioned the House of Commons, stating that she had been 26 months in prison, and would have starved but for the charity of the benevolent. The subject led to a lively debate, in the course of which it was stated that a man in the West of

England had been shortly before excommunicated and imprisoned for refusing to pay a church rate. A promise was made by the Government to deal with the Consistory Courts with a view to their reform, but nothing was effectually done until thirty years later. The fate of Mary Ann Dix is unknown.

The position of a common councillor named Joseph Love (sheriff, 1750) caused some embarrassment to his colleagues about this period. On the 24th March, 1764, the Chamber ordered that a present of 50 guineas be made to Mrs. Love, "towards her present subsistence." Mr. Love continued to attend the Council until March, 1765. A few months later his son petitioned for help to maintain himself at the University of Oxford, when a vote of 20 guineas was accorded; a similar grant was also passed in each of the three following years. At length, in July, 1769, "formal complaint" was made that Love had quitted England four years previously; and a summons was issued requiring him to attend to show cause why he should not be removed from office. As he naturally made no response, his deposition was ordered at the next sitting. Mr. Love was not the only member under a financial cloud. In June, 1764, Joseph Daltera (sheriff, 1761) sent in his resignation, and, "being reduced through a series of misfortunes to very low circumstances," the House granted him a life annuity of £40.

Felix Farley's Journal, of April 28th, 1764, records the death of "Dr. [George] Randolph, a physician of great eminence, well known... as the chief person who first brought the Bristol Hot Well into such public esteem by his judgment in directing the use of the waters, and his ingenious dissertation on the subject." (Dr. Randolph's "Enquiry into the medicinal virtues of Bristol Water" was published in 1745.) The spring continued in great repute. The author of "The Beauties of England," published in 1767, noted when in Bristol that the water was "not only drunk on the spot at the pump-room, but every morning cried in the streets, like milk."

The urgency of port improvement increased with the development of trade after the Seven Years' War. A mere extension of the quays, the stop-gap invented by the non-progressive party, ignored the difficulties and losses arising from the tidal phenomena of the Avon. Vessels lying in the harbour, being left aground for some hours twice a day, were liable to be severely strained, especially when laden, and the possibility of an outbreak of fire whilst the crowded shipping lay immovable was a constant danger. The commerce of the port was still much superior to that of any provincial rival, the net receipts of Customs in 1764 being £195,000, while those at Liverpool were only £70,000; but the rapid growth of the Lancashire town excited apprehension. After much private discussion, a numerously attended meeting of merchants was held in the Guildhall on the 25th July, 1764, when it was resolved that an efficient scheme for keeping vessels afloat would be highly beneficial, and that the sum of £30,000 should be raised by subscription, in £100 shares, for carrying out the design under the approval of the Corporation. Only one third of the proposed capital was, however, subscribed, and many wealthy men refused their co-operation. The promoters nevertheless applied to Smeaton, the celebrated engineer, to furnish a plan, which was produced in the following January. Mr. Smeaton proposed to convert the lower course of the Froom into a floating dock, to be connected with the Avon by a canal through Canons' Marsh. The cost of the works was estimated at £25,000, exclusive of compensation for the land required for the canal. Extraordinary as it now appears, the engineer's scheme took away the breath of the improvement party. Barrett, who was a witness of its effects, briefly notes in his history that the proposed outlay "was so great as to quash the enterprise." In January, 1767, Mr. William Champion proposed a still bolder plan, by which lock gates would have been thrown across the Avon opposite Red Clift House, and both rivers converted into a floating harbour, capable of containing a thousand ships, at an estimated cost of £30,000. The anti-improvement party thereupon employed an engineer named Mylne to write down the scheme, and as the critic positively asserted that £60,000 would scarcely suffice to carry out the design, capitalists held aloof, and the whole matter went to sleep again.

The absence of an organ in the Mayor's Chapel having been complained of, the Common Council, in June, 1764, purchased of Mr. Edmund Broderip, for 300 guineas, the organ then standing in the Assembly Room, Prince's Street, and appointed him organist, at a salary of £25 a year.

The city was horrified on the 27th September by the murder of Mrs. Frances Ruscombe, a lady living in College Green, and of her servant, Mary Sweet. The crime was brought to light by a female relative who had been invited to dinner, and who, on entering the house, found the body of the lady on the stairs, with the head mutilated, while that of the servant, with the head nearly cut off, was lying in the back parlour. The murders had been perpetrated only a short time, the bodies being still warm. The murderer, who had carried off a bag and purse containing about £90 in gold coin, was never detected, although Mr. Nugent, M.P., offered a reward of £500, supplemented by one of £100 by the Corporation, of 50 guineas by Mrs. Ruscombe's sisters, and of £10 more by her husband. Many persons were arrested, and amongst those vehemently suspected was the baker, Peaceable Robert Matthews (see p. 272); but no evidence could be discovered against any one. De Quincy, who learnt the details of the case during one of his visits to Bristol, refers to it in his well-known essay on " Murder as a Fine Art." The house in which the deed was committed was afterwards demolished and rebuilt by Sir Jarrit Smith.

Owing to the demand for lodgings at the Hot Well, the houses known as Dowry Parade were erected about this time. The " third house on the New Parade, newly built, and let at £80 a year," was advertised to be sold in September. "A Tour through Great Britain," issued in 1761, states that " there are magnificent lodgings in the beautiful village of Clifton, on the top of the hill, for such as have carriages, and whose lungs can bear a keener air"; but the road down to the well is described as "far from commodious." It was in fact a rocky precipice, afterwards converted into Granby Hill. The down, however, odoriferous and brilliant with " heath, eyebright, wild thyme, marjoram, maiden-hair, wild sage, geraniums, &c.," and pasturing " cows, horses, sheep and asses," afforded a delightful place of recreation.

When a well-connected clergyman thought himself unjustly treated if his friends did not provide him with at least two livings, pluralities became pardonable in the lower offices of the church. From a marriage notice in the Bristol papers of October 18th, 1764, it appears that one Mr. Ganthony, the father of the bride, was a lay-vicar of the Cathedral, parish clerk of St. Augustine's, and parish clerk of St. John's. The clerkship of St. Augustine's was very profitable, owing to the fees received from wealthy parishioners at marriages and burials. One of the contemporary lay-vicars improved his income by keeping a public-house; but the chapter was offended at the innovation, and the man was dismissed. Mr. Ganthony's lucrative arrangement passed unrebuked by a body of pluralists. Indeed in June,

1765, when a place of lay-vicar became vacant, the chapter presented it to the organist of the Cathedral.

St. Philip's Church underwent a partial reconstruction during the closing months of 1764. The ancient roof of the nave was preserved, but the arches supporting it were removed, and the number of piers diminished one half, thus increasing the accommodation at the sacrifice of architectural harmony. The walls were also rebuilt, and the old window tracery disappeared. The expense incurred amounted to about £1,600. Of this amount, £1,030 were raised by a church rate, to which the in-parish contributed £345, and the out-parish £685.

The laws prohibiting the entry into England of Irish food products were suspended in October, 1764, owing to domestic scarcity. They had, to that date, been rigorously executed, a quantity of Irish butter having been confiscated in 1763. The relaxation caused a sensible increase in the local trade with Ireland.

At a period when nearly all the wealthy families in the city inhabited Queen Square and the neighbourhood of St. James's Barton, the inconveniences attending a visit to the theatre at Jacob's Wells were naturally a subject of much complaint. Early in 1764 a movement was started for the erection of a theatre worthy of the city; and in a short time a body of proprietors was formed, consisting of 50 gentlemen, contributing £50 each. Amongst the promoters were Alexander Edgar, John Jones, John Vaughan, jun., Roger Watts (see p. 65), Michael Miller, Thomas Symons, John Cave, Jas. Laroche, jun., Henry Cruger, Wm. Sedgley, Henry Bright, Ezekiel Nash, George Weare, George Daubeny, John Lambert (Chatterton's master), Thomas Eagles, Jeremy Baker, Paul Farr, and Thomas Harris. Strangely enough, three prominent Quakers, Joseph Harford, and William and Richard Champion, figure in the list of shareholders. In addition to the share capital, the sum of £1,400 was subscribed by various admirers of the drama. Some old property in King Street, having gardens in the rear, together with a piece of ground belonging to the Coopers' Company, was purchased; a design by James Patey, a local architect, was adopted; and the foundation stone of the theatre was laid on the 30th November, 1764. (The houses in King Street were retained, the upper storeys being intended to serve as a dwelling for the manager.) The new place of amusement was finished in the spring of 1766, at a cost of about £5,000, when an unforeseen difficulty presented itself.

The members of the Society of Friends, strongly disapproving of the stage, availed themselves of an Act passed in 1737, by which any person acting in a dramatic piece, in an unlicensed theatre, was liable to be convicted as a rogue and vagabond; and it was intimated that the provisions of the statute would be rigorously enforced. Mr. Champion, the potter, was one of the most ardent of the Quaker opposition, his chief objection to a theatre being the facility for amusement which it offered to the working classes. Another of the dissidents—or perhaps Mr. Champion himself—produced a poem entitled "Bristol Theatre," printed by the Quakeress, Sarah Farley, in which it was affirmed that the stage tempted men to break all laws, human and divine, and that the results of establishing a theatre would be to entice Bristolians into the paths of misery and vice; truth, trade, and industry would decay together; honest men would turn highwaymen; and the gaol would need enlargement to accommodate the horde of criminals and debtors who would clamour for food at its portal! To avoid the penalties of the law, the manager resorted to a shift that had been invented by Foote in London; and the theatre was opened on the 30th May, 1766, with what was styled "A Concert of Musick and a Specimen of Rhetorick"—the concert being simply the ordinary performances of the orchestra, and the rhetoric (professedly offered "gratis"), the comedy of "The Conscious Lovers" and the farce of "The Miller of Mansfield." The net receipts (£63) were presented to the Infirmary. An opening address was written by Garrick, who declared the theatre to be, for its dimensions, the most complete in Europe. (Its semicircular auditorium was the first constructed in England.) The proprietors then took measures to obtain letters patent legalising the theatre, which the Crown was unable to grant without the consent of Parliament. Obstinate opposition was offered in the House of Commons to this and similar measures for other towns, and the necessary Act was not passed until 1778. Immediately afterwards the royal license was granted to George Daubeny, the nominee of the proprietors, who paid £275 for the letters patent. From its opening to the close of the century, the theatre was one of the most prosperous in the provinces. A Londoner, writing in 1792, remarked that "it was no uncommon thing to see 100 carriages at the doors" of the house. Every great actor of the time, Garrick excepted, appeared upon its boards; and some distinguished players were indebted to

it for their early training. The ordinary charges were :—
boxes, 3s. 6d.; pit, 2s.; gallery, 1s. 6d. The performances
commenced at half-past six; and in some of the early play
bills ladies and gentlemen were requested " to send their
servants at 5 o'clock to keep places." Although the house
was open only about three months during the summer, the
rent was £300 per annum. The original proprietors each
received a silver medal, entitling the holder and his assigns
to admission to the house in perpetuity. These tokens were
frequently sold, and in the prosperous days of the theatre
were worth £30 each. On one occasion a medal was disposed
of by raffle, but the lessee of the house, alleging that the
ticket was a counterfeit, refused the winner admission. The
latter—a High Street silk mercer named David—thereupon
applied for advice to Mr. Henry Davis, a sharp attorney
(brother to Mr. R. Hart Davis, afterwards M.P.). The lawyer
obtained the medal from his client, and three years later he
sent him in a bill of 15 guineas, for "many attendances at
the theatre to assert your right" (R. Smith's MSS.).

In the autobiography of Bishop Newton is an account of
an incident which must have occurred between September,
1764, when Henry Swymmer became mayor, and the fall of
the Grenville Ministry in July, 1765. The bishop being in
London, the mayor made a journey to town to complain to
him of the steps that were being taken "for opening a Mass
House at the Hot Wells under the protection of the Duke of
Norfolk." The alarmed bishop, with the approval of the
Primate, forthwith applied to Mr. Grenville, who promised
to prevent a violation of the law, but advised a previous
resort to persuasion. Bishop Newton accordingly convened
a meeting of civic officials at the mayor's house in Bristol,
at which the resident Romanist priest (Father Scudamore)
and the proprietor of the house intended for a chapel were
also present. The two latter were admonished that their
action was illegal, that their conduct was the more pro-
voking inasmuch as their building stood upon Church land,
being leased under the dean and chapter, and that they
already had been allowed "a private Mass House in Bristol,
where this same priest had officiated many years." The
opening of a public chapel in so frequented a place was
declared to be too contemptuous a defiance of the law to
be permitted by the Government, who, if they persisted,
would prosecute them with the utmost rigour. The ad-
monition had the desired effect, the culprits begging the
bishop's pardon, and promising that their design should be

for ever abandoned. Dr. Newton concludes by observing that they were as good as their word. "Only a bastard kind of popery, Methodism, has troubled Bristol since that time."

Unusual enterprise is visible at this period in the local coaching trade. In the summer of 1764 a coach to Exeter was started, which, setting out early in the morning from the George inn at Temple Gate, succeeded in accomplishing a journey of under 77 miles in the afternoon of the following day. The fare was a guinea. On the 30th March, 1765, it was announced that another public vehicle would reach Exeter "in one day," starting at 4 a.m., "the first attempt of the kind ever set on foot in this city." The adventure was unprofitable, for the two-days coach alone held the road in subsequent years. In April, 1765, a summer coach to Birmingham made its first appearance. It set off from the Lamb inn, Broadmead, twice a week, at 4 in the morning, and reached its destination at noon on the following day. This enterprise stirred up the owners of the old Gloucester coach, who gave notice that its "flying" journeys over 34 miles of road would be performed in the surprisingly short period of ten hours!

Although a stately house had been built for the reception of the City Library, the old theological works given by Archbishop Mathew offered no attraction to the inhabitants, and successive librarians turned the building to their own advantage. By some the house was let to private persons. Mr. Benjamin Donn, the librarian in 1765, resolved to establish a mathematical school in the premises (*Bristol Journal*, April 20th). In the following year the library was increased by a bequest of several hundred volumes by Mr. John Heylyn, of College Green, a collateral descendant of Dr. Peter Heylyn; but the books remained unpacked for some years, and Mr. Donn's office continued a sinecure. A contemporary note states that not more than two or three persons visited the library in a twelvemonth, and these were generally strangers. In 1769 Mr. Donn published a beautifully-executed map of the environs of the city, for which the Council complimented him with a gift of 20 guineas.

During a visit to Bath, in October, 1765, the Dukes of York and Gloucester, brothers of George III., honoured Lord Botetourt by spending a few days at Stoke House, Stapleton. On the 14th they attended a civic ball at the Assembly Room, Prince's Street, which was opened by the Duke of York and Miss Baugh, daughter of the mayor. In the following year the Duke of York resided some time at Clifton for the purpose of drinking the Hot Well water. The prince died in 1767.

During the year 1765, Mr. William Champion, whose scheme for a floating harbour has been recorded, constructed a large dock for repairing ships on the bank of the Avon, near Rownham. The adventure proved unfortunate, and the place, commonly known as the Great Dock, was purchased by the Merchants' Society in 1770 for £1,420. The premises, with "the little dock" adjoining, were advertised to be let in May, 1772. Subsequently, a plan for deepening the large dock, to enable it to accommodate large vessels, was approved and carried out by the Society, and Parliamentary powers were obtained in 1776 to enlarge the dock and erect warehouses. The additional outlay is stated in the Bush MSS. to have been £1,500. A local pamphlet published in 1790 stated that "the dock......is capable of containing 36 of the largest ships belonging to the port......and it has never yet been completely filled."

The progress of the new Bristol Bridge forced the Corporation to consider the crying necessity of further improvements for facilitating traffic in the narrow and crowded thoroughfares of the city. At a meeting of the Council in December a committee was appointed to prepare a scheme to be laid before Parliament, and its recommendations were adopted at another meeting in February, 1766. The suggestions, the comprehensiveness of which astounded conservative-minded citizens, included the removal of Lawford's Gate, the demolition of ten adjoining houses in order to widen the road; the widening of the narrow lanes connecting Christmas Street with Broadmead; the destruction of ten dwellings so as to broaden Blind Steps, between Nicholas and Baldwin Streets; the removal of Small Street Gate and adjoining buildings; the taking down of St. Leonard's Church and vicarage, which blocked the western end of Corn Street; and the clearing away of a number of hovels around Newgate gaol, which, owing to the increased number of prisoners and the want of ventilation, was stated to be frequently scourged by disease. Minor improvements were also proposed in other thoroughfares, and the widening of the road to the Hot Well formed another detail of the plan. But its crowning feature remains to be mentioned. In order to open a commodious approach to the Bridge from the eastern and northern parts of the city, the committee recommended the destruction of the whole of the Shambles and Bull Lane, and the erection on their site (under the direction of the Bridge trustees) of a handsome street (Bridge Street), the formation of another street (Dolphin Street) from the east end of the new thoroughfare to Wine Street, involving the removal of St. Peter's Cross and Pump, and of a quantity of old property in Dolphin Lane and Peter Street; and finally the making (by the Corporation) of a new street, 40 feet wide (Union Street), from Wine Street to Broadmead, which would necessitate the sweeping away of numerous buildings standing on the proposed roadway. The committee added that another great improvement had been brought before them—a new street from Corn Street to the Drawbridge—which they admitted would be " very ornamental and of great utility "; but 54 houses and cellars then stood on the ground, and owing to the great outlay involved, they advised the Chamber to decline this responsibility. To encourage private persons to undertake the work, however, powers for its execution were included in the Bill. A scheme for a new street from Stoke's Croft to an intended square (Cumberland Street and Brunswick Square) was dealt with in a similar manner. It was further determined to insert clauses in the Bill to remedy defects in previous Acts; to require the streets to be lighted throughout the year; to remove projecting signs; to compel the erection of water-spouts; to improve the system of scavenging, paving, etc. The Bill embodied all the above suggestions, with the exception of that authorising the removal of St. Leonard's Church, some hitch having occurred with the ecclesiastical authorities. A few weeks later (when the difficulty was overcome by the incumbent being promised the incumbency of St. John's), the Corporation prayed for the insertion of the omitted item, stating that the bishop had sanctioned the union of the parish with that of St. Nicholas. The request was acceded to, and the Bill received the Royal Assent in May.

Considering the responsibilities thus assumed, one might suppose that the Council would have had neither leisure nor relish for additional obligations. Nevertheless, having received a memorial from certain clothiers and traders of Wiltshire, praying that it would undertake to extend the inland navigation of the port of Bristol, the Chamber bravely resolved to apply to .Parliament for powers to make the Avon navigable to Chippenham, under the direction of the mayor and aldermen. The scheme, however, came to a speedy end. The Council minutes of February 5th, 1766, contain the following entry: "It appearing to the House that several indecent and ungenteel resolutions have been lately agreed upon at a meeting held at Melksham, highly reflecting on the undertaking...it is resolvèd that the [previous] order be discharged."

The Hon. Daines Barrington having resigned the recordership, the office was conferred, in February, 1766, upon John Dunning, who had just gained lasting fame for his arguments against the legality of general warrants in the case of John Wilkes. Dunning would have attained the office of Lord Chancellor in 1782, but for the obstinate resistance of George III. As a consolation, he was created a peer under the title of Baron Ashburton, whereupon the Common Council requested him to sit for his picture, "to be placed in the Council Chamber, as a testimony of the very great respect which this Corporation bears to his lordship." The picture, one of the treasures of the Council House, was painted by Sir Joshua Reynolds, who received 100 guineas for it. The portrait is a triumph of art, for the great lawyer was remarkably ugly. Lord Thurlow once stated that his countenance closely resembled the knave of spades.

As has been already recorded, the mayors of Bristol, by ancient custom, were severally entitled to nominate one person to the freedom of the city without payment of a fine. The privilege for some reason became unpopular, and the Chamber abolished it in February, 1766, but ordered that the sum of 40 guineas should be paid to each future mayor, and to each past mayor who had failed to nominate, in compensation for the abrogated right. Several ex-mayors claimed the prescribed equivalent.

The policy of the Government in 1765 in imposing taxation on the American colonists, and the menacing protests offered by the latter against this stretch of power, excited great anxiety in the local mercantile community. The Society of Merchants and many shipowners and commercial firms petitioned the House of Commons in 1766, urging the great benefit derived from the trade with the colonies, and the serious consequences likely to flow from the discontent of the settlements. The Corporation did not co-operate in this movement. It may have been embarrassed by the compliment it had paid to the Premier, Mr. Grenville, shortly before the production of his Stamp scheme, in presenting him with the freedom of the city for what was termed his "steady attention to the promotion and security of commerce." This step was doubtless taken at the instance of Mr. Nugent, M.P., who had remained in office on the fall of the Newcastle Ministry, and so strongly supported Grenville in his American policy that he would have been burnt in effigy at Richmond, Virginia, in July, 1765, if the authorities had not interfered. Nugent was dismissed from his place when Lord Rockingham became Premier. The repeal of the Stamp Act, which followed, gratified the mercantile interest, and the Corporation ordered the bells to be rung when the change of policy was accomplished. At a meeting of the Society of Merchants in September, a letter was ordered to be sent by the master (William Reeve) to Lord Rockingham, expressing the company's grateful and unanimous sense of his lordship's eminent services, especially in securing the abrogation of an Act "injudicious and detrimental to the colonies as well as to the trade and manufactures of the mother country." The letter is said to have been drafted by Richard Champion, the china maker, though he did not become a member of the company until 1767, when he paid a fine for admission of £150.

Evidence as to the character of the vessels in which the West Indian trade was carried on is furnished by petitions presented to Parliament in 1766 by the merchants of Bristol and Liverpool. These documents expressed apprehension that the commerce with the islands would be "much injured, if not entirely ruined," by an Act of the previous year, prohibiting the import and export of rum in vessels of less than 100 tons burden, and praying that the restriction should be applied only to ships of under 70 tons. No action followed, and the transatlantic voyages of many Lilliputian barques came to an end.

The increasing demand for dwelling houses within the city led to the offer for sale, in March, 1766, of the Bowling Green House in St. James's Barton, and the billiard room and bowling green attached to it. The green, a popular place of recreation, had a frontage of 184 feet in Montagu Street. A few weeks later John Berkeley, "of the Coffee Pot in St. James's Barton," announced that he had put the bowling green in excellent order. This is the latest mention of the green, which fell soon afterwards into the hands of some speculative builder, who erected the sordid dwellings now covering the site.

Disputes in reference to wages were never recorded by the timid newsmongers of the time, but occasional information is obtained from advertisements. Thus, in the *Bristol Journal* of the 29th March, we read:—"The master of the Company of Carpenters having received a paper signed by a number of journeymen, desiring their wages to be advanced to 12s. a week...the said Company has resolved that every master should pay them according to what they earned or deserved, and no more." (The orders of the county magistrates, applying to Clifton and other suburbs, and fixing carpenters' wages at 1s. 2d. per day, were still in force.)

One of the schemes embraced in the great city improvement Act of 1766 was started before that measure became law. *Felix Farley's Journal* of April 19th stated that " the plan for building a handsome street from just below the Full Moon was put in execution Wednesday last by beginning the first house. The street is to run back through the gardens, and at the further end of it will be built a most elegant square." The street received the name of Cumberland in honour of one of the king's brothers, and the thoroughfare connecting it with Milk Street was for a similar reason dignified with the name of York. The first house in Brunswick Square, another loyal appellation, was begun in 1769, but the supply of new dwellings in the district already exceeded the demand. The eastern row of the square was deferred for nearly twenty years, while half the western and the whole of the northern rows were never built at all. At an early date, indeed, the promoters demised a large plot of land to a body of trustees acting for the congregation of Lewin's Mead Chapel, who converted it into a cemetery. The first interment there took place in October, 1768. The rural character of the locality may be imagined from the terms of an advertisement in the *Bristol Journal* of February 15th, 1772. A house, " adjoining Brunswick Square," was offered to be let, " with a prospect of two miles from the ground floor."

A silk manufactory existed in Bristol at this time. *Felix Farley's Journal* of the 24th May, 1766, records that, a few days before, " the workmen employed in the silk manufactory in this city and its environs assembled at the Bull tavern in High Street, where they illuminated the windows and gave other public testimonies of joy for the stop put to the importation of foreign silk." Another extinct industry is incidentally mentioned by the *Journal* in reporting the death, through drowning, of a man near Temple Backs, whilst placing his " fishing pots " in the Avon. Before the construction of the floating harbour immense quantities of young eels, called elvers, were yearly caught in the river.

About this period, Miss Hannah More, when in her twenty-third year, received an offer of marriage from Mr. William Turner, of Belmont, near Wraxall, a gentleman of large fortune, but nearly twenty years her senior. Having accepted the proposal, Miss More renounced her share in the Park Street school, and made preparations to take her expected position in fashionable society. Mr. Turner, however, was a man of peculiar disposition, and although he twice or thrice fixed a day for the marriage, he on each occasion postponed the event in a manner tending to cast ridicule upon the young lady. After the curious courtship had extended over six years, Miss More's sisters refused to allow her to be further trifled with, and the engagement was broken off, to the regret of the vacillating lover, who proposed to redeem his conduct by settling a large annuity on his lost bride to enable her to live in independence. Miss More was at length induced to accept a settlement of £200 a year for life, and turned her attention to literature. Her first work, "The Search after Happiness: a pastoral drama," published in 1773, achieved a great success, and she was speedily admitted into the first literary society of the day, having the good fortune to be admired and flattered by its autocrat, Dr. Johnson. Miss More's friendship with Mrs. Garrick, with whom she spent several months yearly, led to the production of her tragedy of "Percy," in 1778, for which Garrick wrote the prologue and epilogue, and which had a long and prosperous "run." After writing another tragedy, she ceased to consider the stage as "becoming the countenance of a Christian," and her numerous subsequent works were of a religious character. Of one of them, "The Shepherd of Salisbury Plain," upwards of a million copies are said to have been printed, and by her entire writings Miss More was estimated to have realised over £30,000. When at the height of her reputation, she had a second amatory flirtation with the Rev. Dr. Langhorne, rector of Blagdon, then a poet of some repute, but whose intemperate habits soon ended the affair. Her old lover, who remained her admirer through life, eventually bequeathed her a legacy of £1,000.

Although the improvement Act of this year marked a growing appreciation of the needs of the city, the civic authorities had occasional relapses into superannuated ideas. Bridewell Bridge, a wooden structure connecting St. James's parish with the quays, having been reported ruinous, it was resolved in May to replace it by "a substantial stone bridge," the width of which was fixed at 8 feet 6 inches! The edifice cost £55.

At a meeting of the Council on the 7th June, Sir William Draper, K.B., who, amongst other distinguished services, had commanded the English forces at the capture of Manilla in 1763, was presented with the freedom of the city. Sir William, whose father had been an officer in the Bristol Custom-house, occupied a large mansion at Clifton, and decorated the ground in front of it with a cenotaph to the memory of his companions in arms of the 79th regiment, and with a pyramidical column in honour of Lord Chatham, of whom he was a devoted admirer. The latter work was to have borne a pompous adulatory inscription, which at Chatham's entreaties was omitted. (It was however engraved on the monument after its recent removal to Clifton Down.) Another of Draper's idols was the Duke of Grafton, whom he was venturesome enough to defend against the attacks of "Junius." The results were disastrous, Draper being so trampled in literary mud and held up to public ridicule that he fled to America to conceal his mortification. Sir William eventually died at Bath on the 8th January, 1787.

The meeting of the civic body on June 7th initiated a remarkable, not to say scandalous, transaction in reference to two of the endowed schools entrusted to the Corporation by philanthropic founders. The Grammar School was then settled in the old buildings of St. Bartholomew's Hospital, near the bottom of Christmas Steps, expressly purchased for that purpose by the executors of Robert Thorne. A good playground was attached to the premises, on which several hundred pounds had been laid out in improvements in 1759-60, when the place, according to the ideas of the age, was deemed in every way suitable for the purposes of a dayschool. In 1764, however, on the preferment of the Rev. Samuel Seyer to the rectory of St. Michael, the headmastership was conferred on the Rev. Charles Lee, who soon afterwards won the affections of the only daughter of Alderman Dampier, one of the leaders of the Council; and this apparently insignificant event was destined to have unforeseen results. The original parent of the design about to be described cannot now be identified. Mr. Lee may have pined for a more imposing abode, with more agreeable surroundings. Miss Dampier or her worshipful parent may have thought dingy premises in a vulgar street an unsuitable residence for a young lady brought up in the aristocratic air of College Green. In any case, Alderman Dampier became the prime mover in a scheme designed for the benefit of his future son in law. The affair was put in motion with great astuteness. At the meeting already referred to, some one proposed the appointment of a committee to consider what additions should be made to the Grammar School "for the better accommodation," not of the master, but "of the scholars." The motion was adopted, and Mr. Dampier and a few other gentlemen were nominated to make the inquiry. A month later the committee reported, as the result of their deliberations, that "it would be a great public benefit if the masters and scholars belonging to the Grammar School were removed to the building called Queen Elizabeth's Hospital, and the master and boys belonging to that hospital removed to the Grammar School." It is scarcely possible that disinterested members of the Chamber can have really approved of this proposal. The Corporation, in the sixteenth century, had given the buildings of St. Mark's Hospital to be "for ever" used by the boys of Queen Elizabeth's Hospital. The stately premises near College Green had been erected by subscription in 1703, on the suggestion of Colston, who had given £500 for the purpose, expressly for the accommodation of the boys of the hospital; and the removal of the boarding-school to a less healthy locality in order to convert its property into a day-school for boys of a wealthier class was an obvious and flagrant breach of trust. It was nevertheless resolved "that the committee be empowered to do therein as they shall think proper." On the 6th September they accordingly presented another report. The Grammar School premises, they alleged, were not spacious enough to accommodate all the day scholars whose parents were desirous of a home education for their boys, while they were "fit for all the purposes" of the boarding-school. The College Green buildings, on the other hand, would "accommodate more than twice the number of young gentlemen" then in the Grammar School. Unfortunately an Act of Parliament, passed in the reign of Elizabeth, had confirmed the Corporation's donation of St. Mark's to Carr's school "for ever," and various subsequent bequests had been specifically made to the hospital near College Green. But the committee thought it was indifferent in what part of the town the charitable purposes of the school were "effectuated" providing the endowments were properly applied, and they therefore recommended that the sanction of Parliament should be obtained for carrying out the proposed exchange. The Chamber not only confirmed this report, but coolly ordered " that the said exchange do take place immediately." On the 3rd November it was resolved that alterations should be made "in the building lately called Queen Elizabeth's Hospital" to fit it for the master and boys of the Grammar School, Messrs. Dampier and Laroche being charged with the direction of the work. In May, 1767, the chamberlain's accounts contain this item: "Paid for bricks used at the late hospital called Queen Elizabeth's, now the Grammar School, £28 14s." A few weeks later there is a charge of £51 6s. 6d. for "altering the late Grammar School for the reception of the city blue boys, removed there." Other similar disbursements occurred about the same time, the aggregate outlay exceeding £725. The respective schools having exchanged places in the sp n of 1767, and the mansion in St. Mark's having been duly swept and garnished, on the 7th January, 1768, the head-master's happiness was crowned by his marriage with Miss Dampier. About a twelvemonth later, the Council resolved to apply to Parliament for power to alter the times of holding the great fairs, and the opportunity was seized to carry out the suggestion of the schools' committee. The framers of the Bill had the effrontery to make it allege that an exchange of schools would be of reciprocal advantage to the two institutions, but that this could not be done without the authority of Parliament; and the measure went on to enact that the Corporation, " from and after" the passing of the Act, should be empowered to remove the respective schools, and to vest the building at St. Bartholomew's in the governors of Queen Elizabeth's Hospital, and that at St. Mark's in the governors of the Grammar School. The Act having passed, the Council played the final scene of a solemn farce on the 6th May, 1769—two years after the revolution had taken place—by ordering that the master and scholars of the Grammar School "do immediately remove" to College Green, and that the master and scholars of Queen Elizabeth's Hospital "do immediately" betake themselves to Christmas Street! A few words will suffice to prove the falseness of the assertion that the exchange of schools would prove beneficial to the citizens. Lee held his office for forty-seven years. Being permitted to take boarders, who paid him well, he discouraged the attendance of Bristol boys, whose fees were low, and he eventually succeeded in getting rid of them altogether. The average number of city pupils under former masters was about a hundred.

For some years before his death, Lee had only one Bristol boy under his tuition—accepted, it was supposed, to guard against legal action as to the shameful misappropriation of Thorne's endowment.

At a meeting of the Bristol Bridge trustees, on the 7th July, 1766, it was resolved that St. Peter's Cross and Pump should be removed "with all expedition," and that a new pump should be erected in Peter Street, having "a feather from the present well." The intended removal of the Cross, which had been renovated in the reign of Charles I., came to the ears of Mr. Henry Hoare, who, thinking it a fitting companion for its old neighbour, the High Cross, already in his park at Stourhead, proffered to take it down provided the trustees would make him a present of the stones. The trustees accepted this proposal with alacrity, giving Mr. Hoare permission to at once remove the structure. A pump was subsequently placed in the ground floor of a house at the corner of Peter and Dolphin Streets. The gateway at Newgate was partially demolished about the same time, the gate itself, as well as two interesting medieval statues on each side of it, being removed. The figures were secured by Mr. Reeve, who placed them on the inner side of the entrance to "Black Castle."

The literary and archæological fribble, Horace Walpole, condescended to cast a glance upon Bristol in October, 1766, during a sojourn at Bath. In a letter to a friend, shortly after leaving the latter town, he wrote: "My excursions were very few...the city is so guarded with mountains. I did go to Bristol, the dirtiest great shop I ever saw, with so foul a river that, had I seen the least appearance of cleanliness, I should have concluded they washed all their linen in it, as they do at Paris. Going into the town, I was struck with a large Gothic building, coal black, and striped with white [Black Castle]. I took it for the devil's cathedral...I found it was an uniform castle, lately built, and serving for stables and offices to a smart false Gothic house on the other side of the road. The real cathedral is very neat...There is a new church besides, of St. Nicholas, neat and truly Gothic." (!)

The poor were suffering under almost unprecedented distress at this period, owing to the dearness of bread, caused by a bad harvest. In ordinary years England produced more corn than could be consumed at home, but an embargo was now placed on exportations. Vigorous steps were taken by the Council for the relief of poor Bristolians.

Bounties were not only offered on imported cargoes of corn, but all the bakers of the city and suburbs were subsidised. The chamberlain records:—" Paid sundry bakers in and about the city 2s. per sack on 2358 sacks of flour baked from the 20th October to the 8th November, in consideration of their making the bread larger the the (sic) price of corn would admit of at that time, £235 16s." This allowance being deemed insufficient, it was raised to 5s. per sack, and £408 10s. were disbursed during the following fortnight. As the money had to be borrowed, the Corporation abandoned a system which would have rapidly exhausted its resources; but bounties on imports continued to be paid. The country labourers attempted to prevent the removal of corn, and violent rioting occurred in Gloucestershire and Wilts, for which seven men were executed. The Chamber had to provide "for 22 pensioners going to newnam [Newnham] to protect the corn and flour destined for Bristol." Altogether the Council expended over £800 on account of the dearth. Owing to the lack of grist mills, the Corporation proposed to build two or three wind-mills, and Brandon Hill, where it had been contemplated to erect an astronomical observatory, was selected for their site; but the design was soon after abandoned.

The Chamber, moreover, had sympathy to spare for a distant island, though it may be suspected that in this case the West India interest benevolently drew out of the civic pocket what should have come out of its own. It was resolved in October that 100 guineas be contributed "towards relieving the unhappy sufferers by a dreadful fire which lately happened at Bridgetown, Barbadoes."

On the fall of the Rockingham Ministry, Mr. Nugent (who had married the Dowager Countess of Berkeley, and joined the ranks of the "King's friends") was appointed First Lord of Trade, and created an Irish peer under the title of Viscount Clare. His seat was vacated by his acceptance of office, but he was re-elected in December, without opposition. The usual copious feasting followed. *Felix Farley's Journal* of December 20th grumbles:—" We are credibly informed that in Trinity Ward, out of the four houses opened for general entertainment, three of them were kept by people not free of this city, notwithstanding there were so many burgesses who ought to have had the preference." Assuming that the other wards were treated with similar liberality, there must have been forty-eight inns opened "for general entertainment." Lord Clare gained much applause in courtly circles soon after this date by some verses he addressed to the Queen, accompanied by a present of Irish poplin.

On the 28th January, 1767, a man calling himself Hickson, and living at Frenchay in the style of a country gentleman, was arrested near Lawford's Gate, on suspicion of having committed several capital offences. The man's story, both before and after his apprehension, would have served the author of "Jack Sheppard" for the foundation of a romance. He was the son of a Worcestershire farmer named Higgins, and had led, with his brothers, a vicious life from boyhood. In 1754 he was convicted of a robbery at Worcester, and, being sentenced to transportation, was shipped at Bristol for America. Within a month of his being sold there into temporary slavery, he broke into a merchant's office at Boston, and stole sufficient money to enable him to secure a berth in a ship bound for England, which he reached within three months of his departure. He then resumed his former career of crime in Worcestershire; but after one of his brothers had been hanged there in 1763, for returning from transportation, he removed into Gloucestershire, and finally took a mansion at Frenchay, set up a pack of dogs and a stable of remarkably fine hunting horses, and lived in what the *Bristol Journal* termed "a splendid manner." Suspicions having arisen that his hunters were really kept for the perpetration of highway robberies, he was carried before Sir Abraham Elton, committed for trial, and removed to Gloucester. But at the April assizes no evidence as to robberies could be obtained against him, and as the charge of returning from transportation could be tried only at Worcester, the judge liberated him upon two sureties of £50 each. Higgins then retired to Carmarthenshire, where he committed two daring burglaries before again falling into the hands of justice. In July he was conveyed in irons to Worcester, where his previous conviction was made clear; but the Crown neglected to prove his shipment at Bristol, and the judge ordered his acquittal. However, at the following assizes at Carmarthen he was sentenced to death for his latest crimes. Executions generally took place about a week after conviction; but powerful influences were exercised to rescue the "gentleman" rogue, an "Earl of ——" being referred to in the newspapers as especially active in his behalf. The execution, repeatedly postponed, took place in November—a respite received a few days before having turned out to be a forgery. Higgins's exploits, as magnified by tradition, are recorded in Mr. Leech's "Brief Romances from Bristol History;" but the cleverly-told story of the highwayman's presence at a Hot Well ball, and of his subsequent robbery of a Bristol banker on the road to London, is the product of a lively imagination.

The prosperity of the slave trade, the ferocity of the men engaged in it, and the loss of life it entailed are graphically indicated in the following extracts from a letter from Old Calabar, dated August 12th, 1767, addressed by a ship captain to his employers at Liverpool:—" There are now seven vessels in the river, each of which expects to purchase 500 slaves, and I imagine there was seldom ever known a greater scarcity of slaves than at present. The natives are at variance with each other, and in my opinion it will never be ended before the destruction of all the people at Old Town, who have taken the lives of many a fine fellow. [It will be seen hereafter that an iniquitous bombardment of the town actually took place.] The river of late has been very fatal. There have been three captains belonging to Bristol died within these few months, besides a number of officers and sailors." The ships lay an enormous time on the pestiferous coast, for the writer adds:—"I do not expect that our stay here will exceed eight months." In a subsequent report of a committee of the House of Commons it is incidentally asserted that about 1766-7 a Bristol slaving ship was two years upon her voyage to the West Indies, having had to lie off the African coast until slaves were brought down from the interior.

The harvest of 1767 was again deficient, and the Corporation renewed its efforts to mitigate the sufferings of the poor. In September £269 were paid to Messrs. Lloyd, Elton, and Co, bankers, "the balance of an account for wheat and flower," sold to the bakers below prime cost. In November, at the instance of Lord Clare, who made a handsome donation, a cargo of 6,000 bushels of wheat was purchased and dealt with in the same manner, the Corporation contributing £140. The distress continuing, the Council, in July, 1768, adopted another policy, advancing £1,000, free of interest, to the board of guardians. The money, which had to be borrowed, was not repaid by the guardians until 1779.

The increase of pauperism caused by the dearth induced the poor law authorities to revive the odious law requiring persons receiving relief to wear a badge of their misfortune.

An order of the guardians, dated September 7th, required every pauper to "wear on the right shoulder, in an open and visible manner, on the uppermost garment, a Badge, with the initial letters of the name "of their parish. The churchwardens were liable to a penalty if they gave relief to unbadged persons. The unpopular order was rescinded in November, 1773.

Clifton Church being no longer capable of accommodating the residents and visitors, the erection of a south aisle was begun in the autumn of 1767. Although the addition cost only £419, the church was not reopened until October, 1768. Fifteen persons, having subscribed 25 guineas each, were severally allotted pews in perpetuity in the new aisle. Sir William Draper and members of the Goldney, Elton, and Hobhouse families were amongst those contributors.

In consequence of frequent prosecutions of barbers for shaving on Sundays, "the master and company of barbers and peruke makers" gave notice in 1767 that they would close their shops on that day, and warned recalcitrant journeymen that the parish constables would take note if they failed to attend divine service.

At a meeting of the Council in December, 1767, John Berrow, sheriff in 1758, and son of a mayor of the same name, resigned his seat in the Chamber. "Being reduced to very low circumstances by a series of misfortunes," he was granted a pension of £40 per annum.

The existence of a hitherto unknown china manufactory in Bristol in 1750 has been recorded under that year. Nothing is known of the history of the place after 1751, and no specimens of its productions are known to exist. But a porcelain bowl, dated January 9th, 1762, was discovered by Mr. Owen, F.S.A., at Devizes, the owner of which stated that it was sent to one of his ancestors by a relative connected with a Bristol pottery; from which it may be inferred that a factory was in operation at that date. In February, 1766, Richard Champion, writing to the Earl of Hyndford, a connection by marriage, who had sent him some porcelain clay from Carolina, stated that he had "had it tried at a manufactory set up here some time ago on the principle of the Chinese porcelain, but not being successful is given up." The works appear to have been in Castle Green, and as Champion, soon after he commenced china-making, removed his factory to that place, he may have availed himself of the abandoned plant. Champion, who was then a merchant engaged in the American trade, started the new enterprise in or about February, 1768. His capital being chiefly engaged in commerce, he was joined by Mr. Edward Brice, a sugar refiner, who advanced £1,000; by Mr. Joseph Harford, iron merchant, who ventured £3,000; and by Mr. Thomas Winwood, fruit merchant, whose subscription is unknown. Soon after, Mr. Joseph Fry, chocolate maker, contributed £1,500, Mr. Mark Harford, £1,500, and Mr. Thomas Frank, grocer, a member of a family of Bristol potters already mentioned, £1,000. Champion was from the outset closely connected with William Cookworthy, who had been experimenting at his porcelain factory at Plymouth on Cornish clay, and who was not improbably concerned in the previous enterprise in Castle Green, where the same clay was also used (see p. 286). He was at all events designated by Sarah Champion " the first inventor of the Bristol China Works," and Champion's productions were made, under license, from the Cornish materials of which Cookworthy had obtained a monopoly by letters patent. In 1770 Cookworthy entered into negotiations with his licensee, which resulted in the Plymouth works being abandoned, their proprietor removing his plant to Bristol and joining Champion, and the firm, from 1771 to 1773, was styled William Cookworthy & Co. An advertisement in the *Bristol Journal* of June 10th, 1773, shows the character of the porcelain produced at this period :—" Complete Tea Sets in the Dresden taste, highly ornamented, £7 7s. to £12 12s. and upwards. Tea Sets, 43 pieces, of various prices as low as £2 2s. Cups and Saucers from 3s. 6d. to 5s. 6d. per half dozen, and all other sorts of useful Ware proportionately cheap." In October, 1773, the patent rights passed into Champion's hands, and Cookworthy's name disappeared. The works soon afterwards attained their highest development. Some of Champion's productions were such admirable imitations of Dresden ware as to deceive the skilfullest connoisseurs; whilst the articles turned out, especially the vases and flower plaques, displayed singular artistic delicacy and beauty. How justly Champion claimed for his china the name of " true porcelain " was proved after the disastrous destruction by fire of the Alexandra Palace, near London, in 1873. Several thousand specimens of English ceramics, produced at Bow, Chelsea and Worcester, were reduced to a molten mass. But the Bristol China, being of hard paste, issued comparatively unscathed, the fashions of the figures and their painted decorations remaining nearly intact. In bringing the manufacture to a state of almost perfect excellence a heavy outlay had been necessary, and in the hope of securing an ultimate return for his outlay and personal labour, Champion, in 1775, applied to Parliament for an extension of Cookworthy's patent. Through the wily manœuvring of Wedgwood, who had powerful friends amongst the peers, the Act obtained, however, was practically valueless, the opaque potters being allowed the free use of the Cornish earths. The cost of the conflict at Westminster was a heavy blow to the Bristol works, already seriously menaced by the revolt of the American colonies, where Champion had expected to find a market for his cheaper products. In a letter to William Burke, in June, 1776, Champion described his manufactory as "the greatest ever known in England," adding that his capital was insufficient to make it a thorough commercial success. "Bristol is not the place to find a man of fortune and spirit to give it its due extent, so as to supply the market. We have no such men, and to divide it out into shares I do not like....... £10,000 additional would make a capital concern." Money was not to be found, owing, perhaps, to the severe commercial depression caused by the American war. Financial embarrassments followed, and Wedgwood, writing to a partner in August, 1778, exultingly announced that Champion was "quite demolished," and hoped that the Cornish material might thus be got on easy terms. The mean-spirited joy was somewhat premature, for the manufactory in Castle Green was not closed until 1781, when the patent rights were sold to a Staffordshire company, and Mr. Champion removed to Tunstall to superintend the new works. In the following year, however, he held for a few months the office of joint-deputy paymaster of the forces, under Burke; and he again occupied that post from April, 1783, to January, 1784. Further public service having become hopeless, he resolved on emigrating with his family to America, and arrived in South Carolina in December, 1784. He died at Camden, in that State, on the 7th October, 1791, in his 48th year.

A general election took place in March, 1768, when Lord Clare again offered his services. Sir Jarrit Smith retired, owing to advancing age, and two Tory candidates came forward to supply the vacancy—Mr. Richard Combe, of College Green, who held a minor office in the Government; and Mr. Matthew Brickdale, once a woollen draper in High Street. On the eve of the nomination day, Combe retired, finding that many Whigs would vote for his rival; and Lord Clare and Mr. Brickdale were thereupon elected. "Many houses," says the *Bristol Journal*, "were opened in the several parishes for the general entertainment of the friends of all parties" whilst a contest seemed imminent; and "the poor freemen and their families" were bountifully regaled after the members were returned. Mr. Laroche, jun., a member of the Corporation, was elected for Bodmyn, and Mr. Dickenson, of College Green, for another borough. Mr. Combe soon after found a seat in Somerset, when he sold his house in Bristol, and left the city. (The following paragraph in *Felix Farley's Journal* of March 19th is not strictly local, but it is too racy to be omitted:— "We hear there is so great a demand for provisions in a certain borough in the West [probably Bridgwater] that 300 guineas have been given for half an ox, and 'tis yet expected to be at a more advanced price." A fortnight later the same paper said it was confidently stated that the losing parties had expended nearly £20,000. "One opulent elector was offered £50 a year and £700 in money for his vote and interest, which he nobly refused.") In the following June, Lord Clare's seat was vacated by his appointment as one of the Vice-Treasurers of Ireland; when he was re-elected without opposition.

An advertisement issued by the Chandlers' and Soap Boilers' Company, dated from their "hall," and offering a reward for the discovery of frauds in the trade, appeared in the Bristol papers in April, 1768. The locality of the hall, of which no later record has been found, is unknown. The "frauds" referred to smuggled imports of Irish soap and candles, then tabooed from this country.

An illustration of a practice already referred to is offered by the following advertisement in the *Bristol Journal* of May 7th, 1768:—"Whereas certain ill-disposed persons in and about Frenchay have propagated a report that Captain John Read of that place had murdered his negro servant, and that Thomas Mountjoy, of Whiteshill, surgeon, had dissected the body." The announcement goes on to offer a reward of £10 for the discovery of the author of the report, adding that, in order "to clear his character," Captain Read had been "at the expense of returning to Frenchay (from London), and bringing the negro with him, notwithstanding he had made him the property of another person by sale." (In November, 1771, at a sale near London, a negro boy was put up to auction, and knocked down at £32.)

A disturbance occurred on the quays on the 13th May,

through a number of sailors having tried to force their comrades to strike for an advance of wages—then 25s. a month. The discontented men demanded 30s., but were unsuccessful. Arthur Young, in the inquiry he made this year into the agricultural condition of the South of England, found that the labourers' earnings in some parts of Gloucestershire were from 4s. to 5s. per week in winter, and 6s. in summer. "The stoutest fellows," he says, "often want work for 9d. a day, and cannot readily get it."

On October 1st, 1768, just a fortnight after the newly-erected Bristol Bridge had been opened for traffic on foot, a short contribution appeared in *Felix Farley's Journal*, styled a "description of the Mayor's first passing over the Old Bridge, taken from an old manuscript." The narrative, which described in spurious antique diction and orthography the rejoicings alleged to have taken place in the city upwards of five hundred years before, excited much interest amongst the few Bristolians of antiquarian tastes, and led to inquiries for the name of the contributor. It then appeared that the manuscript had been handed in anonymously, together with two short poems, also professing to be ancient, but which had been laid aside. The author of the three pieces was, in fact, the gifted but misguided genius, Thomas Chatterton, who was the posthumous son of a master of Pyle Street school bearing the same name, and was born under the shadow of Redcliff Church on the 20th November, 1752. The boy was in infancy so unusually dull that he was dismissed from Pyle Street school as incapable of even learning his letters. When in his seventh year his slumbering intellect was awakened by a singular incident. His mother, who kept a sewing school near the church, was tearing up an old music book that had belonged to her husband, when its illuminated capitals attracted her son's admiration, and by its help she succeeded in teaching him the alphabet, and soon after taught him to read in an old black-letter Testament. About a year later (August 3rd, 1760) Chatterton was admitted into Colston's School on the nomination of John Gardiner, vicar of Henbury, and remained there until July 1st, 1767, on which day he was apprenticed as a scrivener to Mr. John Lambert, attorney, Corn Street. Although the training afforded in Colston's Hospital was limited to the mere rudiments of education, the blue-coat boy at an early age became known at the circulating libraries and second-hand book shops as a greedy hunter after old world literature, which he read during play hours; whilst on Saturday afternoons he returned to his mother's, and spent the holiday in drawing heraldic and architectural subjects. One of his youthful feats, probably completed at Mr. Lambert's, was to compile a glossary of old English words, chiefly extracted from John Kersey's Dictionary, from which it may be inferred that the idea of which the Rowley Poems were the remarkable fruit had germed at an early period. In Mr. Lambert's office library, moreover, was an old edition of Camden's "Britannia," to which the base of many of the lad's future fictions can be clearly traced. (Mr. Nicholls's statement that Chatterton was largely indebted for medieval knowledge to the City Library is certainly inaccurate.) Soon after leaving school, the boy made a discovery peculiarly to his taste. Over the north porch of Redcliff Church was a chamber known as the muniment room, amongst the contents of which, in the time of Chatterton's father, was a large chest, called Canynges' coffer, stored with deeds and ancient parochial papers. In 1727 this coffer, secured with six locks, of which the keys had been lost, was broken open by order of the vestry, and such of the documents as were considered of value were removed, whilst a quantity deemed worthless, contained in that and other chests, were left loose and unprotected. Old church documents were regarded in that age with little respect, and there is nothing surprising in the fact that the Pyle Street schoolmaster subsequently obtained permission to take away large bundles; a number of parchments being afterwards used in covering Bibles and other books for his scholars. After his death, his store of unused manuscripts still filled two boxes, from which his widow supplied her sewing pupils with patterns and thread papers. Whilst her son was one day on a visit, he examined one of the fragments of parchment, then being used as a silk winder, and exclaiming that he had found a treasure, he collected all the remaining morsels that could be found in the house, and carried them off. Mr. Lambert's office hours extended from 8 in the morning until 8 at night; but the attorney's practice was not extensive, and the clerk had long intervals of leisure, which were devoted to poetry and the cultivation of his curious tastes. The prose narrative relating to the Bridge was his first published effort in the manufacture of spurious antiquities. On being shortly afterwards identified at the newspaper office as the contributor, Chatterton alleged that he had found the original, together with some poems, amongst the manuscripts obtained by his father from Redcliff porch. The youth, who was still under 16 years of age, was thereupon introduced to Mr. George Catcott, a pewterer near Bristol Bridge, and a bustling but futile amateur in archæology; and a few days later that gentleman was presented with the "Bristowe Tragedie," shortly afterwards supplemented by an epitaph on Robert Canynges, the "Challenge to Lydgate," and the "Song of Ella," some being so-called originals and some copies, but all alleged to have been composed by Thomas Rowley, a monk or priest, in the fifteenth century. Catcott, overwhelmed with delight, carried one of the poems, written on scraps of parchment, to Mr. William Barrett, an eminent Bristol surgeon, then zealously collecting materials for his contemplated history of the city; and the "discoverer" of the treasures was forthwith introduced to this important personage. Chatterton, who appears to have soon gauged the character of his new patron, lost no time in supplying him with what was styled an "Account of Bristol," written by a monk named Turgot, living in the reign of the Conqueror, and "translated by Rowley from Saxon into English." The prize was at once accepted as genuine, and when the gullible surgeon acquainted his young friend from time to time with his difficulties as to the early history of various Bristol churches, the "relics" that were opportunely furnished to meet his needs were received and made use of with the same unquestioning credulity, the boy being at intervals rewarded with small gifts of money as incentives to further "researches." Though the weakness of the dupe was unscrupulously played upon, it must be remembered that the victimiser was very young, and had, like many boys, a mischievous pleasure in deception. He was, moreover, almost penniless, receiving no wages from his master, and was strongly tempted into wrong-doing by an innate fondness for fine clothing. Mr. Barrett's valuable library having been opened to him, Chatterton obtained from it materials for a less important and more amusing imposture. George Catcott had a partner in trade named Henry Burgum, a man of humble birth, but puffed with a little worldly success, and absurdly ambitious to be thought of good family. To this tradesman Chatterton announced that he had found amongst the Redcliff parchments the armorial bearings of the De Berghems, with proofs of their descent from one of the companions of William I. The pedigree further pretended to be verified by references to ancient charters, the Roll of Battle Abbey, and the works of various antiquaries.

(All the books quoted were in Barrett's collection.) The vain and credulous pewterer having testified his delight by bestowing five shillings on his informant, the latter soon concocted a continuation of the pedigree, cautiously closed at about 1685, accompanied by a piece of poetry alleged to have been written in 1320 by one John de Berghem; and for these the forger was rewarded with another crown. A more daring attempt at deception was made about the same time. Horace Walpole's "Anecdotes of Painting" having recently appeared, Chatterton addressed a letter to the author, enclosing, amongst other manuscripts, the fictitious Rowley's "Ryse of Peyncteyne in England" and some verses about Richard I. Walpole courteously acknowledged the papers, whereupon he received, by return of post, further particulars as to Rowley, with additional manuscripts, including the "Historie of Peyncters yn England," and a significant intimation that the writer was a lover of literature in needy circumstances. The MSS. were submitted to the poets Gray and Mason, who pronounced them to be spurious, and after further correspondence Chatterton met with a mortifying but not undeserved repulse. In the meantime he had sought to better his narrow resources by contributing verses and prose essays to a London magazine. Later on, embittered by what he considered the parsimony of his local patrons, he satirised many prominent Bristolians, to some of whom, especially to Barrett and Catcott, he was under personal obligations. At length, in the spring of 1770, the unhappy youth avowed an intention to commit suicide, and one morning Mr. Lambert found on his desk the document now preserved in the Bristol Museum, entitled his "last will," written "in the utmost distress of mind, 14th April," and bitterly expressive of his forlorn misery. The attorney having at once dismissed his apprentice, Chatterton, aided by the subscription of a few friends, and with only £5 in his pocket, started on the 24th April for London. His miserable career in the capital is described by his biographers. It is sufficient to say that he displayed almost incredible industry, overtaxing his strength by the production of a prodigious pile of prose and verse, literary and political, dramatic and satirical. During one brief gleam of success, he purchased and sent off some little presents to his mother, sister, and grandmother, his affection for whom was unabated. On another occasion, a timely political essay brought him into communication with Lord Mayor Beckford, who seems to have promised to befriend him, for the sudden death of the politician soon afterwards plunged him in despair. The magazines, again, were sordidly conducted. For 250 lines of the "Consuliad" the poet received only 10s. 6d., which indicates the general scale of his rewards. The last and most exquisite of the Rowley poems, the ballad on Charity, was rejected by the editors. The noblest poet of the age, in short, was literally starving, although he was always content to make a dinner on cakes and water. For the last three days of his life, according to the statement of the woman with whom he lodged (at 39, Brook Street, Holborn), he was wholly without food, but proudly rejected her assistance. His mind gave way under his sufferings, and he died from the effects of poison on the 25th August, 1770, aged seventeen years and nine months, and was buried in a pauper's grave. The publishers at that time owed him about £12 for accepted contributions. Such are the main incidents of the poet's life, which it has not been easy to disentangle from the web of fiction and confusion woven around them by the lying stories of Thistlethwaite, the fables engendered by the senile imagination of Mrs. Edkins, the gossip-inspired twaddle of Cottle, and the impudent fabrications of Dix. All that need be said here respecting the Rowley controversy that arose after the boy's death is that, in spite of the thinness of the veil which Chatterton threw over his inventions—a veil that modern schoolboys can easily pierce—many influential writers of the time, with the President of the Antiquarian Society at their head, acrimoniously contended for the antiquity of the poems, whilst all the Bristol acquaintances of Chatterton, with the solitary exception of the Rev. Alexander Catcott, scoffed at the supposition that the works were his own creation. The Rowleyites practically disappeared before the end of the century. Chatterton's lyrics are now ranked amongst the finest in the language, and the brilliant genius and intellectual precocity of "Bristol's marvellous boy" have been sung with admiration and pity by almost every English poet from Coleridge to Rossetti.

The public-house "at Passage Leaze, opposite Pill, commonly called Lamplighter's Hall," was offered to be let in the *Bristol Journal* of December 17th, 1768. This is the first mention of a house that subsequently became a favourite resort of pleasure parties. In 1772, when the property was offered for sale, it was described as "some time the estate of Joseph Swetnam, tinman, of Small Street, deceased."

Swetnam had at one period contracted to light the lamps in some of the city parishes. He was probably the son of another tinman, James Swetnam, who traded at the Three Ship Lanterns on the Back in 1740, and is believed to have been the first Bristol tradesman who used an engraved billhead for making out his invoices.

The minutes of the corporation of the poor for the year 1768 contain the following entry :—" Mr. John Peach, one of the guardians, discharged in consequence of his having convicted a felon." The minute, which led Mr. Nicholls to assume that Mr. Peach was himself a felon, is explained by a statute of 1698, which enacted that burglars, horse stealers, or thieves robbing shops to the value of five shillings, should on conviction be hanged, and that every person successfully prosecuting such a felon should be entitled to exemption from parochial and ward offices in the place where the crime was committed. This singular Act was not repealed until 1818.

In January, 1769, the Corporation presented a petition to the House of Commons, setting forth that the two ancient city fairs, beginning respectively on the 25th January and the 25th July, " did not answer the good ends of their institution, by reason that the times of the year at which they were held were extremely inconvenient to the manufacturers and traders resorting thereto ; " and praying for power to alter the dates to " more convenient parts of the year." A Bill fixing the opening of the fairs on the 1st March and 1st September (and also empowering the Common Council to carry out the arrangements already recorded respecting the Grammar School and Queen Elizabeth's Hospital) passed without opposition.

The *St. James's Chronicle* of July 1st contains an interesting paragraph in reference to Clifton :—" We hear from the Hot Wells that there is a good deal of very good company already ; seldom less than 200 at the public breakfasts with cotillons, and fuller balls than were last year at the height of the season, which is generally about the third week in July." The writer adds that owing to the nearness of Bath, entertainments were given at each place alternately all the year round, and this attraction, combined with the excellence of the play-house, the choice of lodging-houses, the purity of the air, and the virtues of the Hot Well water at all seasons, had " induced several persons of independent fortune either to purchase or take houses in order to live there winter and summer. The inhabitants met twice a week last winter to drink tea and play at cards, which encreased its sociability."

Mr. William Powell, manager of the Bristol theatre, and one of the patentees of Covent Garden theatre, London, died in this city on the 3rd July, aged 33. He had displayed such distinguished talent as a tragedian that he was regarded by his friends as the indicated successor of Garrick. His remains were buried in the Cathedral, the dean (Dr. Barton) performing the funeral service in the presence of a great concourse of influential citizens.

At a meeting of the Council on the 8th July a committee recommended the removal of Lawford's Gate, and the purchase and destruction of three adjoining houses, by which "a very convenient passage would be there opened for persons, horses, and carriages." The Chamber ordered the work to be executed forthwith. The two ancient statues ornamenting the Gate were secured by Mr. Reeve, who placed them on the outside of the entrance arch to "Black Castle." The demolished houses—one of which, it is said, was originally a lodge of one of the keepers of Kingswood chase, who was entitled to demand toll from every packhorse entering the city during the fairs—belonged to Trinity Hospital, and brought in £27 yearly. The Corporation granted the charity a perpetual annuity of £15 per annum. Five more old dwellings were demolished in 1792 to widen the street at this point.

A great pugilistic contest took place in the new Riding School on the 19th June between Stephens "the nailer" and a Kingswood collier named Milsom. The latter was successful, but it was generally suspected that his opponent "sold the fight." Some thousands of spectators were present, including many gentry, and "two noblemen."

During the summer, the treatment of John Wilkes by the House of Commons aroused a strong feeling in his favour. A dinner took place in June at the Cock inn, St. James's churchyard, at which, in honour of the famous number of the *North Briton*, 45 gentlemen sat down to a feast comprised of 45 fowls, a 45lb. ham, a 45lb. rump of beef, 45 cabbages, 45 cucumbers, 45 loaves and 45 tarts, to which were added 45 gallons of ale, 45 glasses of brandy, and 45 papers of tobacco. A meeting was held in the Guildhall in the following month, Mr. Henry Cruger presiding, at which a strongly-worded protest against the action of the Commons was adopted unanimously. It was stated during the proceedings that several attorneys and others had been employed to prevent the meeting, by industriously alleging that those who took part in it would be summoned to Westminster and flung into prison.

On the 13th December, 1769, Thomas Lawrence, innholder (he had just become tenant of the White Lion in Broad Street), was admitted a freeman on payment of a fine of 12 guineas. His distinguished son, Thomas, afterwards President of the Royal Academy, was then an infant, having been born in Redcross Street on the 5th May. In April, 1772, Lawrence announced that the American coffee-house, adjoining the inn, had been united to his establishment; but the adventure was unprofitable, and at midsummer, 1773, he removed to the Black Bear inn at Devizes. The White Lion was at this time a favourite resort of Bristolians who approved of the king's policy towards America. An old citizen informed Mr. Tyson that he remembered having seen effigies of Hancock and Adams, two prominent founders of the United States, ignominiously hanged before the American coffee-house, after having been first " tarred and feathered." After the defeat of the Government, the title of the house became offensive to its political patrons, and " American " was changed to " British " about 1785.

The Corporation, although accumulating a heavy debt, was generally disposed to protect the pockets of the wealthy interest by which it was dominated. In December, 1769, the Council voted a subscription of 100 guineas for the relief of the sufferers by a fire in the island of Antigua. There is no evidence that the West India merchants contributed a shilling towards the same object. The attention of the Chamber was directed at the same meeting to the devoted ministerial services rendered by the Rev. James Rouquet to the prisoners in the gaol for nearly twenty years. It was determined that a gift of £20 would be a sufficient compensation.

The earliest notice of a third Bristol Bank occurs in 1769, when the partners were Henry Bright, Thomas Deane, Jeremiah Ames, Thomas Whitehead, Edward Harford and Samuel Munckley. Business was carried on in Small Street, in a large mansion once belonging to Edward Colston. (The site is now occupied by the Post Office.) After a secession, which will be recorded under 1786, this bank was carried on for some years by Messrs. Deane, Whitehead, Harford, Son, and Aldridge. In 1799, when a removal took place to No. 8, Corn Street, the concern was styled Messrs. Harford, Davis and Company.

An advertisement, dated February 14th, 1770, announced in the local newspapers that the New Bristol Fire Office had opened for business. The company, which had a capital of £108,000, had been formed some years previously by the local sugar refiners for mutual protection against fire. Another local insurance office, styled the Bristol Universal, commenced business in September, 1774, with a subscribed capital of £50,000, undertaking to pay for losses of plate, china, glass, carved work, wainscot of rooms, etc. (which the older offices refused to insure), and to charge no more for large insurances than for small ones, namely, 2s. per cent. The senior offices were soon compelled to follow the example of their new rivals. In 1790 the New Bristol company increased its capital to £240,000, and changed its name to the Bristol Fire Office.

An Act was obtained in 1770 empowering the Bishop of Bristol to dispose, on lease, of the "park" adjoining his palace, for building purposes. Similar powers were conferred on the dean and chapter as regarded "White's Garden." Mr. Samuel Worrall obtained a lease of the Bishop's Park for 90 years, at a rent of £60 per annum, and soon after offered the land in building plots, "in the new street called College Street." The chapter land was covered with low tenements, the inmates of which soon contributed to increase not merely the pauperism but the vice of the city; but the cathedral authorities, content to receive their reserved rents, long ignored the immorality that prevailed. The period was a lucrative one for the chapter. In June, 1770, it obtained £1,000 from two ladies named Clement for inserting a new life in their lease of Canons' Marsh. In April, 1772, another life in the same lease dropped, and £1,050 was paid for adding a fresh one; and two years later the same process had to be gone through again, at a further cost of £1,050.

A petition having been presented to the Council in 1769, urging the Corporation to exercise the powers conferred upon it for the removal of St. Leonard's Church and the laying out of a street from Corn Street to the Quay, the matter was referred to a committee, which, after consideration, declined to advise the Council to undertake the work. A petition was subsequently presented to the Chamber by Daniel Harson, John Fowler, Edward Harford, jun., William Hart, John Deverell, Cranford Becher, Wm. James, Edward Nicholas, John Powell, and John Anderson, praying that the Corporation would assign the powers to private citizens willing to carry out the improvement, and would assist in the work by giving up the site of a public-house, and by a donation of £2,000, which was estimated to be the net loss likely to be incurred in destroying the old property. At a meeting of the Council on the 22nd May, 1770, the requests of the petitioners were unanimously assented to, and it was resolved that the new thoroughfare should be called Clare Street. The promoters lost no time in buying up the old property, the materials of nine houses "at Pyle End, near St. Leonard's Church," and of various tenements in Marsh Street being offered for sale in November. In January, 1771, the church of St. Leonard's, with the dark and tortuous passage called Blind Gate on which it stood, communicating with Marsh Street, Fisher Lane (St. Stephen Street), and Baldwin Street, was demolished, and soon after building operations commenced in earnest. The street was nearly completed in 1775, when Sketchley compiled his Directory. The improvement was effected at a cost greatly below the estimates, and the undertakers reaped a large profit from their enterprise. An advertisement in *Felix Farley's Journal* of July 6th, 1776, stated that subscribers might receive back their subscriptions, "and also receive the final dividends of profits arising from said concern."

Complaint having been made that the city was inadequately supplied with the better sorts of fish, the Corporation, in May, 1770, granted a bounty of 7s. 6d. per cwt. to a Welshman named James, for all the turbot, cod, and soles which he sent into the local market from places west of the Holmes.

An order issued by the Court of Quarter Sessions in August, 1770, offers amusing testimony as to the leisurely business habits of the age. Complaint having been made as to the blocking of the quays, the court decreed as follows:—"All vessels laden with tobacco [it was shown under 1766 that some of these ships were of only about 100 tons burden] to discharge their cargo in 40 working days; all vessels from other foreign parts in 21 working days....All vessels bound to foreign parts to take in their loading in 80 working days." From seventeen to twenty weeks were therefore allowed each ship between her arrival and departure. The following regulation was also made:—"No candle to be lighted on board any vessel at the keys on any night after the Candle Bell shall be rung," on pain of a fine of 10s. The Candle Bell figures in some old engravings of the Drawbridge.

Tea was still an expensive luxury. Mrs. James, of High Street, announced in November that she had just opened "several chests of her so-much-admired bloom and hyson teas," which she continued to sell at the old prices, namely, 11s., 14s., and, for best hyson, 16s. per lb. (Another tradesman sold fine gunpowder tea at 20s., and Mocha coffee at 6s.)

Reference has been already made to the haphazard system under which postal business was conducted early in the century. It would seem from the following paragraph in the *Bristol Journal* of November 3rd that the arrangements had undergone but little improvement in 1770:—"The London mail did not arrive so soon by several hours as usual on Monday, owing to the postman's getting a little intoxicated on his way between Newbury and Marlborough, and falling from his horse into a hedge, where he was found asleep by means of his dog."

The improvements in and around Newgate prison, contemplated by the Act of 1766, were effected this year at a cost of £838.

A healing spring, of which few living Bristolians have perhaps ever heard, solicited the attention of bathers in the local journals of April 20th, 1771. "The Cold Bath, in Castle Ditch," said the advertisement, had a neat drawing room for public accommodation. It was an exceeding fine spring, constantly overflowing, and its salutary qualities had been happily experienced by many afflicted with rheumatic, paralytic, and other nervous disorders. It moreover provoked lost appetites, and elevated sinking spirits. The bath was surrounded with gravel walks and pleasant flowery turfs for after recreation, and the subscription was 6s. per quarter, or a guinea per annum. The institution was in existence in 1820, when Mr. Seyer was compiling his history. It appears to have excited rivalry, for the local *Gazette* of October 17th, 1772, recorded that on the previous Monday "part of the wall against the Avon, belonging to St. Peter's Hospital, fell down, together with a new-erected Cold Bath, which stood near it, into the river."

The Common Council, in June, 1771, resolved to set about the construction of the street (Union Street) from Dolphin Lane to Broadmead. Owing to the costliness of the undertaking, it was determined to reduce the proposed width of the thoroughfare from 40 to 30 feet. The butcher market at the Exchange being overcrowded, it was resolved to erect a market on the eastern side of the new street. The undertaking presented considerable difficulties, many thousand tons of earth having to be carted to the spot, and a lofty bridge constructed over the Froom. St. James's Market was opened on the 1st May, 1776. The outlay of the Corporation far exceeded the original estimate of about £4,000. In 1776, the Chamber ordered that £2,500, in addition to £5,000 already borrowed, be raised by means of life annuities, "for defraying the expence of making Union Street and the market there."

The growing inconvenience to traffic caused by Redcliff Gate at length overcame the conservative instincts of the Corporation. On the 8th June, 1771, the Chamber unanimously ordered that the obstruction should be forthwith taken down. As already stated (p. 175), the gate had been rebuilt so recently as 1731. Redcliff Parade, on a site previously known as Adderclift, belonging to the dean and chapter, but held under lease by Mr. Sydenham Teast, was under construction at this time. In 1776 the capitular lease was renewed on payment of a fine of £650.

A great public improvement was determined upon in the autumn. The impetus came from London, where the corporation had just introduced flagged footways for pedestrians. The Common Council of Bristol resolved, on the 28th September, that a paved way, seven feet wide, should be made before the Exchange, to which it was also determined to remove the four brass pillars that had long stood before the Council House. This resolution must have been come to in view of the action taken in reference to footways by the paving authorities; for a writer in *Felix Farley's Journal* of October 26th, referring to various local improvements, applauds "the paved foot passages so commendably begun in several of the streets." In the following June a letter appeared in the *Bristol Journal*, in which "the Ladies of Bristol return thanks to the magistrates for encouraging the accommodation of their feet with smooth paved streets"; but complain that "four wheeled carriages called trucks" were allowed to be driven along the footways.

The removal of the brass pillars, just recorded, put an end to a singular annual ceremony, described by a London observer as follows:—"On the 5th November the eldest scholar of the city grammar school, standing on a brass pillar in the street, at the Tolzey, commemorates the deliverance in a Latin oration to the mayor, who attends to him at the Council-house door; and when the declaimer dismounts, rewards him with a piece or pieces of gold, as Mr. Mayor thinks proper; but the throng is always so great that very little is heard." The oration was afterwards delivered in the Council House, but was discontinued in 1780, and was only at intervals revived.

On the 7th November, John Shoals was tried at the Admiralty Court, London, for the murder of one M'Coy on board the Bristol ship Black Prince, in January, 1769. Shortly after the ship left Bristol on a slaving voyage, the sailors resolved to seize the vessel and become pirates. The captain and nine officers were accordingly forced into a boat, which soon after sank. M'Coy, who acted as cook, having incurred the displeasure of the crew, was tried by a mock court-martial, of which Shoals was a member, and, having been sentenced to be hanged, was suspended to the yard arm; but the rope broke, and the poor fellow fell into the sea and perished. The prisoner was acquitted of the murder, but was sentenced to death for piracy, and subsequently executed. The Black Prince was eventually stranded on the coast of Hispaniola.

On the 2nd January, 1772, the famous John Wilkes, having been invited by Sir William Codrington, Bart., Mr. Samuel Peach, Mr. Henry Cruger, and other influential citizens to pay a visit to Bristol, arrived at the White Lion inn, Broad Street, amidst the cheers of a vast crowd of admirers. The bells of St. Stephen's and St. Maryleport were rung in his honour; but many of the clergy, according to the *Bristol Journal*, prevented the ringing of a peal. Wilkes was entertained to dinner in Tailors' Hall, where about eighty gentlemen sat down, and 24 toasts were afterwards drunk, that of "the legal representative of Middlesex" being received with enthusiasm. Sarah Farley was venturesome enough to publish in her newspaper the speech of the gentleman who welcomed Wilkes's arrival; but his name, as well as the demagogue's after-dinner oration, was carefully suppressed.

Handel's oratorio of "Judas Maccabæus" was performed on the 25th March in the theatre in King Street, to which the admission was five shillings. Master Linley, then a musical prodigy, was "first violin" in the orchestra.

An advertisement dated April 8th, 1772, appeared in the *Bristol Journal*, announcing that "Robert and Thomas Southey, linen drapers, mercers, and lace-men, have this day opened shop, next door to the Plume of Feathers, in Wine Street." The premises were distinguished by "the sign of the Hare." The senior partner, in the following September, married a Miss Hill, of Bedminster, daughter of Edward

Hill, attorney, deceased, and from this union was born, over
the Wine Street shop, on the 12th August, 1774, Robert
Southey, many years poet laureate, but better known as the
biographer of Nelson and the author of "The Doctor."
The draper brothers dissolved partnership about 1778,
Thomas migrating to Corn Street; but both became bankrupt in 1791. At the latter date the shop in Wine Street,
since divided into two, was let for £44 a year.

On the 15th May, 1772, a man named Jonathan Britain
was hanged at St. Michael's Hill for forging a bill of exchange for the sum of £10. The case excited much public
attention. Britain had been an usher in the school kept by
Mr. Donn in the City Library in King Street, and had also
been a frequent contributor to an anti-ministerial paper
called the *Whisperer*. In July, 1771, whilst at Reading, he
attempted to obtain cash for four bills of exchange to the
total value of £45; but doubts as to their genuineness
having been aroused, he was arrested, and ultimately committed for trial on suspicion of forgery. Apparently in
dread of the result, Britain soon afterwards declared that he
was one of the persons concerned in setting fire to Portsmouth dockyard a short time previously, and that it was his
intention to avail himself of the royal pardon promised in
the *London Gazette* to any one making a full discovery of
that crime. He followed up this statement by publishing
in the *Whisperer* virulent attacks on members of the Government, and on the king's favourite, Lord Bute. These articles,
which were continued for several months, and insinuated
criminal charges against many prominent personages, excited
attention all over the country. In the meantime, a Bristol
firm acquainted the prosecutors at Reading that Britain had
absconded from this city, after obtaining payment of three
forged bills, amounting together to £35. This fact came to
the knowledge of the Rev. William Talbot, vicar of St.
Giles's, Reading, who had taken an inexplicable antipathy
to Britain from the outset, and who, as he afterwards
avowed, had resolved to rid the world of "an execrable
villain." It was foreseen that the charge of forgery at
Reading could not be sustained, the prosecutors having neglected to retain the evidence of the fraud. It appeared also
that the injured persons in Bristol had no intention of prosecuting the prisoner. Mr. Talbot therefore determined to
prosecute the Bristol cases at his own expense, and made
several journeys to the city to engage legal assistance and
collect evidence, having stooped, it was alleged, to gross

dissimulation for the purpose of extracting information from Britain's friends. Two or three journeys were also made to London with the object of strengthening the case. Finally, on the Berkshire grand jury rejecting the Reading indictments, Britain, at Mr. Talbot's instance, was arrested by officers from Bristol, where he was brought up for trial on the 2nd May, 1772, on one of the three indictments laid against him. The prisoner had practically no defence, and his claim to be entitled to pardon under the *Gazette* notice referred to above was, of course, set aside. After conviction, Britain confessed that he really knew nothing about the Portsmouth fire, and that his articles on the subject were a tissue of falsehoods. The man was undoubtedly a vicious and heartless scoundrel; but the extraordinary manner in which he was dragged to the scaffold by a clergyman gave great offence, and Mr. Talbot's solemn assurances that his time and money had been lavished solely in the service of the public were received with general incredulity.

A letter in the *Bristol Journal* of the 13th June, addressed to the mayor by "a great number of the citizens liable to serve as jurors," throws light on the accommodation provided for the due administration of justice. The writers suggested that seats should be placed in the Crown Court at the Guildhall for the use of the jurors, who, being obliged to stand throughout the trial of a prisoner, sometimes lasting for three or four hours, were often so much fatigued as to be unable to perform their functions. The appeal was unnoticed.

A great improvement near St. Stephen's Church was proposed during the summer, namely, the demolition of a number of old hovels which blocked up the approach to the church from the newly-constructed Clare Street. The Corporation subscribed £200 towards the fund raised for clearing the ground. Subsequently the vestry extended the design, and in 1774 an Act of Parliament was obtained to remove old buildings, including the former rectory, to widen the narrow streets in the neighbourhood, and to extend the churchyard. A witness deposed before the House of Commons that, owing to the confined area of the cemetery and the number of burials, the ground had become raised five feet above the natural level. Considerable alterations were also made in the church itself, though they are scarcely referred to by Mr. Barrett, whose indifference to the freaks of contemporary churchwardendom showed his lack of good taste, and caused marked defects in his history. In November, 1776, the vestry resolved on the immediate erection of a new vestry room at the east end of the church, and this building caused the destruction of the east window of the south aisle. In the following May, it was resolved that "the foundation of the north aisle be built and brought up window high, so as to make it of an equal length with the south aisle." It is probable that much of the old tracery of the windows was replaced about this time by work of a debased character. The cost of carrying out the improvements far exceeded the estimates, and, as will be seen hereafter, the parochial authorities were saved from insolvency only by the help of the Corporation.

Felix Farley's Journal of June 20th, 1772, acquainted the public that Thomas Boyce had completely fitted up "three large and elegant lodging houses on Clifton Hill," which appear to have been built by himself at a cost of about £8,000, and received the name of Boyce's Buildings. Attached to the houses were a pleasure garden, three summer-houses, ten coach-houses, and stabling for 34 horses. The projector became bankrupt in the following November.

A coach to Leicester—an unprecedented enterprise—started in June, the owners undertaking to make the journey bi-weekly in two days. By intercepting the London coaches to Liverpool and Lancaster at Coventry, Bristolians were offered greatly increased facilities for reaching that part of the kingdom.

On the 4th September, Elizabeth Inchbald, who had not then completed her nineteenth year, appeared at the King Street theatre in the part of Cordelia; a play-bill of the evening, preserved in R. Smith's MSS., adds "being her first appearance on any stage." The performance was for the benefit of her husband, an actor and painter, whom she had married a few weeks before. Mrs. Inchbald afterwards acquired a lasting reputation and a handsome competence by her dramas and novels. In the summer of 1774 the leading female performer on the local stage was Mrs. Canning (*née* Costello), widow of George Canning, an Irishman claiming descent from the renowned Canynges of Bristol, and mother of a four year old boy of the same name, destined to become Prime Minister. Mrs. Canning, who was much admired for her beauty, married an actor of repute, named Reddish, then manager of Bristol theatre, and frequently acted during three seasons. Reddish dying, his widow married one Hunn, who, according to Mr. Smith, was a liquor dealer in Tucker Street, but by another account was a draper at Plymouth, whom she also outlived

The lady continued on the stage till 1801, when her son, who had been adopted by a banker uncle (father of Lord Stratford de Redcliffe), and had then been Under-Secretary of State for four years, arranged to have his pension of £500 a-year settled on his mother and sisters.

"Mr. Astley, performer of horsemanship, from London," a man destined to attain fame as a circus proprietor, but who at this period picked up a precarious living as a showman at Bristol and other fairs, gave several equestrian entertainments on Durdham Down during the month of October, depending for his reward upon the liberality of the spectators. The chief attractions were the performances of his son, five years old, and of his wife, upon two barebacked horses. The first local equestrian performance indoors seems to have taken place in June, 1786, when a troupe of Astley's company occupied the "new riding school in the Borough Walls, leading from Thomas Street to Temple Street."

The bakers of the city were greatly irritated about this time by the proceedings of an interloper in the trade, named Jenkins, who persisted in selling bread at a lower price than that agreed upon by the Bakers' Company, and thereby gained great popular support. The publication of violent attacks on his character having proved ineffectual, the Company, in October, resolved to prosecute him under the law of Elizabeth, forbidding any one from pursuing a trade to which he had not served seven years' apprenticeship; but the grand jury ignored the indictment, and Jenkins triumphantly opened a shop in Wine Street, started a mill at St. Anne's to defeat a combination of millers, and sold more bread than ever. His family, who succeeded him, eventually acquired a fortune. This appears to have been the last attempt to enforce the old Act by which trade monopolies had been so long defended.

The local theatrical season had been hitherto limited to the summer months, during which the Hot Well was attended by fashionable and pleasure-seeking visitors. In November, 1772, an attempt was made by a band of comedians to supply a series of winter entertainments, and the Coopers' Hall was engaged for that purpose. The Act of 1737, branding players as rogues and vagabonds, being still in force, the company were reduced to the usual expedient for evading the law. The *Bristol Journal* of November 21st cautiously announced:—" We hear that the first theatrical concert at the Coopers' Hall will be on Wednesday next." No opposition having been offered, the following week's *Journal* says :—" We hear the next theatrical concert (between the parts of which will be introduced, gratis, Othello and the Lying Valet) will be on Monday next." Growing bolder, the next number announced that three "concerts" a week would be given, and similar advertisements were continued in later issues. The proceedings were doubtless very aggravating to the proprietors of the neighbouring theatre, but their hands were tied by the fact that the performances in their own house were as illegal as those at the hall. A correspondent of the *Journal* joyfully announced in January that the magistrates had at length put the law in operation against the intruders, and a few days afterwards four of the principal performers were fined £50 each; but the "concerts" nevertheless continued until the 3rd April. In the following winter, to the wrath of the theatre owners, the interlopers reappeared, the "concerts" being resumed on the 17th November, 1773. Three weeks later, however, the Council resolved to crush them, and on the 18th December the managers, Messrs. Booth and Kennedy (both either in hiding or in prison), announced their benefits, hoping that "their present situation," which prevented them from personally waiting on their friends, would not deprive them of public support. A promise was added that the hall would be reopened after Christmas; but the luckless players were unable to fulfil the pledge.

In addition to the annual gift of wine to the two members for the city, the Council, in December, 1772, made a similar present to Mr. James Laroche, one of the Common Council, and M.P. for Bodmyn, " for his services in Parliament." The gift was repeated in the five following years, the recipient having in the meantime been created a baronet for his zealous support of the King's American policy; and, though the present was withheld in 1778, it was resumed in 1779. Owing to commercial misfortunes, Sir James then retired from Parliament.

At a meeting of the Council in December, a pension of £30 a year was granted to William Stevens, an insolvent linen draper. The only claim for sympathy put forward on his behalf was that he had married a daughter of "John Bartlett, Esq., late a member of this House." When Stevens died, in 1780, his widow was granted a pension of the same amount. In 1790 a pension of £20 was proposed to be conferred on the widow of Bartlett's son. The motion was negatived; but the daughter of the widow forthwith petitioned again, alleging that her mother had not sufficiently described her distressed state, and the House thereupon granted £30 a year to the daughter, for life!

On the 15th December, 1772, at a meeting of a few leading citizens, it was resolved to form an association under the title of the Bristol Library Society, having for its purpose the promotion of literature in the city. The original promoters of the movement were John Peach, John Ford, Joseph Harford, Samuel Farr, M.D., John Pryor Estlin, Richard Champion, Mark Harford, William Buller, Abraham Ludlow, M.D., and Joseph Smith. Bishop Newton accepted the office of president. The subscription was fixed at a guinea, with an entrance fee of the same amount. (The latter was afterwards largely increased.) The society from the outset coveted the acquisition of the "Library House" erected by the Corporation in 1740 for the free use of the citizens, and private negotiations to attain that end soon took place, for in January, 1773, at the annual election of civic officials, Mr. Donn, the schoolmaster, who had been librarian for some years, was not reappointed. At the Council meeting in the following March, the Rev. Thomas Johnes petitioned for the vacant office of library keeper, and a memorial was presented from the society "for increasing the library and rendering the same more useful to the publick," begging for the free use of the building, and for Mr. Johnes' appointment. Both requests were granted (Mr. Johnes's salary was soon after raised to 12 guineas with rent-free apartments), and Mr. Donn was directed to quit the premises at Midsummer. The sum of £162 was next paid by the Chamber for renovating the premises and repairing the books. These preparations completed, the library was opened on the 1st July, 1773, the books belonging to the city, though kept apart from those of the society, being, of course, available to the members. Although the house was built for a free library, no reservation of the citizens' rights was made by the civic body, and the entrance of a non-subscriber into the building was soon treated by Mr. Johnes as an impertinent intrusion. In 1775 the Common Council rendered a further service to the new institution. In 1728 the Corporation had permitted Ezekial Longman, ancestor of the great London publishers, to erect a stable and coach-house in King Street, in front of the library, on his paying a rent of 20s. These constructions, with others added by the tenant, being found inconvenient, the Chamber purchased the whole for £392, and had them demolished "to lay open the library house and widen the public way," the Merchant Venturers contributing £100 towards the improvement. The Society was well supported, and being helped by various donations (the Society of Arts subscribed 10 guineas annually for upwards of half a century), its literary treasures rapidly increased. In 1785 it applied to the Common Council for a piece of void ground adjoining the library, upon which to build an additional wing. The land was granted at a rent of 2s. 5d., and a subscription of £100 was voted towards the intended building. The addition was completed in 1789. The restoration of the Library House to its original purpose was not effected until half a century later. See "Annals of the Nineteenth Century," p. 333.

If travelling was slow during the eighteenth century, it was at least comparatively cheap. An advertisement in the *Bristol Journal* of the 13th February, 1773, intimates that a post chaise and pair of horses to Bath or Sodbury could be hired for 9s., or to Wells, 15s. These charges were about fifty per cent. higher than had been usual a few years earlier. In 1760 the price to Wells was half a guinea, and the average rate on level roads was then sixpence a mile in summer. The ordinary rate of travelling by post chaises was thirty miles per day.

At a meeting of the Council on the 27th March, 1773, a petition was read from owners of property on Kingsdown and St. Michael's Hill, representing that they had within a few years built many new houses there, but were discouraged from making further improvements owing to the great damage done to their property by the populace during the execution of criminals, and praying that the gallows be removed to Brandon Hill. On the margin of the minute book is written:—"Nothing done herein."

A strike of tailors took place in April. The workmen, alleging that their weekly earnings averaged only 8s., demanded that the rate for the summer months, 12s., should be raised to 14s. The dispute was maintained for four months, and seems to have ended in the success of the men, for in 1777 there was another strike, caused by the employers reducing the rate from 14s. to 12s. In 1781, and again in 1790, the masters advertised for journeymen, offering 14s., their hands having demanded 15s. On both the latter occasions the workmen were defeated.

The weakness of rich Bristolians in reference to turtle was a theme for much sarcasm down to the first quarter of the present century. Mr. Nugent has been shown describing the civic dignitaries as "full of turtle," and from his time to that of Byron, who said much the same thing, many jokes were cracked at the expense of the citizens. Of late years, thanks to Mr. Punch, the stream of banter has been diverted upon the Corporation of London, and the witticisms upon Bristol turtle eaters have been almost forgotten. The trade appears to have attained its highest point at the period now under review. The *Bristol Journal* of July 17th, 1773, announces:—"Just imported, several large and small turtle from 2 to 120 lb., and from 1s. to 2s. per lb. To be sold at the Old Turtle Warehouse, next door to All Saints' Conduit, Corn Street"—a convenient locality for the dignitaries at the opposite Council House. At this time a famous victualler, John Weeks, had just become tenant of the Bush tavern, fronting the Exchange, where he dressed turtle with such remarkable success that his soup became celebrated throughout the country, large quantities being prepared for distant consumption. In July, 1776, he advertised "turtle ordinaries every Tuesday, Thursday, and Saturday during the turtle season," at 5s. a head. Weeks's renown as a caterer extended over thirty years, and he is said to have enjoyed the patronage of the Prince of Wales (George IV.). In 1781 the Corporation accounts contain the following item:—"Paid for a small turtle sent to the Recorder (Dunning) as a present, £6 16s. 4d." In 1796 the proprietors of the Bush, White Lion, Talbot, and Montague hotels announced that fresh turtle was dressed by them every day during the season.

At a meeting of the Council in December, 1773, the master of Queen Elizabeth's Hospital and the mistress of the Red Maids' School were voted an extra sum of £42 each (£1 per scholar) on account of the high price of provisions. The children in the two charities were "farmed" by their teachers, the master of the Hospital being allowed at this time £10 per boy for clothing, food, and instruction, whilst the mistress of the girls received £7 per head, together with the profits derived from the needlework at which the children were almost constantly employed—their school lessons being confined to reading.

The Council, at the same meeting, ordered that a hogshead of wine should be forwarded to the recorder, as an acknowledgment "for his advice." The fee of the recorders from the time of Sir Michael Foster had been £50 for each gaol delivery. It was now probably thought that this honorarium was insufficient. At all events, the gift of wine was renewed annually, and continued until the reform of the Corporation.

In the session of 1774 a Bill was promoted by the Bristol turnpike trustees for a renewal of their powers, then about to expire, and for the inclusion in the trust of Gallows Acre Lane, of the road from the top of Park Street to the bottom of Clifton Hill, of the lane from Stoke's Croft to the Blackbirds Inn Gate, Stapleton Road, and of the road from Gallows Acre Lane to Whiteladies' Road. The two last-named proposals excited much local agitation, and petitions against them were adopted by the poor law guardians and by a public meeting of the citizens, on the ground that the large traffic between the Hot Well and Bath, as well as that between Wales and the South of England, then passing through Bristol, would be diverted, to the great loss of the inhabitants. The opposition was successful in forcing the trustees to modify their scheme. Power to make a turnpike road from the top of Stoke's Croft to Stapleton Road was, however, obtained a few years later, and Ashley Road was opened in 1786.

On the 22nd February, 1774, the philanthropic John Howard paid his first visit to Bristol in the course of his remarkable exertions for the promotion of prison reform. It is difficult for later generations to render full justice to Howard's dauntless labours, inasmuch as the horrors he had to encounter have long passed away. That he ran no trifling risk is attested by the facts relating to Somerset prison recorded at page 172, and by the circumstance that a lord mayor, an alderman, two judges, and the greater part of a London jury perished from gaol fever caught in court in 1750. These and many other warnings had produced no effect on the authorities when Howard began his mission. The Castle prison at Gloucester, which he had visited before reaching Bristol, was found in a wretched condition. The floor of the main ward was so ruinous that it could not be washed; the male and female felons were herded together in a single day-room; a large dunghill lay against the steps leading to the dormitories; and the gaoler, having no salary, made his living out of the profits of the liquor sold to the prisoners, and by taxing the debtors brought under his charge. "Many prisoners," Howard noted, "died there in the course of the year." Newgate prison, in Bristol, was overcrowded with inmates, but was in a better sanitary state than that of Gloucester, though the "dungeon," or night room for male felons, often densely crowded, was eighteen steps underground, and only 17 feet in diameter. "No bedding, nor straw." In the yard the criminals of all ages and both sexes mingled with the insolvent debtors, even the poorest of the latter class paying the gaoler, who had no salary, 10½d. a week for the lodgings in which they were incarcerated by their creditors. There were 38 felons and 58 debtors in Newgate at the time of Howard's inspection. Bridewell was in a worse state than the gaol, the rooms being very dirty, and the air offensive from open sewers. There was no bedding, no employment, insufficient water, and the only food was two pennyworth of bread per head daily. At Lawford's Gate bridewell there was "a dark room, the dungeon, about 12 feet by 7, in which the felons slept, except those who could afford to pay for beds. The rooms were without chimneys, and yet the inmates were never allowed to leave them. A prisoner had no allowance for food, except he was very poor, when he had twopence a day." Howard paid repeated visits to Bristol, where he generally stayed for some time at the Hot Well. He noted in December, 1775, that he had released a woman from Bridewell, who had been acquitted at the quarter sessions, but was detained for nonpayment of fees, 3s. 6d. Some improvements were effected in Newgate after the publication of Howard's reports; but he describes it in 1787 as "white without and foul within; the dungeon and several rooms very dirty. The allowance still to felons only a penny loaf before trial, and a twopenny loaf (1½lb.) after conviction." At his last inspection, May, 1788, the gaol was found "much cleaner," and Bridewell "perfectly clean." The improvement, however, was of brief duration (See "Annals of the Nineteenth Century," p. 66).

A musical festival took place in the Cathedral on the 31st March, 1774, for the benefit of the Infirmary. During the morning service, to which the admission was free, the performances consisted of "the grand Dettingen Te Deum, a manuscript Anthem, and the Coronation Anthem, all composed by the late Mr. Handel." In the evening "The Messiah" was given, "between the parts of which Master Charles Wesley performed a concerto on the organ." The vocalists and instrumentalists were ninety-one in number. "Tickets, 5s. 3d. each"; and the committee promised that the Cathedral should be "well-aired" for the occasion. The festival realised a profit of £100.

The progress of the quarrel between the American colonies and the mother country suspended the white slave trade, so long carried on under the name of emigration, to which repeated reference has been made. The latest record of the traffic has been found in the *New York Gazette* of May 10th, 1774, an advertisement notifying that a number of "servants" had just arrived, and were then for sale on board the Commerce, "amongst whom are a number of weavers, taylors, blacksmiths, masons, joiners, ... and spinsters from 14 to 35 years of age. Apply to ... the master, on board." A letter in the *Bristol Journal* about a fortnight earlier quotes the price of these imports at New York and Philadelphia at about £15 currency per head. The trade revived after the colonies had gained their independence. In November, 1800, William Cobbett, in his *Porcupine*, stated that he had personally seen a cargo of emigrants put up for sale at Wilmington, and treated as mere cattle, in 1793; adding that an Irishman offered him a little girl, seven years of age, for six guineas, her servitude to last until she reached twenty-one years. The child, with her sisters, was to be sold to pay for the passage of her sick, and therefore valueless, mother.

At a meeting of the Council on the 13th August, 1774, an order was made for the demolition of Froom Gate, Christmas Street, "in order to make the way there more commodious." A committee also reported that the removal of Small Street Gate would greatly improve the locality, and that certain inhabitants had offered to undertake the work, as well as to demolish some projecting tenements adjoining the barrier. On the recommendation of the committee, the Chamber voted £300 towards the estimated outlay of £500. (A further subscription of £50 was made in 1776.) Another street improvement was ordered three weeks later. A committee reported that Blind Steps, between Nicholas and Baldwin Streets, were very narrow, dark, and dangerous, and that it was desirable to make a better thoroughfare, by removing some old hovels and lofts, the property of the Corporation. The report was adopted, and orders were given for carrying out the work.

On the 29th August the rector and churchwardens of St. Michael's published a circular stating that the fabric of the church had been condemned by Mr. Thomas Patey, architect, as being in a ruinous condition. As it provided accommodation for only 550 persons out of an estimated population of 2,000, it was deemed inadvisable to repair the old structure, and Mr. Patey having reported that a "roomy, elegant, and commodious new church" could be erected for £1,800 or £2,000, the authorities solicited subscriptions to carry his suggestion into effect. The parishioners responded liberally to this appeal; the Corporation contributed £300 and the Merchants' Society £150; and, the fund soon amounting to £2,400, the old church, with the exception of the tower, was demolished in the spring of 1775. In the following July the foundation stone was laid of the new edifice, and the building—a striking specimen of the bad taste of the age—was finished at an outlay of £3,100. The church was reopened on the 22nd June, 1777.

The dissolution of Parliament in the autumn of 1774 brought about the most interesting election that ever took place in Bristol. Lord Clare and Mr. Brickdale offered themselves for re-election; but the Whig party was much discontented with the conduct of the former, who was charged with having become an obsequious supporter of the King's American policy; and Mr. Henry Cruger, by birth an American, and an advocate of conciliatory measures towards the colonies, came forward in opposition to the once popular peer. A meeting of Whigs was held on the 5th October, when Mr. Cruger's action was unanimously approved. Some of the more zealous opponents of American taxation being desirous that both the seats should be claimed, the name of Edmund Burke was brought forward by two influential Quakers, Joseph Harford and Richard Champion, but the proposal was disapproved by Mr. Cruger's friends, and was not pressed to a vote. Burke was then at Bath, awaiting the decision of the party. Upon learning the result, he proceeded to Malton, where he was returned without opposition. The formal nomination of candidates for Bristol took place on the 7th October, when Lord Clare, Mr. Brickdale, and Mr. Cruger presented themselves; and after about a dozen votes had been recorded for each, the proceedings were adjourned. Lord Clare, mortified by the discovery that his popularity was at an end, and that many of his former supporters were working zealously for Cruger, left the city in the evening, after intimating that he should not continue the contest. His retreat revived the hopes of Burke's friends, who held a hurried meeting in the middle of the night, drew up a letter to the great orator pressing him to return, and despatched a messenger with it to Malton. Polling on the 8th was practically suspended owing to the announcement of Lord Clare's determination and to the excitement caused by the prospect of another candidate, only twenty votes being tendered during the day. On the 10th (Monday) Burke was proposed by Richard Champion, in the midst of vehement protests by the friends of Brickdale, and the contest now fairly set in, the poll of the day being:—Cruger, 95; Burke, 71; Brickdale, 46. Mr. Burke reached Bristol from Malton in the afternoon of the 13th, after what was regarded as a break-neck journey of 270 miles in 44¼ hours. Upon his arrival he proceeded to the Guildhall, and was cordially received upon offering his services. He subsequently, for several successive days, addressed numerous meetings of the electors, until he lost his voice through hoarseness. Hannah More, hearing of his mishap, sent him a wreath of flowers with the following couplet attached, conveying her mediocre esteem of her fellow citizens:—

Great Edmund's hoarse, they say; the reason's clear,
Could Attic lungs respire Bœotian air?

The poll remained open 23 days, although the number of voters during the last week did not average much more than a hundred daily. At the close of the contest on the 2nd November, the numbers were:—for Mr. Cruger, 3,565; Mr. Burke, 2,707; Mr. Brickdale, 2,456; Lord Clare, 283. The formal declaration of the result was made on the 3rd; after which, says a local journal, "the members were carried through the principal streets in chairs richly ornamented, amidst an incredible number of people, whose acclamations were beyond everything of the kind that was ever seen or heard in this city." The bells were, however, silent, by express order of the clergy. A series of private entertainments followed. Burke, writing to his wife on the 8th November, said:—"I begin to breathe, but my visits are not half over. ...The dinners would never end. But we close the poll of engagements next Saturday"—(the 12th). Peculiar ideas as to freedom of election were then prevalent. Cruger's committee publicly thanked the mayor (C. Hotchkin) "for his great liberality in permitting the publicans in his ward to vote as they thought proper." The aldermen of six other wards voted for Brickdale; it is significant that no similar compliment was offered to them. Only two aldermen supported Burke and Cruger. Not a single beneficed clergyman in the city supported Burke, and only one did not vote against him. Upwards of 400 freemen were brought from London; one came from Guernsey, two from Ireland, and one is recorded as "John Lloyd, merchant, Charlestown, South Carolina." In addition to these, an immense number of men (nearly 2,100) were placed on the freemen's roll, the fees being paid by the committees of the rival candidates. The right of no small portion of these persons was derived from their having summarily married the daughters of freemen for the mere purpose of obtaining a vote, the newly-united couples often separating for ever on leaving the church. (One of the devices for divorce imagined by such couples was to stand on each side of a grave in the churchyard, and to separate after repeating the words "Death us do part.") The fees of these weddings were of course defrayed by the election agents. As the constituency was also copiously regaled throughout the contest, the gross outlay of the contending parties must have been enormous. Burke, in a letter to his wife's sister, stated that he had been returned at no expense to himself; but six years later, in a letter to Joseph Harford, he referred with "horror" to the burden he had entailed on his friends. Mr. Brickdale petitioned against the return, contending that the nomination of Burke after the poll had been opened was illegal, that great numbers had been allowed to vote whose freedoms had been granted after the issue of the writ, and that his defeat had been due to corruption. The last charge was withdrawn; the committee of the Commons decided that the post-nomination was valid; and as the petitioner's agents admitted that 772 of Brickdale's voters had been admitted freemen during the contest, the sitting members were declared duly elected. After the dismissal of the petition, Burke was requested to return to Bristol to take part in a triumphal procession, but he declined to neglect his "duty for such a foolish piece of pageantry." Cruger accepted the invitation, and on the 27th February, 1775, he was met at Keynsham by about a thousand citizens on horseback and fifty private carriages, and escorted amidst cheering crowds to his house in Great George Street, a gay triumphal arch being reared in the newly-opened Clare Street. The story that Mr. Cruger was so incapable of public speaking as to be forced to cry at the declaration of the poll, "I say ditto to Mr. Burke," is a silly fiction. Cruger, as senior member, was the first to return thanks, and made an appropriate address. He subsequently spoke so ably in the House of Commons on American affairs as to be complimented by his party leaders.

Shortly after the election, a satire was published entitled "The Consultation, A Mock Heroick Poem," written by James Thistlethwaite, who had served an apprenticeship to a stationer in Corn Street, and claimed to be a friend of

Chatterton. The author appears to have been utterly destitute of principle, but he was a not unskilful imitator of the style of Churchill, and excelled that master of invective in the vulgarity of his abuse. There are strong reasons for asserting that Thistlethwaite, after printing the book, in which upwards of a hundred Tory citizens were libelled, endeavoured to wring money out of his victims by offering to suppress it if he were compensated for his trouble. This trick meeting with slender success, the satire was published, and as personalities are always agreeable to certain minds, it had a rapid sale; and the slanderer jubilantly produced a second edition, with additional vituperation. A copy of the original pamphlet, annotated by Mr. Richard Smith, of gossipping fame, is in the Jefferies Collection. Some of the notes are amusing. Thus, in a reference to Sir Abraham Isaac Elton, the town clerk, Mr. Smith alleges that it was said the corporate functionary was all jaw and no law, while one Vernon, a contemporary local barrister, was described as all law and no jaw, and Rowles Scudamore, judge of the sheriff's court, neither law nor jaw. Speaking of Daniel Harson, collector of Customs, Smith says he was "formerly a dissenting minister"; while John Powell, who succeeded Harson, was "formerly a medical man on board a slave ship." As to Henry Burgum, the pewterer, to whom Thistlethwaite dedicated the satire in vilifying terms, the note-maker states that twenty men whom Burgum brought up to vote for Cruger and Burke were decorated by him with pewter hats. Thistlethwaite, who walked about "with the butt ends of two horse pistols peeping out of his coat pockets," produced another lampoon in 1775, styled "The Tories in the Dumps," savagely commenting on the failure of the election petition. The author afterwards removed to London, where he was for some years a hack to booksellers and law stationers.

A more agreeable literary souvenir of the election is to be found in Thompson's Life of Hannah More. During the contest a party of Cruger's friends halted before the house of the Mores in Park Street (next door to Cruger's) and gave "three cheers for Sappho"—whom some of the assisting mob imagined to be a new candidate. Burke was a frequent visitor at the house, and, when his success was assured, the Misses More sent him a cockade, adorned with myrtle, bay and laurel, and enriched with silver tassels, which Burke wore on being "chaired."

During the four weeks that Burke remained in Bristol, he was entertained by Mr. Joseph Smith, a merchant residing at 19, Queen Square, but paid occasional visits to Blaize Castle, then belonging to Mr. Thomas Farr, and to the house at Henbury to which Richard Champion had shortly before removed. Grateful for the kindness of the Smith family, the new member requested Champion to exert his utmost skill in the manufacture of a china tea-service for presentation to his host's wife. Champion was preparing a still more exquisite specimen of his art in the shape of a service destined for Mrs. Burke. The result was the production of works which, for the purity of the material and the splendour of the ornamentation, have never been surpassed. For an adequate description of the services the reader must be referred to Mr. Owen's "Ceramic Art in Bristol," pp. 95-98. The tea-pot of the Burke service was sold by auction in 1876 for £215 5s., a cup and saucer at the same time bringing £91— more than thrice the value of their weight in gold. The cream jug was sold for 115 guineas some years previously. The teapot of the Smith set was sold in 1876 for £74 10s., and a cup and saucer have realised £55.

A special meeting of the Council was held in November, for the purpose of passing a vote of thanks to Lord Clare for his lengthy services to the city, and for conferring the freedom upon Mr. Burke. Lord Clare, in responding to the compliment, boasted of his "dutiful attachment" to the king, and of his "inflexible resolution to co-operate in maintaining the sovereign authority of the legislature over the colonies." His lordship's devotion to the king and his policy was rewarded in 1776 by a further elevation in the peerage, the earldom of Nugent being bestowed upon him.

The Corporation, in December, voted a grant of £80 "to assist the inhabitants of Queen Square in removing the middle row of trees on each side of the square, and throwing the double walks there into one." At the same meeting, the Council resolved to give £20 yearly to a chaplain to the Infirmary, and the Rev. Thomas Johnes, the newly-elected city librarian, was nominated to this post also.

In 1774 the Jamaica legislature passed two Acts to restrict the trade in slaves. But the Bristol and Liverpool merchants petitioned the Government not to sanction the measures, and their appeal was successful. The colonists remonstrated, but the President of the Board of Trade replied that "we cannot allow the colonists to check or discourage in any degree a traffic so beneficial to the nation." In a History of Jamaica published in 1774, the author estimates that the yearly number of fresh slaves required to keep up the stock in the British plantations was 6,000, which at the prices of that day involved an outlay of £360,000. The value of negroes had doubled in the previous 15 years. It was the practice, he adds, of speculators to buy slaves, for the purpose of hiring them to poor or thriftless planters, who not only paid from £8 to £12 a year for them, but made good losses by death, the proprietors thus earning a profit of about 16 per cent.

According to calculations made in 1775, when the first blood was spilt in the war with the revolted colonies in America, the yearly value of the produce imported into England from the thirteen settlements before the struggle began was upwards of three millions, while that of the home manufactures taken by the colonists sufficed to balance the account. Of this great trade Bristol possessed a very considerable share, and the effects of the quarrel, long before the actual outbreak of hostilities, was painfully felt in many branches of business. From casual notices in the newspapers, it appears that a single firm in the city employed 400 hands in making serges for America, and that the manufacture came wholly to an end. Another house was accustomed to purchase every spring, for export across the Atlantic, 3,000 pieces of stuff made at Wiveliscombe, but the quantity fell in 1774 to 200 pieces, and afterwards to nothing. Until the quarrel arose, the tobacco-pipe makers of Bristol—a numerous body—each sent 500 or 600 boxes of pipes yearly to the colonies, but the exports ceased after 1774. These facts, though not very important in themselves, indicate the depression caused in many industries by the disruption. In January, 1775, before the last fatal measures of the Government had been taken, a meeting of merchants trading with America at all the chief ports was held in London, to remonstrate against the proceedings of the Ministry, and to petition for a repeal of the Acts prohibiting trade with the colonies. Petitions to a similar effect were forwarded by the Merchants' Society and a numerous body of Bristol citizens. The appeals, however, fell upon deaf ears; and within a few weeks 8,000 tons of shipping had to return from America unloaded, the blockade preventing them from landing their cargoes. The Bristol West India merchants joined with their brethren of Liverpool and London in holding another meeting in the metropolis, and a strong remonstrance was again adopted with practical unanimity. It was stated at this gathering that the amount of English capital invested in the West

Indies was 60 millions sterling; that 20,000 hogsheads of sugar were taken by the American settlements, besides 10,000 hogsheads of refined sugar from England; and that the West Indies were dependent on the revolted States for food and timber. No effect was produced on the Cabinet, or rather on the Crown, which persisted in its attempt to trample down the "rebels" and to realise the merchants' predictions of wide-spread commercial disaster. Mr. Baines, in his History of Liverpool, states that the condition of that town so greatly deteriorated during the war that "not less than 10,000 out of the 40,000 inhabitants became dependent on charity for their daily support." In Bristol the poor rates increased about 150 per cent., and great distress prevailed. The general depression, however, did not abate the determination of the influential local supporters of the Government to defend its policy. On the 18th September a memorial was addressed to the mayor by Thomas Tyndall, Michael Miller, John Vaughan, Slade Baker, and other leading Tories, asking him to summon the Council to address the King in support of the Ministerial policy. A meeting was accordingly convened for the 21st, but a quorum did not attend. The agitators then asked the mayor for the Guildhall to hold a public meeting, which took place on the 28th, when an address, expressing abhorrence of the rebellion and a wish for its forcible suppression, was adopted. Some opposition was manifested by American merchants and others, but a reporter notes that "numbers prevailed, and they were silenced." The address, which was signed by nearly all the local clergy and many merchants, was "very graciously" received by the king. An address praying for conciliatory measures was, however, drawn up by John Fisher Weare, Richard Champion, and others, and was numerously signed. A few weeks later Mr. Burke attempted to introduce a Bill into the Lower House to lay the grounds for reconciliation, but was defeated by an immense majority. During the autumn the Americans began to fit out privateers, which were soon preying upon English merchantmen in all parts of the Atlantic, and even on our own coasts. The step provoked measures of retaliation, and the energies of the two nations were vigorously devoted to the destruction of commerce through the remaining years of the war. The foreign trade of Bristol rapidly declined, until it sank to a small fraction of its previous dimensions. In 1775 the number of ships paying mayor's dues was 529; in 1781 it shrank to 191.

(This, however, was partially due to the refusals to pay the dues about to be recorded.) The African trade was virtually suspended, and the ships laid up. Even the number of privateers was insignificant as compared with the ships sent out in previous wars. In January, 1778, it was stated in the House of Lords that the number of British ships destroyed or taken by the enemy was 559, of a computed value of £1,800,000; that of the vessels thus lost (many of which belonged to Bristol), 247 were engaged in the West India trade; and that all imports from America had risen enormously in price—tobacco from 7½$d.$ to 2$s.$ 6$d.$ per lb., and other articles in proportion.

The extent of the Bristol postal establishment at this date is accidentally brought to light by a paragraph in the *Liverpool Advertiser* of February 17th, 1775. A memorial had been sent to the Postmasters General, complaining that there was only one letter-carrier for the delivery of all the letters received in Liverpool. The answer of the authorities was that only one letter-carrier was maintained in any provincial town, and that they did not think themselves justified in incurring for Liverpool the expense of another. An additional Bristol postman was, however, appointed previous to January, 1778.

A melancholy accident occurred on the 17th March to the Rev. Thomas Newnham, one of the minor canons of the Cathedral. The reverend gentleman, who was about 25 years of age, had gone with his sister and two friends to visit a singular cavern near Brentry, known as Pen Park Hole. Endeavouring to ascertain the depth of the cave, Mr. Newnham hung over the opening for the purpose of throwing down a line, when the small branch of an ash tree to which he was clinging suddenly broke, and he was precipitated to the bottom—nearly 200 feet—into a deep pool of water. Although repeated efforts were made to recover the body, it was not rescued until the 25th April.

A number of the inhabitants of St. Augustine's parish having offered to carry out the clauses of the Improvement Act of 1766 in reference to the removal of old houses standing on the Butts, or Quay, from opposite the end of Denmark Street to the end of Trinity Street, and to supplement this work by widening the narrow and dangerous road from St. Augustine's Back to College Green, the Common Council, on the 1st April, acceded to the proposal. The expense was estimated at £2,400, one third of which had been promised by the Merchant Venturers' Society; and the Corporation contributed the same amount. The improvement was completed in 1776.

At a meeting of the Council in April, 1775, a committee recommended the prosecution of all persons, "particularly members of this House," who had refused to pay the town dues, that is the local tax on goods imported and exported, payable to the Corporation. The report was confirmed, and actions were soon after commenced against Mr. William Miles and Mr. Henry Cruger, two leading merchants, who contended that the dues were illegal, and who both served the office of mayor whilst the matter at issue remained unsettled. In January, 1778, the defendants published an appeal to their fellow merchants in *Felix Farley's Journal*. "The fee in dispute," they wrote, "has within 50 years advanced more than treble, and still the body corporate are not satisfied, which growing evil necessarily alarms us, and is of such a nature that, if established, must put a stop in a great degree to the trade of the city." The writers requested the citizens to attend a meeting in the Guildhall during the following week, "to consider of a proper mode to resist this attack." No report of the gathering is to be found in the local journals, beyond the fact that Mr. Cruger presided and that Mr. Miles made a vigorous speech against the obnoxious burden. What pecuniary support they obtained from other merchants is unknown; but the civic records show that many firms refused to pay the dues. The Corporation seems to have been lethargic in pursuing the litigation, the actions not being brought to trial for more than twelve years. The matter excited much bitterness of feeling. A writer in *Felix Farley's Journal* of November 5th, 1785, asked, if Strafford was punished, "what punishment ought to fall on a Whig C—— in exercising a despotism under the pretence of prescription?"

The miserable condition of the unhappy people incarcerated in Newgate for non-payment of their debts led to the establishment of a local society for the relief of insolvent prisoners, a meeting of which was held on the 11th April The report stated that during the previous year 72 debtors had been released from gaol on payment by the society of £132 10s.—of which sum £32 12s. were demanded by the gaoler for fees. Many people were flung into prison for non-payment of only a few shillings, and, as they were compelled to provide their own food, some would have perished from hunger but for relief obtained from the charitable. The box provided for this purpose at the door of the gaol was, in seasons of extremity, carried about the city. On at least one occasion, this was turned to account by heartless knaves, complaint being made in the newspapers that through the hawking of "false boxes" the debtors had been defrauded of many donations. The "true gaol box" afterwards bore the name of the governor as a security against imposition.

The coaching enterprise of John Weeks, the landlord of the Bush inn, excited much attention at this period. In April, 1775, he advertised that "the original Bristol Diligence, or Flying Post Chaise," would thenceforth make the journey to London in sixteen hours—a feat which plunged old-fashioned travellers in equal astonishment and terror. The fare was 3d. a mile, and luggage was limited to 10lb. a head. The coaches carried only four passengers each. Soon afterwards, Weeks started a fast coach to Birmingham, setting off early in the morning and completing the journey in the evening. The owners of the two-days coach tried to beat their rival off the road by reducing their fares, but Weeks lowered his rates also, and gave his passengers a dinner, with wine, into the bargain. One-day coaches to Exeter and Oxford followed, and the Bush soon attained the first rank amongst local coaching houses.

Amongst the curiosities of English taxation, the duty levied in the last century upon starch is entitled to a place. In July, 1775, the excise officers discovered an illicit starch factory in St. James's Back, and brought the owner before the magistrates, who fined him £500 for breaking the law. The custom of powdering the hair with starch was universal amongst the upper and middle classes at this period, causing a great consumption.

A now very scarce work, in two volumes, styled "The Philosopher in Bristol," was published in July by George Routh, "printer, in the Maiden Tavern, Baldwin Street." The book, which is a collection of desultory essays, was from the pen of a singularly prolific writer, William Combe, born in this city in 1741, and supposed to have been the illegitimate son of a wealthy merchant. Educated at Eton and Oxford, with a handsome person and engaging manners, Combe studied with a view to becoming a barrister, but soon floated into fashionable society, and rapidly spent all his means. Falling into complete destitution, he was by turns a common soldier, a waiter at a Swansea inn, a cook at Douai College, and a private in the French army. In 1772 he was again in England, and, probably through the receipt of some legacy, he soon after mingled with the fashionable company at the Hot Well, amazing the public by his profuse mode of living, his couple of chariots, and his grand retinue of servants; from which he was commonly known as Count Combe. "The Philosopher in Bristol," one of his earliest works, must have been written during this blaze of magnificence. A comedy called "The Flattering Milliner," of which he was also the author, was played at the Bristol theatre on the 11th September, 1775. Having returned to London almost as poor as ever, he sought to gain a precarious living by literary labour, and produced a number of versified satires and other fugitive essays, which like all his works were published anonymously. In the eventful year 1789, when political discussions became a mania, he started as a party pamphleteer, and is alleged to have had no scruples in serving either camp. He gained, however, the favour of Mr. Pitt, and enjoyed a pension of £200 until the resignation of his patron. Later on he became one of the chief conductors of the *Times*. But although he was one of the few men of his age who totally abstained from intoxicants, his taste for extravagance was inveterate, and for the last forty years of his life he was compelled to live within the "rules" of King's Bench prison. His chief literary work was the "Tour of Dr. Syntax in Search of the Picturesque," which originally appeared in Ackermann's *Poetical Magazine*, and won its author both reputation and profit. Combe also wrote histories of Westminster Abbey, Oxford, and Cambridge, finely illustrated. The list of his works in the "Dictionary of Biography" enumerates eighty-six publications, besides which he is known to have written over two hundred biographical sketches, seventy-three sermons, and an immense quantity of fugitive articles. Mr. Combe, whose private life seems to have been far from creditable in despite of his religious professions, died at Lambeth on the 19th June, 1823, in his 82nd year, leaving no legitimate descendants.

An enterprising local shopkeeper, dealing in tea, china and glass, announced in a local paper of August 19th, 1775, that a stock of "silk and other umbrellas" was also on sale. An umbrella was then a great novelty. Southey's mother, born in 1752, stated that when she was a child, a person displaying one in Bristol would have been hooted by the populace. (So late as 1778, a footman who had brought one from Paris was followed by jeering crowds in the streets of

London.) £1 14s. was paid in 1785 for an umbrella "for the use of the Council House."

The old Assembly Room at St. Augustine's Back, having been taken on lease by Selina, Countess of Huntingdon, and fitted up at her expense as a chapel, was opened for divine service in August. Although the building was not consecrated, the Common Prayer Book was adopted, and the pulpit was supplied for several years by clergymen of the Church of England. The attendance was generally large, and many distinguished families, during their visits to the Hot Well, were accustomed to attend. Subsequently, a chapel at Clifton was thought desirable, and the building known as Hope Chapel, erected at the joint expense of Lady Henrietta Hope and Lady Glenorchy (neither of whom lived to see it completed), was opened on the 31st of August, 1788, "under the patronage of Lady Maxwell." The patroness seems to have been a lady of "exclusive" ideas, for a local journal of August 7th, 1790, eulogises "the Rev. Mr. Collins, for asserting so nobly the rights of the public" on the previous Sunday, by "ordering admission for the multitude, who are excluded from that place of worship, now devoted to mercenary purposes."

The Common Council, in December, granted a pension of £20 a year to the widow of Henry Casamajor, she being a daughter of Anthony Whitehead, a former member of the Chamber. A chaplain for Newgate was appointed at a salary of £35 a year. A subscription of 100 guineas was voted to the local movement for the relief of the troops engaged in America (the amount raised by the anti-American party for this purpose was about £2,000); and to denote more strongly the political views of the majority, the freedom of the city was conferred upon Lord North, the head of the Government responsible for driving the Americans into revolt. A similar compliment was paid to the Earl of Berkeley, lord lieutenant, and to the Duke of Beaufort.

The first Bristol Directory was published about the end of the year by James Sketchley, printer and auctioneer, 27, Small Street; who, it is said, not merely collected the names of all the upper class and commercial residents, but also numbered their dwellings throughout the city, and placed the figures on their doors for the consideration of one shilling per house. Copies of his book are so rare that it has escaped the attention of local historians. The commercial directory extends over 110 pages, and contains the names of about 4,400 citizens. A list of 167 merchants, filling six pages, is appended to facilitate reference to that class. The list of the Corporation is interesting as showing the localities still in good repute. Alderman Morgan Smith resided at 78, Lewin's Mead, and had as next door neighbour Alderman William Barnes. Alderman Jeremiah Ames lived in Maudlin Street, and Alderman Mugleworth in Orchard Street. Two others dwelt in Prince's Street, two in St. James's Square, one in Park Street, one at Clifton, and two were non-resident. Of the Common Council, one gentleman resided in the Old Market, one in Nicholas Street, one in Back Lane, St. Philip's, two in Maudlin Street, one in Dove Street, six in Queen Square, four in College Green, one at Clifton, and the rest in various localities. Sir Abraham Elton, Bart., town clerk, lived in St. James's Barton. Dr. Tucker, Dean of Gloucester, lived in Trenchard Lane, and other beneficed clergymen in Wilder and Culver Streets. One of the striking features of the directory is the number —nearly a hundred—of " ship captains " recorded as householders. The textile industries common at the beginning of the century had nearly disappeared, but the city was well supplied with gunsmiths and pewterers, a great many tobacco-pipe makers, four buckle makers, as many patten makers, two workers in horn, and scores of peruke makers. Two "limners" and a miniature painter were the only representatives of art, with the exception of a china painter. One tradesman described himself as a harpsichord and spinnet maker, another as organ builder, and a third as organ builder and harpsichord maker. There were two old book shops on St. James's Back. Only one commercial traveller, described as a "rider and bookkeeper," appears in the list. Some men cumulated trades: one was a gardener and schoolmaster, another a breeches and glue maker; a music-seller kept an alehouse in the Pithay, a ship captain relieved the tedium of life on shore by retailing beer and spirits, and John Cole, victualler and apothecary, invited patronage at the Pestle and Mortar, Prince Eugene Street. The most old-world tradesman in the Directory was Thomas Bennett, hour-glass maker, Wilder Street. About twenty distinctively French names, such as Daltera, Bonbonous, Laroche, and Peloquin, mark the Huguenot element in the population. Sketchley included Clifton in his work, but only 36 houses were numbered " on the hill " (Mr. Goldney's house being " No. 2 "), and the number of merchants residing there was no more than four. In some notes descriptive of

Bristol the author states that a survey of the city, Clifton, and Bedminster had shown the total number of houses to be 6,570 (exclusive of 348 unoccupied), with a population of 35,440. Similar surveys, he adds, had credited Birmingham with a population of 30,804, and Liverpool with 34,407. It is certain, however, that the population of Bristol was greatly underrated in this return. The next Bristol Directory—printed at Birmingham—was published in 1783, and was followed by local works dated 1785, 1787, and 1792.

An Act of Parliament was passed in 1776, " to remove the danger of fire amongst the ships in the port of Bristol," and for other purposes. The preamble recited that owing to the large importations of timber and other inflammable articles, the quays were often encumbered with such goods, and the danger of fire was much dreaded; that the Merchants' Company, to provide a remedy, had purchased certain (Champion's) docks at Clifton, and that it was desirable to enlarge these docks and erect warehouses for storing dangerous materials. The Act empowered the Company to carry out the works, prohibited timber, tar, etc., from being landed at the public quays, and permitted the customary dues to be collected at the docks. It being desirable that the property should be under civic jurisdiction, it was enacted that all that part of Clifton lying to the south of Hotwell Road (between " a little brook anciently called Woodwell Lake, but now a sluice carried under ground near a place where a lime-kiln stood...and a certain ferry called Rownham Passage "), should be separated from the county of Gloucester and become part of the city and county of Bristol; except as regarded local taxes and freeholders' votes at county elections.

In consequence of the complaints made by the parishioners of St. Nicholas of the inconvenience caused by the open markets on the Back, the Council, in April, 1776, gave orders for the erection (at a cost not exceeding £340) of a market house there, " for the sale of poultry, fruit, and other provisions brought from Wales."

On the 29th April, Dr. Johnson, whilst sojourning with the Thrales at Bath, paid a visit to Bristol, accompanied by his faithful companion and biographer, for the purpose of inquiring into the authenticity of the so-called Rowley Manuscripts produced by Chatterton, over which a fierce battle was then raging in the literary world. Johnson had never doubted that the boy poet was the author of the works, and only marvelled how the "young whelp" could have written them. The visitors were met at their inn by the steadfast Rowleian, George Catcott, who predicted to Boswell that he would make a convert of the doctor, but was doomed to disappointment. "We called," adds the biographer, "on Mr. Barrett, the surgeon, and saw some of the originals, as they were called, but...*we* were quite satisfied of the imposture." The enthusiastic Catcott, however, urged Dr. Johnson to visit St. Mary Redcliff, and inspect "with his own eyes the chest in which the manuscripts were found." In spite of his asthma, the lexicographer goodhumouredly toiled up to the old chamber over the north porch; but to the immense mortification of his guide, he remained as sceptical as before. Boswell's account of the Bristol visit is scanty and incomplete. The explanation is that he had a "tiff" with Hannah More whilst preparing his great work, and that he shabbily cancelled his account of the visit which Dr. Johnson paid to the Misses More. The visitors were much dissatisfied with the (unnamed) inn at which they stayed; Johnson jocularly describing it as so bad that Boswell wished himself in Scotland.

The open-air entertainments given during the summer season at "New Vauxhall," near the Hot Well, have been already noticed. In 1761 the garden was offered for sale in building sites, and visitors had thenceforth to content themselves with the in-door amusements offered in the evening at the two assembly rooms near Dowry Square. At length, on the 23rd May, 1776, a few enterprising persons opened another Vauxhall on an estate "formerly called the Red Cliff," and promised, in return for a moderate subscription, to give a grand concert every Monday and Thursday evening during the summer season. "Admission to non-subscribers, one shilling." Handel's "Acis and Galatea" was performed in the following August, when there was "a transparency on the bowling green." The place was extensively patronised at the outset, and occasioned the publication of a satirical poem entitled "A Trip to Vauxhall," professedly written by a Bristolian "lately returned from Madeira" to a friend in that island. The author begins by lamenting the degeneracy of the citizens. Scarcely a trace of the downright honest trading class, he says, remains; Folly has taken possession of all, and the modest shopkeepers that formerly contented themselves with decent bob-wigs now parade about with tails down their backs, like monkeys, while their wives, starched out in silk and lace, rattle along in fine coaches. As if a playhouse in the middle of the city did not offer sufficient scope for dissipation, a Vauxhall was opened by the limpid waters of the Avon.

> They have here furnished up an old family seat,
> And built a saloon, in length seventy-five feet.
> The gardens were luckily laid out before,
> So some lamps stuck about there now needed no more.
> Six days out of seven in business begun
> Is ended in jollity, feasting, and fun.

On Sundays, he continues, the vanity-stricken throng to College Green to display their fine dresses. The nights are given up to fine suppers, upon which tradesmen squander all their profits. After this denunciatory exordium, the author proceeds to describe his visit to Vauxhall, where he beholds a breeches maker defending his fair cheeks from the sun with a pink silk umbrella, and another shopkeeper, renowned for his drinking, mirth and sorg, swaggering

> With a large oaken stick, a slouch'd hat, and black stock,
> Cropt hair, leather breeches, and jockey-cut frock.

A drunken parson, a gouty alderman dubbed Turtle, and other personages receive similar irreverent treatment; the illuminations are ridiculed; and the voices of the singers are said to have been drowned by the uproar made by "the Bucks" in the neighbouring bowling-green. The satire can have had little effect on the fortunes of Vauxhall. The site, however, was inconvenient, as the garden could be reached from Clifton only by crossing the Avon (Vauxhall ferry still exists), and although the subscription concerts were continued in 1777, the speculation was soon after abandoned as unprofitable.

In the course of 1776 the rector of Christ Church, whose fixed income was only £25 or £30 a year, besought the vestry of the parish to contribute, out of the revenue derived from church lands, the sum of £100, which, with a similar subscription expected from the Corporation, would entitle him to a benefaction of £400 from Queen Anne's Bounty, and thus secure an increased rectorial income of £30 a year. The application having been refused, the rector was induced to enquire into his right to the meagre stipend granted him as a boon; and as his claim to a larger share of the estate seemed conclusive, and the vestry haughtily rejected his offers of accommodation, he filed a bill in Chancery in October, 1776. The cause was not heard until May, 1780, when judgment was given in the rector's favour. Finally, in June, 1782, to the great irritation of the parochial authorities, whose fund for feasting was much curtailed, the amount to be paid to the incumbent out of the church estate was fixed at £80 a year, the court also awarding him ten years' arrears. The suit cost the vestry £1,400 in law costs.

The Common Council, in December, granted a lease of upwards of an acre of ground, "part of Brandon Hill," to one Joseph Farrell, then building a house in Great George Street. The appropriation of this slice of public property excited no remark. In December, 1785, another lease of "part of Brandon Hill" was granted to Lowbridge Bright, then living in Great George Street. It is possible, however, that the two leases dealt with the same plot of ground.

In the year 1776, a woman, described as extremely young, of prepossessing appearance and graceful manners, but obviously of disordered intellect, entered a house at Flax Bourton, and asked for a little milk. After obtaining refreshment, she wandered about the fields, and finally took shelter under a haystack, where she remained three or four days. Some ladies in the vicinity having become acquainted with her condition, she was supplied with food, but neither solicitations nor threats induced her to sleep in a house, and as her mental derangement increased she was removed to St. Peter's Hospital in Bristol. How long she was detained there is unknown, but she regained her liberty in 1777 or 1778, and immediately returned to the stackyard at Bourton, where, strange to say, she remained nearly four years, receiving food from the neighbouring gentry, but obstinately refusing the protection of a roof, even in winter. Throughout this period, "Louisa," or "the Maid of the Haystack," as she was called, declined to give any account of her birthplace, parentage, or past life, though from casual remarks it was inferred that her family was of high distinction. A peculiar accent led observers to suppose that she was a foreigner, but there is no trustworthy evidence that she either spoke or understood any language except English. In 1781, the condition of the poor woman excited the interest of Miss Hannah More, who, with the assistance of friends, had her removed to a private lunatic asylum at Hanham; while the mystery of her antecedents was sought to be cleared up by the publication of "A Tale of Real Woe" in a London newspaper. Although no pains were spared to elicit information by publishing translations of this story in the chief towns of France and Germany, the results for some years were wholly negative. But in 1785

lace, rattle along in fine coaches.... French but probably
middle of the city did not offer... ...nce under the title of
tion, a Vauxhall was opene... According to the writer,
Avon. ...tions paid to her by the
...personages, was believed to be
...Emperor Francis I., had lived in a
...from 1765 to 1769; she had
...instance of the Empress, carried
...eventually conducted to the coast near
...were put into her hands, and she was
...wretched destiny." The purpose of the
...did not produce a vestige of evidence in
...story, was to identify the Bristol "Maid of
...with the alleged half-sister of the Queen of
...And in spite of the improbabilities surrounding
...assumptions (Louisa, for example, could not have been
...old when she was supposed to have set up a
...establishment at Bordeaux) Miss More and others
...to have firmly believed in the bare assertions of a
...libeller of the house of Austria, whose work was
...translated into English, and went through three editions.
In the meantime the alienation of Louisa degenerated into
helpless idiocy, and she was removed to a lunatic house connected with Guy's Hospital, London, where she died in December, 1800. Miss More continued to the last to contribute towards her maintenance, and paid the expenses of her funeral. The mystery surrounding the lunatic was never cleared up. The most probable supposition is that Louisa was of gipsy parentage, and had either escaped or been driven from her tribe.

A villainous scheme for destroying the shipping in the harbour was attempted on the morning of the 16th January, 1777. A vessel named the Savannah La Mar, loading for Jamaica, had been daubed during the night with pitch and other combustibles, and had finally been set on fire; but assistance being speedily at hand, the flames were extinguished before much damage was done. The Fame privateer and the ship Hibernia, lying at about an equal distance above and below the Savannah, had been also visited by the incendiary, but the fire he had lighted in each of them failed to communicate to the woodwork. The attempt was made at low water, when all the ships in port were aground, so that the devastation would have been immense had not the flames been suppressed at the outset. A few hours later, whilst the excitement caused by the affair was at its height, it was discovered that a warehouse occupied by Mr. James Morgan, druggist, Corn Street, had narrowly escaped destruction. The incendiary, after forcing an entrance into the building, had filled a large box with tow moistened with spirits of turpentine, and after placing it against some casks of oil, had applied a light to the materials. Through the dampness of the box, however, the match had failed in its purpose. Three days later (Sunday) a more successful attempt caused a general panic. Shortly before daybreak the warehouses of Messrs. Lewsley and Co., in Bell Lane, stored with Spanish wool, grain, etc., burst into flames, and in spite of vigorous exertions six buildings were destroyed in two or three hours. The premises had been fired by large torches, one of which, surrounded with inflammable material, was found when the firemen entered. Similar torches were picked up during the day in different parts of the city; and the sugar house of Alderman Barnes in Lewin's Mead was twice attempted to be destroyed by them. The inhabitants, now thoroughly alarmed, organised patrols in each parish, a rigorous watch being maintained day and night. "The town," as Champion wrote to Burke, "had the appearance of a siege, and people in general were frightened out of their senses." It is lamentable to add that political capital was sought to be made out of the matter by party fanatics. Tories, forgetting that some of the principal merchants were Americans, and that an American was the chief sufferer by the fire, taunted the Whigs with having instigated the outrages; while the latter as foolishly retorted that the whole affair was a factious manœuvre of the Ministerialists. Walpole alleges, moreover, that the Government was much less alarmed by the fires than ready to turn them into matter of clamour against the "rebels." A reward of 500 guineas, to which the king added £1,000, and Mr. Burke £50, was offered for the discovery of the incendiary, but for some weeks the mystery remained impenetrable. Suspicion was at length directed to a Scotchman who had lodged at various houses in the Pithay, but had suddenly disappeared; and a description of him having been circulated, he was arrested in Lancashire, where he had just committed a burglary. (The expenses of his apprehension, £128, were paid by the Corporation and the Merchants' Society.) On being taken to London, proofs were obtained (and in fact he ultimately confessed) that he was the man named James Aitken, *alias* Jack the Painter, who had set fire to the rope-house at Portsmouth dockyard in December, 1776. Being convicted of that crime at Hampshire assizes, he was hanged at Portsmouth on a gallows 67 feet high. In his confession Aitken stated that the Bristol fires were devised solely by himself, and that he had made several other attempts, but had been thwarted by the vigilance of the patrols. Although only 25 years of age, he acknowledged having committed many burglaries, robberies, and outrages. (An extraordinary popular delusion in reference to this criminal's head shows that legends can arise from malefactors as well as from saints. At the time of Aitken's execution, a warehouse was being erected in Quay Street by a mason named Rosser, who, having purchased part of the ruins of Keynsham Abbey, stuck a corbel thus obtained into the front of the new building. For some inexplicable reason, many people firmly believed that the ornament in question was the veritable skull of Jack the Painter. The error was not confined to the lower classes. On the illumination of the city on the king's recovery in 1789, *Sarah Farley's Journal* recorded as a " good thought " that " a light was affixed on the head of John the Painter," in Quay Street. The warehouse has since been rebuilt, and the fate of the corbel is unknown.)

On the 18th January, 1777, whilst the city was still panic stricken by the outrages, the Common Council resolved to present a congratulatory address to George III. on the success of his arms in America, expressing a hope that " the seeds of rebellion would speedily be eradicated." The Chamber was nearly equally divided on the American question. Previous attempts to forward a " loyal " address had been defeated by the inability of its promoters to obtain a quorum. On this occasion, according to a letter of Champion to Burke, two weak-kneed Whigs went over to the Ministerialists, and the address was voted by a House of 22 members, 20 being absent. The majority, which succeeded after a warm debate in carrying a similar address in Merchants' Hall, did not content itself with paper sympathy. The Council offered bounties to sailors volunteering into the Navy, and although the Corporation was embarrassed by a heavy and increasing debt, £592 were thus distributed in less than a year. In August, moreover, the freedom of the city was conferred on the Earls of Suffolk and Sandwich, two Ministers notorious for their rancorous hostility towards the colonists. This compliment was voted just after the Newfoundland trade had been lost to local merchants, and several ships had been captured in the English Channel by American privateers. Burke, in a letter to Champion, wrote:—"To choose the very moment of our scandalous situation as a season of compliment to Ministers seems to me the most surprising instance of insanity that ever was shewn out of the college [madhouse] of Moorfields."

The Bristol newspapers were much too timid to criticise, or even to record, the amusements of the fashionable company that assembled every summer at the Hot Well, but contented themselves with publishing a list of the aristocratic arrivals. In May, 1777, however, *Felix Farley's Journal*, prompted by some sarcastic visitor, startled its readers by publishing "Bon Ton Intelligence" from the healing fountain. One paragraph says:—"We are informed from the Hotwells that it is there the prevailing *ton* for gentlemen to go and drink the waters at the Pump-room with their nightcaps on; and that this innovation of the head-dress somewhat alarms the ladies." A fortnight later, under the same heading, appeared the following:—"We are informed that no considerable alteration in dress has taken place since the Revolution of the Nightcap, except the seemingly extravagant appendage of an extraordinary watch; as the gentlemen of the true *ton* wear one in each fob." (The wearing of two watches by young men of fashion was often noticed by contemporary caricaturists.) Another paragraph refers to some passing folly of the fair sex:—"The season at the Hotwells is now truly brilliant, but no considerable alteration in polite amusements has taken place, except that the ladies and gentlemen have formed a resolution of going to the balls undressed." This was the last quip of the *Journal's* "polite" contributor prior to his departure, and unfortunately he never reappeared.

Statistics showing the precise effects of the American war on local commerce are unfortunately unobtainable. That the decline in the shipping trade was very great is, however, beyond question. At a meeting of the Council, on the 16th August, a resolution was passed to the effect that, as the amount of the mayor's dues (40s. per vessel above 60 tons) had considerably fallen off during the previous year, as the expense of discharging the office of chief magistrate was considerable, and as the dignity of the Corporation was concerned in that office being duly supported, it was desirable that the mayor's income should not fall below £1,000. The chamberlain was accordingly ordered to pay Mr. Farr (mayor in 1775-6) such a sum as would raise his receipts from dues and fees to that amount. As the product of the dues was expected to fall off still more seriously in the current civic year, a similar order was made in favour of Mr. Pope, and also of future mayors. By another resolution, Messrs. Edward Brice and John Noble were ordered to be paid such sum, not exceeding £1,000, as the mayor and aldermen should consider proper, for having served as sheriffs a second time in 1775-6; and the allowance of each future sheriff was fixed at £420.

A carrier named Somerton surprised the city in October by announcing that his "flying wagons," carrying passengers and goods to London three times a week, would thenceforth accomplish the journey in forty-eight hours. Large bets were laid that the conditions would not be fulfilled, and there was much astonishment when Somerton carried out his pledge.

On the 30th October, during a gale, a windmill for grinding snuff on Clifton Down (on the site of the present Observatory) took fire, owing to the rapidity with which it was set in motion by the storm, and the building was gutted. No attempt was made to reconstruct the mill, which had been in existence only a few years.

Owing to the severe distress which prevailed amongst the poor at this time, highway robberies were extremely frequent. One evening during the autumn, the Birmingham coach was stopped within a hundred yards of Stoke's Croft by two footpads armed with blunderbusses, who robbed the passengers of about £5. The carriage of Mr. and Mrs. Trevelyan was attacked in Park Street, probably by the same thieves, and the inmates were stripped of their money and a gold watch. Highwaymen swarmed on all the great roads. A man eventually identified as John Caldwell, who kept the Ship tavern in Milk Street, and a companion robber named Edward Boulter, were so successful in their daring raids as to become for a time the terror of the western counties. Boulter had been previously sentenced to death for robbery, but pardoned on condition of entering the army. He soon deserted from his regiment, and concealed himself in the cellar of Caldwell's house, from whence he and his host, after having stolen two valuable horses near the city, sallied at intervals to prey upon travellers. Several marauding excursions, extending from Cheshire to Dorsetshire, were successful, and the plunder thus acquired was concealed in a deep hole made in Caldwell's cellar. Early in 1778 they were arrested in Birmingham, whilst trying to convert some of their spoil into cash, and were sent to

London for identification. Boulter, however, escaped from Clerkenwell prison, and had the audacity to return to Bristol, where he was soon after recaptured. At the summer assizes at Winchester, the two men were convicted of a robbery in Hampshire, for which they were executed at Winchester. Owing to confessions made by them before death, the police authorities in Bristol made a descent upon the Milk Street tavern, still occupied by Caldwell's wife. The hiding place must have been difficult to find, for the "sundry expenses" of the search, paid by the Corporation, amounted to £4. At length the hoard was brought to light, and several persons recovered their stolen watches and jewellery.

The dean and chapter, in December, 1777, granted leave to the Corporation "to erect a portico at the front door of the Mayor's Chapel," on payment of an acknowledgment of 2s. 6d. annually. A sham Gothic structure was accordingly erected by order of the Corporation in 1778, at a cost of £92 10s. 6d. The abortion was removed in 1888.

The respect of the capitular body for pluralism on the part of their servants is exemplified in a minute which follows the foregoing. It being reported that one of the singing men was parish clerk of St. Stephen's, whilst another held the same office in All Saints', the chapter ordered that one shilling weekly should be allowed to each of them, "to get a clerk to officiate for them every Sunday morning."

On the 19th January, 1778, a meeting of citizens approving of the Ministerial policy towards America was held in the Guildhall, the mayor (John Durbin) presiding, when a subscription was started "to strengthen the hands of the Government." Thirty-nine gentlemen subscribed £200 each, and the fund eventually amounted to upwards of £21,000. A meeting of the opposite party had been held a few days previously, Mr. Joseph Harford in the chair, to raise money for the relief of the numerous distressed Americans detained as prisoners of war; but the total sum subscribed amounted to under £363. The mayor's zeal on behalf of the king's coercive policy was promptly recognised, the honour of knighthood being conferred upon him before the end of the month. Burke, writing to Champion in April, asserted that the local subscription in support of the war had "made America abhor the name of Bristol." The promoters, after all their professions, were by no means so zealous as they wished the country to believe. According to an account published by their committee in May, 1779, only £4,668 of the fund had been expended (in obtaining 1,146 recruits for the army), and £758 were said to remain on hand. The residue of the subscription, £16,500, was not accounted for, and was in fact never paid up.

A cock-fight on the largest scale took place at the Ostrich inn, Durdham Down, in February, 1778, and was attended by great numbers of West country squires, the match having been arranged between the gentry of Somerset and Devon. Fifty-one birds contended on each side, for prizes amounting to about 350 guineas.

At a meeting of the Council in March, the freedom of the city was ordered to be forwarded to the Earl of Sussex, "he being entitled to the same by having married the daughter of a free burgess." The Bristol lady thus referred to was Mary, daughter of John Vaughan, goldsmith and banker. Lady Sussex died childless.

The mode in which ecclesiastical patronage was administered is illustrated by another minute made at the above meeting. The Bishop of Bristol had just conferred the vicarage of Almondsbury and also the rectory of Filton upon the Rev. John Davie, vicar of St. John's, and the recipient petitioned the Corporation to be permitted to retain his city incumbency, to which the Chamber at once consented. Mr. Davie, however, resigned it in the following year, on being presented to Henbury.

Early in April, Earl Nugent, the rejected representative of Bristol, gave notice in the House of Commons on behalf of the Government of a motion for considering the laws regulating the trade and commerce of Ireland. His views as to the impolicy of existing restrictions were immediately applauded by Mr. Burke. A few days later, Lord Nugent brought forward resolutions dealing with the subject, his chief proposals being that all goods produced in Ireland (woollens excepted) should be allowed to be exported to the colonies, and that colonial products (indigo and tobacco excepted) should be permitted to enter Ireland direct. Under regulations then in force Irish imports and exports had to be first landed in England. Permission to export Irish glass to foreign countries, and to import Irish cotton yarn into England were minor features of the scheme, to which Burke added a proposal that Irish sailcloth and cordage should be permitted to enter England. Although the resolutions were received with approval on both sides of the House, they excited a tempest of indignation amongst merchants and traders, and nowhere did the storm blow more fiercely than in Bristol, where the panic was as great as during the outrages of Jack the Painter. Lord Nugent's action in the matter was ascribed to a diabolical spite against the city on account of his rejection in 1774, whilst Burke was charged with a design to promote the interests of his native country by injuring those of England. The Corporation, the Society of Merchants, and the trading classes hastened to forward petitions to Parliament declaring that the proposed concessions to the Irish would have ruinous consequences to local commerce. The Common Council deputed two of its members to organise opposition against the scheme in the lobby of the House of Commons. No feature of the resolutions excited more passionate predictions of injury than did Burke's proposal to admit Irish sailcloth and ropes into England, although, as it was afterwards discovered, the prohibition of these imports had been abolished many years before. Every leading merchant who had supported Burke, with the exception of Richard Champion, seems to have been offended by his conduct, and some electors sent him positive orders to vote against the scheme in its future stages, whatever might be his private opinions. His replies to the Merchants'. Company and to some personal friends may be found in his correspondence. In spite of the clamour, he was more energetic in support of the measure than were the Ministers themselves. Indeed Lord North, quailing before the wrath of the Tory boroughs, gradually withdrew all the important provisions, until little was left of the original scheme save the clauses favouring Irish linens. In the spring of 1779, a Bill introduced to allow Ireland to import her own sugars excited renewed irritation in Bristol, whence a deputation was again sent by the Common Council, and Lord North delighted local merchants by procuring the rejection of the measure. In a few months, however, the scene changed. The islands of St. Vincent and Grenada were captured by the French, whose navy held the mastery of the English Channel; American privateers threatened Hull and Edinburgh; whilst the Irish, invited to prepare for defence against invasion, had raised an army of volunteers, and threatened to follow the example of the Americans unless their grievances were redressed. Covered with humiliation, Lord North, on the 13th December, offered to concede to Ireland full liberty to trade with all the colonies, to remove the restrictions on her glass trade, and, hardest sacrifice of all, to permit the export of her woollen manufactures. A Bill giving effect to this capitulation passed rapidly through Parliament, the opposition of Bristol and other ports becoming lukewarm when the measure was urged forward by the "king's friends." Burke's advocacy of free trade was not, however, forgotten by his constituents, and his dismissal at the next election was already practically certain.

A writ of inquiry was opened at Gloucester on the 9th April, 1778, to assess damages in an action brought by David Lewis, a Bristol merchant, against the mayor and Corporation. It appeared that the water bailiff had demanded illegal fees of the plaintiff, and that, on his refusal to pay them, his goods had been seized and sold by order of the Corporation. A verdict, with £50 damages and costs, was given for the complainant. About eighteen months later an action was tried at Gloucester assizes, Lewis being again the plaintiff, whilst the defendants were Sir John Durbin and other commissioners of the Court of Conscience. The ground of the action was the assault and imprisonment of Lewis after an illegal judgment delivered against him. For some inscrutable reason, the Corporation paid the damages and costs (£115) in this case also.

A frigate of 32 guns, the Medea, was launched from Hilhouse's dock on the 28th April. Ship-building for the navy had been so long suspended in Bristol that the *Journal* very erroneously asserted that this was "the first king's frigate ever built in this port." Four other frigates were then building in local yards.

After a slumber of forty years the question of establishing a Mansion-house was revived at a meeting of the Council on the 13th June. It was unanimously resolved that a committee of the whole Chamber should be appointed to consider "of the taking some convenient house to be constantly occupied and used as a Mayoralty House." On the 22nd August the committee advised that a mansion should be provided forthwith, and suggested that the house of Sir Abraham Isaac Elton, in St. James's Barton, together with the adjoining dwelling, would be most eligible for the purpose. Sir A. Elton had made an offer of his house for £1,500, and the committee recommended its acceptance, provided he would sell the other house for £500. The report was confirmed. For some unexplained reason, however, the Chamber abandoned its intention, and in December it voted £300 to Sir A. Elton, as compensation for breaking the agreement with him.

Mary Ann Peloquin, sister of David Peloquin (mayor 1751), and last survivor of one of the Huguenot families that took refuge in Bristol in the previous century, died on the 23rd July, 1778. By her will, the sum of £19,000, lent by her some years before to the Corporation, was devised to that body, in trust to pay the interest, at 3 per cent., in yearly doles to 156 poor men and women—chiefly to decayed freemen or their widows, not paupers, or keeping alehouses. The testatrix left to the rector of St. Stephen's for the time being the sum of £5 per annum, and her residence in Queen Square, to be used as a parsonage. Dr. Tucker, dean of Gloucester, then incumbent of St. Stephen's, forthwith removed from his house in Trenchard Street. Neither the rector nor the Corporation felt so much gratitude to the benefactress as to inscribe even her name upon the Peloquin monument in her parish church. (The omission was repaired by the churchwardens of St. Stephen's in 1892.)

Owing to commercial disasters caused by the quarrel with America, the picturesque estate of Blaize Castle came into the market in August, 1778. The property, about 110 acres in extent, had been purchased about sixteen years previously from Sir Jarrit Smith by Mr. Thomas Farr, merchant (mayor 1775-6), one of Burke's most zealous supporters. Mr. Farr spent several thousand pounds in laying out drives and walks, affording access to striking points of view, and in erecting a castellated building on an eminence commanding the Bristol Channel. The estate also comprised a windmill (the ruins of which still exist) held of the trustees of Henbury School, subject to the yearly payment "of £4, two turkeys, and a chine." The property was purchased by a gentleman named Skeate, who disposed of it a few years afterwards to Mr. John Scandrett Harford, by whom the mansion was rebuilt.

Mr. John Bull was elected mayor on the 15th September, but declined the office owing to illness, and the fine for refusal was remitted. This is said to have been the first time that a person elected mayor of Bristol repudiated the honour. Mr. Bull's action was anticipated, for the recorder's opinion had been previously taken as to the course to be pursued, several of the gentlemen who stood below Mr. Bull on the roll having positively declined to act until a Mansion-house was provided. It was pointed out that the charter of Anne required that a new mayor should be sworn-in by his predecessor, but supposing, as was probable, that the existing mayor could be induced to serve again, he obviously could not swear-in himself. The recorder eluded the difficulty by advising that, if Mr. Bull refused to serve, the Council should not proceed to a new election, but allow Sir John Durbin to continue in the performance of his functions. This course was adopted, Sir John retaining office for another twelvemonth.

The *Bristol Journal* of September 26th, 1778, contains the following list of privateers belonging to the port. The number of those vessels had largely increased during the year, in consequence of the alliance concluded by France with the Americans. The contrast presented by the list with the roll of 1756 (see p. 320) is highly significant.

	Guns.	Men.		Guns.	Men.
Lyon	32	180	Jackall	14	50
Vigilant	30	180	Hero	12	70
Lord Cardiff	20	150	True Briton	10	50
Old England	20	120	LETTERS OF MARQUE.		
Cato	18	120	Hercules	30	150
Rover	18	100	Levant	28	150
Ranger	18	100	Saville	20	80
Revenge	18	100	Chambers	20	80
Tartar	16	120	Britannia	18	60
Alexander	16	120	Ann	18	100
Valiant	16	50	Albion	16	70

With but two or three exceptions, the owners of the above vessels sustained disastrous losses. Only one important prize, in fact, was captured—a richly laden French East Indiaman, brought into Kingroad in September, 1778, by the Tartar and Alexander, and which, acccording to the *Bristol Journal*, had been insured by London underwriters for £100,000.—Great difficulty being encountered in reinforcing the troops in America, an Act was passed in 1779, by which able-bodied men who could not prove themselves to be exercising a lawful industry were liable to be impressed, and compelled to serve in the army for five years. The Government offered a bounty of three guineas a man for volunteers, to which the Corporation added a guinea to men joining in Bristol.

A minute of the proceedings of the Common Council on the 9th December affords testimony as to the family relations which existed between many members of the Chamber. A pension of £40 a year was voted to Rachel Hilhouse, widow of the late swordbearer, and grand-daughter of Alderman Barnes, deceased, "and being otherwise related to several other late as well as present members of this corporation." This remark appears to have been objected to as more true than felicitous, and the phrase was struck through with a pen. In August, 1780, a daughter of Alderman Barnes was also voted a pension of £40 a year.

The *Bristol Gazette* of December 24th reported that a journeyman shoemaker had just been publicly whipped in the market, having been convicted of substituting inferior leather for that given out to him by his employer.

In 1778, William Fry, a distiller in Redcliff Street, and several years churchwarden of the parish, erected an Almshouse, which he styled "The Mercy House," on Colston's Parade, for the reception of eight aged widows or spinsters. He subsequently endowed the institution with a yearly sum of about £50.

In February, 1779, during one of his visits to the city, John Howard inspected the French prisoners of war, detained in "a place which had been a pottery" (probably at Knowle). He found the arrangements better than those at Plymouth, the men, 151 in number, being at work. In March, 1782, Howard noted that a new prison had been built (at Fishponds). There was no chimney in the wards, which were very dirty, being never washed. The inmates consisted of 774 Spaniards and 13 Dutchmen. "Here was painted on a board that an open market is allowed from 10 to 3."

An Act of Parliament was passed in 1779 authorising the enclosure of that part of Kingswood situated within the parish of Stapleton—in other words the modern parish of Fishponds. The locality of the New Pools, as it was called in the Kingswood map of 1610, was inhabited chiefly by colliers and quarrymen, living in cottages built by themselves. The landowners, with a liberality unusual at the time, allotted half an acre of land to each of these squatters, who were thus encouraged to convert their mud huts into comfortable stone dwellings.

For many years after steam-engines had come into extensive use for mining purposes, their manufacturers were unable to devise any method of producing a circular motion in machinery except by pumping water on the floats of a water-wheel. On the 10th March, 1779, however, a patent was granted to Matthew Wasbrough, brass-founder, Narrow Wine Street (the place of his birth), for converting a reciprocal into a rotary motion by a combination of pulleys and wheels, one of the objects being to adopt the principle " for moving in a direct position any ship or vessel." The inventor had not brought his design into practical operation when, in August, 1780, another patent was obtained by one Pickard, who proposed to attain the same end by means of a crank; and Wasbrough, by an arrangement with the inventor, adopted the improvement. The famous engineer, James Watt, who disliked his Bristol rival in trade, vehemently asserted at the time that Pickard had stolen an idea which he was himself about to carry into execution ; but at a later period he admitted that the real inventor of the crank was the man who, in the infancy of civilisation, contrived the potter's wheel. The engines made down to this period had served only for pumping. By Pickard's ingenuity the steam-engine became capable of employment in a hundred other directions. In 1781 Wasbrough received an order from the Government to erect one of his engines for grinding flour at Deptford. Subsequently, however, the Navy Board asked the celebrated Smeaton for his advice as to the best engine for a flour mill, and upon his reporting that no rotary motion could ever produce such excellent results as those derived " from the regular efflux of water in turning a water wheel," the order to Wasbrough was countermanded. The distress caused by this disappointment, aggravated by bodily indisposition, and anxiety arising from pecuniary losses, threw the unfortunate mechanician into a fever, of which he died on the 21st October in the same year, aged 28. Previous to this unhappy termination of what had promised to be a brilliant career, Wasbrough had used one of the new engines for the purpose of driving the lathes in his manufactory; a second was set up in Birmingham, to the intense irritation of Watt ; and a third was made for the flour mill of Messrs Young and Co., in Lewin's Mead. In all of these he had introduced a "flywheel," in conformity with the specification of his patent of 1779. And although this important feature of an engine had been previously suggested by other projectors, Wasbrough is undoubtedly entitled to the merit of having been the first to bring it into practical use.

As two aldermen were noted in Sketchley's Directory as inhabiting Lewin's Mead in 1775, the fact that a high class boarding school for boys and girls was established in that thoroughfare can cause little surprise. The proprietor, a Quaker named Charles Sawyer, announced the reopening of the school after the (Easter) recess in *Sarah Farley's Journal* of April 3rd, 1779. The fee for boarders—who were taught the classical tongues, Hebrew, Spanish, French, and Italian —was 14 guineas per annum. Day boys and girls were instructed in the ordinary elements, with Latin or French, for 10s. a quarter, and they might have three months' dinners for 25s. a head. A superior school for " young gentlemen" was established about this date in Back Street.

A vacancy having occurred in the lesseeship of the theatre, a proposal was made to the proprietors by Mr. John Palmer, the manager of the Bath house, who will soon present himself as the great reformer of the postal system of his time. Palmer having undertaken to make important alterations in the building, the proprietors, in April, granted him a lease for twenty years, at £200 per annum, and gave up the first three years' rent as a contribution towards his intended outlay. "The future plan," says *Felix Farley's Journal*, "is to play once a week in the winter, three times a week part of the summer, and to have oratorios in Lent." The chief feature of the alterations was the erection over the centre of the dress circle of a second tier of boxes. The theatre was reopened in October, 1779, but Palmer's name does not re-appear, as he had confided the property to Messrs. Dimond and Keasberry, who held the management for several years. Six oratorios were produced during Lent, 1780, a guinea being charged for admission to the series. Two oratorios were also given in 1781 and 1782. From 1779 to 1781 Mrs. Siddons and her husband were members of the theatrical company throughout each season, and the gifted actress on one occasion performed the part of "Hamlet" with great success. Her salary is said to have been £3 a week.

The dearth of entertainments during the summer encouraged a roving company to open the old "hut at Jacob's Wells" for a short season. Dreading the law against "rogues and vagabonds," the conductors offered the traditional "concert" for the price of admission, adding a "Pantomime," rope-dancing, etc., gratis. Bristol pantomimes up to this date had always been given during the summer, and some of them were received with favour for three and even four successive years. The above performances closed the history of the Jacob's Wells house.

At a meeting of the Merchants' Society, June 26th, 1779, an address to the King was adopted, offering "the utmost assistance and support" to his Government in its policy towards America, and a subscription of £1,000 was voted to encourage enlistments in the forces. An amendment, introduced by Mr. Joseph Harford and Mr. Richard Bright, praying the king for a change of Ministry, was negatived by a majority of three. The Common Council was convened on the same day, in the hope that it would adopt similar resolutions, but a sympathetic quorum could not be obtained. At another gathering, a week later, when much dread prevailed of an invasion by the French, then masters of the Channel, Mr. G. Daubeny moved that the Chamber should subscribe £2,000 for the purpose of raising soldiers; but he was vigorously opposed by the Whigs, especially by Mr. Cruger, M.P., who asserted that the supporters of the war were convinced of its hopelessness. The motion was withdrawn by the friends of the Government to avoid the discredit of a defeat. On the 28th August, a public meeting was held to promote the formation of a volunteer corps. The movement met with slender support, but about the same time the anti-American committee reported that they had raised 1,306 men for the service of the Government. A new subscription was started to obtain 1,000 more infantry and marines, and about £2,000 were contributed. The local bounty paid to every able seaman entering the navy was 12 guineas.

Sailors, nevertheless, shunned the fleet, and the press-gangs were constantly on the alert to snap up victims. An impudent outrage occurred on the 12th July, in the Exchange, at the hour when merchants were accustomed to assemble; a press-gang entering the building and seizing Mr. James Caton, a retired ship captain and the owner of several vessels. The magistrates being set at defiance by the commander of the gang, application was made for a *habeas corpus*, which was granted, while Mr. Burke made remonstrances to the Admiralty. Mr. Caton, who was released in a few days, sued the officers of the press-gang for damages, and obtained a verdict for £150.

The sanitary advantages of sea-bathing appear to have been first urged by a London physician named Richard Russell, about 1750. For some years his converts were chiefly drawn from fashionable circles, but the pleasures and advantages of a change of air began to be recognised by all well-to-do people as soon as Weymouth was honoured by the patronage of George III. As that village was the nearest spot at which wealthy Bristolians could meet with clear water, it had been, even before the king's first visit, their favourite resort. At length an advertisement in *Felix Farley's Journal* announced that "the new Bristol and Weymouth Diligence, in one day," would begin to run twice a week on the 9th August, 1779. The service was of course suspended on the approach of winter. It was not until twenty years later that citizens thought of bathing in the troubled waters of the Bristol Channel. In April, 1797, an advertisement announced that Jane Biss and Son had fitted up two commodious houses at Uphill for the reception of families or single persons "for health or sea bathing." Weston-super-Mare was then a scanty hamlet of labourers' hovels. Minehead next attempted to attract visitors, a lodging-house being first announced there in 1800.

Coffee-houses lost their early popularity about this date. The once famous Foster's Coffee-house, the site of which is absorbed in the corporate buildings in Corn Street, ceased to be a place of entertainment in 1779, and was purchased by the Corporation in 1782 for £650. The London Coffee-house, in Corn Street, and probably others, disappeared about the same time, leaving no record in the newspapers. A victualler announced in August that he had taken the West India Coffee-house, fitted up commodious drinking rooms, and provided himself with an ample stock of liquors.

The newspapers of November, 1779, announced the arrival of "the surprising Irish Giant, only 19 years of age, yet measuring 8 feet high. To be seen at Mr. Safford's, watchmaker, Clare Street." O'Brien, the phenomenon in question, who attained a height of 8 feet 3 inches, visited the city annually at fair time, and eventually died at the Hotwells in September, 1806. His body was buried in the lobby of the Romanist chapel in Trenchard Street, in a grave cut 12 feet deep in the rock, and secured by iron bars, these precautions being taken to defeat the acquisitive intentions of certain local anatomists.

The price of tar having greatly increased owing to the American war, ingenuity was taxed to discover a substitute for an article indispensable to shipping. In *Sarah Farley's Journal* of April 29th, 1780," the family of a person deceased" offer for sale his invention of a method of making English tar, information respecting which was to be obtained of Mr. William Champion. Works were shortly afterwards established in the city for extracting tar from coal.

The financial condition of the Corporation for some years previous to this date had been one of increasing embarrassment. Permanent loans being not always obtainable, a custom grew up of borrowing on promissory notes; and in 1778 and 1779, to meet liabilities, some civic property was sold. In February, 1779, a loan of £1,500 was obtained from Alderman Pope. Repayment being called for in 1780, a number of ground rents and plots of building land were disposed of for £5,100, but little more than half the amount was applied to the liquidation of debt. Similar transactions took place in several subsequent years, yet the civic liabilities largely increased, in spite of the alienations of property. The increased receipts from town dues, towards the end of the century, at length arrested the Corporation in its downward course.

The No Popery riots which took place in London in June, 1780, produced some popular effervescence in Bristol. Great alarm was caused by an outbreak at Bath, where the Romanist chapel and five adjoining houses were burnt; and on the 10th June, on intelligence that a Bath mob was preparing to march westward, the Duke of Beaufort took the command of the Monmouthshire militia, then stationed here. The chapel in St. James's Back being threatened, a number of volunteers and constables were placed on guard until the danger had passed away, the magistrates sitting for several nights at the Council House. *F. Farley's Journal* of the 17th stated that "the proprietor of the Romish chapel in this city has taken part of it down in order to convert the building to another use, and also to remove any pretence of evil-disposed persons to destroy the same." The Corporation voted £105 for distribution amongst the militia men; and "sundry expenses on account of a threatened and expected riot" amounted to £85 12s. 5d.

The Common Council was convoked on the 15th August in consequence of the death of the mayor, Michael Miller, jun. Mr. John Bull was elected to fill the office for the few weeks that remained of the civic year.

At a meeting of the Council on the 23rd August, Mr. Joseph Smith, merchant (the host of Burke in 1774), was admitted a freeman on payment of a fine of £10. He was on the same day appointed a common councilman, and three weeks later he was elected sheriff. This method of "pitchforking" members subsequently became common.

At the above meeting Alderman Thomas Harris artfully introduced a scheme destined to make his name memorable. When pressed by financial difficulties, the Corporation had often found it convenient to borrow money from the revenues of Queen Elizabeth's Hospital, of which it was trustee. At this time £4,715 had been so appropriated, and £2,400 were due for interest on the bonds—some of them outstanding for 35 years—given for the loans. Mr. Harris's proposal, which was adopted, was that a committee should be appointed to examine as to whether any and what sum of money was due to the charity by the Chamber. The cause of what appeared to be an extraordinary motion was shortly after explained by the alderman. He had discovered that, soon after the death of John Carr, the founder of the school, the Corporation, in order to hasten its establishment, made advances of money, amounting to about £3,000, for the purpose of clearing off debts and legacies forming a prior charge on the estate. These advances, he alleged, had never been repaid, and by charging interest on the principal at rates varying from £10 to £3 per cent. per annum, the debt of the hospital to the Corporation was asserted to be £27,160. Mr. Harris did not mention that the Corporation, after speaking of those advances in the school charter, obtained from Queen Elizabeth, as money bestowed for charitable purposes, had, in 1600 and 1601, sold a large parcel of the hospital estates, for the purpose, as the minute books state, of paying off "all" the debts to which they were liable. The further fact that the Council had from time to time increased the number of scholars as the hospital income improved, and thus practically admitted that the charity was unencumbered, was also conveniently ignored. Mr. Harris's committee, accepting his statements and calculations, reported that the hospital was indebted to the Chamber in the large sum just mentioned, that the £4,715 drawn from the funds of the school should have been treated as instalments of debt repaid, and not as loans, and that consequently no interest was due upon the bonds. They further recommended a reduction in the number of boys in the school, so that its liabilities might be more speedily reduced. The report (signed by Wm. Miles, mayor, Thomas Harris, Nat. Foy, and others) was confirmed by the Council on the 4th August, 1781; when the bonds were ordered to be cancelled, and the number of scholars reduced to 36. The latter change was a practical violation of a pledge made by the Chamber to Edward Colston, in 1698, when the philanthropist endowed the hospital with an estate sufficient to educate six boys, upon the Corporation undertaking that not less than 36 scholars should in future be maintained. Subsequent to the donation of Colston, bequests had been made for the education of seven additional boys, so that either the pledge to him was broken or the later endowments were misappropriated. The pecuniary results of Mr. Harris's financial legerdemain were very agreeable to the Corporation. Instead of interest being paid on the £4,715 borrowed from the charity, £14,044 of the hospital income were appropriated between 1781 and 1820; at which latter date an account was presented to the Charity Commissioners, claiming £46,499 as still due from the school estate! The final explosion of this impudent claim is related in the Annals of the present century (p. 233).

A dissolution of Parliament took place in September, 1780, when Mr. Henry Cruger and Mr. Burke solicited reelection. An intention to oppose them had been announced in the previous spring by two staunch supporters of the king's American policy — Mr. Richard Combe, the candidate of 1768, who had just been appointed Treasurer of the Ordnance, and Mr. Matthew Brickdale, who sought to avenge his defeat in 1774. A contribution of £1,000 towards the election expenses of the Tory candidates was made, as will presently be shown, by George III. The issue of the contest, as regarded Burke, was foreseen by many of his friends. Lord Clare, during his long membership, paid court to the city during every recess, and made himself welcome to the lower class of voters by copious entertainments. Burke had been absent for four years, and his means did not permit him to treat the poor freemen. In despite of the indignation of the inhabitants, moreover, he had supported the repeal of the laws which crushed Irish commerce and manufactures to the profit of English shipowners and clothiers, and had assisted in passing the free trade measures of 1779. He had given offence to local shopkeepers, again, by ignoring their disapproval of a Bill affording some relief to the wretched people confined in prison for debt, and by speaking in its favour after they had petitioned against the measure. And Protestant feeling had been irritated by his avowed hostility to the political disqualifications imposed on Roman Catholics. The friends of Mr. Cruger consequently refused to coalesce with those of Burke, and maintained an attitude which indicated hostility rather than sympathy. It must be added that many of Burke's influential supporters in 1774 had been ruined by the suicidal rupture with America. In the face of these menacing circumstances, Burke on the 6th September met his supporters in the Guildhall, and uttered a vindicatory address, styled by one of his biographers the greatest speech ever delivered on an English hustings, in which he boldly challenged the approbation of the citizens for the very conduct they had disapproved. On the 8th, fixed for the formal nomination of candidates, Mr. Combe died suddenly at the house of a friend in College Green. His partisans thereupon nominated Sir Henry Lippincott, Bart., who, in right of his wife, represented the old Bristol families of Cann and Jefferis. On the following morning, Mr. Burke, in a brief speech, announced his withdrawal from the contest, having become convinced of its hopelessness. (His action was doubtless largely inspired by a desire to save his friends from the enormous expense of a contest.) The death of Mr. Combe was characteristically seized by the orator to point a lesson on the vanity of human passions. The fate of the lamented gentleman, he said, snatched away " while his desires were as warm and his hopes as eager as ours, has feelingly told us what shadows we are and what shadows we pursue." The poll continued open for nine days, although the issue was never in doubt. The sinister conduct of Mr. Cruger's committee was resented by many Whigs, more than a thousand of whom refused to record their votes, and Mr. Cruger withdrew on the 19th September, alleging that the majority against him was due to bribery and undue influence. At the declaration of the poll, on the 20th, the numbers were given as follows:—Mr. Brickdale, 2771; Sir H. Lippincott, 2518; Mr. Cruger, 1271; Mr. Samuel Peach, 788, Mr. Burke, 18. Mr. Peach, a wealthy linen-draper in Maryleport Street, had been nominated in the interest of his son-in-law, Cruger. Some of the ignorant freeman objecting to "plump" for that gentleman, Mr. Peach was set up to receive their second votes. The scurrilous Thistlethwaite seized the occasion to produce another local satire, entitled "Corruption, a Mock Heroick," but the work, although as virulent as its forerunners, was treated with deserved neglect. A placard was issued by the Crugerites soon after the election, professing to be a playbill of performances "for the benefit of a weak Administration." The assumed players in "All in the Wrong: or The Tories Distracted," include "Dupe, by Sir H. L—p—tt; Orator Mum, by Mr. B—k—le; Sir George Woodbe, by Mr. Da—b—ny (Daubeny); Counsellor Clodpate, by Mr. H—b—se (Hobhouse); and Judas Iscariott, by Mr. F—y (Foy)." "End of the Second Act, an Interlude, intitled The Poll Books, or a new method of securing a Majority. The part of Close 'em by Sir Henry Laughing Stock, from the Theatre at Gloucester. This is reckoned the first exhibition of the kind, and for his peculiar excellence therein the Performer was rewarded with a Title." Lippincott was sheriff of Gloucestershire in 1776-7, during a fierce bye-election, in which he was charged with partiality. He was created a baronet in 1778, and as his only known merit lay in his adherence to the "king's friends," the sarcasm of the Crugerites was not without plausible foundation.

At a meeting of the Council in October, an offer was made, on behalf of the vestry of All Saints' parish, to take down the Merchants' Tolzey, opposite the Council House, and to rebuild "the late London Coffee-house," at the east angle of the Exchange, in a style similar to that of the Post Office at the western corner (by which improvement Corn Street would be widened 5½ feet), provided the Corporation would subscribe £400 towards the outlay, and grant a lease of certain rooms, "formerly the Exchange Tavern," at a rent of £100. The Chamber consented to both conditions. The plan involved the removal of the cistern of All Saints' Conduit, which was to be placed on the first floor of the new house, while the fountain itself was removed from Corn Street into All Saints' Lane.

Sir Henry Lippincott, Bart., M.P., whose election has just been recorded, died on the 1st January, 1781. On the following day, the Union (Whig) club addressed a letter to the Constitutional club of their opponents, proposing that an agreement should be made for dividing the representation between the two parties, and so restoring "peace and good neighbourhood"; but the Tories, assured of pecuniary assistance from the Crown, and counting upon continued discord in their enemies' camp, declined to comply. Their foresight was justified by events. The friends of Burke, although he had been elected for Malton, were anxious to reinstate him in his former seat; but the chief supporters of Cruger declared that unless that gentleman was promised the representation of Malton, they would bring another candidate forward for Bristol, and spare neither money nor labour to defeat Mr. Burke. A few days later, Mr. Cruger took the field, while Mr. George Daubeny was selected by the Ministerial party, and obtained, as will presently be seen, the approval of George III. The contest was of a virulent character, the Tories expatiating on the fact that Mr. Cruger was a "foreigner" (he was a native of New York) whose sympathies were wholly with the "rebels"; whilst it was alleged by the other camp that Mr. Daubeny and some of his prominent friends had openly avowed sympathy with the Jacobites during the rebellion of 1745. Both parties squandered large sums in "entertaining" the electors. One of Daubeny's handbills invited "all true Britons" to a dinner at the Full Moon inn, Stoke's Croft, "to try the difference between American bull beef and the roast beef of Old

England," and "to drink a health to the Friend of the King and the Constitution." In retort the Crugerites assured the freemen that "without Cruger we should have had no beef nor ale," their placard concluding with "A large loaf, a full pot, and Cruger for ever." Many collisions occurred in the streets between the hired mobs of the two parties, and it was alleged by the Crugerites that the press-gang was under the orders, if not in the pay, of their antagonists. The election, which began on the 31st January, was not concluded until the 24th February, when the poll was declared to be: for Mr. Daubeny, 3143; for Mr. Cruger, 2771. A deadly affray marked the close of the contest. A party of Crugerites, passing along the quays, took offence at some flags displayed by a Swansea vessel, and ordered the crew to lower them. The demand being accompanied by some stone-throwing, the sailors fired several swivel guns upon the crowd, killing two men instantly, and wounding many other persons, including three children. The verdict of the coroner's jury on the bodies of the victims was "justifiable homicide"; but there is in Temple churchyard an inscription to their memory, alleging that they were "inhumanly murdered" by three men, whose names appear on the tombstone. Mr. Cruger petitioned against the return, but his case was ultimately withdrawn.

A singular proof of the manner in which employers considered themselves entitled to deal with their workmen at election times is unconsciously revealed in an abusive letter addressed to Mr. Cruger by an opponent, in one of the Tory journals. The writer says:—"At the election in 1774 you ruined so many of the labouring freemen by inveigling them to vote in opposition to their masters, and you were so constantly teased with the cries of their wives and children, that you removed from Park Street to Weston, near Bath, to prevent their craving solicitations from reaching your ears. You are now again spiriting up the journeymen freemen to disoblige their masters, and thereby to reduce them and their families to the same miserable situation." The writer's inability to perceive the discredit he was heaping upon his friends is both amusing and edifying. Party spirit raged at this period with almost unexampled virulence. Mr. R. Smith states that many men regarded their political opponents as personal enemies, and that candidates for vacancies in the Infirmary staff had no chance of success unless they had the approval of the Tory club at the White Lion (Smith MSS.).

The assistance rendered by George III. to Mr. Daubeny, as a supporter of his American policy, was first brought to light by the publication of the king's letters to Lord North. Additional evidence has been produced by the Historical MSS. Commission (10th Report). The king, it appears, had an election manager in the person of Mr. John Robinson, Secretary to the Treasury, for whom he reserved £20,000 yearly to aid suitable candidates. The Premier, Lord North, in a letter to Robinson, dated April 13th, 1781, says: —"I suppose we must comply with the requests of Lord Sheffield [then contesting Coventry] and Mr. Daubeny . . . I suppose the following sums will do. Lord S. £2000, Mr. D. £1500, being £500 more than he asked for at first. But perhaps Mr. D. will not be satisfied, and it will be necessary to give him more. The demands on this occasion are exorbitant beyond the example of any former time." As it turned out, Mr. Daubeny was so far from being satisfied with £1,500 that he applied for £5,000 from the royal bounty, and actually got them. Lord North, in sending the king an account of election charges just paid (in addition to the above they included £2,000 for Gloucestershire), pleaded that "only £1000" had been sent to Bristol at the general election, and that the Tory merchants, having contributed largely on that occasion, "as well as to many loyal subscriptions," had thought it not improper to ask for help in the second contest. Lord North's letter shows that the king's outlay for the promotion of electoral corruption had reached in a few months to about £63,000, exclusive of two pensions amounting to £1,500 a year.

The Arethusa, a 44 gun frigate, one of five war vessels then being built on the Avon, was launched on the 10th April, 1781. The Arethusa for many years enjoyed a special popularity amongst Bristolians.

On the death, in April, 1781, of the Rev. Carew Reynell, minister of Redland Chapel, an unexpected dispute arose respecting the patronage attached to the building. Mr. Cossins, who built and endowed the chapel, and added a handsome house for the chaplain, appointed the first incumbent, and subsequent vacancies had been filled by his representatives, one of whom, Mr. John Innys, his brother-in-law, devised the chapel and advowson to Mr. Jeremy Baker, who appointed Reynell, and now proposed to select his successor. The chapel, however, had never been consecrated, and the Hon. Henry Fane, the patron of Westbury, in which parish it was situated, in conjunction with the Rev. John Whetham, incumbent of the parish, refused to permit Baker's nominee to officiate. The chapel was accordingly closed, and the yearly income was transferred to the Infirmary, in accordance with Mr. Cossins's foundation deeds. Several years elapsed before further steps were taken. At length, Mr. Samuel Edwards, of Cotham Lodge, a friend of Baker's, purchased the advowson of Westbury, and Whetham was induced, no doubt for a satisfactory consideration, to resign the living. The new patron then nominated his nephew, the Rev. Wm. Embury Edwards, to the incumbency, and Mr. Baker presented the same person to Redland. And as it was clear that the incumbent of Westbury could at any future time prevent a minister from officiating in the latter building, it was agreed between the two patrons that the advowson of the chapel should be annexed to that of the parish, and that the nomination to both should be exercised alternately by themselves and their heirs, trustees being appointed to carry out the compact. Manuscripts narrating the above facts are preserved in the Consistory Court. Petition was next made to the Bishop for the consecration of the chapel and burial ground, and the ceremony took place on the 12th November, 1790. [The account of this dispute by the author of the Chronological History is a pure fiction.] Whetham, through the influence of the Fane family, was appointed Dean of Lismore in 1791.

At the Gloucestershire summer assizes in 1781, an action brought at the instance of the Society of Merchants against the lessee of the Hot Well, who had imposed a charge upon Bristolians taking water from the spring, contrary to the conditions of his lease, came on for trial, and resulted in a verdict for the plaintiff. It will afterwards be shown, however, that upon the lease being renewed at a greatly increased rent, the occupier was allowed to resume exactions on the local public, and raised at the same time the charges imposed on visitors, with disastrous effects on the popularity of the Well.

The long pending design of establishing a civic Mansion House was definitively approved at a corporate gathering on the 4th August, 1781. The Chamber, which had that day adopted Alderman Harris's scheme for despoiling Queen Elizabeth's Hospital, resolved, "unanimously, that a messuage in Queen Square in the occupation of Mr. James Harford be forthwith purchased at the price of £1,350, in order that the same may be used as a Mayoralty House." The house in question—standing at the eastern end of the north row—

belonged to Miss Susanna Calwell, by whom it was let at £105 per annum. It was originally built by Alderman Shuter (mayor, 1711). A committee was appointed to conclude the purchase, and to arrange for the suitable furnishing of the house. Possession, however, was not obtained until March, 1783, and the alterations were conducted with extreme deliberation, £800 being spent in 1784 and £1,600 in 1785. The work of furnishing followed. The Council was at first in an economical mood, and restricted the furnishing committee to an outlay of £800. An additional sum of £350 was voted to supply the great room with chandeliers, etc.; and in August, 1786, the chamberlain was ordered to pay further charges incurred by the reckless committee, amounting to £3,400 (including £20 8s. 8d. for "crown glass for the windows in the Great Room," £1 16s. for an umbrella, and £4 for a "large turtle tubb"). Whilst this outlay was going on, the Corporation was compelled to sell property to the value of £3,500, and to increase the city debt by nearly £6,300, in order to meet its expenditure. The Mansion House was occupied in the spring of 1786, when the scavenging authorities, desirous of getting a little profit out of the institution, raised the assessed value of the house from £70 to £400. On appeal, however, the rating was reduced to £90.

A maltster, named Joseph George Pedley, was the subject of much local objurgation about this period. According to his creditors, he raised about £10,000 by means of fraudulent representations, secreted a large portion of the money, and sought to conceal his knavery by setting fire to his premises in Little King Street, the books and papers in which were destroyed. Being declared a bankrupt, and suspected of arson, he was committed to Newgate, from which he escaped, but was again captured at Newcastle. A second attempt to break out of Newgate was detected and foiled. On a third occasion he filed through heavy fetters, and broke through the floor of his cell, but was unable to escape from the room below. At length he confessed that he had concealed upwards of £2,500 of his plunder in the western suburbs, and *Felix Farley's Journal* of the 24th Sept., 1781, announced that £1,000 in notes were found buried near "Tinkers' place," Tyndall's Park, and 600 or 700 guineas near Gallows Acre Lane. The prisoner, who guided the searchers to the latter hoard, alleged that a third had been rifled. In April, 1782, Pedley was found guilty of destroying his house; but on the indictment being laid before the judges they declared that the law did not prohibit the lessee of a dwelling from setting fire to it. The rogue was then committed for burning the adjoining houses. After lying in prison for more than a year, he was acquitted of this charge in May, 1783. His liberation as an insolvent did not take place until June, 1785. He was then immured for defalcations under the excise laws; and Mr. R. Smith saw him in the King's Bench prison in 1794, keeping a coal-shed. He was released only by death.

Sarah Farley's Journal of February 2nd, 1782, contains an advertisement offering the "Enterprise of the Bristol Water Works Company to be sold or let." No adventurer coming forward to continue the undertaking, the service of water was soon after discontinued.

The wasteful system under which the Customs department was administered is illustrated by a letter from George III. to Lord North, dated February 11th. The king requests the Prime Minister to nominate Mr. Barnard, the royal librarian, to a sinecure employment of either comptroller or collector of the Custom-house at Bristol, held for above forty years by a Mr. Bowman, just dead at Egham. His Majesty habitually relieved the Civil List from pensions to dependents by throwing them in this manner on the ordinary revenue. Owing to the destruction of the Custom-house archives in 1831, the result of the king's letter cannot be discovered.

The killing of a refractory Spaniard by a sentinel in March, 1782, occasions the first mention in the local press of the Government buildings at Fishponds for the safe custody of prisoners of war. The place became so extensive that an engraved view of it was published in the *Gentleman's Magazine* (vol. 84). Relics of the prison—converted into a workhouse for the Bristol Union in 1833—may still be seen.

By this time the country had become weary of the inglorious war against the revolted Americans which the Prime Minister was waging, against his own judgment, in deference to George III. Early in 1782, the Corporation of Bristol, repudiating its former sympathy with the Government, unanimously addressed a petition to the House of Commons against the further continuance of the contest, and prayed the House " to advise the King to a total change of the unhappy system which has involved the nation in such complicated misfortunes." A similar petition was adopted at a public meeting of the citizens in the Guildhall. On the 27th February, on the motion of General Conway, an Address, in which the above sentiments were practically embodied, was carried in the House of Commons, and three weeks later the Ministry resigned. At a meeting of the Common Council in April (17 members being absent), it was resolved to present the freedom of the city to General Conway for his exertions to hasten peace, and a similar compliment was paid to eight members of the new Rockingham Ministry. A vote of thanks was also passed to Burke for his great scheme of economical reform. A deputation of five gentlemen set off for London to convey these compliments, and were paid £92 for the expenses of their journey. About the same time, the war with France was marked with a naval triumph that flung Bristol into transports of joy. Five of the English plantations in the West Indies had been captured by the French, and as a commanding fleet under De Grasse was cruising in the neighbourhood, awaiting the junction of a Spanish flotilla, the loss of Jamaica was deemed only too probable. At this critical moment Admiral Rodney challenged the French navy to combat, and on the 12th April a desperate battle resulted in a decisive English victory. Intelligence of this great event arrived in Bristol on the 18th May, and as the fortunes of many wealthy citizens were involved in the fate of Jamaica, the demonstrations of joy were universal. In September, Rodney, who had won a peerage by his success, disembarked at Kingroad, and, on the invitation of Mr. Tyndall, spent a night at the Royal Fort. The only token of rejoicing that could be improvised was a torchlight procession of several hundred citizens, in which a prominent figure was John Weeks, of the Bush inn, who kept open house in honour of the occasion, and distributed liquor gratuitously to the assembled populace. Lord Rodney, in thanking the citizens for the demonstration, promised to return; and when he did so, on the 15th November, he met with a reception never before accorded to a subject. On reaching Totterdown he was welcomed by the sheriffs in a laudatory address, to which he briefly replied. An imposing procession was then organised. Equestrians and private carriages, forming a long line, were headed by a figure of Britannia, "supported by four javelin men," seated in a car drawn by six horses, the drivers in the dress of sailors. Representatives of Mars and Minerva followed in similar state, together with three boats placed upon wheels, accommodating bands of music embowered in laurels, while from a ship of 40 tons burden, also on a carriage drawn by horses, the crew fired at intervals salutes from swivel guns.

Flags, insignia, and trophies of every kind added additional variety to the scene. The cavalcade passed through the principal streets to the Merchants' Hall, where the distinguished guest, before sitting down to a grand dinner, was presented with the freedom of the company. The day concluded with a general illumination. John Weeks, who was the leading spirit in preparing the manifestations, afterwards boasted that they had cost him £447. On this account, perhaps, Weeks " claimed the honour " of becoming one of Lord Rodney's postboys, on his departure next morning for Bath. This was the last local incident of note in connection with the war. The formal proclamation of peace took place on the 13th October, 1783, with the usual formalities.

An advertisement in *Felix Farley's Journal* of May 25th, 1782, affords a final glimpse of the famous Bristol China works of Richard Champion :—"Now selling, by hand, at the late manufactory in Castle Green, the remaining stock of Euamel Blue and White, and White Bristol China. The manufactory being removed into the north."

At a meeting of the Common Council in May, a proposal of the St. Stephen's Improvement trustees was produced, offering to widen the thoroughfare on the Quay, near the church, from twenty-four to forty-four feet, provided the Corporation surrendered the site of the Fish-market. The Chamber accepted the terms; and gave orders for the removal of the market to a site between Nicholas and Baldwin Streets. The purchase of the required land, however, was not effected until 1786, and the retail dealers in fish long resorted to St. James's market.

At another meeting, in December, the Council resolved to present the freedom of the city to Lord Rodney for "his glorious and decisive victory, which saved Jamaica from an attack, and protected in an eminent degree the commercial interests of this city." It seems strange that the Chamber did not discover this when Lord Rodney was in Bristol. The freedom was also voted to Lord Howe for his gallant relief of Gibraltar, and a similar compliment was paid in 1783 to Lord Hood " for his important services."

In December, 1782, a patent was granted to a Bristol plumber named William Watts, for his newly invented process for the manufacture of shot. The invention (said to have been inspired by a dream) consisted in causing the liquid lead to fall from a considerable height, the metal assuming a spherical form in the air. Watts constructed a "shot-tower" on Redcliff Hill, and his products soon acquired celebrity. A local journal of December, 1786, announced that the inventor was about to extend his works by building a new Gothic tower, which, with the old one, was expected to remind a spectator of "the prospect of Westminster Abbey." In a few years Watts amassed about £10,000, which he invested in an unlucky building speculation at Clifton—the construction of Windsor Terrace. Owing to a peculiarity of the strata, the whole of the owner's capital was sunk in securing the foundation of the house overlooking the Avon, and in October, 1792, the building was advertised for sale in an unfinished state. In February, 1794, Watts was declared a bankrupt, and lost his interest in a discovery by which others made ample fortunes. In September, 1794, it was announced that the manufactory on Redcliff Hill would thenceforth be carried on by "Philip George and Patent Shot Company." No later reference to Watts has been found. The statement made in some local works that he became a hosier in High Street is incorrect.

The civic accounts for March, 1783, record the payment of £3 17s. 11d. to a messenger despatched into Herefordshire to obtain the signature of Alderman Durbin to a number of corporate leases. A similar item occurs in 1784. The alderman, repudiating the duties of his office, which included a daily supervision of the constables of his ward, had taken up his residence near Hereford, and refused to resign his gown. His example was followed by other aldermen, nearly all of whom had ceased to reside in the city in the later days of the unreformed Corporation.

The spring of 1783 was a period of great distress amongst the poor owing to the high price of food. One of its consequences was a series of disorders, extending over three days, amongst the sailors of the port, who complained that their families could not subsist upon their earnings. The mayor at length allayed the discontent by promising to recommend the shipowners to pay 30s. a month to each man when at sea, and half that sum when in Kingroad. A few days later, the felons confined in Newgate prayed for relief through the newspapers, stating that they had nothing to live upon saving twopence a day. Untried prisoners received only a penny daily, and many must have starved but for the relief offered by the public. The misery caused by the dearth led to a frightful increase of crime, especially of burglaries and highway robberies. No protection being afforded to the new suburb of Kingsdown, the inhabitants, in April, advertised for " a few able-bodied young men, to be employed as a nightly patrole" in that locality. This watch was continued, at intervals, for several years. The inhabitants of College Green were also compelled to take special measures against footpads and burglars, and in March, 1790, the dean and chapter gave them permission to erect a watch-box in the middle of the green "for their safety and protection."

The Common Council, in May, presented the freedom of the city to the Earl of Surrey, son and eventually successor to the tenth Duke of Norfolk. His lordship took much interest in West Country affairs, and was thrice mayor of Gloucester. For the honour conferred upon him in Bristol he was indebted to his Whig politics, and to his fame as a gastronomist.

The Council, at the above meeting, admitted Mr. Thomas Daniel, jun., as a freeman on the payment of a fine of 12 guineas. Mr. Daniel was in 1785 elected a common councillor, was chosen mayor in 1796, and eventually became the famous alderman who, from his complete omnipotence in corporate affairs, was sometimes called King of Bristol.

A subscription on the tontine principle was started in July for completing a range of warehouses near St. Stephen's church, which the parochial trustees had begun, but were unable to finish. The number of subscribers was 195, and the estate was to be divided amongst the last survivors. (The final division did not take place until about 1850.) In March, 1784, an attempt was made to form a tontine for the building of houses in Great George Street, near Brandon Hill, but the scheme was unsuccessful.

The curious brass pillars in front of the Exchange once formed only a part of a numerous collection. The city chamberlain, in September, 1783, debits himself with £12 17s. 6d., "received for the metal tops of the ancient pillars removed from All Saints' Penthouse, and the Bridgwater slip on the Back." Immediately afterwards, 17s. 6d. is obtained "for the top of a small pillar" removed from the former place. In 1784, there was a receipt of £8 6s. "for a pot metal pillar and cap, taken down under the Tolsey;" and £8 13s. 4d. was obtained in 1795 "for the cap or top of an old pillar supposed formerly to stand at the Bridgwater Slip, and which for many years last past lay useless in the Council House cellars. Weight, 2 cwt. 3 qr. 12lb. of pot brass at 6½d. per lb."

On the 10th December, 1783, the Council appointed Mr. Richard Burke, brother of the great orator, to the recordership of the city, in the place of Lord Ashburton, deceased. Unable to foresee the imminence of events destined to transform the Burkes into ultra conservatives, the Tory councillors voted against the appointment.

The hackney carriages maintained in the city were still kept in the stable yards of their proprietors. On the 26th December, 1783, however, a coach took its stand near the Exchange, and it was styled "No. 1" by the civic officials. The adventure meeting with favour, "No. 2" coach made its appearance three months later, and also stood at the Exchange. The charge made to any place within the limits of the city was a shilling, and for half a mile beyond the boundaries 1s. 6d. By the summer of 1786 the coaches had increased to 18; but the Corporation had imposed no regulations in reference to fares, and there were loud complaints of imposition. The Chamber at length drew up a table of rates in September, 1787, when 20 vehicles were permitted to ply.

The local journals of March, 1784, announced that the extensive gardens appertaining to the Red Lodge were to be disposed of in building sites. Part of the ground was devoted to laying out a street, originally styled Red Lodge Street, connecting Park Row with Trenchard Street.

A dissolution of Parliament in the spring of 1784 gave rise to the longest and closest contest ever known in Bristol. Mr. Cruger's resolve to attempt a reversal of the decision of 1781 was well known, and although he was in America when the Houses were dismissed, his claims were strenuously championed by his father-in-law, Mr. Peach, and his brother, Colonel Cruger. The late members, Mr. Brickdale and Mr. Daubeny, jointly solicited re-election. It was the custom of that age for the voters to be brought up in "tallies," or batches, by the agents of the respective candidates. In order to prevent Cruger's opponents from bringing up two tallies for one, and so giving them a large majority in the early days of the struggle, Mr. Peach was also nominated as a candidate. Cruger being absent, the opportunity was seized to publish a copious store of calumnies against him. A charge that he had torn down and trampled upon the English flag in New York was especially pressed, in spite of clear evidence as to its falsehood. The polling commenced on the 3rd April, and was continued until the 8th May—a period of five weeks and a day. For more than a month the competition between the friends of Daubeny and Cruger was so close as to leave the issue in doubt. Nearly a thousand persons were admitted as freemen during the contest. The ultimate result was as follows:—Mr. Brickdale, 3458; Mr. Cruger, 3052; Mr. Daubeny, 2982; Mr. Peach, 373. Brickdale refused to be "chaired," to the great wrath of the lower class of freemen, who were bountifully treated on such occasions. At the chairing of Colonel Cruger many gentlemen appeared "in blue coats, with pink capes, being the party colour." In the evening, the White Lion inn—the Tory headquarters—was sacked by a Crugerite mob, after a battle with a Tory mob assembled in Broad Street. Mr. Daubeny petitioned against his opponent's return, alleging that Mr. Cruger had ceased to be an English subject, but the House of Commons affirmed the election.

One of the favourite relaxations of the trading class at this period was a Sunday excursion to one or other of the neighbouring villages, where the innkeepers provided a two o'clock "ordinary" for the entertainment of visitors. Almondsbury, Henbury, Shirehampton, and Brislington enjoyed especial popularity in this way. Owing to the number of excursionists, a Sunday coach to Shirehampton, *vid* Henbury, was started in July, 1784.

The changing customs of city life during the century are illustrated by the fact that the Common Council, which assembled at nine o'clock in the morning in 1701, fixed the hour of meeting at noon in June, 1784. Perhaps an equally significant symptom of the later time is that the old fine of one shilling for non-attendance was increased to half a guinea. A week or two later, the fines for refusing the offices of mayor, sheriff, and councillor were again fixed at £400, £300, and £200 respectively, though, as will be seen afterwards, with no practical effect. In June, 1798, the hour of meeting was further postponed until one o'clock.

The Corporation announced in July that hay and straw would be permitted to be brought by carts into Broadmead for sale every Monday, Tuesday, and Friday. The old haymarket there, which had become obsolete, was formally revived in the following September.

Down to July, 1784, the conveyance of letters between the principal English centres was generally effected in conformity with the system established in the reign of Charles II.; namely, by means of "post-boys" (generally sleepy old men), who travelled on wretched horses at an average rate of under four miles an hour. On the London and Bristol road, it had been found necessary to provide the post-boys with light carts for carrying the mail bags, but the arrangement effected no acceleration in the time of transit—from thirty to forty hours, according to the state of the roads. An important reform in the service was at length accomplished at the instance of John Palmer, already mentioned in connection with the Bristol Theatre. In submitting his proposal in 1783 to Mr. Pitt, the Prime Minister, Palmer pointed out that the post, instead of being the quickest, was almost the slowest conveyance in the country, that robberies were frequent, that the mails were generally entrusted to idle " boys " without character, mounted on worn-out hacks, and that these men, so far from attempting defence or flight if attacked by a highwayman, were more likely to be in league with him. A letter despatched from Bristol or Bath on Monday was not delivered in London until Wednesday morning. On the other hand, a letter confided to the fast coach of Monday reached its destination on Tuesday morning, and the consequence was that Bristol traders and others sent letters of value or urgency by the coach, although the proprietors charged 2s. for each missive, or six times the ordinary postage. Palmer therefore urged the Government to establish mail coaches, protected by well-armed guards, the working cost of which would be defrayed by travellers desirous of increased speed and security, while the post office revenue would benefit by the recovery of the business that had fallen into private hands. Although his scheme was vehemently condemned by the leading officials of the Post Office, who alleged that it would prove not only costly but impracticable, and that robberies would greatly increase if the transit of letters took place daily at fixed hours, the Premier gave orders that it should be tried, as an experiment, on the road from London to Bristol. The coaches started on the 2nd August, 1784, the vehicles being timed to perform the journey in sixteen hours. Only four passengers were carried by each two horse " machine," and the fare was £1 8s. The immediate effect was to accelerate the delivery of letters by a day. Palmer was installed in the London office to superintend the working of his scheme, and had to fight single-handed against the staff, which eagerly strove to expel the intruder and thwart his reforms. One of Palmer's proposals was that all the mails out of London should be despatched at the same hour. This the clerks protested against as impossible, and their mutinous behaviour threatened to bring the establishment to a deadlock, when new blood was imported into the office in the person of Francis Freeling, son of a journeyman sugar-baker on Redcliff Hill, who, after being educated at Colston's School, had displayed unusual capacity as a subordinate member of the Bristol postal staff. Freeling soon succeeded in accomplishing the "impossible," and was eventually rewarded by being raised to the head of the department. In the meantime the old-fashioned officials continued to conspire against Palmer's plan, and must have been nearly successful at one moment, for in February, 1785, the Bristol Common Council, the Society of Merchants, and the trading community addressed memorials to the Treasury, representing the great benefits derived from the new system, and praying for its continuance and extension. The financial results of the reform were soon so satisfactory as to secure its general adoption. In July, 1787, the mails from Bristol to Birmingham and the north, previously three per week, were ordered to run daily. A mail coach started about the same time from London to Edinburgh, being only three nights and two days upon the road (see p. 309). Lord Campbell, who made his first visit to the capital by this conveyance, states in his Diary that the speed of the journey was regarded as extremely dangerous, and that he was strongly advised to stay a day at York, "as several passengers who had gone through without stopping had died of apoplexy from the rapidity of the motion." Palmer was ultimately driven out of office by his implacable enemies, and although the Ministry had promised him a commission of 2½ per cent. on the increased revenue that might be produced by his reform, it broke its engagement, and awarded him a fixed pension of £3,000 a year, being only a small fraction of his rights. After frequently claiming redress from the House of Commons, a grant of £50,000 was voted to him in 1813, about five years before his death.

The manufacture of lime was at this period a not unimportant local industry. A correspondent of *F. Farley's Journal*, commenting in August, 1784, upon a case tried at the assizes, remarked:—"There have been in this neighbourhood for upwards of 25 years past upwards of 28 lime-kilns, and they may on a fair calculation have been reckoned to draw on an average 240 bushels a week each," making the yearly output nearly 350,000 bushels. About one third of the total was exported to the West Indies.

Although large sums had been expended from time to time in repairing old Christ Church, the edifice was condemned in 1784 as hopelessly ruinous. The vestry, which had to face the task of raising funds for a complete reconstruction, showed considerable tact in easing the shoulders of those chiefly concerned, by claiming general help towards carrying out an important public improvement. Their appeal for assistance opened as follows:—"Many accidents having happened, and great inconveniences being daily experienced from the narrowness of the upper parts of Broad Street and Wine Street, the latter of which is only 17 feet in breadth," etc. The south and west walls of the church, in fact, were covered with excrescences in the shape of houses and sheds; and the vestry offered to surrender some of the projections on being liberally compensated for the loss. In December the Common Council promised to contribute £1,500 towards rebuilding the church, provided the parish undertook to widen the two streets in the manner proposed. The Society of Merchants subscribed £500 and the Tailors' Company £100 on the same condition. The old church was a commonplace building, and possessed no exterior feature of interest save two figures placed near the clock, which struck the quarter hours upon a bell. An Act authorising its rebuilding, at an estimated cost of £4,200, of which about one half was to be raised by church-rates, was obtained in 1785; and the edifice was soon after removed. Southey, whose dwelling was close to the church, stated long afterwards that "sad things were said of the indecencies that occurred in removing the coffins, for the new foundations to be laid." Some of the old monuments, however, were preserved. The foundation stone of the new church was laid on the 30th October, 1786, when Southey (then 12 years old), whose father was a churchwarden, deposited a few copper coins, amidst the indulgent smiles of the civic dignitaries. Barrett, whose history was being prepared for the press whilst the building was in hand, extolled the preposterous spire as "beautiful," and described the whole edifice as "a great ornament to the city."

A movement for the promotion of Sunday schools became general in 1784, and found warm patrons in Bristol. At a meeting held on the 17th November, Henry Hobhouse presiding, it was resolved to divide the city and suburbs into ten districts, local committees being desired to superintend the work. A few weeks later it was reported that the vestry of St. Nicholas refused to co-operate. Four parochial schools were, however, soon after established, and their success led to the general adoption of the system.

A glimpse of the costume of youthful citizens is afforded by a censorious writer in *Felix Farley's Journal* of the 20th

November. He states that he remembers when apprentices and attorneys' clerks were accustomed to dress in plain clothes. "But now, gold laced waistcoats, ruffled shirts, and silk stockings are become the ordinary wear of every shop-boy in the city." The critic is silent respecting juvenile wigs; but no doubt he compounded for his own weaknesses by condemning those of others.

The Common Council gave orders in December, 1784, that the mayor's and sheriffs' sergeants, the sheriffs' yeomen, and the mayor's marshals (fourteen in all) should thenceforth provide themselves yearly with new uniforms. The Corporation undertook to furnish them with silver-laced hats. In 1789 the garments were ordered to be paid for by the chamberlain. But in 1790 it was again determined that the officers should provide their own clothes (blue coat, red waistcoat, and black velvet breeches), an allowance of £2 being granted to each.

During the year 1784 some local interest was excited by the poetic effusions of a woman named Anne Yearsley, who earned a scanty living by retailing milk. One of her poems having been brought under the notice of Hannah More, that lady made inquiries, the results of which were communicated on the 20th October in a letter to Mrs. Montagu. Anne Yearsley, she said, was 28 years old, the daughter of an old milkwoman, and had herself followed that calling from childhood; she had never received any schooling, but her brother had taught her to read. Having been married very young to a labourer, she had six children, and had been reduced to extreme distress in consequence of repeated misfortunes. In fact, the family were on the point of starvation, for they had concealed their misery, when a gentleman accidentally heard of their destitution, and afforded them relief. Miss More was struck with the simplicity of manners and good taste of the poor woman; and, in concert with Mrs. Montagu and her extensive literary circle, she resolved to "bring to light a genius buried in obscurity" by publishing by subscription a quarto volume of the milkwoman's poems. Through the exertions of Miss More, who afterwards declared that she had written a thousand pages of letters on the subject, upwards of £500 were obtained for the authoress, part of which sum was applied to paying off debts and restoring comfort to the family, while the remainder was invested by Miss More and Mrs. Montagu, who were constituted trustees, with power of control over the interest. One of Hannah More's biographers asserts that upon Anne Yearsley being made acquainted with this arrangement, she charged her benefactress with envy and covetousness, and flung a sum of ten guineas, the balance of the fund, at that lady's head. The latter assertion was warmly contradicted by the accused in a later edition of her works, in which she reflected bitterly on her patroness. She refused, in short, to be kept in the tutelage which the trustees sought to impose upon her; and, with many exclamations on her ingratitude, they paid her the amount placed in their hands. With this money Mrs. Yearsley set up a circulating library at the Colonnade, near the Hot Well, where she published a second volume of poems in 1787. In 1789, her "historical play, Earl Goodwin," was performed for four nights at the theatre, the proceeds of one evening being paid to the author. A novel, "The Man in the Iron Mask," brought her in a further sum of £200. Being unsuccessful in business, she removed to Melksham, where she died, insane, in 1806.

Undeterred by the failure of their predecessors in 1712, the clergy of the city parishes, in January, 1785, determined on making a fresh application to Parliament for power to increase their incomes by imposing a rate upon the inhabitants. The intention of the promoters was to keep the project a secret whilst their Bill was being pressed forward at Westminster; but Dean Tucker, rector of St. Stephen's, was opposed to the scheme, and covered his colleagues with confusion by divulging their tactics. The indignation excited by the discovery led to the immediate retreat of the clergy; but a public meeting was held in the Guildhall on the 24th February "to perpetuate the feeling of the city."

In *Bonner's Bristol Journal* of January 8th, 1785, is a communication from an old Bristolian professing to specify the fortunes left by eminent local merchants and traders deceased "within these fifty years, who had but small beginnings, but died rich." Although the figures were probably founded only on the gossip of the Exchange, they clearly denote a remarkable period of prosperity. William Miller, grocer and banker, is entitled to the first place on the golden roll, his estate being valued at £190,000. Next follow John Brickdale and Zachary Bayley, with £100,000 each, John Andrews, with £90,000, and David Peloquin, with £80,000. Joseph Percival, Henry Hobhouse, Michael Atkins, Jeremiah Ames, and Gough and Burgess, drapers, are credited with £70,000 each; Henry Combe, Henry Tonge, John Lidderdale, and Henry Bright, with £50,000 each; John Turner, Thomas Foord, James Reed, James

Calwell, Stephen Nash, Thomas Evans, L. Richard, and R. Chamberlayne, £40,000 each; John Curtis and John Collet, £35,000 each; and William Matthews, James Hilhouse, Walter Loghan, William Jefferis, Wm. Gordon, Rich. Meyler, Joseph Loscombe, Manassah Whitehead, Sydenham Teast, R. Frampton, P. Wilder, and Richard Blake, £30,000 each.

The repugnance of the Puritans to ecclesiastical fasts and festivals affected national customs long after Puritanism itself was repudiated. Down to about 1780, Good Friday appears to have been as little regarded by the trading classes as Ascension Day is by the present generation. A movement, however, sprang up in London to promote the religious observance of the great fast, and the *Bristol Journal* of March 19th, 1785, shows that the agitation had spread westward:—"It is humbly requested that every shop and warehouse will be closed on Good Friday next. It has been too generally observed that the inhabitants of this city are more regardless of that day than in any other part of England. However, it is never too late to reform." The revived custom gradually became general, Quakers alone refusing to recognise it. In 1798, Bristolians are recorded to have observed the day with "great and rather unusual solemnity," while in 1800, says *Felix Farley's Journal*, "business appeared to be more universally suspended than we recollect it ever to have been on this occasion."

Advertisements announcing that a new lessee was wanted for the Hot Well and the New Hot Well had appeared during the closing months of 1784, but without success. On the 5th March, 1785, the Merchants' Society issued a fresh notice, intimating that they proposed to let both the springs for a term of from 40 to 60 years, the precise period to depend on the amount which the lessee would undertake to lay out in improvements. The Society required £1,000 to be spent in rearing a quay wall, and £500 in fencing the old spring from the tide; and they further desired that the pump-room should be made more commodious for visitors. This proposal falling still-born, the springs were again fruitlessly offered to be let by auction. At length, on the 1st June, Thomas Perkins was appointed by the Society as caretaker for five years, and extensive repairs and improvements were soon after commenced at the Old Well. To insure the genuineness of the water, which was exported in large quantities, the Society had a seal engraved, bearing their arms and the words "Bristol Hot Well," and this was impressed upon every bottle. The New Well was abandoned (see p. 265).

The success of the two Frenchmen named Montgolfier in constructing balloons caused a prodigious excitement in England. In January, 1784, a small balloon, similar to the toys of the present day, was launched at Bath, and to the astonishment of the public it travelled a distance of nearly ten miles, descending at a spot in Kingswood which still bears the name of Air Balloon Hill. The first ascent of an aeronaut in this country took place in September, 1784, in London. A few months later a Mr. Decker announced his intention to ascend at Bristol, provided tickets were taken to the amount of £150, the cost of hydrogen gas, etc., and his feat was eventually performed on the 19th April, 1785, from a field in St. Philip's. A correspondent of a London periodical stated that "the county of Somerset and all the parts adjacent seemed to be emptied of their inhabitants into this city, which perhaps never exhibited so incredible a concourse of people. [Another writer says that some persons travelled sixty miles to witness the sight.] Two guineas for a horse and three for a chaise were offered at Bath for 12 miles conveyance; and the best of the joke was that the thousands who marched hither from Bath marched back again with like rapidity, as the balloon bent its way to Lansdown." The balloon descended near Chippenham, the journey being completed in what was thought the marvellously short space of 67 minutes. On the aeronaut returning to Bristol, his carriage was dragged through the streets by the enthusiastic populace. For some time after balloons were the rage of the day; they were figured on crockery, glasses, handkerchiefs, fans, head dresses, clock-faces, and copper tokens; and John Weeks, of the Bush, started a "balloon coach" to London.

The local newspapers of the 30th April, 1785, contain a notification by the poor law guardians, complaining that many "housekeepers" lodged and entertained strangers, who ultimately claimed relief as paupers, and giving notice that no strangers would be permitted to lodge for the future unless their places of settlement were first communicated to the authorities. The penalty for refusing compliance with this warning was 40s. From an explanatory note appended to the document, it appears that the "amazing increase of the poor rate" had roused the board into action. The charge for the poor had grown from £6,842 in 1763 to £16,548 in 1783, and unless strangers were prevented from renting houses, and so securing settlements, it was alleged that the evil could not be remedied. Country overseers, it was added, frequently bribed poor families to enter Bristol, and sometimes rented houses for them in the city, in order to secure a settlement. The notice having failed to answer its purpose, a more peremptory advertisement was published in September, in which a reward of five shillings was offered to any one giving information respecting those who harboured strangers. The guardians next resorted to corporal punishment. On the 30th November, eight men and six women, chiefly from the suburban parishes (one from the out-parish of St. Philip), " were flogged, and sent home by a pass "; five other men were " flogged, seen out of the city, and ordered never to return," and five women and two men, who had gained settlements, were " flogged and discharged." A woman from St. Philip's out-district, on promising never to enter the city again, was dismissed, as were several who pleaded illness. These high-handed proceedings were continued weekly for some time.

During the session of 1785 a duty on female servants and a tax on shops were proposed in the Budget, and received assent in despite of the petitions of the trading classes. The impost on shops (10 per cent. on rentals of £25 and upwards) came into operation on the 5th July, on which day nearly every shopkeeper in Bristol closed his place of business, and surrounded its doors and windows with emblems of mourning. Many inscriptions were also exhibited condemning the conduct of Mr. Pitt (whose effigy, in many towns, was hanged and burnt). The bells of the various parish churches rang muffled peals throughout the day. As an illustration of the fiscal system then in favour, a local newspaper stated that a village shopkeeper, whose returns did not exceed 40s. per week, paid a license duty to deal in hats, a second for retailing tea, a third for selling patent medicines, a fourth for keeping a horse, and a fifth for a cart; "his little hut is now assessed to the shop tax." The tax was reduced in the following year. In 1787 the product of the burden was only £108,000, of which London paid £42,000, Bristol and Bath £1,000, and the entire kingdom of Scotland £800. The duty was abolished in 1789.

At a meeting of the mayor and aldermen in August, 1785, the county of Gloucester was granted a piece of land in Wells Close, near Lawford's Gate, for the site of a new county house of correction, in consideration of the surrender of the old Bridewell (see p. 112). Powers for constructing the new prison had been comprised in the Gloucester Gaol Act of 1784. Howard noted in 1787 that the architect of the new building was "the ingenious Mr. Blackburn." It was finished and opened in 1790. A writer in *Felix Farley's Journal* of Dec. 2nd, 1826, describes it as " a vile doghole, without light or air." It was destroyed in 1831 (see Annals, p. 161).

The Nassau frigate, pierced for 64 guns, one of the largest vessels ever built on the Avon, was launched from Mr. Hilhouse's yard on the 20th September, 1785. Amongst the crowds gathered to witness the ceremony were great numbers of " peasants, with red cloaks "—then very popular in the rural districts. " Three Irish bishops "—visitors at the Hot Well—were also present at the launch.

In the session of 1786, the Bristol Bridge trustees, in despite of the opposition of a number of citizens, obtained an Act for making a new street from Bridge Parade to the bottom of Temple Street, at a cost not exceeding £12,000. The new thoroughfare (Bath Street) ran for the most part over the site of the ancient Tucker Street—one fragment of which still remains to attest its narrow and sinuous character. Tucker Street Chapel was swept away under the powers of this Act, which also enabled the trustees to demolish Temple Cross, and to remove from the centre of Temple Street to another site the figure of Neptune and the fountain on which it was placed. The last named change took place in December, 1787, when the fountain and figure were erected at the corner of Bear Lane. The site, now occupied by an extension of Dr. White's almshouse, cost the trustees £45. The Cross, which had been used as a preaching cross by the vicar of Temple down to the close of the previous century, and perhaps later (Tucker's MS.), but had been in 1775 converted into a " commodious watchbox," was suffered to remain for some years; but in January, 1794, the trustees ordered that it should be taken down. Private expostulation was probably the cause of delay in carrying out this destruction. The Cross—the last of many Bristol Crosses—was eventually removed in a quasi-surreptitious manner during the night of the 13th August following. The above statute repealed the clause in the Bridge Act requiring the trustees to build a bridge over the Avon, to connect Dolphin Lane with Temple Street.

The condition of the streets, described as " ruinous and dangerous" by two local journals in November, 1785, at length forced itself on the attention of the corporate body.

At a meeting of the Council in February, 1786, a committee that had been previously appointed to consider the defects in the paving and lighting regulations reported that the existing laws were feeble and inadequate, and that it was desirable to obtain legislative powers for confiding the maintenance and lighting of the streets to a body of commissioners. Statutory powers were also alleged to be necessary for the removal of houses obstructing the streets, for preventing losses through fire by means of party walls, for erecting proper offices for public business, and for regulating hackney coaches. Measures were thereupon taken for obtaining an Act. The Corporation proposed that the commissioners should consist of the whole of the aldermen and councillors, with an equal number (43) of persons elected by such of the citizens as were rated at or above £20 a year. The elected commissioners were each to be owners of property to the value of £300 per annum. The oligarchic character of the scheme excited disapproval, and delegates were appointed by the ratepayers in the various parishes to press for modifications. Some trifling concessions were thereupon offered; but the request of the delegates that the number of corporate commissioners should be reduced one third was rejected, and the Bill was postponed for a year. In 1787 the controversy was renewed, the inhabitants manifesting great want of confidence in the self-elected corporators, while the latter haughtily refused to abate their pretensions. The request of a public meeting that the elected commissioners should be increased to 60 having been rejected by the Council, the inhabitants resolved to lay their case before Parliament. The Corporation thereupon withdrew the Bill a second time. At length, in 1788, when the opposition of the citizens to the measure was again displayed, the Chamber abandoned its proposals in reference to paving and lighting. Its schemes dealing with encroachments, licensing public carriages, regulating party walls, widening Broad Street, and enlarging the Council House and Guildhall were embodied in three Bills, which passed into law without opposition. (The Corporation had spent nearly £1,600 in its Parliamentary campaign.) The police of the streets thus remained unimproved.

For reasons explained at page 181, many of the incorporated trading companies silently disappeared during the closing years of the century. The Coopers' Hall was offered for sale by auction in February, 1785. In January, 1786, a similar fate befell the extensive premises—part of the old

Dominican Friary—belonging to the Smiths' Company. The estate consisted of "a very large new-built warehouse, with two lofts, three stables, an accounting house, a large yard, 100 feet by 80 feet, and the erection called the Smiths' Hall, a spacious building," the whole being held for 999 years at a rental of £3. The hall, a medieval building supposed to have been the dormitory of the friars, was purchased in 1845 by the Society of Friends, and has been carefully preserved. The Bakers' Hall was also in the Black Friars, the company having been granted a portion of the cloisters. It now forms part of the Friends' premises.

On the 1st February, 1786, a banking house, styled the New Bank, was opened at No. 15, Corn Street, by Messrs. Levi Ames, John Cave, Joseph Harford, George Daubeny, and Richard Bright, the first and last-named of whom had been previously partners in the "Bristol Bank" of Deane, Whitehead, and Company, Small Street. A few years later, the partners in the New Bank were Messrs. Ames, Bright, Cave, and Daniel. At length, in June, 1826, the "Old Bank" coalesced with the junior institution.

A letter in *Felix Farley's Journal* of February 18th, 1786, contains some instructive facts concerning the spiritual condition of several of the Somerset parishes in this neighbourhood. The writer, the Rev. W. Baddily, ex-curate of Clevedon, stated that he had frequently but vainly represented to the Bishop (Dr. Moss) the state of many of the adjacent parishes. Mr. Goddard, of Long Ashton, held two livings, yet drove a "scandalous trade by preaching at Wraxall, Bourton, and Barrow, at the same time living among none of them." The poor inhabitants of Nailsea were "obliged to go eight or nine miles through rain, frost, or snow, to a curate at Chew Stoke to bury their dead. The incumbent, one Simpkinson, never comes near the parish but once a year, to receive the farmers' money." Bishop Moss had dismissed the writer from his curacy for exposing these abuses. The condition of the above parishes was by no means exceptional. Hannah More, writing to a friend from Cowslip Green in 1789, says:—"We have in this neighbourhood thirteen adjoining parishes, without so much as even a resident curate." Again, "Mr. G. (incumbent of Axbridge) is intoxicated about six times a week, and very frequently is prevented from preaching by two black eyes, honestly earned by fighting." As the labouring population of Bristol was largely recruited from the neglected districts, the above facts can scarcely be regarded as out of place.

The criminal law at this period well deserved the title of draconian. After the spring assizes of 1786 no less than nineteen criminals were executed in Gloucestershire and Somerset. There was no conviction for murder in either county, but many for highway robberies, some of which occurred in the neighbourhood of Bristol. Two of the Gloucestershire convicts, named Fry and Ward, lived in that portion of Kingswood included in the parish of Bitton, and raised to ten the number of criminals from that district executed within three years. The gang to which they belonged, said the *Bristol Gazette*, of April 23rd, kept the neighbourhood in such dread that the inhabitants consented to pay a yearly fee to save themselves from being robbed. The blackmail varied from 5s. to half a guinea, according to the position of the victims, and was regularly and openly collected at Lansdown fair.

One of the greatest cock-fighting tournaments ever held in Bristol took place at the Angel inn cockpit, Redcliff, in April, 1786. The contest was waged between the gentry of Gloucestershire and those of Dorset. The stakes were £350, and the betting was proportionably heavy. Another " main," between Devon and Gloucestershire, took place at Temple Back, in July, 1794, there being 30 battles at 4 guineas each, and a final one for 60 guineas.

The freedom was presented, in May, to the Hon. George C. Berkeley for " his great attention to the Act lately passed for regulating the Newfoundland fishery, in which the commercial interest of this city is materially concerned."

In deference to the suggestions of the fashionable visitors to the Hot Well, who were inconvenienced by the want of a covered promenade in inclement weather, the erection of a " Colonnade " near the pump-room was commenced in the spring of 1786, and the double row of trees along the bank of the Avon was considerably lengthened. A protected walk of some kind had existed previously. A tradesman, in May, 1760, advertised that his warehouse was " under the Piazzas, near the Pump Room."

Great difficulties arose after the loss of the American colonies in reference to the transportation of condemned felons. In October, 1786, the mayor and aldermen, taking into consideration that two women had been immured in Newgate since April, 1783, from want of opportunity to carry out their sentences (seven years' transportation), resolved to recommend the Crown to pardon them. The first deportation of local felons to Botany Bay took place in the spring of 1787. One of the convicts had been sentenced to death for robbery a few years before, but had been pardoned on volunteering to serve in the army. Having forthwith deserted, he was known to have committed forty-two burglaries in and near the parish of St. James before he was captured and tried for a similar crime in Gloucestershire. The new transportation system was more costly than its predecessor. In the civic accounts is the following item:—1789, June 27th, "Paid Daniel Burges, what he advanced in London to pay the passage of 9 female convicts to New South Wales, and his law charges thereon, £83 1s. 6d." Four days later is the extraordinary entry:—"Paid for conveying a convict on board a ship in Kingroad bound to Ireland, 15s. 6d."

A congratulatory address to the King, on his escape from the knife of a lunatic, was voted by the Corporation in August, 1786. A small deputation proceeded to London to present the document, and was paid £79 18s. 8d. for its expenses. Mr. Stephen Nash, one of the sheriffs, was knighted on this occasion. Mr. Nash was a woollen draper, but had been educated at Oxford, and was probably the only dignitary of the Corporation ever honoured with the degree of LL.D.

The Weavers' Company in 1786 had become so diminished in numbers that they ceased to maintain a hall. The building was transferred to the Jews, who decorated it in what Mr. Barrett terms "a neat expensive manner," and opened it on the 15th September as a synagogue.

The Council House erected in 1704 (see p. 59) had been condemned some years before this date owing to the scantiness of its accommodation, but the authorities were long unwilling to face the main difficulty attending the work of reconstruction. The church of St. Ewen, of which the south aisle had been already absorbed in the civic buildings, stood immediately behind them; and no satisfactory extension could be effected unless the edifice were swept away. In 1784 the aldermanic body had treated with the rector for the union of his parish with that of Christ Church; but the incumbent seems to have refused his assent. In November, 1786, the living became vacant, whereupon it was determined that it should be united to Christ Church, and clauses legalising the junction, and permitting the demolition of St. Ewen's, were introduced into one of the Acts obtained in 1788. The Council House scheme was soon afterwards shelved, and beyond the purchase in 1795, for £1,337, of two adjoining houses in Broad Street, belonging to the vestry of St. Ewen's, nothing more was done for nearly thirty years.

The Council, in November, 1786, empowered the city surveyors to remove "the gateway near the gaol of Newgate" for the greater convenience of traffic. About the same date, the salary of the gaoler was increased from £100 to £200, in compensation for the loss he had incurred from a new Act of Parliament forbidding the sale of intoxicating liquors within prisons. The gaoler's lost profits denote the dissipation that had prevailed.

A new item in the chamberlain's accounts makes its appearance about this time. As usually worded, it reads:— "Paid sundry coachmen belonging to the gentlemen of the corporation for attending with their masters' carriages on public days." The amount varied considerably. For the six months ending September, 1786, the charge was £17 12s., while in a similar period in 1789 the outlay was £41 7s. The wide difference in the eyes of the Chamber between dignity and utility is brought out by another item. Highway robberies were then of constant occurrence. After having handsomely "tipped" the coachmen, the chamberlain paid two guineas each to two men "for parading the roads round Bristol to prevent robberies." How long the paraders were on duty does not appear. They received no further reward.

After the death of the Earl of Hardwicke in 1764, the office of Lord High Steward of Bristol had remained vacant. On the 29th November, 1786, it was conferred upon the Duke of Portland. Soon afterwards his grace was made a freeman of the city, and was requested to pay it a visit. Accordingly, on the 11th April, 1787, the Duke made an entry in great parade, and was received at the Mansion House (being its first distinguished visitor) by the mayor, Mr. Daubeny. A grand banquet and a ball took place at the civic mansion, and £350 were afterwards voted to the mayor for the extra expenditure incurred.

The laying out of Berkeley Square, in 1786, gave evidence that some wealthy Bristolians at length appreciated the advantages of the western suburb. The square, however, like the adjoining Charlotte Street, commenced soon afterwards, remained long unfinished, several half-built houses being offered for sale in August, 1799.

The corn market between Wine and Maryleport Streets having been long deserted, the Council resolved to convert the ground floor into a cheese market, and it was opened for that purpose on the 3rd January, 1787. Cheese tasting being provocative of thirst, the Chamber permitted the landlord of the Raven alehouse, in Maryleport Street, to open a passage from his house into the market. The latter was never successful, the receipts being generally insufficient to meet the cost of collection and repairs. The upper room of the building was opened as a school in July, 1793.

The extent of the burial ground attached to Clifton Church was originally proportionate to the scanty population of the parish. As the residents increased, however, the insufficiency of the area became painfully manifest, and in 1779 the vestry applied to the Society of Merchants for the grant of " a piece of ground at the foot of Honey Pen Hill," adding the interesting topographical fact that the site in question was on " the ancient road to Clifton before the present road was laid out." The application was then unsuccessful, but the demand for enlarged accommodation continued to be urged by the inhabitants, who alleged that the state of the cemetery was dangerous to public health. (The number of burials in 1783 was 55, indicating a resident population of about 1,400.) The Merchants' Company at length conceded the above-mentioned plot of ground—part of the site of an extensive quarry—and in 1787 the vestry took measures to have it covered with earth, properly fenced, and consecrated.

In March, 1787, the *Bristol Gazette* published an interesting communication from an aged citizen, giving an account of the West India trade of the port in the first half of the century, from the recollections of the writer and of friends still older than himself. The letter states that many of the leading merchants had resided in the plantations, for the purpose of gaining experience, before commencing business in Bristol. About 1726, for example, Harington Gibbs, after making acquaintance in Jamaica with the great planters, " Beckford, Dawkins, Pennant (now Lord Penryn), Morant and others," returned home and became their Bristol agent for the sale of sugar. This house was subsequently carried on by Mr. Atkins, and then by his nephew, John Curtis, both of whom had resided in Jamaica. About 1726, Mr. William Gordon returned from the same island, and opened the house " which was afterwards carried on by his nephew, the late alderman, and supported by the family, all of whom have been there." Mr. Davis came from Jamaica in 1740, and set up the firm " still conducted by his son." The principal tobacco importers about 1730 or

1740 were "Alderman King, Mr. Innys, Mr. Chamberlayne, and Mr. Farrell, all having resided in Virginia;" they were succeeded by Lidderdale, Farmer, and others, "who had also resided there." "The principal traders to Carolina were Alderman Jefferis and others who had resided there." "About 1750, Mr. Bright, who had resided in St. Kitts and Jamaica, returned from the latter, and opened the channel which is continued by his family, one of whom also resided in Jamaica. About 1750, Mr. Miles returned from Jamaica, the extent of whose intercourse is well known. The imports from Barbadoes are principally carried on by Mr. Daniel and his son, who have resided there." From the writer's remarks he apparently attributed the declining prosperity of the trade to the unwillingness of young men to follow the example of their forerunners. How rapidly this branch of commerce fell off will be shown at a later date. Attention must for the present be directed to incidents destined to inspire the commercial classes of the port with mingled astonishment and fury.

One evening in June, 1787, the Rev. Thomas Clarkson, who had resolved to devote his life to the work of destroying the slave trade, rode into Bristol for the purpose of investigating the evils of the traffic. On coming within sight of the city, just as the curfew was sounding, he says (History of the Abolition, p. 293), "I began to tremble at the arduous task I had undertaken of attempting to subvert one of the branches of the commerce of the great place which was then before me;" but his despondency subsided, and he entered the streets "with an undaunted spirit." He first introduced himself to Mr. Harry Goady, who had been engaged in the slave trade, but had repented, and become a Quaker. The visitor next became acquainted with James Harford, John Lury, Matthew Wright, Philip Debell Tuckett, Thomas Bonville, and John Waring, all zealous sympathisers. He subsequently obtained warm assistance from Dean Tucker— who in a pamphlet issued in 1785 declared that the number of murders committed under the slave trade "almost exceeded the power of numbers to ascertain"—and also from the Rev. Dr. Camplin; but some other clergymen were indifferent, if not hostile. (It is a remarkable fact that the Society for the Propagation of the Gospel, having had two plantations in Barbadoes bequeathed to it in 1710 by Governor Codrington, a Gloucestershire man, not only maintained the system of slavery upon the estates, but, down to 1793, purchased yearly a certain number of fresh negroes from the importers to keep up the original stock of 300. Edwards' West Indies, ii. 36.) In conversing about the human traffic with the citizens generally, "everybody seemed to execrate it, but no one thought of its abolition." It was admitted on all hands that the captains and officers of the slave ships were noted for their brutality, and that crews could be obtained only with extreme difficulty. In respect to the ship Brothers, then lying in Kingroad, unable to get seamen, Clarkson ascertained that the sailors had been so dreadfully ill-treated during the previous voyage that thirty-two of them had died. As to one of the survivors, a negro, it was found that for a trifling circumstance the captain "had fastened him to the deck, poured hot pitch upon his back, and made incisions in it with hot tongs." This story was confirmed by Mr. Sydenham Teast, one of the principal shipbuilders of the port. It was next discovered that similar barbarities had been practised by the officers of the slaver Alfred, which had just returned to Bristol, and Clarkson obtained shocking testimony from some of the crew as to the cruelty of the captain, who had been previously tried for murdering a sailor at Barbadoes, but had escaped justice by bribing the principal witness to abscond—an act of which he delighted to boast. In two of the Alfred cases, the captain's brutality had caused the death of his victims, and Clarkson, with a view to a prosecution, communicated with Mr. Burges, then deputy town clerk, who had privately expressed his sympathy. "I say privately," adds Clarkson, "because, knowing the sentiments of many of the corporate body, he was fearful of coming forward in an open manner." Mr. Burges's advice was that no prosecution should be attempted. The witnesses, he said, could not afford to stay on shore; it would be necessary to maintain them for some months pending the trial; in the meanwhile the merchants would inveigle them away by offering to ship them as petty officers, and when the hearing came on they would have disappeared. It would be an endless task, moreover, to deal with all the charges of cruelty that were reported, for Mr. Burges "only knew of one captain from the port in the slave trade who did not deserve long ago to be hanged." As regards the sentiments of the shipowners, it is enough to say that the captains of the Brothers and of the Alfred were maintained in the command of those vessels in spite of atrocities that were the common talk of the city. Yielding to Mr. Burges's advice, Clarkson pursued his inquiry in a new direction—

the manner in which sailors were seduced to enter into the trade; and as three or four slavers were then preparing for the African coast, information was easily obtained. By the help of a respectable innkeeper, Clarkson paid numerous visits, between midnight and two o'clock in the morning, to drinking dens frequented by seamen. "These houses were in Marsh Street, and most of them were kept by Irishmen. The scenes witnessed were truly distressing. Music, dancing, rioting, and drunkenness were kept up from night to night." The mates of the slavers allured the young sailor by offering high wages and various other temptations, and enticed him to the boats kept waiting to carry recruits to Hungroad. If he could not be caught in this way, he was often drugged with liquor until impotent to offer resistance, when a bargain was made between the landlord and the mate. Sailors, again, often lodged in these sties, where they were encouraged to run into debt, and then offered the alternative of a slaving voyage or a gaol. They were never permitted to read the articles they signed on entering a ship, and by the insertion in those documents of iniquitous clauses, empowering payments in colonial currency, etc., wages in the slave trade (30s. per month), though nominally higher, were actually lower than in other trades. Clarkson found, moreover, on examining the slavers' muster rolls, that more persons died "in three slave vessels in a given time than in all the other Bristol vessels put together, numerous as they were." As to the conditions of the voyage from Africa, an idea of its horror may be formed from Clarkson's description of two little sloops then being fitted out in the Avon. One of them, of the burden of only 25 tons, was to carry seventy human beings. The other, of 11 tons burden, "was said to be destined to carry thirty slaves." The sloops, on reaching the West Indies, were to be sold as yachts, the smaller one having been originally built as a pleasure boat, for the accommodation of six persons. In both, the space allotted to each slave was so contracted that a captive could not have stretched at full length throughout the voyage. Personal testimony respecting the working of the traffic was sought for; but the retired slaving captains avoided Clarkson "as if I had been a mad dog," while those engaged in the commerce were silent from self-interest. At length, evidence was forthcoming against the mate of the ship Thomas, who had killed one of the crew by brutal ill-usage. When the offender was brought up for examination, "one or two slave merchants were on the bench," and one of the owners of the Brothers and the Alfred insolently addressed the mayor before the evidence was taken, declaring' that the "incredible" charge had been "hatched up by vagabonds." The evidence as to the murder was, however, clear, and the prisoner was committed for trial before the Admiralty Court. But before the day of hearing, Mr. Burges's warning proved to be well grounded; for two of the witnesses had been bribed and sent to sea. Two others, who had resisted temptation, were working in a Welsh colliery to support themselves until the trial, and Clarkson, going in search of them, nearly lost his life in crossing the Severn in an open boat during a storm. The witnesses were found at Neath and despatched to London, but the guilty mate had been brought up a few hours before their arrival, and acquitted through want of evidence. The true character of the traffic now began to affect public opinion, and in 1788 a Bill was brought before Parliament to mitigate the sufferings of the negroes during their passage to the colonies by the prevention of overcrowding. The measure was vehemently opposed by the African merchants in London, Bristol, and Liverpool, who were heard by counsel and witnesses in both Houses. A Liverpool trader declared that he had invested £30,000 in the traffic, and would be ruined if the Bill became law. (Sir James Picton, in his history of Liverpool, estimated that the town was then making £300,000 a year by the slave trade.) Another witness, a ship captain, admitted that he had lost by disease, in a single voyage, 15 seamen out of 40, and 120 out of 360 slaves. It was proved that the space allotted to each slave during the voyage across the Atlantic did not generally exceed 5½ feet in length by 16 inches in breadth! Mr. Brickdale, M.P. for Bristol, seconded the motion for rejecting the Bill, but the opposition was ineffectual, and the measure became law. The protracted debates on this scheme, provoked by the merchants, intensified the public horror, it having been proved that 74,000 unhappy Africans were yearly torn from their country; and an agitation was started for the complete abolition of the trade. The first provincial committee formed to further this result was instituted at Bristol, Mr. Joseph Harford being chairman, and Mr. Peter Lunell secretary. Indignant at this movement, the local West India planters and merchants held a meeting at Merchants' Hall in April, 1789, Mr. William Miles presiding, when an influential committee was appointed to defend a traffic "on which the welfare of the West India islands and the commerce and revenue of the kingdom so essentially depend." Amongst the members of this committee, comprising a majority of the Corporation, were Aldermen Miles, Harris, Daubeny, Anderson, and Brice, Sir James Laroche, Thomas Daniel, Evan Baillie, John and William Gordon, Lowbridge and Richard Bright, John Fisher Weare, Robert Claxton, John Pinney, James Tobin, Philip Protheroe, Richard Vaughan, John Cave, James Morgan, James Harvey, Samuel Span, and Henry and Robert Bush. (Alderman Anderson had been for some years the captain of a slaving ship.) About the same time Mr. Wilberforce moved resolutions pointing to abolition in the House of Commons; when petitions against the proposals were presented by Mr. Cruger on behalf of the Corporation and of the principal merchants and traders of Bristol. Mr. Cruger urged that the trade should be regulated and gradually abolished; but if repression were determined upon, he contended that the injured interests should receive compensation, estimated at from 60 to 70 millions sterling. The resolutions were withdrawn, but the Act of the previous year was amended and renewed. From that time the number of Bristol slaving ships steadily declined, though the slave interest remained very powerful. During a debate in 1791, Lord Sheffield, one of the local members, declared that the arguments of the abolitionists were "downright phrensy," and even denied the right of Parliament to suppress the traffic. The majority in favour of his views was 163 against 88. In the same year an extraordinary affair occurred on the African coast. The captains of six English ships, of which three, the Thomas, the Wasp, and the Recovery, belonged to Bristol, thinking that the native dealers asked too much for their slaves, sent a notice to the town of Calabar that they would open fire upon the place if the price were not reduced. No answer being received, the guns of the six vessels were brought to bear upon the defenceless town, and the bombardment was continued for several hours, until the natives submitted. In denouncing this transaction in the House of Commons, Mr. Wilberforce said that twenty negroes had been killed and many cruelly wounded in order that some Bristol and Liverpool merchants might make several hundred pounds additional profit. The facts, he added, were no secret in the two towns, where the conduct of the captains was considered so meritorious that they had been furnished with new appointments! At this period, according to Edwards's History of Jamaica, the price of slaves in that island was about £50 for able-bodied adults, and from £40 to £47 for boys and girls. The price paid on the African coast being under £22 per head, the profit on a voyage was immense, and it is scarcely surprising to learn from Clarkson's biographer that the bells of the Bristol churches rang merry peals on the news being received of the rejection of one of Wilberforce's motions. About the same time, the Reverend Raymond Harris, of Liverpool, produced his "Scriptural Researches on the licitness of the slave trade, showing its conformity with the Sacred writings of the Word of God;" and the work was liberally patronised. Allowance must, of course, be made for sentiments and customs that had long been common to the whole commercial community, and had been applauded by eminent statesmen. It cannot be doubted, however, that there was a latent consciousness that the trade was inconsistent with reason, religion, and humanity; and that the suppression of right principles for the sake of profit lowered, to a certain extent, the tone of society in Bristol during the later years of the century.

"The Jacob's Wells Water Works," held under a lease from the dean and chapter, were offered for sale in the local journals of April 7th, 1787. The water supplied the houses of the capitular body, and a few dwellings in or near College Green. The lease expired in 1800, when the owners granted a new demise of the spring and pipes, "together with the house in the Cloisters in which the cisterns are situate," to George Rogers, chapter clerk, in trust for the dean and chapter.

The refusal of two leading merchants to pay the dues on imports demanded by the Corporation was recorded under 1775. At a meeting of the Council on the 30th June, 1787, it was reported that the actions against Messrs. Cruger and Miles had been heard in the Court of Exchequer, where the legality of the dues had been affirmed, and the defendants had been ordered to pay the amounts demanded from them, with costs. Nothing more was recorded respecting the matter until December, 1789, when the Council ordered that Elton, Miles and Co., Coghlan, Peach and Co., Bush, Elton and Bush, Jer. Hill and Sons, Ames, Hellicar and Son, and other leading firms that had also refused to pay the dues, should be forthwith prosecuted for arrears, Messrs. Miles and Cruger having submitted to the judgment delivered against them. The threatened firms at once surrendered.

The effect of the judgment was to put an end to the financial embarrassment under which the Corporation had been long labouring. In 1785 the dues produced only £291. In 1790 they brought in (exclusive of arrears) £2,448, in 1791, £2,973, while in 1800 the receipts were no less than £3,851. The impost, however, being very burdensome, afterwards crippled the commerce of the port, and diverted much traffic to Liverpool and other rivals.

The creation of a new suburb around Brunswick Square having aroused an agitation in St. James's parish for a new church, the Common Council approved of the division of the parish, subscribed £400 towards the endowment of a new incumbency (of which it claimed the patronage), and undertook to pay the cost of the needful Act of Parliament. The Chamber subsequently voted £1,000 towards the building fund. At a meeting of the parishioners, in June, 1787, it was resolved to build the new church "in the gardens behind the new tontine buildings in Brunswick Square "— where the square named after the Duke of Portland was already in contemplation. In the autumn, Mr. James Allen, architect, produced a design in the Greek style, which the parochial committee accepted; but in December, in consequence of some occult manœuvring, Mr. Allen was dismissed, and a plan of a so-called Gothic church, produced by Daniel Hague, an "eminent mason," was definitively approved. The secret of this intrigue has never been clearly explained; but the belief of contemporaries seems to have been that the Rev. Joseph Atwell Small, D.D., the incumbent of St. James's, was the real inventor of the semi-Chinese tower that the mason fathered and carried out. The foundation stone of St. Paul's was laid by the mayor on the 23rd April, 1789. The church, which was as costly as it was ugly, and burthened the parish with a rate of 1s. 8d. in the pound for twenty years, was consecrated on the 22nd September, 1794, and opened for service on the 25th January following.

The original Infirmary building had been condemned, for some years previous to this time, as inconvenient and inadequate. In 1782, the medical staff strongly urged that the institution should be removed to the Red Lodge, but through the energetic opposition of Mr. T. Tyndall, who objected to the hospital being placed so near his park, the subscribers finally resolved to retain the old site (R. Smith's MSS.). After a long delay occasioned by want of funds, the foundation stone of the east wing was laid in June, 1784, and the work was completed in May, 1786. On the

24th June, 1788, the foundation stone was laid of the central building, the cost being chiefly defrayed out of invested capital. In December, 1792, it was determined to complete the house by adding another wing, at an estimated expense of £7,000, but the work was delayed for several years from lack of funds. For some inexplicable reason, the walls of the whole building were coated with black plaster, which gave it an extremely lugubrious appearance.

Henry Burgum, the pewterer, whose vanity and ignorance during prosperity were so artfully duped by Chatterton, suffered from painful reverses of fortune in the decline of life. In 1786, when he had lost the use of his limbs from gout, he was lodged as an insolvent debtor in a London prison, but was rescued by the subscriptions of sympathising friends. Having returned to Bristol, he arranged for a performance of the oratorio of "Judas Maccabæus" in September, 1787, from which he netted a handsome profit. The ticket of admission to this performance (price five shillings) was beautifully engraved by Bartolozzi, and is now a great rarity. Another oratorio, "The Messiah," was given in April, 1788, also for the benefit of Burgum, who died in the following year. Handel's greatest work was again performed in St. James's church in April, 1791.

A loose sheet of paper, containing a detailed account of the expenses incurred by Mr. Thomas Daniel in serving the office of sheriff in the year ending Michaelmas, 1787, has been preserved in one of the account books of the Corporation. Amongst the items are:—Sheriffs' dinner, £269 16s. 1d. A chariot, £149 2s. Trumpeters, £9 1s. 4d. French wines, £51 3s. Half of cost of plate given to the mayor, £38 12s. 11d. Ribbons for the Judge, £7 12s. 4d. Servants' hats, £15 8s. A variety of other items raises the total to £992 15s. 9d.; while the net allowance for serving the office is set down at £408 3s., showing that Mr. Daniel was nearly £600 out of pocket. His fellow-sheriff, Mr. Baillie, was a sufferer to the same extent. The preservation of the account in the corporate archives indicates that Mr. Daniel had complained of the inadequacy of the allowance, but the Chamber took no action in the matter.

After an interval of twenty years, the question of improving the accommodation offered to shipping frequenting the port again excited public attention. In September, the Merchants' Company instructed Mr. Joseph Nickalls, a London engineer, to make a survey, and that gentleman, on the 22nd November, produced a lengthy report narrating the results of his inspection. A copy of this paper is in the Jefferies' Collection, and after its perusal it seems impossible to doubt that if Mr. Nickalls' advice had been followed the subsequent commercial history of Bristol would have been changed to an extent now hardly conceivable. The engineer pointed out the fatal defect of any scheme for a dock constructed at or above Rownham, namely the impossibility of the larger class of vessels entering it except at spring tides, owing to the rise of about ten feet in the bed of the Avon near St. Vincent's Rocks. He was therefore of opinion that the most desirable place for erecting locks for a floating harbour was near the foot of the Black Rock, by which an additional depth of several feet of water would be gained, and the navigation of the narrow and tortuous portion of the Avon would be rendered easy. The river bottom, at the point in question, being of rock, the task of construction would be inexpensive, while owing to the increased breadth of the stream the arrangements for dealing with land floods by hatches and "cascades" would be greatly facilitated. Ships of the greatest draught could ascend to Black Rock at the lowest tides, the depth there being nearly 40 feet; and thus, if a lock were constructed, instead of a large vessel being detained at Kingroad for nearly a fortnight, as often happened, it could at once proceed to Bristol even at neaps; and a similar saving of time would be secured on departures. The scheme possessed the additional advantage that no purchases of land would be necessary. Bridewell mill would be rendered useless, but its value was inconsiderable, and Mr. Nickalls suggested the erection of mills of vastly greater power at the proposed locks. In the following May another proposal was made by Mr. Jessop, the engineer who in the result so unhappily gained the confidence of the citizens. He proposed the building of a dam near Mardyke, with a cut for carrying off flood water through Rownham Meads, at an estimated outlay of £32,300; observing in his report:—"On the head of expence I have no conception that Mr. Nickalls' dam at the Black Rock can be executed for less than £30,000." Trifling as was the amount even by the admission of a rival, selfish interests and sluggishness stood obstinately in the way, and the question of port improvement was once more indefinitely postponed.

Compulsory church-going was in favour amongst Clifton vestrymen in 1787. On the 10th October the vestry resolved that, "As the poor of the parish do not frequent the service of the church, but loiter in idleness and are most probable guilty of offences during the time of such service," the able-bodied paupers should thenceforth be required to attend prayers every Friday before receiving relief, "and in default of attending shall not receive the usual pay for that week." It was further determined to build a gallery in the church for the use of the paupers, so that they should be compelled to attend twice every Sunday, under pain of forfeiting their allowances. The vestry, two years later, passed a new order, requiring the overseer to withhold the parochial pittance from such of the poor as did not attend divine service twice every Sunday preceding the usual payday. A few days later, a Sunday School was established for the youthful poor of the parish.

In December, 1787, the local society for the relief of poor insolvent debtors secured the release from Newgate of a Frenchman calling himself F. C. M. G. Maratt Amiatt, who had practised in various English towns as a teacher and quack doctor, and had finally been incarcerated for petty debts in Bristol. The man forthwith disappeared, and it was not until some years later that he was identified in the person of the fanatical democrat, Jean Paul Marat, who was accustomed to howl in the French Convention for the heads of 100,000 nobles, and whose infamous career was cut short in 1793 by the knife of Charlotte Corday.

An advertisement in a local journal of January 26th, 1788, offers the cotton mill, "opposite the Hotwell," to be sold or let, the proprietors being about to remove their manufactory to Keynsham. The mill, sometimes called the Red Mill, was afterwards used for grinding logwood.

John Wesley made one of his periodical visits to the city in March, 1788, and preached on the 6th upon the burning question of the slave trade. His sermon was interrupted by what he deemed a supernatural occurrence. "A vehement noise arose, and shot like lightning through the whole congregation. The terror and confusion were inexpressible. The benches were broken in pieces, and nine-tenths of the congregation appeared to be struck with the same panic. In about six minutes the storm ceased. None can account for it without supposing some preternatural influence. Satan fought lest his kingdom should be delivered up." Ten days later Wesley preached at the Mayor's Chapel, and afterwards dined at the Mansion House. The indefatigable missionary paid his last visit to Bristol in July and August, 1790, when he was in his 87th year. At his chapel one morning, he records, he was without assistance, "so I was obliged to shorten the service within the compass of three hours." He preached during the afternoon of the same day near King's Square. Wesley preached at Temple Church as usual during his stay, and incidentally noted the energy of the Rev. Joseph Easterbrook, the vicar, who "had preached in every house in his parish."

The Presbyterian (Unitarian) chapel in Lewin's Mead, having become insufficient for the accommodation of its supporters, was removed in the spring of 1788. Some adjoining property, belonging to the Bartholomew Hospital estate, was acquired, and a large chapel in a semi-classical style was opened on the 4th September, 1791. The congregation was then the wealthiest in the city, many of the aldermen and common councillors being members. Owing to the number of suburban families that drove to the chapel in coaches, a mews was built in the chapel yard for sheltering their horses.

A remarkable illustration of the slow gestation of some public questions in the corporate body is afforded by a minute of the Common Council, dated the 12th April, 1788. "A proposal" was then laid before the Chamber—it is not said by whom—for the conversion of the Drawbridge into a stone bridge. The project was "unanimously negatived," and was not heard of again for nearly a century. The Corporation, shortly before the above date, forbade all carts to cross the Drawbridge, and the bridge was ordered to be drawn up for two days every year.

The lengthened popularity of the feast of the 29th May, in honour of the restoration of Charles II., can only be accounted for by the fact that the holiday was peculiarly cherished by the Jacobites, and served as a cloak for seditious manifestations. So late as 1788, there were influential Bristolians who dressed the front of their dwellings with oak boughs, and huge branches were brought into the city to meet the demand. A writer in *Sarah Farley's Journal* of the 24th May complains warmly of the injury done in the suburbs by persons who mutilated oak trees to supply decorations, and recommends the mayor to stop the practice. The outbreak of the French Revolution gave a new turn to popular demonstrations.

On the 13th June, 1788, the Rev. Joseph Easterbrook, vicar of Temple, assisted by six Wesleyan preachers and eight "serious persons," held an extraordinary service in Temple Church, for the professed purpose of delivering a man named George Lukins, a tailor, of Yatton, from a demoniacal possession. According to the account authenticated by Mr. Easterbrook, Lukins was violently convulsed upon the exorcists singing a hymn, and the voices of various invisible agents proceeded from his mouth uttering horrible blasphemies—a "Te Deum to the Devil" being sung by the demons in different voices whilst the ministers engaged in prayer. However, when the vicar formally ordered the evil spirits to depart, they obeyed with howlings, and the patient was delivered after a two hours' struggle. This account of the proceedings appeared in *Sarah Farley's Journal* of the 21st June, and gave rise to a vehement controversy. The exorcists were covered with ridicule by Mr. Norman, a surgeon, of Yatton, who stated that Lukins, who was a clever ventriloquist, had begun his imposture in 1770 by alleging, in the course of fits of howling and leaping, that he was bewitched, and had from time to time renewed his exhibitions of pretended torture, causing several infirm old people to be cruelly persecuted for bewitching him. Lukins's latest and most impudent fraud was attributed to a natural fondness for mystification, stimulated by the simplicity of his dupes.

The journey of George III. to Cheltenham in the summer of 1788, being the first royal visit to the West since the reign of Queen Anne, caused much excitement in the district. At a meeting of the Council, on the 25th July, a deputation was appointed to invite his Majesty to Bristol, and in the following month the mayor, recorder, and other dignitaries proceeded to Cheltenham in great pomp, to present an address. The king (whose mental infirmity a few weeks later has been attributed to his inordinate consumption of the aperient waters) was unable to respond to the invitation, but promised to visit Bristol at some future time.

The fame for good cheer of John Weeks, the landlord of the Bush hotel, reached its climax in September, when a complaisant London journal held up his hostelry to the admiration of the kingdom. "Any person who calls for three-penny worth of liquor," says the writer, "has the run of the larder, and may eat as much as he pleases for nothing. Last Christmas Day he sold 3000 single glasses of punch before dinner." The usual Christmas bill of fare at the Bush, indeed, would have done honour to the table of Gargantua. For casual visitors—such as the 3,000 punch drinkers— there was a mighty baron of cold beef, weighing about 350lb., flanked by correspondingly liberal supplies of mutton, ham, etc. For orthodox diners, the larder was piled with gastronomical dainties, the list of which occupied half a column in the newspapers.

With the year 1788 commenced a series of bad harvests and a long period of distress. With a view to reducing the price of meat, the Corporation offered bounties upon fish brought into the port. Upwards of £250 were spent in this way during the month of November, 1788, and £309 in the corresponding period of 1789. The bounty was continued until 1791. The increase of pauperism provoked a cry for relief from some of the central parishes, which were still contributing the share of the charge fixed by the first local poor Act of 1695, when the new suburban districts were mere fields. The matter was brought before the Court of King's Bench, which directed the local authorities to make a new assessment; and in the result the central parishes, previously paying nearly two-thirds of the poor rate, were charged little more than one half; the difference being thrown chiefly upon St. James's, St. Augustine's and Redcliff.

The building ground in Wine Street adjoining the reconstructed Christ Church was sold by auction on the 2nd March, 1789, when the ardour of purchasers excited astonishment. The four lots were of a total length of 101 feet, with a very shallow depth. For the whole a perpetual ground-rent was obtained of £224 4s. 10½d., being about £2 5s. per running foot, equivalent to a fee-simple value of about £170 per yard frontage.

The king's recovery from mental alienation was celebrated early in March by a general holiday. The rejoicings cost the civic purse about £150. The Council deputed six gentlemen to present an address at St. James's, and the expenses of the deputation amounted to £189. The Merchants' Society not only forwarded an address, but presented the freedom of the company to Lord Thurlow, Lord Camden, and Mr. Pitt, the leading members of the Government. The fact is of historical significance, as it denotes that the predominance which the Whigs long possessed in the society had been wrested from them by their political opponents.

The Common Council, in March, increased the yearly payment made to the master of Queen Elizabeth's Hospital for feeding, clothing, and educating the boys from the modest sum of £10 to £12 per head. At a later meeting, the Chamber arranged the dietary of the scholars. Dinner was to consist of meat for five days, and of milk pottage for two days weekly. Breakfast all the year round was limited to bread and table beer ; for supper the provision was bread and cheese, with beer. Malt liquor figured at all the meals. The boys were to rise at 6 o'clock in summer and 7 in winter, and go to bed at 8 every evening.

A visitor to the Hot Well addressed a letter to a local journal in June, suggesting that a few stands for hackney coaches should be established in Clifton. As there was " no proper footpath " in the road to Bristol, strangers, he said, suffered much inconvenience. About the same time, a quarrel broke out between the lessees of the New Long Room and the Old Long Room, and as most of the visitors supported one or the other of the disputants the place was unusually animated. The question at issue was as to the days on which breakfasts and promenades should be held at the respective rooms. It was at length resolved that there should be a public breakfast and dance every Monday, a ball every Tuesday, and a promenade with dancing every Thursday, alternately at the two rooms. Admission to the breakfasts and promenades cost 1s. 6d. per head. For the balls a gentleman paid a guinea at each room for the season, and could introduce two ladies. The Bristol residents in Clifton received a vote of thanks from the visitors for having allowed the dispute to be arranged by the latter.

Owing to an augmentation of the stamp-duty on newspapers, the price of the local journals was advanced in July to 3½d., and shortly afterwards to 4d. The duty on advertisements, however short, was fixed at 2s. 6d. (increased in 1797 to 3s. 6d.). A clause in the Act imposing those burdens inflicted a penalty of £10 on any person lending a newspaper for hire. The tax on newspapers was repeatedly increased, and about the close of the century the price of each tiny journal was advanced to sixpence.

Little information has been preserved respecting the numerous glass manufactories carried on in the city during the century. In a local journal of August 22nd, 1789, Messrs. Wadham, Ricketts and Co. announced that they had entered upon " the Phœnix flint-glass works, without Temple Gate (late the Phœnix inn)," a place which was subsequently converted into a bottle manufactory. Fourteen glass works were in operation in 1797, to some of which strangers and sight-seers were admitted twice a week.

In the autumn of 1789 the Misses More retired from the prosperous boarding-school conducted by them for upwards of thirty years. The sisters removed to Cowslip Green,

Somerset, where they had built a commodious retreat, and applied themselves with exemplary devotion to establishing Sunday schools in the benighted parishes around them. The boarding-school was continued by Selina Mills (who had been a teacher in the establishment), assisted by her sisters, one of whom married Mr. Zachary Macaulay, and became the mother of the historian, Lord Macaulay. Miss Mills's charge for boarders in 1789 was only 20 guineas a year per head.

The outbreak of the French Revolution this year seems to have inspired the corporate body with a desire to celebrate the centenary of a more wisely conducted incident in English history. The 4th November " being the anniversary of the Glorious Revolution," was commemorated with unexampled rejoicing, £177 11s. 8d. being expended by the chamberlain, chiefly for liquor, to render fitting honour to William III. Animated, probably, by the same motive, the Common Council, in December, requested the Duke of Portland, the descendant of the Dutch King's favourite, to sit for his portrait. His Grace having assented, the commission was entrusted to Thomas Lawrence, the Bristol-born artist then fast rising into celebrity, who received 100 guineas for the picture and £44 for the frame.

Shiercliffe's Guide to Bristol, published in 1789, contains some information in reference to the winter balls held at the Assembly Rooms. Those reunions took place on alternate Thursdays, when "menuets" commenced at half-past six, and gave place at 8 o'clock to country dances. "No ladies to be admitted in hats. No children admitted to dance menuets in frocks." The ladies were to draw for places in country dances, or to go to the bottom. No citizen was admitted unless he became a subscriber of two guineas, which freed himself and two ladies. Non-residents paid 5s. each evening, the fund arising from visitors being devoted to a cotillon ball at the end of the season. The master of the ceremonies, James Russell, Esq., had orders to close the balls at 11 o'clock precisely.

An Act of Parliament was obtained in 1790 for rebuilding the church of St. Thomas, then in a ruinous condition. The cost of reconstruction was estimated at £5,000. The Act empowered the trustees to appropriate a fund of £1,470 belonging to the parish, to borrow £700 on the parochial estates, including the tolls of St. Thomas's market, and to raise £3,500 on security of a church-rate. The original intention was to destroy the tower as well as the church, but the former by some means escaped. Of the church, said to have been one of the finest in the city, not a fragment was preserved. On the 21st December the foundation stone was laid of the present edifice, which was opened for service precisely three years later.

Dr. Hallam, dean of Bristol, and other influential inhabitants·addressed a memorial to the Corporation early in 1790, pointing out the defects of the city gaol, and urging the adoption of Mr. Howard's suggestions for the better management of felons and other prisoners. The Council, in February, resolved to apply for powers to build a new gaol, and a Bill for that purpose was soon after laid before the House of Commons; but its provisions were no sooner discovered by the citizens than they raised a storm of indignant protests. Newgate, just a century old, had been built at the expense of the inhabitants, by means of a rate, yet the Bill declared it to be the sole property of the civic body. The Corporation had hitherto borne the expense of maintaining the gaol and bridewell, and this charge represented almost the only benefit which the inhabitants derived from the property of the municipality; but the Bill proposed to relieve the corporate estates from the burden (save a grant of £150 yearly), and to lay it upon the citizens in the shape of a county rate. The aldermen, as justices, were to have uncontrolled power in fixing the amount of the rate, while the Common Council was to be left equally unrestricted in its administration of the proceeds. Against these propositions, as well as against various details—notably the site of the new prison, which it was proposed to build in the crowded Castle Precincts—a formidable opposition was organised, and the Corporation withdrew the Bill. The scheme was revived in 1791, only to be again hotly opposed and to be again withdrawn—as it was supposed, definitively. The civic body, however, resorted to a manœuvre. In 1792 the Bill, with all its unpopular features, was hurriedly passed through the House of Commons, and had been read a first time in the Upper House before its existence became known to the citizens. Petitions with 4,000 signatures were forthwith presented, and the objections of the opponents were heard by the Lords' committee; but after a brief delay the measure became law. The discontent of the citizens was intensified by the sharp practice of the Corporation. The mayor and several prominent civic personages were insulted in the streets, riots were threatened, and the parishes raised a fund of nearly £4,000 to prevent the Act being put in operation. The attitude of the inhabitants at length alarmed the Corporation, and some leading members of the Council privately gave an assurance that the powers of the Act should be allowed to expire by afflux of time (seven years). The expenses of the delegates nominated to oppose the Bill, £680, were defrayed by subscription. The scandals of Newgate remained unreformed for another quarter of a century.

Stoke's Croft still retained a semi-rural character. At a meeting of the Council in March, 1790, a committee recommended that the local surveyors should view the trees and the Cross, or centre posts, in Stoke's Croft, and report on their condition. At the suggestion of the surveyors, the Council, in November, ordered the trees and posts in the Croft and North Street to be removed. The task was thrown upon the inhabitants, who displayed no zeal in undertaking it, for in the following year the Chamber issued a fresh order, requiring the tenants to remove the trees as "nuisances." Double rows of trees ornamented King Square at this time, and St. James's Square, St. James's churchyard, Wilder Street, and part of Broadmead, were luxuriantly leafy in the summer months.

Mr. Henry Cruger, M.P., for many years one of the most influential of local politicians, sailed on the 8th April, to spend the remainder of his life in his native city of New York. He had previously issued a retiring address, in which he significantly referred to the commercial reverses caused by the disruption with America. He also surrendered his aldermanic gown, but continued a member of the Council until his death, thirty-seven years later. By his first wife, Miss Peach, Mr. Cruger had an only son, who assumed his mother's surname on succeeding to the estate of her father, Mr. Samuel Peach, of Bristol and Tockington.

The local newspapers of the 8th May contain an announcement that Mr. Samuel Powell had entered into occupation of "the Hotwells." The terms of his lease from the Merchants' Society are unknown, but it is certain that the owners, wishing to profit from the outlay they had incurred for improvements, greatly increased the former rent. The tenant, in consequence, resorted to expedients for raising the receipts which not only defeated themselves, but brought about the complete loss of the spring's reputation. The fee for drinking the water was increased from a nominal sum to 26s. per month for each individual. Many upper-class families that had flocked to the pump-room in the pursuit of pleasure rather than of health declined to pay the enhanced charge, and betook themselves to other watering places, and their example soon became contagious. Down to 1789 the Hot Well was crowded during the season by the aristocracy and gentry. Between noon and two o'clock the pump-room was generally so thronged that it was difficult to reach the drinking tables. In the afternoon the Downs were alive with carriages and equestrians. Three large hotels were fully occupied; two assembly rooms were kept open (a third, on Clifton Hill, was added in August, 1790); while lodging-house keepers (although charging only 5s. per room weekly in winter and 10s. in summer) frequently retired from business with comfortable fortunes. In a few years the place was deserted except by a slender band of invalids; the fashionable company had disappeared; one of the hotels and two of the assembly rooms were closed by the bankruptcy of the occupiers; many of the lodging-house keepers became insolvent; and the value of houses near the well greatly decreased. Short-sighted rapacity, in fact, had been emphatically punished. Powell's exactions, it must be added, were not confined to strangers. Soon after he entered upon the premises, the right of Bristolians to visit the well was denied, the pump previously reserved for them was shut up, and a charge of 3d. per bottle was demanded for the water. In spite of complaints, the Merchants' Company tolerated the proceedings of their tenant, and it was not until March, 1793, that the Common Council resolved to vindicate the public rights. Procrastination was successful in defeating those rights for a considerable further period, but in September, 1795, the Merchants' Company recognised the privilege of the inhabitants to drink the water at the "back pump," and to carry it away in bottles if marked with their owners' names.

The Ostrich inn, Durdham Down, was occupied in the summer of 1790 by an enterprising landlord, who turned the advantages of the house to good account. Breakfasts were provided for visitors from the Hot Well, many of whom rode over to play on the bowling green; dinners, with turtle soup, could be had at short notice, and on Sunday there was an ordinary at 2 o'clock (at one shilling per head) for excursionists from Bristol. The house became so popular a resort that Evans, the tenant, erected lamps on the Down, and undertook to light them nightly during the winter. In 1793 Evans removed to the York House hotel, Gloucester Place, Clifton (originally opened in August, 1790, by one John

Dalton), and the popularity of the rural inn declined with that of the Hot Well.

A general election took place in June, 1790. The sitting members, Messrs. Cruger and Brickdale, having retired, the local party leaders, to avoid the expense of a contest, had come to an understanding, the Tories bringing forward the Marquis of Worcester, while the Whigs selected Lord Sheffield. The latter, as has been already shown, was one of the persons who received a grant from the king's secret election fund in 1781. He was, in fact, a Tory in all but the name, but had made himself acceptable to the West India interest by his advocacy of the slave trade. He is now chiefly remembered as the literary executor of Gibbon. The party truce was distasteful to the lower class of freemen, who were deprived of a month's saturnalia, and their griefs were espoused by a clique of extreme Tories, led by a Rev. Dr. Barry, who were opposed to a compromise with the Whigs. Instigated, probably, by this coterie, Mr. David Lewis, an eccentric Welsh tradesman, came forward as a candidate. Unhappily, Mr. Lewis, as one of his friends put the matter, "laboured under a little disadvantage respecting the English language." He was, in fact, grossly illiterate, and his attempts at oratory excited general ridicule. The official candidates were received by imposing processions, Lord Sheffield being met at Keynsham and Lord Worcester on Durdham Down by their respective partisans. The polling opened on the 19th June, and the result of the first day's voting was so emphatic that Mr. Lewis at once withdrew, charging the freemen with having falsified their promises and bartered their liberty for liquor. The numbers polled were as follows :—Lord Worcester, 544 ; Lord Sheffield, 537 ; Mr. Lewis, 12 ; Wm. Cunninghame (nominated without his consent), 5. The freedom of the city was soon afterwards presented to the new members.

A useful improvement was determined upon by the Council on the 9th June, when the aldermen of the various wards were directed to see that the name of each street and lane was set up in a conspicuous place. From some doggrel lines in a local journal, the work seems to have been completed in the spring of 1791. The writer notes that out of the numerous thoroughfares dedicated to saints, the only one complimented with its full name was St. John Street, which had then been recently opened.

A chapel in Trenchard Street dedicated to St. Joseph, the first building erected in the city since the Reformation for

Roman Catholic worship, was opened by Father Robert Plowden on the 27th June, 1790. Mr. Plowden was a Jesuit, and the chapel had been built under the directions of the Order, who had undertaken to serve the "Bristol mission." The house on St. James's Back, previously used as a chapel, was disposed of, and was for a short time occupied by a few Swedenborgians.

In despite of public disapproval, and of the emphatic judgment of Lord Mansfield in the Somerset case, the practice of keeping negroes as domestic slaves was still not uncommon. In a letter to Horace Walpole, dated July, 1790, Hannah More wrote:—"I cannot forbear telling you that at my city of Bristol, during church-time, the congregations were surprised last Sunday with the bell of the public crier in the streets. It was so unusual a sound on that day that the people were alarmed in the churches. They found that the bellman was crying the reward of a guinea to any one who would produce a poor negro girl who had run away because she would not return to one of those trafficking islands, whither her master was resolved to send her. To my great grief and indignation, the poor trembling wretch was dragged out from a hole in the top of a house where she had hid herself, and forced on board ship." *Bonner's Bristol Journal* of December 8th, 1792, stated that a citizen had recently sold his negro servant girl, who had been many years in his service, for £80 Jamaica currency, and that she had been shipped for that island. "A byestander who saw her put on board the boat at Lamplighter's Hall says, 'her tears flowed down her face like a shower of rain.'"

An "Equestrian Theatre," or in modern parlance a circus, was erected in 1791, in Limekiln Lane, for the accommodation of the travelling companies that usually visited the city once a year. The eastern part of the building, which is described as of large dimensions, was fitted up as an amphitheatre for the spectators.

Much unwillingness having been shown by various members of the Common Council to serve the office of sheriff, an edifying by-law was enacted in March, 1791. The fine for non-acceptance of the dignity was fixed at £300. If all the members of the Corporation had served the office, an election was to be made out of the councillors by seniority, excepting those who had already served a second time, and also excepting any "gentleman who hath become bankrupt or hath compounded with his creditors, and not afterwards paid twenty shillings in the pound." There is reason to believe that persons entitled to the second exemption were by no means rare. Mr. J. B. Kington, the author of numerous letters signed "A Burgess," published in the *Bristol Mercury* in 1833-4, asserted that " at one time a sixth part of the Council" consisted of insolvents, " each paying about 5s. in the pound, except one, who left the country without paying anything."

On the 19th March the gossip mongers of the city were entertained by the romantic elopement of one of the pupils confided to the care of Miss Mills, of Park Street. The girl in question, Clementina Clerke, was under 15 years of age, and was the heiress of an uncle named Ogilvie, who had made a fortune of £6,000 a year in Jamaica. Her wealth having come to the knowledge of a dissipated but handsome apothecary named Richard V. Perry, he furtively sought her attention whilst she and her companions made their daily promenades. The precocious heiress offering tokens of affection, Perry one day slipped a note into her hand proposing that she should go off with him to be married at Gretna Green, and the evasion was facilitated by the bribing of a servant. The lovers had never spoken to each other when the girl joined Perry in the post-chaise which hurried them to Scotland, in company with an attorney named Baynton. Miss Clerke's schoolmistress followed the couple to Belgium and elsewhere, but without success. On returning to England, Perry was arrested on a charge of abduction, preferred by Mr. W. Gordon, the guardian of his child wife, but the latter, at the trial in April, 1794, swore that she had eloped of her own accord, and the prisoner was acquitted. Baynton, who disappeared for many months, was not prosecuted. He afterwards informed Mr. Richard Smith that he had lost £3,000 by the affair, but was never able to extract a guinea from his client, who had promised him £3,500. Mrs. Perry separated from her husband, and died in poverty at Bath about 1812. Her husband transported himself to Jamaica, where he took the name of Ogilvie, lived in magnificent style, and was a candidate for the House of Assembly in 1816 (R. Smith's MSS.).

The building trade of the city was possessed at this period with a speculative mania destined to end in widespread and prolonged disaster. The "rage for building" was first noticed by the local press in November, 1786, but was then chiefly confined to Clifton, where Sion Row was being constructed. In May, 1788, a letter in *Sarah Farley's Journal* stated that houses were rising fast near Brandon Hill and in

Great George Street, Park Street, and College Street, while preparations for others were being made in Lodge Street, various parts of Kingsdown, Portland Square, Milk Street, Bath Street, and elsewhere. Shortly after, the erection was noticed of houses in Berkeley Square and Rodney Place. In April, 1791, *Felix Farley's Journal* observed:—" So great is the spirit of building in this city and its environs that we hear ground is actually taken for more than 3000 houses, which will require some hundreds more artificers than are already employed." Amongst the designs then proposed was the construction of the two imposing lines of dwellings afterwards known as Royal York and Cornwallis Crescents. In October *Bonner's Journal* announced that the Royal Fort and its parks (about 68 acres in area), late the property of Mr. Thomas Tyndall, who had died in the previous April, had been purchased (it was said for £40,000) by a party of gentlemen, who intended to convert the whole into building sites. A plan for a gigantic terrace in the park was soon afterwards designed by Wyatt, the fashionable London architect, but operations were suspended for a time in order that an Act might be obtained to empower the dean and chapter to grant a lease for 1,000 years of that portion of the land held under a capitular lease. The Act passed in 1792, when preparations were made for the erection of the terrace. At the same period, Mr. Samuel Worrall, who had a large estate adjoining Clifton Down, produced plans for the construction of a stately line of mansions, and urged the superiority of the site over that of Tyndall's Park. A terrace of 60 houses, to cost £60,000, was proposed to be built near Ashley Down about the same time. The mania had scarcely burst into full bloom before it evinced signs of coming decay. In December, 1792, an attempt was made to complete the erection of York Crescent, on which £20,000 had been spent, by the creation of a tontine, with a capital of £70,000 in £100 shares. A similar association, with a capital of £14,000, was proposed to finish King's Parade, where £8,000 had been laid out by the builder. Both these schemes proved abortive. On the breaking out of the French war, in 1793, there was a financial panic throughout the kingdom, and the failure of Messrs. Lockier, McAulay, and Co., the most extensive of the local speculators, heralded the ruin of a crowd of minor firms. More than 500 houses in course of construction were left unfinished, and the appearance of the suburbs, for many years after this collapse, reminded strangers of a place that had undergone bombardment. The shells of thirty-four roofless houses stood in York Crescent, dominating similar ruins in Cornwallis Crescent, the Mall, Saville Place, Belle Vue, Richmond Place, York Place, and other localities. Kingsdown and St. Michael's Hill presented many mournful wrecks; Portland Square and the neighbouring streets were in the same condition; and Great George Street and its environs were in no better plight. Mr. T. G. Vaughan, the chief promoter of the Tyndall's Park scheme, became bankrupt before much progress had been made with the proposed terrace, the foundations of which were levelled when the estate returned into the hands of the Tyndall family in 1798. Many years elapsed before other traces of this calamitous mania disappeared. Mr. Malcolm, the historian of London, in a work published in 1807, described the "silent and falling" houses in Clifton and the tottering ruins in Portland Square as the most melancholy spectacle within his recollection.

Mr. Matthew Brickdale, ex-M.P. for the city, and a common councillor, had been repeatedly pressed to take the office of mayor, but had hitherto succeeded in evading the dignity. On the 15th September, 1791, he sent in a resignation of his office, but the Council, refusing to accept it, elected him chief magistrate. He, however, declined either to be sworn or to pay the fine. John Noble was thereupon elected mayor, and an action was commenced against Brickdale, who was eventually compelled to pay the penalty of £400 and the Corporation's costs.

Mr. Noble had a high sense of the dignity of his office, and availed himself of an ancient privilege to astonish the judges of the Court of Admiralty. On the 7th June, 1792, while the court was trying prisoners at the Old Bailey, London, the mayor of Bristol, in his state robes, proceeded to the bench, and claimed a seat with the other commissioners. An explanation being demanded, his worship showed that by an ancient charter the successive mayors and recorders of Bristol were constituted judges of the court. The claim having been admitted, Mr. Noble stated that his object was merely to assert a right, and, after saluting the judges, he withdrew. The mayor, who appears to have travelled to London expressly for this purpose, notified the result a few days later to the Common Council, who passed a vote of thanks to him for his conduct, and the matter was registered in the civic minutes. (Mr. Nicholls recorded this incident as having taken place in 1762.)

The powers obtained in 1766 for widening the narrow

alleys connecting Christmas Street and Broad Street with Broadmead remained in suspension until September, 1791, when the Council resolved to obtain estimates for the work; but the authorities proceeded languidly in obtaining possession of the old hovels in Halliers' Lane and Duck Lane. In February, 1796, it was reported that property had been purchased at a cost of £8,860, and that the remaining houses required could have been had for £7,500 if the cash had been in hand; but the owners now demanded more, owing to a rise in the value of money. About the same time, a bridge over the Froom, known as Needless Bridge, connecting Broadmead and Duck Lane, was replaced by a more convenient structure. After some additional outlay, the street, one of the ugliest in the city, was opened in 1799, when the Chamber, in honour of the great naval hero of the age, ordered it to be styled Nelson Street.

On the recovery of the corporate finances after the revival of the town dues, the state of the accounts of Whitson's charities seems to have shamed the authorities into action. The sum of £4,000 had been borrowed for civic purposes from the charity funds on bonds, one of which had been outstanding for 31 years, another for 28, and six from 15 to 20 years, while interest had never been paid on any of them. The sum of £1,938 was now transferred to the charity, as interest on the loans.

The question of harbour improvement was temporarily resuscitated in October, the Council holding a special meeting to discuss a project "for floating the ships at the Quay." A committee was appointed to report, and did so in December. After stating that the future prosperity of the port largely depended on the creation of improved facilities for commerce, so as to place the city on fairer terms with its rivals, and avoid the heavy losses to shipping caused by existing defects, they recommended the design of Messrs. Smeaton and Jessop for damming the Avon at Red Clift, and cutting a canal through Rownham Meads. The subject was soon after allowed to go to sleep again, notwithstanding the frequent occurrence of disasters in the harbour.

The mayor informed the Council in December that possession had been taken of St. Ewen's church on behalf of the Corporation, in whom the property was vested by the Act of 1788. The woodwork, bell, etc., were sold soon afterwards. The upper part of the tower (a mean structure built in the reign of Charles I.) was taken down in 1795, when some of the vaults and graves were "arched over": but the rest of the fabric remained standing until about 1820.

Down to this period, the aldermanic body claimed the right of filling up vacancies in its own number, independent of the Common Council. A death having occurred early in 1792, Jeremy Baker was elected an alderman in the customary manner, but for the first time in the history of the Corporation the dignity was rejected. A "case" having been sent to the recorder for his opinion, the learned gentleman replied in September that elections of aldermen ought to take place in the Common Council, though the mayor and aldermen were alone entitled vto ote. This course was thenceforth adopted.

The embarrassments of the St. Stephen's improvement trustees have been already noticed. To assist in discharging their debts, the Common Council, in March, 1792, offered a subscription of £500, provided the parish would reconvey to the Corporation, for the sum of £1,000, the cemetery at the south end of Prince's Street. (This burial ground was granted to the parish by the civic body in 1676, at a fee farm rent of 3s. 4d. yearly.) The trustees made no response to this proposal for two years and a half. At length, in September, 1794, at a meeting of the landowners and inhabitants of the parish, when the debt of the trustees amounted to upwards of £3,000, it was resolved to assent to the offer, the meeting being moved thereto by the fact that "the said churchyard, owing to the numerous interments there, will in a short time be rendered of no use to the parish, and has long been considered and indicted as a nuisance." The site of the cemetery is now partially covered by warehouses.

A letter in a local newspaper of April, 1792, reporting a carriage accident in Hotwell Road, sarcastically compliments the Society of Merchants upon the manner in which the highway was maintained. So long as the mud remains, says the writer, coaches will fall on a soft surface, "consequently nothing but smothering remains to be dreaded."

Owing to the great activity in the local building trades, disputes as to wages were numerous about this time. At the summer assizes at Gloucester, two brickmakers, of St. Philip's parish, were each sentenced to two years' imprisonment, for having combined, with others, to demand an advance of wages. Strikes were nevertheless common, and in some cases successful. It is worth observing that whilst the employers denounced workmen's combinations, and put the law against them in operation when they could, they published advertisements announcing that they had themselves combined to maintain the old rates of wages, and to refuse work to strikers.

The population in the northern suburbs having become numerous, the Wesleyans were encouraged to build a chapel in Portland Street, Kingsdown, which was opened on the 19th August. The chief promoter was Thomas Webb, a lieutenant in the army, who frequently preached in his uniform to large congregations.

Bonner's Journal of November 10th announced that "a society is now forming in this city for promoting the happiness of blind children by instructing them in some useful employment, and the meeting-house in Callowhill Street is fitting up for their reception." The building was a disused chapel belonging to the Friends, who were the most zealous promoters of the infant Blind Asylum.

The "canal mania" of 1792, though productive of less important results than the railway mania of 1845, was in many respects a counterpart of that memorable delirium. On the 20th November a meeting to promote the construction of a canal from Bristol to Gloucester was held in the Guildhall, when the scheme was enthusiastically supported by influential persons, and a very large sum was subscribed by those present, who struggled violently with each other in their rush to the subscription book. A few days later, a Somerset paper announced that a meeting would be held at Wells to promote a canal from Bristol to Taunton. The design had been formed in this city, but the promoters strove to keep it a secret, and bought up all the newspapers containing the advertisement. The news nevertheless leaked out on the evening before the intended gathering, and a host of speculators set off to secure shares in the undertaking, some arriving only to find that the subscription list was full. The third meeting was at Devizes, on the 12th December. Only one day's notice was given of this movement, which was to promote a canal from Bristol to Southampton and London, but the news rapidly spread, and thousands of intending subscribers rushed to the little town, where the proposed capital was offered several times over. The "race to Devizes" on the part of Bristolians, who had hired or bought up at absurd prices all the old hacks that could be found, and plunged along the miry roads through a long wintry night, was attended with many comic incidents. A legion of schemes followed, Bristol being the proposed terminus of canals to all parts of the country, and some of the projected water-ways running in close proximity to each other. A pamphlet published in 1795, narrating the story of the mania, states that the passion for speculation spread like an epidemical disease through the city, every man believing that he would gain thousands by his adventures. The shares which were at 50 premium to-day were expected to rise to 60 to-morrow and to 100 in a week. Unfortunately for these dreams, the financial panic to be noticed presently caused a general collapse; and the only local proposal carried out was the comparatively insignificant scheme for uniting the Kennet with the Avon.

The closing weeks of 1792 were marked by an outburst of loyal enthusiasm, provoked by the insolent threats of the French revolutionary leaders and the frothy talk of a handful of Republican enthusiasts in London. At a city meeting in the Guildhall a declaration of attachment to the Constitution was cordially approved, and was subsequently signed by many thousands. Effigies of Tom Paine were burnt by the populace in every parish, and for several days the bells rang loyal peals.

A correspondent of a local journal of January 12th, 1793, complained that there were no public warm baths in the city, notwithstanding its wealth and population. A hot bath at Baptist Mills is, however, casually mentioned in a newspaper of the previous April.

War with France was declared in February, a few days after the execution of Louis XVI. Placing faith in the predictions of Burke as to the effects of the revolution, a vast majority of politicians believed that the defeat of the Anarchists would be speedily effected. It is remarkable, however, that the ardour for privateering manifested by Bristolians in previous wars was on this occasion entirely lacking. The newspapers do not record the fitting out of even a single cruiser. The heavy losses incurred during the American struggle may have contributed to this inaction, but it was doubtless chiefly due to commercial disasters unprecedented in local history. As has been shown, the years preceding the war had been marked in Bristol, in common with other mercantile centres, by excessive speculation, encouraged by the numerous banks, which prodigiously increased their issues of paper money. At the moment when credit was dangerously strained, the French Government declared war, and a violent financial revulsion at once took place all over this country. About one hundred provincial banks stopped payment, two of them in Bath, and for a few days crowds of Bristolians possessing bank-notes rushed to the issuers to demand payment in cash. The banks met every claim, and confidence in them soon revived, but the sudden restriction of credits necessitated by the state of the country brought about an extent of misery and insolvency till then unknown in Bristol. Nearly fifty considerable local bankruptcies occurred within two or three months, and the aggregate losses were enormous. The effects of the panic on the building trade have been already noticed.

The Corporation manifested its zeal in supporting the Government at this crisis by largely increasing the bounties offered to sailors on joining the navy. Upwards of £700 were paid out of the civic purse in this manner at the beginning of the war. An amusing incident occurred about this time in the Common Council. Mr. Joseph Harford, for many years an influential Quaker, had been noted for his advanced Whig principles. His admiration of Burke, however, caused him to secede from his party, as he had already done from his sect, and he not only became an ardent champion of the war, but displayed an eager desire to push a near relative into the struggle. At a meeting of the Council on the 12th June, he moved that the Corporation " do recommend Lieut. John Harford, now on board H.M.S. St. George, to the Lords of the Admiralty for promotion, and that Mr. Mayor be requested to make such recommendation." Although many members must have stared at the impudence of the proposal, it was carried without dissent. In December, 1794, no notice having been taken of the mayor's application, the ex-Friend, who had just actively promoted the embodiment of a local regiment, induced the Chamber to direct that the mayor should write to the Duke of Portland (to whom a butt of sherry was ordered to be sent at the same meeting) pressing the interests of the young lieutenant upon his attention. Probably to Mr. Harford's extreme annoyance, the second supplication was as fruitless as the first.

A penny postal system for letters and small parcels was established in July, 1793, for the accommodation of local business. Several parishes around the city were included in the arrangement, but the selection was capricious. In some cases a four-ounce packet was transmitted eighteen miles for a penny, while to other places within that distance such a parcel incurred a postage of 6s. 8d.

The most tragical local incident of the century, the Bristol Bridge riots, has been so fully narrated by Mr. Pryce and others that it seems unnecessary to enter into lengthy details. Although the popular rising cannot be justified, it is equally clear that the conduct of the bridge trustees deserved severe condemnation. Under the provisions of the Act of 1785, the authorities were entitled to collect tolls on vehicles, horses, etc., until the money borrowed had been paid off, and a balance of £2,000 secured, the interest on which was to be devoted to lighting and maintaining the bridge. In September, 1792, when the debt had been reduced to £5,500, the trustees had a sum of £4,400 to their credit, and the net income of the following year was estimated at £3,000. The auctioneer employed to let the tolls and the solicitor to the trustees consequently informed the lessee that the tolls would cease in September, 1793; and this statement, which gave satisfaction to the citizens, was never contradicted. Shortly before the close of the lease, however, the trustees announced that the tolls would be let for another twelvemonth. As a matter of fact, the required balance of £2,000 had not been obtained, and the authorities, under a belief that the interest of that sum would be insufficient to keep the bridge in repair, wished to increase the capital fund, and so avoid the expense of another Act. Had this been explained to the city, the plan might have won a certain measure of approval. But the acting trustees, most of whom were members of the Common Council, had all the Corporation's contempt for popular feeling, as well as its abhorrence of popular control. Although administering revenues entirely drawn from the pockets of the inhabitants, they had refused for 25 years to produce their accounts. They now haughtily refused to enlighten the city as to their purposes, and persisted in a step exceeding their lawful powers. On the 21st September the tolls were leased for another year, for £1,920, to Wintour Harris, an underling of the Corporation. The proper method of defeating the illegal proceeding would have been an appeal to the law courts. Unfortunately a small body of citizens, who had already taken action, resolved to meet usurpation by stratagem. Believing that if the toll were once suspended it could not be reimposed, they made a bargain with the lessee of the previous year for a relinquishment of his rights during the last nine days of the term; and on the 19th September the bridge was thrown open and traffic passed toll-free amidst the clamorous joy of the assembled populace, which made a bonfire of the gates and toll-boards during the evening. The trustees, greatly exasperated, offered a reward on the 20th for the discovery of the offenders, pointing out that the destruction of the tollboards was a capital crime; their placard further asserted that the liabilities of the trust still amounted to £2,500, which they did not offer to prove, and which was in substance untrue. On the 28th workmen were employed to erect new gates, to the great irritation of the lower classes, who gathered in increasing numbers as the day advanced; and at night, when a large mob had assembled, the new barriers were set on fire and destroyed. The magistrates now appeared on the scene, and warned the rabble as to the consequences of further rioting; but the justices were roughly hustled about, and their remonstrances were received with derision. The Riot Act was consequently read, and a party of the Herefordshire militia was sent for to keep order; but as great crowds followed the troops in their march to the spot, the tumult soon became greater than ever, and the justices and soldiers were assailed with volleys of stones. At length the militia received orders to fire, and one man was killed and two or three others wounded by a volley, which put an immediate end to the disorder. At noon on the 29th (Sunday), when the old lease expired, and men were posted on the bridge to collect tolls, assisted by the civil power, the spot was for many hours a scene of uproar and confusion, those who refused to pay the charge being seized by the constables, and often incontinently rescued by crowds of excited spectators. At length a few soldiers were brought down to support the toll-takers, and further resistance was abandoned. On Monday morning, however, the populace gathered in great numbers, and the disorders of the previous day were renewed with increased violence. Some of the magistrates were early in attendance, and the Riot Act was read three times, a warning being given at the third reading that the populace must disperse within an hour. The notice being disregarded, the militia were again summoned, and the magistrates superintended the collection of the tolls until about six o'clock, when, the mob having diminished in number, they withdrew, accompanied by the troops and constabulary, toll-collecting being abandoned for the night. Their retreat was almost immediately signalised by renewed rioting, one of the toll-houses being speedily sacked, and the furniture burnt in the street; while a few militiamen sent back to protect the building were driven off by volleys of oyster shells. The attitude of the mob now became very threatening, and when the magistrates, supported by the troops, again repaired to the bridge, they encountered a storm of missiles, accompanied with yells of defiance. The justices, after commanding the populace to disperse, and being answered by more stone-throwing, ordered the soldiers to fire, the front rank discharging their muskets at their assailants on the bridge, while the rear, changing front, swept the crowd that was attacking them from High Street. The effects of repeated volleys, followed by a bayonet charge, were naturally tragical. Eleven persons were killed or mortally wounded, and 45 others were injured; and as is always the case in such calamities, several of the sufferers were harmless lookers-on, two being respectable tradesmen and one a visitor. The riot, however, was at an end, the mob flying in every direction. Judging from the opinions expressed by the coroners' juries on the following day (October 1st), the conduct of the bridge trustees and the magistrates was condemned by many citizens, verdicts of wilful murder by persons unknown being delivered upon ten of the bodies. Possibly excited by this decision, a large mob assembled in the evening, and destroyed the windows of the Council House and Guildhall. Further tumults were happily obviated by the public spirit of a few leading citizens, amongst whom Messrs. John Thomas, William Elton, Matthew Wright and John Bally were most prominent. Those gentlemen, raising the needful amount by private subscription, purchased an assignment of Harris's lease, paying over three months' rent to the trustees, who were thus enabled to purchase £2,230 in Consols after discharging all their liabilities. The tolls, never collected after Monday's bloodshed, were thus definitively abolished. The Corporation condemned this arrangement as a dangerous concession to the populace, but its opposition was ineffectual. The civic body, however, successfully thwarted the efforts of Dr. Long Fox, an eminent local physician, to bring the conduct of the trustees before the bar of public opinion. His request that the Guildhall might be granted for a meeting of the citizens was refused by the court of aldermen, all of whom were themselves trustees. Dr. Fox then obtained leave to use the Coopers' Hall, but through corporate intimidation the permission was withdrawn, and a similar result attended his engagement of a large warehouse. The Corporation next successfully exerted itself to prevent a public subscription for the families of the victims, starting at the same time a fund to provide shoes and stockings for the British troops in Holland. It next commenced an action for libel against the printer of a London newspaper called the *Star*, which had published a letter from Bristol accusing Alderman Daubeny of brutal conduct during the disturbances ; but the only apparent result of this step was the expenditure of about £189 in law costs. As will shortly be shown, the Chamber became so unpopular in consequence of the riots that it was found almost impossible for several years to induce respectable inhabitants to accept civic honours.

The first and only reference to street watering throughout the century occurs in the civic accounts for September, 1793, when ten shillings were paid for two years' watering before the Council House.

During the year 1793, Dr. Thomas Beddoes, who had distinguished himself as Reader in Chemistry at the University of Oxford from 1788 to 1792, but had found further residence there impracticable owing to his sympathy with the French Republicans, settled in Clifton, with a view to establishing a Pneumatic Institute for the treatment of diseases by inhalation. The reputation of the new comer as a vigorous and original thinker was already considerable in cultivated circles, and his fame amongst the visitors to Clifton—amongst whom the Marquis of Lansdowne, Earl Stanhope, and Mr. Lambton, father of the first Earl of Durham, were then conspicuous—soon spread amongst the Whig inhabitants. The apparatus for the intended experiment was constructed by James Watt, £1,500 of the outlay being contributed by Mr. Lambton, and £1,000 by Thomas Wedgwood, who removed to Clifton to enjoy Beddoes's society. Southey and Coleridge were also close friends of the doctor, whose talents and philanthropy they warmly eulogised. The institution was at length opened in Dowry Square in 1798, and, though it failed in its professed object, it is memorable for having fostered the genius of young Humphry Davy, who was engaged as assistant, and who there discovered the properties of nitrous-oxide gas in 1799, to Southey's enthusiastic delight. Dr. Beddoes closed the institution in 1801, and died in December, 1808, at a moment, says Davy, when his mind was purified for noble affections and great works. " He had talents which would have raised him to the highest pinnacle of philosophical eminence if they had been applied with discretion."

In a treatise entitled " Of the Hotwell Waters, near Bristol," by John Nott, M.D., published in 1793, the writer briefly refers to " the newly discovered hot spring . . . discovered some few years since on Clifton hill." The water of Sion Spring, as it was called, was obtained by driving a shaft through the limestone to the depth of about 250 feet, at a great expense to the adventurer, an attorney, named Morgan. A copious store being, however, reached (the spring yielded nearly 34,000 gallons daily), a steam engine was erected on the premises, supply pipes were laid to many neighbouring houses, and more distant customers were served by carts. Clifton had been previously deficient in springs, and Mr. Morgan proved a local benefactor. As the temperature of the water was 70 degrees, or nearly as high as that of the Hot Well, a pump-room was erected for visitors, and in June, 1798, Thomas Bird announced that he had fitted up the premises at a great expense, and had also provided his patrons with hot baths and a reading room. Although some physicians had declared the Sion water to possess all the healing properties of the lower well, and although the spring was not disturbed, like its more famous rival, by the spring tides of the Avon, the place was never successful in attracting visitors. In 1803 the pump room, "calculated for any genteel business," was advertised to be let. The baths were continued for some years. The proprietor, moreover, obtained a considerable income from private dwellings, over 300 being eventually furnished with a supply from his property.

A duel was fought on the 10th December, 1793, in a field near the Montague inn, Kingsdown, between two officers of the army. Three shots were fired on each side, and one of the combatants nearly lost his life from a wound in the leg. The newspaper report states that the encounter was witnessed by a number of spectators.

Another attempt was made about this time to establish cotton weaving as a branch of local industry. An advertisement of the Bristol Cotton Manufactory, published in January, 1794, stated that the proprietors were offering for sale at their warehouse, adjoining the factory in Temple Street, a large stock of calicoes, bed ticks, etc. The concern employed about 250 persons, and seventy looms were at one time in operation. A small factory for spinning cotton yarn then existed at Keynsham. The Temple Street works were abandoned in 1805.

Mr. Burke, the recorder, the " honest Richard " of Goldsmith's " Retaliation," having died in February, 1794, the Common Council, in the following month, appointed Mr. Vicary Gibbs to the vacant office. The new functionary, who was knighted on becoming one of the law officers of the Crown, and subsequently attained the chief justiceship of the Common Pleas, gained the name of "Sir Vinegar" from the acrid.ty of his temper and the sourness of his language, which spared neither litigants, barristers nor criminals. (The unfortunate Spencer Perceval asserted on one occasion that Gibbs's nose would remove iron-moulds from linen.) Soon after his election, the Common Council raised the annual honorarium of the recordership from 50 to 100 guineas.

On the 29th April, when much alarm prevailed owing to the French threats of invasion, a meeting was held in the Guildhall, to promote measures for increasing the security of the country. A subscription was opened, which soon reached nearly £5,000, and it was resolved to raise a regiment of infantry, to be called the Loyal Bristol Regiment—subsequently the 103rd of the Line. By offering a bounty of 5 guineas a head, 684 men were soon under the colours, and the Government appointed Lord Charles Somerset lieutenant-colonel. The accounts afterwards published showed the following disbursements:—Bounty, £3,591; extra accoutrements, 20s. per man, £684; colours and drums, £92; drink to men on embarking at Pill, £30; flags and ribbons for recruiting sergeants, £22.

Although the French revolutionists seemed irresistible on land, they were no match for the English navy. During the year, to the great joy of Bristolians, the principal West India colonies of the enemy fell into British hands. About the end of April the capture of Martinico was announced; a few weeks later the bells rang a whole day in honour of the conquest of Guadaloupe, and early in July there were similar rejoicings at the fall of Port-au-Prince. But the crowning naval event of the year was Lord Howe's famous victory over the French fleet on the 1st June, intelligence of which arrived on the 12th, and excited transports of enthusiasm. John Weeks, of the Bush inn, in the costume of a sailor, proposed loyal toasts through a speaking trumpet from the balcony of his house, drinking innumerable bumpers in their honour, while his servants distributed liquor amongst the delighted populace below. In the evening the city was illuminated.

The local journals of the 28th June announced that Mr. T. Davis had fitted up a pump-room at the mineral spring at the Tennis Court house, Hotwell Road. The medicinal qualities of the spa, originally discovered about 1785, were alleged to be superior to those of Cheltenham water, and astonishing cures were said to have been effected. Hot and cold baths were subsequently constructed—to the annoyance of the renter of the neighbouring cold baths at Jacob's Wells, who invited public attention to the superior advantages of his establishment. In July, 1808, the spa, with its "pleasant garden bordering on the river," was advertised to be let, and in January, 1810, the premises were converted into "the Mineral Spa coal wharf," by J. Poole, coal wharfinger. The Jacob's Wells baths survived their rival for half a century.

The Corporation account books record a loan, in July, 1794, from a local bank of which no previous mention has been found. The proprietors—all men of high standing—were James Ireland, Philip Protheroe, Henry Bengough, Joseph Haythorne, and Matthew Wright. The Bristol City Bank, as it was called, was carried on at 46, High Street, until 1837, when the goodwill was purchased by the National Provincial Bank, which opened a branch in the old premises.

Until the death of the Rev. John Wesley, the services at the local Methodist chapels had been held at hours which permitted the congregations to attend their parish churches also. In the autumn of 1794, many Wesleyans, disapproving of the arrangement, urged that the services should be held simultaneously with those of the churches, while others protested against any change in Mr. Wesley's system. The denomination was also divided on another point—the celebration of the Communion—which had hitherto been conducted by clergymen who had received episcopal ordination, though many young Wesleyans contended that the ordinary ministers of the society were competent for its performance. In the result, the more fervent followers of Wesley's precepts continued to observe them at Broadmead and Guinea Street chapels, whilst their opponents assembled at Portland Chapel and other meeting houses. A dispute followed with the trustees of the chapel in the Horsefair, which was abandoned in 1795 for the newly erected Ebenezer in King Street, and Wesley's first edifice was opened in December, 1800, for "preaching the Gospel in the Welsh language."

The Common Council, in September, elected Mr. John Fisher Weare to the office of mayor. On his refusal to accept the dignity, Mr. Joseph Harford was appointed, but also declined. Mr. Joseph Smith then consented to serve. It is probably significant that during his term of office the yearly allowance made to each mayor was raised from £1,000 to £1,200. In the course of a few months, three influential citizens, George Gibbs, Stephen Cave, and Robert Bush, jun., were severally elected councillors, but declined to enter the Chamber. In September, 1795, Mr. William Weare was elected mayor, but followed the example of his relative. Mr. James Harvey was then induced to assume the dignity. So great was the difficulty encountered in filling vacancies in the Council that a committee was appointed early in 1796 to consider the matter, and in conformity with its suggestion the fine for refusing office was increased to £300. The reluctance of the citizens, however, was not overcome, for Benjamin Baugh, Philip John Miles, James Brown, Henry King, and John Pinney soon afterwards refused to serve as councillors after being elected. A new embarrassment arose about the same time, several councillors declining to vote when questions were brought to a division. A case was laid before the new recorder, to elicit his opinion as to how the dumb might be made to speak, and the recalcitrants appear to have submitted to Mr. Gibbs's implied rebuke. In September, 1796, Mr. Richard Bright and Mr. Evan Baillie respectively paid the fine of £400 rather than assume the office of mayor, and Mr. Harvey remained in the civic chair for another twelvemonth. A little later, Thomas Pierce, Michael Castle, and Samuel Edwards refused to become councillors. The unpopularity into which the Corporation had fallen is sufficiently indicated by this imperfect summary of its perplexities.

Early in 1794 a thin quarto pamphlet made its appearance entitled, "Bristol, a Satire." The anonymous author, Robert Lovell, was a young Quaker of some talent, who had married one of three ladies named Fricker, carrying on business as milliners in Wine Street, his two sisters-in-law, as will presently be seen, becoming the helpmates of poets of more lasting fame. Lovell's satire is marked rather by spleen than force. One of the chief complaints which he formulated against

Bristol's matchless sons,
In avarice Dutchmen, and in science Huns,

was that when they assembled in places of business resort, their conversation rolled exclusively upon business topics and commercial news, which does not seem a striking proof of unintelligence. He rates their stinginess, however, in permitting the reconstruction of the Infirmary to linger on from year to year; he mocks their stupidity in still assembling on 'Change in Corn Street, regardless of the elegant building raised close by for their accommodation; and he sneers at the want of taste of a community that refused to enliven its dulness by supporting winter concerts, though six entertainments had been offered for a guinea a head. Some scathing lines follow, denouncing the oppression practised by the self-elected Corporation, which claimed by chartered right the privilege of doing wrong. In 1795, Lovell, in conjunction with his brother-in-law, Southey, published another volume of "Poems," now much prized for its rarity.

The coinage in 1794 was in a state of utter disorganisation. The silver currency having become worn down to mere slips of metal, the manufacture of counterfeit coin became the easiest of processes, and false shillings were sold wholesale to knavish traders, waiters, etc., at the rate of 4s. 6d. for twenty. The counterfeiting of halfpence had been going on for some years, but received a new impulse from the silver frauds. Unscrupulous employers, buying largely from the coiners, paid away the worthless metal in wages to their workmen, and similar iniquity was only too common amongst low shopkeepers, turnpike men, and others. The evil became so great that the Bristol newspaper proprietors announced that halfpence would not be accepted by their newsmen. Some local tradesmen adopted an opposite course, offering to receive payments in any coin, but of course protecting themselves from loss by an unavowed increase of prices. Two shopkeepers, again, Mr. Niblock, draper, Bridge Street, and Mr. Bird, tea-dealer, Wine Street, issued halfpence bearing their respective names. Genuine silver coins showing any trace of the royal effigy were hoarded, or sold at a premium, until at length, in 1796, there was such a scarcity of change as to impede ordinary business. The production by forgers then became immense. On the 11th March, 1796, a meeting was held in the Guildhall to take measures to meet the evil. There being reason to believe that some inhabitants had leagued themselves with the coiners in order to plunder the public, it was resolved to offer rewards for the discovery of the offenders. The device was fruitless, and the frauds increased enormously during the year, the London *Times* remarking in October that scarce a waggon or coach left the capital that did not carry boxes of base coin to the provincial towns, "insomuch that the country is deluged with counterfeit money." A large supply of new copper coin was at length furnished in 1797.

In July or August, 1794, Samuel Taylor Coleridge, who had just conceived a sublime scheme for the regeneration of humanity, and had inoculated a few youthful associates with his own enthusiasm as to its success, visited Bristol with some of his disciples, for the purpose of starting the enterprise. It was proposed to establish a philosophical and social colony, or Pantisocracy, on the banks of the Susquehanna, in the United States, where a select body of incorruptible and cultivated men and women would secure felicity for themselves, whilst striving to regenerate an effete civilisation by a revival of the communism of primitive Christianity. (The choice of the locality, it is said, was mainly due to the poetical beauty of the river's name.) Amongst the propounder's most zealous supporters were the Bristol-born Robert Southey, then an Oxford student disgusted with the Toryism and orthodoxy of his university, the young Bristol Quaker, Robert Lovell, already noticed, and George Burnett, the son of a Somerset farmer. Other converts were expected to arrive from the universities. Coleridge, with Southey and Burnett, lodged in the meantime at 48, College Street. [The numbering of the street has been altered, but the house in question now bears a tablet commemorating Coleridge's visit.] The dreams of the youthful philosophers were soon roughly disturbed by an encounter with the harsh realities of life. They had come to Bristol to provide themselves with the needful equipage for their proposed Elysium, the hire of a ship and the outlay for stores being calmly estimated by Coleridge at about £1,200. Their combined funds, however, were so limited that, in order to pay a lodging bill for seven weeks, they were compelled to ask for a loan of £5 from Joseph Cottle, poet and bookseller, who then occupied an old house (afterwards burnt down) at the corner of High Street and Corn Street. Cottle's liberality to the enthusiasts will be remembered long after his prosy poetry is forgotten. He not only relieved their immediate distress, but, with a generosity uncommon in his trade, offered to give Coleridge and Southey—then unknown to the public—the sum of £30 each for two volumes of poems, following up this proposal by promising Southey 100 guineas (in money and books) for "Joan of Arc," from which the author—a lifelong victim of self-admiration—anticipated immortal fame. Coleridge and Southey next proposed to improve their resources by delivering lectures in Bristol, the former choosing political and moral subjects, whilst his friend discoursed on history. Coleridge's first two lectures were delivered at the Plume of Feathers inn, Wine Street; others were given at the Cheese Market, and in a room in Castle Green; and several at the

Assembly Room Coffee-house, on the Quay. Southey's twelve lectures (" tickets for the whole course 10s. 6d.") were delivered in the Assembly Room, and were, like the others, well attended, in spite of the unpopular political and religious opinions of the two orators. Although Coleridge gladly availed himself of advances from Cottle, the manuscript of his poems was not forthcoming for many months. The dreamy philosopher, in fact, was in love, so far as was compatible with his peculiar nature. Every Pantisocratist, indeed, was to be married, for in the ideal society the women were to busy themselves with material affairs, in order to leave the men at leisure to philosophise and versify at their ease. A sort of matrimonial epidemic accordingly broke out in the family of Mrs. Fricker, a schoolmistress on Redcliff Hill, who had five marriageable daughters. Lovell had already married one of the young ladies, Southey was engaged to another, an unnamed Pantisocratist had laid siege to a third, who was too practical-minded to accept him, and in October, 1795, Coleridge was married at St. Mary Redcliff church to a fourth, named Sarah. A cottage at the then secluded village of Clevedon had been engaged for the young couple at a rent of £5 yearly, but Coleridge treated the question of furnishing with characteristic contempt, and two days after the marriage Cottle received a hurried epistle requesting him to buy and forward an assortment of domestic necessaries, including a tea-kettle, a couple of candlesticks, a dust-pan, two tumblers, two spoons, a cheese toaster, a pair of slippers, a keg of porter, and some groceries. Even a bit of carpet would have been wanting but for the thoughtfulness of a friend. A Pantisocratic life was thus lived for the first time in beautiful simplicity. But a residence twelve miles from books and society was soon found untenable, and Coleridge removed to Redcliff Hill in December. Robert Southey had already followed the example of his companion, having married Edith Fricker in November; but in this case the couple separated at the door of Redcliff Church, and the young husband—so poor as to be unable to buy a wedding ring without Cottle's help—immediately sailed for Lisbon. His desertion gave the finishing blow to the Pantisocratic system, for Coleridge's promise of a book in defence of his social reform—like many other similar promises—was never fulfilled. He was temporarily diverted, indeed, from his dreams by the action of the Ministry, who, by their own admission, determined to revive the despotic legislation of the Tudors. Two Bills were brought into Parliament and speedily passed, by one of which any person who, by speech or writing, should incite "contempt" of the Government or of the unreformed House of Commons was rendered liable to transportation for seven years; while by the other the right of public meeting was practically set aside, and the penalty of death was incurred by any twelve persons who remained assembled, even in a peaceable manner, for one hour after a magistrate had ordered them to disperse. Against proposals which he deemed monstrous, Coleridge was aroused to protest warmly. He delivered an address on the 26th November " in the Great Room, at the Pelican inn, Thomas Street; admission, one shilling;" and followed this up by two pamphlets, " Conciones ad Populum," and " The Plot Discovered," in which he emphatically denounced the tyrannical policy of Mr. Pitt. (According to Mr. Fitzgerald, the ablest authority on the subject, Coleridge was at this period constantly "overshadowed" by one of the army of spies maintained by the Government.) Various literary projects were next contemplated, Coleridge eventually resolving to publish a periodical miscellany, "to supply the places of a review, newspaper and annual register." About 370 subscribers were obtained in Bristol; the roll was increased to 1,000 by a canvass made by the author himself in the great manufacturing towns; and on the 1st March, 1796, the first number was issued of *The Watchman*, price four-pence, which was to appear every eighth day, in order to avoid the heavy tax on newspapers. About half the subscribers, however, were lost by the publication in the second number of an article on public fasts, containing an unlucky Scriptural quotation ("My bowels shall sound like a harp," Isaiah xvi.); the two next alienated the admirers of the French Republic; and the tenth intimated that *The Watchman* had run its course, as "the work did not pay its expenses." The loss entailed by the publication was chiefly borne by Cottle. Coleridge, in the meantime, had removed from Redcliff Hill to Kingsdown, where his son Hartley was born. He was at this period an occasional preacher in Unitarian chapels, and Cottle gives an account of two characteristic performances in a Bath pulpit, where the philosopher, attired in a blue coat and white waistcoat, scared away the congregations by discoursing on the corn laws and the new tax on hair powder. During the summer, urged by his friend Mr. Thomas Poole, of Nether Stowey, he removed to a cottage at that place, and his preaching came to an end. In 1797, Cottle published a second edition of Coleridge's poems, to which were added several pieces by his young friends, Charles Lamb and Charles Lloyd. In the same year, Coleridge published in a Bristol newspaper a poem on the death of Burns, which resulted in a handsome local contribution to the fund for the relief of the poet's family. In 1798, Mr. Thomas Wedgwood, then residing at Cote House, Durdham Down, determined, in conjunction with his brother Josiah, to allow Coleridge £150 yearly for life, and the munificent gift led to the recipient's departure from the West of England. Before leaving for Germany with Wordsworth, who had also been living near Stowey, Coleridge induced Cottle to give 30 guineas for another volume of poems, containing the Lyrical Ballads of his new friend (Wordsworth's first work), and his own immortal "Ancient Mariner." The book fell almost still-born from the press, and the enterprising publisher, who soon afterwards retired from business, was informed by Messrs. Longman that the copyright was valueless. The sufferer presented it to Wordsworth, and afterwards consoled himself for his loss by reminding the public that he, a Bristol tradesman, had secured himself the fame—rejected by the great London houses—of publishing the first works of four of the most eminent writers of his generation.

An accident illustrating the dangers of the harbour occurred on the 24th September, 1794. The Esther, a new ship, which had just arrived from Barbadoes with a cargo of 519 hhds. of sugar and other goods, fell on her beam ends at ebb tide, and the whole of her contents, valued at many thousand pounds, was practically destroyed. The captain and crew had displayed remarkable gallantry a few days before reaching Kingroad. The Esther, which had only 18 men and 3 boys, was attacked by a French privateer with 20 six-pounders and about 140 men, but after an engagement lasting from 5 o'clock in the evening until 9 the following morning, the determined resistance of the Englishmen forced the enemy to sheer off.

A curiously shaped coach, running upon eight wheels, was introduced into the district about this time. Two of the vehicles were running daily between Bristol and Bath in November, 1794, carrying outside passengers at 1s. and inside at 2s. each, and performing the journey in 2½ hours. Southey mentions a Bristol coach to Birmingham carrying 16 persons inside, which must have been constructed on the same principle.

The Incorporation of the Poor, in spite of former failures, determined in 1794 to establish a manufactory at the workhouse for the employment of the youthful inmates. The making of flannels having been resolved upon, a building for the purpose was erected at St. Peter's Hospital. In 1799 it was reported that raw material had been purchased at a cost of £1,660, while the total sum obtained for the manufactured goods was only £1,394. The factory was thereupon closed, the premises being converted into wards for the greatly increased number of paupers.

The refusal of sailors to enter the navy led to an unusual stretch of power in February, 1795. By an Order in Council an embargo was placed on the merchant shipping and trows lying in the ports, and an Act was passed in the following month, ordaining that no British vessel should be permitted to clear outwards until the port at which it lay had furnished the navy with the number of seamen prescribed in the statute. The numbers fixed for the chief ports afford only too striking evidence of the comparative decline of Bristol shipping. London was required to find 5,704 men; Liverpool, 1,711; Newcastle, 1,240; Hull, 731; the Clyde ports, 683; Sunderland, 669; Bristol, 666. It may be interesting to show the relative positions of the other local ports. Gloucester was required to furnish 28 men; Chepstow (of which Newport was a creek), 38; Cardiff, 14; Bridgwater, 26; Minehead, 18; Swansea, 85; and Ilfracombe, 49. To quicken the recruiting, the Admiralty offered bounties of 25 guineas a head to able seamen, 20 guineas to ordinary seamen, and 15 guineas to landsmen. The Bristol contingent (half of the men being landsmen) was completed in May, when the embargo was removed. By another Act, passed in the same session, a further levy of men was made upon the kingdom generally, Gloucestershire, including Bristol, being required to produce 201. (The Corporation was greatly offended at the city being included in the shire, and refused to co-operate with the county authorities.) The manner in which the demand was met is shown by the minutes of the vestry of St. Stephen's parish, the clerk being ordered on the 10th September to make a rate to raise £50 13s. 6d. "to pay bounties to three seamen raised by the parish for the use of his Majesty's Navy." The recruitment of the army presented similar difficulties. The Crown debtors in Bristol and other gaols were offered their liberty provided they would join a marching regiment, and in October a number of felons awaiting transportation were treated in the same manner. The unpopularity of the forces was largely due to the abuses that prevailed. In the course of the year the Duke of York, commander in chief, issued a circular to the colonels of regiments, demanding a return to be made of the number of captaincies held by boys under 12 years of age—many commissions being in fact sinecures enjoyed by lads at school.

The manufacture of cloth, once the most important of local industries, rapidly declined during the later years of the century, scarcely any attempt having been made to compete with the Yorkshire clothiers in the production of more popular fabrics. A Bristol cloth mill "at the One Mile Stone, Stapleton Road," was offered for sale in March, 1795, and is the last mentioned in the newspapers.

The following amusing illustration of the lawlessness of the Kingswood district has been found in the London *Times* of April, 1795. "Monday last, two bailiffs' followers made a seizure for rent at a house in Kingswood, near Bristol. An alarm being given, they were surrounded by a number of colliers, who conveyed them to a neighbouring coal-pit, and let them down, where they were suffered to remain till about 2 the next morning, when they were had up, and, each having a glass of gin and some gingerbread given him, were immersed again in the dreary bowels of the earth, where they were confined, in all, nearly 24 hours. On being released they were made to pay a fine of 6s. 8d. each for their lodging, and take an oath never to trouble, or molest, any of them again."

The use of starch or flour for "powdering" the hair was long universal amongst the upper and middle classes of both sexes. A duty of $3\frac{1}{4}d.$ per lb. was imposed on starch in 1787, and produced a considerable sum. In 1795, Mr. Pitt, fancying that he could raise a still greater revenue out of hair powder, placed a tax on those who adopted it; but merely hastened a reform which was already imminent. Powdering having been dropped in France at the Revolution, many youthful Englishmen followed the example; and when a succession of bad harvests raised flour to a famine price, the absurdity of diminishing the food supply for the sake of disfiguring a natural ornament was soon widely recognised. A correspondent of *Felix Farley's Journal* of the 16th May estimated the cost of powder to be at least 3 guineas per head yearly, and suggested that the amount saved by giving it up should be devoted to the relief of the distressed poor. Strangely enough, the military authorities persisted for some years in requiring the infantry and militia to powder their heads, and when volunteering became popular, in 1797, the Government sought to encourage the movement by exempting citizen soldiers from the tax on hair powder.

The distress caused by the dearth was exceeding great, and every class was required to make sacrifices happily unknown to a later age. The harvest of the year proved even more deficient than that of 1794, and George III. gave orders that the bread used in his household should be made of mixed wheat and rye, an example extensively followed. The families of small tradesmen and working men were reduced to eat a bread composed of equal proportions of flour and potatoes. But even food of this kind was above the reach of the poor, who were occasionally driven to desperation by hunger, and on June 6th the populace attacked the butchers' shops in the High Street Market, carried off a quantity of meat, and sacked a (baker's?) shop. Riots also occurred in the eastern suburbs, and the Kingswood colliers seized several cartloads of corn on the way to market. But all these incidents were unreported in the newspapers, from a foolish dread that publicity might tend to increase the disorders. Our information on the subject is chiefly derived from the civic minute books:—" June 26: Expenses incurred during the late riots in the neighbourhood of this city, £119 6s. 9d."; "Sept. 5, Resolved that an additional sum of £500 be paid to the mayor in consideration of extra expenses by a military force being called in to suppress the riots caused by the high price of provisions." In July a public meeting was held to take measures for relieving the distress, at which it was announced that the sheriffs would curtail the entertainments given at the assizes, and contribute the cost of one banquet (£120) to the fund. Large subscriptions were offered, and daily distributions of rice and other grain at reduced prices were soon after established. The Corporation ordered the purchase of several cargoes of wheat and flour, which were sold to bakers at prime cost, the loss incurred by these transactions being more than covered by sales at market price to the distressed inhabitants of the adjoining counties. In August the average price of wheat rose to the unprecedented sum of 106s. 9d. per quarter. The magistrates had already forbidden the manufacture of bread made from fine flour, and for nearly two years more (the harvest of 1796 being also a failure) wheat had to be largely supplemented by barley, peas, rice, and potatoes.

One of the consequences of the dearth was a great advance

in the charges of boarding schools. In September, 1795, Mr. George Pocock opened a boarding school on St. Michael's Hill, where his fee for boys was 25 guineas each per annum. Pocock was a man of great mechanical ingenuity. His kite carriage is described in the Annals of the Nineteenth Century. Southey states that he also invented a machine for thrashing his scholars, which they called a "royal patent self-acting ferule."

The ill-fated marriage of George, Prince of Wales, seems to have provoked little rejoicing. The corporate cash book, however, records a payment of £124 6s. 10d., "expenses attending the presentation of an address to the King, and compliments to the Prince on the occasion." The cost of the civic deputations was mainly due to the mode in which they travelled. Three post chaises, each with four horses, were engaged for the aldermen, sheriffs, and chief officers, and a mysterious chariot followed. The journey each way occupied three days, and as turtle was carried in the chariot, the aldermen could not trust the delicacy to the country kitchen-maids, and the fish kettle was accompanied by a skilful cook and all his implements.

The commerce of the country was still largely carried on in vessels the dwarfishness of which would now excite astonishment. Many of the Bristol ships that conveyed emigrants to America did not exceed 100 tons registered burden. *Felix Farley's Journal* of July 25th, 1795, reports the arrival in Kingroad of a vessel "called the Jenny, of 75 tons, the property of S. Teast, Esq., after making a voyage round the world in one year and ten months." The commerce of the port diminished greatly during the early years of the war. In 1792 the vessels paying mayor's dues numbered 480. In 1796 the total was only 304.

On the 27th November the Duke of York, after reviewing two militia regiments on Durdham Down, paid a visit to Bristol, and was presented with the freedom of the city. A grand dinner followed at the Mansion House, for which the mayor was voted an additional allowance of £212.

Mention was made at page 256 of the gunpowder magazine at Tower Harritz, from which privateers and merchant vessels obtained supplies of ammunition. In despite of its perilous character, the magazine existed down to the close of the century, and was so carelessly guarded that in April, 1796, its owners, Messrs. Elton, Ames and Co., offered a reward for the discovery of thieves who had broken into the premises and stolen four barrels of powder.

A dissolution of Parliament took place in May, 1796, when the Marquis of Worcester withdrew from Bristol to offer himself for Gloucestershire. Mr. Charles Bragge came forward in the Tory interest. Lord Sheffield solicited reelection, but had lost the confidence of many Whigs owing to his support of all the Government measures, especially those for suspending the Habeas Corpus Act and restricting the liberty of the press. The dissidents accordingly brought forward M.. Ben'amin Hobhouse, a native of Bristol, and member of the Merchants' Company. [Mr. Hobhouse's son, long afterwards created Baron Broughton for distinguished political services, was at this time being educated in the famous school conducted by the Rev. Dr. Estlin on St. Michael's Hill]. A coalition was immediately formed between the Tory leaders and the friends of Lord Sheffield, who were numerous in the Corporation. The nomination took place on the 27th May, and the poll opened on the same day, when Mr. Bragge received 364 votes, Lord Sheffield 340, and Mr. Hobhouse 102. The last named gentleman withdrew the same evening, but the eccentric David Lewis, for whom two votes had been tendered, kept the poll open for several hours on the following day. The final figures were—Mr. Bragge, 714; Lord Sheffield, 679; Mr. Hobhouse, 102; Mr Lewis, 4. The freemen were afterwards feasted at the joint expense of the new members. Lord Sheffield was unpopular amongst the labouring classes, and, in consequence of the prominent part taken on his behalf by the mayor and some of the aldermen, a mob demolished the windows of the Mansion House, of the Council House, and of the Bush hotel (Lord Sheffield's headquarters).

Trinity Chapel, appertaining to Barstaple's Hospital in Old Market Street, was rebuilt during the summer at a cost of £454. The mean and ugly structure produced for this sum has been since demolished in its turn.

An illustration of the ecclesiastical abuses of the time occurs in the minutes of a Common Council meeting held on the 3rd October. A memorial was presented by the Rev. Joseph Atwell Small, D.D., incumbent of St. James's and vicar of St. Paul's, representing that he had been offered two vicarages in Monmouthshire, but that his acceptance of them would not only cause him to vacate the rectory of Burnsall, Yorkshire, but jeopardise his right to hold his two livings in Bristol. He therefore prayed the Chamber to guarantee him against this further deprivation, and the Council complaisantly resolved that no advantage should be taken of the possible avoidance of the two incumbencies. Dr. Small, who also held a prebend at Gloucester, presented another modest petition in June, 1799. It set forth that he desired to exchange the living of St. James's for the vicarage of Congresbury and chapelry of Wick St. Lawrence (held by the Rev. T. T. Biddulph). If permission to do so were granted, he undertook to exchange his two Monmouthshire livings for the rectory of Whitestaunton, Somerset, and he prayed the Chamber to permit him to remain in possession of the vicarage of St. Paul's, Bristol. The Corporation assented to all the requests of the reverend pluralist. Moreover, when he subsequently died insolvent, his "dilapidations" at Congresbury were defrayed out of the civic purse.

The West India trade of the port fell off to a surprising extent during the later years of the century. Out of a fleet of a hundred Jamaica merchantmen convoyed by the Royal Navy in 1796, only 7 vessels belonged to Bristol, 66 hailing from London, and 28 from Liverpool. In the Leeward Islands fleet of 97 ships in the same year, the Bristol vessels numbered only 14. In 1797 the Jamaica fleet comprised 144 merchantmen, of which 17 were bound for Bristol, while in 1798 the Bristol ships numbered 16 out of 150. Owing to the amazing decline in imports, the local sugar refineries had to look for supplies in other markets. *Felix Farley's Journal* of March 29th, 1800, records that "several cargoes of West Indian and American produce have been recently imported into this city from Liverpool."

Previous to 1796, the difficulty of adequately lighting churches and chapels with candles or smoky lamps rendered evening services uncommon. The newly invented Argand burner, however, reached England about this time, and worked a little social revolution, brilliant lighting being thenceforth only a question of expense. An evening lectureship was soon after established at St. Werburgh's. Evening services were nevertheless rare until a quarter of a century later.

The threats of the French Directory to spread republican principles by fire and sword, and to crush English opposition by a conquest of the island, were continuous throughout 1796. An army was drawn up on the coast of Normandy, where extensive preparations were made for the menaced invasion. The English Government raised an additional militia force of 60,000 to meet this peril, but the successes of the French in Italy inspired apprehensions as to the national security, and a feeling gradually arose in favour of a general armament of the country. *Felix Farley's Journal* of February 18th, 1797, stated that a body of "provisional cavalry" was being formed, and that a number of merchants and tradesmen, who had entered into an association with a view to guarding the prisoners of war at Stapleton in case the militia should be called away for active service, would hold a meeting that day to extend the movement. A numerously attended gathering consequently took place in the Guildhall, Evan Baillie, Esq., in the chair, when it was resolved to establish a "Military Volunteer Association." The proposed corps was to be of infantry, 1,000 strong, and to be called the Bristol Volunteers, commanded by two lieutenant colonels, two majors, ten captains, ten lieutenants, and ten ensigns, the whole force to serve without pay. (The lieutenants were afterwards increased to twenty-two.) The Government were expected to furnish muskets, field pieces, ammunition, and drums; also the pay of an adjutant, ten sergeants, and ten drummers; and it was stipulated that in no exigency should the corps be removed above one day's march from Bristol. The mayor for the time being was nominated honorary colonel; Messrs. Evan Baillie (Park Row) and William Gore (Brislington) were recommended to the Crown as suitable lieutenant colonels, and Thomas Kington (Rodney Place) and Thomas Haynes (Castle Green) were designated majors. The opening of a subscription, to provide uniforms for the less wealthy Volunteers, closed the proceedings. The movement received a powerful stimulus by the landing of 1,400 French troops, four days later, in Pembrokeshire, for although the incapable commander surrendered in a few hours, the incident showed that the navy was an uncertain security against invasion. On the 2nd March, when the Volunteers were still without arms, a lively sensation was caused by a report that another French force had landed in South Wales, and was advancing on Bristol. The Bucks Militia and a few regular troops, quartered in the city, received immediate orders to march to Pill, where they embarked in pilot skiffs for Tenby. Many citizens volunteered wagons and horses for the conveyance of the baggage, others liberally regaled the soldiers, and to provide them with comforts during the voyage nearly £100 were collected from the crowd assembled in College Green to witness their departure. A few militiamen had been reserved to guard the 2,000 French prisoners at Stapleton, but the Volunteers prevailed upon Lord Buckingham to despatch those men also, undertaking to perform the necessary duty. (When the alarm was at its height, it was proposed that the prisoners should be lowered into the Kingswood collieries of the Duke of Beaufort and Lord Middleton, and this would probably have been done if the city had been seriously menaced.) In the evening, however, the reported invasion proved a hoax, and the troops returned to their quarters. The Government, through the Duke of Portland, eulogised the patriotic zeal of the citizens, and the ranks of the Volunteers rapidly increased. Mr. Evan Baillie was afterwards gazetted as acting colonel, when Capt. Thomas Tyndall was promoted to the vacant lieutenant colonelcy. As the list of officers published in a local history is exceedingly incorrect, it may be as well to give the names of the gentlemen originally nominated by the corps and appointed by the Crown as captains and lieutenants:—No. 1 Company; Ralph Montague (Montague Street) and Azariah Pinney (Great George Street). No. 2 Comp.; Robert Claxton (Park Street) and Ralph Montague, jun. (Park Street). No. 3 Comp.; John Lambert (Clifton) and Henry King (St. Augustine's Back). No. 4 Comp.; John Span (Clifton) and J. S. Riddle (Portland Square). No. 5 Comp.; Gabriel Goldney (Clifton) and Thomas Corser (Redcliff Street). No. 6 Comp.; Charles Payne (Queen's Parade) and Thomas Hill (Orchard Street). No. 7 Comp.; Joseph Bisset (Clifton) and George Gibbs (Park Street). No. 8 Comp.; Robert Bush (College Green) and H. Tobin (Berkeley Square). No. 9 Comp.; Thomas Tyndall (Berkeley Square) and John Gordon (Cleeve Hill). No. 10 Comp.; Philip John Miles (Clifton) and John Foy Edgar (Park Row). Mr. Stephen Cave (Brunswick Square) was quartermaster. Mr. W. B. Elwyn (Berkeley Square) was captain of a cavalry corps, called the Bristol Light Horse Volunteers, subsequently formed into two troops under Richard Pearsall and Levi Ames, John Vaughan and John Wedgwood being lieutenants. Both corps were presented with colours by the ladies of Bristol, and at their first review on Durdham Down the steadiness of the citizen soldiers won general applause. The corps at one time numbered nearly 1,500 effectives, exclusive of a Clifton corps of 132 and a Westbury corps of 136 men. The dress of the Volunteers has been preserved to posterity by two life-size marble figures sculptured upon the monument in the Cathedral to the memory of Lieutenant Colonel Gore. Many influential citizens served in the ranks, and somewhat fabulous statements have been made as to the personal wealth represented by some of the companies.

Southey states in his Common Place Book that during the alarm of invasion the Rev. Samuel Seyer, the Bristol historian, furnished the boys in his boarding school with arms, and that the lads seriously thought of shooting their master, whose fondness for excessive punishments was abnormal even in those days. Their design was, however, discovered, and the affair was hushed up.

The French landing in Wales, in spite of its ludicrous failure, caused a financial convulsion throughout the country. The hoarding of gold had become prevalent in the later months of 1796, in consequence of the invasion alarms, and when news arrived of an actual descent, a rush was made on the banks for repayment of their notes. On Saturday, the 25th February, the bullion in the Bank of England was reduced to £1,272,000, with every prospect of being exhausted on the following Monday. The Privy Council, however, met on Sunday, and ordered the Bank to suspend cash payments. As the step was calculated to increase the panic and augment the demands on private bankers, a meeting, hurriedly convened by the mayor at the suggestion of the Government, was held at the Mansion House, Bristol, on Monday morning, when about seventy leading citizens (including many bankers) passed a resolution earnestly recommending the citizens to receive local bank notes in lieu of cash, and advising the banks to make no payments in specie, and to demand none in discharge of bills. The excitement afterwards gradually died away.

The Common Council, in March, 1797, presented the freedom of the city to Sir John Jervis, afterwards Earl St. Vincent, in honour of his brilliant victory over the French and Spanish fleets. In September a similar compliment was paid to Admiral Nelson, and in the following month to Lord Duncan for his triumph at Camperdown.

General Kosciusko, the celebrated Polish patriot, arrived in Bristol on the 13th June on his way to the United States, and was received with enthusiastic tokens of sympathy. The sheriffs tendered the congratulations of the civic body, but he became the guest of the American Consul until his embarkation. On the 17th, the general was presented by a deputation of citizens with an address eulogising his character and heroism, accompanied by a piece of plate, value 100 guineas. The exile sailed on the 19th amidst renewed demonstrations of respect.

The newspapers of the 24th June announced that Edward Bird, portrait, historical and landscape painter, had opened an evening drawing-school for young gentlemen—the first, so far as is known, attempted in the city. The academy was situated in what would now be deemed a strange locality, "Temple Back, near the Passing Slip" (a much frequented ferry). Mr. Bird's terms were as humble as was his residence. His fee for each pupil was one guinea a quarter for three lessons a week "from 5 to 7 o'clock." The talented artist attained the rank of Royal Academician, but his merits were ignored by the city of his adoption, and he died, as he had lived, in poverty.

The ordnance officers charged with the first trigonometrical survey of the kingdom (commenced in 1784) pitched their tents on Dundry hill about the end of July, and commenced their work in this district. Three weeks later the camp—which caused great disquietude in the agricultural community, to whom the supposed magical powers of the surveying instruments suggested alarming intentions on the part of the Government—was removed to Lansdown. The local maps formed upon this survey were not published until twenty years afterwards.

The Common Council, in October, granted permission to the Rev. T. Broughton, rector of St. Peter's, to hold with that living the incumbency of Westbury, the chapelry of Redland and the chapelry of Shirehampton.

The defenceless state of the Bristol Channel naturally created much uneasiness at a time when the French Government was constantly threatening invasion. At a meeting of the aldermanic body, in October, it was resolved to address the Admiralty, drawing attention to the fact that between Lundy Island and Kingroad there was not a single fortified point of land, and praying that a gunboat be stationed off Portishead and another in the Bristol Channel. It was also resolved to make an appeal to the Duke of York for the erection of signal posts to guard against a surprise, and for the fortifying of certain points for the security of the harbour. The authorities held a deaf ear to these applications, apparently in the hope that the citizens would protect themselves. In April, 1798, the Admiralty recommended that all the serviceable long-boats in the port should be armed with cannon for the purpose of being used as gunboats at Kingroad, but neither men, arms nor ammunition were offered by the Government. A Pill row-boat and a ship's long-boat were shortly afterwards armed by a local committee. A battery at the mouth of the Avon appears to have been constructed about the same time, and the old works at Portishead were repaired and garrisoned.

The local newspapers of the 18th November announced that two well-known surgeons, Mr. Francis C. Bowles and Mr. Richard Smith, were about to deliver a course of anatomical lectures at the Red Lodge. The movement was initiated by Dr. Beddoes, who induced the Marquis of Lansdowne, Earl Stanhope, and other friends then sojourning at Clifton to guarantee the lecturers from loss. The course, however, was so popular that, including £50 presented by the guarantors, a profit was made of about £140. The two surgeons subsequently determined to found a permanent School of Anatomy, and, having purchased a house in Trinity Street, they built a theatre on the stables behind it. But Mr. Bowles having died soon afterwards, the premises were transferred to a Philosophical Society; on the breaking up of which they were purchased by Dr. Kentish, who fitted them up for hot baths—the first, apparently, in the city. In 1806 Mr. Thomas Shute built an anatomical theatre at the end of College Street, where he lectured for nine years, thus practically founding the Bristol Medical School. In 1813, Mr. Frank Gold opened a rival establishment over part of the cloisters of the Cathedral. (The site is identified in O'Neil's view of the cloisters, a skeleton being depicted as looking out of the window of Gold's room.) After Mr. Shute's death, in 1816, Dr. Wallis occupied his theatre until 1822, when new rooms were built in the Bishop's Park, behind College Street. In the meantime Mr. Goodeve began lecturing over the cloisters in 1819, and continued to do so until about 1827. The extraordinary attachment of the professors for the Cathedral precincts will be remarked throughout these changes. In 1826 Mr. Clarke began to lecture in King Square. About 1830, a new school was erected in Park Square, behind College Street. Finally the long continued rivalry gave place to co-operation, and the Bristol Medical School was opened in Old Park on the 14th October, 1834, when Mr. Richard Smith delivered an opening address, from which the above facts have been derived.

On the 17th November, 1797, an obstinately fought duel took place near Durdham Down between Lieut.-Colonel Sykes, of the Berkshire Militia, and Mr. Charles F. Williams, a barrister, and one of the Bristol Volunteers. Four shots were exchanged on each side at ten paces distance, and on each occasion one or other of the combatants had his clothes pierced by a ball. Eventually both were wounded, though not seriously, and the affair terminated with mutual apologies. The encounter arose out of some remarks made by Williams in a newspaper on the rude conduct of a militia officer at a concert.

On the 23rd February, 1798, at a time when Consols had fallen to 48, and the Government were extremely embarrassed to find means for maintaining the war, a meeting was held in the Guildhall to consider the best means of supporting the Ministry. To stimulate the enthusiasm of the citizens, *Felix Farley's Journal* of the 17th published the orders alleged to have been issued by General Hoche, the commander of the French troops that landed in Wales, to Colonel Tate, one of his subordinates. "The destruction of Bristol," said this document, "is of the very last importance, and every possible effort should be made to accomplish it." Tate was directed to sail up the Avon at night, land about five miles from the mouth on the right bank, and set fire to the quarter lying to windward, which would produce the total ruin of the town, the port, the docks and the vessels. The mayor, who presided at the meeting, reminded his hearers of the patriotic exertions of the citizens in 1745, when they raised such a sum for the defence of the country as excited the surprise of the whole kingdom. It was resolved to open a voluntary subscription. The list was headed by the Corporation, which voted £1,000, "after taking into consideration the low state of its finances." The mayor gave £500, the Society of Merchants £600, Messrs. J. Hill and Sons £600, Mr. J. Powell, Messrs. A. Drummond and Son, Mr. T. Tyndall, Mr. L. Ames, Mr. Jos. Harford, and Messrs. W. Miles and Son £500 each, the Dean and Chapter, Mr. Evan Baillie, Mr. J. Ireland, and Mr. S. Worrall, £400 each, and Messrs. J. Cave and Co. promised £300 annually during the war. The vestry of St. Stephen's, partaking in the enthusiasm, deprived itself of the Easter feast usually given by one of the churchwardens, and the official in question subscribed 20 guineas to the fund "in lieu of the dinner." Another item in the subscription list was:— "Nancy Bendall, out of her parish pay, 2*d*." The newspapers of April 7th stated that the fund then amounted to £31,300. At the same date the Liverpool subscription stood at £17,000, that at Manchester £20,000, and that at Birmingham £10,000. The local fund ultimately reached £33,260, but £4,070 of that sum were offered "in lieu of assessed taxes."

Sir William Sydney Smith, who had been captured by the French during the siege of Toulon, but had escaped from prison after two years' ill-treatment, arrived in Bristol on the 26th May, 1798, and took up his quarters at the White Hart hotel, Broad Street, which was surrounded by thousands of citizens. "It is impossible," says a local journalist, "to describe the ecstacy of the populace for many hours." Sir Sydney posted himself at a window, where he proposed and drank numberless patriotic toasts amidst the acclamations of the crowd. Before his departure, three days later, the future "hero of Acre" was magnificently entertained at the Mansion House.

Felix Farley's Journal announced in June, 1798, that Traitor's Bridge, Wade Street, had been rebuilt, and was to be thenceforth called Froom Bridge. Popular appellations are rarely altered by authority, but the above order was not without some effect. Half a century later, although the term Traitor's Bridge was still remembered, many residents in the locality applied the name to another bridge, originally known as Quakers' Bridge from its propinquity to the Quakers' Almshouse.

Peculiar ideas as to recruiting the army and navy still lingered in magisterial minds. At the gaol delivery in 1798 a man named Thomas Brown was sentenced to death for forgery; but the mayor and aldermen, deeming it absurd to deprive the country of an able-bodied man when such men were hard to catch for the forces, besought the Duke of Portland to pardon the felon on condition of his entering the army. The Government manifested unusual squeamishness in responding to this application. As already stated, convicts under sentence of transportation had been permitted to enter the army in 1795. The Duke, however, now replied that the War Office objected to enroll convicts: but if the magistrates approved he would direct Brown to be pardoned. The mayor and aldermen declined to ask for the criminal's discharge, and he was probably transported. As three men were hanged in the city for forgery only six months later, without the justices stirring a finger to save their lives, it is clear that their action in Brown's case was not inspired by any antipathy to the sanguinary punishments of the age.

The dirty and ill-regulated condition of even the most frequented streets of the city was noticed in the records of the earliest years of the century, and continued with little improvement until its close. Frequent complaints were raised in the newspapers of this period respecting the heaps of mud permitted to encumber the thoroughfares, the absence of foot pavements in many streets, and the pitiful lighting arrangements through which the lamps often became extinguished before 8 o'clock in the evening. A local journal of October 27th, 1798, stated that a man had just been convicted for suffering seven pigs to wander in the streets. In the following week three men were fined for a similar offence, and three more cases occurred a week later. On the last occasion *Felix Farley's Journal*, which had previously complained of the filthiness of the thoroughfares, added:—" The city and its environs are much infested by such irregularities. Pigs, goats, and other animals are suffered to wander about the streets with impunity." A writer in the *Monthly Magazine* (May, 1799) condemns another local nuisance, "the barbarous custom of using sledges in the public streets for the carriage of goods, which are continually endangering the limbs both of men and cattle." The inefficiency of the lighting arrangements, producing only " a visible obscurity," was repeatedly urged on the authorities by the newspapers. Reforms were constantly postponed, however, owing to the distrust in which the Corporation was held by the citizens, and to the arrogance of the former in maintaining its ancient rights. The inhabitants were willing to be taxed for carrying out an efficient system of police, but they required the money to be administered by elected commissioners. The civic body demanded that the control of the arrangements should remain, as before, in itself. The dispute, which excited much bitterness of feeling, continued for many years.

It may possibly have been to the dangers and difficulties of the streets that another social shortcoming was attributable. *Felix Farley's Journal* of December 15th, 1798, observes:—" The deficiency of public amusements in this populous and opulent city is not only a constant source of complaint to persons visiting it, but is also the subject of frequent regret to a great number of the respectable inhabitants." The writer in the *Monthly Magazine* referred to in the last paragraph uttered a similar reproach:—" Perhaps there is no place in England where public and social amusements are so little attended to as here." He added that the inhabitants had been in consequence stigmatised for their want of taste, and described as sordid devotees of Plutus, but that a more plausible reason for the monotonous dulness was to be found in the number of dissenters in Bristol.

Whatever may have been the cause of the singularity, so strikingly in contrast with contemporary descriptions of life in Norwich, York, Newcastle, and other towns, its existence is beyond question. Nevertheless, in Mr. Seyer's MSS. is a paper in the historian's handwriting, penned about the end of the century, which shows that a fashionable gathering known as a "rout," invented in London, had its local devotees. With a commendable regard for readers of the present day, Mr. Seyer wrote:—"It is possible that a hundred years hence an account of that species of entertainment called a Rout may be curious to those who take a pleasure in watching the passing manners of a nation. A Rout is a large assembly of ladies and gentlemen meeting by invitation at the house of some friend, *so that Assembly Rooms are ruined.* The tickets of invitation are usually sent out near a month before the time appointed, in which tickets the expression is 'to tea and cards,' or 'for the evening,' or the like, the word Rout being a word of Undress, and never used formally though in every one's mouth. A company of less than forty would scarcely be called a rout, and there have been some here at which 200 persons have assembled; and as not many houses can furnish accommodations for such a party, some ladies have removed partitions and taken down beds in order to gain a room or two, for the greater the crowd the more honoured the entertainment; and sometimes you can scarce stir, and find no place to sit in but a staircase. The carriages begin to drive up to the door about 8 o'clock; a servant at the door of the first apartment announces the name of each visitor as they enter; and the mistress of the house (and perhaps the master too) is at hand to receive them. Every room is spendidly lighted with wax and coloured lamps. The visitors sit down to cards, usually at whist, but many of the younger people crowd to a large table, and play a round game. . . Presently the servants on silver salvers carry round biscuits, sweet cakes, &c., with glasses of wine, lemonade, ices, and the like, and this is repeated every half hour or thereabouts during the evening. . . Some stay only a few minutes, and depart, perhaps, to another rout in some other part of the town. In general the company gradually separates without supper before 11 o'clock, unless the invitations were for supper also, which is not the usual practice. Of this kind of assembly there have been in Bristol for several years past about a dozen every winter, besides one or two at the Mansion House."

In view of the dearth of public amusements, it is surprising to learn that the magisterial hatred of billiard playing revived at this date. In the MS. diary of a citizen, in the Jefferies Collection, is the following entry dated November 13th, 1798:—"Mr. Claxton, mayor, caused two billiard tables to be destroyed in the Exchange; a measure which he intended to take with all, but did not pursue his purpose." The destructive intentions of the magistracy were warmly approved in *Bonner's Journal*.

At a meeting of the Common Council on the 12th January, 1799, it was announced that Alderman John Merlott, who had died shortly before, had bequeathed £3,000 to the Corporation, in trust, and that the money had been invested in Consols. (Owing to the low price of securities at that time, the amount of stock secured was £6,114.) The Chamber undertook the administration of the income, which Alderman Merlott directed should be paid, in sums of £10 each yearly, to blind persons of 50 years or upwards. Subsequently Miss Elizabeth Merlott contributed £4,000 and the philanthropic Richard Reynolds nearly £2,450 to the charity, the income eventually sufficing to provide annuities for about 45 afflicted persons.

The heavy tax on salt imposed about this time was met by the manufacturers by so enormous an increase in its price as to cause suffering amongst the poor. The remedy devised by the Government was to pass an Act authorising the magistrates to fix the price of salt, and the mayor and aldermen of Bristol, in February, 1799, accordingly published a scale of prices at which dealers were compelled to supply the public. The bushel of 56lb. of rock or Bristol salt was to be sold at 13s. 6d. (the cost price of that quantity was then about a shilling). For a single pound the charge was not to exceed 3½d. Any person demanding higher prices, or refusing to sell at the fixed rates, was liable to a penalty of £20. The tariff was raised a few years later, when the tax was increased to 15s. per bushel, or about 3¼d. per lb.

The Government made a tempting proposal in the spring of 1799 to the owners of landed property for the redemption of the land tax by the contribution of a lump sum, liquidated by instalments. The Corporation resolved on availing itself of this offer in order to relieve the whole of the civic estates, and the first payment was made in July. The amount it expended in this way was nearly £14,800.

Readers of the present day are unable to realise the devastation committed a century ago by the smallpox. In spite of attempts to check the malady by inoculation, every town in the kingdom was repeatedly swept by outbreaks of the scourge during the reigns of the first three Georges. At such seasons the last sound heard at night was a funereal knell, and the first tidings of each morning was the death of a neighbour or a friend. A man could hardly walk the streets without being a terror to those he encountered. On some occasions the rural population would neither send in supplies of food to towns, nor enter to make purchases. During an especial deadly visitation at Cirencester, in 1758, farmers and dealers held markets outside the town, business in the borough being practically suspended for three months. The local authorities finally announced in the newspapers that the sickness was greatly on the decline, adding the remarkable assurance that it must soon cease, "there being but few people remaining to have it." The mortality in Bristol in that and other years is known to have been great, but the newspapers, in the interests of trade, suppressed disquieting details, and the statistics have perished. The disease was never so rife or so destructive as during the last ten years of the century, when 92 per 1,000 of the population—nearly one-tenth—are recorded to have died from smallpox alone, whilst at least twice that proportion narrowly escaped from the scourge, and were disfigured for life. A discovery which vastly diminished the amount of domestic sorrow and extended the average term of human life was at length made by Edward Jenner, born in 1749 at Berkeley. After a prolonged study of a disease called cowpox, found by experience to protect dairy servants from smallpox, Jenner published in 1798 the result of his researches, which, in spite of the derision of many medical practitioners, soon produced a sensation throughout Europe. In May, 1799, the Bristol journals announced that Mr. Henry Jenner, surgeon, Berkeley, would visit the city once a week "for the purpose of inoculating for the vaccine disease." Ignorance and prejudice impeded the diffusion of the discovery, but the prodigious diminution of mortality in some continental States, where vaccination was made compulsory, at length silenced hostile critics. In 1802, before a committee of the House of Commons, it was stated that Jenner, whose experiments had suspended the profitable exercise of his profession, might easily have earned from £10,000 to £20,000 a year had he kept his discovery a secret. A vote to him of £20,000 was proposed, but through the influence of the then Premier (Addington) it was reduced to £10,000.

Another bad harvest occurred in 1799, and the distress amongst the poor in that and the following year exceeded even the miseries experienced in 1795 and 1796. For a considerable time the price of coarse household bread was fixed by the magistrates at fourpence per pound, a rate implying semi-starvation amongst thousands of families. At the close of February, 1800, a subscription was opened for the purchase of food, to be distributed under cost price to the poor, and a fund amounting to £15,500, of which £2,000 were contributed by the Corporation, was raised in a few days. The Court of Aldermen, in May, offered bounties to encourage the importation of fish, the effect of the step being to largely increase the supply. Public and private benevolence, however, could make little appreciable impression on the vast mass of suffering, and in autumn, when the crops again failed, and prices rose higher than ever, there were alarming symptoms of popular discontent. A serious riot occurred on the 18th September. A baker near the Stone Bridge had promised to sell some damaged flour to the poor at 2s. 6d. per peck, but on receiving a higher offer privately he rejected the money of a crowd of applicants. A mob thereupon broke into his house, seized the flour, and threw a quantity of it into the Froom. The rioters, charged by the military, were with difficulty dispersed. The affair was wholly unreported in *Felix Farley's Journal*, the editor avowing that he invariably suppressed such intelligence, but the civic minute book shows that the justices sat in permanence for three days through fear of further disturbances. Wheat continued to rise, and in December, though an unprecedented importation of foreign grain had taken place, and though the ordinary consumption of bread was said to have diminished by one fourth, the average price of wheat in the markets of Bristol and Gloucestershire reached the appalling sum of 159s. 10d. per quarter, and the civic authorities fixed the minimum weight of the shilling loaf of standard wheat bread at 2lb. 10½oz.! After a vote of £50,000 by the House of Commons for relieving the famishing poor, the Government purchased a number of cargoes of herrings in Scotland, one of which, consigned to Bristol, arrived about the close of the year. It was so gratefully received that another shipload was ordered by the mayor and other gentlemen. The dearth was accompanied by a terrible outbreak of fever amongst the underfed labouring classes, and the mortality was for many months enormous.

The Corporation's annual gifts of wine became greatly more expensive towards the end of the century, though it may be doubted whether the liquor had improved in quality. In 1709 the two pipes sent to the members for the city cost £50 5s. In April, 1800, Alderman Noble, for a similar consignment, to which was added a butt for the Lord High Steward and a hogshead to the recorder, received £227 17s., besides £25 2s. 6d. additional for the bottling of the previous year's presents, for which he had received £210. The yearly outlay subsequently rose to nearly £300. In despite of the increased prices intemperance was never more fashionable. "Heroic drinking" was patronised by the princes of the royal family, and men of the best education and social position drank like the northern barbarians of olden times—the "three bottle man" being an object of admiration. At the Colston banquets, it was the custom to drink about thirty toasts, and the festivity was kept up by determined topers until after breakfast on the following morning.

A musical festival took place at the Assembly Rooms on the 31st May, when Handel's "Messiah" was performed. Incledon, the greatest singer of the time, was engaged for the occasion. This appears to have been the tenth local performance of the oratorio, though Mr. Nicholls' history infers that the work was not attempted here until 1803.

The Common Council's difficulty in finding a gentleman willing to accept the chief magistracy again became acute at this period. Mr. Philip Protheroe was elected on the usual day, but refused the honour. Mr. John Gordon was next chosen, but declined the office. After further delay, Mr. William Gibbons was appointed. It may be suspected that his acceptance was not unconditional, for the allowance made to the mayor was increased by the Chamber to £1,500. This profligate expenditure at a period of intense distress provoked severe criticism out of doors. Perhaps to allay discontent, the new mayor announced that the second course of the Mansion House dinners would be given up, and other efforts made to ensure economy. Thrift, however, was not a virtue much admired in civic circles. Soon afterwards the allowance to each chief magistrate was raised to £2,000.

In spite of the distress caused by bad harvests and the war, the theatre continued to be so well patronised that the manager was encouraged to increase its accommodation. The old gallery, which was erected over the dress boxes, was removed, a tier of upper boxes taking its place; and a new gallery was constructed over the "undress circle" by raising the roof. The appearance of the interior was said to be improved by the alterations.

A great flood occurred in the valley of the Froom on the 9th November. Part of Stapleton Bridge was carried away, and along the whole of the lower course of the river, especially in the neighbourhood of the Broad Weir and Broadmead, there was a serious destruction of property.

Lethargy and selfishness marked too many ecclesiastical dignitaries during the eighteenth century, and, so far as the capitular body of Bristol was concerned, the latest minute of its proceedings coming under review betrays even greater demerit than the earliest. At a meeting of the chapter on the 1st December, 1800, it was resolved to empower the dean (Dr. Layard) "to see what he thinks wanting in the choir, and to dispose of the brass Eagle and the bell towards the expense of the same." The prebendaries, in fact, determined to despoil the Cathedral of part of its requisites rather than slightly curtail their own incomes to provide for trivial repairs. The lectern, which weighed 6 cwt. 20 lb., was actually sold as old metal in the following year, realising about £27. The fate of the bell is not recorded.

A brief paragraph in the *Bristol Gazette* affords a glimpse of the state of the prison at Fishponds, occupied by Frenchmen captured during the war. Upwards of 3,000 soldiers and sailors were immured in December. They were said to be fairly fed, but disease was rife in the crowded wards, and 78 men died during the last six weeks of the year. Gambling was pursued with frenzied eagerness, and to pay their losses many prisoners sold their beds, their clothes, and even their food for several successive days, being sometimes found absolutely naked and famishing.

It is characteristic of the century whose annals have now been traced that the last incident to be recorded was a prize fight. On the 23rd December a battle for £100 was fought on Wimbledon Common between "the noted Jem Belcher, of Bristol" (then 21 years of age, and of remarkable muscular vigour), and an Irishman named Gamble. The combat was witnessed by several noble lords and members of Parliament, and upwards of £8,000 had been betted upon the issue. Belcher won an easy victory, and was for some years one of the most popular of pugilistic heroes. Two other Bristol men famed for their prowess about this time were "Bill Warr" and "Bob Watson."

CATHEDRAL AND CIVIC DIGNITARIES.

BISHOPS.

1691 John Hall, died February 4, 1709.
1710 John Robinson, translated to London, 1718; died 1723.
1714 George Smalridge, died September 27, 1719.
1719 Hugh Boulter, translated to Armagh, 1723; died 1742.
1724 William Bradshaw, died December 16, 1732.
1732 Charles Cecill, translated to Bangor, 1734; died 1787.
1734 Thomas Secker, translated to Oxford, 1737; to Canterbury, 1758; died 1768.
1737 Thomas Gooch, translated to Norwich 1738; to Ely, 1748; died 1754.
1738 Joseph Butler, translated to Durham, 1750; died 1752.
1750 John Conybeare, died July 13, 1755.
1756 John Hume, translated to Oxford, 1758; to Salisbury, 1766; died 1782.
1758 Philip Yonge, translated to Norwich, 1761; died 1783.
1761 Thomas Newton, died February 15, 1782.
1782 Lewis Bagot, translated to Norwich, 1783; to St. Asaph, 1790; died 1802.
1783 Christopher Wilson, died April 18, 1792.
1792 Spencer Madan, translated to Peterborough, 1794; died 1813.
1794 Henry Reginald Courtenay, translated to Exeter, 1797; died 1803.
1797 Foliot H. W. Cornwall, translated to Hereford, 1802; to Worcester, 1808; died 1831.

DEANS.

1698 George Royse, died April, 1708.
1708 Robert Booth, died 1730.
1730 Samuel Creswicke, promoted to Wells, 1739.
1739 Thomas Chamberlayne, died September 15, 1757.
1755 William Warburton, Bishop of Gloucester, 1759; died 1779.
1760 Samuel Squire, Bishop of St. Davids, 1761.
1761 Francis Ayscough, died August 15, 1763.
1763 Cutts Barton, died December 10, 1780.
1781 John Hallam, resigned 1800, died 1811.
1800 Charles Peter Layard, died May 11, 1803.

MAYORS AND SHERIFFS.

The civic year, under the old charters, began and ended on the 29th September. (The occupations of the mayors have been obtained from a curious Calendar in the library of Mr. Alderman Fox.)

MAYORS.	SHERIFFS.
1700 Sir William Daines, merchant	Robert Bound, Isaac Davies
1701 John Hawkins, brewer (knighted)	Samuel Bayly, Richard Bayly
1702 William Lewis, soapboiler (knighted)	Abraham Elton, Christopher Shuter
1703 Peter Saunders, merchant	Thomas Hort, Henry Whitehead
1704 Francis Whitchurch, grocer	Anthony Swymmer, Henry Walter
1705 Nathaniel Day, soapboiler	Morgan Smith, Nathaniel Webb
1706 George Stephens, draper	Abraham Hooke, Nicholas Hicks
1707 William Whitehead, distiller	Onesiphorus Tyndall. Thomas Tyler
1708 James Holledge, merchant	Philip Freke, John Day
1709 Robert Bound, shipwright	James Haynes, Thomas Clement

MAYORS AND SHERIFFS.

MAYORS.
1710 Abraham Elton, merchant
1711 Christopher Shuter, grocer
1712 Thomas Hort, merchant
1713 Anthony Swymmer, merchant
1714 Henry Whitehead, salt-maker
1715 Henry Walter, woollen draper
1716 Nicholas Hicks, mercer
1717 John Day, merchant (see p. 121)
 Thomas Clement, shipwright
1718 Edmund Mountjoy, soap-maker
1719 Abraham Elton, jun., merchant
1720 Henry Watts, merchant (see p. 128)
 Sir Abraham Elton, Bart.
1721 John Becher, merchant
1722 Henry Swymmer, merchant
1723 James Donning, merchant
1724 Joseph Jefferis, merchant
1725 Robert Earle, merchant

1726 Peter Day, merchant
1727 Henry Nash, distiller
1728 John Price, merchant
1729 Samuel Stokes, soapboiler
1730 Edward Foy, merchant
1731 Arthur Taylor, distiller
1732 John King, merchant
1733 Jacob Elton, merchant
1734 John Rich, merchant
1735 Lionel Lyde, merchant
1736 John Blackwell, merchant
1737 Nathaniel Day, merchant
1738 William Jefferis, merchant
1739 Stephen Clutterbuck, tobacconist
1740 Henry Combe (linen draper)
1741 Richard Bayley (see p. 238)
 John Bartlett
1742 Sir Abraham Elton, Bart.
1743 John Berrow
1744 John Day, merchant
1745 William Barnes, sugar-baker
1746 Edward Cooper, merchant
1747 John Foy, merchant
1748 Buckler Weekes, draper
1749 Thomas Curtis, merchant
1750 James Laroche, merchant
1751 David Peloquin, merchant
1752 John Clement, shipwright
1753 Abraham Elton, merchant
1754 Morgan Smith, sugar-baker
1755 Henry Dampier, merchant
1756 Giles Baily, druggist
1757 William Martin, tobacconist
1758 Henry Mugleworth, upholder
1759 Jeremiah Ames, sugar-baker
1760 John Durbin, drysalter

SHERIFFS.
Edmund Mountjoy, Ab. Elton, jun.
William Bayly, Poole Stokes
Richard Gravett, Henry Watts
John Becher, Henry Swymmer
William Whitehead, Richard Taylor
James Donning, Joseph Jefferis
Robert Earle, Peter Day
Henry Nash, John Price

Samuel Stokes, Edward Foy
Arthur Taylor, John King

Robert Addison, Jacob Elton

John Rich, Noblet Ruddock
Robert Smith, Lionel Lyde
John Blackwell, Nathaniel Wraxall
Nathaniel Day, William Jefferis
Michael Puxton, Stephen Clutterbuck
Ezekial Longman, Henry Combe
Richard Bayley, John Bartlett
Henry Lloyd, Abraham Elton
John Berrow, John Day
Edward Buckler, William Barnsdale
Edward Cooper, William Barnes
John Foy, Buckler Weekes
Michael Pope, Benjamin Glisson
Thomas Curtis, James Laroche
David Peloquin, John Clement
Morgan Smith, Abraham Elton
Joseph Iles, Henry Dampier
John Combe, Giles Bayly
Michael Becher, David Dehany

Walter Jenkins, William Martin
John Chamberlayne, Henry Mugleworth
William Cossley, Jeremiah Ames
Isaac Elton, John Durbin
John Foy, Buckler Weekes
Thomas Marsh, John Noble
Henry Swymmer, Richard Farr, jun.
John Berrow, Giles Bayly
John Daltera, Isaac Baugh
William Barnes, jun., John Curtis
George Weare, Joseph Love
Henry Dampier, Isaac Baugh
Daniel Woodward, Edward Whatley
Henry Bright, Thomas Harris
Thomas Knox, Thomas Deane
Henry Weare, James Hilhouse
Nathaniel Foy, Austin Goodwin
Robert Gordon, Isaac Piguenit
Samuel Webb, John Berrow
Charles Hotchkin, John Noble
Isaac Piguenit, Samuel Sedgley

	MAYORS.	SHERIFFS.
1761	Isaac Elton, merchant	Joseph Daltera, William Barnes, jun.
1762	John Noble, merchant	William Weare, Thomas Farr
1763	Richard Farr, merchant	Andrew Pope, John Durbin, jun.
1764	Henry Swymmer, merchant	James Laroche, jun., John Bull
1765	Isaac Baugh, gentleman	Isaac Elton, jun., Michael Miller, jun.
1766	William Barnes, jun., sugar-baker	William Miles, Henry Cruger
1767	George Weare, grocer	Edward Brice, Alexander Edgar
1768	Edward Whatley, sugar-baker	John Crofts, Henry Lippincott
1769	Thomas Harris, merchant	John Merlott, George Daubeny
1770	Thomas Deane, merchant	Isaac Elton, jun., Henry Lippincott
1771	Henry Bright, merchant	Levi Ames, Jeremy Baker
1772	Nathaniel Foy, brewer	John Noble, John Anderson
1773	Robert Gordon, merchant	Andrew Pope, Thomas Pierce
1774	Charles Hotchkin, gentleman	John Durbin, jun., James Hill
1775	Thomas Farr, merchant	Edward Brice, John Noble
1776	Andrew Pope, sugar-baker	John Farr, John Harris
1777	John Durbin, jun., gentleman (knighted)	John Fisher Weare, Philip Protheroe
1778	Sir John Durbin	Benjamin Loscombe, James Morgan, jun.
1779	Michael Miller, jun., merchant (see p. 442) John Bull	Edward Brice, John Harford
1780	William Miles, merchant	Samuel Span, Joseph Smith
1781	Henry Cruger, merchant	Robert Coleman, John Collard
1782	Edward Brice, sugar-baker	Rowland Williams, William Blake
1783	John Anderson, merchant	John Garnett, Anthony Henderson
1784	John Farr, rope-maker	John Fisher Weare, John Harvey
1785	John Crofts, esquire	Joseph Harford, Stephen Nash (knighted)
1786	George Daubeny, sugar-baker	Evan Baillie, Thomas Daniel, jun.
1787	Alexander Edgar, esquire	John Morgan, Robert Claxton
1788	Levi Ames, drysalter	James Hill, John Harris
1789	James Hill, linen draper	Henry Bengough, John Gordon, jun.
1790	John Harris, hosier	James Morgan, Rowland Williams
1791	John Noble, merchant	Joseph Harford, Samuel Span
1792	Henry Bengough, attorney	William Gibbons, Joseph Gregory Harris
1793	James Morgan, druggist	Charles Young, John Page
1794	Joseph Smith, merchant	Robert Castle, Joseph Edye
1795	James Harvey, iron merchant	David Evans, John Wilcox
1796	James Harvey, iron merchant	John Foy Edgar, Azariah Pinney
1797	Thomas Daniel, merchant	Edward Protheroe, John Span
1798	Robert Claxton, merchant	Daniel Wait, William Fripp
1799	John Morgan, druggist	Henry Bright, Worthington Brice
1800	William Gibbons, ironmonger	Robert Castle, Samuel Birch

MASTERS OF THE SOCIETY OF MERCHANT VENTURERS.

(The compiler is indebted for this list to the *Bristol Times and Mirror* of July 22, 1885.)

1700 James Holledge.
1701 James Holledge.
1702 Thomas Hort.
1703 Thomas Hort.
1704 William Clarke.
1705 William Clarke.
1706 John Batchelor.
1707 John Batchelor.
1708 Abraham Elton.
1709 Anthony Swymmer.
1710 Thomas Moore.
1711 George Mason.
1712 Abraham Hooke.
1713 Philip Freke.
1714 Henry Watts.
1715 Sir John Duddleston (died); Henry Watts.
1716 John Day (mayor).
1717 William Swymmer.
1718 Henry Swymmer.
1719 Abraham Elton, jun. (mayor).
1720 James Downing.
1721 Joseph Earle.
1722 John Becher.
1723 Thomas Longman.
1724 Samuel Hunt.
1725 Jeremy Innys.
1726 John Blackwell.
1727 John Norman.
1728 Jacob Elton.
1729 Abel Grant.
1730 James Hilhouse.
1731 Edmund Baugh.
1732 Peter Day.
1733 Robert Earle.
1734 John Holledge.
1735 James Day.
1736 John Duckinfield.
1737 John Coysgarne.
1738 Richard Lougher.
1739 Thomas Eston.
1740 William Challoner.
1741 Lionel Lyde.
1742 John Day.
1743 Richard Henvill.
1744 Walter Lougher.
1745 Arthur Hart.
1746 Robert Smith.
1747 Christopher Willoughby.
1748 John Foy.
1749 Michael Becher.
1750 Henry Dampier.
1751 James Laroche.
1752 William Hare.
1753 Nathaniel Foy.
1754 Edward Cooper.
1755 Henry Swymmer.
1756 Cranfield Becher.
1757 Abraham Elton.
1758 Henry Casamajor.
1759 Isaac Baugh.
1760 Joseph Daltera.
1761 William Hart.
1762 Richard Farr.
1763 Samuel Smith.
1764 Isaac Elton.
1765 William Reeve.
1766 James Bonbonous.
1767 Sir A. I. Elton.
1768 Samuel Munckley.
1769 Andrew Pope.
1770 William Jones.
1771 Thomas Farr.
1772 James Daltera.
1773 Isaac Elton, jun.
1774 Robert Smith.
1775 Paul Farr.
1776 Henry Garnett.
1777 Samuel Span.
1778 Michael Miller, jun.
1779 John Powell.
1780 Thomas Perkins.
1781 Henry Cruger (mayor).
1782 Sir James Laroche.
1783 John Fowler.
1784 George Daubeny.
1785 Jeremiah Hill.
1786 Edward Brice.
1787 John Vaughan.
1788 Henry Hobhouse.
1789 John Daubeny.
1790 George Gibbs.
1791 Jeremiah Hill, jun.
1792 Richard Bright.
1793 James Martin Hilhouse.
1794 John Garnett.
1795 Joshua Powell.
1796 Joseph Harford.
1797 Charles Hill.
1798 John Scandrett Harford.
1799 Samuel Whitchurch.
1800 Timothy Powell.

INDEX.

Abbey gateway, 345.
Addison, Jos., in Bristol, 122.
Admiralty Court, Mayor and the, 495.
African trade, extent of, 89; defended, 89, 270-2; suspended, 416.
Ague, charm for, 294.
Aitken, James, 426.
Aldermen, absentee, 454.
Ale, *see* Beer. [235, 268.
Alehouses, number of, 18, 57, 199,
Algerine corsairs, 188, 281.
Almshouses, Tailors', 43; Foster's, 46; Stokes Croft, 134; Stevens', 116; Blanchard's, 134; Ridley's, 188; Old Maids', 218; Fry's, 487.
Almondsbury, 267, 359, 457.
Amelia, Princess, visit of, 164.
America, trade restraints, 205, 414; Stamp Act, 370; war, 415, 420, 428, 431, 439, 451; local trade with, 414, 429.
Ames family, 462, 468, 517.
Amusements, 24, 333, 487, 527.
Anchor Society, 280.
Anne, Queen, coronation, 43; visit, 44; portrait, 45; gift to, 56; death, 106.
Apple brandy, 101.
Army, recruited from gaol, 41, 69, 272, 514; desertions, 246; bounties, 270, 432, 436, 440; billeting, 235; vagrants impressed, 436; regiments raised, 256, 506.
Arno's Vale, 285, 359.
Art School, first, 523.
Ashburton, Lord, 370, 405, *ib.*
Ashley Road, 406.
Assembly Rooms, 26, 208, 283, 307, 420, 487.
Assizes, soldiers during, 223.
Augustine's, St., theatre in, 61; Assembly Room, 64, 420; great house, 84; improvements, 416.
Aurora Borealis, 114.
Aust, road to, 331.
Avon, nuisances in, 87, 254; Navigation schemes, 94, 369; boats to Bath, 161, 164; obstructions, 117, 254, *ib.*; proposed floating harbour, 316, 362, 480, 496; defences, 523.

Baber's Tower, 244.
Back Gate removed, 211.
Backsword fighting, 27, 314.
Baggs, Richard, 148, 185.
Baillie, Evan, 477, 508, 520.
Baker, Slade, 415; Jer., 448, 497.
Bakers' Company, 272, 401, 468; "foreign," 22, 79; subsidised, 378, 516.
Baker, a rebellious, 214; knavish, 272; cheap, 401.
Balloon, first, 464.
Balls, early, 26, 208; 487.
Banking, early, 224, 282.
Banks, Bristol, 282, 297, 392, 468, 507.
Baptisms, local, 8.
Baptist Mills brass works, 66, 71.
Barbers' Company, 219, 240, 381; charges, 309.
Barrett, William, 387.
Barrington, Daines, 341, 370; Lord, 312-3.
Barton, Dean, 347, 354.
Barton Hundred, 359. [161, 164.
Bath, coaches to, 140, 513; boats to,
Bath Street opened, 466.
Bathavon ferry, 246.
Baths, 269, 315, 395, 499, 524.
Bathing, sea, 24, 249, 440.
Bayley, Richard, 238.
Beaufort, Dukes of, 86, 110, 420.
Becher family, 179, 210, 268, 307, 393.
Beckford, Rich., 310, 318.
Beddoes, Thomas, 504, 524. [120.
Bedford, Rev. Arthur, 61, 62, 80, 86,
Bedminster, 2, 274; gibbet at, 227; Bridewell, 227, 250; revel, 189; cunning woman, 350; clerical innkeeper, 159, 383; colliery, 318.
Beer, consumption of, 13, 16, 285; price of, 14, 235, 309, 356.
Bellman, city, 73, 492.
Bengough, Henry, 360, 507.
Berkeley Square, 471.
Berkeley, Norborne, 352; G.C., 469.

INDEX.

Berkeley, Earls of, 69, 111-2, 256, 313, 420.
Billiard tables, 26, 116, 371, 529.
Bird, Edward, R.A., 523.
Births and burials tax, 41.
Bishopric, poverty of, 85, 122, 816, 347.
Bishops, list of, 534; Hall, 36, 88; Robinson, 88, 100; Smalridge, 103, 119, 123; Boulter, 127; Secker, 206; Gooch, 207; Butler, 202, 207, 283; Conybeare, 316; Hume, 316; Yonge, 345; Newton, 345, 366.
Bishops' palace, 86, 283; park, 393; orchard, 185.
Bisse, Rev. Edw., Jacobite, 121.
Bitton parish, crime in, 469.
Black Castle, 68, 285, 329, 877, ib., 391.
Blackmail in Kingswood, 469.
Blacksworth, manor of, 141.
Blaize Castle, 413, 485.
Blenheim, victory of, 65.
Blind, Asylum for, 498; Merlott's charity, 529.
Blind steps, 368, 408.
Bonny, Wm., printer, 21, 48, 61.
Books, scarcity of, 11, 163; pedlars, 71.
Boulter, Bishop, 127.
Boundaries, city, 24; extended, 422; parish, 243.
Bowles, Francis C., 524.
Bowling-greens, 25, 202, 371.
Boyce's buildings, 400.
Bragge, Charles, 518.
Branding thieves, 69.
Brandon Hill, 378, 425.
Brandy, apple, 101; French, 101.
Brass works, 14, 66; extent of trade, 96. [455.
Brass pillars, Corn St., 162, 183, 396,
Bread, dear, *see* Dearth.
Breakfasts in 1700, 16.
Brice, Edward, 382.
Brickdale, John, 63, 304-5, 462; Matthew, 3, 383, 409, 444, 456, 491,
Bricks, early, 43, 59. [495.
Bridewell rebuilt, 125; enlarged, 225; sacked, 304; state of, 407.
Bridge, great house at, 45, 163.
Bridge Street, 369.
Bridges, James, 336, 352.
Bridges, Bristol, rebuilt, 334, 353; riots, 500; Bridewell, 373; St. John's, 327; Stone, 290; Needless, 196; Traitor's, 92, 526; Drawbridge, 99, 483.
Bridgwater elections, 246, 384.
Briefs, Church, 74, 266, 329.
Bright family, 392, 425, 439, 462, 468, 473, 477, 508.
Brislington, gibbet at, 227.

Bristol, Satires on, 221, 411, 423, 508.
Bristol in 1700, 1-36; in 1727, 161; in 1789, 222; views of, 3, 121; poetical description of, 96; plan of, 285; population, 6, 194, 292, 422; French designs on, 525.
Bristol regiments, 256, 506.
Bristol milk, 17, 104, 161.
Bristol manners censured, 8, 161, 377.
Bristol Channel defenceless, 528.
Britain, Jonathan, hanged, 398.
Broad Street, market, 4, 193; width of, 460, 467. [tery, 372.
Brunswick Square, 372, 479; cemeBrutality, popular, 192, 278.
Bubb, John, 68.
Building mania, 493.
Bull, John, 435, 442.
Bullbaiting, 27.
Burges, Daniel, 474.
Burgum, Henry, 387, 412, 480.
Burials, tax on, 41; in woollen, 9, 302; in churches, 182, 357.
Burial grounds, 264, 355, 358, 372, 399, 497.
Burke, Edmund, 409-13, 428, 431, 432, 444; tea service, 413; Richard, 455, 505.
Bush family, 477, 507.
But and Cudgel playing, 314.
Butchers' ordinances, 211.
Butler, Bishop, 202, 207, 283.
Butter, Irish, seized, 112, 306.
Buttons, law respecting, 125.
Byng, Admiral, mania, 322.

Caldwell, J., highwayman, 430.
Calendar reformed, 298.
Callowhill Street, 318.
Cambric prohibited, 278.
Camplin, Rev. John, 315, 348, 478.
Canada, conquest of, 339.
Canal mania, 498.
Candle bell, 394.
Cann, Sir William, 251.
Canning's monument, 345; his coffer, 386.
Canning, Mrs., at theatre, 400.
Canons' Marsh, 36, 393.
Carbry, Capt., bravery of, 281.
Carpenters, rules, 21, 181, 268; wages, 182, 268, 372.
Carriers, 73, 269, 288, 430.
Carts forbidden, 68, 175, 252.
Cary, John, 32, 49.
Castelman, Rev. J., 326.
Castle Gate removed, 351.
Castle Ditch bath, 395. [389, 423.
Catcott family, 119, 126, 353, 387,

540 INDEX.

Cathedral injured by storm, 57; candlesticks, 77; penitent in, 94; chapter house mutilated, 180; library, 315; services, 345; graves in, 357; lay pluralists, 151, 363, 431; choir, 151, 364; sale of lectern, 533.
Cave family, 468, 477, 507, 521.
Cemeteries, *see* Burial grounds.
Chamberlayne family, 463 473.
Champion, William, 67, 244, 289, 362, 368; Richard, 364–5, 371, 381–3, 408, 409, 418, 453.
Chandlers' Company, 384.
Chapels: St. Clement's, 42; Dowry, 260; French, 155; Holy Spirit, 358; Lady Huntingdon's, 420; Hope, 420; Lewin's Mead, 483; Mayor's, *see* St. Mark's Church; Quakers', 270; Redland, 173, 448; Romanist, 115. 366, 442, 491; Tabernacle, 306; Trinity, 518; Tucker Street, 466; Wesleyan, 204, 498, 507.
Charity School, first, 12; *see* Schools.
Charlotte Street, 471.
Charter of Queen Anne, 86; Charters printed, 195.
Chatterton, Thomas, 199, 358, 385.
China dinner ware, 188; Bristol, 286, 381, 413, 453.
Chocolate, Bristol, 177.
Christ Church great lamp, 38; cemetery, 264; living, 424; ground rents, 485.
Christmas Day. "Old," 298.
Churches: All Saints', 91; Christ Church, 228, 306, 459, 485; St. Ewen's, 470, 496; St. Leonard's, 368-9, 393; St. Mark's, 126, 305, 324, 362, 431; St. Michael's, 408; St. James', 154; St. Mary Redcliff, 73, 198, 321, 345, 358; St. Nicholas's, 40, 119, 179, 215, 266, 326, 352: St. Peter's, 281; St. Paul's, 479; St. Philip's, 283, 364; St. Stephen's, 57, 169, 181-2, 400, 435; Temple, 483; St. Thomas, 487; St. Werburgh's, 329, 519.
Church, absentees from, 326; compulsory attendance, 481.
Churchyards, 249, 264, 358, 399, 497.
Churchman, Walter, 177.   [357.
Cider, consumption of, 235; tax on, Circus, first, 401; 492.
Clare, Lord, *see* Nugent.
Clare Street built, 393, 399.
Clarkson, Thomas, in Bristol, 473.
Clergy: Incomes of, 92, 109; attempts to levy clergy rate, 98, 462; disloyal, 19, 119, 121; pluralist, 351, 432, 518, 523; non-resident, 468; credulous, 348, 483.
Clerke, Clementina, 498.
Clevedon, traffic with, 325.
Clifton (*see* Hot Well): In 1700, 2; in 1710, 87; in 1723, 139; in 1750, 245; in 1764, 363; in 1775, 421; in 1790, 490; church, 116, 381; churchyard, 472; value of living, 93, 109; grotto, 139; foxes, etc., killed, 140; whipping post, 140; rateable value, 313; tithes, 141, 351; first boarding school, 190; population, 87, 472; Dowry Square, 158, 245, 368; Boyce's buildings, 400; Windsor terrace, 454; building mania, 493; the Crescents, 494; York hotel, 490; Vauxhalls, 245, 423; Sion Spring, 504; Hotwell Road spa, 506; turnpikes, 406; Hope Chapel, 420; proposed bridge, 309; part of included in city, 422; windmill burnt, 430; treatment of paupers, 481; volunteers, 521; Assembly room, 490.
Clothing trade, 41; decline, 81, 209, 236, 515.
Coaches, private, 8, 274; first public, 22; mail, 458; eight wheeled, 513; "flying," 140, 172, 260, 309, 338, 359, 367, 400, 418, 464.
Coal famine, 156.
Coal tar discovered, 441.
Cobweb, wonderful, 106.
Cockfighting, 25, 140, 170, 179, 432, 469.
Cockthrowing, 294.
Cocoa manufacture, 177.
Coffee, price of, 82, 395.
Coffee houses, 17, 97, 240, 392; decline of, 241, 441.
Coinage, state of, 323, 509.
Coleridge, Sam. Taylor, 503.
College Green, 79, 325' 353; road to, 199, 416; watchbox, 455.
College Street built, 393.
Collieries, Bedminster, 313.
Collins, Emanuel, 159, 338.
Colston, Edward, in Bristol, 46, 84, 85; his school schemes, 46, 80, 83; elected M.P., 85, 102; conduct to a low churchman, 86; gifts, 92, 199; death, 129; portraits, 46, 130.
Colston, Francis, 110.
Colston Dinners, first, 85, 102, 111; Parent Society, 153; Loyal, 299; Dolphin, Grateful, and Anchor, 280, 532.

INDEX. 541

Combe, Henry, 213, 224; Rich., 383, 444; William, 418.
Companies, trading, 21; decline of, 181, 467; carpenters, 181, 268; coopers, 208, 239, 467; smiths, 468, bakers, 272, 401, 468; chandlers, 384; innholders, 189; barbers, 219, 240, 381; mercers, 181; tailors, 181, 460; weavers, 470.
Conduits. Temple, 185; St. Nicholas, 141, 353; St. Peter's Pump, 377; All Saints', 446; St. Stephen, 88.
Conjurer, travelling, 300.
Consistory Court, 94, 359.
Convicts forced into army, etc., 41, 69, 272, 514, 526; pardoned, 90; transported, 150, 153; murderous plot, 180.
Conybeare, Bishop, 316.
Cook's Folly, 266.
Cooks, strike of, 21.
Coopers' Hall, 208, 239, 401.
Copper works, 66–8, 162.
Corn Street improved, 446.
Coroners, salaries of, 129.
Corporation: in 1700, 29; debt, 58, 441, 450; love of feasting, 81, 226; book of orders, 56, 232; pensions to members, etc., 69, 120, 128, 187, 206, 219, 288, 243, 263, 302, 361, 381, 402, 420, 436; fee farm rents, 70; payments to M.P.s, 77; citizens refuse to enter, 86–7, 219, 508; presents of wine, 77, 86, 87, 104, 209, 281, 311, 402, 582; defence of the slave trade, 89, 90, 249, 271, 477; dissenters disqualified, 94; mayor's chapel, 126, 305, 324, 362; hours of meeting, 16, 196, 457; state swords, 100, 291; civic maces, 134; mansion house, 191, 434, 449; defaulting chamberlain, 218; non-attendance, 237, 258, 457; secrecy of debates, 253; waits, 26, 114, 239; country jaunts, 31, 246, 255; entertainments, 300, 528; love of turtle, 328, 404, 517; quarrels with dean and chapter, 29, 126, 171, 340; insolvent members, 287, 361, 492; charity to West Indies, 378, 392; treatment of endowed schools, 374; and of city library, 403; American war policy, 420, 428, 440, 451; official salaries, 429–30, 507; illegalities of officials, 434; pitchforking members, 422; absentee aldermen, 454; family cliques in, 436; sales of property, 441, 450; appropriates charity funds, 443, 496; clothing of sergeants, etc., 461; opposed by city, 467, 488; fees to coachmen, 471; receipts from town dues, 479; refusals of the mayoralty, 435, 495, 507–8, 532; unpopularity of, 488, 504, 508, 527: election of aldermen, 497; costly deputations, 485, 517.
Corsairs, ships taken by, 188, 281.
Cossins, John, 173, 448.
Coster, Thomas, 66, 188, 224, 239.
Cotham, disorders at, 281, 404; tower, 303.
Cottle, Joseph, 510–13.
Cotton factories, 123, 196, 482, 505.
Cotton dresses forbidden, 42, 125, 196.
Council House rebuilt, 59; a free club, 217; proposed rebuilding, 467, 470.
Courtney, Stephen, 75, 146.
Crediton, subscription for, 249.
Credulity, see Superstition.
Creswick family, 243.
Creswicke, Dean, 170, 201.
Crewes Hole brass works, 67; water works, 88.
Cricket, early, 297.
Criminal law, state of, 347.
Crosses: High, 186, 325, 358; Temple, 466; Redcliff, 358; St. Peter's, 377.
Cruger, Henry, 391, 397, 409–11, 417, 440, 444, 446–7, 456, 477, 478, 489.
Cumberland Street, 372.
Cursing, profane, 169, 268.
Custom House, 60; new, 82, 107; strange collectors, 68, 412; sinecures, 451.

Daines, Sir Wm., 42, 66, 85, 102, 108, 124, 130–1.
Dampier, Ald. Henry, 291, 374.
Daniel, Thomas, 455, 468, 478, 477, 480, 525.
Darby, Abraham, 71; Mary, 336.
Daubeny, George, 440, 446–8, 456, 468, 477, 504.
Davis family, 366, 392, 472.
Davy, (Sir) Humphry, 504.
Day family, 45, 58, 121, 144, 168 206, 333; great house, 45, 163.
Deans: Royse, 36; Booth, 170; Creswicke, 170, 201; Chamberlayne, 276, 825; Warburton, 327; Squire, 328–9; Barton, 347, 354; Hallam, 488; Layard, 533.
Dean and Chapter, 36; estates, 141, 185, 393, 396; quarrels, 276, 325; negligence, 352, 345, 347; treat-

ment of quire, 151, 364, 431; dispose of High Cross, 325; and of lectern, 533.
Deane, Thomas, 268, 350, 392.
Deanery repaired, 328.
Dearth and distress, 78, 87, 166, 209, 225, 303, 823, 377, 380, 454, 485, 516, 531.
Debtors, imprisoned, misery of, 225, 308, 355, 417; impressed into army and navy, 69, 514; released, 169, 247, 279, 417.
Defence, National, funds, 256, 506, 525.
Delaval. ship, 117.
Demoniac, Yatton, 483.
Denmark Street, 115.
Dicker, Samuel, 267.
Dineley murder, 228; Lady, 232; Edward, 233.
Directory, first local, 420.
Dissenters, treatment of, 91, 103.
Distilling trade, 7, 101, 290.
Dock, Champion's (Merchants'), 368, 422; Sea Mills, 98, 171, 296,; proposed floating, 317, 362, 480, 496.
Dolman, John, 265.
Dolphin Street, 369.
Dolphin Society, 280.
Donn, Benjamin, 367, 398, 403.
Dover, Dr. Thomas, 74, 76.
Dowry Square, 158, 245, 363.
Draper, Sir William, 374, 381.
Drawbridge, 99; proposed fixed bridge, 483.
Drawing school, first, 523.
Dress of citizens, 300, 423, 460.
Drinking habits, 18, 31, 40, 309, 532.
Drunkenness, 18, 27; punishment for, 169.
Ducie, Lord, 313.
Duckhunting day, 24, 128.
Ducking Stool, 27, 131.
Duddleston, Sir John, 57, 149.
Duels, local, 168, 505, 524.
Duke and Duchess privateers, 74.
Duncan, Lord, freedom to, 522.
Dunning, John, recorder, 370, 405, *ib.*
Durbin family, 330, 348, 431, 436, 454.
Durdham Down, mines, 105; races, 24, 122, 278; murders, 104, 248; Wallis's wall, 266; Ostrich inn, 25, 122, 279, 314, 432, 490.

Earle, Joseph, 85, 102, 108, 130, 160; Giles, 226, 334.
Early rising, 16-18.
Earthenware, early, 7, 14, 82, 287.

Easterbrook, Rev. J., zeal and credulity, 483, *ib.*
Easton, inn at, 359.
Ecclesiastical Court, 94, 359.
Education, state of, 11. [449.
Edwards, Thomas, 102, 108; Sam., Elbridge, John, 199, 218.
Elections, parliamentary:—(1701) 42; (1702) *ib.*; (1705) 66; (1710) 85; (1713) 102; (1715) 108; (1722) 130; (1727) 159; (1734) 188; (1739) 224; (1741) 234; (1742) 239; (1747) 267; (1754) 309; (1756) 318; (1759) 340; (1761) 344; (1766) 378; (1768) 383; (1774) 409; (1780) 444; (1781) 446; (1784) 456; (1790) 491; (1796) 518.
Elections, abuses at, 20, 224, 378, 447; excessive cost, 109, 384, 411.
Elopement case, curious, 493.
Elton, Sir Ab., 95, 130, 160, 162; family, 127, 160, 184, 188, 235, 239, 282, 381, 412, 434, 503, 517.
Embargo on shipping, 514.
Emigration, early, 152, 326, 408.
Entertainments, 300, 333, 401, 528.
Equestrianism, 333, 401, 492.
Esther, ship, gallantry of, 513.
Estlin, Rev. Dr., 518. [117.
Evil, King's, touching for, 55, 56, Exchange, proposed, 118, 180, 218, 226; opened, 247; plate found, 238; brass pillars, 396; outrage at, 440.
Excise scheme, Walpole's, 183.
Excommunication of scolds, 360.
Executions, 27; list of, 136, 295; excessive number of, 469; survivals after hanging, 197; Capt. Goodere, 231; clergy at, 209; for trivial crimes, 347; curious case, 237; scenes at, 262, 294.

Fairs, the great, 64, 178, 390; West Street, 166.
Fane, Thomas, 261, 354.
Farley, family, 50, 51, 292.
Farr, family, 408, 413, 435.
Fecham, Stephen, 167.
Felons, made soldiers, 41, 69, 272, 514; pardoning of, 90; transported, 150, 153.
Fencing master, unlucky, 116.
Fillwood forest, 191.
Fire, precautions against, 58, 225, 356.
Fire Insurance offices, 54, 398.
Fires, fatal, 340, 356; incendiary, 171, 426.
Fish, supply, 394, 485, 531.

INDEX.   543

Fishing in Avon, 372.
Fishponds, prison, 437, 451, 520, 533; common, 437. [480, 496.
Floating harbours, proposed, 316, 362,
Flogging, punishment by, 180, 315, 356, 465.
Floods, great, 125, 208, 533.
Flower, Joseph, 288.
Food, cheapness of, 48; excessive dearness, 531.
Forlorn Hope Estate, 40.
" Foreigners," treatment of, 20, 116, 176, 186, 197, 215, 327, 356.
Foreign Protestants' Bill, 289.
Fortune telling, 224.
Fortunes, mercantile, 462.   [341.
Foster, (Sir) Michael, 192, 197, 224.
Foundlings, disposal of, 336.
Fox, Dr. Long, 508.
Frank, Richard, 287; T., 382.
Franklyn, Joshua, 98.
Freedom, admissions to, 21, 128, 213, 260, 313, 340, 370, 374, 413, 420, 428, 452, 453, 455, 469, 491, 517, 522; excessive fees, 260, 356.   [482.
Freedom acquired by marriage, 411,
Freeling, (Sir) Francis, 458.
Freeman's Copper Co., 67.
Freke family, 108, 145.
French Chapel, 155.
French man of war taken, 332.
French prisoners, 250, 339, 437, 451, 520, 533.
French wars, 42, 100, 343, 499.   [525.
French invasions menaced, 339, 519,
Frenchay highwayman, 379.
Frigates built, 434, 448, 466.
Fripp, family, 178, 331.
Froom, fishing in the, 24; floods, 125, 176, 208, 533.
Frost, remarkable, 78.
Fry, Joseph, 177, 382.
Fry, William, Mercy House, 437.
Funeral customs, 8, 122, 129, 163, 169, 208.

Gallows, *see* Executions; disorders near, 281, 404.
Gambling, 116, 223.
Gaol, the, *see* Newgate.
Gardens, city, 25, 301.
Gates: Abbey, 345; Temple and Redcliff, 175, 211, 396; Newgate, 57, 377, 471; Back, 211; St. Nicholas, 3, 215, 225, 266, 335, 352; Needless Bridge, 341; Queen and Castle Street, 351: Pithay, 359; Blind, 394; Froom, 408; Small Street, 368, 408; Lawford's, 3, 175, 268, 391.

Gentry, county, and turnpikes, 156, 275.
George I., accession, 106; coronation riot, 106; dinner, 120; portrait, 114.
George II., accession, 159; portrait, *ib.*; quarrel with his son, 236; death, 342.
George III., accession, 342; election gifts, 444, 448; attempted murder, 470; at Cheltenham, 484; recovery, 485.
German Protestant exiles, 80.
Gibbets, 104, 227, 248, 290, 350.
Gibbs, (Sir) Vicary, 505; Geo., 507.
Giles, Richard, 269, 348.
Gin drinking, 198, 290, 300.
Glass, table, 14, 45; price of, 313; local works, 168, 486.
Gloucester Journal, 162.
Gloucestershire. elections, 42; wages in, 182; society, 45, 183.
Goldney, Thomas, 72, 74, 139, 297.
Goldwin, Rev. Wm., 96, 119.
Good Friday neglected, 463.
Goodere, Capt., murderer, 228.
Goods, rates of carriage, 78, 269.
Gordon family, 463, 472, 477, 493, 582.
Gore, Col. William, 520.
Grateful Society, 280.
Great George Street, 425, 494.
Greep, Henry, 50.
Grenville, Geo., a freeman, 370.
Greville, Giles, 205.
Ground rents, valuable, 485.
Gunpowder magazine, 256, 517.
Gunpowder Plot Day, 310, 396.

Hackney coaches, first, 130; 277, 456, 467, 486.
Hair powder, 342, 418, 448, 515.
Hallam, Dean, 488.
Hangman, a, hanged, 237.
Hanover Street built, 115.
Hardwicke, Lord, 209.
Harford, Joseph, 364, 382, 403, 409, 431, 439, 468, 476, 500, 507; family, 382, 392, 435, 478.
Harford's Brass works, 67.
Harris, Thomas, 412, 477.
Harson, Daniel, 393, 412.
Hart family, 77, 107, 111, 130, 160, 194, 330.
Harvest, a plentiful, 246.   [154.
Hawkins, John, knighted, 45-6, 74,
Hawksworth family, 67, 74, 175.
Haystacks in city, 26.
Haystack, Maid of the, 425.
Haythorne, Joseph, 507.

Henbury, excursions to, 457.
Heylyn, John, 307, 367.
High Street, 97, 225; market, 4, 193, 253.
Highwayman, "gentleman," 379; Bristol, 430. [471.
Highway robberies, 210, 227, 430, Hill, Rev. Rowland, 307.
Hippisley, John, 15, 63.
Hobbs, John, 95, 117.
Hobhouse, Isaac, 135, 142-5, 152; H., 462; Ben., 518.
Hoblyn, Robert, 239, 267, 281, 310.
Hogarth, Wm., pictures, 321.
Holledge, James, 74, 218.
Holmes, lighthouse at, 200.
Holworthy, Lady, 99.
Hooke, Andrew, 51, 240, 279; Abraham, 92, 94.
Horfield, living, 93, 109.
Horseback, travelling on, 48, 246, 255.
Hospitals, *see* Poor and Schools.
Hospital, proposed sailors', 269.
Hot Well in 1703, 57; theatre, 62; fashionable life at, 139, 244, 245, 390, 429, 490; Pope's description of, 222; water sold in London, 151; poems on, 139, 288; Lebeck inn, 311; Lisbon earthquake, 316; lead works near, 321; Dr. Randolph on, 361; water hawked in streets, 361; Romanist scare, 366; Duke of York at, 367; Vauxhalls, 245, 423; public refused a supply, 449, 490; well to be let, 463; road to, 486, 497; inn quarrels, 486; high charges and decline, 489; Sion Spring, 504; spa near, 506; Colonnade built, 469.
Hot Well, the New, 264, 464. [10.
Houses, timber, 3; meanly furnished, Howard, John, on prisons, 406, 437, 466.
Howe, Lord, his victory, 506, 453.
Huguenots, the, 126, 155, 421.
Hume, David, in Bristol, 189.
Huntingdon, Lady, 279, 420.

Impressment, *see* Press-gangs.
Improvement scheme, great, 368.
Incendiaries, Bristol, 171-2, 426.
Informers, common, 207, 278.
Inchbald, Mrs., 400.
Infirmary erected, 199; state of, 318; chaplaincy, 413; rebuilt, 479.
Innkeeper, a clerical, 159, 333.
Inns: White Lion, 17, 257, 392; Bear, 263; Lamb, 269; Ostrich, 25, 122, 279, 314, 432, 490; Guilders,

180; Three Tuns, 180, 280; Exchange, 248; Montague, 205; Barton Hundred, 359; Bush, 405, 485; York House, 490; carriers, 288.
Insolvents, *see* Debtors.
Insurance offices, 54, 393.
Intelligence office, 242.
Invasions, threatened, 389, 519, 525.
Irish leather, 96; butter, etc., prohibited, 7, 112, 306, 364, 384; copper coinage, 138; wool trade, 195, 432; vagrants, 227; trade opened, 324, 432-3; giant, 441.
Iron: early founder, 71; price of, 315; local trade, 205; American, 205.

Jack the Painter's fires, 426.
Jacobites: local, 19; riot, 107; plots to seize Bristol, 110, 113; arms seized, 118; disloyal clergy, 19, 119, 121; Lovell's case, 117; local demonstrations, 139, 164, 193, 257-8; capture of a warship, 256.
Jacob's Wells theatre, 63, 489; water works, 478; baths, 507.
Jamaica, prosperity of, 234.
James', St., Square, 114; Barton, 421, 434. [473.
Jefferis, Wm., 150, 191, 208, 209, 463,
Jenkins' cheap bread, 401.
Jenner, Henry, 530.
Jessop, William, 481, 496.
Jews' Naturalisation Bill, 299.
Jews' burial ground, 337; synagogue, 470.
John Street, 491.
Johnson, Dr., in Bristol, 422.
Jones, John, 128, 242. [165.
Judges, entertainment of, 32, 48, 59,
Juries, accommodation of, 399.

Kennet and Avon Canal, 499.
Kentish, Dr., 524.
Kidnapping, local, 56, 152.
King, John, 101.
Kingsdown, 2, 205, 343; patrol, 454.
King's Evil, magical cures, 55, 56, 117.
King's Parade, 494.
King's Square, 318. [224.
Kingsweston road, 65, 331; House, Kingswood, lawless colliers, 78, 156, 211, 219, 303, 469, 515; rangership, 190; Whitefield at, 201; schools, 203, 272; fire at, 267, church, 288; Common, 487, blackmail paid, 469.
Knight, Sir John, 77, 120, 290; Anne, 120; John, 78.

INDEX. 545

Knowle, prison at, 389, 487.
Kosciusko in Bristol, 522.

Labour, hours of, 72, 182, 351.
Ladies, illiteracy of, 12; ill-treated in streets, 278.
Lamb inn, witchcraft at, 348.
Lambton, Wm. Henry, 504.
Lamplighters' Hall, 389.
Land tax redeemed, 529. [477.
Laroche, (Sir) James, 268, 884, 402,
Lawford's Gate, 8, 175, 268; removed, 891; prison, 112, 407, 465.
Lawrence, (Sir) Thomas, 892, 487.
Leadworks nuisance, 821.
Leather, sales of, 297; bad, 154.
Lee, Rev. Charles, 874-6.
Leicester, a journey to, 89.
Levant trade, 305.
Lewdness, punishment of, 27, 170.
Lewin's Mead, residents in, 421, 488.
Lewis, Sir Wm., 56, 68; David, 484, 491, 518.
Library, City, rebuilt, 210, 367, 408; circulating, 168; Chapter, 815; Library Society, 408.
Licensing system, 268; *see* Alehouses.
Lighting, public, 5, 18, 80; new Act, 87; defects, 82; Bill, 217; Act, 277, 369; improvement Bill, 467; deficient, 527.
Lime trade, 459.
Lippincott, Sir Henry, 444-6. [531.
Living, cheapness of, 88; dearness,
Lock-out, early, 851.
Lodge Street, 456.
Lodgings, bill for, 88.
Logwood mills, 482.
London, first coach to, 22; wagons, 78, 269, 288. [420.
Lord Lieutenants, 69, 110, 818, 852,
Louisa, Story of, 425.
Lovell, Chris., 117; Robert, 508, 510.
Loyalty demonstrations, 287, 499.
Lukins, Geo., imposture of, 488.
Lunell, Peter, 476.

Macaulay, Lord, 487.
Maces, civic, 184.
Madagascar slave trade, 127.
Mail robberies, 210.
Mails: London, 17, 285; to Chester, 38; accelerated, 855; first coaches, 458; to Birmingham, 459.
Man of War, French, captured, 882; English recaptured, 259, 832.
Mansion House, civic, 191, 484, 449.
Manufactures, local, 7, 89, 414.
Map of environs, 867.

Marat, J. P., in Bristol, 482.
Markets: in streets, 4, 88, 198, 258; corn, 151, 471; hay, 176, 457; Exchange, 198, 258; St. James's, 895; on Back, 97, 422; fish, 88, 458; cheese, 152, 471; regulations, 198, 258.
Marriages, early hour of, 16; clandestine, 158, 285, 333, 498; notices of, 239, 880.
Marsh, Bristol, 25, 42; Canon's, 86, 398; Dean's, 185.
Mayor's dues, 194, 415, 517.
Mayors: list of, 584; attempt to obtain a lord mayor, 29: an unpopular, 65; deaths of, 121, 128, 288, 442; refusals to accept office, 485, 495, 507-8, 582; salary, 429, 507, 582; Chapel, 126, 305, 824, 362, 481; carriage, 209, 291; holiday, 196; scabbard, 86, 291; cursing a mayor, 117; freemen, 870; right to sit as judges, 495.
Meat, regulations touching, 211, 254; price of, 191, 844.
Medical schools, early, 264, 524; costumes, 178; licenses granted by Church, 258.
Members of Parliament: *see* Elections; payments to, 58; gifts of wine, 77, 86, 281, 811.
Mendicants, treatment of, 121.
Mercantile incomes, 7.
Merchants, fortunes of local, 462.
Merchant Venturers Society: List of Masters, 587; defence of the slave trade, 89; wharfage dues, 81, 99, 817; hall, 42, 99, 218; taboos Quakers, 91; politics of, 189; policy towards America, 870, 428, 489; change of politics, 485; dock, 368, 422; treatment of the Hot Well, 489.
Merchant Tailors Company, 181, 460; almshouse, 48.
Merlott, John, his charity, 529.
Methodism in Bristol, early, 200.
Michael's, St., the fashionable suburb, 97, 166.
Miles family, 298, 417, 448, 478, 476, 478, 508.
Militia musters, 69, 79, *ib.*, 85, 824.
Miller, Michael, 190, 268, 305, 415, 442; Wm., 282, 297, 462.
"Mint," the, 88. [224.
Money, difficulty in remitting, 180,
Montague Street, 871.
More, Hannah, 881, 878, 410, 412, 428, 425, 461, 468, 492.
Morocco, envoy from, 225.

N N

Murders: Maccartny's, 104; by ship captains, 151, 193; by Capt. Goodere, 228; Cann's coachman, 248; White Ladies', 279; of a woman, 280; of the Warner, 351; Mrs. Ruscombe, 862.
Murderer's body destroyed, 192.
Musical Festivals, 161, 308, 327, 407, 480, 582; in theatre, 397, 489.

Nash, Stephen, 63, 468, 470.
Naturalisation Bill, 289.
Navigation School, 99.
Navy, recruited from gaol, 69; impressments, *see* Press-gangs; Bristol ships, 434, 448, 466; bounties for men, 69, 428, 440, 500, 514; successes of, 452-3, 506, 522.
Nelson (Lord), a freeman, 522.
Nelson Street opened, 496.
Neptune figure, 135, 466.
Newcastle, Duke of, freedom to, 340.
Newfoundland trade, 469.
Newgate, closed on Sundays, 57.
Newgate: the city gaol, 31; epidemics in, 126, 164; treatment of suspected criminals, 172; charges of keeper, 237, 279; drinking in, 355, 471; physician, 209; chaplain, 392, 420; repaired, 395; Howard's account of, 406; distress during dearth, 308, 454; proposed new gaol, 488. And *see* Debtors.
Newnham, Rev. T., killed, 416.
Newspapers, early, 48, 50; later, 292; restrictions on, 267; taxes on, 486.
Newton, Bishop, 345, 366.
Nicholas Street: narrowness of, 131; passage through crypt, 215; through tower, 353; conduit, 141, 353.
Nicholas', St., vestry, 326.
Noble, John, and the judges, 495.
Non-jurors, local, 19, 119.
Norfolk, Duke of, a freeman, 455.
North, Lord, a freeman, 420.
Northington, Lord, anecdote, 284.
Norton's Folly, 266.
Nott, Dr. John, 504.
Nugent, Robert (Lord Clare, Earl Nugent), 309, 311, 340, 344, 378, 388, 409, 413, 432.

Oar, silver, 263.
O'Brien, Patrick, 441.
Offices, meanness of business, 40.
Old style abolished, 298.
Oliffe, John, 128.

Orange, Prince of, visit of, 187.
Orchard Street built, 115.
Ordnance Survey, 523.
Ormond, Duke of, 104, 110.
Osborne, Jeremiah, 260.

Packhorses, traffic by, 68, 73, 325.
Palatines. poor, 80.
Palmer, John, 439, 457-9.
Panics, financial, 499, 522.
Paper hangings, 332.
Pardons for criminals, 90.
Parish clerks, 363, 431.
Parish feasts, 116, 525; boundaries, beating, 243.
Park Street built, 227, 332, 333.
Parliament, members of, *see* Elections; payments to, 77; gifts of wine, 77, 86, 281, 311; reporting debates, 162.
Patriotic funds, 256, 506, 525.
Patronage, Government, 124, 451.
Pauper badges, 78, 380.
Pauperism, *see* Poor.
Paving Act, 277; new Bills, 467.
Peace of 1713, 100; of 1749, 274; of 1763, 357; of 1783, 458.
Peach family, 63, 190, 390, 397, 403, 445, 456, 489.
Pedley, J. G., frauds, 450.
Peloquin, Mary Ann, charity, 435.
Penance in the cathedral, 94.
Penn Street, 318.
Penn, William, 77, 318.
Pen Park Hole fatality, 416.
Penpole, excursions to, 331.
Perry, Richard, and his wife, 493.
Peter Street Cross and Pump, 377.
Pewter platters, 14, 45, 164, 188, 214.
Philip's, St., and militia, 79; hedgehogs in, 140.
Philipps, Sir John, 310, 311.
"Philosopher in Bristol," The, 418.
Pigs in the streets, 4, 527.
Pill, road to, 325. [396, 455.
Pillars, Brass, Corn Street, 162, 183.
Pillory, the, 27; riotous scenes, 148, 207.
Pine, William, 177, 294.
Piracy by Bristol crews, 351, 397.
Pitt, W. (Earl of Chatham) a freeman, 340.
Pitts, Capt. Sam., gallantry of, 165.
Plan of Bristol, Rocques', 285.
Plate, silver, local stores, 18; corporate, 78; discovery of, 238.
Playbills, early, 61.
Pluralism, clerical, 351, 432, 518, 523; lay, 151, 368, 431.
Pneumatic Institute, 504...

Pocock, George, 517.
Podmore, John, 180.
Pointz Pool fair, 166.
Police constables, 172.
Political bitterness, 18, 103, 107, 447.
Poor, Corporation of: founded, 32; early troubles, 54, 81, 103; buys a farm, 55; credulity of guardians, 55; infant labour, 72, 514; educational views, 72, 80; gift to, 73; pauper badges, 78, 380; increase of pauperism and rates, 81, 103, 236, 252–3, 380, 464, 485; churchwardens become guardians, 108; party feeling, 108, 123; treatment of vagrancy, 121; debts, 124; whipping paupers, 465; redistribution of rates, 485; factory in workhouse, 514; Baggs' fraud, 185.
Pope, Alex., in Bristol, 222.
Popery, anti, riots, 442.
Population of city, 6, 194, 292, 422.
Port, danger from fire, 361; float schemes, 316, 362, 480, 496; regulations, 394; defences of, 523; *see* Mayor's dues and Town dues.
Port wine, first appearance, 101.
Portishead, manor, 31; battery, 524.
Portland, Duke of, visit of, 471; portrait of, 487.
Portland Square, 494.
Post chaise travelling, 262, 404.
Posts from London, 17, 235, 395; to Chester, 38; Exeter, 39; Salisbury, 355; rates of postage, 78, 344; Palmer's acceleration, 457; to Birmingham, 459; penny post, 500.
Post Office, early, 39, 242; in Corn Street, 268; extent of staff, 416; Francis Freeling, 458.
Potteries, Bristol, 7, 287–8.
Powell, William, 391,
Press-gang brutalities, 168, 216, 314, 322, 337, 440.
Pretender, the, in Bristol, 257, 319.
Prince's Street built, 149.
Prisoners of war, *see* French.
Prisoners for debt, *see* Debtors.
Privateering: ships Duke and Duchess, 74; (1739) 216; (1744) 249; (1747) 267; (1756) 320, 338; (1762) 351; (1775) 415, 436; Royal Family priv., 255, 259; local losses, 338, 436; gallant feats of, 234, 247, 250–1, 256, 259, 268, 332, 343; crew turned pirates, 351.
Privateers, foreign, captured, 83, 268, 332.
Prizefighting, 27, 159, 273, 313, 341, 391, 533; by women, 168.

Profanity punished, 169, 263.
Protestants, foreign, 80, 289.
Protheroe, Philip, 477, 507, 532.
Public-houses, *see* Alehouses.
Publican, a clerical, 159, 388.
Pugilists, *see* Prizefighting. [465.
Punishments, excessive, 27, 315, 347,
Quakers persecuted, 19; boarding-school, 48; loan to Penn, 77; tabooed, 85, 91; decline and revival of sect, 178; fighting Quakers, 178, 285; tithe-owners, 178, 286; penitents, 278.
Quays, new, 149, 317.
Quay dues, 317.
Quebec taken: rejoicings, 339.
Queen Square, 25, 42, 45; nuisances in, 98; trees, 117, 418.
Race meetings, 24, 122, 278.
Randall, Joseph, 136, 257.
Randolph, Dr., 361. [264.
Rebellion (1715) 110; (1745) 255,
Recorders: Eyre, 123; Scrope, 166, 192; Foster, 192, 341; Barrington, 341, 870; Dunning, 370; Burke, 455, 505; Gibbs, 505; fees of, 123, 192, 341, 405, 506.
Recruiting tricks, 270.
Red Book of Orders, 56. 252.
Redcliff Cross and churchyard, 358.
Redcliff Gate, rebuilt, 175, 211; removed, 896.
Redcliff Parade, 396.
Redland Court, 178; Chapel, 178, 448; value of land, 284.
Red Lodge, 456, 479.
Reeve, William, anecdote of, 285, 370; *see* Black Castle.
Regiments, Bristol, 256, 506.
Rennison's Baths, 269.
Rents, 344, 398.
Revolution, centenary of, 487.
Reynolds, Richard, 72, 529.
Riding School, first, 344.
Ring, Joseph, 287–8.
Rings, funeral, 18
Riots: (1709) 78; (1714) 107; (1726) 156; (1728) 167; (1738) 212; (1749) 274; (1753) 308; (1766) 378; (1780) 442; Bristol Bridge, 500; Food, 516, 531.
Roads: state of, 23, 40, 155, 170, 214, 270, 313, 497; Kingsweston, 65, 331; Pill, 325; Whiteladies, 331, 333; cleansing, 340.
Robinson, Mrs., *see* Darby.
Rodney, Lord, in Bristol, 452–3.
Rogers, Woodes, Capt., 74–7.
Roman Catholics, 115, 366.

Romsey, John, 54, 74, 77.
Roquet, Rev. J., 392.
Routs described, 528.
Royal Oak Day, 164, 488.
Royal Family privateers, 255, 259.
Ruddock, Noblet, 142, 287.
Rum trade, 101, 102.
Ruscombe, Mrs., murdered, 362.

Sailors, *see* Seamen.
St. Vincent, Earl, freedom to, 522.
Sallee corsairs, 188, 225.
Salt refining, 289; tax on, 529.
Sansom, John, 54.
Savage, Richard, in Bristol, 219.
Scavenging, 80, 38, 82; gratuitous, Schoolmasters, 12, 128. [340.
Schools: Queen Eliz. Hospital, 12, 16, 46; new school-house, 47; removed, 374; cost of boarding, 405, 485; funds misappropriated, 442; dietary, 485. Colston's, 80, 88. Grammar, 16, 119; removed, 374; speech day, 396. Red Maids', 12, 134; cost of boarding, 134, 405. Charity, 12, 80, 134, 198, 218; Navigation, 99. Redcliff Grammar, 12, 358. Boarding, 43, 241, 272, 438, 517, 518. Misses More's, 331, 486. Day, 242, 367, 438.
Scolds, treatment of, 27, 132, 359.
Scrope, John, 160, 166, 188, 354.
Seafights, gallant, 234, 250, 259, 268, 332, 518.
Seamen, wages, 385, 454; forging their wills, 261; required for navy, 514; proposed hospital, 269; *see* Press-gangs.
Sea Mills dock, 98, 171, 296.
Sea walls, 266.
Sectarian divisions, 18, 103, 204.
Sedan chairs, 324.
Selkirk, Alexander, found, 75–6.
Sermons, fee for, 9, 99, 126.
Servants, domestic, 10, 182. [528.
Seyer, Samuel, 243, 348, 374, 522,
Shambles, the, 208, 385.
Shaving, Sunday, 27, 306, 336, 381.
Sheffield, Lord, 448, 491, 518.
Sheriffs, list of, 534; gloves, 87; dinners, 226, 251; allowance, 251, 430; expenses, 430; fine for refusing office, 87, 492.
Sherry trade, 104.
Shipping, Bristol, 6, 89; seized by corsairs, 188, 281; size of vessels, 6, 188, 371, 517; regulations, 394; ship sunk by a press-gang, 322; sunk in harbour, 117, 513; embargo on, 514.

Shirehampton, road, 65, 331; Sunday coach, 457.
Shoes, bad, destroyed, 155.
Shops, signs, 4, 278, 369; open, 3, 264, 827; tax on, 465.
Shot factory, 458.
Shrove Tuesday sports, 188.
Siddons, Mrs., at theatre, 489.
Signs, tradesmen's, 4, 278, 369.
Silk imports prohibited, 42, 101, 372; local works, 372.
Simmons, John, 342.
Sketchley's Directory, 420.
Slander, actions for, 359.
Slave dealing: Assiento treaty, 100; extent of local trade, 89, 249, 271-2, 343, 380, 416, 477; with Madagascar, 127; defended by Corporation, 89, 249, 271; enormous profits of, 142, 476–8; slave ship captains, 146, 380, 474; tragedies, 145, 301, 343; gin trade, 300; restrictions on, 418; value of negroes, 414, 478; Clarkson's crusade, 473–8; local agitation, 476–7; atrocities, 477.
Slaves in Bristol, 15, 146, 384, 492.
Slaves, Christian, 188.
Sledges, street, 8, 252, 527.
Small, Dr. J. A., 479, 518.
Small pox, ravages of, 529.
Smalridge, Bishop, 103, 119, 123.
Smith, Sir Sydney, 526.
Smith, Jarrit, 185, 228, 257, 318, 380, 344, 388; Joseph, 408, 412, 442; Richard, 524.
Smiths' Hall, 306, 468. [214, 217.
Smoking, prevalence of, 9, 48, 52,
Snuff trade, local, 269, 302, 430.
Soap, Irish, seized, 312. [183.
Somerset, wages in, 182; Society,
South Sea Company, 90, 127.
Southey, Robert, 397, 460, 510.
Southwell, Edward, 104, 224, 285, 267, 281, 310.
Southwell Street, 205.
Spain, irritation against, 174, 215; wars, 216, 351; losses of Bristolians, 175, 216, 286; peace, 274.
Spelter works, 67, 289.
Spencer, Hon. John, 318.
Spider's web, enormous, 106.
Sports, suburban, 27, 140.
Stables, circular, 344.
Stamp Office, 261. [487.
Stapleton living, 98, 109; common, Starch, illicit, 418; duty, 515.
Steam engines, early, 244, 273; improvements, 437.
Steep Street, 331.

INDEX.   549

Stephen's, St., lamp-rate, 38, 82; constables, 305; windfalls, 306; Peloquin's gift, 485; vestry, 244, 514, 525; improvements, 399, 458, 497.
Stewart, James, 242. [471.
Stewards, Lord High, 87, 111, 209,
Stocks, the, 27, 169, 207, 268.
Stoke Park, 352, 867. [64.
Stokes Croft, 2, 166, 489; theatre, 61,
Storm, great, the, 57.
Streets, narrowness of, 8, 131, 460; pigs in, 4, 527; nuisances, 169; encroachments, 83; fighting in, 355; footways in, 396, 527; bad condition, 356, 466, 526; names posted up, 491; watering, 504.
Strikes, 21, 70, 315, 385, 404, 497.
Styles, Old and New, 154, 298.
Sugar trade, extent of, 142, 302, 519.
Sunday restrictions, 56, 60, 306, 336; excursions, 359, 457, 490; schools, 460, 482; evening services, 519.
Superstition, popular, 56, 117, 224, 294, 348.
Sussex, Earl of, freedom to, 432.
Swetnam, J., 389.
Swimming baths, 269, 315.
Swords, state, 100, 291.

Tabernacle account book, 306.
Tailors' bill, early, 109; wages, 315; 404; hours, 351.
Tailors Company, 181, 460; almshouse, 48.
Talbot, Rev. Wm., 398.
Tanners' grievances, 96.
Tar, Coal, discovered, 441.
Tarring and feathering, 207.
Tea-drinking, 82, 314; price of tea, 82, 395.
Teast, Sydenham, 396, 463, 474, 517.
Temple Street, 97, Gate rebuilt, 175, 211; schools, 80; gardens, 98; Cross, 466; churchyard, 249; conduit, 185.
Tennis courts, 25, 318, 359, 506.
Theatres, early, 26; agitation against, 60; suppressed, 61-3; Jacob's Wells, 63, 439; at fairs, 64; Theatre Royal, 364, 400, 439, 582; at Coopers' Hall, 401.
Thistlethwaite, James, 411, 445.
Thomas, John, 71.
Thorne, Nich., monument, 329.
Tobacco, *see* Smoking and Snuff; trade, 185; price of, 416.
Tokens, local, 509.
Tolzey, Mayor's, removed, 59; merchants, 17, 118, 446; brass pillars, 162, 188, 396; St. Nicholas', 60.
Tontines, Brunswick Square, 479;

circular stables, 344; warehouses, 455; projected, 455, 494.
Tower, Great, on Quay, 119.
Town Clerk, insane, 251.
Town dues, 251, 417, 478; receipts from, 479.
Trade Unions, early, 21, 70.
Trade, restraints on, 21, 176, 181, 195, 260, 268, 401 (and *see* Foreigners); old, 128, 421.
Trading frauds, 154, 197, 272, 437.
Train bands, *see* Militia.
Traitor's Bridge, 92, 526.
"Translator," A, 128.
Transportation system, 91, 150-8, 237, 326, 469. [ness, 404.
Travelling discomforts, 22; cheapTrees in the streets, 489.
Trinity Street built, 185.
Trucks, street, 68, 396.
Trumpeters, city, 59, 114.
Tucker. Josiah, 118, 288, 283-4, 289, 319, 322, 328, 435, 462, 478.
Tucker Street, 466.
Tuckett, Philip D., 473.
Turner, William, 378.
Turnpike roads, 155, 274, 381, 406; riots, 156, 274; cleansing, 340.
Turtle, civic love of, 323, 404, 517.
Tyburn ticket, 390.
Tyndall, Onesiphorus, 94, 145; family, 190, 219, 334, 415, 479, 521.
Tyndall's Park, 334, 494.
Type factory, 177.

Umbrellas, early, 134; Church, 187; modern, 419.
Underhill, John, 58.
Union with Scotland, 73.
Union Street, 369, 395.
Unity Street, 237.

Vaccination discovered, 530.
Vagrancy, treatment of, 121.
Vaughan, John, 186, 224, 282, 297, 415, 432; R., 477.
Vauxhall gardens, 245, 423.
Vernon, Admiral, 241; privateer, 217.
Vick, William, 63, 308.
Visitors, distinguished: Queen Anne, 45; Prince of Wales, 212; Dukes of York, 350, 367, 517; Princess Amelia, 164; Prince of Orange, 187; Jos. Addison, 122; T. Clarkson, 473; Edward Colston, 46, 85; J. Howard, 406, 437, 466; Lady Huntingdon, 279, 420; Mrs. Inchbald, 400; Dr. Johnson, 422; Kosciusko, 522; Marat, 432; Pope, 222; Duke of Portland, 471; Lord Rod-

ney, 452; Admiral of Sallee, 225;
R. Savage, 219; Scheck Schidit,
192; Sir S. Smith, 526; Admiral
Vernon, 241; H. Walpole, 377;
John Wilkes, 397.
Volunteer corps, 113-4, 256, 440, 516,
520; cavalry, 521.

Wade, Nathaniel, 78, 92.
Wade Street and Bridge, 92, 526.
Wade, General, in Bristol, 112.
Wages, rates of, 59, 168, 182, 268, 315, 372, 385, 404, 454.
Wagons, travelling, 73, 148, 268, 288, 430; forbidden in streets, 175.
Waits, city, 26, 114, 239.
Wales, Fred., Prince of, 196, 212, 236, 290; George, 336, 517.
Wales, French landing in, 520.
Wallis, John, 208, 266.
Walpole, Horace, 377, 388.
War proclaimed, 216, 249, 320, 499; losses by, 286, 258, 415.
War ships launched, 434, 448, 466.
Warburton, Dean, 327.
Ward, Edward, 52.
Wasbrough, Matthew, 437.
Watching Act, 80, proposed Bill, 217; Act, 311.
Watchman, newspaper, 512.
Watchmen, city, 18, 80, 172, 197, 311, 340.
Water Bailiff's oar, 263.
Water Company, 82, 237, 451.
Watering places, seaside, 440.
Watts's patent shot, 453.
Weare, John Fisher, 415, 477, 507; Wm., 508.
Weavers, trade union, 70; assault women in streets, 125; washing place, 125; fatal riots, 166; wages, 168; Company, 470; truck system, 71, 209; decline of trade, 81, 209, 286, 515.
Wedgwood, Thomas, 504, 513.
Weeks, John, 405, 418, 458, 464, 484, 506.
Wesley, John, first visit, 208; at Hot Well, 265; at election. 319; his school, 272; at French prison, 389; alleged miracles, 266, 482; last visit, 482.
Wesley, Charles, 204.
Wesleyan Conferences, 204; disputes, 507.
West India trade, 6, 89, 142; prosperity of, 284; vessels, 371; French islands taken, 348; corporate sympathy, 378, 392; decline, 415, 519; names of merchants, 472.
West Street fair, 166.
Westbury, living of, 98, 109, 448, 528; volunteers, 521.
Westmoreland, Earl of, *see* Fane.
Weston-super-Mare, 441.
Weymouth, coach to, 440.
Whale, ship struck by, 208; fishing. 296.
Wharfage dues, 81, 99, 317.
Wheat, price of. 246, 516.
Wheelage toll, 252.
Whipping, public, 27, 65, 180, 224 315, 356, 437; paupers, 465.
Whipping posts, 27, 140, 268.
Whitefield, Geo., in Bristol, 200, 306.
Whitehall, 38, 124, 225.
Whitehead's poem, 288.
Whiteladies Road, 331, 338.
Whitson's charity funds, 496.
Whitsuntide sports, 314.
Wigs worn by boys, 158.
Wild, Jonathan, 130.
Wilkes, John, 391, 397.
William III., statue, 178, 193, 278.
Williams, (Sir) Charles F., 524.
Wills, W. and H. O., 308.
Wills, local, 14; forgery of, 261.
Wiltshire Society, 183.
Wine, civic gifts of, 77, 86, 87, 104, 209, 281, 311, 402, 582; price of, 188, 319, 329, 356, 582; change of taste in, 100; "Shampeighn," 214.
Wine Street, scenes in, 4, 148; width of, 460; value of sites in, 485.
Witchcraft, 28, 249, 484; at Lamb inn, 348.
Women, treatment of, 27-8, 65; boxing by, 168; races by, 122, 279.
Wood's pence, 133.
Woollen, burials in, 9, 302.
Worcester, Marquis of, 491, 518.
Wordsworth, Wm., 513.
Worrall family, the, 261, 308, 351, 393, 494.
Wotton-under-Edge, post to, 39.
Wraxall family, 234, 308.
Wrestling, 314.
Wright, Matthew, 473, 503, 507

Yate, Robert, 42, 58, 66, 85, 203.
Yearsley, Anne, 461.
Yonge, Bishop, 345.
York. Dukes of, 350, 367, 517.
York Street, 372.

Zinc works, *see* Spelter.

Lightning Source UK Ltd.
Milton Keynes UK
UKHW02f2004030918
328275UK00004B/23/P